Programming Boot Sector Games

Includes a crash course on 8086/8088 programming

Óscar Toledo Gutiérrez

Programming Boot Sector Games

Copyright © 2019 Óscar Toledo Gutiérrez

ISBN: 978-0-359-81631-6

Official website: **http://nanochess.org/**

The author welcomes your comments, suggestions and errata reports. Please send them to: **biyubi@gmail.com**

You can also follow him on Twitter as **@nanochess**

First published in 2019.

Dedicated to my beloved wife Rosa Nely and our little fairies Myriam Sofía and Samantha.

For Elisa, keep smiling.

For my mother and my father, thanks for all.

Contents

The Book

Foreword

All in 510 bytes

A boot-sector in an IBM-compatible environment is intended to hold 510 bytes (the last two bytes being a signature for validation) of code and data sufficient to locate and load the next stage for the boot. For a standard DOS disk, the code would parse the FAT12 file-system in order to detect the presence of the files named IBMBIO.COM or IO.SYS, and IBMDOS.COM or MSDOS.SYS, and then to load IBMBIO.COM or IO.SYS file (which in turns loads the IBMDOS.COM or MSDOS.SYS file). There was very little spare space in the boot sector for a detailed error message if either file could not be located. Non-DOS systems were free to perform direct disk activity or parse their own file-systems, of course, but the size limit remained.

Given such a constrained environment, it's often overlooked as a target for a function other than booting the system. However, over the years, two particular groups of people found alternative uses for it. One group was the virus writer. The other group is the demo maker.

Virus writers created "boot-sector" viruses that activated when the infected disk was booted, resided in memory, and then infected other floppy disks as they were inserted into the floppy drive. It was common for boot-sector viruses to copy the original boot-sector to another location on the disk, and then to replace the original code with the virus-specific code. Early boot-sector viruses would copy the original boot-sector to the end of the disk, hoping that it was not in use already. This technique was not used for very long because booting such an infected floppy disk would have a noticeable delay and unusual sound while the drive arm moved to the end of the disk and then back again to resume loading.

The replacement technique relied on the fact that regular DOS disks carry two copies of the File Allocation Table (FAT), one immediately after the other, and both within the first track of the disk. The first copy of the FAT is used as the master version. The second is a back-up which can in some cases enable undeletion of files and repair of certain disk errors. Virus writers decided that the back-up copy of the FAT would not be used very often, and claimed the copy as free space. That became the location for storing the original boot-sector, along with any additional code that the virus needed as its second stage. Using this location avoided the drive arm movement during the boot, making the boot seem very similar between an uninfected disk and an infected one.

As hard disks became more common and larger capacity, they were often "partitioned" into sections with particular purposes, or to avoid a limitation of the BIOS disk-capacity description. The partitions could allow multi-boot systems – one environment per partition. Each of the partitions carried its own boot sector which knew how to parse the format of the data in its partition. Virus writers often targeted the hard disk's Master Boot Record (MBR) rather than the boot sector of individual partitions. The MBR is used to select the partition of interest and then to pass control to that partition's boot sector to boot the contents of that partition, so it is the first code that runs, and it is always executed. In contrast, a partition's boot-sector might be executed only rarely, or potentially not at all if the partition shares the same disk format as another partition which is booted instead. A virus in a MBR could still infect floppy disk as they were inserted to the floppy drive.

Boot-sector viruses spread freely and widely among pirated disks, since it was not common for a copied disk to be write-protected. They survived until floppy drives ceased to be shipped with new PCs. Despite that, the MBR lives on. As I write this in 2019, the BIOS in IBM-compatible PCs still carries the code to allow a system to boot from the MBR.

That leaves the demo maker. For almost as long as there have been computers, there have been demos (short for demonstration programs) for computers. As hardware improved in speed and capability, the size of demos increased as more assets could be manipulated and take advantage of what was offered. Many demos moved from real-time generation of objects with tracked music, to essentially videos with pre-generated textures and MP3 music of multiple-megabytes in size. However, there has always been smaller groups of demo makers who target older machines or older environments.

The interest in size-coding has been heightened by demo competitions. PC 64kb competitions appeared in 1991, followed by Amiga 40kb competitions in 1992, and PC 4kb competitions in 1994. It wasn't until 2012 that PC 1kb competitions appeared. 1kb files are still suitable for Windows environments, or an Amiga boot-block. Sub-1kb competitions are effectively limited to a .COM file in the DOS environment, which presents some difficulties to get them to run on modern hardware. Conveniently, though, the DOS environment is a very close match to the MBR environment, the primary difference being the initial value of the segment registers and general-purpose registers. Thus, the MBR is the perfect place for a small demo which does not require booting DOS.

It might sound easy to target smaller file sizes, since there's less code to write, but in fact it can be extremely challenging. The difficulty comes from the fact that such small programs are still expected to demonstrate amazing effects, so instead of taking the easy way and carrying huge assets, these small demos have to rely on coding tricks to generate visual elements on-the-fly. The smaller the program, the harder it gets.

So what can we do in an MBR? It turns out that it's both a little and a lot. When the code in the MBR is executing, there is no operating system present. It means that there are no corresponding services offered, so we have no easy access to the GPU or the sound card or high-resolution video modes. Instead, we have only the most basic hardware support – there are built-in functions to place text and pixels on the screen in various lower-resolution video modes, read low-resolution timers, and read additional data from the disk (but that would be cheating). We can interact directly with the hardware, so we have access to high-resolution timers, and we can operate the speaker. From there, we can draw pictures and play music, so we can make demos.

In 510 bytes, we can display rotating flat-shaded vector balls, explore dot-vector landscapes, fly over cityscapes, be hypnotized by raster bars, zoom into fractals, or experience the illusion of movement created by color cycling... but wait! That's not all. We can interact with the user. In short, we can make games! Not just any games, but *good* games. We can make variations of Tetris, Space Invaders, Puck-Man, Robotron, Snake...

All in 510 bytes.

Peter Ferrie
Distinguished Engineer.
Symantec Corp.

July 24, 2019.

Preface

Why this book?

This book started as a way to document the tricks I've used in my boot sector games, but as I read the comments on my games, I've noticed lots of people telling me: okay, we have the source, we have the comments, it's nice, but we don't know 8088!

Unfortunately, in the good old days I never found a book that could satisfy my hunger for knowledge. At most it was an instruction reference book with two example programs developed at the author's whim. I had to discover myself the way to use the instructions, and I learned from others how to use certain esoteric instructions (now described for your delight in appendix D).

In my learning path I found very useful the DEBUG command included with MS-DOS. I could enter the instruction I didn't understand and see the result in the registers and flags.

So I wrote this book thinking of the type of book that I would like to have read.

Why boot sector games? I think that millions of PC computers have been manufactured since its introduction in 1981 with the original IBM PC, have been upgraded multiple times through different processors: 8088, 80286, 80386, 80486, Pentium, etc. Many millions are still lurking in homes. So these are easily accessible, and why not put these to good use?

We aren't wasting time. Every PC still boots with the old 8088 instruction set. Almost every PC still has floppy disk code in its guts, and if it doesn't have support for floppy disk drive, it emulates a floppy disk reading from a CD-ROM.

And if it's too modern for even having a CD-ROM, you can still install a free emulator and develop your creativity, even if Intel removes the boot sector support by 2020.[1]

There are hobbies for everything. We can make statues with kids' clay, we can build machines with cardboard, and we can also challenge our creativity doing games for computers that essentially (and literally) we have in every corner!

So in this book we are going through a crash course on 8086/8088 assembly language. We will fly fast and try to practice each thing as we learn it. And no example exceeds 512 bytes of machine code!

Also you'll see how you can build small games using assembly language speaking directly to the heart of the computer. I've included 4 of my best examples of boot sector games: F-Bird, Invaders, Pillman, and Toledo Atomchess. For learning purposes I've also included screen art programs in sections 4.3 (text mode) and 5.6 (Mandelbrot set).

For this book I assume you have previous knowledge of programming in any high-level language that includes hexadecimal numbers, like C, C++, PHP, Java, Javascript, etc., and how to use command-line on Windows, Linux or Mac OS X.

I strongly recommend to enter each program using the keyboard, because it's a great practice to read the instructions as you type them. No real warrior can learn only from copy & paste.[2]

If I can do it, then you can do it.

Welcome to a world of possibilities.

Óscar Toledo G.

July 2019

---

[1] https://arstechnica.com/gadgets/2017/11/intel-to-kill-off-the-last-vestiges-of-the-ancient-pc-bios-by-2020/

[2] Although if you get stuck, all the programs are available for download at my git: https://github.com/nanochess/book8088

Acknowledgments

No man is an island

I want to give special thanks to Michael Hayes (Zendocon). He went through the Herculean task of proofreading this book and testing all the examples. He also suggested the batch file for section 1.6.

I'm deeply grateful to Peter Ferrie (qkumba) who contributed a lot of optimization tricks to early versions of Toledo Atomchess, and Atomchess 6502. He also contributed the foreword to this book.

To HellMood who suggested translating Toledo Atomchess to *nasm* syntax and gave me some optimization suggestions. This fact helped a lot of people to assemble the game into their machines all around the world.

qu1j0t3 for providing a Makefile to Toledo Atomchess. Although I know both Windows and UNIX, sometimes I forgot that a Makefile eases the work at UNIX-like operating systems.

John Tsiombikas (jtsiomb) also contributed to Invaders with a Makefile (again I forgot doing one) and made some suggestions.

At Reddit, nils-m-holm made the suggestion to change Invaders keyboard input to use the service 0x02 (Get modifier keys), and this enhanced significantly the spaceship movement, and the extra bytes allowed me to add barriers between the invaders and the spaceship.

Special thanks to William M. Moeller.

Chapter 1

What's inside your PC

First fact: your PC computer has deep inside its guts an 8088 processor, no matter how advanced it is or how many gigahertz it runs at.

Second fact: your 8088 processor is an idiot. It takes its instructions from boxes (known as memory), reads them and does the indicated operation, then (if the instruction doesn't tell otherwise) it will advance to next box and so on, until the end.

The instructions in fact are bytes read from RAM or ROM memory (the basic system that boots your machine to run Windows or Linux). Some instructions take 1 byte, others take 2 bytes, and so on. An instruction to put a data value inside an address can take 6 bytes.

The instructions are something like this:

```
90
A0 55
B8 AA 55
C7 06 44 33 AA 55
```

Stop the press! Only a machine could understand this. Many years ago, after the creation of the first processor made with vacuum tubes, the engineers building these computers thought of a better way of helping the programmers, so assemblers were invented.

An assembler is a program that receives instruction mnemonics and outputs the hexadecimal data we saw before. So instead of the hexadecimal mumbo-jumbo we have seen, we can write this:

```
NOP
MOV AL,0x55
MOV AX,0x55aa
MOV WORD [0x3344],0x55aa
```

Now that's actually easier to read, although somewhat incomprehensible yet.

Apart from reading memory, the 8088 processor itself contains some data in the form of registers, so it can save the intermediate data of operations before writing them again to memory as required by the programmer.

The registers of the 8088 processor are each 16-bit, and are these:

AX	Accumulator
BX	Common use (address)
CX	Common use (counter)
DX	Common use (32-bit extension of AX)
SI	Common use (source address)
DI	Common use (target address)
BP	Base pointer (used along SP)
SP	Stack pointer
Flags	State of last instruction affecting flags.

Typically the registers (with the exception of Flags) are free to use, but some have dedicated functions with certain instructions.

Besides, AX, BX, CX and DX can be used in 8-bit halves: AH, BH, CH, DH and AL, BL, CL, DL.

So if we save 0x55aa in AX, then AH contains 0x55 and AL contains 0xaa.

AH	AL	= AX
CH	CL	= CX
DH	DL	= DX
BH	BL	= BX

Too many words – let's try this out!

1.1 Tools setup.

Let us download the Netwide Assembler (NASM) from *www.nasm.us*. This is a command-line utility.

Uncompress it to some directory where you can work. My suggestion for Windows: *My documents/nasm/*

For Linux and Mac OS X, I suggest to create a *nasm* directory under your home directory.

You must edit your source code somehow. I typically use EDIT from MS-DOS under Windows XP (not included with it, but easy to search and download), but you can resort to your daily editor, like *emacs, vi, vim, Notepad ++, nano* or even the original *Notepad* included with Windows.

Testing your programs will require some extra tools. If you are using Windows 10 or Mac OS X, then you'll need DosBox available from *http://www.dosbox.com* or VirtualBox from *http://www.virtualbox.org* to test your programs.

Notice that the Netwide Assembler works on any modern PC with Windows, Linux, and also under Mac OS X. It has the advantage that its syntax for the 8086/8088 processor is similar to the recommended one by Intel. Other free assemblers like *gas* (from the GNU toolchain) use the AT&T syntax, that unfortunately is too complicated for our learning purposes.

The documentation for *nasm* is available online at the following address: *https://nasm.us/docs.php*

1.2 Practice.

Create your first assembler program. Name it anything like *first.asm* and put it inside the same directory as *nasm*:

```
      org 0x0100
start:
      mov bx,string
repeat:
      mov al,[bx]
      test al,al
      je end
      push bx
      mov ah,0x0e
      mov bx,0x000f
      int 0x10
      pop bx
      inc bx
      jmp repeat

end:
      int 0x20

string:
      db "Hello, world",0
```

Then using the command-line (*cmd.exe* in Windows, or your current shell in Linux or Mac OS X), go to *nasm* directory/folder and assemble the program with this command (where ↵ appears I mean to press the Enter key):

```
nasm -f bin first.asm -o first.com↵
```

If everything went right, it should assemble without an error, and no message will be output to command-line. It simply will end and you now should have a file in your current directory named *first.com* that is 36 bytes in size. And you can run it using (MS-DOS/Windows only; for the other platforms you need an emulator as previously described):

```
first↵
```

The message "Hello, world" will appear in the console.

I would suggest changing the message (just make sure to stay within the double quotes), so you can get a grasp of how things change once you start continuously assembling a program.

What does the *.com* extension mean? It means COMmand, and it has been used since the creation in 1974 of CP/M, which was an operating system running over 8080 processors, and a predecessor to MS-DOS.

1.3 Comments.

There are two things that we have used in the program: labels and mnemonics.

The labels begin with a letter or underscore (_) and continue with digits, letters or underscores, completed with a colon. A label marks a point for the assembler, and the assembler takes note of the address where the label appears (more on this soon).

Mnemonics are the names for the instructions of the 8088 processor, but we also have pseudo-ops. These give special instructions to the assembler. We use two pseudo-ops (**org** and **db**).

The **org** directive indicates to the assembler that every instruction coming after this will start at the indicated address. The **db** directive indicates that the assembler should put literal bytes into the output.

Actually there is a third thing important in shaping the source code: comments. It's enough to add a semicolon within a line, and everything from that point until the end of line will be a comment. Let us add comments to our little program.

```
;
; The incredible Hello, World program
;
    org 0x0100      ; Start point of program for a COM file
start:
    mov bx,string ; Load register BX with address of 'string'
repeat:
    mov al,[bx]     ; Load a byte in AL from address pointed by BX
    test al,al     ; Test AL for zero
```

```
        je end        ; Jump if equal to 'end' label (jump if zero)
        push bx       ; Save BX register in stack
        mov ah,0x0e   ; Load AH with code for terminal output
        mov bx,0x000f ; BH is page zero, BL is color (graphic mode)
        int 0x10      ; Call the BIOS for displaying one letter
        pop bx        ; Restore BX register from stack
        inc bx        ; Increase BX register by 1 (next letter)
        jmp repeat    ; Jump to 'repeat' label

end:
        int 0x20      ; Exit to command-line.

string:
        db "Hello, world",0
```

Essentially the sequence of steps of this program (or algorithm) is:

1. Get the address of string in BX

2. Get a letter from the string in AL

3. If it's zero then program finishes.

4. Output letter to the screen

5. Repeat

Notice that we cannot use AX to keep the address of the string because no instruction exists to read the memory using AX as source. Also we read the letter into the AL register (the low part of AX)

We are using BIOS interrupts. Using **int 0x10** we call a "service" that displays a letter on the screen, and also **int 0x20** to return to the command-line. A list of commonly used interrupts is listed in Appendix A.

The thing that makes a processor more than a glorified calculator are the *jump* instructions.

We used **je** and **jmp** there, along the label where the jump should go. The instruction **je** is a conditional jump because it only jumps if a condition is met, in this case when the result of the previous operation is zero. The instruction **jmp** is an unconditional jump, because it jumps always.

What does jumping mean? The 8088 processor executes instructions sequentially. A jumping instruction breaks that sequence, and makes it to go to another place. That place can be before or after the current instruction, in this way creating loops to repeat interesting operations.

1.4 Input.

A non-interactive program isn't so useful; it can do only one task. So let us see how to read the keyboard. Save this as *second.asm*:

```
;
; The incredible keyboard reading program
;
    org 0x0100
start:

    mov ah,0x00    ; Keyboard read
    int 0x16       ; Call the BIOS to read it

    cmp al,0x1b    ; ESC key pressed?
    je exit_to_command_line
    mov ah,0x0e    ; Load AH with code for terminal output
    mov bx,0x000f  ; BH is page zero, BL is color (graphic mode)
    int 0x10       ; Call the BIOS for displaying one letter
    jmp start

exit_to_command_line:
    int 0x20
```

Then go to the command-line and assemble it with NASM (where ↵ appears we mean to press the Enter key):

```
nasm -f bin second.asm -o second.com↵
second↵
```

The two lines following the *start* label call a BIOS service to read the keyboard. It waits for a key to be pressed, and puts a code into register AL.

The code in register AL follows the ASCII standard (see appendix B). For example, pressing the uppercase A letter returns 0x41, while the lowercase A letter returns 0x61.

If the pressed key value is 0x1b, then the Esc key has been pressed (the instruction **cmp** does this CoMParison), and then the **je** (Jump if Equal) instruction jumps to exit the program.

Otherwise, it calls the same routine of the previous program to display the letter on the screen, and JuMPs again to the *start* label.

1.5 Viewing the machine code.

You can see the machine code generated by the *nasm* assembler. In order to do this, you need to add a command-line option to generate a listing.

For example, for the keyboard reading program:

```
nasm -f bin second.asm -l second.lst -o second.com↵
```

And the listing will look like this (the comments were amended to fit the width of this book):

```
 1                              ;
 2                              ; The incredible keyboard reading
 3                              ;
 4                              org 0x0100
 5                      start:
 6 00000000 B400             mov ah,0x00   ; Keyboard status
 7 00000002 CD16             int 0x16      ; Call the BIOS.
 8 00000004 3C1B             cmp al,0x1b   ; ESC key pressed?
 9 00000006 7409             je exit_to_command_line
10 00000008 B40E             mov ah,0x0e   ; Load AH with code
11 0000000A BB0F00           mov bx,0x000f ; Load BH with page
12 0000000D CD10             int 0x10      ; Call the BIOS
13 0000000F EBEF             jmp start
14
15                      exit_to_command_line:
16 00000011 CD20             int 0x20
17
```

1.6 Batch file.

For MS-DOS and Windows command-line, you can accelerate the assembly of your programs using a batch file like this one (save it as *m.bat*):

```
@echo off
if "%1"="" goto error
nasm -f bin %1.asm -l %1.lst -o %1.com
goto end
:error
echo What do you want to Make?
:end
```

Then it would be a matter of entering only this to assemble each program:

```
m first↵
```

1.7 Instructions learned.

The instructions we learned in this chapter were:

1. **inc**, increment by one.
2. **int**, interruption (call service vector).
3. **je**, jump if equal (also can be **jz**, jump if zero)
4. **jmp**, jump always.
5. **pop**, restore data from stack.
6. **push**, save data into stack.
7. **test**, test register for mask or zero (same as **and** but without modifying test register, as we'll see in the next chapter).

Chapter 2

Arithmetic

The 8088 is especially able to do simple calculations. These include adding, subtracting, doing multiplication, division and remainder, also bit-shift to left and right.

You can do most operations with register and register, register and memory, memory and register, register and immediate, and memory and immediate (a constant).

Unless otherwise indicated, the registers can be 16 bits or 8 bits. The 16-bit registers are AX, BX, CX, DX, SI, DI, BP and SP. While the 8-bit registers are AH, AL, BH, BL, CH, CL, DH and DL.

You cannot do operations with memory and memory, except for some special instructions that we'll see later.

For the purposes of this crash course, we'll create a subroutine that we should include in each program at the end of the code (only for chapters 2 and 3).

A subroutine is a piece of code that does a task and is called with **call**, and ends with **ret** (RETurn). There are some other things that we'll learn like the stack pointer, but for the purpose of this discussion, if we need to display a letter we only need to put this instruction in our code:

```
CALL display_letter
```

This is the small library routine:

```
; Save this library as library1.asm
int 0x20      ; Exit to command line.

; Display letter contained in AL (ASCII code, see appendix B)
display_letter:
    push ax
    push bx
    push cx
    push dx
    push si
    push di
    mov ah,0x0e   ; Load AH with code for terminal output
    mov bx,0x000f ; Load BH page zero and BL color (graphic mode)
    int 0x10      ; Call the BIOS for displaying one letter
    pop di
    pop si
    pop dx
    pop cx
    pop bx
    pop ax
    ret           ; Returns to caller

; Read keyboard into AL (ASCII code, see appendix B)
read_keyboard:
    push bx
    push cx
    push dx
    push si
    push di
    mov ah,0x00   ; Load AH with code for keyboard read
    int 0x16      ; Call the BIOS for reading keyboard
    pop di
    pop si
    pop dx
    pop cx
    pop bx
    ret           ; Returns to caller
```

For each of the following examples, you should copy and paste *library1.asm* at the end of each example. This means each example will finish exiting to command-line, and it will include support for displaying a letter (sending the contents of register AL to the screen as a letter), and reading the keyboard (into the register AL).

2.1 Addition.

For addition, we'll use the AL register, and immediate **add**:

```
    ; add1.asm
    org 0x0100
start:
    mov al,0x04    ; Load register AL with 0x04
    add al,0x03    ; Add 0x03 to register AL
    ;
    add al,0x30    ; Convert to ASCII digit
    call display_letter
    ; Add library1.asm here
```

This program after being assembled will output a single digit '7'. (because 4 + 3 = 7)

2.2 Subtraction.

For subtraction, we'll use the AL register, and immediate **sub**:

```
    ; sub1.asm
    org 0x0100
start:
    mov al,0x04    ; Load register AL with 0x04
    sub al,0x03    ; Subtract 0x03 to register AL
    ;
    add al,0x30    ; Convert to ASCII digit
    call display_letter
    ; Add library1.asm here
```

This program after being assembled will output a single digit '1'. (because 4 - 3 = 1)

2.3 Multiplication.

Multiplication allows you to multiply AL by any register or memory byte, or AX by any register or memory word (a word is a combination of two bytes).

```
    ; mul1.asm
    org 0x0100
start:
    mov al,0x03    ; Load register AL with 0x03
    mov cl,0x02    ; Load register CL with 0x02
    mul cl         ; Multiply AL by CL, result into AX
    ;
    add al,0x30    ; Convert to ASCII digit
    call display_letter
    ; Add library1.asm here
```

This program after being assembled will output a single digit '6'. (because 3 x 2 = 6)

Note that this is unsigned multiplication. If you want signed multiplication then you must use **imul**.

2.4 Division.

Division allows you to divide AX by any register or memory byte, putting the result in AL, and the remainder in AH. Or DX:AX (32 bits) divided by any register or memory word (again a word is a combination of two bytes), putting the result in AX, and the remainder in DX.

Caveat! This instruction can generate a system error (exiting to command-line), if the result doesn't fit into AL or AX, or the divisor is zero.

```
    ; div1.asm
    org 0x0100
start:
```

```
mov ax,0x64    ; Load register AX with 0x64 (100 decimal)
mov cl,0x21    ; Load register CL with 0x1e (33 decimal)
div cl         ; Divide AX by CL, result->AL, remainder->AH
;
add al,0x30    ; Convert to ASCII digit
call display_letter
; Add library1.asm here
```

This program after being assembled will output a single digit '3'. (because 100 / 33 = 3)

You can test that the remainder (100 % 33 = 1) is generated adding this instruction in the line after **div**:

```
mov al,ah      ; Copy AH (remainder) into AL for displaying.
```

Note that this is unsigned division. If you want to do signed division, then you must use **idiv**.

2.5 Shift.

Shift and rotation to left or right by one bit are essential tools when working with the core of a processor. In the early days of 8088, it was pretty costly to do multiplication. It was faster to use an arithmetic shift to left (operator << in high-level languages).

Same for division; it was faster to use an arithmetic or logical shift to right (operator >> in high-level languages).

```
; shift1.asm
    org 0x0100
start:
    mov al,0x02    ; Load register AL with 0x02 (2 decimal)
    shl al,1       ; Shift AL left by one bit
    ;
    add al,0x30    ; Convert to ASCII digit
    call display_letter
    ; Add library1.asm here
```

If we see the value of register AL like a binary value, then **shl** moves every bit one position to left, and the new bit at right is always zero, while the bit coming out at left is kept in the Carry flag (more on this later).

The other instructions that deserve mention here are **shr** and **sar**. The instruction **shr** moves every bit one position to right, and the bit coming out through the right goes into the Carry flag. The bit introduced at left is put to zero.

The instruction **sar** is same as **shr**, except that the bit introduced at left is a copy of the original bit. Like in the C language, **sar** is the equivalent of using the operator >> over signed integers, while **shr** is the equivalent of using the operator >> over unsigned integers.

All shift operations of the 8088 work by moving data by one place, or by several places, but this value should be in register CL.

This means that if we need to do **shl ax,2** then we must do:

```
SHL AX,1
SHL AX,1
```

Or alternatively:

```
MOV CL,2
SHL AX,CL
```

There are also the instructions **ror**, **rcr**, **rol** and **rcl**, that rotate the bits in the source data to the right or the left directly (**ror/rol**) or through the carry flag (**rcr/rcl**). As a final note, **shl** has a synonym called **sal**, so both are interchangeable but generate the same machine code.

2.6 Logical operations.

The logical instructions available in 8088 are **and**, **or** and **xor**:

```
    ; logical1.asm
    org 0x0100
start:
    mov al,0x32    ; Load register AL with 0x32 (50 decimal)
```

```
and al,0x0f    ; Logical AND AL with 0x0f
;
add al,0x30    ; Convert to ASCII digit
call display_letter
; Add library1.asm here
```

The instruction **and** is equivalent to the operator & from C and Javascript, **or** is the operator |, and **xor** is the operator ^.

There is also the **not** instruction that works without an operator, reversing all bits in the register (**not al** would be the C/Javascript equivalent of AL = ~AL).

```
; logical1.asm
    org 0x0100
start:
    mov al,0xfc    ; Load register AL with 0xfc (-4 decimal)
    not al         ; Logical NOT with AL
    ;
    add al,0x30    ; Convert to ASCII digit
    call display_letter
    ; Add library1.asm here
```

And also we have the **neg** instruction, pretty similar to **not**, except it is 2's complement. That means it reverses the integer value of its operand (AL = -AL is the C/Javascript equivalent of **neg al**).

2.7 Increment and decrement.

The increment and decrement instructions allow you to increase or decrease by one the value of a register or memory position. These instructions can work as byte (8-bit) or word (16-bit).

```
; inc1.asm
    org 0x0100
start:
    mov al,0x30
count1:
    call display_letter
    inc al
    cmp al,0x39
```

```
    jne count1
count2:
    call display_letter
    dec al
    cmp al,0x30
    jne count2
    ; Add library1.asm here
```

It loads AL with the code for ASCII digit zero equal to 0x30, displays it, increases the value of AL, and repeats until AL becomes 0x39.

Then it displays the letter, and decreases the value of AL, until AL becomes 0x30.

The result is a string of numbers in the output:

```
012345678987654321
```

There is a new instruction in this program: **cmp** (CoMParison). It is the same as the subtraction instruction, but with an important difference: it doesn't alter the register. So it becomes a comparison, as it alters the processor Flags register.

We have been using so far the **je** and **jne** instructions, Jump if Equal, and Jump if Not Equal.

2.8 Guess the number.

With our knowledge of these instructions we can make a small game, bending the rules a little and inserting a new instruction:

```
    ; guess.asm
    ; Guess a number between 0 and 7.
    org 0x0100

    in al,(0x40)   ; Read the timer counter chip
    and al,0x07    ; Mask bits so the value becomes 0-7
    add al,0x30    ; Convert into ASCII digit
    mov cl,al      ; Save AL into CL
game_loop:
    mov al,0x3f    ; AL now is question-mark sign
```

```
call display_letter    ; Display
call read_keyboard     ; Read keyboard
cmp al,cl      ; AL equals CL?
jne game_loop ; No, jumps (Jump if Not Equal)
call display_letter       ; Display number
mov al,0x3a               ; Display happy face
call display_letter
mov al,0x29
call display_letter
; add library1.asm here
```

Run it and a question-mark sign will appear. That means it's waiting for your answer.

If the number you enter isn't the one chosen by the computer, then it will repeat the question-mark sign.

Once you successfully guess the number, it will display the number and a happy face emoticon (the colon and right parenthesis sign). Feel free to replace 0x3a and 0x29 with 0x01 and 0x03 (see appendix B).

How does it choose a pseudo-random number? It reads port 0x40 of the PC. This port is connected internally to a chip called Timer, and one of its ports is counting continuously, so any time you read this port, you'll get a different value between 0x00 and 0xff.

So far we have been using hexadecimal codes for each ASCII letter, but *nasm* provides us with a powerful feature: an apostrophe operator that gives us the ASCII code directly without using hexadecimal.

Let us rewrite the program using this feature:

```
; guess.asm
; Guess a number between 0 and 7.
org 0x0100

in al,(0x40)  ; Read the timer counter
and al,0x07   ; Mask bits so the value becomes 0-7
add al,0x30   ; Convert into ASCII digit
mov cl,al
game_loop:
mov al,'?'
call display_letter
call read_keyboard
```

19

```
cmp al,cl
jne game_loop
call display_letter
mov al,':'
call display_letter
mov al,')'
call display_letter
; add library1.asm here
```

As you can see, it is more readable now.

And by the way, we are on a good path to write small games. This one is only 70 bytes in size.

2.9 Useful trivia.

If you know C, Java or Javascript, then the following equivalents will be useful for you:

- **xor** instruction = operator ^
- **or** instruction = operator |
- **and** instruction = operator &
- **not** instruction = unary operator ~
- **neg** instruction = unary operator -
- **shl** instruction = operator <<
- **shr/sar** instruction = operator >>

There is also an instruction that does nothing. You can insert it anywhere in your program and it won't have any effect in the operation of your program, except of course making it slightly slower. It is **nop**. You can try it in the *guess.asm* program. Insert it anywhere after the **org** directive, and you can see how the program grows by one byte (the size of the No Operation instruction), but otherwise runs unaffected.

The **nop** instruction resolves to the opcode 0x90 (search for it in Appendix C). The true instruction's operation is that it does: nothing.

2.10 Instructions learned.

The instructions we learned in this chapter were:

1. **add**, addition.
2. **and**, bitwise operation.
3. **call**, call subroutine.
4. **cmp**, comparison.
5. **dec**, decrement.
6. **div**, division (unsigned division).
7. **idiv**, integer division (signed division operation).
8. **imul**, integer multiplication (signed multiplication operation).
9. **in**, read port.
10. **mul**, multiplication (unsigned multiplication).
11. **neg**, negation.
12. **nop**, no operation.
13. **not**, bitwise operation.
14. **or**, bitwise operation.
15. **rcl**, rotation to left through carry flag.
16. **rcr**, rotation to right through carry flag.
17. **ret**, return from subroutine.
18. **rol**, rotation to left circular.
19. **ror**, rotation to right circular.
20. **sar**, shift arithmetic to right.
21. **shl/sal**, shift logical to left, or shift arithmetic to left.
22. **shr**, shift logical to right.
23. **sub**, subtraction.
24. **xor**, bitwise operation.

Chapter 3

Variables

So far we learned the 8088 processor has several registers like AX, BX, CX, DX, SI, DI, BP, SP and Flags. Also that these registers are read as 16-bit (word), and some as 8-bit (byte) using AH, AL, BH, BL, CH, CL, DH and DL.

That's good, but there's not enough space in the processor registers to keep info of complex tasks. In our case, a complex task is a game.

So we need to keep variables in memory. Our variables can use 8-bit, 16-bit or more. There could be a few variables or many variables. There even could exist arrangements of several variables, also known as arrays.

Why would we use an array? It could contain a game board, like one needed in Chess, Checkers, Tic-Tac-Toe or Go.

3.1 Space to keep things.

How can we tell the assembler where to put data?

So far we know that a program starts at address 0x0100 inside a *.com* file. The 8088 processor in this basic level doesn't distinguish code from data. In fact it can happily run over data doing non-sense operations.

This means we can put data almost anywhere! But we shouldn't use the area 0x0000-0x00ff because in that area is saved information from the command-line processor.

In the first chapter, we have put data inside our program in the "Hello, World" program using a label.

The advantage of using an assembler program is that if we insert or remove instructions, then it recalculates automatically the position of the label.

```
var1:          db 5      ; My variable contains 5
```

Another *nasm* directive that we can use is:

```
var1:          resb 1    ; Reserve one byte
```

But we can also use fixed positions in this way:

```
var1:          equ 0x0400    ; My variable is at address 0x0400
                             ; but I must initialize it.
```

Notice that you shouldn't put data in a position where code is going to be executed, or the processor will become crazy, and probably become stuck forever in an infinite loop.

For example, this is absolutely wrong:

```
        mov ax,[var1] ; Read var1 into AX
var1:   dw 5          ; Initialize var1 to 5
        add ax,5      ; Add 5 to AX
  ...                 ; Code continues
```

The label *var1* must be outside the executable code, after the last **int**, **jmp** or **ret** in your code.

3.2 Enhancing our library.

Before going deeper into the subject, we need to enhance our support library *library1.asm* (the one we've been adding at the end of every program). Let us call it *library2.asm* and add this subroutine at the end:

```
        ;
        ; Display the value of AX as a decimal number
        ;
display_number:
        mov dx,0            ; Makes DX = 0
        mov cx,10           ; Makes CX = 10
        div cx              ; AX = DX:AX / CX
        push dx
        cmp ax,0            ; If AX is zero...
        je display_number_1 ; ...jump
        call display_number ; else calls itself
display_number_1:
        pop ax
        add al,'0'          ; Convert remainder to ASCII digit
        call display_letter ; Display in the screen.
        ret
```

This subroutine displays the value of AX as a decimal number. It works by dividing AX by 10 using the **div** instruction, and it saves the remainder in DX and the result in AX. Before printing the remainder it checks if AX is non-zero, then calls itself and prints the remainder after returning.

For example, if AX is 5 then after the division the routine won't call itself, but display the remainder 5.

But if AX was 17, then after the division AX is 1 and the routine will call itself, displaying 1, and on return it will display the 7.

Tricky, isn't it? If you have trouble grasping the concept, assign AX a value of 42, and follow each line as if you were the processor, and annotate each instruction on a squared notebook.

When you call *display_number*, move the following lines one place at right, and when reaching **ret**, move the following lines one place at left.

Finally, notice this subroutine destroys the original value in AX.

3.3 Prime numbers.

Prime numbers are those that can only be evenly divided by 1 and themselves.

An incredibly inefficient way of generating these is using the Sieve of Eratosthenes:[3] once we get a prime number, we mark all the multiples of each prime, so these aren't taken as prime, and we continue number by number. The algorithm for this would be:

1. Start with 2.

2. Is this number marked non-prime? Go to step 5.

3. If so, show it as prime.

4. Mark all multiples as non-prime.

5. Increment current number.

6. If we haven't reached the limit, go to step 2.

Where will we mark numbers as prime? A memory area.

Let us work on this. Save this as *sieve.asm*:

```
;
; Sieve of Eratosthenes
;
    org 0x0100

table:        equ 0x8000
table_size:   equ 1000

start:
    mov bx,table
    mov cx,table_size
    mov al,0
p1:
    mov [bx],al    ; Write AL into the address pointed by BX
    inc bx         ; Increase BX
    loop p1        ; Decrease CX, jump if non-zero
```

This first part of the code will initialize the table to zero. We've put the table at an arbitrary address that doesn't collide with our code.

---

[3] It's inefficient because it requires a bit array as big as the largest prime to be generated to flag the non-prime numbers. The current largest known prime number (as of January 2019) is $2^{82,589,933} - 1$ and it would require the same number of memory bits (or half of these if we optimize for even numbers). A larger memory capacity than today's computers can handle, and probably larger that computers will be able to handle for the next 100 years!

Notice the usage of square brackets. This means to write AL at the address pointed by BX. It doesn't mean to copy AL value into register BX.

Let us continue the program:

```
      mov ax,2       ; Start at number 2
p2:   mov bx,table   ; BX = table address
      add bx,ax       ; BX = BX + AX
      cmp byte [bx],0    ; Is it prime?
      jne p3
      push ax
      call display_number
      mov al,0x2c    ; Comma
      call display_letter
      pop ax
```

This part of code starts with AX set to 2. Then it loads BX with the table address, and adds the value of AX. Then it checks if the new address contains zero (remember we initialized all the table to zero). If it isn't zero (because it has been marked) then it jumps to label *p3*, or else it calls *display_number* to show the prime number, and adds a comma to display.

Notice the **byte** indicator in **cmp.** It indicates to the assembler that we are doing a comparison of a byte (8-bit), not a word (16-bit).

Now add this to the code:

```
      mov bx,table
      add bx,ax
p4:   add bx,ax
      cmp bx,table+table_size
      jnc p3
      mov byte [bx],1
      jmp p4
```

It does the same operation as before, but adds AX to BX again because it needs the following address of memory that is a multiple. Before marking it as a multiple (and non-prime by the way), it checks that BX value doesn't exceed the table size *table+table_size* (CoMParison). The **jnc** instruction means Jump if Not Carry, meaning the left operand of **cmp** is greater than or equal to the operand value at right.

If the BX value is still inside the table limits, then we write a 1 into the memory position. Notice the square brackets. It means to write 1 at the address pointed by BX, not copying 1 to register BX.

Again we used the **byte** indicator in **mov** to warn the assembler to generate code for storing one byte (8-bit), and not a word (16-bit).

And now the final step:

```
p3:  inc ax
     cmp ax,table_size
     jne p2
     ; Add library2.asm
```

It goes to the next number using **inc ax**, and does a comparison to see if AX reaches the end of table (*table_size*), and jumps back to *p2* if it still hasn't finished. If everything goes right, now you can assemble this without any problems, and when executing it you'll have a list of prime numbers.

If something goes wrong, then you'll need to revise the source code you've entered.

As an option, you can modify the number assigned to label *table_size*, so you can see shorter or longer lists of prime numbers.

Trivia: our sieve program uses 123 bytes.

Exercise: modify the program so instead of emitting a comma to display, it emits the bytes 0x0d and 0x0a (meaning one extra call to display_letter). See what happens.

3.4 Tic-Tac-Toe.

This is the old game played by kids in school. Simple, but you need to learn how to program it, so you can build the basic foundations for board games.

We'll opt for a direct implementation:

1. Setup the initial board (3x3 squares)
2. Show the current board.

3. Check for a line and exit if one is found.

4. Wait for movement (key 1-9) and put the letter for the turn X/O

5. Go to 2

We'll do the game in steps. At any time you can add *library1.asm* at the end of the program in order to get an executable version, and see the current progress. If the text reads "add this at the end of the program," it means adding it before *library1.asm* contents.

Let us start with board initialization. Save this as *tictac.asm*:

```
;
; Tic-Tac-Toe
; by Oscar Toledo G.
; Creation date: Jun/21/2019
;
    org 0x0100

board:  equ 0x0300

start:
    mov bx,board    ; Put address of game board in BX
    mov cx,9        ; Count 9 squares
    mov al,'1'      ; Setup AL to contain 0x31 (ASCII code for 1)
b09:
    mov [bx],al     ; Save it into the square (one byte)
    inc al          ; Increase AL, this gives us next digit
    inc bx          ; Increase direction
    loop b09        ; Decrement CX, jump if non-zero
```

This initializes the game board. Internally the content for memory data will be:

Address	Data								
0x0300	0x31	0x32	0x33	0x34	0x35	0x36	0x37	0x38	0x39

Now let us continue with displaying the board. Add this call after the LOOP instruction:

```
b10:
    call show_board
    int 0x20

show_board:
    mov bx,board
    call show_row
    call show_div
    mov bx,board+3
    call show_row
    call show_div
    mov bx,board+6
    jmp show_row

show_row:
    call show_square
    mov al,0x7c
    call display_letter
    call show_square
    mov al,0x7c
    call display_letter
    call show_square
show_crlf:
    mov al,0x0d
    call display_letter
    mov al,0x0a
    jmp display_letter

show_div:
    mov al,0x2d
    call display_letter
    mov al,0x2b
    call display_letter
    mov al,0x2d
    call display_letter
    mov al,0x2b
    call display_letter
    mov al,0x2d
    call display_letter
    jmp show_crlf

show_square:
    mov al,[bx]
    inc bx
    jmp display_letter
```

Because we'll be calling the game board displaying routine twice, we make it a subroutine called *show_board*.

The subroutine *show_board* calls *show_row* to display 3 squares, then *show_div* to display a separator between lines, and repeats the calls.

The subroutine *show_row* displays square contents separated by vertical bars, and then calls *display_letter* with the special codes 0x0d and 0x0a.

The 0x0d means CR (Carriage Return), and its name comes from ancient times when the output was a physical printer, so CR made the print head to return to the start of the current row.

On the other hand 0x0a means LF (Line Feed), and it made the printer to advance one line in paper (feeding the paper). For the screen this means the cursor will jump to the following row and scroll the screen as necessary.

The game is now reading the board kept in memory and displaying its content in a readable way. If we execute now the program (of course, adding *library1.asm* at end), then we'll see the following on the screen:

```
1|2|3
-+-+-
4|5|6
-+-+-
7|8|9
```

Let us enter movements into it! Replace the **int 0x20** just below **call show_board** with this:

```
call get_movement  ; Get movement
mov byte [bx],'X'  ; Put X into square

call show_board    ; Show board

call get_movement  ; Get movement
mov byte [bx],'O'  ; Put O into square

jmp b10
```

```
get_movement:
    call read_keyboard
    cmp al,0x1b          ; Esc key pressed?
    je do_exit           ; Yes, exit
    sub al,0x31          ; Subtract code for ASCII digit 1
    jc get_movement      ; Is it less than? Wait for another key
    cmp al,0x09          ; Comparison with 9
    jnc get_movement     ; Is it greater than or equal to? Wait
    cbw                  ; Expand AL to 16 bits using AH.
    mov bx,board         ; BX points to board
    add bx,ax            ; Add the key entered
    mov al,[bx]          ; Get square content
    cmp al,0x40          ; Comparison with 0x40
    jnc get_movement     ; Is it greater than or equal to? Wait
    call show_crlf       ; Line change
    ret                  ; Return, now BX points to square

do_exit:
    int 0x20             ; Exit to command-line
```

The *get_movement* subroutine reads the keyboard, and the key pressed gets into AL register. We don't accept any key but digits 1 to 9. The ASCII codes for these digits is 0x31 to 0x39, so we subtract 0x31 from AL. If it underflows the value in AL, then the 8088 processor will set the Carry flag, or else the flag will be cleared.

So any value under 0x31 sets Carry flag, and **jc** (Jump if Carry) jumps in consequence so it expects another key. After this AL will contain 0x00 to 0x08.

The comparison with 0x09 again sets the Carry flag if AL is less than 0x09, so if Carry isn't set then the key is invalid and **jnc** (Jump if Non-Carry) is invoked.

Then we use the **cbw**[4] instruction to convert AL from a signed byte to a 16-bit word in AX, because we cannot directly add AL to BX. But we can add AX to BX so we can get the address of the square in the game board. (BX = *game_board* + AX)

_____

[4] Trivia: Stephen P. Morse, the original designer of the 8086 microprocessor, had used SEX (Sign EXtend) as mnemonic for this instruction, but Intel documentation writers changed it to CBW. https://www.pcworld.com/article/146917/article.html?page=3

Then it reads the byte at that position, and if it is less than 0x40 then it is valid (no X or O at that position), or else it returns to wait for another key.

To complete the routine, it goes to the next line on the screen.

Notice how we use **mov byte [bx],'X'** and **mov byte [bx],'O'** to put the letter inside the square of the game board. The **byte** qualifier indicates to the assembler it is writing a single byte, not a word. There's also a **word** qualifier because the assembler wouldn't admit the instruction without the qualifier as it would be ambiguous.

You can now play the game and exit it using the Esc key, but it doesn't stop once a line is done. Can we implement a line detection?

There are 8 possible lines in Tic-Tac-Toe: three horizontal lines, three vertical lines, and two diagonal lines (from corner to corner).

Our clever algorithm will read a square and compare with the other 2 squares of the line. If all three have the same value, then we have a line. Notice it doesn't take in account what is inside the square, so it can work both for the X and the O.

Let us add this at the end of the program:

```
find_line:
    ; First horizontal row
    mov al,[board]      ; X.. ... ...
    cmp al,[board+1]    ; .X. ... ...
    jne b01
    cmp al,[board+2]    ; ..X ... ...
    je won
b01:
    ; Leftmost vertical row
    cmp al,[board+3]    ; ... X.. ...
    jne b04
    cmp al,[board+6]    ; ... ... X..
    je won
b04:
    ; First diagonal
    cmp al,[board+4]    ; ... .X. ...
    jne b05
    cmp al,[board+8]    ; ... ... ..X
    je won
b05:
```

```
    ; Second horizontal row
    mov al,[board+3]    ; ... X.. ...
    cmp al,[board+4]    ; ... .X. ...
    jne b02
    cmp al,[board+5]    ; ... ..X ...
    je won
b02:
    ; Third horizontal row
    mov al,[board+6]    ; ... ... X..
    cmp al,[board+7]    ; ... ... .X.
    jne b03
    cmp al,[board+8]    ; ... ... ..X
    je won
b03:
    ; Middle vertical row
    mov al,[board+1]    ; .X. ... ...
    cmp al,[board+4]    ; ... .X. ...
    jne b06
    cmp al,[board+7]    ; ... ... .X.
    je won
b06:
    ; Rightmost vertical row
    mov al,[board+2]    ; ..X ... ...
    cmp al,[board+5]    ; ... ..X ...
    jne b07
    cmp al,[board+8]    ; ... ... ..X
    je won
b07:
    ; Second diagonal
    cmp al,[board+4]    ; ... .X. ...
    jne b08
    cmp al,[board+6]    ; ... ... X..
    je won
b08:
    ret

won:
    ; At this point AL contains the letter which made the line
    call display_letter
    mov al,0x20    ; space
    call display_letter
    mov al,0x77    ; w
    call display_letter
    mov al,0x69    ; i
    call display_letter
    mov al,0x6e    ; n
    call display_letter
    mov al,0x73    ; s
```

```
call display_letter
int 0x20
```

Notice how the first 5 lines of the subroutine *find_line* are dedicated to detect a line in the first horizontal row of the board, then the value of AL is reused to detect a line in the left vertical row of the board, and then again reused to detect a diagonal line starting in top left of the board.

For it to work, don't forget to add **call find_line** after each of the two **call show_board** lines.

You can now play a Tic-Tac-Toe game for two players, and it will stop when a line is made. A case it doesn't detect is when the board is filled (a tie), but we leave this as an exercise for you. It would be a matter of revisiting each square, and if there are no squares containing less than 0x40 (initialization digits) then the board is filled and the "Tie" message could be shown.

By the way, our Tic-Tac-Toe game is 338 bytes in size.

It could be more optimal, but we are using a basic subset of 8088 instructions so the program can be more easily understood.

Feel free to replace the character code 0x7c with 0xb3 inside *show_row*, and try the character codes 0xc4 and 0xc5 inside *show_div* to show the lines as graphical characters instead of text characters (see appendix B).

3.5 Addressing modes.

So far we've been using the **[bx]** idiom in **mov** instructions to access the address indicated by BX. In fact we could code our programs using only **mov [bx],al** and **mov al,[bx]**, but it would be inefficient because the 8088 allows more addressing modes.

The commonly available addressing modes for **mov** and all the arithmetic instructions are:

```
[BX]        [BX+d8]        [BX+d16]
[mem]       [BP+d8]        [BP+d16]
[SI]        [SI+d8]        [SI+d16]
[DI]        [DI+d8]        [DI+d16]
[BX+SI]     [BX+SI+d8]     [BX+SI+d16]
[BX+DI]     [BX+DI+d8]     [BX+DI+d16]
[BP+SI]     [BP+SI+d8]     [BP+SI+d16]
[BP+DI]     [BP+DI+d8]     [BP+DI+d16]
```

These can appear at the left operand or the right operand. When we say d8, it means an 8-bit signed displacement ranging from -128 to 127, and for d16 it means a 16-bit displacement, typically from 0 to 65535, but it can be seen also as signed, but because for the internal 16-bit addition the result is the same.

The instructions adding two registers are especially useful to save bytes, because you avoid using an **add** instruction. For example:

```
MOV BX,board   ; 3 bytes
ADD BX,SI ; 2 bytes
ADD BX,5  ; 3 bytes
MOV AL,[BX]    ; 2 bytes
     ; total = 10 bytes
```

Can be optimized as:

```
MOV BX,board   ; 3 bytes
MOV AL,[BX+SI+5]   ; 3 bytes
     ; total = 6 bytes
```

The fact that the memory addressing can be used in the other operand is useful because we can do this:

```
; ... we did operations with AL...
MOV [BX+SI+5],AL   ; Save result
```

Another example: in the Tic-Tac-Toe game, we could have replaced BX with DI (or even SI or BP):

```
start:
    mov di,board   ; Put address of game board in DI
    mov cx,9       ; Count 9 squares
    mov al,'1'     ; Setup AL to contain 0x31 (ASCII code for 1)
b09:
    mov [di],al    ; Save it into the square (one byte)
    inc al         ; Increase AL, this gives us next digit
    inc di         ; Increase direction
    loop b09       ; Decrement CX, jump if non-zero
```

There's no direct **[bp]** addressing, but if you use it the assembler will generate **[bp+0]** using a d8 displacement. This is because that code is reserved to access a position of memory directly as 16-bit. For example:

```
    mov al,[var1]
    sub al,[var2]
    mov [var3],al
```

For your programming efforts you can always take a look at the list of instructions of 8088 that accept these addressing modes in Appendix C.

3.6 Jump instructions.

Until now we have used the **jmp**, **je**, **jne**, **jc** and **jnc** instructions, but the 8088 processor offers more conditional jump instructions.

The conditional jump instructions have a limitation in the jump range of 128 bytes backward and 127 bytes ahead. But don't worry about it because *nasm* will generate an extra jump if the conditional jump goes too far.

This is the list of instructions provided by the 8088. Notice there are several mnemonics that generate the same instruction, but you can use the most appropriate one for your source code:

```
; All these are pretty useful with CMP/SUB
JE d8          ; Jump if equal
JZ d8          ; Jump if zero

JNE d8         ; Jump if not equal
JNZ d8         ; Jump if not zero

JC d8          ; Jump if Carry set (unsigned less than)
JB d8          ; Jump if unsigned less than.

JNC d8         ; Jump if Carry not set (unsigned greater equal)
JAE d8         ; Jump if unsigned greater than or equal.

JBE d8         ; Jump if unsigned less than or equal
JA d8          ; Jump if unsigned greater than

JL d8          ; Jump if signed less than
JG d8          ; Jump if signed greater than
JLE d8         ; Jump if signed less than or equal
JGE d8         ; Jump if signed greater than or equal

; These are more useful with AND/OR/XOR/TEST
JS d8          ; Jump if result is negative
JNS d8         ; Jump if result is non-negative

JPE d8         ; Jump if parity is even
JPO d8         ; Jump if parity is odd

; These are more useful with arithmetic operations
JO d8          ; Jump if overflow
JNO d8         ; Jump if non-overflow

; General use
JCXZ d8        ; Jump if CX is zero

LOOP d8        ; Decrement CX and jump if non-zero
```

Most of these instructions relate directly to comparison operators in high-level languages.

Notice the flags aren't affected by every instruction of the 8088 processor. For example, the **mov** instructions don't affect Flags (see appendix C for a full list of instructions affecting the Flags register). This means you could have a bunch of instructions between the last instruction that affected Flags and the conditional jump.

So you can do something like this:

```
    CMP AX,5         ; AX is 5?
    MOV BX,0x3333    ; Load BX with 0x3333
    JZ label         ; Jump if zero (equal)
    MOV BX,0x5555    ; Load BX with 0x5555
label:
```

It does a comparison of AX with 5 and then loads BX with 0x3333 *before* jumping. If AX wasn't 5 then it loads BX with 0x5555. Technically it's slow but it is shorter than this:

```
    CMP AX,5
    JZ label1
    MOV BX,0x5555
    JMP label2

label1:
    MOV BX,0x3333
label2:
```

It's your decision to choose the best instruction sequence for the job.

By the way, the C, JavaScript or PHP equivalent for this code would be:

```
    BX = (AX == 5) ? 0x3333 : 0x5555;
```

3.7 Instructions learned.

The instructions we learned in this chapter were:

1. **cbw**, expand 8 bit signed AL into 16-bit AX.

2. **jcxz**, jump if CX register is zero.

3. **loop**, decrement CX and jump if non-zero.

Chapter 4

All your memory belongs to us

Before we dive into direct access to the screen memory and the boot sector, we need to know about segment registers.

The 8088 is able to address 1 megabyte of memory. You can now start to laugh, because modern computers typically come with 4 gigabytes of memory, or 4096 megabytes.

All registers in the 8088 have 16-bit capacity or 64K, so how does it address 1 megabyte of memory? The answer is: segment registers.

There are four segment registers: CS, DS, ES and SS, and each one is 16-bit.

CS is the segment register for code execution. It is used each time the processor reads an instruction opcode.

DS and ES are the segment registers for data. These are used whenever an instruction reads or stores data (DS is used more than ES).

And finally, SS is the segment register for the stack pointer; the stack pointer is the place where **push**, **pop**, **call** and **ret** save its information.

All the values inside the segment registers of an 8088 processor are the base address divided by 16. If the CS register contains 0x0000, then it's reading opcodes for instructions from memory area 0x00000 to 0x0ffff. If the CS register contains 0x1000, then it's reading opcodes for instructions from memory area 0x10000 to 0x1ffff.

The DS register is used each time there is a memory access, except SS is used for addressing using the BP register.

The string instructions use ES for all access to addresses pointed by register DI.

If you need to address another segment, you can use the segment prefixes CS, DS, ES and SS before the instruction. For example:

```
CS MOV AL,[BX] ; Read from CS:BX instead of DS:BX

ES MOV [BX],AL ; Write to ES:BX instead of DS:BX

               ; Assembler generates 1 extra byte
DS MOV AL,[BX] ; Read from DS:BX (prefix is unneeded)
```

You cannot write directly to segment registers. Instead you use instructions like **mov** to segment register, **push/pop** or **lds/les**:

```
MOV AX,0xa000
MOV DS,AX          ; Copy AX into DS (also can be ES and SS)

MOV AX,0xa000
PUSH AX            ; Save AX into stack
POP DS             ; Load DS from stack (also can be ES)

LDS BX,[0x0200]    ; Read from address 0x0200 into BX.
                   ; Read from address 0x0202 into DS.

LES BX,[0x0200]    ; Read from address 0x0200 into BX
                   ; Read from address 0x0202 into ES
```

Although in 8088 you can do **pop cs**; it immediately changes the code segment and the next instruction would be read from a new place. This disrupting **pop cs** isn't supported in 80286 and higher.

So changing the segment registers (basically DS and ES) allows you to access the complete first megabyte of memory of a PC computer.

4.1 The memory map.

We need to know the memory map of the standard PC in order to do more interesting things:

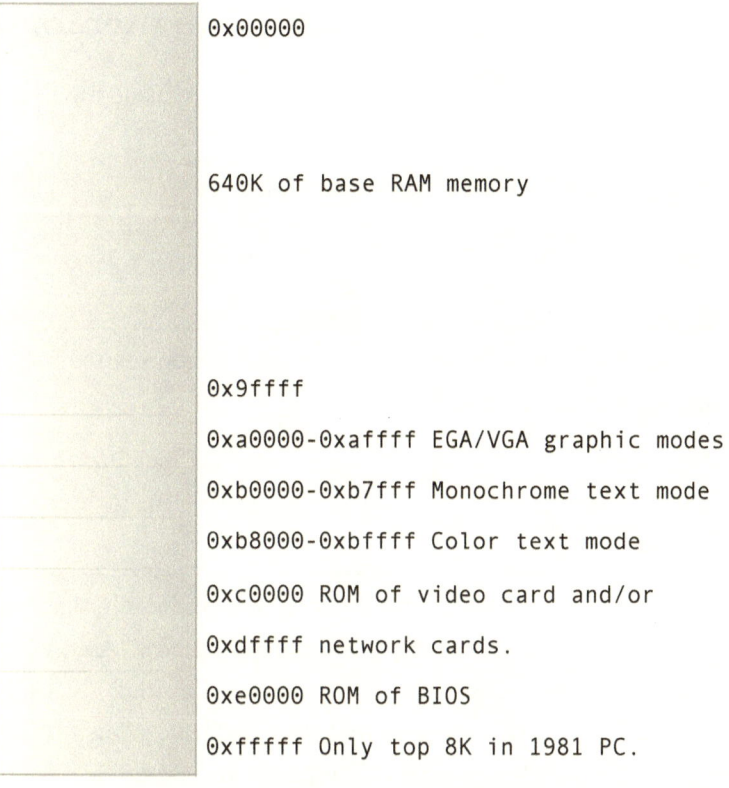

```
0x00000




640K of base RAM memory




0x9ffff

0xa0000-0xafff EGA/VGA graphic modes

0xb0000-0xb7fff Monochrome text mode

0xb8000-0xbffff Color text mode

0xc0000 ROM of video card and/or

0xdffff network cards.

0xe0000 ROM of BIOS

0xfffff Only top 8K in 1981 PC.
```

A standard thing between PC machines is that all boot into text mode. This is 80 columns by 25 rows in color mode, and the text screen is available at addresses 0xb8000 - 0xb8fff.

The first byte is the first letter in top left of the screen. It is followed by the attribute byte that contains background and foreground colors, then follows the next letter at right and it continues this way until filling 80 columns, then the next byte corresponds to 2nd line, 1st column, and it continues this way until filling 25 rows.

The IBM PC in 1981 would boot in monochrome mode (address 0xb0000) or color mode (address 0xb8000), depending on the card that you were able to buy, but this has been forgotten for many years now. In fact some pretty old games wrote a byte at 0xb8000, and read it back to see if there was memory in order to work in color or monochrome mode.

4.2 Direct access to text-mode memory.

In order to directly access the screen memory (not using the BIOS services), we must set the current video mode.

For a standard text mode we can use:

```
MOV AX,0x0002      ; AH = 0x00 Set mode, AL = 0x02 80x25x16 text
INT 0x10
```

In this mode the screen is available at address 0xb8000. You can easily access it using:

```
MOV AX,0xB800
MOV DS,AX
MOV ES,AX
```

Notice that now you cannot access the variables in the same segment of code as we were doing in the example programs. Anyway, in order to save space, we won't be switching values on DS and ES; we'll stay with fixed values. Although if you were working in a program with its own data segment, then in selected parts of your code you would do this:

```
PUSH DS            ; Save current data segment
MOV AX,0xB800
MOV DS,AX
… Your subroutine …
POP DS             ; Restore data segment to previous one
```

The organization of the screen memory is as follows:

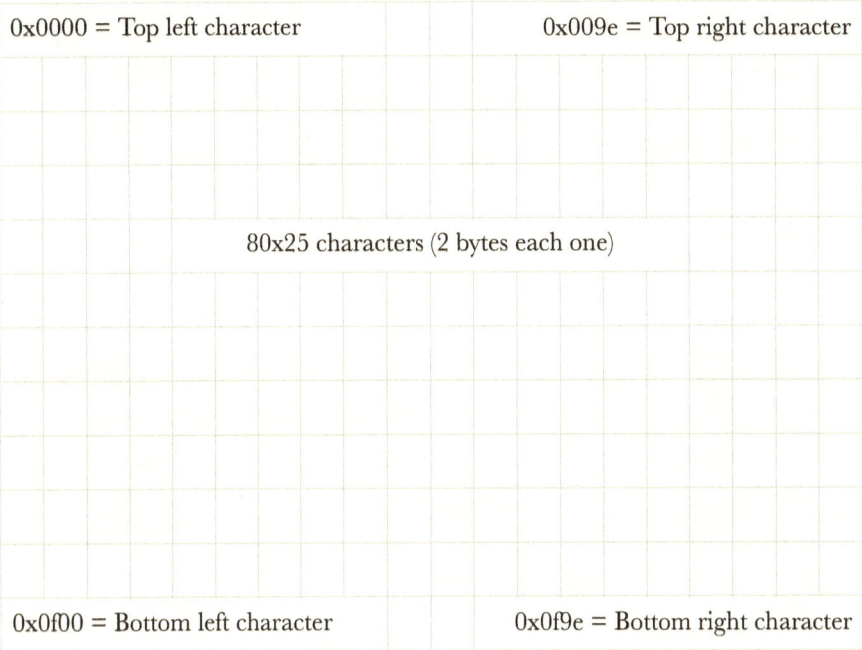

0x0000 = Top left character   0x009e = Top right character

80x25 characters (2 bytes each one)

0x0f00 = Bottom left character   0x0f9e = Bottom right character

Each character is represented by two bytes. The first byte is the ASCII code for the letter (also PC-850 if you just have booted from BIOS, or a code page selected by MS-DOS if you are inside MS-DOS). The second byte has this format:

7	6	5	4	3	2	1	0
Background color				Foreground color			

And the available colors are:

0 = Black	8 = Gray
1 = Blue	9 = Light blue
2 = Green	A = Light green
3 = Aqua	B = Light aqua
4 = Red	C = Light red
5 = Purple	D = Light purple
6 = Yellow	E = Light yellow
7 = White	F = Bright white

Let us make an example with this. You can call this *hello.asm*:

```
ORG 0x0100

MOV AX,0x0002
INT 0x10
MOV AX,0xB800
MOV DS,AX
MOV ES,AX
CLD
XOR DI,DI
MOV AX,0x1a48
STOSW
MOV AX,0x1b45
STOSW
MOV AX,0x1c4c
STOSW
MOV AX,0x1d4c
STOSW
MOV AX,0x1e4f
STOSW
INT 0x20
```

We introduced a pair of new instructions: **cld** and **stosw**. The instruction **cld** clears the "direction" flag. It signals for some advanced instructions to increase or decrease the SI and/or DI registers.

The instruction **stosw** writes the value of AX at the address ES:DI, and increments DI by 2 (the size of a word). Notice that it would decrement DI by 2 if the direction flag is set (could be done with instruction **sed**). Because of that we used **cld** at start, as we don't know the initial state of the D flag (Direction).

Each time we load AX, AL contains the letter to be put on the screen (one letter of HELLO), and AH contains the color for the letter (blue background and a different color for each letter).

When writing a word to memory, the low byte is always written first (in this case the AL value) and the high byte is written in the following byte (the AH value).

So the screen memory contents after writing all the text is:

0x0000		0x48	0x1a	0x45	0x1b	0x4c	0x1c	0x4c	0x1d	0x4f	0x1e

Now you are able to draw text screens with color, and also use some of the predefined graphics available inside the BIOS.

As a side note, there exists the **stosb** instruction that writes the value of AX at the address ES:DI and increments DI by 1 (or decrements if the flag D is 1).

4.3 Pseudo-graphics in text mode.

Let us do some pseudo-graphics in the basic text mode of 80 columns by 25 rows and 16 colors for foreground and background.

First the steps required to initialize the video mode are done. Name this file as *circles.asm*:

```
        ;
        ; Colorful circles
        ; by Oscar Toledo G.
        ; Creation date: Jun/21/2019.
        ;
        org 0x0100

        mov ax,0x0002    ; Setup text 80x25 mode color
        int 0x10         ; Call BIOS

        mov ax,0xb800    ; Segment for video data
        mov ds,ax        ; ...load into DS
        mov es,ax        ; ...load into ES
```

Now it waits for the internal clock of the PC:

```
        ;
        ; Main loop
        ;
main_loop:
        mov ah,0x00      ; Service to read clock
        int 0x1a         ; Call BIOS
        mov al,dl        ;
        test al,0x40     ; Bit 6 is 1?
        je m2            ; No, jump
```

```
            not al              ; Complement bits for reverse effect
m2:
            and al,0x3f         ; Separate lower 6 bits
            sub al,0x20         ; Make it -32 to +31
            cbw                 ; Extend to word
            mov cx,ax           ; Save in CX
```

The internal service 0x1a of BIOS is dedicated to time and clock. In this case the service 0x00 (loaded into AH) reads the number of ticks counted since the system booted up as a 32-bit number into CX:DX.

Since we need a number increasing from 0x00 to 0x3f and then going back to 0x00, it checks bit 6 (0x40) and reverses the bits for getting the reverse count.

Then **and al,0x3f** separates the lower 6 bits, and a subtraction makes it a signed 8-bit value in the range -32 to +31, which then is extended to a word into CX.

```
            mov di,0x0000       ; Point to the screen
            mov dh,0            ; Row
m0:         mov dl,0            ; Column
m1:         push dx             ; Save DX (DH and DL)
            mov bx,sin_table

            mov al,dh           ; Take the row
            shl al,1            ; Multiply by 2 (because aspect ratio)
            and al,0x3f         ; Limit to 0-63
            cs xlat             ; Extract sin value
            cbw                 ; Extend to 16 bits
            push ax             ; Save in stack

            mov al,dl           ; Take the column
            and al,0x3f         ; Limit to 0-63
            cs xlat             ; Extract sin value
            cbw                 ; Extend to 16 bits
            pop dx
            add ax,dx           ; Add with previous sin
            add ax,cx           ; Add with clock time
            mov ah,al           ; Use as color background/foreground
            mov al,0x2a         ; Use asterisk as letter
            mov [di],ax         ; Put in display (word)
            add di,2            ; Go to next letter (word)
```

Here the DI register is initialized to point at the start of the screen, while DH and DL contains the row and column number. Then BX is initialized to contain the address of a sine table.

Then it takes the row from DH, multiplies by 2 (because of the aspect ratio of the screen; it's only 25 rows and there are 80 columns) and uses **xlat**.

The instruction **xlat** mnemonic means TRANSLATE. It adds internally the AL value to BX, and reads the byte pointed by the result into AL. It doesn't alter BX.

So technically **xlat** is something like a fictitious **mov al,[bx+al]**.

But we have used the prefix CS. This is an extra instruction that commands the 8088 to use the code segment as the segment for reading the data. Without it, **xlat** reads from DS segment that points to the screen, instead of the CS segment where our sine table is contained.

The read value is saved on the stack (the **push ax** instruction).

Then it takes the column from DL and does the same operation, so we now have two sine values. It restores the saved value from the previous operation into DX (the **pop dx** instruction).

It adds the two sine values, including the current clock time value, and uses the low byte as the color for the screen (background+foreground), while using an asterisk.

The resulting value is displayed on the screen with **mov [di],ax** and increases DI by 2 to go to next letter. (Remember each letter is a word, 16-bit or 2 bytes).

Finally, the last step of the program:

```
pop dx          ; Restore DX
inc dl          ; Increment column
cmp dl,80       ; Reached 80 columns?
jne m1          ; No, jump

inc dh          ; Increment row
cmp dh,25       ; Reached 25 rows?
jne m0          ; No, jump
```

```
        mov ah,0x01      ; BIOS service. Get keyboard state
        int 0x16         ; Call BIOS
        jne key_pressed  ; Jump if key pressed.
        jmp main_loop    ; Repeat

key_pressed:
        int 0x20         ; Exit to command-line


        ;
        ; Sin table of 360 degrees in 64 bytes
        ; Also -1.0 is -64 and +1.0 is 64
        ;
sin_table:
    db 0,6,12,19,24,30,36,41
    db 45,49,53,56,59,61,63,64
    db 64,64,63,61,59,56,53,49
    db 45,41,36,30,24,19,12,6
    db 0,-6,-12,-19,-24,-30,-36,-41
    db -45,-49,-53,-56,-59,-61,-63,-64
    db -64,-64,-63,-61,-59,-56,-53,-49
    db -45,-41,-36,-30,-24,-19,-12,-6
```

It restores the DX value from the stack, because it contains the row and column counters. Then it increases DL and if it isn't 80 (the number of columns), then it repeats the cycle, or else it increases DH and if it isn't 25 (the number of rows) then it repeats the cycle (notice it jumps to label *m0* in order to set DL to zero).

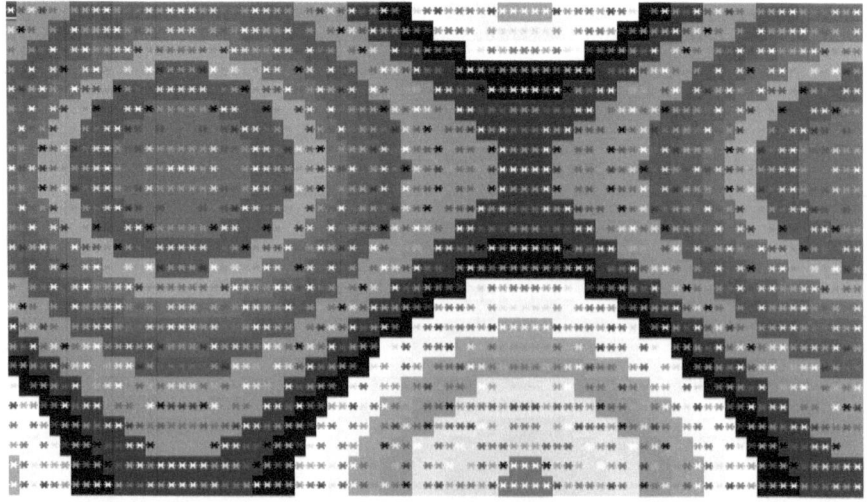

Finally, the loop repeats waiting for the next clock cycle of PC. This means the circles will appear to grow and shrink.

Notice *sin_table*. This is the table from where the values used by the program are taken.

Also the program will exit to the command-line if any key is pressed.

4.4 Boot sector.

When the original IBM PC is reset, the 8088 processor is directed to jump to FFFF:0000 (CS:IP, CS is Code Segment and IP is Instruction Pointer), or the address 0xffff0, from where it starts executing instructions.

Typically the first instruction inside a BIOS ROM (Basic Input/Output System, Read Only Memory) is a **jmp far** instruction to another place inside the BIOS.

The **jmp far** instruction looks like:

```
EA dd cc bb aa     JMP FAR aabb:ccdd
```

It sets the CS and IP registers at the same time. This is needed because the last 16 bytes of ROM memory aren't enough to contain a meaningful program.

Notice that in *nasm* the **jmp far** instruction needs to be only entered as **jmp**.

The BIOS does a revision and a check list of all the basic items in the PC motherboard, like memory, ports, timers and counters, floppy disk, and so on. In fact, in some PCs, there was a beep code so you could know where the problem was. Or if the screen was working, it would show an error code.

The final step of the BIOS is to try to boot from floppy disk, reading the first sector (512 bytes) of the floppy disk inside the RAM at address 0x07c00, checking whether the last two bytes of the sector (at 0x07dfe) are 0x55 and 0xaa, and then doing a **jmp far** 0000:7c00, which essentially sets the CS register to 0 and the instruction pointer to 0x7c00. Most BIOS are like this.

But afterwards there would come BIOS that would include things like **jmp far** 07c0:0000, so you cannot trust the value in CS register.

Let us re-translate our first example program from chapter 1 into something that can be used inside a boot sector.

Now, this won't be a *.com* file. It would crash the computer if you attempt to run it. You should name the source code as *boot.asm* and the output file as *boot.img* for easy reference (I tend to always use the *img* extension for peace of mind).

```
      org 0x7c00
start:
      push cs        ; Assumes CS contains 0x0000
      pop ds
      mov bx,string
repeat:
      mov al,[bx]
      test al,al
      je end
      push bx
      mov ah,0x0e
      mov bx,0x000f
      int 0x10
      pop bx
      inc bx
      jmp repeat

end:
      jmp $          ; Jump over itself ($ gives current address)

string:
      db "Hello, world",0

      times 510-($-$$) db 0  ; Fills boot sector (510 bytes)

      db 0x55,0xaa  ; Signature so BIOS detects it as bootable.
```

We did several things in order to translate it into a bootable sector:

1. Change the **org** directive to point to 0x7c00.

2. Load the DS register so the string can be accessed.

3. Change the **int 0x20** instruction to **jmp $** (infinite loop because the instruction jumps over itself)

4. Fill the program to 510 bytes using **times 510-($-$$) db 0**

5. Add the bootable signature with **db 0x55,0xaa**

5 ¼" and 3 ½" floppy disks.

We now have several options for assembling it:

1. Writing it to the boot sector of a real floppy disk.[5] This means that you have a floppy disk drive installed in your computer (probably of the 3 ½" variety, although Windows 98 still supports 5 ¼" ones, but don't forget to put the write protection tab because Windows has the bad taste of rewriting the boot sector or recommending a full format of the disk if it doesn't

---

[5] The first floppy disk for IBM PC had the size 5 ¼" and could keep the amazing quantity of 180K bytes (single density), and then it became double density for 360K bytes. There also appeared 3 ½" floppy disks with 720K bytes, and later a mixture of 5 ¼" at 1.2 MB and 3 ½" at 1.44 MB. There even appeared briefly a 2" floppy disk with a capacity of 2.88 MB but it never grew popular.

recognize the boot sector as standard). I recommend using *Rawrite32* for Windows.[6] Or Linux command-line: `sudo dd if=boot.img of=/dev/fd0 count=1 bs=512`

2. Creating a file filled with zeroes of length 1474560 (1.44 MB), put `boot.img` at the start of the file and record an empty CD with El Torito specification.[7] For Windows, Nero and EasyCD support the option for creating a bootable CD. For Linux see: `https://www.tldp.org/HOWTO/Bootdisk-HOWTO/cd-roms.html`

3. Writing it to the boot sector of a USB memory, same as step 1 but replacing target device with the USB drive (Windows) or the device file (Linux). But beware that you will destroy the important partition information of the USB memory, so you need a means to read the boot sector and save it so you can reuse the USB memory later. Saving the boot record with Linux would be (don't forget to replace */dev/fd0* with the correct one for the USB memory): `dd if=/dev/fd0 of=saved.img count=1 bs=512`

4. Feeding an emulator or virtual machine with the *boot.img* file as bootable disk. *VirtualBox* allows you to set up a floppy disk drive with a file as the image (applies for Windows, Mac OS X and Linux). While *qemu* can be run from the Linux command line: `qemu-system-x86_64 -fda boot.img`

Intel plans to remove altogether the support for boot sector by 2020, but this still means every PC manufactured before that year continues to support boot sectors the same way since 1981.

---

[6] https://www.netbsd.org/~martin/rawrite32/

[7] As CD-ROM was created and standardized, it came up El Torito specification in 1995. It made it possible to embed a 1.44 MB. boot image inside a CD-ROM.

4.5 Instructions learned.

The instructions we learned in this chapter were:

1. **cld**, clear direction flag.

2. **lds**, load register and DS register.

3. **les**, load register and ES register.

4. **sed**, set direction flag.

5. **stosb**, store AL into ES:DI address. Increase DI by 1 (if direction flag is zero) or decrease DI by 1 (if direction flag is zero).

6. **stosw**, store AX into ES:DI address. Increase DI by 2 (if direction flag is zero) or decrease DI by 2 (if direction flag is one).

Chapter 5

Advanced instructions

What we do with the 8088 instruction set is build *super-instructions*. These super-instructions are typically called subroutines. The instruction **call** is in reality our way to these blocks of instructions that do the required work.

Before the compilers were widely distributed, it was considered that processors should have "big" instructions that would do the "big" work the "fastest" way.

The 8088 includes instructions for handling blocks of data, like copying one block of data to another place. Also the adding, subtraction and multiplication instructions can be put together to work for bigger numbers.

5.1 Reading memory.

Typically we have been using **BX** as an example for reading memory in this way:

```
MOV BX,address
MOV AL,[BX]
INC BX
```

But we could made it this way:

```
MOV SI,address
LODSB
```

The instruction **lodsb** tells the 8088 to load a byte from the address pointed by DS:SI and store it into AL, then increment SI by 1 (if D flag is zero; see section 4.2).

There also exists the instruction **lodsw**, that loads from DS:SI address into register AX, then increments SI by 2.

5.2 Copying memory.

Given the existence of **lodsb/lodsw** and its counterpart **stosb/stosw** (see section 4.2), we could write a subroutine to copy memory:

```
    MOV SI,source_address
    MOV DI,target_address
    MOV CX,byte_count
label:
    LODSB          ; 1 byte
    STOSB          ; 1 byte
    LOOP label     ; 2 bytes
```

The inner loop uses 4 bytes. But the 8088 has the instructions **movsb** and **movsw** that do exactly the same operation but without modifying the register AL or AX.

```
    MOV SI,source_address              ʹ
    MOV DI,target_address
    MOV CX,byte_count
label:
    MOVSB          ; 1 byte
    LOOP label     ; 2 bytes
```

Now the inner loop uses 3 bytes, but even better, there is an instruction for doing the repeat without using the instruction **loop**:

```
    MOV SI,source_address
    MOV DI,target_address
    MOV CX,byte_count
    REP MOVSB      ; 2 bytes
```

Notice that **movsb** does the combined operations of **lodsb/stosb**. There also exists **movsw** to do a combined **lodsw/stosw**, but without using AL or AX, and it remains unaffected.

5.3 Comparison with strings.

The 8088 also provides instructions to do comparison of strings (**cmps**) and comparison of AX or AL (**scas**).

These instructions affect the flags, so you can use the conditional jump instructions to handle the conditions.

The instruction **cmpsb** does the comparison of the byte pointed by DS:SI against the byte pointed by ES:DI, then increments both DI and SI by 1 (or decrements if the D flag is set).

The instruction **cmpsw** does the same thing but using word comparison and increments/decrements by 2.

Notice that both instructions don't need AL or AX and it remains unaffected.

The instruction **scasb** does the comparison of AL against the byte pointed by ES:DI, then increments DI by 1 (or decrements by one per the D flag).

The instruction **scasw** does the same thing but using AX and increments/decrements by 2.

All four instructions can be combined with the **repe/repne** prefix, that means to repeat the instruction while the condition is met (E = Equal, NE = Not Equal).

5.4 Arithmetic with 32-bit.

So far we know that the register size of the 8088 processor is 16-bit, but we can use these registers to do arithmetic with 32-bit or even more.

The processor already includes the **mul** instruction that does multiplication of AX by 16-bit register and puts the result into DX:AX.

There is also the **div** instruction that does a division of DX:AX by 16-bit register and puts the result into AX and the remainder in DX.

With these examples from the processor itself, it is logical to preserve a 32-bit number into DX:AX (DX being the high word and AX being the lower word).

A secondary 32-bit number could be kept into CX:BX.

Then, we could use the **adc** and **sbb** instructions of 8088 to create 32-bit arithmetic:

```
; Add two 32-bit numbers DX:AX = DX:AX + CX:BX
ADD AX,BX
ADC DX,CX
```

It works because the **add** instruction affects the Carry flag to indicate if we should "carry" one to next operation.

The **adc** instruction does the operation DX = DX+CX+Carry. So it includes the Carry flag into the operation as one extra digit.

```
; Subtract two 32-bit numbers DX:AX = DX:AX - CX:BX
SUB AX,BX
SBB DX,CX
```

Here it works the same, because the **sub** instruction affects the Carry flag to indicate if we should "borrow" one to next operation.

The **sbb** instruction does the operation DX = DX - CX - Carry. So it includes the Carry flag into the operation as an extra digit to subtract.

If we need the logical **not** operation (one's complement), it would be:

```
NOT AX
NOT DX
```

While the **neg** instruction (two's complement) would be almost the same except for the addition of one:

```
        NOT AX
        NOT DX
        ADD AX,1
        ADC DX,0
```

There exists a single instruction to convert a signed 16-bit number inside register AX to a 32-bit number into DX:AX.

```
        CWD         ; Signed 16-bit AX expanded into DX:AX
```

The multiplication instructions are more tricky, but it depends on the things we learned in basic school:

```
              15    multiplicand
        x     29    multiplier
        _____
             135    result of 15x9
              30    result of 15x2 (shifted left one place)
        _____
             435    result
```

We replace each of the digits of the multiplicand and multiplier with a multiplication. This means we need to do 4 multiplications to create a full result. We can see each digit as a byte, or a word. Given the 8088 processor has a 16-bit multiplication instruction, it is a better resource usage to approach it using the 16-bit **mul**.

The routine to do a 32x32 bit multiplication is as follows:

```
        mov [v_s1],ax     ; Save multiplicand (S1)
        mov [v_s1+2],dx

                          ; In this diagram each point and letter
                          ; is a word.
                          ;    . = not calculated
                          ;  · + = calculated
                          ;    A = AX value
                          ;    B = multiplier
                          ;    C = step's result
                          ; rightmost column of result goes into v_s2
                          ; next to last goes into v_s2+2
```

```
                        ; next into v_s2+4

                        ;          .A
                        ;        x .B
                        ;        ----
                        ;          .C
                        ;          ..

    mul bx              ; S1:low * BX = DX:AX
    mov [v_s2],ax       ; Save provisional result.
    mov [v_s2+2],dx

                        ;          A.
                        ;        x B.
                        ;        ----
                        ;          .+
                        ;          C.

    mov ax,[v_s1+2]     ; S1:high * CX = DX:AX
    mul cx
    mov [v_s2+4],ax     ; Save next word of result.
                        ; Notice it doesn't need DX.

                        ;          A.
                        ;        x .B
                        ;        ----
                        ;          C+
                        ;          +.

    mov ax,[v_s1+2]     ; S1:high * BX = DX:AX
    mul bx
    add [v_s2+2],ax     ; Adds to previous result.
    adc [v_s2+4],dx

                        ;          .A
                        ;        x B.
                        ;        ----
                        ;          ++
                        ;          +C

    mov ax,[v_s1]       ; S1:low * CX = DX:AX
    mul cx
    add [v_s2+2],ax     ; Adds to previous result.
    adc [v_s2+4],dx
                        ; The result is in [v_s2+2]:[v_s2]
```

It looks a little complicated, but it's easier if you see that the process is divided into 4 steps, one step for each 16-bit word.

When moving to a 32-bit processor like the 80386, this exact same routine using the 32-bit instructions multiplies 32-bit x 32-bit and generates a 64-bit result.

5.5 Graphics video mode.

Let us see a practical result of these operations doing a graphical program.

So far we only have used the text mode (80 columns by 25 rows) but now we will use the VGA graphics mode of 320x200 pixels and 256 colors.

Let us recall that the basic IBM PC only had a monochrome text adapter with optional CGA adapter (320x200 pixels and 4 colors or 640x200 pixels monochrome).

Later in early 1985 appeared the EGA adapter (adding 320x200 with 16 colors, 640x200 in 16 colors and 640x350 in 16 colors).

The VGA graphic adapter appeared in early 1988 for high-end IBM machines, adding support for 640x480 in 16 colors and 320x200 in 256 colors.

The use of the screen color in 16 colors modes is complicated and not within the reach of this tutorial, but the 320x200x256 mode is easy to use because the graphic screen is planar. What does that mean? It means that every pixel is represented by a single byte in memory, so 320x200 means we have 64000 bytes to represent the screen.

The written value for each byte is passed through a "palette" chip that's programmed on mode setup to a default set of colors using 18-bit colors (6 bits for red, 6 bits for green and 6 bits for blue). So it is common to call 320x200x256 a "palletized" mode.

Also because of the VGA standard we can be sure that the memory screen is located at 0xa0000-0xaffff. This is easy to access loading DS and ES registers with 0xa000.

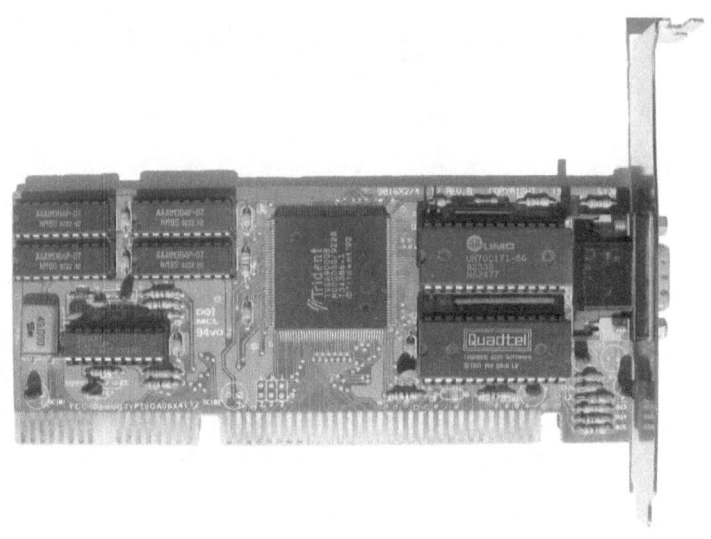

Trident VGA card with 16-bit ISA interface (Industry Standard Architecture), circa 1992. This card is also compatible with ISA 8-bit slots used by original PC and PC XT. Public domain picture by George Shuklin.

The following programs can be run on an original IBM PC, but you'll need to get a VGA video card with support for 8-bit ISA connector. Remember the original IBM PC didn't have the video on board.

Let us see the default palette that the VGA BIOS provides:

```
        ;
        ; Show the VGA palette
        ; by Oscar Toledo G.
        ; Creation date: Jun/27/2019.
        ;

        cpu 8086

        org 0x0100

        ;
        ; Memory screen uses 64000 pixels,
        ; this means 0xfa00 is the first byte of
        ; memory not visible on the screen.
        ;
v_a:    equ 0xfa00
v_b:    equ 0xfa02
```

```
start:
        mov ax,0x0013    ; Set mode 320x200x256
        int 0x10         ; Video interruption vector

        mov ax,0xa000    ; 0xa000 video segment
        mov ds,ax        ; Setup data segment
        mov es,ax        ; Setup extended segment

m4:
        mov ax,127       ; 127 as row
        mov [v_a],ax     ; Save into v_a
m0:     mov ax,127       ; 127 as column
        mov [v_b],ax     ; Save into v_b
```

This first part of the source code sets up the video mode, the segment registers, and the two variables we are using to keep the current pixel position over the screen.

```
m1:
        mov ax,[v_a]     ; Get Y-coordinate
        mov dx,320       ; Multiply by 320 (size of pixel row)
        mul dx
        add ax,[v_b]     ; Add X-coordinate to result
        xchg ax,di       ; Pass AX to DI
```

Now it reads the Y-coordinate, multiplies it by 320 (the size of a pixel row), and then adds the X-coordinate. So it now addresses the current pixel over the screen (0-63999 or 0x0000-0xf9ff).

```
┌──┬──────────────────────────────────────────────────────────┬──┐
│  │ top-left pixel at 0x0000          top-right pixel at 0x013f│  │
│  ├──────────────────────────────────────────────────────────┘  │
│  │ 2nd row left pixel at 0x0140                                 │
│  │                                                              │
│  │                                                              │
│  │                                                              │
│  │                  320x200 pixels 256 colors.                  │
│  │                  Video segment 0xa000                        │
│  │        The value of each byte maps to a color on the screen  │
│  │                                                              │
│  │                                                              │
│  ├──────────────────────────────────────────────────────────┐  │
│  │ bottom-left pixel at 0xf8c0     bottom-right pixel at 0xf9ff│  │
└──┴──────────────────────────────────────────────────────────┴──┘
```

It uses the instruction **xchg** to interchange AX and DI, but we forget about the DI value and only intend to put AX into DI. Notice this saves one byte in comparison to **mov di,ax** that uses 2 bytes. It always saves one byte when one of the operands is AX and the other is a 16-bit register.

```
        mov ax,[v_a]      ; Get current Y-coordinate
        and ax,0x78       ; Separate 4 bits = 16 rows
        add ax,ax         ; Value between 0x00 and 0xf0

        mov bx,[v_b]      ; Get current X-coordinate
        and bx,0x78       ; Separate 4 bits = 16 columns
        mov cl,3          ; Shift right by 3 places
        shr bx,cl
        add ax,bx         ; Combine with previous value
        stosb             ; Write AL into address pointed by DI
```

Now it takes the current Y-coordinate, and the two instructions **and** and **add** have the same effect as doing division by 8 and multiplication by 16, in order to have a palette index in steps of 16. The value stays in AX register.

66

Then using the BX register it gets the current X-coordinate and does a division by 8 to get a value between 0-15, and adds it to AX.

This means that as the program walks through the screen it will generate the index values 0-255, then it writes the byte onto the screen using **stosb**.

```
dec word [v_b]    ; Decrease column
jns m1            ; Is it negative? No, jump

dec word [v_a]    ; Decrease row
jns m0            ; Is it negative? No, jump

mov ah,0x00       ; Wait for a key
int 0x16          ; Keyboard interruption vector.

mov ax,0x0002     ; Set mode 80x25 text.
int 0x10          ; Video interruption vector.

int 0x20          ; Exit to command-line.
```

This is the last step, decreasing the coordinates to advance over the screen. Instead of increasing them and doing comparison with a value, we decrease them and jump if still positive.

After displaying the palette over the screen, now it waits for a key press, in order to restore to text-mode and return to command-line.

This program is very useful to choose a color even if it doesn't have numbers or letters alongside. Because if you want to use a single color, then you must count from top to bottom in hexadecimal starting from zero until the desired row; that's the left digit. Then you count from left to right in hexadecimal starting from zero, and that's the right digit.

The top-left corner black color is pixel value 0x00, while the top-right corner white color is pixel value 0x0f. The whole row of gray scale pixel values goes from 0x10 to 0x1f. And the rainbow colors start at 0x20.

5.6 Mandelbrot set.

Benoît Mandelbrot was a French Mathematician that discovered the Mandelbrot set in 1980 while working at IBM's Thomas J. Watson Research Center. But it wasn't his only discovery; he coined the word "fractal" and made many other important mathematical discoveries.

The Mandelbrot set itself is a fractal, a kind of mathematical equation that when "zoomed" repeats itself.

When preparing the Mandelbrot program for this book (yes, I wanted you to learn to do something beautiful) I was very worried that there wouldn't be enough precision in integer arithmetic, but fortunately I was able to complete it fully.

Essentially the pseudo-algorithm sequence is:

```
x = 0
y = 0
Repeat while iteration < 100 and x²+y² < 4
    t = x² - y² + ix
    y = 2xy + iy
    x = t
    iteration = iteration + 1
```

Or in C language:

```
/* ix and iy are fractions for offset and zoom */
iteration = 0;
x = 0.0;
y = 0.0;
while (iteration < 100 && x * x + y * y < 4.0) {
    t = x * x - y * y + ix;
    y = 2 * x * y + iy;
    x = t;
    iteration++;
}
/* Now use 'iteration' variable as color */
```

We will translate this now into assembler code to use it. We need to be aware of the following things:

1. The x and y variables are saved as 32-bit integers, *with* 8-bit fraction. So 1.0 is saved internally as 0x00000100 (256 decimal).

2. The multiplication of two fractional numbers doubles the number of bits of fraction, so the result must be divided by 256. For example, 0x0100 x 0x0100 = 0x010000, and after division by 256 the result appears correctly as 0x0100. (1.0 x 1.0 = 1.0)

Let us see the assembler source code for displaying a Mandelbrot set:

```
;
; Draw a Mandelbrot set
; by Oscar Toledo G.
; Creation date: Jun/24/2019.
;

cpu 8086        ; NASM warns us of non-8086 instructions

org 0x0100      ; Start of code

;
; Working in VGA 320x200x256 colors
;
; 0xfa00 is the first byte of video memory
; not visible on the screen.
```

```
          ;
v_a:      equ 0xfa00      ; Y-coordinate
v_b:      equ 0xfa02      ; X-coordinate
v_x:      equ 0xfa04      ; x 32-bit for Mandelbrot 24.8 fraction
v_y:      equ 0xfa08      ; y 32-bit for Mandelbrot 24.8 fraction
v_s1:     equ 0xfa0c      ; temporal s1
v_s2:     equ 0xfa10      ; temporal s2 (48-bit or 6 bytes)

start:
          mov ax,0x0013   ; Set mode 320x200x256
          int 0x10        ; Video interruption vector

          mov ax,0xa000   ; 0xa000 video segment
          mov ds,ax       ; Setup data segment
          mov es,ax       ; Setup extended segment

m4:
          mov ax,199      ; 199 is the bottommost row
          mov [v_a],ax    ; Save into v_a
m0:       mov ax,319      ; 319 is the rightmost column
          mov [v_b],ax    ; Save into v_b
```

We are using a new directive of *nasm*. The **cpu** directive allows us to be sure that we will be using only instructions that exist in the 8086 processor (and its cousin, the 8088).

We setup the addresses for the variables. Notice the v_x and v_y variables are setup in addresses separated by 4, because these occupy 4 bytes.

The temporary variable v_s2 occupies 6 bytes due to the large result of 32-bit x 32-bit multiplication.

The program starts by setting the graphics mode 320x200x256 colors, then loads the segment registers to point to the screen data.

Again like the palette program, it starts drawing at the bottom right pixel of the screen. The x,y coordinates are 319,199, and named *a* and *b*. Don't confuse this with the *x* and *y* values used internally by Mandelbrot mathematics.

Now the first step of the algorithm, setup *x* and *y*, and the iteration counter:

```
m1:      xor ax,ax
         mov [v_x],ax    ; x = 0.0
         mov [v_x+2],ax
         mov [v_y],ax    ; y = 0.0
         mov [v_y+2],ax
         mov cx,0        ; Iteration counter
```

Notice how the variables *v_x* and *v_y* are setup using two **mov** each, because both are 32-bit.

Now it tests for the exit condition:

```
m2:      push cx         ; Save counter
         mov ax,[v_x]    ; Read x
         mov dx,[v_x+2]
         call square32   ; Get x² (x * x)
         push dx         ; Save result to stack
         push ax
         mov ax,[v_y]    ; Read y
         mov dx,[v_y+2]
         call square32   ; Get y² (y * y)

         pop bx
         add ax,bx       ; Add both (x² + y²)
         pop bx
         adc dx,bx

         pop cx          ; Restore counter
         cmp dx,0        ; Result is >= 4.0 ?
         jne m3
         cmp ax,4*256
         jnc m3          ; Yes, jump
```

We didn't talk before about stack ordering. Now it's time. The **push** instruction saves the data into the stack as adding a dish to the top of a pile, and the **pop** instruction restores the data from the stack as taking the first dish from the top of a pile.

This stack setup is known as LIFO (Last in - First out).

The effect in our program is that we save DX and AX (the result of x^2) and then the first **pop bx** get us the old value of AX into BX, and the

71

second **pop bx** get us the old value of DX into BX, in the right order to do a 32-bit addition.

Finally we do a comparison with 4.0, but if DX is non-zero we know already it is bigger than 4.0 so it jumps. Only if DX is zero does it proceed to do a comparison of AX with 4.0 (4 multiplied by 256).

Next step is the inner loop of the Mandelbrot set:

```
push cx
mov ax,[v_y]      ; Read y
mov dx,[v_y+2]
call square32     ; Get y² (y * y)
push dx
push ax
mov ax,[v_x]      ; Read x
mov dx,[v_x+2]
call square32     ; Get x² (x * x)

pop bx
sub ax,bx         ; Subtract (x² - y²)
pop bx
sbb dx,bx

;
; Adding x coordinate like a fraction
; to current value.
;
add ax,[v_b]      ; Add x coordinate
adc dx,0
add ax,[v_b]      ; Add x coordinate
adc dx,0
sub ax,480        ; Center coordinate
sbb dx,0

push ax           ; Save result to stack
push dx
```

Now it does the operation $x^2 - y^2 + ix$.

Again it does the same trick with the stack because we don't have enough registers to contain the intermediate values, and adds the current screen X coordinate, so it displaces over the Mandelbrot set plus an adjustment of -480 to center it properly. Notice how it adds v_b to a 32-bit value, but as it is 16-bit, it then does **adc dx,0** to complete the operation.

The same is done with the constant 480.

Now the second mathematical operation $y = 2xy + iy$:

```
        mov ax,[v_x]      ; Get x
        mov dx,[v_x+2]
        mov bx,[v_y]      ; Get y
        mov cx,[v_y+2]
        call mul32        ; Multiply (x * y)

        shl ax,1          ; Multiply by 2
        rcl dx,1

        add ax,[v_a]      ; Add y coordinate
        adc dx,0
        add ax,[v_a]      ; Add y coordinate
        adc dx,0
        sub ax,250        ; Center coordinate
        sbb dx,0

        mov [v_y],ax      ; Save as new y value
        mov [v_y+2],dx
```

Notice a new operation formed by **shl ax,1 + rcl dx,1**. It's a 32-bit multiplication by 2, using a left shift. The first operation displaces AX by one bit to left inserting a zero; the leftmost bit comes out into the Carry flag. And the second operation displaces DX to left, inserting the Carry bit at the rightmost bit.

Again it adds the current y coordinate and adjusts the offset. The final result is saved into v_y variable.

Now to complete the Mandelbrot algorithm:

```
        pop dx            ; Restore value from stack
        pop ax

        mov [v_x],ax      ; Save as new x value
        mov [v_x+2],dx

        pop cx
        inc cx            ; Increase iteration counter
        cmp cx,100        ; Attempt 100?
        je m3             ; Yes, jump
        jmp m2            ; No, continue
```

What value did we have in the stack? The new one for the *x* variable. If you lost track, go back and search for **sub ax,480.** After this instruction it saves the 32-bit value into the stack.

Notice it couldn't have been written directly into *x*, because the old value of *x* was going to be used again for calculating *y*.

At the end, it increases the iteration counter (CX) and does a comparison with 100. When it reaches 100 it exits the loop, or else it continues jumping to M2.

All this mathematics and we still don't display anything. Let us resolve that:

```
m3:     mov ax,[v_a]      ; Get Y-coordinate
        mov dx,320        ; Multiply by 320 (size of pixel row)
        mul dx
        add ax,[v_b]      ; Add X-coordinate to result
        xchg ax,di        ; Pass AX to DI

        add cl,0x20       ; Index counter into rainbow colors
        mov [di],cl       ; Put pixel on the screen

        dec word [v_b]    ; Decrease column
        jns m1            ; Is it negative? No, jump

        dec word [v_a]    ; Decrease row
        jns m0            ; Is it negative? No, jump

        mov ah,0x00       ; Wait for a key
        int 0x16          ; Keyboard interruption vector.

        mov ax,0x0002     ; Set mode 80x25 text.
        int 0x10          ; Video interruption vector.

        int 0x20          ; Exit to command-line.
```

Almost the same as the palette program, except the CL value (0-99) is added with 32 to index it into the rainbow colors predefined by the VGA display.

Of course we forgot the adjusted 32-bit multiplication routine. It has been modified to work with signed values and to divide by 256.

```
        ;
        ; Calculate a squared number
        ; DX:AX = (DX:AX * DX:AX) / 256
        ;
square32:
                        ; Copy multiplicand to multiplier
        mov bx,ax       ; Copy AX -> BX
        mov cx,dx       ; Copy DX -> CX
        ;
        ; 32-bit signed fractional multiplication
        ; DX:AX = (DX:AX * CX:BX) / 256
        ;
mul32:
        xor dx,cx       ; Look for different signs
        pushf
        xor dx,cx       ; Restore DX (pair of XOR = unaffected)
        jns mul32_2     ; If multiplicand is positive then jump.
        not ax          ; Negate multiplicand
        not dx
        add ax,1
        adc dx,0
mul32_2:
        test cx,cx      ; Test if multiplier is positive
        jns mul32_3     ; Is it positive? Yes, jump.
        not bx          ; Negate multiplier
        not cx
        add bx,1
        adc cx,0
mul32_3:
        mov [v_s1],ax   ; Save multiplicand (S1)
        mov [v_s1+2],dx

                        ; In this diagram each point and letter
                        ; is a word.
                        ;    . = not calculated
                        ;    + = calculated
                        ;    A = AX value
                        ;    B = multiplier
                        ;    C = result
                        ; rightmost column of result goes into v_s2
                        ; next to last goes into v_s2+2
                        ; next into v_s2+4

                        ;         .A
                        ;       x .B
                        ;       ----
                        ;         .C
                        ;         ..
```

```
        mul bx              ; S1:low * BX = DX:AX
        mov [v_s2],ax       ; Save provisional result
        mov [v_s2+2],dx


                    ;           A.
                    ;         x B.
                    ;         ----
                    ;          .+
                    ;           C.

        mov ax,[v_s1+2]  ; S1:high * CX = DX:AX
        mul cx
        mov [v_s2+4],ax  ; Save next word of result
                         ; Notice it doesn't need DX


                    ;           A.
                    ;         x .B
                    ;         ----
                    ;           C+
                    ;           +.

        mov ax,[v_s1+2]  ; S1:high * BX = DX:AX
        mul bx
        add [v_s2+2],ax  ; Adds to previous result
        adc [v_s2+4],dx


                    ;           .A
                    ;         x B.
                    ;         ----
                    ;           ++
                    ;           +C

        mov ax,[v_s1]    ; S1:low * CX = DX:AX
        mul cx
        add [v_s2+2],ax  ; Adds to previous result
        adc [v_s2+4],dx

        mov ax,[v_s2+1]  ; Reads result shifted by 1 byte
        mov dx,[v_s2+3]  ; equivalent to divide by 256

        popf             ; Restore flags
        jns mul32_1      ; Different signs? No, jump.
        not ax           ; Negate result.
        not dx
        add ax,1
        adc dx,0
mul32_1:
        ret              ; Return.
```

And now we can see the beautiful result:

Feel free to play with the offset adjustment constants 480 and 250, and also try removing the duplicated **add** instructions for v_a and v_b. If it doesn't add two times, you effectively will get a zoomed Mandelbrot set.

5.7 Brief discussion of stack.

The instructions **push**, **pop**, **call** and **ret**, all depend on the SP register (abbreviation of Stack Pointer).

The stack pointer saves its information using the SS register (Stack Segment).

Whenever you *push* data inside the stack, the register SP is decremented by 2, and the data word is written at the memory address pointed by SP.

Whenever you *pop* data from the stack, the data word is read from the memory address pointed by SP, and SP is incremented by 2.

5.8 Instructions learned.

The instructions we learned in this chapter were:

1. **adc**, does addition with the Carry flag.

2. **cmpsb**, does comparison of one byte of DS:SI against ES:DI, increment/decrement both SI and DI by 1.

3. **cmpsw**, does comparison of one word of DS:SI against ES:DI, increment/decrement both SI and DI by 2.

4. **cwd**, does expansion of signed value inside AX to a 32-bit value inside DX:AX.

5. **lodsb**, read one byte into AL from DS:SI, increment/decrement SI by 1.

6. **lodsw**, read one word into AX from DS:SI, increment/decrement SI by 2.

7. **movsb**, copy one byte from DS:SI into ES:DI, increment/decrement both SI and DI by 1.

8. **movsw**, copy one word from DS:SI into ES:DI, increment/decrement both SI and DI by 2.

9. **sbb**, does subtraction with the Carry flag.

10. **scasb**, does comparison of one byte of AL against ES:DI, increment/decrement DI by 1.

11. **scasw**, does comparison of one word of AX against ES:DI, increment/decrement DI by 2.

12. **xchg**, interchange content of register and register or memory. It uses a single byte when interchanging AX with any register.

Chapter 6

F-Bird

F-Bird is a game I've made about a bird that flies between sets of pipes, and must pass through the hole between the two pipes.

The bird keeps falling down (gravity) and you must press a key in order to make it "flap". The trick is to keep flapping at the right rhythm to keep flying horizontally, or a little faster to go up, or a little slower to go down.

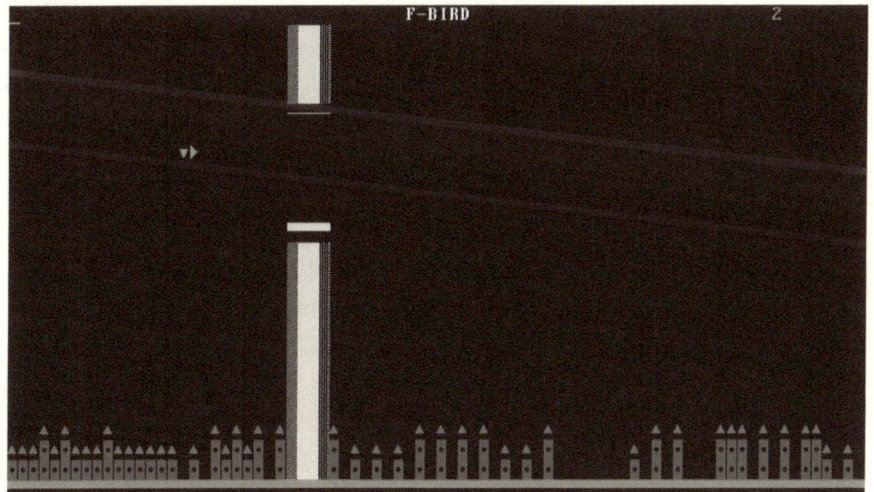

The game scrolls the screen horizontally and draws "buildings" at the bottom. It also keeps the current score and displays its name at the top of the screen.

The bird is made with letters and symbols that are available in text
mode.

```
        ;
        ; F-bird text game in a bootsector
        ;
        ; by Oscar Toledo G.
        ; http://nanochess.org/
        ;
        ; Creation date: Jun/04/2017.
        ; Revision date: Jun/05/2017.
        ;

        use16

pipe:   equ 0x0fa0
score:  equ 0x0fa2
grav:   equ 0x0fa4
next:   equ 0x0fa6
bird:   equ 0x0fa8
tall:   equ 0x0faa
frame:  equ 0x0fac

        mov ax,0x0002    ; Set 80x25 text mode
        int 0x10         ; Call BIOS
        cld              ; Reset direction flag
        mov ax,0xb800    ; Point to video segment
        mov ds,ax        ; Both the source (common access)
        mov es,ax        ; and target segments
```

It resets the video to a standard setting of 80x25 text mode, clears
the direction flag, and resets DS and ES to 0xb800 to point to the screen.

It also sets up the addresses for the variables used inside the game.
The addresses are inside the remaining bytes of memory, non-visible on the
screen.

```
        ;
        ; Game restart
        ;
fb21:
        mov di,pipe      ; Init variables in video segment
        xor ax,ax        ; AX = 0
        stosw            ; pipe
        stosw            ; score
        stosw            ; grav
```

```
mov al,0xa0
stosw           ; next
mov al,0x60
stosw           ; bird
```

Now it resets the variables for the game. Notice the usage of **stosw** to save many bytes while storing 3 times the register AX (initialized to zero using **xor ax,ax**).

Then instead of doing **mov ax,0x00a0** it uses **mov al,0xa0** to save one byte (assuming that AH is zero as we already know).

Also the position of the bird is initialized as 0x0060.

```
mov di,0x004a   ; Game title
mov ax,0x0f46   ; 'F' in white, good old ASCII
stosw
mov al,0x2d     ; '-'
stosw
mov al,0x42     ; 'B'
stosw
mov al,0x49     ; 'I'
stosw
mov al,0x52     ; 'R'
stosw
mov al,0x44     ; 'D'
stosw
```

It shows the game's title (as we did in section 4.2). Remember the ASCII code for each letter goes into AL (lower byte of AX). Notice also that AH remains constant as white color for each **stosw**.

```
    mov cx,80       ; Introduce 80 columns of scenery
fb1:
    push cx
    call scroll_scenery
    pop cx
    loop fb1
```

We have a subroutine to insert a new column of the scenery at the right side of the screen. As the text screen has a width of 80 columns, we call 80 times the subroutine *scroll_scenery*. (we'll see it later)

```
fb23:
    mov ah,0x01      ; Check if key pressed
    int 0x16
    pushf
    xor ax,ax        ; Wait for a key
    int 0x16
    popf
    jnz fb23         ; Jump if key was accumulated ;)
```

Then as it is at the "title screen", it waits for a key to be pressed before going ahead. It "eats" any key accumulated in keyboard buffer.

For this it calls **int 0x16** with AH = 0x01. This function verifies if there's a key in the buffer and returns Z=0. These flags are saved using **pushf/popf** (Push Flags / Pop Flags).

And then it calls **int 0x16** with AH = 0x00 to read the key in the buffer. If there's no key, it will wait until a key is pressed.

If there wasn't a key pressed, Z will be 1 and the loop will exit.

```
    ;
    ; Main loop
    ;
fb12:
    mov al,[bird]    ; Bird falls...
    add al,[grav]    ; ...because of gravity...
    mov [bird],al    ; ...into new position.

    and al,0xf8      ; Row is a 5.3 fraction, nullify fraction
    mov ah,0x14      ; Integer is x8, multiply by 20 for 160 x row
    mul ah           ; Row on the screen
    add ax,$0020     ; Fixed column
    xchg ax,di       ; Pass to DI (AX cannot be used as pointer)
    mov al,[frame]
    and al,4         ; Wing movement each 4 frames
    jz fb15
    mov al,[di-160]  ; Get character below
    mov word [di-160],0x0d1e ; Draw upper wing
    add al,[di]      ; Add another character below
    shr al,1         ; Normalize
    mov word [di],0x0d14 ; Draw body
    jmp short fb16

fb15:
```

```
    mov al,[di]              ; Get character below
    mov word [di],0x0d1f     ; Draw body
fb16:
    add al,[di+2]            ; Get character below head
    mov word [di+2],0x0d10   ; Draw head
```

Now comes the main loop.

The bird falls continuously because of "gravity." It does the operation *bird = bird + grav*. But it keeps the result inside AL in order to calculate position on the screen. Given *bird* is a fractional integer 5.3 (5 bits of integer and 3 of fraction), it then erases the fraction using **and al,0xf8**.

Then it multiplies by 20. Given row 1 is value 8 (because fraction 5.3) then 8 * 20 = 160, the width of each video row.

Now it adds 32 to the result, in order for the bird to be slightly at right, and not "glued" to the left border.

And the final result is put into DI using **xchg ax,di**.

The display frame number is used to detect if the bird should flap its wings. Before drawing using **mov word [di]** (remember: low byte is character and high byte is color), it reads the content of video at that address using **mov al,[di]** (some are with offset displacement in order to read the video under the parts of the bird).

But as a clue, the 0x0d is the color of our bird (magenta). The codes for symbols can be seen in Appendix B.

Bird made with symbols   [DI-160] Code 0x1e

▲

[DI] Code 0x1f   ✇▶   [DI + 2] Code 0x10

The value read from the screen memory is put into AL and it serves to detect if the bird has crashed against the background.

```
    cmp al,0x40         ; Collision with scenery?
    jz fb19
    ;
    ; Stars and game over
```

85

```
    ;
    mov byte [di],$2a     ; '*' Asterisks to indicate crashing
    mov byte [di+2],$2a
    mov di,0x07CA
    mov ax,0x0f42         ; 'B' in white, good old ASCII
    stosw
    mov al,0x4F           ; 'O'
    stosw
    mov al,0x4E           ; 'N'
    stosw
    mov al,0x4B           ; 'K'
    stosw
    mov al,0x21           ; '!'
    stosw
    mov cx,100            ; Wait 100 frames
fb20:
    push cx
    call wait_frame
    pop cx
    loop fb20
    jmp fb21             ; Restart
```

The comparison of AL with 0x40 (two ASCII spaces 0x20 + 0x20 = 0x40) does the verification. If AL isn't 0x40 then the game is over, and it shows "BONK!" on the screen, then it waits 100 frames before jumping to game restart.

```
fb19:
    call wait_frame       ; Wait for frame
    mov al,[frame]
    and al,7              ; 8 frames have passed?
    jnz fb17              ; No, jump
    inc word [grav]       ; Increase gravity
fb17:
    mov al,$20
    mov [di-160],al       ; Delete bird from the screen
    mov [di+2],al
    stosb
    call scroll_scenery   ; Scroll scenery
    call scroll_scenery   ; Scroll scenery
    cmp byte [0x00a0],0xb0 ; Passed a column?
    jz fb27
    cmp byte [0x00a2],0xb0 ; Passed a column?
fb27:
    jnz fb24
```

```
        inc word [score]       ; Increase score
        mov ax,[score]
        mov di,0x008e          ; Show current score
fb25:
        xor dx,dx              ; Extend AX to 32 bits
        mov bx,10             ; Divisor is 10
        div bx                ; Divide
        add dx,0x0c30   ; Convert remaining 0-9 to ASCII, also put color
        xchg ax,dx
        std
        stosw
        mov byte [di],0x20     ; Clean one character of prev. score
        cld
        xchg ax,dx
        or ax,ax              ; Score digits still remain?
        jnz fb25              ; Yes, jump
fb24:
```

The main game now waits for a frame. When eight frames have passed, it increases the gravity variable (*grav*).

Then it deletes the bird from the screen, otherwise it would leave trash as the screen scrolls horizontally.

And it calls the *scroll_scenery* subroutine twice, so the bird appears to advance horizontally.

It checks also if the characters of a column are at position 0x00a0 of the screen. If so it means it should increment the current score doing **inc word [score]** and copies it into AX to update the score on the screen.

To display the score it sets up DI to point to 0x008e. Then it divides AX by 10, and adjusts the remainder to be an ASCII digit, and at the same time adds the color light red (0x0c30), then it sets the D flag and stores the word using **stosw** (it decrements DI by 2 because D flag is set), and then clears the D flag.

While the result of division isn't zero, it continues drawing digits on the screen (**jnz fb25**)

```
        mov ah,0x01           ; Any key pressed?
        int 0x16
        jz fb26              ; No, go to main loop
        mov ah,0x00
```

```
        int 0x16            ; Get key
        cmp al,0x1b         ; Escape key?
        jne fb4             ; No, jump
        int 0x20            ; Exit to DOS or to oblivion (boot sector)
fb4:
        mov ax,[bird]
        sub ax,0x10         ; Move bird two rows upward
        cmp ax,0x08       ; Make sure the bird doesn't fly outside screen
        jb fb18
        mov [bird],ax
fb18:
        mov byte [grav],0   ; Reset gravity
        mov al,0xb6         ; Flap sound
        out (0x43),al
        mov al,0x90
        out (0x42),al
        mov al,0x4a
        out (0x42),al
        in al,(0x61)
        or al,0x03          ; Turn on sound
        out (0x61),al
fb26:
        jmp fb12
```

Now it checks for a keypress (AH = 0x01 **int 0x16**). If not, it jumps to *fb26* that goes to *fb12*, repeating the whole game loop.

Otherwise it reads the key in the buffer (AH = 0x00 **int 0x16**). If the Esc key is pressed then it returns to the command-line.

Any other key moves the bird 2 rows upward, and resets gravity to zero (variable *grav*).

At the same time it tries to do a flap sound, but it will work only on a very old PC. It sets up the connection to the PC speaker using port 0x43, then the frequency is written two times into port 0x42, and finally turns sound on, using port 0x61.

6.1 Scrolling scenery.

This doesn't complete the game. Still we need to scroll the scenery, and add pipes and buildings.

The first step is to scroll the whole screen except the top row:

```
      ;
      ; Scroll scenery one column at a time
      ;
scroll_scenery:
      ;
      ; Move whole screen
      ;
      mov si,0x00a2    ; Point to row 1, column 1 in SI
      mov di,0x00a0    ; Point to row 1, column 0 in DI
fb2:
      mov cx,79        ; 79 columns
      repz             ; Scroll!!!
      movsw
      mov ax,0x0e20    ; Clean last character
      stosw
      lodsw            ; Advance source to keep pair source/target
      cmp si,0x0fa2    ; All scrolled?
      jnz fb2          ; No, jump
```

The SI register is made to point at row 1, column 1 on the screen, while the DI register is made to point at row 1, column 0. This means that when we do a **movsw**, it will move a whole character from SI to DI (code and color). Repeating it 79 times moves the whole row one character to left!

Of course, it should clean the last character using **mov ax,0x0e20 + stosw** (increases DI) and align the source using **lodsw** (increases SI).

When SI register reaches the value 0x0fa2 it means all the screen has been scrolled horizontally to the left.

```
      ;
      ; Insert houses
      ;
      mov word [0x0f9e],0x02df    ; Terrain
      in al,(0x40)     ; Get "random" number
      and al,0x70
      jz fb5
      mov bx,0x0408    ; House of one floor
      mov [0x0efe],bx
      mov di,0x0e5e
      and al,0x20      ; Check "random" number
      jz fb3
      mov [di],bx      ; House of two floors
      sub di,0x00a0
```

```
fb3:
    mov word [di],0x091e ; Add roof
```

Now is time to insert houses. Some terrain is always drawn (a fat green line at the bottom of the screen in row 24, column 79 = address 0x0f9e)

It reads the port 0x40 using **in al,(0x40)**. As you may recall, this is a counter of the internal timer chip of the PC; it always contains a different value. Based on the value it draws a house of one or two floors. The floors are based on reversed bullet (character 0x08) in red color (0x04) so these look like windows.

The roof is a triangle (character 0x1e) in blue color (0x09).

```
    ;
    ; Check if is it time to insert a column
    ;
fb5:
    dec word [next] ; Decrease time (column really) for next pipe
    mov bx,[next]
    cmp bx,0x03     ; bx = 3,2,1,0 for the four columns making the
pipe
    ja fb6
    jne fb8
    in al,(0x40)    ; Get "random" number
    and ax,0x0007   ; Between 0 and 7
    add al,0x04     ; Between 4 and 11
    mov [tall],ax   ; This will tell how tall the pipe is
fb8:
    mov cx,[tall]
    or bx,bx        ; Rightmost?
    mov dl,0xb0
    jz fb7          ; Yes, jump
    mov dl,0xdb
    cmp bx,0x03     ; Leftmost?
    jb fb7          ; No, jump
    mov dl,0xb1
fb7:
    mov di,0x013e   ; Start from top of the screen
    mov ah,0x0a
    mov al,dl
fb9:
    stosw
    add di,0x009e
```

```
        loop fb9
        mov al,0xc4
        stosw
        add di,0x009e*6+10
        mov al,0xdf
        stosw
        add di,0x009e
fb10:
        mov al,dl
        stosw
        add di,0x009e
        cmp di,0x0f00
        jb fb10
        or bx,bx
        jnz fb6
        mov ax,[pipe]
        inc ax          ; Increase total pipes shown
        mov [pipe],ax
        mov cl,3
        shr ax,cl
        mov ah,0x50     ; Decrease distance between pipes
        sub ah,al
        cmp ah,0x10
        ja fb11
        mov ah,0x10
fb11:
        mov [next],ah   ; Time for next pipe
fb6:
        ret
```

The *next* variable is decremented, and contains a counter that is used to check if it is time to draw a new pipe.

When *next* is 3, 2, 1 or 0, then it is time to draw a new pipe. A value of 3 reads the time counter, and creates a number between 4 and 11 that is saved on the variable *tall* for using it on future values of *next*.

Then based again on the value of *next*, it chooses the graphic character to use and saves it into DL. It can be 0xb1 (lightly filled block), 0xdb (fully filled block), or 0xb0 (barely filled block). See appendix B.

Then it starts at row 1 right side (DI = 0x013e), and draws the first part of column (CX = contents of *tall*), draws a bottom cap (**mov al,0xc4**), jumps 6 rows down (the space between pipes), draws a top cap (**mov al,**

0xdf), and keeps drawing another pipe, until it reaches the land row. (**cmp di,0x0f00**)

If *next* was zero, then it increases the total number of pipes shown, and creates an expression *0x50 - pipes / 8* until a minimum of 0x10 to derive the new time for the next pipe. So it increases the difficulty of the game over time.

6.2 Synchronization of gameplay.

There are many speeds of PC computers out there, from 4.77 mhz. up to 3 ghz. How we can synchronize the timing for all?

The answer is the service 0x1a (**int 0x1a**) that allows us to read the number of ticks since the machine is booted.

This number saved into **CX:DX** increases each 18.2 hz.

```
    ;
    ; Wait for a frame
    ;
wait_frame:
    mov ah,0x00      ; Use base clock tick
    int 0x1a
fb14:
    push dx
    mov ah,0x00      ; Read again base clock tick
    int 0x1a
    pop bx
    cmp bx,dx        ; Wait for change
    jz fb14
    inc word [frame] ; Increase frame count
    in al,(0x61)
    and al,0xfc          ; Turn off sound
    out (0x61),al
    ret
```

This reads the current time value, and then compares again indefinitely with the new current time value until it changes.

Then increases the frame number (used in other parts of the game) and turns off sound (again only in old PC). Notice the **out** instruction sends data to the internal chip indicated by the port number between parentheses.

To make it bootable, just add the following and we are finished with this game.

```
db "OTG"     ; 3 unused bytes

db 0x55,0xaa    ; Bootable signature
```

This is bad programming practice. It depends upon checking the size of the program by ourselves in order to add or remove unused bytes. But we'll see later other examples about how to fill the complete boot sector.

Chapter 7

Invaders

Invaders from a faraway galaxy were over Earth taking a walk. Unfortunately, someone shot fireworks to welcome them, and they saw it as an attack! So now the last ship on Earth must defend the whole planet.

The invaders come in an ordered army of 11x5 aliens. They will walk to left, descend, walk to right, descend, and repeat. An interesting thing of the aliens is that only one is needed to touch the border in order to start a descent, so it's a good strategy to remove invaders by columns. The invaders also throw bullets at the player randomly.

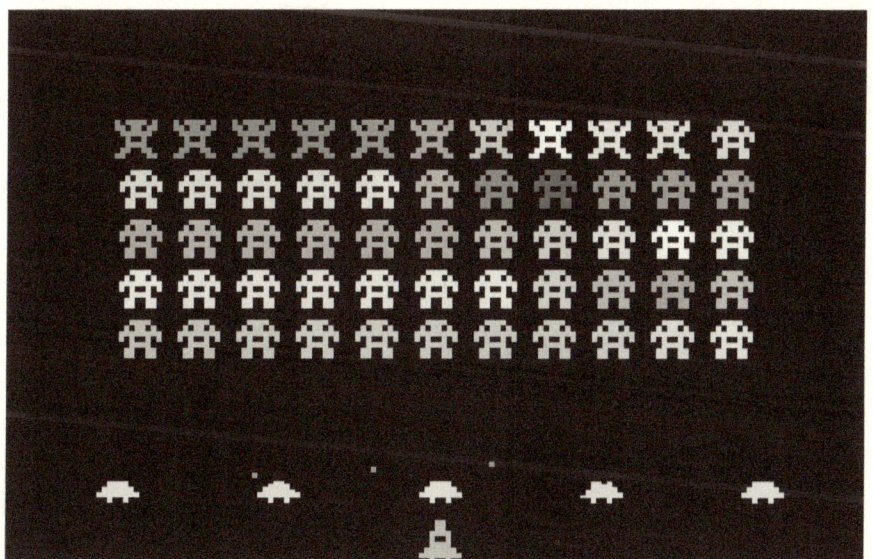

The player only moves left and right, and can only shoot one bullet at a time. So you better make sure it hits an invader!

As a side note, this game took 4 years to develop. Started in October, 2015, it was delayed by unexpected things and was finished by June, 2019.

It had great feedback on the Internet because it was the first Invaders game to fit into a boot sector (512 bytes).

7.1 Preparation.

The first step is to initialize the system for the game. This means setting the VGA 320x200x256 mode and the segment registers.

```
        ;
        ; Invaders in 512 bytes
        ;
        ; by Oscar Toledo G.
        ;
        ; (c) Copyright 2015-2019 Oscar Toledo G.
        ;
        ; Creation: Oct/27/2015.
        ; Revision: Jun/29/2019.

    %ifndef com_file        ; If not defined create a boot sector
com_file:   equ 0
    %endif


base:       equ 0xfc80      ; Memory base (same segment as video)

shots:      equ base+0x00   ; Space for 4 shots (2 bytes each one)
                            ; Plus space for an ignored shot (full table)
                            ; Notice (sprites + SPRITE_SIZE) - (shots + 2)
                            ; must be divisible by SPRITE_SIZE.

old_time:   equ base+0x0c   ; Old time
level:      equ base+0x10   ; Current level number
lives:      equ base+0x11   ; Current lives
sprites:    equ base+0x12   ; Space to contain sprite table

SHIP_ROW:     equ 0x5c*OFFSET_X       ; Row of spaceship
X_WIDTH:      equ 0x0140    ; X-width of video
OFFSET_X:     equ X_WIDTH*2 ; X-offset between screen rows (2 pixs)
SPRITE_SIZE:  equ 4         ; Size of each sprite in bytes
```

```
        ;
        ; All colors different (important to distinguish things)
        ;
SPACESHIP_COLOR:           equ 0x1c    ; Must be below 0x20
BARRIER_COLOR:             equ 0x0b
SHIP_EXPLOSION_COLOR:      equ 0x0a
INVADER_EXPLOSION_COLOR:   equ 0x0e
BULLET_COLOR:              equ 0x0c
START_COLOR:    equ ((sprites+SPRITE_SIZE-(shots+2))/SPRITE_SIZE+0x20)

    %if com_file
        org 0x0100      ; Start position for COM files
    %else
        org 0x7c00      ; Start position for boot sector
    %endif
        mov ax,0x0013   ; Set mode 0x13 (320x200x256 VGA)
        int 0x10        ; Call BIOS
        cld             ; Clear direction flag.
        mov ax,0xa000   ; Point to the screen memory
        mov ds,ax       ; Both DS...
        mov es,ax       ; ...and ES
        mov ah,0x04
        mov [level],ax  ; Level = 0, Lives = 4
```

There are many variables needed in a game of this complexity.

First, the address where the variables are saved is 0xfc80 inside the video segment (0xa000), DS and ES are set at the bottom of this piece of code.

There is a small table for five shots (three for invaders, one for player and one ignored).

Position on the screen	shots + 0 (player shot)
Position on the screen	shots + 2 (first invader shot)
Position on the screen	shots + 4 (second invader shot)
Position on the screen	shots + 6 (third invader shot)
Ignored	shots + 8 (trash shot)

The variable *old_time* contains the last value returned by **int 0x1a** service 0x00 (clock time) in order to do a comparison, while *level* contains the current level (in each level the invaders descend a little more before starting its horizontal movement), and *lives* contains the number of ships remaining.

Finally there is a *sprites* table. This table contains position, shape number and color for each item over the screen. It uses 4 bytes per entry and it is only used for invaders and the spaceship, for a total of 56 entries.

We are using directives of *nasm* to allow a certain grade of flexibility while assembling the game. **%ifdef** means to only assemble the following code if the label is defined, and the block is finished with **%endif**.

The directive **%if** means to test an expression for non-zero. If it is non-zero then the following code is assembled. The block is finished with **%else** for another assembler code branch and **%endif**.

This is done so we can assemble the same program for boot sector and for *.com* executable file with some differences.

```
restart_game:
        xor ax,ax
        mov cx,level/2   ; Clear screen and vars (except level/lives)
        xor di,di
        rep
        stosw            ; ch is zero from here

        ;
        ; Setup descend state
        ;
        mov ax,[di]      ; al now contains level, ah contains lives
        inc ax           ; Increase by 2 (so invaders descend right)
        inc ax
        stosw            ; Advance level number
        mov ah,al
        xchg ax,dx       ; It shouldn't modify DX starting here

        ;
        ; Setup the spaceship
        ;
        mov ax,SPACESHIP_COLOR*0x0100+0x00
        stosw
        mov ax,SHIP_ROW+0x4c*2
        stosw
```

```
        ;
        ; Setup the invaders
        ;
        mov ax,0x08*OFFSET_X+0x28
        mov bx,START_COLOR*0x0100+0x10
in1:    mov cl,0x0b              ; Eleven invaders per row
in5:    stosw                    ; Set invader position
        add ax,0x0b*2            ; Go to next column
        xchg ax,bx
        stosw                    ; Set invader color and shape
        inc ah                   ; Go to next color
        xchg ax,bx
        loop in5                 ; Loop and make sure ch is zero
        add ax,0x09*OFFSET_X-11*0x000b*2    ; Go to next row
        cmp bh,START_COLOR+55    ; Whole board finished?
        jne in1                  ; No, jump


        ;
        ; Draw the barriers
        ;
        mov di,0x55*OFFSET_X+0x10*2
        mov cl,5
in48:
        mov ax,BARRIER_COLOR*0x0100+0x04
        call draw_sprite
        add di,0x1e*2
        loop in48

        ; CH is zero
```

The first step after label *restart_game* is to clear the whole screen and some variables at the same time. In order to do this it sets up AX to zero with **xor ax,ax**, DI to zero to point at the start of the screen, and CX is carefully set to the address of the *level* variable divided by 2. Why is it made this way? So the **rep/stosw** instructions finish filling the memory with zero immediately before the *level* variable. The division by 2 is required because we are filling with words (2 bytes) instead of bytes. Although nothing prevents us from changing the code to remove the division by 2 and use the **stosb** instruction.

Because of our little trick, now the register CX is zero and the register DI contains the address of the variable *level* (remember **stosw** auto increments DI). It reads into AX the variables *level* and *lives* at the same time with **mov ax,[di]** but is shorter by 1 byte than **mov ax,[level]**.

It increments AX by two (notice it doesn't use **inc al** because it would use 2 bytes more), and saves the result using **stosw**, meaning it saves again. It's like using **mov [di],ax** and **add di,2**, but it saves 4 bytes!

Then it copies AL (level number) into AH and puts it into DX using **xchg ax,dx** for further use much later into the code. In fact it won't use DX again in all this piece of code!

The clever usage of DI means that now it is pointing to the *sprites* array. Remember it was pointing at *level* variable and then we used **stosw** so DI was incremented.

Now because of the heavy optimization going on in this small game, it loads AX with the shape (*0x00*) and color (*SPACESHIP_COLOR*) and saves it into the sprite table, then it loads the position for the screen (*SHIP_ROW+0x4c * 2*) and saves it into the sprite table. This is the only sprite entry that has the position and shape/color words reversed.

To prepare the invaders set, it loads AX with the position of the top-left invader (*0x08 * OFFSET_X + 0x20*), and BX with the shape (*0x10*) and color (*START_COLOR*).

Space between invaders

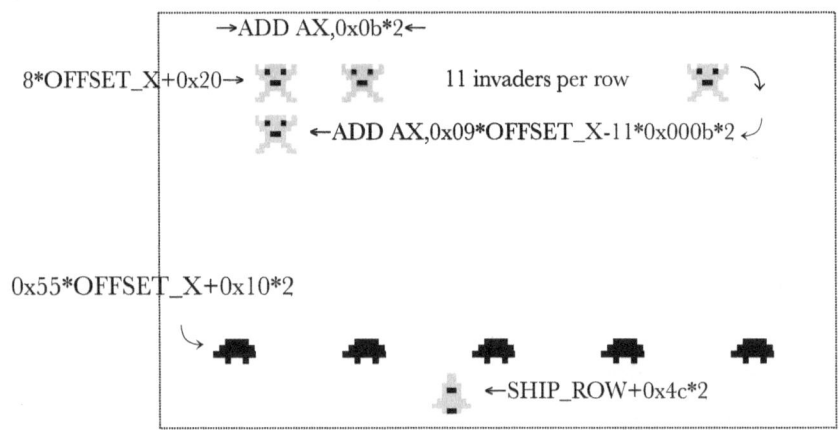

From the previous use of the **rep** instruction, the CX register still contains zero, so it only loads CL to count 11 invaders.

Then the loop writes the position of the invader, moves the coordinate by 0x0b * 2 to right, writes the shape/color of the invader (it uses **stosw** but interchanges registers using **xchg ax,bx** two times) and increases the color number of the invader.

Once it is finished, it adds a constant to AX to make it point to the next row of invaders at the left. Doing a comparison with the color in register BH lets us know when all 55 invaders are ready.

The last step is to draw the barriers that protect the player from invaders' bullets. The register DI is loaded with the screen position: row 0x55 by *OFFSET_X* and column 0x10 multiplied by 2.

The CL register is loaded with 5 (for 5 barriers) and calls *draw_sprite* the same number of times, with AX loaded with *BARRIER_COLOR* and shape 0x04, meaning it will draw half of the spaceship as a barrier. After each cycle of the loop, it will add *0x1e * 2* to the register DI in order to get the position for the next barrier.

7.2 Main game loop.

The main game loop is where everything is controlled. Because of the space constraints there are several things done that *shouldn't be done* in real production code.

One of these things is the use of registers to contain important information, like the next invader to process. It is made in this game because otherwise it wouldn't fit into 512 bytes, but it prevents the easy modification of the code.

```
in14:
        mov si,sprites+SPRITE_SIZE

        ;
        ; Game loop
        ;
        ; Globals:
        ; SI = Next invader to animate
        ; DL = state (0=left, 1=right, >=2 down)
        ; DH = nstate (next state)
        ; CH = dead invaders
```

```
        ; BP = frame counter
        ;
in46:
        cmp byte [si+2],0x20    ; Current invader is cosmic debris?
        jc in2                  ; No, jump
        inc ch                  ; Count another dead invader
        cmp ch,55               ; All invaders defeated?
        je restart_game         ; Yes, jump.
        ;
        ; Yes, invaders speed up
        ;
in6:
        lodsw                   ; Load position in AX
        xchg ax,di              ; Move to DI
        lodsw                   ; Get type of sprite
        cmp al,0x28             ; Destroyed?
        je in27                 ; Yes, jump
        cmp al,0x20             ; Explosion?
        jne in29                ; No, jump
        mov byte [si-2],0x28    ; Don't draw again
in29:   call draw_sprite        ; Draw invader on screen
in27:   cmp si,sprites+56*SPRITE_SIZE    ; Whole board revised?
        jne in46                ; No, jump
        mov al,dh
        sub al,2                ; Going down?
        jc in14                 ; No, preserve left/right direction
        xor al,1                ; Switch direction
        mov dl,al
        mov dh,al
        jmp in14
```

The first register used to contain important information is SI. This register contains the address of the next invader to process; it points to the corresponding *sprite* entry. It is used because it can save us bytes using **lodsw** to load data from it, and increment it at the same time.

It sets the SI register to point to the first invader (*sprites* + *SPRITE_SIZE*, because *sprites* alone points to the spaceship).

Remember that we put *level* into register DX. It contains the current state of invaders and whether these are going left/right or descending.

CH is zero upon entering the main loop, and it is used to count the number of dead invaders in order to trigger level advance.

Finally BP contains the frame counter, but its value isn't important except for the lower 3 bits. In fact we can work with initial trash here, saving bytes because we don't do **mov bp,0** nor **xor bp,bp**.

The first step of the main loop is to access the shape byte **[si+2]** and check if it's less than 0x20. If it is greater than or equal to 0x20 then it means the invaders are in the process of explosion and shouldn't be moved, so it increases CH to count the dead invader, and does a comparison of CH with 55. If all invaders are defeated then it jumps to *restart_game*.

Then comes a shared part of code (it's also used by live invaders), where it loads the screen position into DI and the shape/color into AX.

If the shape is 0x28, it means the invader was destroyed in a previous iteration, and it jumps to *in27* to avoid drawing it.

If the shape is 0x20, it means the invader was exploding before, and now it should erase the explosion. It calls *draw_sprite* but not before changing shape byte to 0x28, so the invader isn't drawn again in later iterations.

For any other value of shape, it simply calls *draw_sprite*.

If the value of register SI isn't equal to the end of *sprites* table, then it repeats the loop, jumping to *in46*.

When all invaders have been handled, it reads DH and subtracts 2. While it's greater than 2 it means the invaders are still descending, or else it does an **xor al,1** to reverse horizontal direction.

```
in2:
        xor byte [si+2],8    ; Invader animation (possible explosion)
        ;
        ; Synchronize game to 18.20648 hz. of BIOS
        ;
        inc bp
        and bp,7                 ; Each 8 invaders
        push dx
        push si
        push bp
        jne in12
in22:
        mov ah,0x00
        int 0x1a                 ; BIOS clock read
```

```
        cmp dx,[old_time]        ; Wait for change
        je in22
        mov [old_time],dx        ; Save new current time
in12:
```

7.3 Player's bullet.

When an invader is alive (shape < 0x20), it jumps to *in2* and animates the shape using **xor byte [si+2],8**. This means the invader alternates between shape 0x10 and shape 0x18, moving arms and legs.

Then it uses BP only this one time, increasing it by 1 and doing **and bp,7**. This sets the Z flag for each of 8 invaders. When this happens, it reads the clock time and waits until 1/18.2 second have elapsed. Also this is a unique use of *old_time* variable.

```
        ;
        ; Handle player bullet
        ;
        mov si,shots                    ; Point to shots list
        mov cx,4                        ; 4 shots at most
        lodsw                           ; Read position (player)
        cmp ax,X_WIDTH                  ; Is it at top of screen?
        xchg ax,di
        jc in31                         ; Erase bullet

        call zero                       ; Remove bullet
        sub di,X_WIDTH+2
        mov al,[di]                     ; Read pixel
        sub al,0x20                     ; Hits invader?
        jc in30                         ; No, jump
        push si
        push di
        mov ah,SPRITE_SIZE              ; The pixel indicates the...
        mul ah                          ; ...invader hit.
        add si,ax
        lodsw
        xchg ax,di
        mov byte [si],0x20              ; Erase next time
        mov ax,INVADER_EXPLOSION_COLOR*0x0100+0x08   ; Explosion now
        call draw_sprite                ; Draw sprite
        pop di
        pop si
```

```
        jmp in31
```

Now it handles the player's bullet. The first step is to initialize the register SI to point to bullets. Also it loads CX with 4 (the maximum number of bullets at the same time inside the game).

It reads the position of bullet using **lodsw**, and does a comparison with *X_WIDTH* (the size of each video row in bytes). If it is less than *X_WIDTH* then it means the bullet reached the top or it is inactive. So it jumps to "erase bullet" routine (*in31*). It is not affected if this is already done as the bullet is erased to black, and the background is black.

If the bullet is active, it removes the bullet with **call zero**, and then subtracts *X_WIDTH+2* from register DI. This causes the bullet to go up. The +2 is because the subroutine *zero* incremented DI by 2.

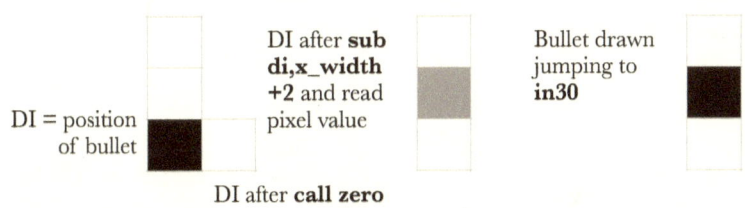

Movement of player's bullet

Before drawing the bullet, it reads the memory location pointed by DI register. If the byte read is less than 0x20 then it didn't hit anything important, and jumps to *in30* to draw the bullet.

But if the byte read is greater than or equal to 0x20 then it uses the value to do a multiplication by *SPRITE_SIZE* (4 bytes), and add to the current value of SI (always *shots* + *2*). So it now has the location of the invader being hit.

It loads the position on the screen of the invader and draws an explosion sprite over it. It also changes the invader shape to contain value 0x20 (for erasing it the next time). Then it jumps to *in31* and erases the players's bullet.

Notice that the pixel value detected by the bullet is exactly the number of the invader being hit. This avoids the overhead of a collision routine, and this allowed the game to fit within 512 bytes.

7.4 Invaders' bullets.

The handling of invaders' bullets is similar to the player's bullet, but these bullets fall down, and should check for player collision.

```
        ;
        ; Handle invader bullets
        ;
in24:
        lodsw                           ; Read current coordinate
        or ax,ax                        ; Is it falling?
        je in23                         ; No, jump
        cmp ax,0x60*OFFSET_X            ; At row of spaceship?
        xchg ax,di
        jnc in31                        ; Yes, remove bullet
        call zero                       ; Remove bullet
        add di,X_WIDTH-2                ; Bullet falls down

        ; Draw bullet
in30:
        mov ax,BULLET_COLOR*0x0100+BULLET_COLOR
        mov [si-2],di                   ; Update position of bullet
        cmp byte [di+X_WIDTH],BARRIER_COLOR    ; Barrier in path?
        jne in7             ; Yes, erase bullet and barrier pixel

        ; Remove bullet
in31:   xor ax,ax                       ; AX = zero (DI unaffected)
        mov [si-2],ax                   ; Delete bullet from table

in7:    cmp byte [di],SPACESHIP_COLOR  ; Check collision with player
        jne in41                        ; No, jump
                                        ; Player explosion
        mov word [sprites],SHIP_EXPLOSION_COLOR*0x0100+0x38
in41:
        call big_pixel                  ; Draw/erase bullet
in23:   loop in24
```

The first step is to load the current position of the bullet using **lodsw**. If it is zero then no bullet is active, and it jumps to *in23*.

It does a comparison of register AX with the spaceship row. If it still hasn't reached that row, it erases the bullet, moves it one row down and redraws it. But before redrawing it, it verifies if it is about to overwrite a pixel with *BARRIER_COLOR* value. If it's true then it erases the bullet, but notice this is done after moving the bullet down, in order to erase one pixel of the barrier.

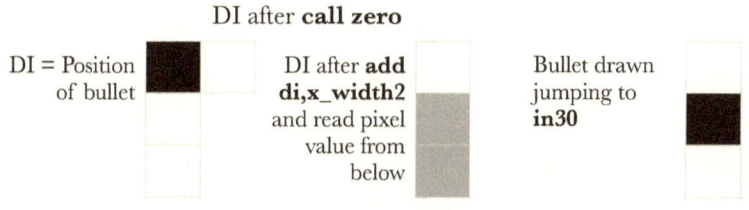

Movement of invader's bullet

When it reaches the spaceship row, it removes the bullet while verifying if the row below the bullet contains any pixel with the value *SPACESHIP_COLOR*. If the spaceship is hit, its shape is replaced with 0x38 and color with *SHIP_EXPLOSION_COLOR*.

Notice each time it deletes a bullet, it already has the position in DI register so it can delete it, but loads AX with zero and stores it in the bullet position at the bullet's table. The same value of zero in AX is used as the pixel value to delete the bullet.

7.5 Spaceship handling.

The spaceship is drawn in a similar way to the invaders.

```
        ;
        ; Spaceship handling
        ;
        mov si,sprites              ; Point to spaceship
        lodsw                       ; Load sprite frame / color
        or al,al                    ; Explosion?
        je in42                     ; No, jump
        add al,0x08                 ; Keep explosion
        jne in42                    ; Finished? No, jump
        mov ah,SPACESHIP_COLOR      ; Restore color (sprite already)
```

```
         dec byte [lives]      ; Remove one life
         js in10                ; Exit if all used
in42:    mov [si-2],ax         ; Save new frame / color
         mov di,[si]           ; Load position
         call draw_sprite      ; Draw sprite (spaceship)
         jne in43              ; Jump if still explosion
```

The register SI is made to point to the spaceship data (*sprites*), and loads the shape and color into AX using **lodsw**.

If AL is zero (shape is 0x00) then the spaceship is normal, and it jumps to *in42*, or else it adds 0x08 in order to generate the explosion timing, and also at the same time uses trash bytes in memory to draw the explosion. When it reaches the value 0x00 then it restores AH to the *SPACESHIP_COLOR* and decrements the number of *lives*. If all lives have been used then it exits the game jumping to *in10*.

The updated shape/color is saved using **mov [si-2],ax**, and then it reads the screen position of the spaceship and calls *draw_sprite*.

The flags are preserved and Z is zero if the spaceship is exploding, so it jumps to *in43* to prevent movement.

```
         mov ah,0x02           ; BIOS Get Keyboard Flags
         int 0x16
    %if com_file
         test al,0x10          ; Test for Scroll Lock and exit
         jnz in10
    %endif

         test al,0x04          ; Ctrl key?
         jz in17               ; No, jump
         dec di                ; Move 2 pixels to left
         dec di

in17:    test al,0x08          ; Alt key?
         jz in18               ; No, jump
         inc di                ; Move 2 pixels to right
         inc di
in18:
         test al,0x03          ; Shift keys?
         jz in35               ; No, jump
         cmp word [shots],0    ; Bullet available?
         jne in35              ; No, jump
```

```
        lea ax,[di+(0x04*2)]          ; Offset from spaceship
        mov [shots],ax                ; Start bullet
in35:
        xchg ax,di
        cmp ax,SHIP_ROW-2             ; Update if not touching border
        je in43
        cmp ax,SHIP_ROW+0x0132
        je in43
in19:   mov [si],ax                   ; Update position
in43:
        pop bp
        pop si
        pop dx
```

It calls **int 0x16** with AH = 0x02. That means to read the state of
the modifier keys. These are Ctrl, Alt, Shift, Scroll Lock, Num Lock and
Caps Lock. Its status is returned into register AL.

The advantage of this is that the BIOS is put in charge of testing if
the key has been pressed *and unpressed*. This is something that the Read Key
or Check for Available Key services don't do.

The bit 4 in AL means if Scroll Lock is in pressed state, it causes the
game to exit (only for *.com* files).

If the Ctrl key is pressed (bit 2 in AL is set), then it moves the current
position of the spaceship 2 pixels to the left. But if the Alt key is pressed (bit
3 in AL is set), then it moves the position of the spaceship 2 pixels to the
right.

If either of the two Shift keys are pressed (bit 0 or bit 1 are set in
register AL), then it verifies if the first entry of the bullet table is non-zero.

If so then it jumps to *in43*, preventing the player from shooting
another bullet when there's already a bullet on the screen. If the entry is
zero, then it sets the bullet to point on the screen just over the spaceship. It
uses the **lea** instruction to get the address pointed by DI plus an offset.
Effectively we use it as a simple addition instruction with the result saved in
AX.

It moves the new spaceship position in register DI to register AX,
and then does a comparison of AX with *SHIP_ROW-2* and *SHIP_ROW*

+0x0132. These are the left and right borders of the screen. If it equals any of these values then it *doesn't save the new position.* This is a good way of preventing the spaceship from exiting the screen to the left or right.

The final instructions of the code restore the global variables contained into registers BP, SI and DX.

7.6 Invaders movement.

Each invader follows the same movement per the state in registers DH and DL.

```
        mov ax,[si]           ; Get position of current invader
        cmp dl,1              ; Going down (state 2)?
        jbe in9              ; No, jump
        add ax,0x0280         ; Go down by 2 pixels
        cmp ax,0x55*0x280     ; Reaches Earth?
        jc in8               ; No, jump
in10:
    %if com_file
        mov ax,0x0003    ; Restore text mode
        int 0x10
        int 0x20         ; Exit to DOS
    %else
        jmp $
    %endif

in9:    dec ax           ; Moving to left
        dec ax
        jc in20
        add ax,4         ; Moving to right
in20:   push ax
        shr ax,1         ; Divide position by 2...
        mov cl,0xa0      ; ...to get column dividing by 0xa0
        div cl           ; ...instead of 0x0140 (longer code)
        dec ah           ; Convert 0x00 to 0xff
        cmp ah,0x94      ; Border touched? (>= 0x94)
        pop ax
        jb in8           ; No, jump
        or dh,22         ; Goes down by 11 pixels (11*2) must be odd
in8:    mov [si],ax
```

The current invader is pointed to by register SI. It reads the current position of invader using **mov ax,[si]**.

110

If register DL is greater than 1, then the invaders descend using **add ax,0x0280**, and if one touches the bottom of the screen then the game exits. Notice the label *in10*, where other parts of code jump to exit the game.

Jumping into *in9* when DL is less than 2 moves the invaders leftward, but if the Carry is set, it reverses the motion to the right using **add ax,4**. Notice it uses the DEC instruction feature of not changing the Carry flag.

Then it divides the position by 2. That allows us to divide the current position by 160 (0xa0). The remainders in AH we are interested in are 0x00 or 0x95, meaning an invader touched the left or right sides of the screen respectively. To do a single border comparison, AH is decremented, so now the values to check are 0x94 or 0xff. A comparison with 0x94 and jumping if lower to *in8* is enough, and it sets DH to 22 using **or** to preserve the lower bit indicating the current horizontal direction.

For the final step, it saves the invader's new position using **mov [si],ax**.

```
        add ax,0x06*0x280+0x03*2        ; Offset for bullet
        xchg ax,bx

        mov cx,3            ; ch = 0 - invader alive
        in al,(0x40)        ; Read timer
        cmp al,0xfc         ; Random event happening?
        jc in4              ; No, jump
        mov di,shots+2
in45:   cmp word [di],0 ; Search for free slot
        je in44             ; It's free, jump!
        scasw               ; Advance DI
        loop in45           ; Until 3 slots searched
in44:
        mov [di],bx     ; Start invader shot (or put in ignored slot)
in4:
        jmp in6
```

Using the recently saved position still contained inside AX, it adds an offset for bullet, and moves the AX value into BX.

It loads 3 into CX, erasing CH to zero at the same time (to indicate the invaders are alive).

It reads the timer counter chip to get a random number, and chooses a time to drop a bullet over the player. If it isn't the right time then it jumps to *in4*, or else it loads the DI register with the address of the bullets table (*shots+2*), and searches for a free slot doing a comparison of memory contents with zero using **cmp word [di],0**. When it finds a zero then it jumps to *in44*, or else it advances DI using **scasw** and using **loop** repeats the loop 3 times (CX was loaded with 3 before entering the loop).

The bullet is then initialized using **mov [di],bx**. If there are already 3 active bullets, then the DI value points to the unused slot in the bullets table, preventing it from writing in another part of memory, and also preventing the invaders from shooting more than 3 bullets at the same time.

Finally the game loop is complete and jumps to *in6* to repeat the cycle.

7.7 The sprites.

The sprites are entered as 8x8-pixel shapes. Given that a byte contains 8 bits, then each shape uses 8 bytes.

We can enter shapes as a hexadecimal table like this:

```
        ;
        ; Bitmaps for sprites
        ;
bitmaps:
        db 0x18,0x18,0x3c,0x24,0x3c,0x7e,0xff,0x24 ; Spaceship
        db 0x00,0x80,0x42,0x18,0x10,0x48,0x82,0x01 ; Explosion
        db 0x00,0xbd,0xdb,0x7e,0x24,0x3c,0x66,0xc3 ; Alien (frame 1)
        db 0x00,0x3c,0x5a,0xff,0xa5,0x3c,0x66,0x66 ; Alien (frame 2)
        db 0x00,0x00,0x00,0x00,0x00,0x00,0x00,0x00 ; Erase
```

Or we can be clearer using binary numbers directly:

```
           ;
           ; Bitmaps for sprites
           ;
bitmaps:
           db 00011000b  ; Spaceship
           db 00011000b
           db 00111100b
           db 00100100b
           db 00111100b
           db 01111110b
           db 11111111b
           db 00100100b

           db 00000000b  ; Explosion
           db 10000000b
           db 01000010b
           db 00011000b
           db 00010000b
           db 01000100b
           db 00000010b
           db 00000001b

           db 00000000b  ; Alien (frame 1)
           db 10111101b
           db 11011011b
           db 01111110b
           db 00100100b
           db 00111100b
           db 01100110b
           db 11000011b

           db 00000000b  ; Alien (frame 2)
           db 00111100b
           db 01011010b
           db 11111111b
           db 10100101b
           db 00111100b
           db 01100110b
           db 01100110b

           db 00000000b  ; Eraser
           db 00000000b
           db 00000000b
           db 00000000b
           db 00000000b
           db 00000000b
```

```
            db 00000000b
            db 00000000b
```

The next step of source code are the drawing routines.

```
        ;
        ; Draw pixel per Carry (use AX if Carry=1 or zero if Carry=0)
        ;
bit:    jc big_pixel
zero:   xor ax,ax
        ; Draw a big pixel (2x2 pixels)
big_pixel:
        mov [di+X_WIDTH],ax
        stosw
        ret
```

The game is designed to double the pixel size. This way the invaders look bigger at 16x16 pixels instead of 8x8 pixels.

The subroutine *bit* draws a pixel in the color indicated by AX if the Carry flag is set, or else it sets AX to zero using **xor ax,ax**.

The subroutine *zero* directly draws a zero 2x2 pixel, technically the color black using AX = 0x0000.

And finally the subroutine *big_pixel* draws a 2x2 pixel using the color inside AX.

The video mode is 320x200x256 colors and each pixel is one byte on the screen memory, but we write **words**. This means we write 2 pixels each time: one time using **mov [di+X_WIDTH],ax**, and another time using **stosw**, for a total of 2x2 pixels. The instruction **stosw** also increases DI by 2, pointing to the pixel immediately to the right.

```
        ; ah = sprite color
        ; al = sprite (x8)
        ; di = Target address
draw_sprite:
        push cx
        push di
        pushf
in3:    push ax
        mov bx,bitmaps
        cs xlat              ; Extract one byte from bitmap
```

```
        xchg ax,bx          ; bl contains byte, bh contains color
        mov cx,10           ; Two extra zero pixels at left and right
        clc                 ; Left pixel as zero (clean)
in0:    mov al,bh           ; Duplicate color in AX
        mov ah,bh
        call bit            ; Draw pixel
        shl bl,1
        loop in0
        add di,OFFSET_X-20  ; Go to next video line
        pop ax
        inc ax              ; Next bitmap byte
        test al,7           ; Sprite complete?
        jne in3             ; No, jump
        popf
        pop di
        pop cx
        ret

    %if com_file
    %else
        times 510-($-$$) db 0x4f
        db 0x55,0xaa        ; Make it a bootable sector
    %endif
```

This is the subroutine *draw_sprite* and the whole game depends on it. It receives the screen position in register DI, the shape number in AL and the color in AH. It also saves a few registers like CX, DI and Flags, and restores them on exit.

It immediately reads the first byte of the shape, using **mov bx,bitmaps** and **cs xlat**. The **cs** qualifier is needed because our segments are pointing to the screen memory, but we need to access the shape data in the code segment. **xlat** does the same operation as a fictitious **mov al,[bx +al]**, getting the byte for the current line of the shape. Then it does **xchg ax,bx** in order to put the shape byte into BL, and as it didn't modify AH, the color gets into BH.

Then it draws 10 pixels. But wait! We only have 8 bits in the shape definition, but the trick is that these are buffered with extra black pixels to the left and right. To achieve this, we use **clc** (CLear Carry flag), then it immediately calls the *bit* subroutine, so it draws a black pixel. Then it starts pulling out pixel data using **shl bl,1**. This puts the next bit of the shape

115

into the Carry flag, at the same time filling BL with zero bits. So when CX reaches the tenth bit, it will draw a final black pixel because BL is all zero.

All the time AX is loaded with duplicated color values from BH, so it keeps the color in both AH and AL for the usage of *bit* subroutine.

The final step is to correct the DI register position for the next row of the shape. Then it increases AX and using **test al,7** verifies if it has drawn the eight rows of the shape.

As a final note, the invaders don't use the top line of its 8x8 bitmap. It's because when moving down it helps to erase its track on the screen.

Finally the boot sector signature is added to the game.

Chapter 8

Pillman

Our little man has a big yellow head and he likes to eat pills. For some reason, someone opened the monsters' cage and these are roaming the maze, trying to catch our little man.

This game is even more complex than Invaders: the monsters actually are trying to catch you. There are pills in the maze, and the monsters shouldn't erase them.

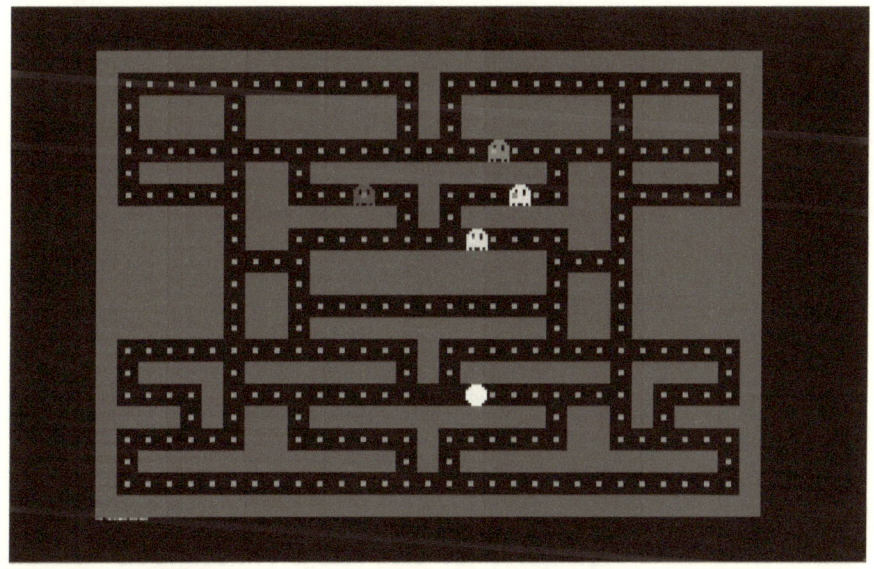

I had to leave certain features out, like power pills, or flashing the screen when the level is completed. There is no completion check. But then, the game is so hard that it's pretty hard to complete a level!

8.1 Initialization.

Here is the initialization code. Same as Invaders, it has an option for *.com* file or boot sector assembly.

```
        ;
        ; Pillman
        ;
        ; by Oscar Toledo G.
        ;
        ; Creation date: Jun/11/2019.
        ; Revision date: Jun/15/2019. Optimized in 509 bytes.
        ;

        %ifndef com_file         ; If not defined create a boot sector
com_file:       equ 0
        %endif

base:           equ 0xf9fe   ; Memory base (same segment as video)
intended_dir:   equ base+0x00
frame:          equ base+0x01
x_player:       equ base+0x02
y_player:       equ base+0x04
old_time:       equ base+0x06


        ;
        ; Maze should start at x,y coordinate multiple of 8
        ;
BASE_MAZE:      equ 16*X_OFFSET+32
pos1:           equ BASE_MAZE+21*8*X_OFFSET

X_OFFSET:       equ 0x0140

MAZE_COLOR:     equ 0x37  ; No color should be higher or equal value
PILL_COLOR:     equ 0x02
PLAYER_COLOR:   equ 0x0e  ; Should be unique


        ;
        ; XOR combination of these plus PILL_COLOR shouldn't
        ; result in PLAYER_COLOR
        ;
```

```
GHOST1_COLOR:    equ 0x21
GHOST2_COLOR:    equ 0x2e
GHOST3_COLOR:    equ 0x28
GHOST4_COLOR:    equ 0x34

    %if com_file
        org 0x0100
    %else
        org 0x7c00
    %endif
restart:
        mov ax,0x0013        ; Set mode 0x13 (320x200x256 VGA)
        int 0x10             ; Call BIOS
        cld
        mov ax,0xa000        ; Video segment
        mov ds,ax            ; Use as source data segment
        mov es,ax            ; Use as target data segment
```

Again, we start selecting the VGA video mode (320x200 in 256 colors), and set the DS and ES segment registers to point to video memory.

Several variables are defined inside the video memory. The variables *intended_dir* and *frame* are indeed inside the visible screen, in order for these to be initialized to zero automatically by the video mode setup.

The variables *x_player* and *y_player* contain the current position of player as x,y coordinates. These aren't used to handle the player, but to give a position clue to the monsters.

The variable *old_time* is used to keep the last time as in Invaders.

The constant *BASE_MAZE* is the position of the maze over the screen. The Y coordinate is 16, and the X coordinate is 32. This gives us an equation of *16 * X_OFFSET + 32*. The constant *X_OFFSET* contains the width in bytes of a pixel row.

Also defined are the colors for the maze, pills, player and monsters, with restrictions for getting smaller code size.

```
        mov si,maze
        mov di,BASE_MAZE
draw_maze_row:
        cs lodsw
        xchg ax,cx
```

```
            mov bx,30*8
draw_maze_col:
            shl cx,1
            mov ax,MAZE_COLOR*0x0100+0x18
            jnc dm1
            mov ax,PILL_COLOR*0x0100+0x38
dm1:        call draw_sprite
            add di,bx
            sub bx,16
            jc dm2
            call draw_sprite
            sub di,bx
            sub di,8
            jmp draw_maze_col

dm2:
            add di,X_OFFSET*8-15*8
            cmp si,setup_data
            jne draw_maze_row
```

The maze is drawn from data at label *maze* pointed to by register SI. It is defined as 21 words of 16-bit, where each bit maps to two tiles on the screen (left side and right side of the screen). At the same time, the register DI is set to the top-left of the maze on the screen.

Remember we set up DS and ES to point to video memory, so it uses **cs lodsw** to load a word of the maze data from the code segment (see section 8.6), and moves it to register CX using **xchg ax,cx**.

The register BX is initialized to point to the rightmost position of the maze, because the right side of the maze is drawn as a mirror.

Then it uses **shl cx,1** to get a tile of the maze. Remember this instruction displaces the register and the expelled bit goes inside the Carry flag. If the Carry flag is unset then it chooses a wall: *MAZE_COLOR * 0x0100 + 0x18*, and if the Carry flag is set then it chooses a pill: *PILL_COLOR * 0x0100 + 0x38*.

It uses the subroutine *draw_sprite*, similar to the Invaders' one, to draw one tile in the maze.

120

Next, it adds BX to DI to get the mirror position, and if there's still the mirror to draw (**sub bx,16** didn't set the Carry flag), then it repeats the tile, and restores the DI value for the next tile on the left side.

When the row is complete, it advances the DI register, and if SI doesn't point to the end of the maze data, then it repeats the loop to draw another row of the maze.

```
        ; CX is zero at this point
        ; DI is equal to pos1 at this point
        ;mov di,pos1
        mov cl,5
        mov ax,2                ; Going to right
dm3:
        cs movsw
        stosw
        loop dm3
```

Because of the space constraints, the monsters' position array is saved on the visible screen memory, just below the bottommost row of the maze, and the constant *pos1* contains that value. The constant *pos1* is equal to *BASE_MAZE+21*8*X_OFFSET*.

Notice that CX is zero at start, so it only loads 5 into CL to copy the data for the player and 4 monsters.

8.2 Main game loop.

The main game loop is relatively small, and comprises: frame rate, keyboard read, player's update, and monsters update.

```
game_loop:
        mov ah,0x00
        int 0x1a                ; BIOS clock read
        cmp dx,[old_time]       ; Wait for change
        je game_loop
        mov [old_time],dx

        mov ah,0x01             ; BIOS Key available
        int 0x16
        mov ah,0x00             ; BIOS Read Key
        je no_key
```

```
            int 0x16
no_key:
            mov al,ah
            sub al,0x48
            jc no_key2
            cmp al,0x09
            jnc no_key2
            mov bx,dirs
            cs xlat
            mov [intended_dir],al
no_key2:
```

The main game loop starts by reading the clock time using service 0x00 of interruption 0x1a (BIOS Clock read), and waits for another clock tick to happen. It saves the new value into the variable *old_time*.

Then it checks if a key is available in the buffer (AH=0x01, **int 0x16**). If it isn't available it jumps to *no_key* with AH register equal to zero, or else it reads the keyboard buffer (AH=0x00, **int 0x16**).

For using fewer bytes, it copies register AH into AL, and then subtracts 0x48. If Carry is set (because the value was less than 0x48) then it jumps to *no_key2*, or else it does a comparison with 0x09. If it's greater than or equal to 0x09 it also goes to *no_key2*. If the value is within 0x00 to 0x08, it is indexed into the table *dirs* using **cs xlat** (because the data is inside the code segment), and it saves the value of AL into variable *intended_dir*.

The variable *intended_dir* is where the player wants to go, but it is kept until the player is actually aligned at a tile, because as it moves smoothly pixel by pixel, it could be unaligned.

```
            mov si,pos1
            lodsw
            xchg ax,di
            lodsw
            xchg ax,bx
            xor ax,ax                    ; Delete pillman
            call move_sprite2            ; Move
            xor byte [frame],0x80
            mov ax,0x0e28                ; Closed mouth
            js close_mouth
            mov al,[pos1+2]
            mov cl,3
```

```
        shl al,cl              ; Open mouth
close_mouth:
        call draw_sprite       ; Draw
```

Now it sets up the SI register to point to *pos1*. It contains the position for each of the five movable things on the screen. It loads the position of the player into DI, then it loads the shape and color into BX.

The first step is to erase the player from its old position. It does **xor ax,ax** to set register AX to zero (black pixel) and calls *move_sprite2*.

Then it counts the current video frame using **xor byte [frame], 0x80**. The value 0x80 has the advantage that *frame* doesn't need to be initialized, and also sets the S flag. It loads AX with 0x0e28, meaning shape 0x28 (closed mouth), and color 0x0e (yellow). This value is used if the S flag is set.

If the S flag is clear, then it takes the current direction from *pos1+2*, multiplies it by 8 (doing a shift to left by 3 bit positions), and this value in AL is the shape of an open mouth in the current direction for the player. Notice it cannot take the value of the variable *intended_dir* because that direction isn't validated yet. For example, our player would look upward while still being displaced to the left.

The last step is to call *draw_sprite*.

```
    mov bh,GHOST1_COLOR
    call move_ghost
    mov bh,GHOST2_COLOR
    call move_ghost
    mov bh,GHOST3_COLOR
    call move_ghost
    mov bh,GHOST4_COLOR
    call move_ghost
    jmp game_loop
```

Granted the 4 monsters have the same behavior, but different color. It loads the color of each monster into the BH register, and calls *move_ghost* for each one. Then it repeats the game loop again.

8.3 Sprite movement.

A big subroutine is in charge of moving the player and monsters over the maze. It verifies if the desired movement is possible and doesn't go over the walls.

```
        ;
        ; DI = address on the screen
        ; BL = wanted direction
        ;
move_sprite3:
        je move_sprite
move_sprite2:
        call draw_sprite          ; Remove ghost
move_sprite:
        mov ax,di
        xor dx,dx
        mov cx,X_OFFSET
        div cx
        mov ah,dl
        or ah,al
        and ah,7
        jne ms0
```

The label *move_sprite3* is used only by monsters, because the first time these shouldn't be "erased". More about this in the next section.

The label *move_sprite2* is used by the player sprite code, in order to remove the player from the screen. AX is zero, so it's overwritten with black pixels, erasing the pills underneath at the same time.

The first step is to take the DI value and divide it by *X_OFFSET* in order to have the *x* and *y* coordinates in DX and AX registers (the remainder and the result of **div**) .

Given the pixel row goes from 0 to 199, then the AH register is always zero, and it is used to do a logical **or** of AL and DL, and separate the lower 3 bits. Technically it tests for the pixel row and column to be aligned at a multiple of 8, or in other words, aligned at a tile if both the register AX modulo 8 and the register DX modulo 8 are zero.

If it is unaligned with a tile, it jumps directly to label *ms0*.

```
    ; AH is zero already
    ;mov ah,0

    mov ch,MAZE_COLOR
    cmp [di-0x0001],ch      ; Left
    adc ah,ah               ; AH = 0000 000L
    cmp [di+X_OFFSET*8],ch  ; Down
    adc ah,ah               ; AH = 0000 00LD
    cmp [di+0x0008],ch      ; Right
    adc ah,ah               ; AH = 0000 0LDR
    cmp [di-X_OFFSET],ch    ; Up
    adc ah,ah               ; AH = 0000 LDRU
```

Given that the player or monster is aligned over a tile, then it loads the register CH with *MAZE_COLOR*, and starts doing comparison with the up direction, the right direction, the down direction, and the left direction, searching for blocked pathways.

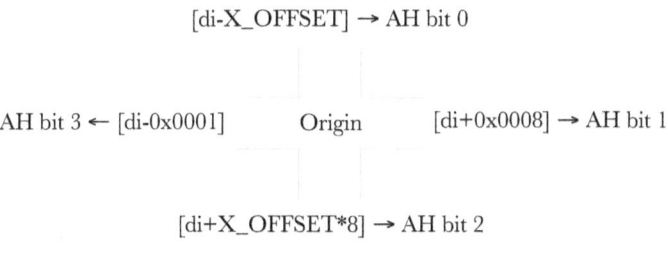

[di-X_OFFSET] → AH bit 0

AH bit 3 ← [di-0x0001]   Origin   [di+0x0008] → AH bit 1

[di+X_OFFSET*8] → AH bit 2

Detection of available directions

For each **cmp**, there is an **adc ah,ah**, because if the result of comparison goes into the Carry flag, then **adc ah,ah** shifts left AH by one bit and inserts Carry at the rightmost bit (bit 0).

If Carry is set to 1, it means the pathway is open, or available to walk in.

This means the bit mask for AH ends up looking like this:

- bit 0 - Up.
- bit 1 - Right.
- bit 2 - Down.
- bit 3 - Left.

8.4 Monster movement.

The shape of the sprite, available at register BH, tells us if we are moving the player or a monster. At the same time, the register BL contains the current direction of movement.

```
            test bh,bh              ; Is it pillman?
            je ms4                  ; Yes, jump


            ;
            ; Ghost
            ;
            test bl,0x05            ; Test BL for .... .D.U
            je ms6                  ; No, jump
            ; Current direction is up/down
            cmp dx,[x_player]       ; Compare X coordinate with player
            mov al,0x02             ; Go right
            jc ms8                  ; Jump if X ghost < X player
            mov al,0x08             ; Go left
            jmp ms8

            ; Current direction is left/right
ms6:        cmp al,[y_player]       ; Compare Y coordinate with player
            mov al,0x04             ; Go down
            jc ms8                  ; Jump if Y ghost < Y player
            mov al,0x01             ; Go up
ms8:
            test ah,al              ; Can it go in intended direction?
            jne ms1                 ; Yes, go in direction

            mov al,bl
ms9:        test ah,al              ; Can it go in current direction?
            jne ms1                 ; Yes, jump
            shr al,1                ; Try another direction
            jne ms9
            mov al,0x08             ; Cycle direction
            jmp ms9
```

If the monster is moving in a vertical direction, then **test bl,0x05** will be non-zero. And the code will compare the current X position (in register DX) with the saved position of the player. If it's less, it will move to the right using **mov al,0x02**, or else it will move to the left with **mov al, 0x08**.

126

If the monster is moving in a horizontal direction, the code will go into label *ms6*. And the code will compare the current Y position (in register AL) with the saved position of the player. If it's less, it will move downwards using **mov al,0x04**, or else it will move upwards using **mov al, 0x01**.

Before using a direction, it checks for validity using **test ah,al**. If the register AH contains the AL bit pattern, it will jump to label *ms1*.

If the direction wasn't valid because there's a wall, then it shifts the current direction one bit to the right, and if the direction becomes 0x00 it is reset to 0x08 and repeats *ms9* until it finds a way.

8.5 Player movement.

```
        ;
        ; Pillman
        ;
ms4:
        mov [x_player],dx       ; Save current X coordinate
        mov [y_player],al       ; Save current Y coordinate

        mov al,[intended_dir]
        test ah,al              ; Can it go in intended direction?
        jne ms1                 ; Yes, go in that direction

ms5:    and ah,bl               ; Can it go in current direction?
        je ms2                  ; No, stops
```

If it is moving the player, then it saves its current X and Y coordinates for further use by monsters.

Then it checks the variable *intended_dir* (the one saved from the keyboard). If it's valid then it jumps to label *ms1*.

If the intended direction is valid, it attempts to go in current direction (register BL), but if it isn't possible then the player stops against the wall (doesn't try another direction like the monsters).

```
ms0:    mov al,bl

ms1:    mov [si-2],al           ; Save new direction
```

```
        test al,5                 ; If going up/down...
        mov bx,-X_OFFSET*2        ; ...bx = vertical movement
        jne ms3
        mov bx,1*2                ; ...bx = horizontal movement
ms3:
        test al,12
        je ms7
        neg bx                    ; Reverse direction
ms7:
        add di,bx                 ; Do move
        mov [si-4],di             ; Save the new screen position
ms2:
        ret
```

The new direction is saved using **mov [si-2],al**.

Then it verifies if it's a vertical direction, and does **mov bx,-X_OFFSET*2** or **mov bx,1*2** for horizontal directions. If the contrary bits are set, then it negates BX. This is a good trick for generating an offset for 4 directions without using a table.

The final direction is added to register DI and saved as the new position using **mov [si-4],di**.

8.6 Bitmaps.

These are the bitmaps used by the game. The shape numbers are assigned taking in account the directions of player (for open mouth). The remaining shapes are used for wall, closed mouth, monster and pill.

Sprites/tiles used for Pillman in the order of source code

```
bitmaps:
        db 0x00,0x42,0xe7,0xe7,0xff,0xff,0x7e,0x3c   ; dir = 1
        db 0x3c,0x7e,0xfc,0xf0,0xf0,0xfc,0x7e,0x3c   ; dir = 2
        db 0xff,0xff,0xff,0xff,0xff,0xff,0xff,0xff   ; Maze
        db 0x3c,0x7e,0xff,0xff,0xe7,0xe7,0x42,0x00   ; dir = 4
        db 0x3c,0x7e,0xff,0xff,0xff,0xff,0x7e,0x3c   ; Closed mouth
        db 0x3c,0x7e,0xdb,0xdb,0xff,0xff,0xff,0xa5   ; Ghost
        db 0x00,0x00,0x00,0x18,0x18,0x00,0x00,0x00   ; Pill
        db 0x3c,0x7e,0x3f,0x0f,0x0f,0x3f,0x7e,0x3c   ; dir = 8
```

The maze is drawn using 16-bit words. It makes it easy to "see" the left side of the maze.

```
maze:
        dw 0b0000_0000_0000_0000
        dw 0b0111_1111_1111_1110
        dw 0b0100_0010_0000_0010
        dw 0b0100_0010_0000_0010
        dw 0b0111_1111_1111_1111
        dw 0b0100_0010_0100_0000
        dw 0b0111_1110_0111_1110
        dw 0b0000_0010_0000_0010
        dw 0b0000_0010_0111_1111
        dw 0b0000_0011_1100_0000
        dw 0b0000_0010_0100_0000
        dw 0b0000_0010_0111_1111
        dw 0b0000_0010_0100_0000
        dw 0b0111_1111_1111_1110
        dw 0b0100_0010_0000_0010
        dw 0b0111_1011_1111_1111
        dw 0b0000_1010_0100_0000
        dw 0b0111_1110_0111_1110
        dw 0b0100_0000_0000_0010
        dw 0b0111_1111_1111_1111
        dw 0b0000_0000_0000_0000
```

And then we have the setup data for the player and monsters. Notice these are only the positions on the screen, added to the base position of the maze.

```
setup_data:
        dw BASE_MAZE+0x78*X_OFFSET+0x78    ; Player
        dw BASE_MAZE+0x30*X_OFFSET+0x70    ; Ghost 1
        dw BASE_MAZE+0x40*X_OFFSET+0x78    ; Ghost 2
        dw BASE_MAZE+0x20*X_OFFSET+0x80    ; Ghost 3
        dw BASE_MAZE+0x30*X_OFFSET+0x88    ; Ghost 4
```

Another small table, *dirs*, contains the direction codes for each scan code of the keyboard, starting at scan code 0x48. So scan code 0x48 = up = 0x01, 0x4b = left = 0x08, 0x4d = right = 0x02, and 0x50 = down = 0x04.

```
        ;
        ; Convert arrow codes to internal directions
        ;
dirs:
        db 0x01         ; 0x48 = Up arrow
        db 0x00
        db 0x00
        db 0x08         ; 0x4b = Left arrow
        db 0x00
        db 0x02         ; 0x4d = Right arrow
        db 0x00
        db 0x00
        db 0x04         ; 0x50 = Down arrow
```

8.7 Support subroutines.

Now, the shared code for moving a monster. It loads the position into the DI register, and the shape and color into the BX register. Notice it uses **xchg ax,bx** so it interchanges color and BH and drops it into AH. At the same time, the color code of the monster is really used to detect if it is the first time it is drawn, by means of setting the Z flag, and the next instructions don't alter this flag.

AL is loaded with the shape 0x30 of the monster. And **mov byte [si-1],0x02** makes sure the monster ends the first-time status.

```
        ;
        ; Move ghost
        ; bh = color
        ;
move_ghost:
        lodsw                       ; Load screen position
        xchg ax,di
        lodsw                       ; Load direction
        test ah,ah
        xchg ax,bx                  ; Color now in ah
        mov al,0x30
        push ax
        mov byte [si-1],0x02        ; Remove first time setup flag
        call move_sprite3
        pop ax
        ; ah = sprite color
        ; al = sprite (x8)
```

```
               ; di = Target address
draw_sprite:
        push ax
        push bx
        push cx
        push di
ds0:    push ax
        mov bx,bitmaps-8
        cs xlat                 ; Extract one byte from bitmap
        xchg ax,bx
        mov cx,8
ds1:    mov al,bh
        shl bl,1                ; Extract one bit
        jc ds2
        xor ax,ax               ; Background color
ds2:
        cmp bh,0x10             ; Color < 0x10
        jc ds4                  ; Yes, jump
        cmp byte [di],PLAYER_COLOR      ; "Eats" player?
        jne ds3                 ; No, jump
        jmp restart     ; It should crash after several hundred games
ds3:
        xor al,[di]             ; XOR ghost again pixel
ds4:
        stosb
        loop ds1
        add di,X_OFFSET-8       ; Go to next video line
        pop ax
        inc ax                  ; Next bitmap byte
        test al,7               ; Sprite complete?
        jne ds0                 ; No, jump
        pop di
        pop cx
        pop bx
        pop ax
        ret

    %if com_file
    %else
        times 510-($-$$) db 0x4f
        db 0x55,0xaa            ; Make it a bootable sector
    %endif
```

This is the subroutine *draw_sprite* and the whole game depends on it for drawing the player, monsters, and maze.

It receives the screen position in register DI, the shape number in AL, and the color in AH. Also it saves to the stack a few registers like AX, BX, CX, and DI, and restores them on exit.

It immediately reads the first byte of the shape, using **mov bx,bitmaps** and **cs xlat**. The CS qualifier is needed because our segments are pointing to the screen memory, but we need to access the shape data in the code segment. **xlat** does the same operation as a fictitious **mov al,[bx+al]**, getting the byte for the current line of the shape. Then it does **xchg ax,bx** in order to put the shape byte into BL, and as it didn't modify AH, the color goes into BH.

Then it draws 8 pixels, and starts pulling out pixel data using **shl bl, 1**. This puts the next bit of the shape into the Carry flag. The register AL is loaded with the current draw color from register BH, and then AL is set to zero if the Carry is unset, so it alternates color and background per the shape in *bitmaps*.

If the pixel value is less than 0x10, then it draws the pixel directly on the screen, overwriting anything below. But if the pixel value is greater than 0x10 (drawing a monster), then it does a comparison of the pixel value at the current position. If it is equal to *PLAYER_COLOR* then the player has been eaten by a monster, and it restarts the game without adjusting the stack pointer!!! This means that after some hundreds of deaths, the game can crash.

And then as it is drawing a monster, it uses **xor** with the current pixel value of the screen, so the monster is pseudo-transparent over the pills.

Repeating this operation with the same screen position causes the monster to disappear *without affecting the pill below*. Because of this the monster must be drawn only once at the first step of the game, or else it would leave trash on the screen.

The final step is to correct the DI register position for the next row of the shape. Then it increases AX and using **test al,7** verifies if it has drawn the eight rows of the shape.

Finally the boot sector signature is added to the game.

Chapter 9

Toledo Atomchess

For the final example of a game that fits in a boot sector, I will show you Toledo Atomchess, a small chess program that fits in 392 bytes, and the computer is capable of giving a response to your movements.

It fits into this size with some small caveats: no promotion of pawns, no castling, and no en passant.

If you feel like you need a full chess program, I have one playing with all the rules at my Github: https://github.com/nanochess

This is one of the most complex programs in this book. If you feel like it's too much for your head, stop reading, and attempt it another day.

This program, being one of my first boot sectors, requires the instructions **pusha/popa**, only available on 80186 processors and higher. These instructions save and restore *all* the registers of the processor. This includes AX, BX, CX, DX, SI, DI, BP, and SP. Also the instruction **push** is used with a constant.

9.1 Initialization.

The game can be assembled both for .*com* file and for boot sector. I've preserved the revision comments so you can see the huge effort that went into it.

```
;
; Toledo Atomchess
;
; by Óscar Toledo Gutiérrez
;
; © Copyright 2015 Óscar Toledo Gutiérrez
;
; Creation: Jan/28/2015 21:00 local time.
; Revision: Jan/29/2015 18:17 local time. Finished.
; Revision: Jan/30/2015 13:34 local time. Debugging finished.
; Revision: Jun/01/2015 10:08 local time. Solved bug where
;     computer bishops never moved over upper diagonals.
; Revision: Oct/06/2015 06:38 local time. Optimized board
;     setup/display, plus tiny bits.
; Revision: Oct/07/2015 14:47 local time. More optimization
;     and debugged.
; Revision: Oct/10/2015 08:21 local time. More optimization.
; Revision: Oct/22/2015 16:59 local time. Now in nasm syntax
;     and uses LEA per HellMood suggestion, 1 byte saved.
;     Relocated sr20 per suggestion of Peter Ferrie (qkumba),
;     saves 2 bytes.
; Revision: Oct/23/2015 10:49 local time. Replaced TEST CL,1
;     with SAL CL,1, and changed AND CL,0x1f CMP CL,0x10 with
;     CMP DL,2. 5 bytes saved.
; Revision: Oct/23/2015 19:52 local time.
;     Integrated Peter Ferrie suggestions: moved subroutines
;     and changed 16-bit load to 8-bit for 4 bytes.
; Revision: Oct/23/2015 20:31 local time.
;     Constants reduced on my own for other 2 bytes.
; Revision: Oct/23/2015 20:45 local time.
;   Removed push cx/pop cx because pusha/popa internally
;   does the job, changed push di/pop ax to xchg ax,di
```

```
;      after confirming INT 0x16 doesn't affect di (Peter Ferrie)
;      4 bytes less.
; Revision: Oct/23/2015 21:09 Solved bug where computer pawn
;      could "jump" over own pawn. Saved two bytes more reusing
;      ch as zero before first "call play"
; Revision: Oct/24/2015 10:09 local time.
;      Reduced another 6 bytes redesigning the next target square
;      calculation.
; Revision: Oct/24/2015 18:21 local time.
;      Changed xlat to xlatb for yasm compatibility. (Peter Ferrie)
;      CL now used for current ply depth, removes ugly SP code so
;      now MOV SP removed for COM file (Oscar Toledo)
;      Integrated offset of movement in table.
; Revision: Oct/25/2015 11:07 local time.
;      Reduced another 1 byte by reordering registers to enable
;      XCHG. (Peter Ferrie)
; Revision: Oct/26/2015 12:48 local time.
;      Reduced 2 bytes more exchanging AH and AL in piece move
;      code and an arithmetic trick with CH. (Oscar Toledo)
; Revision: Oct/26/2015 13:44 local time.
;      Reduced 3 bytes more reusing check comparison.
; Revision: Oct/29/2015 10:58 local time.
;      Reduced another 2 bytes by replacing MOV ,1 with INC
;      replaced ADD+SHL+SUB with IMUL+LEA. (Peter Ferrie)
; Revision: Oct/29/2015 13:05 local time.
;      Reduced another 4 bytes by allowing dummy calculation
;      pass. (Peter Ferrie)
; Revision: Oct/29/2015 16:03 local time.
;      Reduced 2 bytes more merging cmp dl,16+displacement
;       (Oscar Toledo)
; Revision: Oct/29/2015 17:03 local time.
;      Saved 1 byte more redesigning pawn 2 square advance, now
;      bootable 399 bytes (Oscar Toledo)
; Revision: Nov/02/2015 21:55 local time.
;      Saved 1 byte more replacing constant with register, now
;      bootable 398 bytes (Peter Ferrie)
; Revision: Dec/29/2015 12:58 local time.
;      Saved 1 byte more replacing inc dl with inc dx, now
;      bootable 397 bytes. (Oscar Toledo)
; Revision: Feb/24/2016 16:03 local time.
;      Saved 1 byte more in board initialization using mov cx,di,
;      now bootable 396 bytes. (Oscar Toledo)
; Revision: Mar/04/2016 13:36 local time.
;      Saved 4 bytes more saving one CALL instruction and using
;      mov cl in display_board (courtesy of theshich)

   ; Features:
   ; * Computer plays legal basic chess movements ;)
```

```
        ; * Enter moves as algebraic form (D2D4)
        ;   (note your moves aren't validated)
        ; * Search depth of 3-ply
        ; * No promotion of pawns.
        ; * No castling
        ; * No en passant.
        ; * 392 bytes size (runs in a boot sector) or
        ;   383 bytes (COM file)

        use16

        ; Edit this to 0 for a bootable sector
        ; Edit this to 1 for a COM file
    %ifndef com_file
com_file:       equ 0
    %endif

    %if com_file
        org 0x0100
    %else
        org 0x7c00
    %endif

        ; Note careful use of side-effects along all code.

        ; Housekeeping
        cld
    %if com_file
        ; Saves 9 bytes in COM file because of preset environment ;)
    %else
        mov sp,stack
        push cs
        push cs
        push cs
        pop ds
        pop es
        pop ss
    %endif
        ; Create board
        mov di,board-8
        mov cx,di       ; Trick: needs to be at least 0x0108 ;)
sr1:    push di
        pop ax
        and al,0x88     ; 0x88 board
        jz sr2
        mov al,0x07     ; Frontier
sr2:    stosb
        loop sr1
```

```
        ; Setup board
        mov si,initial
        mov di,board
        mov cl,0x08
sr3:    lodsb               ; Load piece
        stosb               ; Black pieces
        or al,8
        mov [di+0x6f],al ; White pieces
        inc byte [di+0x0f]       ; Black pawn
        mov byte [di+0x5f],0x09 ; White pawn
        loop sr3
```

Unlike the other boot sector examples I've shown in this book, it doesn't setup the text mode because the BIOS boots into text mode. This saves 5 bytes.

Also for boot sector it copies the CS segment into DS, ES and SS. Not a safe way, but as of yet I haven't found any evidence of any "live" BIOS jumping into boot sector using CS register with a value different from zero.

Then it creates the chessboard. The register DI points to the chessboard, and the register CX is the counter to create it (it overruns the board, but it doesn't matter).

Using the low byte of DI (copying DI to AX, and doing **and al, 0x88**) it detects the frontier of the chessboard. Each frontier byte is written as 0x07, and all other squares as 0x00.

So it ends with a chessboard looking in memory this way:

0x00	0	0	0	0	0	0	0	0	7	7	7	7	7	7	7	7
0x10	0	0	0	0	0	0	0	0	7	7	7	7	7	7	7	7
0x20	0	0	0	0	0	0	0	0	7	7	7	7	7	7	7	7
0x30	0	0	0	0	0	0	0	0	7	7	7	7	7	7	7	7
0x40	0	0	0	0	0	0	0	0	7	7	7	7	7	7	7	7
0x50	0	0	0	0	0	0	0	0	7	7	7	7	7	7	7	7
0x60	0	0	0	0	0	0	0	0	7	7	7	7	7	7	7	7
0x70	0	0	0	0	0	0	0	0	7	7	7	7	7	7	7	7
0x80	7	7	7	7	7	7	7	7	7	7	7	7	7	7	7	7

The final step is to fill the chessboard with the chessmen. The register SI points to the initial configuration, and the register DI points to the chessboard top-left corner. Given that CX is now zero, it loads CL with 8 because it will be filling the board one column at a time.

It uses **lodsb** to get a copy of a piece into register AL, does **stosb** to write black pieces, then does **or al,8** to generate the code for a white piece and writes it using **mov [di+0x6f],al** (remember DI was incremented by STOSB), does **inc byte [di+0x0f]** to create a black pawn in the 2nd row (converts 0x00 into 0x01 and saves 1 byte), and the white pawn in the 7th row is written using a conventional **mov byte [di+0x5f],0x09.**

Then it does a **loop** instruction to fill all eight columns.

9.2 Main loop.

The main loop is convoluted in order to save bytes.

```
        ;
        ; Main loop
        ;
        ; Note reversed order of calls
        ;
sr21:   push sr21            ; 7th. Repeat loop
        push play            ; 6th. Computer play. ch = 8=White, 0=Black
```

```
            push display_board  ; 5th. Display board. Returns cx to zero
            push sr28            ; 4th. Make movement
            mov si,key2
            push si              ; 3rd. Take coordinate
            push si              ; 2nd. Take coordinate
            ; Inline function for displaying board
display_board:
            mov si,board-8
                                 ; Assume ch=0. It would fail in previous
                                 ; loop if 'play' is called with ch=8
            mov cl,73            ; 1 frontier + 8 rows * (8 cols+1 frontier)
sr4:        lodsb
            mov bx,chars         ; Note BH is reused outside this subroutine
            xlatb
            cmp al,0x0d          ; Is it RC?
            jnz sr5              ; No, jump
            add si,7             ; Jump 7 frontier bytes
            call display         ; Display RC
            mov al,0x0a          ; Now display LF
sr5:        call display
            loop sr4
            ret                  ; cx=0
```

The sequence of steps is like this:

1. Display the chessboard.

2. Read origin coordinate (piece to move).

3. Read target coordinate (where to move).

4. Make movement.

5. Display the chessboard again.

6. Computer plays.

7. Repeat the loop.

Each step is saved on the stack, but in *reverse* order. So after doing 6 **push** instructions, it does the display of the chessboard.

To display the chessboard, the register SI points to *board - 8*, and CL is set to 73, the number of squares to display, more than necessary in order to insert space on the screen.

Then it loads the square contents into register AL using **lodsb**, and translates it into ASCII code using **xlat** (register BX gives the base for the decoding table *chars*).

And if it decodes a 0x0d value (ASCII CR), it adds 7 to register SI, and emits a 0x0a value (ASCII LF) to go to next screen row.

It loops again until all the chessboard is displayed.

9.3 Making a "smart" computer.

If you remember the description of conditional jumps (see section 3.6), these can only jump a small range of -128 to +127 bytes.

In order to save bytes, the final piece of computer A.I. (Artificial Intelligence) code is at the top, but the order of execution is the same:

```
sr14:   inc dx          ; Shorter than inc dl and doesn't overflow
        dec dh
        jnz sr12
sr17:   inc si
sr6:    cmp si,board+120
        jne sr7
        pop di
        pop si
        test cl,cl      ; Top call?
        jne sr24
        cmp bp,-127     ; Illegal move? (any move = always in check)
        jl sr24         ; Yes, don't move
sr28:   movsb           ; Do move
        mov byte [si-1],0    ; Clear origin square
sr24:   ret
```

The **inc dx** increases the whole DX register, but never changes DH because DL never exceeds 255. DL contains the index to the direction offset for the chess piece.

The instruction **dec dh** decreases the count of directions of the chess piece. If it becomes zero then we have finished moving that piece, or else it jumps to *sr12* to move the piece in the next direction.

The instruction **inc si** goes to the next square of the chessboard. If it reaches *board+120* then it has finished searching the chessboard, or else it jumps to *sr7* to read the square and process it.

If register CL is zero it means this is the first call, and it checks the current score inside the BP register, in order to avoid making an illegal movement.

The best move is saved on the stack, SI contains the best move origin square, and DI contains the best move target square. So moving a piece is a matter of doing **movsb** and **mov byte [si-1],0**. This copies origin square into target square, and then empties origin square.

```
        ;
        ; Computer plays :)
        ;
play:   mov bp,-256     ; Current score
        push bp         ; Origin square
        push bp         ; Target square

        mov si,board
```

This is the entry point to computer play code. The BP register contains the current best score. It is setup to a minimum value. It also makes space in the stack pointer for the origin square and target square (whose values are meaningless at this point).

The register SI is made to point to the top-left of the chessboard, or the first square.

```
sr7:    lodsb           ; Read square
        xor al,ch       ; XOR with current playing side
        dec ax          ; Empty square 0x00 becomes 0xFF
        cmp al,6        ; Ignore if frontier or empty
        jnc sr6
        or al,al        ; Is it a pawn?
        jnz sr8
        or ch,ch        ; Current side is black?
        jnz sr25        ; No, jump
sr8:    inc ax
sr25:   dec si
        add al,0x04
        mov ah,al       ; Total movements of piece in ah (later dh)
```

```
            and ah,0x0c
            mov bl,offsets-4
            xlatb
            xchg dx,ax      ; Movements offset in dl
```

It first reads the content of the square using **lodsb**. Doing an **xor al,ch** and **dec ax** detects if the square is valid for the current turn.

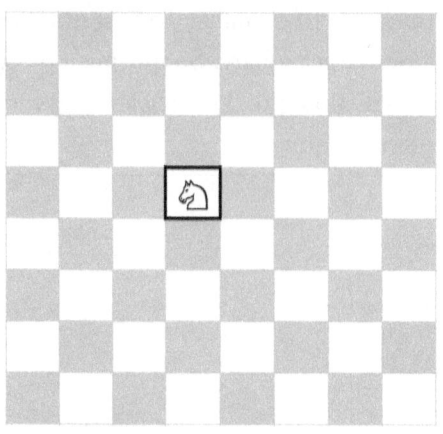

SI points to current square

If AL >= 6 then it jumps to *sr6*, and ignores the current square.

If AL isn't zero then it has a normal piece and jumps to *sr8*, to assign it a value of 2 onwards, or else it has a pawn and will use piece number 0 for white's turn, or 1 for black's turn.

It decrements SI to point again to origin square (remember **lodsb** increments SI), and does arithmetic AH = (AL + 0x04) AND 0x0c to get the number of directions for the current piece: 4 for pawns (implemented as diagonal left, diagonal right, one square ahead, and two squares ahead), 4 also for bishop and rooks, and 8 for knight, queen and king.

Then it uses **xlat** to get the offset into the directions table for the piece, and saves the offset into the DL register.

```
sr12:   mov di,si       ; Restart target square
sr9:    mov bl,dl       ; Build index into directions
        xchg ax,di
        add al,[bx]     ; Next target square
        xchg ax,di
        mov al,[di]     ; Content of target square in al
        inc ax
```

144

```
            mov ah,[si]         ; Content of origin square in ah
            cmp dl,16+displacement
            dec al              ; Check for empty square in z flag
            jz sr10             ; Goes to empty square, jump
            jc sr27             ; If not pawn, jump
            cmp dh,3            ; Straight?
            jb sr17             ; Yes, avoid+cancel any 2 square movement
    sr27:   xor al,ch
            sub al,0x09         ; Valid capture?
            cmp al,0x05         ; Check Z with king, C=0 if invalid
            mov al,[di]
            ja sr18             ; No, avoid
            ; z=0/1 if king captured
            jne sr20            ; Wizard trick, jump if not captured king
            dec cl              ; If not in first response...
            mov bp,78           ; ...maximum score
            jne sr26
            add bp,bp           ; Maximum score (maybe checkmate/stalemate)
    sr26:   pop ax              ; Ignore values
            pop ax
            ret
```

Before going into the loop, it copies the register SI (origin square) into the DI register (target square).

It copies DL into BL (BH already was setup with high-byte of address), so **[bx]** contains the direction offset for the movement.

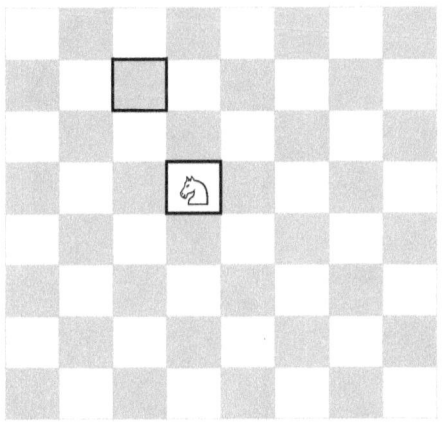

SI points to origin square. DI points to target square adjusted by the value contained at [BX], in this case -33 for first knight movement.

Now it adds the direction offset to the target square, using **xchg ax,di**, **add al,[bx]**, **xchg ax,di** (we cannot directly do **add byte di,[bx]**, because that instruction doesn't exist).

145

Then it reads the content of the target square into AL, and the content of the origin square into AH. Then using the intermixed **inc ax / dec al** it checks for an empty target square (enabling Z flag).

If the square is empty, then it jumps to *sr10*, or else it verifies if it's handling a pawn. A pawn cannot capture pieces going straight (cancels jumping to *sr17*).

It does **xor al,ch / sub al,0x09 / cmp al,0x05** to search for valid capture. It also restores AL to the content of the target square [DI].

If the result is higher than 0x05 then the capture is invalid and it jumps to *sr18*.

If the flag Z is zero (value equal to 0x05) then it has captured the enemy king (check or checkmate), and stops the search by putting a very high score in register BP. It removes the best origin/target squares from the stack, and returns to caller.

```
sr20:   push ax           ; Save for restoring in near future
        and al,7
        mov bl,scores
        xlatb
        cbw
;        cmp cl,4  ; 4-ply depth
        cmp cl,3  ; 3-ply depth
;        cmp cl,2  ; 2-ply depth
;        cmp cl,1  ; 1-ply depth
        jnc sr22
        pusha             ; Save all state (+ current side in ch)
        call sr28         ; Do move
        xor ch,8          ; Change side
        inc cx            ; Increase depth
        call play
        mov bx,sp
        sub [bx+14],bp    ; Subtract BP from AX
        popa              ; Save all state (+ current side in ch)
sr22:   cmp bp,ax         ; Better score?
        jg sr23           ; No, jump
        xchg ax,bp        ; New best score
        jne sr23          ; Same score?
        in al,(0x40)
        cmp al,0xaa       ; Randomize it
sr23:   pop ax            ; Restore board
        mov [si],ah
        mov [di],al
```

```
        jg sr18
        add sp,4
        push si          ; Save movement
        push di
```

The movement is valid, so it saves AX on the stack (contains AH = Content of origin square, AL = Content of target square).

It extracts the lower 3 bits of AL, equivalent to AL = AL modulo 8, and uses it as an index into the *scores* table, to get the value of the piece being captured, or zero if the target square is empty. It then extends the score into 16 bits using the CBW instruction (AL extended into AX).

Then it does a comparison of register CL to 3 (the depth of analysis). If it reaches the maximum depth then it will jump to *sr22*, or else it will save all registers with **pusha**, do the current move calling *sr28* (moving the piece over the chessboard), change sides with **xor ch,8**, increase depth with **inc cl**, and call itself again to analyze the chessboard for the opposite side. The resulting score of the new search (in BP) is subtracted from the AX value that's going to be restored with **popa**.

The new score is in register AX. It does a comparison of BP with AX, and if AX has a better score then it's saved into BP, but if AX has the same score, it reads the timer counter chip to decide if it will take the movement as good. This introduces some movement variability.

The flags are kept while it restores AX (AH = content of origin square, AL = content of target square) and restores the chessboard. Then if the movement was good enough, it will do **add sp,4** and **push si** / **push di** to save the current best movement origin and target squares.

```
sr18:   dec ah
        xor ah,ch       ; Was it a pawn?
        jz sr16         ; Yes, end sequence, choose next movement
        cmp ah,0x04     ; Knight or king?
        jnc sr16        ; End sequence, choose next movement
        or al,al        ; To empty square?
        jz sr9          ; Yes, follow line of squares
sr16:   jmp sr14
```

If it is handling a pawn, the sequence is complete and it goes to the next direction. If it is handling a knight or king, again the sequence is complete and it goes to the next direction. But for all other pieces, if the target square is empty, it can continue moving in the same direction (following the line).

```
sr10:   jc sr20         ; If not pawn, jump,
        cmp dh,2        ; Diagonal?
        ja sr18         ; Yes, avoid
        jnz short sr20  ; Advances one square? No, jump.
        xchg ax,si
        push ax
        sub al,0x20
        cmp al,0x40     ; Moving from the center of the board?
        pop ax
        xchg ax,si
        sbb dh,al       ; Yes, then avoid checking for two squares
        jmp short sr20
```

This code gets executed when the piece is moving to an empty square. If it isn't a pawn, it goes ahead to *sr20* for the scoring calculation and a probable call to another analysis.

If it is a pawn, then it checks for diagonal movement. These cannot be done to an empty square, and so it aborts by jumping to *sr18*.

If it is moving one square ahead, then it checks if the pawn is at the starting rank. If it isn't then it subtracts one from DH (**sbb dh,al**), so it doesn't attempt to move two squares ahead.

9.4 Input/output subroutines.

The input and output routines use the already-known BIOS routines to read a key from the buffer, and output to the screen.

```
        ; Read algebraic coordinate
key2:   xchg si,di
        call key         ; Read letter
        xchg di,ax
                         ; Fall through to read number

        ; Read a key and display it
```

```
key:        mov ah,0        ; Read keyboard
            int 0x16        ; Call BIOS, only affects AX and Flags
```

The *key2* subroutine reads an algebraic coordinate. It first moves the current target square in register DI into register SI. Then it reads the letter (A-H) and puts the column into register DI.

The *key* subroutine actually reads the keyboard using BIOS **int 0x16** with service AH=0x00.

```
display:
        pusha
        mov ah,0x0e     ; Console output
        mov bh,0x00
        int 0x10        ; Call BIOS, can affect AX in old VGA BIOS.
        popa
```

Each key introduced is displayed on the screen. It saves all registers and restores them.

```
        and ax,0x0f     ; Extract column
        imul bp,ax,-0x10; Calculate digit row multiplied by 16
        lea di,[bp+di+board+127] ; Subtract board column
        ret
```

It separates the value (1-8 for letters, and 1-8 for digits) into register AX, and it does a multiplication BP = AX * -0x10 in order to have the right rank (remember that in Chess the rows are the digit), and then does a complex addition to get the square inside the chessboard: DI = BP + DI + board + 127.

So essentially: DI = (AX * -0x10) + DI + board + 127, where DI is the column letter previously introduced, and the new result is the square over the chessboard.

Notice it doesn't modify AX, because if this isn't the row process, it will be used to provide the column number.

9.5 Tables used by the chess program.

```
initial:
        db 2,5,3,4,6,3,5,2
```

The initial setup for the chessboard is (from left to right): 2=Rook, 5=Knight, 3=Bishop, 4=Queen, 6=King, 3=Bishop, 5=Knight, 2=Rook.

```
scores:
        db 0,1,5,3,9,3
```

Per the canonical scores for pieces, a pawn is valued at 1 point, a rook at 5 points, a bishop at 3 points, a queen at 9 points, and a knight at 3 points. The king value is given inside the computer playing code.

```
chars:
        db ".prbqnk",0x0d,".PRBQNK"
```

The ASCII letters for pieces, first black pieces, then white pieces.

```
offsets:
        db 16+displacement
        db 20+displacement
        db 8+displacement
        db 12+displacement
        db 8+displacement
        db 0+displacement
        db 8+displacement
displacement:
        db -33,-31,-18,-14,14,18,31,33
        db -16,16,-1,1
        db 15,17,-15,-17
        db -15,-17,-16,-32
        db 15,17,16,32
```

This is the table of movements for each piece. The *offsets* table points into the *displacement* table. The first row of *offsets* is for white pawns, and the second row is for black pawns. Then it continues the rows for rook, bishop, queen, knight and king. The length of each table is calculated inside the A.I. code.

```
      %if com_file
board:  equ 0x0300
    %else
        ; 118 bytes to say something
        db "Toledo Atomchess. Mar/04/2016"
        db " (c) 2015-2016 Oscar Toledo G. "
        db "www.nanochess.org"
        db " Happy coding! :-) "
        db "Most fun MBR ever!!"
        db 0,0,0


        ;
        ; This marker is required for BIOS to boot floppy disk
        ;

        db 0x55,0xaa

board:  equ $7e00

stack:  equ $8000
    %endif
```

Finally we have the filler data, and the boot sector signature.

When your tiny chess
program is smarter
than you...

Chapter 10

bootBASIC

We have seen how much potential is available using only 512 bytes. So far we've worked with games, but what about a programming language? Although there exist small interpreters for esoteric languages (like Brainfuck[8]), I targeted a more known language and a classic: BASIC (Beginners-All purpose-Symbolic-Instruction-Code), developed in 1964 by John Kemeny and Thomas E. Kurtz at the Darmouth College.

So bootBASIC is an integer BASIC interpreter contained in only 512 bytes, yet it allows us to enter "useful" programs and run them.

It implements several of the classic BASIC commands (like 'print' and 'input'), handles integer expressions with four operators (addition, subtraction, multiplication and division), and has 26 variables (from a to z).

For example, this program displays the numbers from 1 to 10:

```
10 a=1
20 print a
30 a=a+1
40 if a-11 goto 20
run
```

---

[8] Brainfuck is an esoteric programming language created in 1993 by Urban Müller, and is notable for its extreme minimalism. It has only 8 commands. More information at https://en.wikipedia.org/wiki/Brainfuck

It assigns the value 1 to the variable *a*. Prints the value of the variable *a*. Increments *a* by one. And finally if *a* doesn't equal 11, goes to line 20.

10.1 Memory structure.

The memory structure used by bootBASIC is divided into several parts:

- A line buffer for entering data from the keyboard.
- A buffer to keep the BASIC program entered by the user.
- An array to keep the BASIC variables (a-z).
- An indicator of Interactive Mode or Running Mode.

The program starts by defining the memory areas that are going to be used:

```
;
; bootBASIC interpreter in 512 bytes (boot sector)
;
; by Oscar Toledo G.
; http://nanochess.org/
;
; (c) Copyright 2019 Oscar Toledo G.
;
; Creation date: Jul/19/2019. 10pm to 12am.
; Revision date: Jul/20/2019. 10am to 2pm.

        cpu 8086

    %ifndef com_file    ; If not defined create a boot sector
com_file:       equ 0
    %endif

    %if com_file
        org 0x0100
    %else
        org 0x7c00
    %endif

vars:       equ 0x7e00  ; Variables (multiple of 256)
running:    equ 0x7e7e  ; Running status
line:       equ 0x7e80  ; Line input
program:    equ 0x7f00  ; Program address
stack:      equ 0xff00  ; Stack address
```

```
max_line:    equ 1000     ; First unavailable line number
max_length:  equ 20       ; Maximum length of line
max_size:    equ max_line*max_length ; Max. program size

start:
    %if com_file
    %else
        push cs           ; For boot sector
        push cs           ; it needs to setup
        push cs           ; DS, ES and SS.
        pop ds
        pop es
        pop ss
    %endif
        cld               ; Clear Direction flag
        mov di,program    ; Point to program
        mov al,0x0d       ; Fill with CR
        mov cx,max_size   ; Max. program size
        rep stosb         ; Initialize
```

The first step for execution from a boot sector is to copy the CS value (zero in most PC computers, any other value would cause it to fail) into the DS, ES and SS registers.

Then it clears the direction flag so the string instructions work incrementing the register SI and/or the register DI.

The area for BASIC program is filled with 0x0d (CR character or Carriage Return, most known in the PC world as the Enter key).

It doesn't handle a list of lines and moving them accordingly for entering and deleting program lines. Instead, it handles the BASIC program like a bidimensional array of 1000 lines by 20 characters. This means that entering a line is as easy as copying the input data to the line address (*program* + *line* * *max_length*), and deleting a line is as easy as putting the 0x0d byte at the start of the line location in memory. Almost no memory management is needed with this architecture.

program label (line 0)	20 characters (*max_length*)	
+ 20 (line 1)	20 characters (*max_length*)	
+ 40 (line 2)	20 characters (*max_length*)	
...		
+ 19980 (line 999)	20 characters (*max_length*)	*max_line* - 1 = 999

10.2 Interactive Mode.

One of the things that make BASIC very attractive, is the fact that every instruction can be tried at the command prompt without making any program (for example, *print 5+6*). This is known as Interactive Mode and it is different from the Running Mode when a program being executed.

```
        ;
        ; Main loop
        ;
main_loop:
        mov sp,stack     ; Reinitialize stack pointer
        xor ax,ax        ; Mark as interactive
        mov [running],ax
        mov al,'>'       ; Show prompt
        call input_line  ; Accept line
        call input_number    ; Get number
        or ax,ax         ; No number or zero?
        je f14           ; Yes, jump
        call find_line   ; Find the line
        xchg ax,di
        mov cx,max_length
        rep movsb        ; Copy entered line into program
        jmp main_loop    ; Repeat the main loop

f14:    call statement   ; Process statement
        jmp main_loop    ; Repeat the main loop
```

The first step of the *main_loop* is to reinitialize the SP register (Stack Pointer). This is necessary for two reasons: 1. The BIOS set it up to a position that's good for the BIOS but not necessarily for us. 2. This way it is reset to a known position when an error happens inside the BASIC program (the interpreter can locate some errors and exit from some point inside a thread of **call** instructions).

It also sets the variable *running* to zero (this means it is running currently in Interactive Mode). Then it calls *input_line* to read a line from the keyboard (anything including the byte 0x0d or Enter key; also this routine sets the SI register to point to the start of the buffer), and calls *input_number* to verify if the *line* buffer starts with a number (the register AX will be zero if no valid number is found, or if the user entered 0).

If the line number is valid, then it calls *find_line* to locate the position in memory of the program line and puts it on the register DI. Then it copies the full line into the program buffer using **rep movsb**. And it goes to wait another command. This is an example of entering a line for a program:

```
10 print "Hello, world!"
```

Entering the line number without a statement happens to be equivalent to deleting the line.

Notice that exceeding the *max_length - 1* number of characters (equal to 19) means the line can "spill" into the next line. Currently there is no check to avoid this. Just make sure you don't exceed 19 letters per line.

If the line number isn't valid, then it tries to execute the input as a statement calling the subroutine *statement*, and after this it goes to wait for another command.

10.3 Statement handling.

The statements are compared directly with a table of valid bootBASIC statements located at the *statements* label. These statements are stored in lowercase, and the user should enter them also in lowercase for his/her programs, because there is no provision for internal conversion of uppercase to lowercase.

```
        ;
        ; Handle 'if' statement
        ;
if_statement:
        call expr       ; Process expression
        or ax,ax        ; Is it zero?
        je f6           ; Yes, return (ignore if)
statement:
        call spaces     ; Avoid spaces
        cmp byte [si],0x0d  ; Empty line?
        je f6               ; Yes, return
        mov di,statements   ; Point to statements list
f5:     mov cl,[di]     ; Read length of the string
        mov ch,0
        test cx,cx      ; Is it zero?
        je f4           ; Yes, jump
        push si         ; Save current position
        inc di          ; Avoid length byte
f16:    rep cmpsb       ; Compare statement
        jne f3          ; Equal? No, jump
        pop ax
        call spaces     ; Avoid spaces
        jmp word [di]   ; Jump to process

f3:     add di,cx       ; Advance the list pointer
        inc di          ; Avoid the address
        inc di
        pop si
        jmp f5          ; Compare another statement

f4:     call get_variable       ; Try variable
        push ax         ; Save address
        lodsb           ; Read a line letter
        cmp al,'='      ; Is it assignment '=' ?
        je assignment   ; Yes, jump to assignment.


        ;
        ; An error happened
        ;
error:
        mov si,error_message
        call print_2    ; Show error message
        jmp main_loop   ; Exit to main loop

error_message:
```

```
        db "@#!",0x0d    ; Guess the words :P
```

The *statement* label is preceded by the *if_statement* label. It handles the 'if' statement of BASIC. For example:

```
if a-5 goto 20
```

If the expression result is zero, then it returns (ignoring the 'goto' part), or else it executes the 'goto 20'.

The first step in the statement process is to avoid the spaces that can be inserted by the user, then if the line is empty it simply returns.

If the line isn't empty then it starts doing a comparison of the source line to the statements list (*statements* label). The comparison is done as a full chunk, for example, to compare the 'run' statement: it reads the size of the string (3 for 'run'), and then does the comparison using **repe / cmpsb**. If the comparison is valid (all bytes are equal, meaning the input string indeed was 'run'), then the register SI points to the first character after the statement and it avoids the spaces following it, then it jumps to the statement handling using an indirect jump **jmp [di]**. This means to read the word at the address pointed by the register DI and jump to the address indicated by the word (see section 10.10 for the statements table).

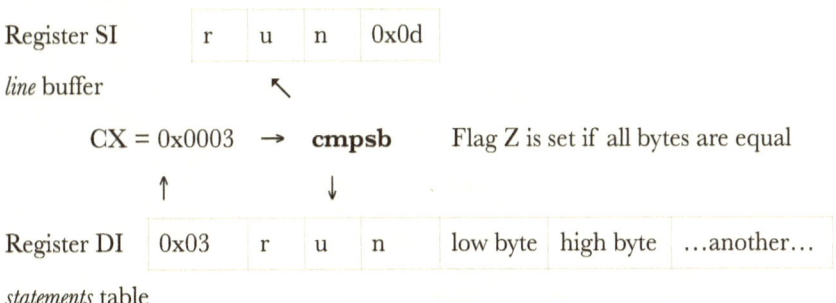

If the comparison fails, it adds the contents of the CX register (count of unchecked letters) to the register DI in order to advance to the next instruction in the *statements* table, plus 2 to avoid the subroutine's address contained in the table. Then it restores the SI register to point again to the start of the statement at the source line and does a comparison with the next statement in the table by means of **jmp f5**.

The end of the table is signaled by a length of zero. This makes the statement parser call *get_variable*, save the address of the variable on the stack, check if there is a '=' character in the input (it generates an error if it isn't present), and jump to *assignment* in order to assign a value to the variable. So this code only processes the 'a' and the '=' characters in the following assignment statement:

```
a=5
```

The error message is printed by the *error* routine (SI points to the address of *error_message*). I've made it to be three characters: @#! The kind of thing that we say when a program doesn't work (not really; it could have been simply 'bad', 'err' or 'bug'). Also it stops the execution and jumps to *main_loop*. You may recall it reinitializes the SP register.

10.4 The 'list' statement.

The 'list' statement allows us to see the program entered into memory:

```
        ;
        ; Handle 'list' statement
        ;
list_statement:
        xor ax,ax       ; Start from line zero
f29:    push ax
        call find_line  ; Find program line
        xchg ax,si
        cmp byte [si],0x0d ; Empty line?
        je f30          ; Yes, jump
        pop ax
        push ax
```

```
        call output_number ; Show line number
f32:    lodsb              ; Show line contents
        call output
        cmp al,0x0d        ; Finish with CR
        jne f32
f30:    pop ax
        inc ax             ; Go to next line
        cmp ax,max_line    ; Finished?
        jne f29            ; No, continue
f6:
        ret
```

The first step is to initialize the register AX to zero (the first line of the program). Then it calls *find_line* to get the respective address and puts it on the register SI. It does a comparison of the first character of the line with 0x0d (CR, Carriage Return), if it is equal then the line is empty and jumps to *f30*, or else it shows the current line number calling *output_number* and then does a loop reading the content of the line until a 0x0d byte is found (again CR, and this means it also goes to the next line on the screen).

Then it restores the register AX, increases it by 1 for the next line, and continues until the *max_line* line number is reached (1000 currently).

10.5 The 'input' statement.

The 'input' statement allows us to enter a number via the keyboard and save it to a variable.

```
        ;
        ; Handle 'input' statement
        ;
input_statement:
        call get_variable  ; Get variable address
        push ax            ; Save it
        mov al,'?'         ; Prompt
        call input_line    ; Wait for line
        ;
        ; Second part of the assignment statement
        ;
assignment:
        call expr          ; Process expression
```

```
        pop di
        stosw                ; Save on the variable
        ret
```

It simply calls the *get_variable* subroutine that reads the input buffer for the variable name and returns the address of the variable into AX. It saves the value of AX, then shows the prompt '?' and waits for a line to be entered. Then it parses the line as an expression, restores the variable's address into the register DI and saves the value of AX using **stosw**.

Notice this statement also contains the missing part of the assignment statement that we discussed in the previous section.

10.6 Expressions handling.

The expressions handling is done in a multi-level process. The first tier handles the addition and subtraction operators, the second tier handles the multiplication and division operators, and finally the third tier handles the expressions between parentheses, variable names and numbers.

```
        ;
        ; Handle an expression.
        ; First tier: addition & subtraction.
        ;
expr:
        call expr1           ; Call second tier
f20:    cmp byte [si],'-'    ; Subtraction operator?
        je f19               ; Yes, jump
        cmp byte [si],'+'    ; Addition operator?
        jne f6               ; No, return
        push ax
        call expr1_2         ; Call second tier
        pop cx
        add ax,cx            ; Addition
        jmp f20              ; Find more operators

f19:
        push ax
        call expr1_2         ; Call second tier
        pop cx
        xchg ax,cx
```

```
        sub ax,cx              ; Subtraction
        jmp f20                ; Find more operators
```

The first step is to get the left-side of the expression calling *expr1*, then it does a comparison of the next character to see if it is a handled operator '-' or '+' (subtraction or addition). If it is, then it saves the current value using **push ax**, gets the right-side of the expression calling *expr1_2*, and restores the left side into the register CX using **pop cx**. Then it does the operation using **add ax,cx** or **sub ax,cx**.

It goes again to *f20*, in order to account for expressions like 1+3+4.

```
        ;
        ; Handle an expression.
        ; Second tier: division & multiplication.
        ;
expr1_2:
        inc si                 ; Avoid operator
expr1:
        call expr2             ; Call third tier
f21:    cmp byte [si],'/'      ; Division operator?
        je f23                 ; Yes, jump
        cmp byte [si],'*'      ; Multiplication operator?
        jne f6                 ; No, return

        push ax
        call expr2_2           ; Call third tier
        pop cx
        imul cx                ; Multiplication
        jmp f21                ; Find more operators


f23:
        push ax
        call expr2_2           ; Call third tier
        pop cx
        xchg ax,cx
        cwd                    ; Expand AX to DX:AX
        idiv cx                ; Signed division
        jmp f21                ; Find more operators
```

The second tier also reads first the left-side expression calling **expr2**, then it does a comparison for '/' or '*' (division and multiplication

163

operators). Same as the previous tier, it saves the current value, reads the right-side expression, restores the previous value and does the operation.

The fact that the second tier is called by the first one accounts for operator precedence. For example 5*6+3*4 is processed as (5*6)+(3*4).

Finally, the third tier handles expressions between parentheses, numbers and variables.

```
        ;
        ; Handle an expression.
        ; Third tier: parentheses, numbers and vars.
        ;
expr2_2:
        inc si                ; Avoid operator
expr2:
        call spaces           ; Jump spaces
        lodsb                 ; Read character
        cmp al,'('            ; Open parenthesis?
        jne f24
        call expr             ; Process inner expr.
        cmp byte [si],')'     ; Closing parenthesis?
        jne error             ; No, jump to error
        jmp spaces_2          ; Yes, avoid spaces

f24:    cmp al,0x40           ; Variable?
        jnc f25               ; Yes, jump
        dec si                ; Back one letter...
        call input_number     ; ...to read number
        jmp spaces            ; Avoid spaces

f25:    call get_variable_2 ; Get variable address
        xchg ax,bx
        mov ax,[bx]           ; Read
        ret                   ; Return
```

The first step is to avoid spaces in the input, then it reads the first character and if it is '(' (left parenthesis) then it calls recursively *expr* to get another expression. It also verifies for the closing parenthesis ')'. If it isn't present it generates an error, or else it avoid spaces and returns happily.

If it wasn't a left parenthesis, it does a comparison with 0x40 (see the Appendix B). If the value is less than 0x40 then it attempts to interpret a number calling *input_number*, but if the value is greater than or equal to

0x40 it means it has a variable, so it gets the variable's address and reads its content with **mov ax,[bx]**.

10.7 Variable handling.

The variables are the basis of the BASIC language and it is what allows us to do operations in multiple steps while saving intermediate values.

```
        ;
        ; Get variable address
        ;
get_variable:
        lodsb                   ; Read source
get_variable_2:
        and al,0x1f             ; 0x61-0x7a -> 0x01-0x1a
        add al,al               ; x 2 (each variable = word)
        mov ah,vars>>8          ; Setup high-byte of address
        ;
        ; Avoid spaces
        ;
spaces:
        cmp byte [si],' '       ; Space found?
        jne f22                 ; No, return
        ;
        ; Avoid spaces after current character
        ;
spaces_2:
        inc si                  ; Advance to next character
        jmp spaces
```

There are two versions of this subroutine. The first one *get_variable* reads the variable letter using **lodsb**, while the second one *get_variable_2* uses the variable name already contained in the register AL.

It doesn't make any check of validity. It just does **and al,0x1f** to extract the variable number (ASCII 0x61-0x7a is converted to 0x01-0x1a), multiplies it by 2 (each variable uses a 16-bit word in memory), and then integrates the variables' table address top with **mov ah,vars>>8**. It means to load the high-byte of the address into AH, making it a complete address into the register AX starting at *vars* address.

The code is combined with the subroutines *spaces* to avoid the spaces following the variable and *spaces_2* that advances the SI register by one character before avoiding spaces.

10.8 Displaying and processing numbers.

The following routines handle the display and processing of numbers entered by the keyboard and already in the line buffer.

```
                ; Output unsigned number
                ; AX = value
                ;
output_number:
f26:
        xor dx,dx           ; DX:AX
        mov cx,10           ; Divisor = 10
        div cx              ; Divide
        or ax,ax            ; Nothing at left?
        push dx
        je f8               ; No, jump
        call f26            ; Yes, output left side
f8:     pop ax
        add al,'0'          ; Output remainder as...
        jmp output          ; ...ASCII digit


        ;
        ; Read number in input
        ; AX = result
        ;
input_number:
        xor bx,bx           ; BX = 0
f11:    lodsb               ; Read source
        sub al,'0'
        cmp al,10           ; Digit valid?
        cbw
        xchg ax,bx
        jnc f12             ; No, jump
        mov cx,10           ; Multiply by 10
        mul cx
        add bx,ax           ; Add new digit
        jmp f11             ; Continue

f12:    dec si              ; SI points to first non-digit
f22:
        ret
```

The first subroutine is a highly-optimized version of the *display_number* subroutine which we saw in section 3.2. Feel free to do a side-by-side comparison in order to see what has been improved.

The second subroutine converts an ASCII decimal number pointed by the register SI into a value inside the register AX. It starts by setting the register BX to zero (the accumulator), then it reads a digit from the buffer using **lodsb**. It subtracts the value of 0x30 (ASCII code for digit 0) and does a comparison with 10 as anything greater than or equal means it isn't a numeric digit and exits.

If the digit is valid then it extends it to a word using **cbw**, does an interchange of the values of the registers AX and BX (accumulator goes to AX, digit goes to BX), multiplies AX by 10 and adds the result to BX so the accumulator stays in BX, and then it repeats the loop looking for another valid digit.

Notice how it exits with a jump to *f12* after doing **xchg ax,bx**, so the final result gets into the register AX.

10.9 Running programs with 'run'/'goto'.

The statement 'run' starts running the program contained in the program buffer from the first line, and the statement 'goto' goes to the indicated line:

```
        ;
        ; Handle 'run' statement
        ; (equivalent to 'goto 0')
        ;
run_statement:
        xor ax,ax
        jmp f10


        ;
        ; Handle 'goto' statement
        ;
goto_statement:
        call expr              ; Handle expression
f10:
        call find_line         ; Find line in program
f27:    cmp word [running],0 ; Already running?
        je f31
```

```
        mov [running],ax      ; Yes, target is new line
        ret
f31:
        push ax
        pop si
        add ax,max_length     ; Point to next line
        mov [running],ax      ; Save for next time
        call statement        ; Process current statement
        mov ax,[running]
        cmp ax,program+max_size ; Reached the end?
        jne f31                 ; No, continue
        ret                     ; Yes, return


        ;
        ; Find line in program
        ; Entry:
        ;    ax = line number
        ; Result:
        ;    ax = pointer to program
find_line:
        mov cx,max_length
        mul cx
        add ax,program
        ret
```

The *run_statement* label simply sets AX to zero and jumps to the second instruction of the *goto_statement* label.

The *goto_statement* label processes the expression following the 'goto' and gets the value into AX as the target line number for jumping inside the BASIC program.

It then proceeds to find the address for the program line calling *find_line*, and it checks if it is in Interactive Mode or Running Mode. For Running Mode it simply saves the pointer into the *running* variable, so the next program line is taken from it, changing the program flow. For Interactive Mode, it saves the pointer to the next line (using **add ax,max_length**) into the *running* variable and it processes the current line calling *statement*, then it verifies if it has reached the maximum number of lines fitting a program and exits.

Notice that if it doesn't check for Interactive Mode, the 'goto' statement would start a new call to *statement* and would enter into a recursive bug, filling the stack continuously.

Finally, the *find_line* subroutine takes the BASIC line number from the register AX and does a multiplication by *max_length* (the maximum length of each program line), and adds the *program* label to get the address in memory of the line into the register AX.

10.10 Input/output.

The bootBASIC interpreter depends on the following subroutines to read a line from the keyboard and output text on the screen.

```
        ;
        ; Input line from keyboard
        ; Entry:
        ;   al = prompt character
        ; Result:
        ;   buffer 'line' contains line, finished with CR
        ;   SI points to 'line'.
        ;
input_line:
        call output
        mov si,line
        push si
        pop di          ; Target for writing line
f1:     call input_key  ; Read keyboard
        cmp al,0x08     ; Backspace?
        jne f2          ; No, jump
        dec di          ; Get back one character
        jmp f1          ; Wait another key

f2:     stosb           ; Save key in buffer
        cmp al,0x0d     ; CR pressed?
        jne f1          ; No, wait another key
        ret             ; Yes, return
```

The *input_line* subroutine outputs the prompt character contained in the register AL (see section 10.2 and 10.5). Then it sets the registers SI and DI to point to the *line* buffer. It then reads the keyboard into register AL.

If the AL register contains 0x08 it means the user pressed the Backspace key, and it decrements the DI register to point to the previous character. Unfortunately, we didn't had enough space to erase the previous character from the screen. Also we didn't put a limit, so you can erase more than possible in the input line (this means the register DI can go <u>before</u> the address of *line*).

If it was any other key then it saves the AL character using **stosb** (remember this saves the AL value into the address pointed by the DI register and increases the DI register). If the character stored was 0x0d (CR, Carriage Return or Enter) then it returns.

This means the line is completed with a 0x0d character. You may recall it is checked in several parts of the interpreter.

```
                ;
                ; Handle "print" statement
                ;
        print_statement:
                lodsb           ; Read source
                cmp al,0x0d     ; End of line?
                je new_line     ; Yes, generate new line and return
                cmp al,'"'      ; Double quotes?
                jne f7          ; No, jump
        print_2:
        f9:
                lodsb           ; Read string contents
                cmp al,'"'      ; Double quotes?
                je f18          ; Yes, jump
                call output     ; Output character
                cmp al,0x0d     ; Unfinished string?
                jne f9          ; No, jump
                ret             ; Return

        f7:     dec si
                call expr       ; Handle expression
                call output_number      ; Output result
        f18:    lodsb           ; Read next character
                cmp al,';'      ; Is it semicolon?
                jne new_line    ; No, jump to generate new line
                ret             ; Yes, return
```

The 'print' statement is multi-syntax. For example:

```
PRINT                Goes to next line on the screen
PRINT "Hello"        Prints Hello and goes to next line
PRINT "Hello";       Prints Hello and cursor stays
PRINT 5              Prints 5 and goes to next line
PRINT 5;             Prints 5 and cursor stays
```

The first comparison **cmp al,0x0d** handles the first case of 'print' without any arguments.

The second comparison **cmp al,'"'** handles the cases of printing a string enclosed by double quotes on the screen. It then proceeds to show all characters on the screen, and it finishes when it detects another double quotes character or the 0x0d byte, meaning the user forgot to enter the double quotes character. It then jumps to *f18* to handle the semicolon case.

At the *f7* label it processes an expression and displays the value as a number, then *f18* checks if there is a semicolon and returns, or else starts a new line on the screen.

```
        ;
        ; Read a key into al
        ; Also outputs it to screen
        ;
input_key:
        mov ah,0x00
        int 0x16
        ;
        ; Screen output of character contained in al
        ; Expands 0x0d (CR) into 0x0a 0x0d (LF CR)
        ;
output:
        cmp al,0x0d
        jne f17
        ;
        ; Go to next line (generates LF+CR)
        ;
new_line:
        mov al,0x0a
        call f17
        mov al,0x0d
f17:
        mov ah,0x0e
        int 0x10
        ret
```

The *input_key* subroutine reads the keyboard using the BIOS Interrupt 0x16 service 0x00. The AL register contains the key pressed in ASCII code (see appendix B). Then it immediately displays the pressed key on the screen.

The *output* subroutine checks first if the register AL contains 0x0d (CR, Carriage Return or Enter). If it is true then it outputs also a 0x0a (LF, Line Feed) to the screen in order to go to the next row at the left. Notice it isn't enough to send the 0x0d character to display, because it would only put the cursor at the left side of the screen.

The display routine is the BIOS Interrupt 0x10, service 0x0e. It receives the ASCII code of letter in the register AL.

```
        ;
        ; List of statements of bootBASIC
        ; First one byte with length of string
        ; Then string with statement
        ; Then a word with the address of the code
        ;
statements:
        db 3,"new"
        dw start

        db 4,"list"
        dw list_statement

        db 3,"run"
        dw run_statement

        db 5,"print"
        dw print_statement

        db 5,"input"
        dw input_statement

        db 2,"if"
        dw if_statement

        db 4,"goto"
        dw goto_statement

    %if com_file
        db 6,"system"
        dw 0     ; Location 0 contains int 0x20 (setup by DOS)
```

```
        %endif

            db 0
```

Finally we have the list of statements accepted by our bootBASIC language. Each entry starts with the length in characters of the statement, followed by the statement's text string, and then a **dw** mnemonic containing the function label where the statement is processed.

Exclusively for the *.com* file, it allows the 'system' statement allowing us to exit to DOS command-line just by typing it and pressing the Enter key. The address is zero. Because of immemorial CP/M compatibility, at the address zero of a *.com* file, there exists an instruction **int 0x20**, that exits to command-line.

```
        ;
        ; Boot sector filler
        ;
        %if com_file
        %else
            times 510-($-$$) db 0x4f
            db 0x55,0xaa              ; Make it a bootable sector
        %endif
```

The boot sector filler completes this program.

10.11 Pascal's Triangle.

The Pascal's Triangle is a triangular array of binomial coefficients. The first number at the top of the triangle is 1, and in the following rows the numbers that appear are the addition of the two numbers of previous row.

Many examples of code use arrays for calculating easily or subroutines to calculate factorials. For this example, I've opted for an iterative solver that doesn't require subroutines or arrays (we have neither in bootBASIC). The only available comparison in bootBASIC is for inequality by means of the subtraction operator; for example: *if a-5 then goto 20*, it jumps if the variable *a* isn't 5.

Here is the bootBASIC source code for it:

```
10 input n
20 i=1
30 c=1
40 j=0
50 t=n-i
60 if j-t goto 80
70 goto 110
80 print " ";
90 j=j+1
100 goto 50
110 k=1
120 if k-i-1 goto 140
130 goto 190
140 print c;
150 c=c*(i-k)/k
160 print " ";
170 k=k+1
180 goto 120
190 print
200 i=i+1
210 if i-n-1 goto 30
run
```

When running it, try entering 5 or 6 and press Enter to see the result.

There are many more things that can be done with the bootBASIC interpreter. You can also try to expand the language, for example, allowing to enter statements in uppercase, or adding the 'cls' statement (CLear Screen), 'gosub' and 'return' for subroutines, and arrays. Or maybe expanding it with graphical statements (like 'screen' and 'pset').

Appendix A

Small BIOS reference

The BIOS provides several services and several subfunctions for each one. We don't intend to cover everything but we will cover the most essential ones. If you are interested in diving more into INT services, you can always search INT 0x10, INT 0x13 or INT 0x16 in any Internet search engine.

A.1 INT 0x10 Video services.

INT 0x10 covers video services. It preserves all registers, except BP in some buggy BIOS.

A.1.1 Set video mode (AH = 0x00)

Sets the current video mode:

AL = Video mode.

The recommended modes are:

- AL = 0x02 = Text 80x25 color. Data segment 0xb800.
- AL = 0x12 = VGA 640x480x16 colors. Data segment 0xa000.
- AL = 0x13 = VGA 320x200x256 colors. Data segment 0xa000.

A.1.2 Display letter in terminal (AH = 0x0e)

Display letter contained in AL to terminal. BH must contain the page number (use 0x00 always) and BL the text color (use 0x0f, only used in graphic modes).

It handles special codes:

- 0x0d = Returns cursor to start of line.
- 0x0a = Advances cursor to next line.
- 0x08 = Cursor back one character.
- 0x07 = Bell.

A.2 INT 0x13 Disk services.

INT 0x13 covers disk services. The registers will probably be trashed.

A.2.1 Read sector (AH = 0x02)

Reads a sector from floppy disk or hard drive. The floppy drive can be trapped by emulation of floppy disk from CD-ROM.

- AL = Number of sectors to read.
- CH = Low byte of cylinder number.
- CL = Sector number (bits 5-0) and high two bits of cylinder (bits 7-6).
- DH = Head number.
- DL = Drive number (0x00 disk drive A, 0x01 disk drive B, 0x80 hard disk 1, 0x81 hard disk 2).
- ES:BX = Data buffer.

On return, if the Carry flag is set, it indicates there was an error (it may be the floppy disk wasn't ready or there is no floppy disk). You can retry the operation.

This service is useful for reading bigger programs from the boot sector.

A.2.2 Write sector (AH = 0x03)

Writes a sector from floppy disk or hard drive.

- AL = Number of sectors to write.
- CH = Low byte of cylinder number.
- CL = Sector number (bits 5-0) and high two bits of cylinder (bits 7-6).
- DH = Head number.
- DL = Drive number (0x00 disk drive A, 0x01 disk drive B, 0x80 hard disk 1, 0x81 hard disk 2).
- ES:BX = Data buffer.

On return, if the Carry flag is set, it indicates there was an error (it may be the floppy disk wasn't ready, was write protected, or there is no floppy disk). You can retry the operation. Guess what's the most-used service by old virus programs.

A.3 INT 0x16 Keyboard services.

It provides keyboard services. All registers are preserved except for AX and Flags.

A.3.1 AH = 0x00 Get key.

If no key is available then it waits for a key to be pressed. It will discard Shift, Alt, Caps and Ctrl keys.

It will return AH = BIOS scan code, AL = ASCII character.

A.3.2 AH = 0x01 Check for available key.

If no key is available then it returns the Z flag set, or else it returns the Z flag clear.

If a key is available, it will return the key available without emptying the buffer. AH = BIOS scan code, AL = ASCII character.

A.3.3 AH = 0x02 Get keyboard flags.

It returns the register AL filled with the following flags:

- bit 0 = 1 = Right shift key pressed.
- bit 1 = 1 = Left shift key pressed.
- bit 2 = 1 = Ctrl key pressed.
- bit 3 = 1 = Alt key pressed.
- bit 4 = 1 = Scroll Lock down.
- bit 5 = 1 = Num Lock down.
- bit 6 = 1 = Caps Lock down.
- bit 7 = 1 = Insert on.

A.4 INT 0x19 Bootstrap loader.

This interrupt makes the BIOS to reboot (it loads again the first boot sector that it can find).

A.5 INT 0x1A Time services.

It provides time services.

A.5.1 AH = 0x00 Get system time.

It returns the number of clock ticks since midnight into CX:DX.

The number of clock ticks per second is approximately 18.2, so every second the value will increase by 18 approximately.

A.6 INT 0x20 Terminate program.

This interrupt makes the operating system to terminate the current program. This only works with MS-DOS, DR-DOS, FreeDOS or the command-line of Windows 7 and previous versions.

Appendix B

ASCII charset

The ASCII charset available by default on booting up a common PC.

```
00-        18- ↑    30- 0    48- H    60- `    78- x    90- É    A8- ¿    C0- └    D8- ╪    F0- ≡
01- ☺      19- ↓    31- 1    49- I    61- a    79- y    91- æ    A9- ⌐    C1- ┴    D9- ┘    F1- ±
02- ☻      1A- →    32- 2    4A- J    62- b    7A- z    92- Æ    AA- ¬    C2- ┬    DA- ┌    F2- ≥
03- ♥      1B- ←    33- 3    4B- K    63- c    7B- {    93- ô    AB- ½    C3- ├    DB- █    F3- ≤
04- ♦      1C- ∟    34- 4    4C- L    64- d    7C- |    94- ö    AC- ¼    C4- ─    DC- ▄    F4- ⌠
05- ♣      1D- ↔    35- 5    4D- M    65- e    7D- }    95- ò    AD- ¡    C5- ┼    DD- ▌    F5- ⌡
06- ♠      1E- ▲    36- 6    4E- N    66- f    7E- ~    96- û    AE- «    C6- ╞    DE- ▐    F6- ÷
07- •      1F- ▼    37- 7    4F- O    67- g    7F- ⌂    97- ù    AF- »    C7- ╟    DF- ▀    F7- ≈
08- ◘      20-      38- 8    50- P    68- h    80- Ç    98- ÿ    B0- ░    C8- ╚    E0- α    F8- °
09- ○      21- !    39- 9    51- Q    69- i    81- ü    99- Ö    B1- ▒    C9- ╔    E1- ß    F9- ·
0A- ◙      22- "    3A- :    52- R    6A- j    82- é    9A- Ü    B2- ▓    CA- ╩    E2- Γ    FA- ·
0B- ♂      23- #    3B- ;    53- S    6B- k    83- â    9B- ¢    B3- │    CB- ╦    E3- π    FB- √
0C- ♀      24- $    3C- <    54- T    6C- l    84- ä    9C- £    B4- ┤    CC- ╠    E4- Σ    FC- ⁿ
0D- ♪      25- %    3D- =    55- U    6D- m    85- à    9D- ¥    B5- ╡    CD- ═    E5- σ    FD- ²
0E- ♫      26- &    3E- >    56- V    6E- n    86- å    9E- ₧    B6- ╢    CE- ╬    E6- µ    FE- ■
0F- ☼      27- '    3F- ?    57- W    6F- o    87- ç    9F- ƒ    B7- ╖    CF- ╧    E7- τ    FF-
10- ►      28- (    40- @    58- X    70- p    88- ê    A0- á    B8- ╕    D0- ╨    E8- Φ
11- ◄      29- )    41- A    59- Y    71- q    89- ë    A1- í    B9- ╣    D1- ╤    E9- Θ
12- ↕      2A- *    42- B    5A- Z    72- r    8A- è    A2- ó    BA- ║    D2- ╥    EA- Ω
13- ‼      2B- +    43- C    5B- [    73- s    8B- ï    A3- ú    BB- ╗    D3- ╙    EB- δ
14- ¶      2C- ,    44- D    5C- \    74- t    8C- î    A4- ñ    BC- ╝    D4- ╘    EC- ∞
15- §      2D- -    45- E    5D- ]    75- u    8D- ì    A5- Ñ    BD- ╜    D5- ╒    ED- φ
16- ▬      2E- .    46- F    5E- ^    76- v    8E- Ä    A6- ª    BE- ╛    D6- ╓    EE- ε
17- ↨      2F- /    47- G    5F- _    77- w    8F- Å    A7- º    BF- ┐    D7- ╫    EF- ∩
```

The ASCII charset is comprised by the symbols 0x20-0x7f. The remaining are known as PC-850 charset. Don't trust the characters in the range 0x80-0xff when running under DOS or Windows command-line, because these can change with the codepage for the default language. Typically the characters almost always available are the bottom set (0x00-0x1f), the single line bars (0xbe-0xc6, 0xcd and 0xd4), and the filler blocks (0xdb-0xdf).

This chart has been generated by booting this program under VirtualBox and doing a screenshot:

```
        ;
        ; Create an ASCII chart
        ; by Oscar Toledo G.
        ; Creation date: Jun/27/2019.
        ;

        cpu 8086

        org 0x7c00      ; Start for boot sector

        mov ax,0x0002   ; Text mode 80x25
        int 0x10        ; Set video mode

        mov ax,0xb800   ; Screen segment
        mov ds,ax       ; Load for using it
        mov es,ax

        xor di,di       ; DI = 0x0000
        mov cx,0x07d0   ; CX = 2000 characters
        mov ax,0xf020   ; AX = Black on white
        rep stosw       ; Fill the screen

        mov di,0x00a4   ; Point to row 1, column 2
        mov al,0x00     ; AL = Character 0x00
al:
        push di         ; Save current address
        push ax         ; Save current letter
        mov cl,4        ; Take high nibble
        shr al,cl
        add al,0x30     ; Convert to ASCII
        cmp al,0x3a     ; Higher than 9?
        jb a3           ; No, jump
        add al,0x07     ; Add 7 to make it a letter
a3:     stosb           ; Put on screen
        inc di          ; Avoid attribute

        pop ax
        push ax
        and al,0x0f     ; Take lower nibble
        add al,0x30     ; Convert to ASCII
        cmp al,0x3a     ; Higher than 9?
        jb a4           ; No, jump
        add al,0x07     ; Add 7 to make it a letter
a4:     stosb           ; Put on screen
        inc di          ; Avoid attribute
```

```
        mov al,0x2d    ; Hyphen
        stosb          ; Put on screen
        inc di         ; Avoid attribute

        inc di         ; Jump one letter
        inc di
        pop ax
        stosb          ; Put current letter
        pop di         ; Restore address
        inc al         ; Next letter
        jz a2          ; Jump if zero (ending)

        add di,0x00a0  ; Go to next line
        cmp di,0x0fa0  ; Reached end of screen?
        jb a1          ; No, jump.
        sub di,0x0f00-14  ; Go back 24 lines
                       ; and move 7 columns to right.
        jmp a1         ; Repeat cycle.

a2:     jmp $          ; Completed.

        times 510-($-$$) db 0x4f   ; Fill boot sector

        db 0x55,0xaa   ; Make it bootable
```

Make code smaller
but not this way...

181

Appendix C

8088 instruction set

This is the full 8088 processor instruction set. Instead of including an abbreviated opcode list with R/M fields, I preferred to show the whole instruction set without some repeated opcodes. This allows you to see the <u>bytes used</u> for each instruction in order to optimize your code, and also to inspire yourself to reorganize your code using the possible variations for addressing and registers.

The list has been generated by an automated tool and verified with *nasm* to make sure each instruction is valid. It accounts for 12485 different instructions! I'm sure some repeated instructions are present, but the opcode is different.

This is the 8088/8086 Flags register with its bits separated:

15	14	13	12	11	10	9	8	7	6	5	4	3	2	1	0
				O	D	I	T	S	Z		A		P		C

O means Overflow: it happens when the result of an operation exceeds the signed capacity of an 8-bit or 16-bit register. D is the Direction flag: it's used for the string operations (MOVS and related). I is the Interruption flag: it's used for low-level hardware. T is the Trap flag: it's enabled when a trap is taken. S is the Sign flag: it takes a copy of the highest bit of the operation. Z is the Zero flag: it is set when the result is zero. A is the Auxiliary Carry: it is set when half of the result sets Carry (not useful because it isn't accessible directly). P is the Parity flag: it is set when the number of bits set to 1 in the result are even. C is the Carry flag: it is set when the result exceeds the capacity of the register.

The other information needed for developing are the flags affected by each instruction:

- SAHF stores the AH register into bits 7-0 of Flags register, while LAHF loads the Flags register bits 7-0 into the AH register.

- ADD, SUB, ADC, SBC, AND, OR, XOR, CMP, TEST, ROL, ROR, RCL, RCR, SHL, SHR, SAR, NEG, MUL, DIV, IMUL, IDIV, CMPS, SCAS, DAA, DAS, AAA, AAS, AAM and AAD. These affect the O, S, Z, A, P and C flags.

- INC, DEC. These affect the O, S, Z, A and P flags, but not the C flag.

- CLC, sets C flag to 0, SEC sets C flag to 1, CMC complements the C flag.

- MOV/LEA/LDS/LES instructions don't affect the flags.

C.1 Instruction set ordered by opcode.

```
ADD [BX+SI],AL .................;00 00        ADD [SI],AH ....................;00 24
ADD [BX+DI],AL .................;00 01        ADD [DI],AH ....................;00 25
ADD [BP+SI],AL .................;00 02        ADD [0x5566],AH ...............;00 26 66 55
ADD [BP+DI],AL .................;00 03        ADD [BX],AH ...................;00 27
ADD [SI],AL ....................;00 04        ADD [BX+SI],CH ................;00 28
ADD [DI],AL ....................;00 05        ADD [BX+DI],CH ................;00 29
ADD [0x5566],AL ...............;00 06 66 55   ADD [BP+SI],CH ................;00 2a
ADD [BX],AL ...................;00 07         ADD [BP+DI],CH ................;00 2b
ADD [BX+SI],CL ................;00 08         ADD [SI],CH ...................;00 2c
ADD [BX+DI],CL ................;00 09         ADD [DI],CH ...................;00 2d
ADD [BP+SI],CL ................;00 0a         ADD [0x5566],CH ...............;00 2e 66 55
ADD [BP+DI],CL ................;00 0b         ADD [BX],CH ...................;00 2f
ADD [SI],CL ...................;00 0c         ADD [BX+SI],DH ................;00 30
ADD [DI],CL ...................;00 0d         ADD [BX+DI],DH ................;00 31
ADD [0x5566],CL ...............;00 0e 66 55   ADD [BP+SI],DH ................;00 32
ADD [BX],CL ...................;00 0f         ADD [BP+DI],DH ................;00 33
ADD [BX+SI],DL ................;00 10         ADD [SI],DH ...................;00 34
ADD [BX+DI],DL ................;00 11         ADD [DI],DH ...................;00 35
ADD [BP+SI],DL ................;00 12         ADD [0x5566],DH ...............;00 36 66 55
ADD [BP+DI],DL ................;00 13         ADD [BX],DH ...................;00 37
ADD [SI],DL ...................;00 14         ADD [BX+SI],BH ................;00 38
ADD [DI],DL ...................;00 15         ADD [BX+DI],BH ................;00 39
ADD [0x5566],DL ...............;00 16 66 55   ADD [BP+SI],BH ................;00 3a
ADD [BX],DL ...................;00 17         ADD [BP+DI],BH ................;00 3b
ADD [BX+SI],BL ................;00 18         ADD [SI],BH ...................;00 3c
ADD [BX+DI],BL ................;00 19         ADD [DI],BH ...................;00 3d
ADD [BP+SI],BL ................;00 1a         ADD [0x5566],BH ...............;00 3e 66 55
ADD [BP+DI],BL ................;00 1b         ADD [BX],BH ...................;00 3f
ADD [SI],BL ...................;00 1c         ADD [BX+SI+0x55],AL ...........;00 40 55
ADD [DI],BL ...................;00 1d         ADD [BX+DI+0x55],AL ...........;00 41 55
ADD [0x5566],BL ...............;00 1e 66 55   ADD [BP+SI+0x55],AL ...........;00 42 55
ADD [BX],BL ...................;00 1f         ADD [BP+DI+0x55],AL ...........;00 43 55
ADD [BX+SI],AH ................;00 20         ADD [SI+0x55],AL ..............;00 44 55
ADD [BX+DI],AH ................;00 21         ADD [DI+0x55],AL ..............;00 45 55
ADD [BP+SI],AH ................;00 22         ADD [BP+0x55],AL ..............;00 46 55
ADD [BP+DI],AH ................;00 23         ADD [BX+0x55],AL ..............;00 47 55
```

```
ADD [BX+SI+0x55],CL .............;00 48 55
ADD [BX+DI+0x55],CL .............;00 49 55
ADD [BP+SI+0x55],CL .............;00 4a 55
ADD [BP+DI+0x55],CL .............;00 4b 55
ADD [SI+0x55],CL ................;00 4c 55
ADD [DI+0x55],CL ................;00 4d 55
ADD [BP+0x55],CL ................;00 4e 55
ADD [BX+0x55],CL ................;00 4f 55
ADD [BX+SI+0x55],DL .............;00 50 55
ADD [BX+DI+0x55],DL .............;00 51 55
ADD [BP+SI+0x55],DL .............;00 52 55
ADD [BP+DI+0x55],DL .............;00 53 55
ADD [SI+0x55],DL ................;00 54 55
ADD [DI+0x55],DL ................;00 55 55
ADD [BP+0x55],DL ................;00 56 55
ADD [BX+0x55],DL ................;00 57 55
ADD [BX+SI+0x55],BL .............;00 58 55
ADD [BX+DI+0x55],BL .............;00 59 55
ADD [BP+SI+0x55],BL .............;00 5a 55
ADD [BP+DI+0x55],BL .............;00 5b 55
ADD [SI+0x55],BL ................;00 5c 55
ADD [DI+0x55],BL ................;00 5d 55
ADD [BP+0x55],BL ................;00 5e 55
ADD [BX+0x55],BL ................;00 5f 55
ADD [BX+SI+0x55],AH .............;00 60 55
ADD [BX+DI+0x55],AH .............;00 61 55
ADD [BP+SI+0x55],AH .............;00 62 55
ADD [BP+DI+0x55],AH .............;00 63 55
ADD [SI+0x55],AH ................;00 64 55
ADD [DI+0x55],AH ................;00 65 55
ADD [BP+0x55],AH ................;00 66 55
ADD [BX+0x55],AH ................;00 67 55
ADD [BX+SI+0x55],CH .............;00 68 55
ADD [BX+DI+0x55],CH .............;00 69 55
ADD [BP+SI+0x55],CH .............;00 6a 55
ADD [BP+DI+0x55],CH .............;00 6b 55
ADD [SI+0x55],CH ................;00 6c 55
ADD [DI+0x55],CH ................;00 6d 55
ADD [BP+0x55],CH ................;00 6e 55
ADD [BX+0x55],CH ................;00 6f 55
ADD [BX+SI+0x55],DH .............;00 70 55
ADD [BX+DI+0x55],DH .............;00 71 55
ADD [BP+SI+0x55],DH .............;00 72 55
ADD [BP+DI+0x55],DH .............;00 73 55
ADD [SI+0x55],DH ................;00 74 55
ADD [DI+0x55],DH ................;00 75 55
ADD [BP+0x55],DH ................;00 76 55
ADD [BX+0x55],DH ................;00 77 55
ADD [BX+SI+0x55],BH .............;00 78 55
ADD [BX+DI+0x55],BH .............;00 79 55
ADD [BP+SI+0x55],BH .............;00 7a 55
ADD [BP+DI+0x55],BH .............;00 7b 55
ADD [SI+0x55],BH ................;00 7c 55
ADD [DI+0x55],BH ................;00 7d 55
ADD [BP+0x55],BH ................;00 7e 55
ADD [BX+0x55],BH ................;00 7f 55
ADD [BX+SI+0x5566],AL ...........;00 80 66 55
ADD [BX+DI+0x5566],AL ...........;00 81 66 55
ADD [BP+SI+0x5566],AL ...........;00 82 66 55
ADD [BP+DI+0x5566],AL ...........;00 83 66 55
ADD [SI+0x5566],AL ..............;00 84 66 55
ADD [DI+0x5566],AL ..............;00 85 66 55
ADD [BP+0x5566],AL ..............;00 86 66 55
ADD [BX+0x5566],AL ..............;00 87 66 55
ADD [BX+SI+0x5566],CL ...........;00 88 66 55
ADD [BX+DI+0x5566],CL ...........;00 89 66 55
ADD [BP+SI+0x5566],CL ...........;00 8a 66 55
ADD [BP+DI+0x5566],CL ...........;00 8b 66 55
ADD [SI+0x5566],CL ..............;00 8c 66 55
ADD [DI+0x5566],CL ..............;00 8d 66 55
ADD [BP+0x5566],CL ..............;00 8e 66 55
ADD [BX+0x5566],CL ..............;00 8f 66 55
ADD [BX+SI+0x5566],DL ...........;00 90 66 55
ADD [BX+DI+0x5566],DL ...........;00 91 66 55
ADD [BP+SI+0x5566],DL ...........;00 92 66 55
ADD [BP+DI+0x5566],DL ...........;00 93 66 55
ADD [SI+0x5566],DL ..............;00 94 66 55
ADD [DI+0x5566],DL ..............;00 95 66 55
ADD [BP+0x5566],DL ..............;00 96 66 55
ADD [BX+0x5566],DL ..............;00 97 66 55
ADD [BX+SI+0x5566],BL ...........;00 98 66 55
ADD [BX+DI+0x5566],BL ...........;00 99 66 55
ADD [BP+SI+0x5566],BL ...........;00 9a 66 55
ADD [BP+DI+0x5566],BL ...........;00 9b 66 55
ADD [SI+0x5566],BL ..............;00 9c 66 55
ADD [DI+0x5566],BL ..............;00 9d 66 55
ADD [BP+0x5566],BL ..............;00 9e 66 55
ADD [BX+0x5566],BL ..............;00 9f 66 55
ADD [BX+SI+0x5566],AH ...........;00 a0 66 55

ADD [BX+DI+0x5566],AH ...........;00 a1 66 55
ADD [BP+SI+0x5566],AH ...........;00 a2 66 55
ADD [BP+DI+0x5566],AH ...........;00 a3 66 55
ADD [SI+0x5566],AH ..............;00 a4 66 55
ADD [DI+0x5566],AH ..............;00 a5 66 55
ADD [BP+0x5566],AH ..............;00 a6 66 55
ADD [BX+0x5566],AH ..............;00 a7 66 55
ADD [BX+SI+0x5566],CH ...........;00 a8 66 55
ADD [BX+DI+0x5566],CH ...........;00 a9 66 55
ADD [BP+SI+0x5566],CH ...........;00 aa 66 55
ADD [BP+DI+0x5566],CH ...........;00 ab 66 55
ADD [SI+0x5566],CH ..............;00 ac 66 55
ADD [DI+0x5566],CH ..............;00 ad 66 55
ADD [BP+0x5566],CH ..............;00 ae 66 55
ADD [BX+0x5566],CH ..............;00 af 66 55
ADD [BX+SI+0x5566],DH ...........;00 b0 66 55
ADD [BX+DI+0x5566],DH ...........;00 b1 66 55
ADD [BP+SI+0x5566],DH ...........;00 b2 66 55
ADD [BP+DI+0x5566],DH ...........;00 b3 66 55
ADD [SI+0x5566],DH ..............;00 b4 66 55
ADD [DI+0x5566],DH ..............;00 b5 66 55
ADD [BP+0x5566],DH ..............;00 b6 66 55
ADD [BX+0x5566],DH ..............;00 b7 66 55
ADD [BX+SI+0x5566],BH ...........;00 b8 66 55
ADD [BX+DI+0x5566],BH ...........;00 b9 66 55
ADD [BP+SI+0x5566],BH ...........;00 ba 66 55
ADD [BP+DI+0x5566],BH ...........;00 bb 66 55
ADD [SI+0x5566],BH ..............;00 bc 66 55
ADD [DI+0x5566],BH ..............;00 bd 66 55
ADD [BP+0x5566],BH ..............;00 be 66 55
ADD [BX+0x5566],BH ..............;00 bf 66 55
ADD AL,AL ......................;00 c0
ADD CL,AL ......................;00 c1
ADD DL,AL ......................;00 c2
ADD BL,AL ......................;00 c3
ADD AH,AL ......................;00 c4
ADD CH,AL ......................;00 c5
ADD DH,AL ......................;00 c6
ADD BH,AL ......................;00 c7
ADD AL,CL ......................;00 c8
ADD CL,CL ......................;00 c9
ADD DL,CL ......................;00 ca
ADD BL,CL ......................;00 cb
ADD AH,CL ......................;00 cc
ADD CH,CL ......................;00 cd
ADD DH,CL ......................;00 ce
ADD BH,CL ......................;00 cf
ADD AL,DL ......................;00 d0
ADD CL,DL ......................;00 d1
ADD DL,DL ......................;00 d2
ADD BL,DL ......................;00 d3
ADD AH,DL ......................;00 d4
ADD CH,DL ......................;00 d5
ADD DH,DL ......................;00 d6
ADD BH,DL ......................;00 d7
ADD AL,BL ......................;00 d8
ADD CL,BL ......................;00 d9
ADD DL,BL ......................;00 da
ADD BL,BL ......................;00 db
ADD AH,BL ......................;00 dc
ADD CH,BL ......................;00 dd
ADD DH,BL ......................;00 de
ADD BH,BL ......................;00 df
ADD AL,AH ......................;00 e0
ADD CL,AH ......................;00 e1
ADD DL,AH ......................;00 e2
ADD BL,AH ......................;00 e3
ADD AH,AH ......................;00 e4
ADD CH,AH ......................;00 e5
ADD DH,AH ......................;00 e6
ADD BH,AH ......................;00 e7
ADD AL,CH ......................;00 e8
ADD CL,CH ......................;00 e9
ADD DL,CH ......................;00 ea
ADD BL,CH ......................;00 eb
ADD AH,CH ......................;00 ec
ADD CH,CH ......................;00 ed
ADD DH,CH ......................;00 ee
ADD BH,CH ......................;00 ef
ADD AL,DH ......................;00 f0
ADD CL,DH ......................;00 f1
ADD DL,DH ......................;00 f2
ADD BL,DH ......................;00 f3
ADD AH,DH ......................;00 f4
ADD CH,DH ......................;00 f5
ADD DH,DH ......................;00 f6
ADD BH,DH ......................;00 f7
ADD AL,BH ......................;00 f8
ADD CL,BH ......................;00 f9
```

```
ADD DL,BH .....................;00 fa
ADD BL,BH .....................;00 fb
ADD AH,BH .....................;00 fc
ADD CH,BH .....................;00 fd
ADD DH,BH .....................;00 fe
ADD BH,BH .....................;00 ff
ADD [BX+SI],AX ................;01 00
ADD [BX+DI],AX ................;01 01
ADD [BP+SI],AX ................;01 02
ADD [BP+DI],AX ................;01 03
ADD [SI],AX ...................;01 04
ADD [DI],AX ...................;01 05
ADD [0x5566],AX ...............;01 06 66 55
ADD [BX],AX ...................;01 07
ADD [BX+SI],CX ................;01 08
ADD [BX+DI],CX ................;01 09
ADD [BP+SI],CX ................;01 0a
ADD [BP+DI],CX ................;01 0b
ADD [SI],CX ...................;01 0c
ADD [DI],CX ...................;01 0d
ADD [0x5566],CX ...............;01 0e 66 55
ADD [BX],CX ...................;01 0f
ADD [BX+SI],DX ................;01 10
ADD [BX+DI],DX ................;01 11
ADD [BP+SI],DX ................;01 12
ADD [BP+DI],DX ................;01 13
ADD [SI],DX ...................;01 14
ADD [DI],DX ...................;01 15
ADD [0x5566],DX ...............;01 16 66 55
ADD [BX],DX ...................;01 17
ADD [BX+SI],BX ................;01 18
ADD [BX+DI],BX ................;01 19
ADD [BP+SI],BX ................;01 1a
ADD [BP+DI],BX ................;01 1b
ADD [SI],BX ...................;01 1c
ADD [DI],BX ...................;01 1d
ADD [0x5566],BX ...............;01 1e 66 55
ADD [BX],BX ...................;01 1f
ADD [BX+SI],SP ................;01 20
ADD [BX+DI],SP ................;01 21
ADD [BP+SI],SP ................;01 22
ADD [BP+DI],SP ................;01 23
ADD [SI],SP ...................;01 24
ADD [DI],SP ...................;01 25
ADD [0x5566],SP ...............;01 26 66 55
ADD [BX],SP ...................;01 27
ADD [BX+SI],BP ................;01 28
ADD [BX+DI],BP ................;01 29
ADD [BP+SI],BP ................;01 2a
ADD [BP+DI],BP ................;01 2b
ADD [SI],BP ...................;01 2c
ADD [DI],BP ...................;01 2d
ADD [0x5566],BP ...............;01 2e 66 55
ADD [BX],BP ...................;01 2f
ADD [BX+SI],SI ................;01 30
ADD [BX+DI],SI ................;01 31
ADD [BP+SI],SI ................;01 32
ADD [BP+DI],SI ................;01 33
ADD [SI],SI ...................;01 34
ADD [DI],SI ...................;01 35
ADD [0x5566],SI ...............;01 36 66 55
ADD [BX],SI ...................;01 37
ADD [BX+SI],DI ................;01 38
ADD [BX+DI],DI ................;01 39
ADD [BP+SI],DI ................;01 3a
ADD [BP+DI],DI ................;01 3b
ADD [SI],DI ...................;01 3c
ADD [DI],DI ...................;01 3d
ADD [0x5566],DI ...............;01 3e 66 55
ADD [BX],DI ...................;01 3f
ADD [BX+SI+0x55],AX ...........;01 40 55
ADD [BX+DI+0x55],AX ...........;01 41 55
ADD [BP+SI+0x55],AX ...........;01 42 55
ADD [BP+DI+0x55],AX ...........;01 43 55
ADD [SI+0x55],AX ..............;01 44 55
ADD [DI+0x55],AX ..............;01 45 55
ADD [BP+0x55],AX ..............;01 46 55
ADD [BX+0x55],AX ..............;01 47 55
ADD [BX+SI+0x55],CX ...........;01 48 55
ADD [BX+DI+0x55],CX ...........;01 49 55
ADD [BP+SI+0x55],CX ...........;01 4a 55
ADD [BP+DI+0x55],CX ...........;01 4b 55
ADD [SI+0x55],CX ..............;01 4c 55
ADD [DI+0x55],CX ..............;01 4d 55
ADD [BP+0x55],CX ..............;01 4e 55
ADD [BX+0x55],CX ..............;01 4f 55
ADD [BX+SI+0x55],DX ...........;01 50 55
ADD [BX+DI+0x55],DX ...........;01 51 55
ADD [BP+SI+0x55],DX ...........;01 52 55
ADD [BP+DI+0x55],DX ...........;01 53 55
ADD [SI+0x55],DX ..............;01 54 55
ADD [DI+0x55],DX ..............;01 55 55
ADD [BP+0x55],DX ..............;01 56 55
ADD [BX+0x55],DX ..............;01 57 55
ADD [BX+SI+0x55],BX ...........;01 58 55
ADD [BX+DI+0x55],BX ...........;01 59 55
ADD [BP+SI+0x55],BX ...........;01 5a 55
ADD [BP+DI+0x55],BX ...........;01 5b 55
ADD [SI+0x55],BX ..............;01 5c 55
ADD [DI+0x55],BX ..............;01 5d 55
ADD [BP+0x55],BX ..............;01 5e 55
ADD [BX+0x55],BX ..............;01 5f 55
ADD [BX+SI+0x55],SP ...........;01 60 55
ADD [BX+DI+0x55],SP ...........;01 61 55
ADD [BP+SI+0x55],SP ...........;01 62 55
ADD [BP+DI+0x55],SP ...........;01 63 55
ADD [SI+0x55],SP ..............;01 64 55
ADD [DI+0x55],SP ..............;01 65 55
ADD [BP+0x55],SP ..............;01 66 55
ADD [BX+0x55],SP ..............;01 67 55
ADD [BX+SI+0x55],BP ...........;01 68 55
ADD [BX+DI+0x55],BP ...........;01 69 55
ADD [BP+SI+0x55],BP ...........;01 6a 55
ADD [BP+DI+0x55],BP ...........;01 6b 55
ADD [SI+0x55],BP ..............;01 6c 55
ADD [DI+0x55],BP ..............;01 6d 55
ADD [BP+0x55],BP ..............;01 6e 55
ADD [BX+0x55],BP ..............;01 6f 55
ADD [BX+SI+0x55],SI ...........;01 70 55
ADD [BX+DI+0x55],SI ...........;01 71 55
ADD [BP+SI+0x55],SI ...........;01 72 55
ADD [BP+DI+0x55],SI ...........;01 73 55
ADD [SI+0x55],SI ..............;01 74 55
ADD [DI+0x55],SI ..............;01 75 55
ADD [BP+0x55],SI ..............;01 76 55
ADD [BX+0x55],SI ..............;01 77 55
ADD [BX+SI+0x55],DI ...........;01 78 55
ADD [BX+DI+0x55],DI ...........;01 79 55
ADD [BP+SI+0x55],DI ...........;01 7a 55
ADD [BP+DI+0x55],DI ...........;01 7b 55
ADD [SI+0x55],DI ..............;01 7c 55
ADD [DI+0x55],DI ..............;01 7d 55
ADD [BP+0x55],DI ..............;01 7e 55
ADD [BX+0x55],DI ..............;01 7f 55
ADD [BX+SI+0x5566],AX .........;01 80 66 55
ADD [BX+DI+0x5566],AX .........;01 81 66 55
ADD [BP+SI+0x5566],AX .........;01 82 66 55
ADD [BP+DI+0x5566],AX .........;01 83 66 55
ADD [SI+0x5566],AX ............;01 84 66 55
ADD [DI+0x5566],AX ............;01 85 66 55
ADD [BP+0x5566],AX ............;01 86 66 55
ADD [BX+0x5566],AX ............;01 87 66 55
ADD [BX+SI+0x5566],CX .........;01 88 66 55
ADD [BX+DI+0x5566],CX .........;01 89 66 55
ADD [BP+SI+0x5566],CX .........;01 8a 66 55
ADD [BP+DI+0x5566],CX .........;01 8b 66 55
ADD [SI+0x5566],CX ............;01 8c 66 55
ADD [DI+0x5566],CX ............;01 8d 66 55
ADD [BP+0x5566],CX ............;01 8e 66 55
ADD [BX+0x5566],CX ............;01 8f 66 55
ADD [BX+SI+0x5566],DX .........;01 90 66 55
ADD [BX+DI+0x5566],DX .........;01 91 66 55
ADD [BP+SI+0x5566],DX .........;01 92 66 55
ADD [BP+DI+0x5566],DX .........;01 93 66 55
ADD [SI+0x5566],DX ............;01 94 66 55
ADD [DI+0x5566],DX ............;01 95 66 55
ADD [BP+0x5566],DX ............;01 96 66 55
ADD [BX+0x5566],DX ............;01 97 66 55
ADD [BX+SI+0x5566],BX .........;01 98 66 55
ADD [BX+DI+0x5566],BX .........;01 99 66 55
ADD [BP+SI+0x5566],BX .........;01 9a 66 55
ADD [BP+DI+0x5566],BX .........;01 9b 66 55
ADD [SI+0x5566],BX ............;01 9c 66 55
ADD [DI+0x5566],BX ............;01 9d 66 55
ADD [BP+0x5566],BX ............;01 9e 66 55
ADD [BX+0x5566],BX ............;01 9f 66 55
ADD [BX+SI+0x5566],SP .........;01 a0 66 55
ADD [BX+DI+0x5566],SP .........;01 a1 66 55
ADD [BP+SI+0x5566],SP .........;01 a2 66 55
ADD [BP+DI+0x5566],SP .........;01 a3 66 55
ADD [SI+0x5566],SP ............;01 a4 66 55
ADD [DI+0x5566],SP ............;01 a5 66 55
ADD [BP+0x5566],SP ............;01 a6 66 55
ADD [BX+0x5566],SP ............;01 a7 66 55
ADD [BX+SI+0x5566],BP .........;01 a8 66 55
ADD [BX+DI+0x5566],BP .........;01 a9 66 55
ADD [BP+SI+0x5566],BP .........;01 aa 66 55
ADD [BP+DI+0x5566],BP .........;01 ab 66 55
```

```
ADD [SI+0x5566],BP .............;01 ac 66 55      ADD AL,[DI] ...................;02 05
ADD [DI+0x5566],BP .............;01 ad 66 55      ADD AL,[0x5566] ...............;02 06 66 55
ADD [BP+0x5566],BP .............;01 ae 66 55      ADD AL,[BX] ...................;02 07
ADD [BX+0x5566],BP .............;01 af 66 55      ADD CL,[BX+SI] ................;02 08
ADD [BX+SI+0x5566],SI ..........;01 b0 66 55      ADD CL,[BX+DI] ................;02 09
ADD [BX+DI+0x5566],SI ..........;01 b1 66 55      ADD CL,[BP+SI] ................;02 0a
ADD [BP+SI+0x5566],SI ..........;01 b2 66 55      ADD CL,[BP+DI] ................;02 0b
ADD [BP+DI+0x5566],SI ..........;01 b3 66 55      ADD CL,[SI] ...................;02 0c
ADD [SI+0x5566],SI .............;01 b4 66 55      ADD CL,[DI] ...................;02 0d
ADD [DI+0x5566],SI .............;01 b5 66 55      ADD CL,[0x5566] ...............;02 0e 66 55
ADD [BP+0x5566],SI .............;01 b6 66 55      ADD CL,[BX] ...................;02 0f
ADD [BX+0x5566],SI .............;01 b7 66 55      ADD DL,[BX+SI] ................;02 10
ADD [BX+SI+0x5566],DI ..........;01 b8 66 55      ADD DL,[BX+DI] ................;02 11
ADD [BX+DI+0x5566],DI ..........;01 b9 66 55      ADD DL,[BP+SI] ................;02 12
ADD [BP+SI+0x5566],DI ..........;01 ba 66 55      ADD DL,[BP+DI] ................;02 13
ADD [BP+DI+0x5566],DI ..........;01 bb 66 55      ADD DL,[SI] ...................;02 14
ADD [SI+0x5566],DI .............;01 bc 66 55      ADD DL,[DI] ...................;02 15
ADD [DI+0x5566],DI .............;01 bd 66 55      ADD DL,[0x5566] ...............;02 16 66 55
ADD [BP+0x5566],DI .............;01 be 66 55      ADD DL,[BX] ...................;02 17
ADD [BX+0x5566],DI .............;01 bf 66 55      ADD BL,[BX+SI] ................;02 18
ADD AX,AX .....................;01 c0            ADD BL,[BX+DI] ................;02 19
ADD CX,AX .....................;01 c1            ADD BL,[BP+SI] ................;02 1a
ADD DX,AX .....................;01 c2            ADD BL,[BP+DI] ................;02 1b
ADD BX,AX .....................;01 c3            ADD BL,[SI] ...................;02 1c
ADD SP,AX .....................;01 c4            ADD BL,[DI] ...................;02 1d
ADD BP,AX .....................;01 c5            ADD BL,[0x5566] ...............;02 1e 66 55
ADD SI,AX .....................;01 c6            ADD BL,[BX] ...................;02 1f
ADD DI,AX .....................;01 c7            ADD AH,[BX+SI] ................;02 20
ADD AX,CX .....................;01 c8            ADD AH,[BX+DI] ................;02 21
ADD CX,CX .....................;01 c9            ADD AH,[BP+SI] ................;02 22
ADD DX,CX .....................;01 ca            ADD AH,[BP+DI] ................;02 23
ADD BX,CX .....................;01 cb            ADD AH,[SI] ...................;02 24
ADD SP,CX .....................;01 cc            ADD AH,[DI] ...................;02 25
ADD BP,CX .....................;01 cd            ADD AH,[0x5566] ...............;02 26 66 55
ADD SI,CX .....................;01 ce            ADD AH,[BX] ...................;02 27
ADD DI,CX .....................;01 cf            ADD CH,[BX+SI] ................;02 28
ADD AX,DX .....................;01 d0            ADD CH,[BX+DI] ................;02 29
ADD CX,DX .....................;01 d1            ADD CH,[BP+SI] ................;02 2a
ADD DX,DX .....................;01 d2            ADD CH,[BP+DI] ................;02 2b
ADD BX,DX .....................;01 d3            ADD CH,[SI] ...................;02 2c
ADD SP,DX .....................;01 d4            ADD CH,[DI] ...................;02 2d
ADD BP,DX .....................;01 d5            ADD CH,[0x5566] ...............;02 2e 66 55
ADD SI,DX .....................;01 d6            ADD CH,[BX] ...................;02 2f
ADD DI,DX .....................;01 d7            ADD DH,[BX+SI] ................;02 30
ADD AX,BX .....................;01 d8            ADD DH,[BX+DI] ................;02 31
ADD CX,BX .....................;01 d9            ADD DH,[BP+SI] ................;02 32
ADD DX,BX .....................;01 da            ADD DH,[BP+DI] ................;02 33
ADD BX,BX .....................;01 db            ADD DH,[SI] ...................;02 34
ADD SP,BX .....................;01 dc            ADD DH,[DI] ...................;02 35
ADD BP,BX .....................;01 dd            ADD DH,[0x5566] ...............;02 36 66 55
ADD SI,BX .....................;01 de            ADD DH,[BX] ...................;02 37
ADD DI,BX .....................;01 df            ADD BH,[BX+SI] ................;02 38
ADD AX,SP .....................;01 e0            ADD BH,[BX+DI] ................;02 39
ADD CX,SP .....................;01 e1            ADD BH,[BP+SI] ................;02 3a
ADD DX,SP .....................;01 e2            ADD BH,[BP+DI] ................;02 3b
ADD BX,SP .....................;01 e3            ADD BH,[SI] ...................;02 3c
ADD SP,SP .....................;01 e4            ADD BH,[DI] ...................;02 3d
ADD BP,SP .....................;01 e5            ADD BH,[0x5566] ...............;02 3e 66 55
ADD SI,SP .....................;01 e6            ADD BH,[BX] ...................;02 3f
ADD DI,SP .....................;01 e7            ADD AL,[BX+SI+0x55] ...........;02 40 55
ADD AX,BP .....................;01 e8            ADD AL,[BX+DI+0x55] ...........;02 41 55
ADD CX,BP .....................;01 e9            ADD AL,[BP+SI+0x55] ...........;02 42 55
ADD DX,BP .....................;01 ea            ADD AL,[BP+DI+0x55] ...........;02 43 55
ADD BX,BP .....................;01 eb            ADD AL,[SI+0x55] ..............;02 44 55
ADD SP,BP .....................;01 ec            ADD AL,[DI+0x55] ..............;02 45 55
ADD BP,BP .....................;01 ed            ADD AL,[BP+0x55] ..............;02 46 55
ADD SI,BP .....................;01 ee            ADD AL,[BX+0x55] ..............;02 47 55
ADD DI,BP .....................;01 ef            ADD CL,[BX+SI+0x55] ...........;02 48 55
ADD AX,SI .....................;01 f0            ADD CL,[BX+DI+0x55] ...........;02 49 55
ADD CX,SI .....................;01 f1            ADD CL,[BP+SI+0x55] ...........;02 4a 55
ADD DX,SI .....................;01 f2            ADD CL,[BP+DI+0x55] ...........;02 4b 55
ADD BX,SI .....................;01 f3            ADD CL,[SI+0x55] ..............;02 4c 55
ADD SP,SI .....................;01 f4            ADD CL,[DI+0x55] ..............;02 4d 55
ADD BP,SI .....................;01 f5            ADD CL,[BP+0x55] ..............;02 4e 55
ADD SI,SI .....................;01 f6            ADD CL,[BX+0x55] ..............;02 4f 55
ADD DI,SI .....................;01 f7            ADD DL,[BX+SI+0x55] ...........;02 50 55
ADD AX,DI .....................;01 f8            ADD DL,[BX+DI+0x55] ...........;02 51 55
ADD CX,DI .....................;01 f9            ADD DL,[BP+SI+0x55] ...........;02 52 55
ADD DX,DI .....................;01 fa            ADD DL,[BP+DI+0x55] ...........;02 53 55
ADD BX,DI .....................;01 fb            ADD DL,[SI+0x55] ..............;02 54 55
ADD SP,DI .....................;01 fc            ADD DL,[DI+0x55] ..............;02 55 55
ADD BP,DI .....................;01 fd            ADD DL,[BP+0x55] ..............;02 56 55
ADD SI,DI .....................;01 fe            ADD DL,[BX+0x55] ..............;02 57 55
ADD DI,DI .....................;01 ff            ADD BL,[BX+SI+0x55] ...........;02 58 55
ADD AL,[BX+SI] ................;02 00            ADD BL,[BX+DI+0x55] ...........;02 59 55
ADD AL,[BX+DI] ................;02 01            ADD BL,[BP+SI+0x55] ...........;02 5a 55
ADD AL,[BP+SI] ................;02 02            ADD BL,[BP+DI+0x55] ...........;02 5b 55
ADD AL,[BP+DI] ................;02 03            ADD BL,[SI+0x55] ..............;02 5c 55
ADD AL,[SI] ...................;02 04            ADD BL,[DI+0x55] ..............;02 5d 55
```

```
ADD BL,[BP+0x55]           ...............;02 5e 55
ADD BL,[BX+0x55]           ...............;02 5f 55
ADD AH,[BX+SI+0x55]        ...............;02 60 55
ADD AH,[BX+DI+0x55]        ...............;02 61 55
ADD AH,[BP+SI+0x55]        ...............;02 62 55
ADD AH,[BP+DI+0x55]        ...............;02 63 55
ADD AH,[SI+0x55]           ...............;02 64 55
ADD AH,[DI+0x55]           ...............;02 65 55
ADD AH,[BP+0x55]           ...............;02 66 55
ADD AH,[BX+0x55]           ...............;02 67 55
ADD CH,[BX+SI+0x55]        ...............;02 68 55
ADD CH,[BX+DI+0x55]        ...............;02 69 55
ADD CH,[BP+SI+0x55]        ...............;02 6a 55
ADD CH,[BP+DI+0x55]        ...............;02 6b 55
ADD CH,[SI+0x55]           ...............;02 6c 55
ADD CH,[DI+0x55]           ...............;02 6d 55
ADD CH,[BP+0x55]           ...............;02 6e 55
ADD CH,[BX+0x55]           ...............;02 6f 55
ADD DH,[BX+SI+0x55]        ...............;02 70 55
ADD DH,[BX+DI+0x55]        ...............;02 71 55
ADD DH,[BP+SI+0x55]        ...............;02 72 55
ADD DH,[BP+DI+0x55]        ...............;02 73 55
ADD DH,[SI+0x55]           ...............;02 74 55
ADD DH,[DI+0x55]           ...............;02 75 55
ADD DH,[BP+0x55]           ...............;02 76 55
ADD DH,[BX+0x55]           ...............;02 77 55
ADD BH,[BX+SI+0x55]        ...............;02 78 55
ADD BH,[BX+DI+0x55]        ...............;02 79 55
ADD BH,[BP+SI+0x55]        ...............;02 7a 55
ADD BH,[BP+DI+0x55]        ...............;02 7b 55
ADD BH,[SI+0x55]           ...............;02 7c 55
ADD BH,[DI+0x55]           ...............;02 7d 55
ADD BH,[BP+0x55]           ...............;02 7e 55
ADD BH,[BX+0x55]           ...............;02 7f 55
ADD AL,[BX+SI+0x5566]      ...........;02 80 66 55
ADD AL,[BX+DI+0x5566]      ...........;02 81 66 55
ADD AL,[BP+SI+0x5566]      ...........;02 82 66 55
ADD AL,[BP+DI+0x5566]      ...........;02 83 66 55
ADD AL,[SI+0x5566]         ...........;02 84 66 55
ADD AL,[DI+0x5566]         ...........;02 85 66 55
ADD AL,[BP+0x5566]         ...........;02 86 66 55
ADD AL,[BX+0x5566]         ...........;02 87 66 55
ADD CL,[BX+SI+0x5566]      ...........;02 88 66 55
ADD CL,[BX+DI+0x5566]      ...........;02 89 66 55
ADD CL,[BP+SI+0x5566]      ...........;02 8a 66 55
ADD CL,[BP+DI+0x5566]      ...........;02 8b 66 55
ADD CL,[SI+0x5566]         ...........;02 8c 66 55
ADD CL,[DI+0x5566]         ...........;02 8d 66 55
ADD CL,[BP+0x5566]         ...........;02 8e 66 55
ADD CL,[BX+0x5566]         ...........;02 8f 66 55
ADD DL,[BX+SI+0x5566]      ...........;02 90 66 55
ADD DL,[BX+DI+0x5566]      ...........;02 91 66 55
ADD DL,[BP+SI+0x5566]      ...........;02 92 66 55
ADD DL,[BP+DI+0x5566]      ...........;02 93 66 55
ADD DL,[SI+0x5566]         ...........;02 94 66 55
ADD DL,[DI+0x5566]         ...........;02 95 66 55
ADD DL,[BP+0x5566]         ...........;02 96 66 55
ADD DL,[BX+0x5566]         ...........;02 97 66 55
ADD BL,[BX+SI+0x5566]      ...........;02 98 66 55
ADD BL,[BX+DI+0x5566]      ...........;02 99 66 55
ADD BL,[BP+SI+0x5566]      ...........;02 9a 66 55
ADD BL,[BP+DI+0x5566]      ...........;02 9b 66 55
ADD BL,[SI+0x5566]         ...........;02 9c 66 55
ADD BL,[DI+0x5566]         ...........;02 9d 66 55
ADD BL,[BP+0x5566]         ...........;02 9e 66 55
ADD BL,[BX+0x5566]         ...........;02 9f 66 55
ADD AH,[BX+SI+0x5566]      ...........;02 a0 66 55
ADD AH,[BX+DI+0x5566]      ...........;02 a1 66 55
ADD AH,[BP+SI+0x5566]      ...........;02 a2 66 55
ADD AH,[BP+DI+0x5566]      ...........;02 a3 66 55
ADD AH,[SI+0x5566]         ...........;02 a4 66 55
ADD AH,[DI+0x5566]         ...........;02 a5 66 55
ADD AH,[BP+0x5566]         ...........;02 a6 66 55
ADD AH,[BX+0x5566]         ...........;02 a7 66 55
ADD CH,[BX+SI+0x5566]      ...........;02 a8 66 55
ADD CH,[BX+DI+0x5566]      ...........;02 a9 66 55
ADD CH,[BP+SI+0x5566]      ...........;02 aa 66 55
ADD CH,[BP+DI+0x5566]      ...........;02 ab 66 55
ADD CH,[SI+0x5566]         ...........;02 ac 66 55
ADD CH,[DI+0x5566]         ...........;02 ad 66 55
ADD CH,[BP+0x5566]         ...........;02 ae 66 55
ADD CH,[BX+0x5566]         ...........;02 af 66 55
ADD DH,[BX+SI+0x5566]      ...........;02 b0 66 55
ADD DH,[BX+DI+0x5566]      ...........;02 b1 66 55
ADD DH,[BP+SI+0x5566]      ...........;02 b2 66 55
ADD DH,[BP+DI+0x5566]      ...........;02 b3 66 55
ADD DH,[SI+0x5566]         ...........;02 b4 66 55
ADD DH,[DI+0x5566]         ...........;02 b5 66 55
ADD DH,[BP+0x5566]         ...........;02 b6 66 55
ADD DH,[BX+0x5566]         ...........;02 b7 66 55
ADD BH,[BX+SI+0x5566]      ...........;02 b8 66 55
ADD BH,[BX+DI+0x5566]      ...........;02 b9 66 55
ADD BH,[BP+DI+0x5566]      ...........;02 ba 66 55
ADD BH,[BP+DI+0x5566]      ...........;02 bb 66 55
ADD BH,[SI+0x5566]         ...........;02 bc 66 55
ADD BH,[DI+0x5566]         ...........;02 bd 66 55
ADD BH,[BP+0x5566]         ...........;02 be 66 55
ADD BH,[BX+0x5566]         ...........;02 bf 66 55
ADD AX,[BX+SI]             ...................;03 00
ADD AX,[BX+DI]             ...................;03 01
ADD AX,[BP+SI]             ...................;03 02
ADD AX,[BP+DI]             ...................;03 03
ADD AX,[SI]                ...................;03 04
ADD AX,[DI]                ...................;03 05
ADD AX,[0x5566]            ...............;03 06 66 55
ADD AX,[BX]                ...................;03 07
ADD CX,[BX+SI]             ...................;03 08
ADD CX,[BX+DI]             ...................;03 09
ADD CX,[BP+SI]             ...................;03 0a
ADD CX,[BP+DI]             ...................;03 0b
ADD CX,[SI]                ...................;03 0c
ADD CX,[DI]                ...................;03 0d
ADD CX,[0x5566]            ...............;03 0e 66 55
ADD CX,[BX]                ...................;03 0f
ADD DX,[BX+SI]             ...................;03 10
ADD DX,[BX+DI]             ...................;03 11
ADD DX,[BP+SI]             ...................;03 12
ADD DX,[BP+DI]             ...................;03 13
ADD DX,[SI]                ...................;03 14
ADD DX,[DI]                ...................;03 15
ADD DX,[0x5566]            ...............;03 16 66 55
ADD DX,[BX]                ...................;03 17
ADD BX,[BX+SI]             ...................;03 18
ADD BX,[BX+DI]             ...................;03 19
ADD BX,[BP+SI]             ...................;03 1a
ADD BX,[BP+DI]             ...................;03 1b
ADD BX,[SI]                ...................;03 1c
ADD BX,[DI]                ...................;03 1d
ADD BX,[0x5566]            ...............;03 1e 66 55
ADD BX,[BX]                ...................;03 1f
ADD SP,[BX+SI]             ...................;03 20
ADD SP,[BX+DI]             ...................;03 21
ADD SP,[BP+SI]             ...................;03 22
ADD SP,[BP+DI]             ...................;03 23
ADD SP,[SI]                ...................;03 24
ADD SP,[DI]                ...................;03 25
ADD SP,[0x5566]            ...............;03 26 66 55
ADD SP,[BX]                ...................;03 27
ADD BP,[BX+SI]             ...................;03 28
ADD BP,[BX+DI]             ...................;03 29
ADD BP,[BP+SI]             ...................;03 2a
ADD BP,[BP+DI]             ...................;03 2b
ADD BP,[SI]                ...................;03 2c
ADD BP,[DI]                ...................;03 2d
ADD BP,[0x5566]            ...............;03 2e 66 55
ADD BP,[BX]                ...................;03 2f
ADD SI,[BX+SI]             ...................;03 30
ADD SI,[BX+DI]             ...................;03 31
ADD SI,[BP+SI]             ...................;03 32
ADD SI,[BP+DI]             ...................;03 33
ADD SI,[SI]                ...................;03 34
ADD SI,[DI]                ...................;03 35
ADD SI,[0x5566]            ...............;03 36 66 55
ADD SI,[BX]                ...................;03 37
ADD DI,[BX+SI]             ...................;03 38
ADD DI,[BX+DI]             ...................;03 39
ADD DI,[BP+SI]             ...................;03 3a
ADD DI,[BP+DI]             ...................;03 3b
ADD DI,[SI]                ...................;03 3c
ADD DI,[DI]                ...................;03 3d
ADD DI,[0x5566]            ...............;03 3e 66 55
ADD DI,[BX]                ...................;03 3f
ADD AX,[BX+SI+0x55]        ...............;03 40 55
ADD AX,[BX+DI+0x55]        ...............;03 41 55
ADD AX,[BP+SI+0x55]        ...............;03 42 55
ADD AX,[BP+DI+0x55]        ...............;03 43 55
ADD AX,[SI+0x55]           ...............;03 44 55
ADD AX,[DI+0x55]           ...............;03 45 55
ADD AX,[BP+0x55]           ...............;03 46 55
ADD AX,[BX+0x55]           ...............;03 47 55
ADD CX,[BX+SI+0x55]        ...............;03 48 55
ADD CX,[BX+DI+0x55]        ...............;03 49 55
ADD CX,[BP+SI+0x55]        ...............;03 4a 55
ADD CX,[BP+DI+0x55]        ...............;03 4b 55
ADD CX,[SI+0x55]           ...............;03 4c 55
ADD CX,[DI+0x55]           ...............;03 4d 55
ADD CX,[BP+0x55]           ...............;03 4e 55
ADD CX,[BX+0x55]           ...............;03 4f 55
```

```
ADD DX,[BX+SI+0x55] ...........;03 50 55
ADD DX,[BX+DI+0x55] ...........;03 51 55
ADD DX,[BP+SI+0x55] ...........;03 52 55
ADD DX,[BP+DI+0x55] ...........;03 53 55
ADD DX,[SI+0x55] ..............;03 54 55
ADD DX,[DI+0x55] ..............;03 55 55
ADD DX,[BP+0x55] ..............;03 56 55
ADD DX,[BX+0x55] ..............;03 57 55
ADD BX,[BX+SI+0x55] ...........;03 58 55
ADD BX,[BX+DI+0x55] ...........;03 59 55
ADD BX,[BP+SI+0x55] ...........;03 5a 55
ADD BX,[BP+DI+0x55] ...........;03 5b 55
ADD BX,[SI+0x55] ..............;03 5c 55
ADD BX,[DI+0x55] ..............;03 5d 55
ADD BX,[BP+0x55] ..............;03 5e 55
ADD BX,[BX+0x55] ..............;03 5f 55
ADD SP,[BX+SI+0x55] ...........;03 60 55
ADD SP,[BX+DI+0x55] ...........;03 61 55
ADD SP,[BP+SI+0x55] ...........;03 62 55
ADD SP,[BP+DI+0x55] ...........;03 63 55
ADD SP,[SI+0x55] ..............;03 64 55
ADD SP,[DI+0x55] ..............;03 65 55
ADD SP,[BP+0x55] ..............;03 66 55
ADD SP,[BX+0x55] ..............;03 67 55
ADD BP,[BX+SI+0x55] ...........;03 68 55
ADD BP,[BX+DI+0x55] ...........;03 69 55
ADD BP,[BP+SI+0x55] ...........;03 6a 55
ADD BP,[BP+DI+0x55] ...........;03 6b 55
ADD BP,[SI+0x55] ..............;03 6c 55
ADD BP,[DI+0x55] ..............;03 6d 55
ADD BP,[BP+0x55] ..............;03 6e 55
ADD BP,[BX+0x55] ..............;03 6f 55
ADD SI,[BX+SI+0x55] ...........;03 70 55
ADD SI,[BX+DI+0x55] ...........;03 71 55
ADD SI,[BP+SI+0x55] ...........;03 72 55
ADD SI,[BP+DI+0x55] ...........;03 73 55
ADD SI,[SI+0x55] ..............;03 74 55
ADD SI,[DI+0x55] ..............;03 75 55
ADD SI,[BP+0x55] ..............;03 76 55
ADD SI,[BX+0x55] ..............;03 77 55
ADD DI,[BX+SI+0x55] ...........;03 78 55
ADD DI,[BX+DI+0x55] ...........;03 79 55
ADD DI,[BP+SI+0x55] ...........;03 7a 55
ADD DI,[BP+DI+0x55] ...........;03 7b 55
ADD DI,[SI+0x55] ..............;03 7c 55
ADD DI,[DI+0x55] ..............;03 7d 55
ADD DI,[BP+0x55] ..............;03 7e 55
ADD DI,[BX+0x55] ..............;03 7f 55
ADD AX,[BX+SI+0x5566] .........;03 80 66 55
ADD AX,[BX+DI+0x5566] .........;03 81 66 55
ADD AX,[BP+SI+0x5566] .........;03 82 66 55
ADD AX,[BP+DI+0x5566] .........;03 83 66 55
ADD AX,[SI+0x5566] ............;03 84 66 55
ADD AX,[DI+0x5566] ............;03 85 66 55
ADD AX,[BP+0x5566] ............;03 86 66 55
ADD AX,[BX+0x5566] ............;03 87 66 55
ADD CX,[BX+SI+0x5566] .........;03 88 66 55
ADD CX,[BX+DI+0x5566] .........;03 89 66 55
ADD CX,[BP+SI+0x5566] .........;03 8a 66 55
ADD CX,[BP+DI+0x5566] .........;03 8b 66 55
ADD CX,[SI+0x5566] ............;03 8c 66 55
ADD CX,[DI+0x5566] ............;03 8d 66 55
ADD CX,[BP+0x5566] ............;03 8e 66 55
ADD CX,[BX+0x5566] ............;03 8f 66 55
ADD DX,[BX+SI+0x5566] .........;03 90 66 55
ADD DX,[BX+DI+0x5566] .........;03 91 66 55
ADD DX,[BP+SI+0x5566] .........;03 92 66 55
ADD DX,[BP+DI+0x5566] .........;03 93 66 55
ADD DX,[SI+0x5566] ............;03 94 66 55
ADD DX,[DI+0x5566] ............;03 95 66 55
ADD DX,[BP+0x5566] ............;03 96 66 55
ADD DX,[BX+0x5566] ............;03 97 66 55
ADD BX,[BX+SI+0x5566] .........;03 98 66 55
ADD BX,[BX+DI+0x5566] .........;03 99 66 55
ADD BX,[BP+SI+0x5566] .........;03 9a 66 55
ADD BX,[BP+DI+0x5566] .........;03 9b 66 55
ADD BX,[SI+0x5566] ............;03 9c 66 55
ADD BX,[DI+0x5566] ............;03 9d 66 55
ADD BX,[BP+0x5566] ............;03 9e 66 55
ADD BX,[BX+0x5566] ............;03 9f 66 55
ADD SP,[BX+SI+0x5566] .........;03 a0 66 55
ADD SP,[BX+DI+0x5566] .........;03 a1 66 55
ADD SP,[BP+SI+0x5566] .........;03 a2 66 55
ADD SP,[BP+DI+0x5566] .........;03 a3 66 55
ADD SP,[SI+0x5566] ............;03 a4 66 55
ADD SP,[DI+0x5566] ............;03 a5 66 55
ADD SP,[BP+0x5566] ............;03 a6 66 55
ADD SP,[BX+0x5566] ............;03 a7 66 55
ADD BP,[BX+SI+0x5566] .........;03 a8 66 55

ADD BP,[BX+DI+0x5566] .........;03 a9 66 55
ADD BP,[BP+SI+0x5566] .........;03 aa 66 55
ADD BP,[BP+DI+0x5566] .........;03 ab 66 55
ADD BP,[SI+0x5566] ............;03 ac 66 55
ADD BP,[DI+0x5566] ............;03 ad 66 55
ADD BP,[BP+0x5566] ............;03 ae 66 55
ADD BP,[BX+0x5566] ............;03 af 66 55
ADD SI,[BX+SI+0x5566] .........;03 b0 66 55
ADD SI,[BX+DI+0x5566] .........;03 b1 66 55
ADD SI,[BP+SI+0x5566] .........;03 b2 66 55
ADD SI,[BP+DI+0x5566] .........;03 b3 66 55
ADD SI,[SI+0x5566] ............;03 b4 66 55
ADD SI,[DI+0x5566] ............;03 b5 66 55
ADD SI,[BP+0x5566] ............;03 b6 66 55
ADD SI,[BX+0x5566] ............;03 b7 66 55
ADD DI,[BX+SI+0x5566] .........;03 b8 66 55
ADD DI,[BX+DI+0x5566] .........;03 b9 66 55
ADD DI,[BP+SI+0x5566] .........;03 ba 66 55
ADD DI,[BP+DI+0x5566] .........;03 bb 66 55
ADD DI,[SI+0x5566] ............;03 bc 66 55
ADD DI,[DI+0x5566] ............;03 bd 66 55
ADD DI,[BP+0x5566] ............;03 be 66 55
ADD DI,[BX+0x5566] ............;03 bf 66 55
ADD AL,0x55 ..................;04 55
ADD AX,0x5566 ................;05 66 55
PUSH ES ......................;06
POP ES .......................;07
OR [BX+SI],AL ................;08 00
OR [BX+DI],AL ................;08 01
OR [BP+SI],AL ................;08 02
OR [BP+DI],AL ................;08 03
OR [SI],AL ...................;08 04
OR [DI],AL ...................;08 05
OR [0x5566],AL ...............;08 06 66 55
OR [BX],AL ...................;08 07
OR [BX+SI],CL ................;08 08
OR [BX+DI],CL ................;08 09
OR [BP+SI],CL ................;08 0a
OR [BP+DI],CL ................;08 0b
OR [SI],CL ...................;08 0c
OR [DI],CL ...................;08 0d
OR [0x5566],CL ...............;08 0e 66 55
OR [BX],CL ...................;08 0f
OR [BX+SI],DL ................;08 10
OR [BX+DI],DL ................;08 11
OR [BP+SI],DL ................;08 12
OR [BP+DI],DL ................;08 13
OR [SI],DL ...................;08 14
OR [DI],DL ...................;08 15
OR [0x5566],DL ...............;08 16 66 55
OR [BX],DL ...................;08 17
OR [BX+SI],BL ................;08 18
OR [BX+DI],BL ................;08 19
OR [BP+SI],BL ................;08 1a
OR [BP+DI],BL ................;08 1b
OR [SI],BL ...................;08 1c
OR [DI],BL ...................;08 1d
OR [0x5566],BL ...............;08 1e 66 55
OR [BX],BL ...................;08 1f
OR [BX+SI],AH ................;08 20
OR [BX+DI],AH ................;08 21
OR [BP+SI],AH ................;08 22
OR [BP+DI],AH ................;08 23
OR [SI],AH ...................;08 24
OR [DI],AH ...................;08 25
OR [0x5566],AH ...............;08 26 66 55
OR [BX],AH ...................;08 27
OR [BX+SI],CH ................;08 28
OR [BX+DI],CH ................;08 29
OR [BP+SI],CH ................;08 2a
OR [BP+DI],CH ................;08 2b
OR [SI],CH ...................;08 2c
OR [DI],CH ...................;08 2d
OR [0x5566],CH ...............;08 2e 66 55
OR [BX],CH ...................;08 2f
OR [BX+SI],DH ................;08 30
OR [BX+DI],DH ................;08 31
OR [BP+SI],DH ................;08 32
OR [BP+DI],DH ................;08 33
OR [SI],DH ...................;08 34
OR [DI],DH ...................;08 35
OR [0x5566],DH ...............;08 36 66 55
OR [BX],DH ...................;08 37
OR [BX+SI],BH ................;08 38
OR [BX+DI],BH ................;08 39
OR [BP+SI],BH ................;08 3a
OR [BP+DI],BH ................;08 3b
OR [SI],BH ...................;08 3c
OR [DI],BH ...................;08 3d
```

```
OR [0x5566],BH .................;08 3e 66 55
OR [BX],BH .....................;08 3f
OR [BX+SI+0x55],AL .............;08 40 55
OR [BX+DI+0x55],AL .............;08 41 55
OR [BP+SI+0x55],AL .............;08 42 55
OR [BP+DI+0x55],AL .............;08 43 55
OR [SI+0x55],AL ................;08 44 55
OR [DI+0x55],AL ................;08 45 55
OR [BP+0x55],AL ................;08 46 55
OR [BX+0x55],AL ................;08 47 55
OR [BX+SI+0x55],CL .............;08 48 55
OR [BX+DI+0x55],CL .............;08 49 55
OR [BP+SI+0x55],CL .............;08 4a 55
OR [BP+DI+0x55],CL .............;08 4b 55
OR [SI+0x55],CL ................;08 4c 55
OR [DI+0x55],CL ................;08 4d 55
OR [BP+0x55],CL ................;08 4e 55
OR [BX+0x55],CL ................;08 4f 55
OR [BX+SI+0x55],DL .............;08 50 55
OR [BX+DI+0x55],DL .............;08 51 55
OR [BP+SI+0x55],DL .............;08 52 55
OR [BP+DI+0x55],DL .............;08 53 55
OR [SI+0x55],DL ................;08 54 55
OR [DI+0x55],DL ................;08 55 55
OR [BP+0x55],DL ................;08 56 55
OR [BX+0x55],DL ................;08 57 55
OR [BX+SI+0x55],BL .............;08 58 55
OR [BX+DI+0x55],BL .............;08 59 55
OR [BP+SI+0x55],BL .............;08 5a 55
OR [BP+DI+0x55],BL .............;08 5b 55
OR [SI+0x55],BL ................;08 5c 55
OR [DI+0x55],BL ................;08 5d 55
OR [BP+0x55],BL ................;08 5e 55
OR [BX+0x55],BL ................;08 5f 55
OR [BX+SI+0x55],AH .............;08 60 55
OR [BX+DI+0x55],AH .............;08 61 55
OR [BP+SI+0x55],AH .............;08 62 55
OR [BP+DI+0x55],AH .............;08 63 55
OR [SI+0x55],AH ................;08 64 55
OR [DI+0x55],AH ................;08 65 55
OR [BP+0x55],AH ................;08 66 55
OR [BX+0x55],AH ................;08 67 55
OR [BX+SI+0x55],CH .............;08 68 55
OR [BX+DI+0x55],CH .............;08 69 55
OR [BP+SI+0x55],CH .............;08 6a 55
OR [BP+DI+0x55],CH .............;08 6b 55
OR [SI+0x55],CH ................;08 6c 55
OR [DI+0x55],CH ................;08 6d 55
OR [BP+0x55],CH ................;08 6e 55
OR [BX+0x55],CH ................;08 6f 55
OR [BX+SI+0x55],DH .............;08 70 55
OR [BX+DI+0x55],DH .............;08 71 55
OR [BP+SI+0x55],DH .............;08 72 55
OR [BP+DI+0x55],DH .............;08 73 55
OR [SI+0x55],DH ................;08 74 55
OR [DI+0x55],DH ................;08 75 55
OR [BP+0x55],DH ................;08 76 55
OR [BX+0x55],DH ................;08 77 55
OR [BX+SI+0x55],BH .............;08 78 55
OR [BX+DI+0x55],BH .............;08 79 55
OR [BP+SI+0x55],BH .............;08 7a 55
OR [BP+DI+0x55],BH .............;08 7b 55
OR [SI+0x55],BH ................;08 7c 55
OR [DI+0x55],BH ................;08 7d 55
OR [BP+0x55],BH ................;08 7e 55
OR [BX+0x55],BH ................;08 7f 55
OR [BX+SI+0x5566],AL ..........;08 80 66 55
OR [BX+DI+0x5566],AL ..........;08 81 66 55
OR [BP+SI+0x5566],AL ..........;08 82 66 55
OR [BP+DI+0x5566],AL ..........;08 83 66 55
OR [SI+0x5566],AL .............;08 84 66 55
OR [DI+0x5566],AL .............;08 85 66 55
OR [BP+0x5566],AL .............;08 86 66 55
OR [BX+0x5566],AL .............;08 87 66 55
OR [BX+SI+0x5566],CL ..........;08 88 66 55
OR [BX+DI+0x5566],CL ..........;08 89 66 55
OR [BP+SI+0x5566],CL ..........;08 8a 66 55
OR [BP+DI+0x5566],CL ..........;08 8b 66 55
OR [SI+0x5566],CL .............;08 8c 66 55
OR [DI+0x5566],CL .............;08 8d 66 55
OR [BP+0x5566],CL .............;08 8e 66 55
OR [BX+0x5566],CL .............;08 8f 66 55
OR [BX+SI+0x5566],DL ..........;08 90 66 55
OR [BX+DI+0x5566],DL ..........;08 91 66 55
OR [BP+SI+0x5566],DL ..........;08 92 66 55
OR [BP+DI+0x5566],DL ..........;08 93 66 55
OR [SI+0x5566],DL .............;08 94 66 55
OR [DI+0x5566],DL .............;08 95 66 55
OR [BP+0x5566],DL .............;08 96 66 55
OR [BX+0x5566],DL .............;08 97 66 55
OR [BX+SI+0x5566],BL ..........;08 98 66 55
OR [BX+DI+0x5566],BL ..........;08 99 66 55
OR [BP+SI+0x5566],BL ..........;08 9a 66 55
OR [BP+DI+0x5566],BL ..........;08 9b 66 55
OR [SI+0x5566],BL .............;08 9c 66 55
OR [DI+0x5566],BL .............;08 9d 66 55
OR [BP+0x5566],BL .............;08 9e 66 55
OR [BX+0x5566],BL .............;08 9f 66 55
OR [BX+SI+0x5566],AH ..........;08 a0 66 55
OR [BX+DI+0x5566],AH ..........;08 a1 66 55
OR [BP+SI+0x5566],AH ..........;08 a2 66 55
OR [BP+DI+0x5566],AH ..........;08 a3 66 55
OR [SI+0x5566],AH .............;08 a4 66 55
OR [DI+0x5566],AH .............;08 a5 66 55
OR [BP+0x5566],AH .............;08 a6 66 55
OR [BX+0x5566],AH .............;08 a7 66 55
OR [BX+SI+0x5566],CH ..........;08 a8 66 55
OR [BX+DI+0x5566],CH ..........;08 a9 66 55
OR [BP+SI+0x5566],CH ..........;08 aa 66 55
OR [BP+DI+0x5566],CH ..........;08 ab 66 55
OR [SI+0x5566],CH .............;08 ac 66 55
OR [DI+0x5566],CH .............;08 ad 66 55
OR [BP+0x5566],CH .............;08 ae 66 55
OR [BX+0x5566],CH .............;08 af 66 55
OR [BX+SI+0x5566],DH ..........;08 b0 66 55
OR [BX+DI+0x5566],DH ..........;08 b1 66 55
OR [BP+SI+0x5566],DH ..........;08 b2 66 55
OR [BP+DI+0x5566],DH ..........;08 b3 66 55
OR [SI+0x5566],DH .............;08 b4 66 55
OR [DI+0x5566],DH .............;08 b5 66 55
OR [BP+0x5566],DH .............;08 b6 66 55
OR [BX+0x5566],DH .............;08 b7 66 55
OR [BX+SI+0x5566],BH ..........;08 b8 66 55
OR [BX+DI+0x5566],BH ..........;08 b9 66 55
OR [BP+SI+0x5566],BH ..........;08 ba 66 55
OR [BP+DI+0x5566],BH ..........;08 bb 66 55
OR [SI+0x5566],BH .............;08 bc 66 55
OR [DI+0x5566],BH .............;08 bd 66 55
OR [BP+0x5566],BH .............;08 be 66 55
OR [BX+0x5566],BH .............;08 bf 66 55
OR AL,AL ......................;08 c0
OR CL,AL ......................;08 c1
OR DL,AL ......................;08 c2
OR BL,AL ......................;08 c3
OR AH,AL ......................;08 c4
OR CH,AL ......................;08 c5
OR DH,AL ......................;08 c6
OR BH,AL ......................;08 c7
OR AL,CL ......................;08 c8
OR CL,CL ......................;08 c9
OR DL,CL ......................;08 ca
OR BL,CL ......................;08 cb
OR AH,CL ......................;08 cc
OR CH,CL ......................;08 cd
OR DH,CL ......................;08 ce
OR BH,CL ......................;08 cf
OR AL,DL ......................;08 d0
OR CL,DL ......................;08 d1
OR DL,DL ......................;08 d2
OR BL,DL ......................;08 d3
OR AH,DL ......................;08 d4
OR CH,DL ......................;08 d5
OR DH,DL ......................;08 d6
OR BH,DL ......................;08 d7
OR AL,BL ......................;08 d8
OR CL,BL ......................;08 d9
OR DL,BL ......................;08 da
OR BL,BL ......................;08 db
OR AH,BL ......................;08 dc
OR CH,BL ......................;08 dd
OR DH,BL ......................;08 de
OR BH,BL ......................;08 df
OR AL,AH ......................;08 e0
OR CL,AH ......................;08 e1
OR DL,AH ......................;08 e2
OR BL,AH ......................;08 e3
OR AH,AH ......................;08 e4
OR CH,AH ......................;08 e5
OR DH,AH ......................;08 e6
OR BH,AH ......................;08 e7
OR AL,CH ......................;08 e8
OR CL,CH ......................;08 e9
OR DL,CH ......................;08 ea
OR BL,CH ......................;08 eb
OR AH,CH ......................;08 ec
OR CH,CH ......................;08 ed
OR DH,CH ......................;08 ee
OR BH,CH ......................;08 ef
```

```
OR AL,DH .................;08 f0        OR [BX+DI+0x55],CX ...........;09 49 55
OR CL,DH .................;08 f1        OR [BP+SI+0x55],CX ...........;09 4a 55
OR DL,DH .................;08 f2        OR [BP+DI+0x55],CX ...........;09 4b 55
OR BL,DH .................;08 f3        OR [SI+0x55],CX ..............;09 4c 55
OR AH,DH .................;08 f4        OR [DI+0x55],CX ..............;09 4d 55
OR CH,DH .................;08 f5        OR [BP+0x55],CX ..............;09 4e 55
OR DH,DH .................;08 f6        OR [BX+0x55],CX ..............;09 4f 55
OR BH,DH .................;08 f7        OR [BX+SI+0x55],DX ...........;09 50 55
OR AL,BH .................;08 f8        OR [BX+DI+0x55],DX ...........;09 51 55
OR CL,BH .................;08 f9        OR [BP+SI+0x55],DX ...........;09 52 55
OR DL,BH .................;08 fa        OR [BP+DI+0x55],DX ...........;09 53 55
OR BL,BH .................;08 fb        OR [SI+0x55],DX ..............;09 54 55
OR AH,BH .................;08 fc        OR [DI+0x55],DX ..............;09 55 55
OR CH,BH .................;08 fd        OR [BP+0x55],DX ..............;09 56 55
OR DH,BH .................;08 fe        OR [BX+0x55],DX ..............;09 57 55
OR BH,BH .................;08 ff        OR [BX+SI+0x55],BX ...........;09 58 55
OR [BX+SI],AX ............;09 00        OR [BX+DI+0x55],BX ...........;09 59 55
OR [BX+DI],AX ............;09 01        OR [BP+SI+0x55],BX ...........;09 5a 55
OR [BP+SI],AX ............;09 02        OR [BP+DI+0x55],BX ...........;09 5b 55
OR [BP+DI],AX ............;09 03        OR [SI+0x55],BX ..............;09 5c 55
OR [SI],AX ...............;09 04        OR [DI+0x55],BX ..............;09 5d 55
OR [DI],AX ...............;09 05        OR [BP+0x55],BX ..............;09 5e 55
OR [0x5566],AX ...........;09 06 66 55  OR [BX+0x55],BX ..............;09 5f 55
OR [BX],AX ...............;09 07        OR [BX+SI+0x55],SP ...........;09 60 55
OR [BX+SI],CX ............;09 08        OR [BX+DI+0x55],SP ...........;09 61 55
OR [BX+DI],CX ............;09 09        OR [BP+SI+0x55],SP ...........;09 62 55
OR [BP+SI],CX ............;09 0a        OR [BP+DI+0x55],SP ...........;09 63 55
OR [BP+DI],CX ............;09 0b        OR [SI+0x55],SP ..............;09 64 55
OR [SI],CX ...............;09 0c        OR [DI+0x55],SP ..............;09 65 55
OR [DI],CX ...............;09 0d        OR [BP+0x55],SP ..............;09 66 55
OR [0x5566],CX ...........;09 0e 66 55  OR [BX+0x55],SP ..............;09 67 55
OR [BX],CX ...............;09 0f        OR [BX+SI+0x55],BP ...........;09 68 55
OR [BX+SI],DX ............;09 10        OR [BX+DI+0x55],BP ...........;09 69 55
OR [BX+DI],DX ............;09 11        OR [BP+SI+0x55],BP ...........;09 6a 55
OR [BP+SI],DX ............;09 12        OR [BP+DI+0x55],BP ...........;09 6b 55
OR [BP+DI],DX ............;09 13        OR [SI+0x55],BP ..............;09 6c 55
OR [SI],DX ...............;09 14        OR [DI+0x55],BP ..............;09 6d 55
OR [DI],DX ...............;09 15        OR [BP+0x55],BP ..............;09 6e 55
OR [0x5566],DX ...........;09 16 66 55  OR [BX+0x55],BP ..............;09 6f 55
OR [BX],DX ...............;09 17        OR [BX+SI+0x55],SI ...........;09 70 55
OR [BX+SI],BX ............;09 18        OR [BX+DI+0x55],SI ...........;09 71 55
OR [BX+DI],BX ............;09 19        OR [BP+SI+0x55],SI ...........;09 72 55
OR [BP+SI],BX ............;09 1a        OR [BP+DI+0x55],SI ...........;09 73 55
OR [BP+DI],BX ............;09 1b        OR [SI+0x55],SI ..............;09 74 55
OR [SI],BX ...............;09 1c        OR [DI+0x55],SI ..............;09 75 55
OR [DI],BX ...............;09 1d        OR [BP+0x55],SI ..............;09 76 55
OR [0x5566],BX ...........;09 1e 66 55  OR [BX+0x55],SI ..............;09 77 55
OR [BX],BX ...............;09 1f        OR [BX+SI+0x55],DI ...........;09 78 55
OR [BX+SI],SP ............;09 20        OR [BX+DI+0x55],DI ...........;09 79 55
OR [BX+DI],SP ............;09 21        OR [BP+SI+0x55],DI ...........;09 7a 55
OR [BP+SI],SP ............;09 22        OR [BP+DI+0x55],DI ...........;09 7b 55
OR [BP+DI],SP ............;09 23        OR [SI+0x55],DI ..............;09 7c 55
OR [SI],SP ...............;09 24        OR [DI+0x55],DI ..............;09 7d 55
OR [DI],SP ...............;09 25        OR [BP+0x55],DI ..............;09 7e 55
OR [0x5566],SP ...........;09 26 66 55  OR [BX+0x55],DI ..............;09 7f 55
OR [BX],SP ...............;09 27        OR [BX+SI+0x5566],AX .........;09 80 66 55
OR [BX+SI],BP ............;09 28        OR [BX+DI+0x5566],AX .........;09 81 66 55
OR [BX+DI],BP ............;09 29        OR [BP+SI+0x5566],AX .........;09 82 66 55
OR [BP+SI],BP ............;09 2a        OR [BP+DI+0x5566],AX .........;09 83 66 55
OR [BP+DI],BP ............;09 2b        OR [SI+0x5566],AX ............;09 84 66 55
OR [SI],BP ...............;09 2c        OR [DI+0x5566],AX ............;09 85 66 55
OR [DI],BP ...............;09 2d        OR [BP+0x5566],AX ............;09 86 66 55
OR [0x5566],BP ...........;09 2e 66 55  OR [BX+0x5566],AX ............;09 87 66 55
OR [BX],BP ...............;09 2f        OR [BX+SI+0x5566],CX .........;09 88 66 55
OR [BX+SI],SI ............;09 30        OR [BX+DI+0x5566],CX .........;09 89 66 55
OR [BX+DI],SI ............;09 31        OR [BP+SI+0x5566],CX .........;09 8a 66 55
OR [BP+SI],SI ............;09 32        OR [BP+DI+0x5566],CX .........;09 8b 66 55
OR [BP+DI],SI ............;09 33        OR [SI+0x5566],CX ............;09 8c 66 55
OR [SI],SI ...............;09 34        OR [DI+0x5566],CX ............;09 8d 66 55
OR [DI],SI ...............;09 35        OR [BP+0x5566],CX ............;09 8e 66 55
OR [0x5566],SI ...........;09 36 66 55  OR [BX+0x5566],CX ............;09 8f 66 55
OR [BX],SI ...............;09 37        OR [BX+SI+0x5566],DX .........;09 90 66 55
OR [BX+SI],DI ............;09 38        OR [BX+DI+0x5566],DX .........;09 91 66 55
OR [BX+DI],DI ............;09 39        OR [BP+SI+0x5566],DX .........;09 92 66 55
OR [BP+SI],DI ............;09 3a        OR [BP+DI+0x5566],DX .........;09 93 66 55
OR [BP+DI],DI ............;09 3b        OR [SI+0x5566],DX ............;09 94 66 55
OR [SI],DI ...............;09 3c        OR [DI+0x5566],DX ............;09 95 66 55
OR [DI],DI ...............;09 3d        OR [BP+0x5566],DX ............;09 96 66 55
OR [0x5566],DI ...........;09 3e 66 55  OR [BX+0x5566],DX ............;09 97 66 55
OR [BX],DI ...............;09 3f        OR [BX+SI+0x5566],BX .........;09 98 66 55
OR [BX+SI+0x55],AX .......;09 40 55     OR [BX+DI+0x5566],BX .........;09 99 66 55
OR [BX+DI+0x55],AX .......;09 41 55     OR [BP+SI+0x5566],BX .........;09 9a 66 55
OR [BP+SI+0x55],AX .......;09 42 55     OR [BP+DI+0x5566],BX .........;09 9b 66 55
OR [BP+DI+0x55],AX .......;09 43 55     OR [SI+0x5566],BX ............;09 9c 66 55
OR [SI+0x55],AX ..........;09 44 55     OR [DI+0x5566],BX ............;09 9d 66 55
OR [DI+0x55],AX ..........;09 45 55     OR [BP+0x5566],BX ............;09 9e 66 55
OR [BP+0x55],AX ..........;09 46 55     OR [BX+0x5566],BX ............;09 9f 66 55
OR [BX+0x55],AX ..........;09 47 55     OR [BX+SI+0x5566],SP .........;09 a0 66 55
OR [BX+SI+0x55],CX .......;09 48 55     OR [BX+DI+0x5566],SP .........;09 a1 66 55
```

```
OR [BP+SI+0x5566],SP ............ ;09 a2 66 55        OR BX,DI ...................... ;09 fb
OR [BP+DI+0x5566],SP ............ ;09 a3 66 55        OR SP,DI ...................... ;09 fc
OR [SI+0x5566],SP .............. ;09 a4 66 55         OR BP,DI ...................... ;09 fd
OR [DI+0x5566],SP .............. ;09 a5 66 55         OR SI,DI ...................... ;09 fe
OR [BP+0x5566],SP .............. ;09 a6 66 55         OR DI,DI ...................... ;09 ff
OR [BX+0x5566],SP .............. ;09 a7 66 55         OR AL,[BX+SI] ................. ;0a 00
OR [BX+SI+0x5566],BP ............ ;09 a8 66 55        OR AL,[BX+DI] ................. ;0a 01
OR [BX+DI+0x5566],BP ............ ;09 a9 66 55        OR AL,[BP+SI] ................. ;0a 02
OR [BP+SI+0x5566],BP ............ ;09 aa 66 55        OR AL,[BP+DI] ................. ;0a 03
OR [BP+DI+0x5566],BP ............ ;09 ab 66 55        OR AL,[SI] .................... ;0a 04
OR [SI+0x5566],BP .............. ;09 ac 66 55         OR AL,[DI] .................... ;0a 05
OR [DI+0x5566],BP .............. ;09 ad 66 55         OR AL,[0x5566] ................ ;0a 06 66 55
OR [BP+0x5566],BP .............. ;09 ae 66 55         OR AL,[BX] .................... ;0a 07
OR [BX+0x5566],BP .............. ;09 af 66 55         OR CL,[BX+SI] ................. ;0a 08
OR [BX+SI+0x5566],SI ............ ;09 b0 66 55        OR CL,[BX+DI] ................. ;0a 09
OR [BX+DI+0x5566],SI ............ ;09 b1 66 55        OR CL,[BP+SI] ................. ;0a 0a
OR [BP+SI+0x5566],SI ............ ;09 b2 66 55        OR CL,[BP+DI] ................. ;0a 0b
OR [BP+DI+0x5566],SI ............ ;09 b3 66 55        OR CL,[SI] .................... ;0a 0c
OR [SI+0x5566],SI .............. ;09 b4 66 55         OR CL,[DI] .................... ;0a 0d
OR [DI+0x5566],SI .............. ;09 b5 66 55         OR CL,[0x5566] ................ ;0a 0e 66 55
OR [BP+0x5566],SI .............. ;09 b6 66 55         OR CL,[BX] .................... ;0a 0f
OR [BX+0x5566],SI .............. ;09 b7 66 55         OR DL,[BX+SI] ................. ;0a 10
OR [BX+SI+0x5566],DI ............ ;09 b8 66 55        OR DL,[BX+DI] ................. ;0a 11
OR [BX+DI+0x5566],DI ............ ;09 b9 66 55        OR DL,[BP+SI] ................. ;0a 12
OR [BP+SI+0x5566],DI ............ ;09 ba 66 55        OR DL,[BP+DI] ................. ;0a 13
OR [BP+DI+0x5566],DI ............ ;09 bb 66 55        OR DL,[SI] .................... ;0a 14
OR [SI+0x5566],DI .............. ;09 bc 66 55         OR DL,[DI] .................... ;0a 15
OR [DI+0x5566],DI .............. ;09 bd 66 55         OR DL,[0x5566] ................ ;0a 16 66 55
OR [BP+0x5566],DI .............. ;09 be 66 55         OR DL,[BX] .................... ;0a 17
OR [BX+0x5566],DI .............. ;09 bf 66 55         OR BL,[BX+SI] ................. ;0a 18
OR AX,AX ...................... ;09 c0                OR BL,[BX+DI] ................. ;0a 19
OR CX,AX ...................... ;09 c1                OR BL,[BP+SI] ................. ;0a 1a
OR DX,AX ...................... ;09 c2                OR BL,[BP+DI] ................. ;0a 1b
OR BX,AX ...................... ;09 c3                OR BL,[SI] .................... ;0a 1c
OR SP,AX ...................... ;09 c4                OR BL,[DI] .................... ;0a 1d
OR BP,AX ...................... ;09 c5                OR BL,[0x5566] ................ ;0a 1e 66 55
OR SI,AX ...................... ;09 c6                OR BL,[BX] .................... ;0a 1f
OR DI,AX ...................... ;09 c7                OR AH,[BX+SI] ................. ;0a 20
OR AX,CX ...................... ;09 c8                OR AH,[BX+DI] ................. ;0a 21
OR CX,CX ...................... ;09 c9                OR AH,[BP+SI] ................. ;0a 22
OR DX,CX ...................... ;09 ca                OR AH,[BP+DI] ................. ;0a 23
OR BX,CX ...................... ;09 cb                OR AH,[SI] .................... ;0a 24
OR SP,CX ...................... ;09 cc                OR AH,[DI] .................... ;0a 25
OR BP,CX ...................... ;09 cd                OR AH,[0x5566] ................ ;0a 26 66 55
OR SI,CX ...................... ;09 ce                OR AH,[BX] .................... ;0a 27
OR DI,CX ...................... ;09 cf                OR CH,[BX+SI] ................. ;0a 28
OR AX,DX ...................... ;09 d0                OR CH,[BX+DI] ................. ;0a 29
OR CX,DX ...................... ;09 d1                OR CH,[BP+SI] ................. ;0a 2a
OR DX,DX ...................... ;09 d2                OR CH,[BP+DI] ................. ;0a 2b
OR BX,DX ...................... ;09 d3                OR CH,[SI] .................... ;0a 2c
OR SP,DX ...................... ;09 d4                OR CH,[DI] .................... ;0a 2d
OR BP,DX ...................... ;09 d5                OR CH,[0x5566] ................ ;0a 2e 66 55
OR SI,DX ...................... ;09 d6                OR CH,[BX] .................... ;0a 2f
OR DI,DX ...................... ;09 d7                OR DH,[BX+SI] ................. ;0a 30
OR AX,BX ...................... ;09 d8                OR DH,[BX+DI] ................. ;0a 31
OR CX,BX ...................... ;09 d9                OR DH,[BP+SI] ................. ;0a 32
OR DX,BX ...................... ;09 da                OR DH,[BP+DI] ................. ;0a 33
OR BX,BX ...................... ;09 db                OR DH,[SI] .................... ;0a 34
OR SP,BX ...................... ;09 dc                OR DH,[DI] .................... ;0a 35
OR BP,BX ...................... ;09 dd                OR DH,[0x5566] ................ ;0a 36 66 55
OR SI,BX ...................... ;09 de                OR DH,[BX] .................... ;0a 37
OR DI,BX ...................... ;09 df                OR BH,[BX+SI] ................. ;0a 38
OR AX,SP ...................... ;09 e0                OR BH,[BX+DI] ................. ;0a 39
OR CX,SP ...................... ;09 e1                OR BH,[BP+SI] ................. ;0a 3a
OR DX,SP ...................... ;09 e2                OR BH,[BP+DI] ................. ;0a 3b
OR BX,SP ...................... ;09 e3                OR BH,[SI] .................... ;0a 3c
OR SP,SP ...................... ;09 e4                OR BH,[DI] .................... ;0a 3d
OR BP,SP ...................... ;09 e5                OR BH,[0x5566] ................ ;0a 3e 66 55
OR SI,SP ...................... ;09 e6                OR BH,[BX] .................... ;0a 3f
OR DI,SP ...................... ;09 e7                OR AL,[BX+SI+0x55] ............ ;0a 40 55
OR AX,BP ...................... ;09 e8                OR AL,[BX+DI+0x55] ............ ;0a 41 55
OR CX,BP ...................... ;09 e9                OR AL,[BP+SI+0x55] ............ ;0a 42 55
OR DX,BP ...................... ;09 ea                OR AL,[BP+DI+0x55] ............ ;0a 43 55
OR BX,BP ...................... ;09 eb                OR AL,[SI+0x55] ............... ;0a 44 55
OR SP,BP ...................... ;09 ec                OR AL,[DI+0x55] ............... ;0a 45 55
OR BP,BP ...................... ;09 ed                OR AL,[BP+0x55] ............... ;0a 46 55
OR SI,BP ...................... ;09 ee                OR AL,[BX+0x55] ............... ;0a 47 55
OR DI,BP ...................... ;09 ef                OR CL,[BX+SI+0x55] ............ ;0a 48 55
OR AX,SI ...................... ;09 f0                OR CL,[BX+DI+0x55] ............ ;0a 49 55
OR CX,SI ...................... ;09 f1                OR CL,[BP+SI+0x55] ............ ;0a 4a 55
OR DX,SI ...................... ;09 f2                OR CL,[BP+DI+0x55] ............ ;0a 4b 55
OR BX,SI ...................... ;09 f3                OR CL,[SI+0x55] ............... ;0a 4c 55
OR SP,SI ...................... ;09 f4                OR CL,[DI+0x55] ............... ;0a 4d 55
OR BP,SI ...................... ;09 f5                OR CL,[BP+0x55] ............... ;0a 4e 55
OR SI,SI ...................... ;09 f6                OR CL,[BX+0x55] ............... ;0a 4f 55
OR DI,SI ...................... ;09 f7                OR DL,[BX+SI+0x55] ............ ;0a 50 55
OR AX,DI ...................... ;09 f8                OR DL,[BX+DI+0x55] ............ ;0a 51 55
OR CX,DI ...................... ;09 f9                OR DL,[BP+SI+0x55] ............ ;0a 52 55
OR DX,DI ...................... ;09 fa                OR DL,[BP+DI+0x55] ............ ;0a 53 55
```

```
OR DL,[SI+0x55]   .............;0a 54 55
OR DL,[DI+0x55]   .............;0a 55 55
OR DL,[BP+0x55]   .............;0a 56 55
OR DL,[BX+0x55]   .............;0a 57 55
OR BL,[BX+SI+0x55] ............;0a 58 55
OR BL,[BX+DI+0x55] ............;0a 59 55
OR BL,[BP+SI+0x55] ............;0a 5a 55
OR BL,[BP+DI+0x55] ............;0a 5b 55
OR BL,[SI+0x55]   .............;0a 5c 55
OR BL,[DI+0x55]   .............;0a 5d 55
OR BL,[BP+0x55]   .............;0a 5e 55
OR BL,[BX+0x55]   .............;0a 5f 55
OR AH,[BX+SI+0x55] ............;0a 60 55
OR AH,[BX+DI+0x55] ............;0a 61 55
OR AH,[BP+SI+0x55] ............;0a 62 55
OR AH,[BP+DI+0x55] ............;0a 63 55
OR AH,[SI+0x55]   .............;0a 64 55
OR AH,[DI+0x55]   .............;0a 65 55
OR AH,[BP+0x55]   .............;0a 66 55
OR AH,[BX+0x55]   .............;0a 67 55
OR CH,[BX+SI+0x55] ............;0a 68 55
OR CH,[BX+DI+0x55] ............;0a 69 55
OR CH,[BP+SI+0x55] ............;0a 6a 55
OR CH,[BP+DI+0x55] ............;0a 6b 55
OR CH,[SI+0x55]   .............;0a 6c 55
OR CH,[DI+0x55]   .............;0a 6d 55
OR CH,[BP+0x55]   .............;0a 6e 55
OR CH,[BX+0x55]   .............;0a 6f 55
OR DH,[BX+SI+0x55] ............;0a 70 55
OR DH,[BX+DI+0x55] ............;0a 71 55
OR DH,[BP+SI+0x55] ............;0a 72 55
OR DH,[BP+DI+0x55] ............;0a 73 55
OR DH,[SI+0x55]   .............;0a 74 55
OR DH,[DI+0x55]   .............;0a 75 55
OR DH,[BP+0x55]   .............;0a 76 55
OR DH,[BX+0x55]   .............;0a 77 55
OR BH,[BX+SI+0x55] ............;0a 78 55
OR BH,[BX+DI+0x55] ............;0a 79 55
OR BH,[BP+SI+0x55] ............;0a 7a 55
OR BH,[BP+DI+0x55] ............;0a 7b 55
OR BH,[SI+0x55]   .............;0a 7c 55
OR BH,[DI+0x55]   .............;0a 7d 55
OR BH,[BP+0x55]   .............;0a 7e 55
OR BH,[BX+0x55]   .............;0a 7f 55
OR AL,[BX+SI+0x5566] ..........;0a 80 66 55
OR AL,[BX+DI+0x5566] ..........;0a 81 66 55
OR AL,[BP+SI+0x5566] ..........;0a 82 66 55
OR AL,[BP+DI+0x5566] ..........;0a 83 66 55
OR AL,[SI+0x5566] .............;0a 84 66 55
OR AL,[DI+0x5566] .............;0a 85 66 55
OR AL,[BP+0x5566] .............;0a 86 66 55
OR AL,[BX+0x5566] .............;0a 87 66 55
OR CL,[BX+SI+0x5566] ..........;0a 88 66 55
OR CL,[BX+DI+0x5566] ..........;0a 89 66 55
OR CL,[BP+SI+0x5566] ..........;0a 8a 66 55
OR CL,[BP+DI+0x5566] ..........;0a 8b 66 55
OR CL,[SI+0x5566] .............;0a 8c 66 55
OR CL,[DI+0x5566] .............;0a 8d 66 55
OR CL,[BP+0x5566] .............;0a 8e 66 55
OR CL,[BX+0x5566] .............;0a 8f 66 55
OR DL,[BX+SI+0x5566] ..........;0a 90 66 55
OR DL,[BX+DI+0x5566] ..........;0a 91 66 55
OR DL,[BP+SI+0x5566] ..........;0a 92 66 55
OR DL,[BP+DI+0x5566] ..........;0a 93 66 55
OR DL,[SI+0x5566] .............;0a 94 66 55
OR DL,[DI+0x5566] .............;0a 95 66 55
OR DL,[BP+0x5566] .............;0a 96 66 55
OR DL,[BX+0x5566] .............;0a 97 66 55
OR BL,[BX+SI+0x5566] ..........;0a 98 66 55
OR BL,[BX+DI+0x5566] ..........;0a 99 66 55
OR BL,[BP+SI+0x5566] ..........;0a 9a 66 55
OR BL,[BP+DI+0x5566] ..........;0a 9b 66 55
OR BL,[SI+0x5566] .............;0a 9c 66 55
OR BL,[DI+0x5566] .............;0a 9d 66 55
OR BL,[BP+0x5566] .............;0a 9e 66 55
OR BL,[BX+0x5566] .............;0a 9f 66 55
OR AH,[BX+SI+0x5566] ..........;0a a0 66 55
OR AH,[BX+DI+0x5566] ..........;0a a1 66 55
OR AH,[BP+SI+0x5566] ..........;0a a2 66 55
OR AH,[BP+DI+0x5566] ..........;0a a3 66 55
OR AH,[SI+0x5566] .............;0a a4 66 55
OR AH,[DI+0x5566] .............;0a a5 66 55
OR AH,[BP+0x5566] .............;0a a6 66 55
OR AH,[BX+0x5566] .............;0a a7 66 55
OR CH,[BX+SI+0x5566] ..........;0a a8 66 55
OR CH,[BX+DI+0x5566] ..........;0a a9 66 55
OR CH,[BP+SI+0x5566] ..........;0a aa 66 55
OR CH,[BP+DI+0x5566] ..........;0a ab 66 55
OR CH,[SI+0x5566] .............;0a ac 66 55
OR CH,[DI+0x5566] .............;0a ad 66 55
OR CH,[BP+0x5566] .............;0a ae 66 55
OR CH,[BX+0x5566] .............;0a af 66 55
OR DH,[BX+SI+0x5566] ..........;0a b0 66 55
OR DH,[BX+DI+0x5566] ..........;0a b1 66 55
OR DH,[BP+SI+0x5566] ..........;0a b2 66 55
OR DH,[BP+DI+0x5566] ..........;0a b3 66 55
OR DH,[SI+0x5566] .............;0a b4 66 55
OR DH,[DI+0x5566] .............;0a b5 66 55
OR DH,[BP+0x5566] .............;0a b6 66 55
OR DH,[BX+0x5566] .............;0a b7 66 55
OR BH,[BX+SI+0x5566] ..........;0a b8 66 55
OR BH,[BX+DI+0x5566] ..........;0a b9 66 55
OR BH,[BP+SI+0x5566] ..........;0a ba 66 55
OR BH,[BP+DI+0x5566] ..........;0a bb 66 55
OR BH,[SI+0x5566] .............;0a bc 66 55
OR BH,[DI+0x5566] .............;0a bd 66 55
OR BH,[BP+0x5566] .............;0a be 66 55
OR BH,[BX+0x5566] .............;0a bf 66 55
OR AX,[BX+SI]  ................;0b 00
OR AX,[BX+DI]  ................;0b 01
OR AX,[BP+SI]  ................;0b 02
OR AX,[BP+DI]  ................;0b 03
OR AX,[SI]  ...................;0b 04
OR AX,[DI]  ...................;0b 05
OR AX,[0x5566] ................;0b 06 66 55
OR AX,[BX]  ...................;0b 07
OR CX,[BX+SI]  ................;0b 08
OR CX,[BX+DI]  ................;0b 09
OR CX,[BP+SI]  ................;0b 0a
OR CX,[BP+DI]  ................;0b 0b
OR CX,[SI]  ...................;0b 0c
OR CX,[DI]  ...................;0b 0d
OR CX,[0x5566] ................;0b 0e 66 55
OR CX,[BX]  ...................;0b 0f
OR DX,[BX+SI]  ................;0b 10
OR DX,[BX+DI]  ................;0b 11
OR DX,[BP+SI]  ................;0b 12
OR DX,[BP+DI]  ................;0b 13
OR DX,[SI]  ...................;0b 14
OR DX,[DI]  ...................;0b 15
OR DX,[0x5566] ................;0b 16 66 55
OR DX,[BX]  ...................;0b 17
OR BX,[BX+SI]  ................;0b 18
OR BX,[BX+DI]  ................;0b 19
OR BX,[BP+SI]  ................;0b 1a
OR BX,[BP+DI]  ................;0b 1b
OR BX,[SI]  ...................;0b 1c
OR BX,[DI]  ...................;0b 1d
OR BX,[0x5566] ................;0b 1e 66 55
OR BX,[BX]  ...................;0b 1f
OR SP,[BX+SI]  ................;0b 20
OR SP,[BX+DI]  ................;0b 21
OR SP,[BP+SI]  ................;0b 22
OR SP,[BP+DI]  ................;0b 23
OR SP,[SI]  ...................;0b 24
OR SP,[DI]  ...................;0b 25
OR SP,[0x5566] ................;0b 26 66 55
OR SP,[BX]  ...................;0b 27
OR BP,[BX+SI]  ................;0b 28
OR BP,[BX+DI]  ................;0b 29
OR BP,[BP+SI]  ................;0b 2a
OR BP,[BP+DI]  ................;0b 2b
OR BP,[SI]  ...................;0b 2c
OR BP,[DI]  ...................;0b 2d
OR BP,[0x5566] ................;0b 2e 66 55
OR BP,[BX]  ...................;0b 2f
OR SI,[BX+SI]  ................;0b 30
OR SI,[BX+DI]  ................;0b 31
OR SI,[BP+SI]  ................;0b 32
OR SI,[BP+DI]  ................;0b 33
OR SI,[SI]  ...................;0b 34
OR SI,[DI]  ...................;0b 35
OR SI,[0x5566] ................;0b 36 66 55
OR SI,[BX]  ...................;0b 37
OR DI,[BX+SI]  ................;0b 38
OR DI,[BX+DI]  ................;0b 39
OR DI,[BP+SI]  ................;0b 3a
OR DI,[BP+DI]  ................;0b 3b
OR DI,[SI]  ...................;0b 3c
OR DI,[DI]  ...................;0b 3d
OR DI,[0x5566] ................;0b 3e 66 55
OR DI,[BX]  ...................;0b 3f
OR AX,[BX+SI+0x55] ............;0b 40 55
OR AX,[BX+DI+0x55] ............;0b 41 55
OR AX,[BP+SI+0x55] ............;0b 42 55
OR AX,[BP+DI+0x55] ............;0b 43 55
OR AX,[SI+0x55]   .............;0b 44 55
OR AX,[DI+0x55]   .............;0b 45 55
```

193

```
OR AX,[BP+0x55] ................;0b 46 55        OR BX,[BX+0x5566] ..............;0b 9f 66 55
OR AX,[BX+0x55] ................;0b 47 55        OR SP,[BX+SI+0x5566] ...........;0b a0 66 55
OR CX,[BX+SI+0x55] .............;0b 48 55        OR SP,[BX+DI+0x5566] ...........;0b a1 66 55
OR CX,[BX+DI+0x55] .............;0b 49 55        OR SP,[BP+SI+0x5566] ...........;0b a2 66 55
OR CX,[BP+SI+0x55] .............;0b 4a 55        OR SP,[BP+DI+0x5566] ...........;0b a3 66 55
OR CX,[BP+DI+0x55] .............;0b 4b 55        OR SP,[SI+0x5566] ..............;0b a4 66 55
OR CX,[SI+0x55] ................;0b 4c 55        OR SP,[DI+0x5566] ..............;0b a5 66 55
OR CX,[DI+0x55] ................;0b 4d 55        OR SP,[BP+0x5566] ..............;0b a6 66 55
OR CX,[BP+0x55] ................;0b 4e 55        OR SP,[BX+0x5566] ..............;0b a7 66 55
OR CX,[BX+0x55] ................;0b 4f 55        OR BP,[BX+SI+0x5566] ...........;0b a8 66 55
OR DX,[BX+SI+0x55] .............;0b 50 55        OR BP,[BX+DI+0x5566] ...........;0b a9 66 55
OR DX,[BX+DI+0x55] .............;0b 51 55        OR BP,[BP+SI+0x5566] ...........;0b aa 66 55
OR DX,[BP+SI+0x55] .............;0b 52 55        OR BP,[BP+DI+0x5566] ...........;0b ab 66 55
OR DX,[BP+DI+0x55] .............;0b 53 55        OR BP,[SI+0x5566] ..............;0b ac 66 55
OR DX,[SI+0x55] ................;0b 54 55        OR BP,[DI+0x5566] ..............;0b ad 66 55
OR DX,[DI+0x55] ................;0b 55 55        OR BP,[BP+0x5566] ..............;0b ae 66 55
OR DX,[BP+0x55] ................;0b 56 55        OR BP,[BX+0x5566] ..............;0b af 66 55
OR DX,[BX+0x55] ................;0b 57 55        OR SI,[BX+SI+0x5566] ...........;0b b0 66 55
OR BX,[BX+SI+0x55] .............;0b 58 55        OR SI,[BX+DI+0x5566] ...........;0b b1 66 55
OR BX,[BX+DI+0x55] .............;0b 59 55        OR SI,[BP+SI+0x5566] ...........;0b b2 66 55
OR BX,[BP+SI+0x55] .............;0b 5a 55        OR SI,[BP+DI+0x5566] ...........;0b b3 66 55
OR BX,[BP+DI+0x55] .............;0b 5b 55        OR SI,[SI+0x5566] ..............;0b b4 66 55
OR BX,[SI+0x55] ................;0b 5c 55        OR SI,[DI+0x5566] ..............;0b b5 66 55
OR BX,[DI+0x55] ................;0b 5d 55        OR SI,[BP+0x5566] ..............;0b b6 66 55
OR BX,[BP+0x55] ................;0b 5e 55        OR SI,[BX+0x5566] ..............;0b b7 66 55
OR BX,[BX+0x55] ................;0b 5f 55        OR DI,[BX+SI+0x5566] ...........;0b b8 66 55
OR SP,[BX+SI+0x55] .............;0b 60 55        OR DI,[BX+DI+0x5566] ...........;0b b9 66 55
OR SP,[BX+DI+0x55] .............;0b 61 55        OR DI,[BP+SI+0x5566] ...........;0b ba 66 55
OR SP,[BP+SI+0x55] .............;0b 62 55        OR DI,[BP+DI+0x5566] ...........;0b bb 66 55
OR SP,[BP+DI+0x55] .............;0b 63 55        OR DI,[SI+0x5566] ..............;0b bc 66 55
OR SP,[SI+0x55] ................;0b 64 55        OR DI,[DI+0x5566] ..............;0b bd 66 55
OR SP,[DI+0x55] ................;0b 65 55        OR DI,[BP+0x5566] ..............;0b be 66 55
OR SP,[BP+0x55] ................;0b 66 55        OR DI,[BX+0x5566] ..............;0b bf 66 55
OR SP,[BX+0x55] ................;0b 67 55        OR AL,0x55 .....................;0c 55
OR BP,[BX+SI+0x55] .............;0b 68 55        OR AX,0x5566 ...................;0d 66 55
OR BP,[BX+DI+0x55] .............;0b 69 55        PUSH CS ........................;0e
OR BP,[BP+SI+0x55] .............;0b 6a 55        ADC [BX+SI],AL .................;10 00
OR BP,[BP+DI+0x55] .............;0b 6b 55        ADC [BX+DI],AL .................;10 01
OR BP,[SI+0x55] ................;0b 6c 55        ADC [BP+SI],AL .................;10 02
OR BP,[DI+0x55] ................;0b 6d 55        ADC [BP+DI],AL .................;10 03
OR BP,[BP+0x55] ................;0b 6e 55        ADC [SI],AL ....................;10 04
OR BP,[BX+0x55] ................;0b 6f 55        ADC [DI],AL ....................;10 05
OR SI,[BX+SI+0x55] .............;0b 70 55        ADC [0x5566],AL ................;10 06 66 55
OR SI,[BX+DI+0x55] .............;0b 71 55        ADC [BX],AL ....................;10 07
OR SI,[BP+SI+0x55] .............;0b 72 55        ADC [BX+SI],CL .................;10 08
OR SI,[BP+DI+0x55] .............;0b 73 55        ADC [BX+DI],CL .................;10 09
OR SI,[SI+0x55] ................;0b 74 55        ADC [BP+SI],CL .................;10 0a
OR SI,[DI+0x55] ................;0b 75 55        ADC [BP+DI],CL .................;10 0b
OR SI,[BP+0x55] ................;0b 76 55        ADC [SI],CL ....................;10 0c
OR SI,[BX+0x55] ................;0b 77 55        ADC [DI],CL ....................;10 0d
OR DI,[BX+SI+0x55] .............;0b 78 55        ADC [0x5566],CL ................;10 0e 66 55
OR DI,[BX+DI+0x55] .............;0b 79 55        ADC [BX],CL ....................;10 0f
OR DI,[BP+SI+0x55] .............;0b 7a 55        ADC [BX+SI],DL .................;10 10
OR DI,[BP+DI+0x55] .............;0b 7b 55        ADC [BX+DI],DL .................;10 11
OR DI,[SI+0x55] ................;0b 7c 55        ADC [BP+SI],DL .................;10 12
OR DI,[DI+0x55] ................;0b 7d 55        ADC [BP+DI],DL .................;10 13
OR DI,[BP+0x55] ................;0b 7e 55        ADC [SI],DL ....................;10 14
OR DI,[BX+0x55] ................;0b 7f 55        ADC [DI],DL ....................;10 15
OR AX,[BX+SI+0x5566] ...........;0b 80 66 55     ADC [0x5566],DL ................;10 16 66 55
OR AX,[BX+DI+0x5566] ...........;0b 81 66 55     ADC [BX],DL ....................;10 17
OR AX,[BP+SI+0x5566] ...........;0b 82 66 55     ADC [BX+SI],BL .................;10 18
OR AX,[BP+DI+0x5566] ...........;0b 83 66 55     ADC [BX+DI],BL .................;10 19
OR AX,[SI+0x5566] ..............;0b 84 66 55     ADC [BP+SI],BL .................;10 1a
OR AX,[DI+0x5566] ..............;0b 85 66 55     ADC [BP+DI],BL .................;10 1b
OR AX,[BP+0x5566] ..............;0b 86 66 55     ADC [SI],BL ....................;10 1c
OR AX,[BX+0x5566] ..............;0b 87 66 55     ADC [DI],BL ....................;10 1d
OR CX,[BX+SI+0x5566] ...........;0b 88 66 55     ADC [0x5566],BL ................;10 1e 66 55
OR CX,[BX+DI+0x5566] ...........;0b 89 66 55     ADC [BX],BL ....................;10 1f
OR CX,[BP+SI+0x5566] ...........;0b 8a 66 55     ADC [BX+SI],AH .................;10 20
OR CX,[BP+DI+0x5566] ...........;0b 8b 66 55     ADC [BX+DI],AH .................;10 21
OR CX,[SI+0x5566] ..............;0b 8c 66 55     ADC [BP+SI],AH .................;10 22
OR CX,[DI+0x5566] ..............;0b 8d 66 55     ADC [BP+DI],AH .................;10 23
OR CX,[BP+0x5566] ..............;0b 8e 66 55     ADC [SI],AH ....................;10 24
OR CX,[BX+0x5566] ..............;0b 8f 66 55     ADC [DI],AH ....................;10 25
OR DX,[BX+SI+0x5566] ...........;0b 90 66 55     ADC [0x5566],AH ................;10 26 66 55
OR DX,[BX+DI+0x5566] ...........;0b 91 66 55     ADC [BX],AH ....................;10 27
OR DX,[BP+SI+0x5566] ...........;0b 92 66 55     ADC [BX+SI],CH .................;10 28
OR DX,[BP+DI+0x5566] ...........;0b 93 66 55     ADC [BX+DI],CH .................;10 29
OR DX,[SI+0x5566] ..............;0b 94 66 55     ADC [BP+SI],CH .................;10 2a
OR DX,[DI+0x5566] ..............;0b 95 66 55     ADC [BP+DI],CH .................;10 2b
OR DX,[BP+0x5566] ..............;0b 96 66 55     ADC [SI],CH ....................;10 2c
OR DX,[BX+0x5566] ..............;0b 97 66 55     ADC [DI],CH ....................;10 2d
OR BX,[BX+SI+0x5566] ...........;0b 98 66 55     ADC [0x5566],CH ................;10 2e 66 55
OR BX,[BX+DI+0x5566] ...........;0b 99 66 55     ADC [BX],CH ....................;10 2f
OR BX,[BP+SI+0x5566] ...........;0b 9a 66 55     ADC [BX+SI],DH .................;10 30
OR BX,[BP+DI+0x5566] ...........;0b 9b 66 55     ADC [BX+DI],DH .................;10 31
OR BX,[SI+0x5566] ..............;0b 9c 66 55     ADC [BP+SI],DH .................;10 32
OR BX,[DI+0x5566] ..............;0b 9d 66 55     ADC [BP+DI],DH .................;10 33
OR BX,[BP+0x5566] ..............;0b 9e 66 55     ADC [SI],DH ....................;10 34
```

```
ADC [DI],DH ...............;10 35            ADC [BP+0x5566],CL ........;10 8e 66 55
ADC [0x5566],DH ...........;10 36 66 55     ADC [BX+0x5566],CL ........;10 8f 66 55
ADC [BX],DH ...............;10 37            ADC [BX+SI+0x5566],DL .....;10 90 66 55
ADC [BX+SI],BH ............;10 38            ADC [BX+DI+0x5566],DL .....;10 91 66 55
ADC [BX+DI],BH ............;10 39            ADC [BP+SI+0x5566],DL .....;10 92 66 55
ADC [BP+SI],BH ............;10 3a            ADC [BP+DI+0x5566],DL .....;10 93 66 55
ADC [BP+DI],BH ............;10 3b            ADC [SI+0x5566],DL ........;10 94 66 55
ADC [SI],BH ...............;10 3c            ADC [DI+0x5566],DL ........;10 95 66 55
ADC [DI],BH ...............;10 3d            ADC [BP+0x5566],DL ........;10 96 66 55
ADC [0x5566],BH ...........;10 3e 66 55     ADC [BX+0x5566],DL ........;10 97 66 55
ADC [BX],BH ...............;10 3f            ADC [BX+SI+0x5566],BL .....;10 98 66 55
ADC [BX+SI+0x55],AL .......;10 40 55         ADC [BX+DI+0x5566],BL .....;10 99 66 55
ADC [BX+DI+0x55],AL .......;10 41 55         ADC [BP+SI+0x5566],BL .....;10 9a 66 55
ADC [BP+SI+0x55],AL .......;10 42 55         ADC [BP+DI+0x5566],BL .....;10 9b 66 55
ADC [BP+DI+0x55],AL .......;10 43 55         ADC [SI+0x5566],BL ........;10 9c 66 55
ADC [SI+0x55],AL ..........;10 44 55         ADC [DI+0x5566],BL ........;10 9d 66 55
ADC [DI+0x55],AL ..........;10 45 55         ADC [BP+0x5566],BL ........;10 9e 66 55
ADC [BP+0x55],AL ..........;10 46 55         ADC [BX+0x5566],BL ........;10 9f 66 55
ADC [BX+0x55],AL ..........;10 47 55         ADC [BX+SI+0x5566],AH .....;10 a0 66 55
ADC [BX+SI+0x55],CL .......;10 48 55         ADC [BX+DI+0x5566],AH .....;10 a1 66 55
ADC [BX+DI+0x55],CL .......;10 49 55         ADC [BP+SI+0x5566],AH .....;10 a2 66 55
ADC [BP+SI+0x55],CL .......;10 4a 55         ADC [BP+DI+0x5566],AH .....;10 a3 66 55
ADC [BP+DI+0x55],CL .......;10 4b 55         ADC [SI+0x5566],AH ........;10 a4 66 55
ADC [SI+0x55],CL ..........;10 4c 55         ADC [DI+0x5566],AH ........;10 a5 66 55
ADC [DI+0x55],CL ..........;10 4d 55         ADC [BP+0x5566],AH ........;10 a6 66 55
ADC [BP+0x55],CL ..........;10 4e 55         ADC [BX+0x5566],AH ........;10 a7 66 55
ADC [BX+0x55],CL ..........;10 4f 55         ADC [BX+SI+0x5566],CH .....;10 a8 66 55
ADC [BX+SI+0x55],DL .......;10 50 55         ADC [BX+DI+0x5566],CH .....;10 a9 66 55
ADC [BX+DI+0x55],DL .......;10 51 55         ADC [BP+SI+0x5566],CH .....;10 aa 66 55
ADC [BP+SI+0x55],DL .......;10 52 55         ADC [BP+DI+0x5566],CH .....;10 ab 66 55
ADC [BP+DI+0x55],DL .......;10 53 55         ADC [SI+0x5566],CH ........;10 ac 66 55
ADC [SI+0x55],DL ..........;10 54 55         ADC [DI+0x5566],CH ........;10 ad 66 55
ADC [DI+0x55],DL ..........;10 55 55         ADC [BP+0x5566],CH ........;10 ae 66 55
ADC [BP+0x55],DL ..........;10 56 55         ADC [BX+0x5566],CH ........;10 af 66 55
ADC [BX+0x55],DL ..........;10 57 55         ADC [BX+SI+0x5566],DH .....;10 b0 66 55
ADC [BX+SI+0x55],BL .......;10 58 55         ADC [BX+DI+0x5566],DH .....;10 b1 66 55
ADC [BX+DI+0x55],BL .......;10 59 55         ADC [BP+SI+0x5566],DH .....;10 b2 66 55
ADC [BP+SI+0x55],BL .......;10 5a 55         ADC [BP+DI+0x5566],DH .....;10 b3 66 55
ADC [BP+DI+0x55],BL .......;10 5b 55         ADC [SI+0x5566],DH ........;10 b4 66 55
ADC [SI+0x55],BL ..........;10 5c 55         ADC [DI+0x5566],DH ........;10 b5 66 55
ADC [DI+0x55],BL ..........;10 5d 55         ADC [BP+0x5566],DH ........;10 b6 66 55
ADC [BP+0x55],BL ..........;10 5e 55         ADC [BX+0x5566],DH ........;10 b7 66 55
ADC [BX+0x55],BL ..........;10 5f 55         ADC [BX+SI+0x5566],BH .....;10 b8 66 55
ADC [BX+SI+0x55],AH .......;10 60 55         ADC [BX+DI+0x5566],BH .....;10 b9 66 55
ADC [BX+DI+0x55],AH .......;10 61 55         ADC [BP+SI+0x5566],BH .....;10 ba 66 55
ADC [BP+SI+0x55],AH .......;10 62 55         ADC [BP+DI+0x5566],BH .....;10 bb 66 55
ADC [BP+DI+0x55],AH .......;10 63 55         ADC [SI+0x5566],BH ........;10 bc 66 55
ADC [SI+0x55],AH ..........;10 64 55         ADC [DI+0x5566],BH ........;10 bd 66 55
ADC [DI+0x55],AH ..........;10 65 55         ADC [BP+0x5566],BH ........;10 be 66 55
ADC [BP+0x55],AH ..........;10 66 55         ADC [BX+0x5566],BH ........;10 bf 66 55
ADC [BX+0x55],AH ..........;10 67 55         ADC AL,AL .................;10 c0
ADC [BX+SI+0x55],CH .......;10 68 55         ADC CL,AL .................;10 c1
ADC [BX+DI+0x55],CH .......;10 69 55         ADC DL,AL .................;10 c2
ADC [BP+SI+0x55],CH .......;10 6a 55         ADC BL,AL .................;10 c3
ADC [BP+DI+0x55],CH .......;10 6b 55         ADC AH,AL .................;10 c4
ADC [SI+0x55],CH ..........;10 6c 55         ADC CH,AL .................;10 c5
ADC [DI+0x55],CH ..........;10 6d 55         ADC DH,AL .................;10 c6
ADC [BP+0x55],CH ..........;10 6e 55         ADC BH,AL .................;10 c7
ADC [BX+0x55],CH ..........;10 6f 55         ADC AL,CL .................;10 c8
ADC [BX+SI+0x55],DH .......;10 70 55         ADC CL,CL .................;10 c9
ADC [BX+DI+0x55],DH .......;10 71 55         ADC DL,CL .................;10 ca
ADC [BP+SI+0x55],DH .......;10 72 55         ADC BL,CL .................;10 cb
ADC [BP+DI+0x55],DH .......;10 73 55         ADC AH,CL .................;10 cc
ADC [SI+0x55],DH ..........;10 74 55         ADC CH,CL .................;10 cd
ADC [DI+0x55],DH ..........;10 75 55         ADC DH,CL .................;10 ce
ADC [BP+0x55],DH ..........;10 76 55         ADC BH,CL .................;10 cf
ADC [BX+0x55],DH ..........;10 77 55         ADC AL,DL .................;10 d0
ADC [BX+SI+0x55],BH .......;10 78 55         ADC CL,DL .................;10 d1
ADC [BX+DI+0x55],BH .......;10 79 55         ADC DL,DL .................;10 d2
ADC [BP+SI+0x55],BH .......;10 7a 55         ADC BL,DL .................;10 d3
ADC [BP+DI+0x55],BH .......;10 7b 55         ADC AH,DL .................;10 d4
ADC [SI+0x55],BH ..........;10 7c 55         ADC CH,DL .................;10 d5
ADC [DI+0x55],BH ..........;10 7d 55         ADC DH,DL .................;10 d6
ADC [BP+0x55],BH ..........;10 7e 55         ADC BH,DL .................;10 d7
ADC [BX+0x55],BH ..........;10 7f 55         ADC AL,BL .................;10 d8
ADC [BX+SI+0x5566],AL .....;10 80 66 55     ADC CL,BL .................;10 d9
ADC [BX+DI+0x5566],AL .....;10 81 66 55     ADC DL,BL .................;10 da
ADC [BP+SI+0x5566],AL .....;10 82 66 55     ADC BL,BL .................;10 db
ADC [BP+DI+0x5566],AL .....;10 83 66 55     ADC AH,BL .................;10 dc
ADC [SI+0x5566],AL ........;10 84 66 55     ADC CH,BL .................;10 dd
ADC [DI+0x5566],AL ........;10 85 66 55     ADC DH,BL .................;10 de
ADC [BP+0x5566],AL ........;10 86 66 55     ADC BH,BL .................;10 df
ADC [BX+0x5566],AL ........;10 87 66 55     ADC AL,AH .................;10 e0
ADC [BX+SI+0x5566],CL .....;10 88 66 55     ADC CL,AH .................;10 e1
ADC [BX+DI+0x5566],CL .....;10 89 66 55     ADC DL,AH .................;10 e2
ADC [BP+SI+0x5566],CL .....;10 8a 66 55     ADC BL,AH .................;10 e3
ADC [BP+DI+0x5566],CL .....;10 8b 66 55     ADC AH,AH .................;10 e4
ADC [SI+0x5566],CL ........;10 8c 66 55     ADC CH,AH .................;10 e5
ADC [DI+0x5566],CL ........;10 8d 66 55     ADC DH,AH .................;10 e6
```

```
ADC BH,AH .....................;10 e7        ADC [BX+SI+0x55],AX ...........;11 40 55
ADC AL,CH .....................;10 e8        ADC [BX+DI+0x55],AX ...........;11 41 55
ADC CL,CH .....................;10 e9        ADC [BP+SI+0x55],AX ...........;11 42 55
ADC DL,CH .....................;10 ea        ADC [BP+DI+0x55],AX ...........;11 43 55
ADC BL,CH .....................;10 eb        ADC [SI+0x55],AX ..............;11 44 55
ADC AH,CH .....................;10 ec        ADC [DI+0x55],AX ..............;11 45 55
ADC CH,CH .....................;10 ed        ADC [BP+0x55],AX ..............;11 46 55
ADC DH,CH .....................;10 ee        ADC [BX+0x55],AX ..............;11 47 55
ADC BH,CH .....................;10 ef        ADC [BX+SI+0x55],CX ...........;11 48 55
ADC AL,DH .....................;10 f0        ADC [BX+DI+0x55],CX ...........;11 49 55
ADC CL,DH .....................;10 f1        ADC [BP+SI+0x55],CX ...........;11 4a 55
ADC DL,DH .....................;10 f2        ADC [BP+DI+0x55],CX ...........;11 4b 55
ADC BL,DH .....................;10 f3        ADC [SI+0x55],CX ..............;11 4c 55
ADC AH,DH .....................;10 f4        ADC [DI+0x55],CX ..............;11 4d 55
ADC CH,DH .....................;10 f5        ADC [BP+0x55],CX ..............;11 4e 55
ADC DH,DH .....................;10 f6        ADC [BX+0x55],CX ..............;11 4f 55
ADC BH,DH .....................;10 f7        ADC [BX+SI+0x55],DX ...........;11 50 55
ADC AL,BH .....................;10 f8        ADC [BX+DI+0x55],DX ...........;11 51 55
ADC CL,BH .....................;10 f9        ADC [BP+SI+0x55],DX ...........;11 52 55
ADC DL,BH .....................;10 fa        ADC [BP+DI+0x55],DX ...........;11 53 55
ADC BL,BH .....................;10 fb        ADC [SI+0x55],DX ..............;11 54 55
ADC AH,BH .....................;10 fc        ADC [DI+0x55],DX ..............;11 55 55
ADC CH,BH .....................;10 fd        ADC [BP+0x55],DX ..............;11 56 55
ADC DH,BH .....................;10 fe        ADC [BX+0x55],DX ..............;11 57 55
ADC BH,BH .....................;10 ff        ADC [BX+SI+0x55],BX ...........;11 58 55
ADC [BX+SI],AX ................;11 00        ADC [BX+DI+0x55],BX ...........;11 59 55
ADC [BX+DI],AX ................;11 01        ADC [BP+SI+0x55],BX ...........;11 5a 55
ADC [BP+SI],AX ................;11 02        ADC [BP+DI+0x55],BX ...........;11 5b 55
ADC [BP+DI],AX ................;11 03        ADC [SI+0x55],BX ..............;11 5c 55
ADC [SI],AX ...................;11 04        ADC [DI+0x55],BX ..............;11 5d 55
ADC [DI],AX ...................;11 05        ADC [BP+0x55],BX ..............;11 5e 55
ADC [0x5566],AX ...............;11 06 66 55  ADC [BX+0x55],BX ..............;11 5f 55
ADC [BX],AX ...................;11 07        ADC [BX+SI+0x55],SP ...........;11 60 55
ADC [BX+SI],CX ................;11 08        ADC [BX+DI+0x55],SP ...........;11 61 55
ADC [BX+DI],CX ................;11 09        ADC [BP+SI+0x55],SP ...........;11 62 55
ADC [BP+SI],CX ................;11 0a        ADC [BP+DI+0x55],SP ...........;11 63 55
ADC [BP+DI],CX ................;11 0b        ADC [SI+0x55],SP ..............;11 64 55
ADC [SI],CX ...................;11 0c        ADC [DI+0x55],SP ..............;11 65 55
ADC [DI],CX ...................;11 0d        ADC [BP+0x55],SP ..............;11 66 55
ADC [0x5566],CX ...............;11 0e 66 55  ADC [BX+0x55],SP ..............;11 67 55
ADC [BX],CX ...................;11 0f        ADC [BX+SI+0x55],BP ...........;11 68 55
ADC [BX+SI],DX ................;11 10        ADC [BX+DI+0x55],BP ...........;11 69 55
ADC [BX+DI],DX ................;11 11        ADC [BP+SI+0x55],BP ...........;11 6a 55
ADC [BP+SI],DX ................;11 12        ADC [BP+DI+0x55],BP ...........;11 6b 55
ADC [BP+DI],DX ................;11 13        ADC [SI+0x55],BP ..............;11 6c 55
ADC [SI],DX ...................;11 14        ADC [DI+0x55],BP ..............;11 6d 55
ADC [DI],DX ...................;11 15        ADC [BP+0x55],BP ..............;11 6e 55
ADC [0x5566],DX ...............;11 16 66 55  ADC [BX+0x55],BP ..............;11 6f 55
ADC [BX],DX ...................;11 17        ADC [BX+SI+0x55],SI ...........;11 70 55
ADC [BX+SI],BX ................;11 18        ADC [BX+DI+0x55],SI ...........;11 71 55
ADC [BX+DI],BX ................;11 19        ADC [BP+SI+0x55],SI ...........;11 72 55
ADC [BP+SI],BX ................;11 1a        ADC [BP+DI+0x55],SI ...........;11 73 55
ADC [BP+DI],BX ................;11 1b        ADC [SI+0x55],SI ..............;11 74 55
ADC [SI],BX ...................;11 1c        ADC [DI+0x55],SI ..............;11 75 55
ADC [DI],BX ...................;11 1d        ADC [BP+0x55],SI ..............;11 76 55
ADC [0x5566],BX ...............;11 1e 66 55  ADC [BX+0x55],SI ..............;11 77 55
ADC [BX],BX ...................;11 1f        ADC [BX+SI+0x55],DI ...........;11 78 55
ADC [BX+SI],SP ................;11 20        ADC [BX+DI+0x55],DI ...........;11 79 55
ADC [BX+DI],SP ................;11 21        ADC [BP+SI+0x55],DI ...........;11 7a 55
ADC [BP+SI],SP ................;11 22        ADC [BP+DI+0x55],DI ...........;11 7b 55
ADC [BP+DI],SP ................;11 23        ADC [SI+0x55],DI ..............;11 7c 55
ADC [SI],SP ...................;11 24        ADC [DI+0x55],DI ..............;11 7d 55
ADC [DI],SP ...................;11 25        ADC [BP+0x55],DI ..............;11 7e 55
ADC [0x5566],SP ...............;11 26 66 55  ADC [BX+0x55],DI ..............;11 7f 55
ADC [BX],SP ...................;11 27        ADC [BX+SI+0x5566],AX .........;11 80 66 55
ADC [BX+SI],BP ................;11 28        ADC [BX+DI+0x5566],AX .........;11 81 66 55
ADC [BX+DI],BP ................;11 29        ADC [BP+SI+0x5566],AX .........;11 82 66 55
ADC [BP+SI],BP ................;11 2a        ADC [BP+DI+0x5566],AX .........;11 83 66 55
ADC [BP+DI],BP ................;11 2b        ADC [SI+0x5566],AX ............;11 84 66 55
ADC [SI],BP ...................;11 2c        ADC [DI+0x5566],AX ............;11 85 66 55
ADC [DI],BP ...................;11 2d        ADC [BP+0x5566],AX ............;11 86 66 55
ADC [0x5566],BP ...............;11 2e 66 55  ADC [BX+0x5566],AX ............;11 87 66 55
ADC [BX],BP ...................;11 2f        ADC [BX+SI+0x5566],CX .........;11 88 66 55
ADC [BX+SI],SI ................;11 30        ADC [BX+DI+0x5566],CX .........;11 89 66 55
ADC [BX+DI],SI ................;11 31        ADC [BP+SI+0x5566],CX .........;11 8a 66 55
ADC [BP+SI],SI ................;11 32        ADC [BP+DI+0x5566],CX .........;11 8b 66 55
ADC [BP+DI],SI ................;11 33        ADC [SI+0x5566],CX ............;11 8c 66 55
ADC [SI],SI ...................;11 34        ADC [DI+0x5566],CX ............;11 8d 66 55
ADC [DI],SI ...................;11 35        ADC [BP+0x5566],CX ............;11 8e 66 55
ADC [0x5566],SI ...............;11 36 66 55  ADC [BX+0x5566],CX ............;11 8f 66 55
ADC [BX],SI ...................;11 37        ADC [BX+SI+0x5566],DX .........;11 90 66 55
ADC [BX+SI],DI ................;11 38        ADC [BX+DI+0x5566],DX .........;11 91 66 55
ADC [BX+DI],DI ................;11 39        ADC [BP+SI+0x5566],DX .........;11 92 66 55
ADC [BP+SI],DI ................;11 3a        ADC [BP+DI+0x5566],DX .........;11 93 66 55
ADC [BP+DI],DI ................;11 3b        ADC [SI+0x5566],DX ............;11 94 66 55
ADC [SI],DI ...................;11 3c        ADC [DI+0x5566],DX ............;11 95 66 55
ADC [DI],DI ...................;11 3d        ADC [BP+0x5566],DX ............;11 96 66 55
ADC [0x5566],DI ...............;11 3e 66 55  ADC [BX+0x5566],DX ............;11 97 66 55
ADC [BX],DI ...................;11 3f        ADC [BX+SI+0x5566],BX .........;11 98 66 55
```

```
ADC [BX+DI+0x5566],BX ..........;11 99 66 55      ADC DX,SI ....................;11 f2
ADC [BP+SI+0x5566],BX ..........;11 9a 66 55      ADC BX,SI ....................;11 f3
ADC [BP+DI+0x5566],BX ..........;11 9b 66 55      ADC SP,SI ....................;11 f4
ADC [SI+0x5566],BX .............;11 9c 66 55      ADC BP,SI ....................;11 f5
ADC [DI+0x5566],BX .............;11 9d 66 55      ADC SI,SI ....................;11 f6
ADC [BP+0x5566],BX .............;11 9e 66 55      ADC DI,SI ....................;11 f7
ADC [BX+0x5566],BX .............;11 9f 66 55      ADC AX,DI ....................;11 f8
ADC [BX+SI+0x5566],SP ..........;11 a0 66 55      ADC CX,DI ....................;11 f9
ADC [BX+DI+0x5566],SP ..........;11 a1 66 55      ADC DX,DI ....................;11 fa
ADC [BP+SI+0x5566],SP ..........;11 a2 66 55      ADC BX,DI ....................;11 fb
ADC [BP+DI+0x5566],SP ..........;11 a3 66 55      ADC SP,DI ....................;11 fc
ADC [SI+0x5566],SP .............;11 a4 66 55      ADC BP,DI ....................;11 fd
ADC [DI+0x5566],SP .............;11 a5 66 55      ADC SI,DI ....................;11 fe
ADC [BP+0x5566],SP .............;11 a6 66 55      ADC DI,DI ....................;11 ff
ADC [BX+0x5566],SP .............;11 a7 66 55      ADC AL,[BX+SI] ...............;12 00
ADC [BX+SI+0x5566],BP ..........;11 a8 66 55      ADC AL,[BX+DI] ...............;12 01
ADC [BX+DI+0x5566],BP ..........;11 a9 66 55      ADC AL,[BP+SI] ...............;12 02
ADC [BP+SI+0x5566],BP ..........;11 aa 66 55      ADC AL,[BP+DI] ...............;12 03
ADC [BP+DI+0x5566],BP ..........;11 ab 66 55      ADC AL,[SI] ..................;12 04
ADC [SI+0x5566],BP .............;11 ac 66 55      ADC AL,[DI] ..................;12 05
ADC [DI+0x5566],BP .............;11 ad 66 55      ADC AL,[0x5566] ..............;12 06 66 55
ADC [BP+0x5566],BP .............;11 ae 66 55      ADC AL,[BX] ..................;12 07
ADC [BX+0x5566],BP .............;11 af 66 55      ADC CL,[BX+SI] ...............;12 08
ADC [BX+SI+0x5566],SI ..........;11 b0 66 55      ADC CL,[BX+DI] ...............;12 09
ADC [BX+DI+0x5566],SI ..........;11 b1 66 55      ADC CL,[BP+SI] ...............;12 0a
ADC [BP+SI+0x5566],SI ..........;11 b2 66 55      ADC CL,[BP+DI] ...............;12 0b
ADC [BP+DI+0x5566],SI ..........;11 b3 66 55      ADC CL,[SI] ..................;12 0c
ADC [SI+0x5566],SI .............;11 b4 66 55      ADC CL,[DI] ..................;12 0d
ADC [DI+0x5566],SI .............;11 b5 66 55      ADC CL,[0x5566] ..............;12 0e 66 55
ADC [BP+0x5566],SI .............;11 b6 66 55      ADC CL,[BX] ..................;12 0f
ADC [BX+0x5566],SI .............;11 b7 66 55      ADC DL,[BX+SI] ...............;12 10
ADC [BX+SI+0x5566],DI ..........;11 b8 66 55      ADC DL,[BX+DI] ...............;12 11
ADC [BX+DI+0x5566],DI ..........;11 b9 66 55      ADC DL,[BP+SI] ...............;12 12
ADC [BP+SI+0x5566],DI ..........;11 ba 66 55      ADC DL,[BP+DI] ...............;12 13
ADC [BP+DI+0x5566],DI ..........;11 bb 66 55      ADC DL,[SI] ..................;12 14
ADC [SI+0x5566],DI .............;11 bc 66 55      ADC DL,[DI] ..................;12 15
ADC [DI+0x5566],DI .............;11 bd 66 55      ADC DL,[0x5566] ..............;12 16 66 55
ADC [BP+0x5566],DI .............;11 be 66 55      ADC DL,[BX] ..................;12 17
ADC [BX+0x5566],DI .............;11 bf 66 55      ADC BL,[BX+SI] ...............;12 18
ADC AX,AX ....................;11 c0              ADC BL,[BX+DI] ...............;12 19
ADC CX,AX ....................;11 c1              ADC BL,[BP+SI] ...............;12 1a
ADC DX,AX ....................;11 c2              ADC BL,[BP+DI] ...............;12 1b
ADC BX,AX ....................;11 c3              ADC BL,[SI] ..................;12 1c
ADC SP,AX ....................;11 c4              ADC BL,[DI] ..................;12 1d
ADC BP,AX ....................;11 c5              ADC BL,[0x5566] ..............;12 1e 66 55
ADC SI,AX ....................;11 c6              ADC BL,[BX] ..................;12 1f
ADC DI,AX ....................;11 c7              ADC AH,[BX+SI] ...............;12 20
ADC AX,CX ....................;11 c8              ADC AH,[BX+DI] ...............;12 21
ADC CX,CX ....................;11 c9              ADC AH,[BP+SI] ...............;12 22
ADC DX,CX ....................;11 ca              ADC AH,[BP+DI] ...............;12 23
ADC BX,CX ....................;11 cb              ADC AH,[SI] ..................;12 24
ADC SP,CX ....................;11 cc              ADC AH,[DI] ..................;12 25
ADC BP,CX ....................;11 cd              ADC AH,[0x5566] ..............;12 26 66 55
ADC SI,CX ....................;11 ce              ADC AH,[BX] ..................;12 27
ADC DI,CX ....................;11 cf              ADC CH,[BX+SI] ...............;12 28
ADC AX,DX ....................;11 d0              ADC CH,[BX+DI] ...............;12 29
ADC CX,DX ....................;11 d1              ADC CH,[BP+SI] ...............;12 2a
ADC DX,DX ....................;11 d2              ADC CH,[BP+DI] ...............;12 2b
ADC BX,DX ....................;11 d3              ADC CH,[SI] ..................;12 2c
ADC SP,DX ....................;11 d4              ADC CH,[DI] ..................;12 2d
ADC BP,DX ....................;11 d5              ADC CH,[0x5566] ..............;12 2e 66 55
ADC SI,DX ....................;11 d6              ADC CH,[BX] ..................;12 2f
ADC DI,DX ....................;11 d7              ADC DH,[BX+SI] ...............;12 30
ADC AX,BX ....................;11 d8              ADC DH,[BX+DI] ...............;12 31
ADC CX,BX ....................;11 d9              ADC DH,[BP+SI] ...............;12 32
ADC DX,BX ....................;11 da              ADC DH,[BP+DI] ...............;12 33
ADC BX,BX ....................;11 db              ADC DH,[SI] ..................;12 34
ADC SP,BX ....................;11 dc              ADC DH,[DI] ..................;12 35
ADC BP,BX ....................;11 dd              ADC DH,[0x5566] ..............;12 36 66 55
ADC SI,BX ....................;11 de              ADC DH,[BX] ..................;12 37
ADC DI,BX ....................;11 df              ADC BH,[BX+SI] ...............;12 38
ADC AX,SP ....................;11 e0              ADC BH,[BX+DI] ...............;12 39
ADC CX,SP ....................;11 e1              ADC BH,[BP+SI] ...............;12 3a
ADC DX,SP ....................;11 e2              ADC BH,[BP+DI] ...............;12 3b
ADC BX,SP ....................;11 e3              ADC BH,[SI] ..................;12 3c
ADC SP,SP ....................;11 e4              ADC BH,[DI] ..................;12 3d
ADC BP,SP ....................;11 e5              ADC BH,[0x5566] ..............;12 3e 66 55
ADC SI,SP ....................;11 e6              ADC BH,[BX] ..................;12 3f
ADC DI,SP ....................;11 e7              ADC AL,[BX+SI+0x55] ..........;12 40 55
ADC AX,BP ....................;11 e8              ADC AL,[BX+DI+0x55] ..........;12 41 55
ADC CX,BP ....................;11 e9              ADC AL,[BP+SI+0x55] ..........;12 42 55
ADC DX,BP ....................;11 ea              ADC AL,[BP+DI+0x55] ..........;12 43 55
ADC BX,BP ....................;11 eb              ADC AL,[SI+0x55] .............;12 44 55
ADC SP,BP ....................;11 ec              ADC AL,[DI+0x55] .............;12 45 55
ADC BP,BP ....................;11 ed              ADC AL,[BP+0x55] .............;12 46 55
ADC SI,BP ....................;11 ee              ADC AL,[BX+0x55] .............;12 47 55
ADC DI,BP ....................;11 ef              ADC CL,[BX+SI+0x55] ..........;12 48 55
ADC AX,SI ....................;11 f0              ADC CL,[BX+DI+0x55] ..........;12 49 55
ADC CX,SI ....................;11 f1              ADC CL,[BP+SI+0x55] ..........;12 4a 55
```

```
ADC CL,[BP+DI+0x55] ............;12 4b 55        ADC AH,[SI+0x5566] ............;12 a4 66 55
ADC CL,[SI+0x55] ...............;12 4c 55        ADC AH,[DI+0x5566] ............;12 a5 66 55
ADC CL,[DI+0x55] ...............;12 4d 55        ADC AH,[BP+0x5566] ............;12 a6 66 55
ADC CL,[BP+0x55] ...............;12 4e 55        ADC AH,[BX+0x5566] ............;12 a7 66 55
ADC CL,[BX+0x55] ...............;12 4f 55        ADC CH,[BX+SI+0x5566] .........;12 a8 66 55
ADC DL,[BX+SI+0x55] ............;12 50 55        ADC CH,[BX+DI+0x5566] .........;12 a9 66 55
ADC DL,[BX+DI+0x55] ............;12 51 55        ADC CH,[BP+SI+0x5566] .........;12 aa 66 55
ADC DL,[BP+SI+0x55] ............;12 52 55        ADC CH,[BP+DI+0x5566] .........;12 ab 66 55
ADC DL,[BP+DI+0x55] ............;12 53 55        ADC CH,[SI+0x5566] ............;12 ac 66 55
ADC DL,[SI+0x55] ...............;12 54 55        ADC CH,[DI+0x5566] ............;12 ad 66 55
ADC DL,[DI+0x55] ...............;12 55 55        ADC CH,[BP+0x5566] ............;12 ae 66 55
ADC DL,[BP+0x55] ...............;12 56 55        ADC CH,[BX+0x5566] ............;12 af 66 55
ADC DL,[BX+0x55] ...............;12 57 55        ADC DH,[BX+SI+0x5566] .........;12 b0 66 55
ADC BL,[BX+SI+0x55] ............;12 58 55        ADC DH,[BX+DI+0x5566] .........;12 b1 66 55
ADC BL,[BX+DI+0x55] ............;12 59 55        ADC DH,[BP+SI+0x5566] .........;12 b2 66 55
ADC BL,[BP+SI+0x55] ............;12 5a 55        ADC DH,[BP+DI+0x5566] .........;12 b3 66 55
ADC BL,[BP+DI+0x55] ............;12 5b 55        ADC DH,[SI+0x5566] ............;12 b4 66 55
ADC BL,[SI+0x55] ...............;12 5c 55        ADC DH,[DI+0x5566] ............;12 b5 66 55
ADC BL,[DI+0x55] ...............;12 5d 55        ADC DH,[BP+0x5566] ............;12 b6 66 55
ADC BL,[BP+0x55] ...............;12 5e 55        ADC DH,[BX+0x5566] ............;12 b7 66 55
ADC BL,[BX+0x55] ...............;12 5f 55        ADC BH,[BX+SI+0x5566] .........;12 b8 66 55
ADC AH,[BX+SI+0x55] ............;12 60 55        ADC BH,[BX+DI+0x5566] .........;12 b9 66 55
ADC AH,[BX+DI+0x55] ............;12 61 55        ADC BH,[BP+SI+0x5566] .........;12 ba 66 55
ADC AH,[BP+SI+0x55] ............;12 62 55        ADC BH,[BP+DI+0x5566] .........;12 bb 66 55
ADC AH,[BP+DI+0x55] ............;12 63 55        ADC BH,[SI+0x5566] ............;12 bc 66 55
ADC AH,[SI+0x55] ...............;12 64 55        ADC BH,[DI+0x5566] ............;12 bd 66 55
ADC AH,[DI+0x55] ...............;12 65 55        ADC BH,[BP+0x5566] ............;12 be 66 55
ADC AH,[BP+0x55] ...............;12 66 55        ADC BH,[BX+0x5566] ............;12 bf 66 55
ADC AH,[BX+0x55] ...............;12 67 55        ADC AX,[BX+SI] ................;13 00
ADC CH,[BX+SI+0x55] ............;12 68 55        ADC AX,[BX+DI] ................;13 01
ADC CH,[BX+DI+0x55] ............;12 69 55        ADC AX,[BP+SI] ................;13 02
ADC CH,[BP+SI+0x55] ............;12 6a 55        ADC AX,[BP+DI] ................;13 03
ADC CH,[BP+DI+0x55] ............;12 6b 55        ADC AX,[SI] ...................;13 04
ADC CH,[SI+0x55] ...............;12 6c 55        ADC AX,[DI] ...................;13 05
ADC CH,[DI+0x55] ...............;12 6d 55        ADC AX,[0x5566] ...............;13 06 66 55
ADC CH,[BP+0x55] ...............;12 6e 55        ADC AX,[BX] ...................;13 07
ADC CH,[BX+0x55] ...............;12 6f 55        ADC CX,[BX+SI] ................;13 08
ADC DH,[BX+SI+0x55] ............;12 70 55        ADC CX,[BX+DI] ................;13 09
ADC DH,[BX+DI+0x55] ............;12 71 55        ADC CX,[BP+SI] ................;13 0a
ADC DH,[BP+SI+0x55] ............;12 72 55        ADC CX,[BP+DI] ................;13 0b
ADC DH,[BP+DI+0x55] ............;12 73 55        ADC CX,[SI] ...................;13 0c
ADC DH,[SI+0x55] ...............;12 74 55        ADC CX,[DI] ...................;13 0d
ADC DH,[DI+0x55] ...............;12 75 55        ADC CX,[0x5566] ...............;13 0e 66 55
ADC DH,[BP+0x55] ...............;12 76 55        ADC CX,[BX] ...................;13 0f
ADC DH,[BX+0x55] ...............;12 77 55        ADC DX,[BX+SI] ................;13 10
ADC BH,[BX+SI+0x55] ............;12 78 55        ADC DX,[BX+DI] ................;13 11
ADC BH,[BX+DI+0x55] ............;12 79 55        ADC DX,[BP+SI] ................;13 12
ADC BH,[BP+SI+0x55] ............;12 7a 55        ADC DX,[BP+DI] ................;13 13
ADC BH,[BP+DI+0x55] ............;12 7b 55        ADC DX,[SI] ...................;13 14
ADC BH,[SI+0x55] ...............;12 7c 55        ADC DX,[DI] ...................;13 15
ADC BH,[DI+0x55] ...............;12 7d 55        ADC DX,[0x5566] ...............;13 16 66 55
ADC BH,[BP+0x55] ...............;12 7e 55        ADC DX,[BX] ...................;13 17
ADC BH,[BX+0x55] ...............;12 7f 55        ADC BX,[BX+SI] ................;13 18
ADC AL,[BX+SI+0x5566] .........;12 80 66 55      ADC BX,[BX+DI] ................;13 19
ADC AL,[BX+DI+0x5566] .........;12 81 66 55      ADC BX,[BP+SI] ................;13 1a
ADC AL,[BP+SI+0x5566] .........;12 82 66 55      ADC BX,[BP+DI] ................;13 1b
ADC AL,[BP+DI+0x5566] .........;12 83 66 55      ADC BX,[SI] ...................;13 1c
ADC AL,[SI+0x5566] ............;12 84 66 55      ADC BX,[DI] ...................;13 1d
ADC AL,[DI+0x5566] ............;12 85 66 55      ADC BX,[0x5566] ...............;13 1e 66 55
ADC AL,[BP+0x5566] ............;12 86 66 55      ADC BX,[BX] ...................;13 1f
ADC AL,[BX+0x5566] ............;12 87 66 55      ADC SP,[BX+SI] ................;13 20
ADC CL,[BX+SI+0x5566] .........;12 88 66 55      ADC SP,[BX+DI] ................;13 21
ADC CL,[BX+DI+0x5566] .........;12 89 66 55      ADC SP,[BP+SI] ................;13 22
ADC CL,[BP+SI+0x5566] .........;12 8a 66 55      ADC SP,[BP+DI] ................;13 23
ADC CL,[BP+DI+0x5566] .........;12 8b 66 55      ADC SP,[SI] ...................;13 24
ADC CL,[SI+0x5566] ............;12 8c 66 55      ADC SP,[DI] ...................;13 25
ADC CL,[DI+0x5566] ............;12 8d 66 55      ADC SP,[0x5566] ...............;13 26 66 55
ADC CL,[BP+0x5566] ............;12 8e 66 55      ADC SP,[BX] ...................;13 27
ADC CL,[BX+0x5566] ............;12 8f 66 55      ADC BP,[BX+SI] ................;13 28
ADC DL,[BX+SI+0x5566] .........;12 90 66 55      ADC BP,[BX+DI] ................;13 29
ADC DL,[BX+DI+0x5566] .........;12 91 66 55      ADC BP,[BP+SI] ................;13 2a
ADC DL,[BP+SI+0x5566] .........;12 92 66 55      ADC BP,[BP+DI] ................;13 2b
ADC DL,[BP+DI+0x5566] .........;12 93 66 55      ADC BP,[SI] ...................;13 2c
ADC DL,[SI+0x5566] ............;12 94 66 55      ADC BP,[DI] ...................;13 2d
ADC DL,[DI+0x5566] ............;12 95 66 55      ADC BP,[0x5566] ...............;13 2e 66 55
ADC DL,[BP+0x5566] ............;12 96 66 55      ADC BP,[BX] ...................;13 2f
ADC DL,[BX+0x5566] ............;12 97 66 55      ADC SI,[BX+SI] ................;13 30
ADC BL,[BX+SI+0x5566] .........;12 98 66 55      ADC SI,[BX+DI] ................;13 31
ADC BL,[BX+DI+0x5566] .........;12 99 66 55      ADC SI,[BP+SI] ................;13 32
ADC BL,[BP+SI+0x5566] .........;12 9a 66 55      ADC SI,[BP+DI] ................;13 33
ADC BL,[BP+DI+0x5566] .........;12 9b 66 55      ADC SI,[SI] ...................;13 34
ADC BL,[SI+0x5566] ............;12 9c 66 55      ADC SI,[DI] ...................;13 35
ADC BL,[DI+0x5566] ............;12 9d 66 55      ADC SI,[0x5566] ...............;13 36 66 55
ADC BL,[BP+0x5566] ............;12 9e 66 55      ADC SI,[BX] ...................;13 37
ADC BL,[BX+0x5566] ............;12 9f 66 55      ADC DI,[BX+SI] ................;13 38
ADC AH,[BX+SI+0x5566] .........;12 a0 66 55      ADC DI,[BX+DI] ................;13 39
ADC AH,[BX+DI+0x5566] .........;12 a1 66 55      ADC DI,[BP+SI] ................;13 3a
ADC AH,[BP+SI+0x5566] .........;12 a2 66 55      ADC DI,[BP+DI] ................;13 3b
ADC AH,[BP+DI+0x5566] .........;12 a3 66 55      ADC DI,[SI] ...................;13 3c
```

```
ADC DI,[DI] ....................;13 3d
ADC DI,[0x5566] ...............;13 3e 66 55
ADC DI,[BX] ...................;13 3f
ADC AX,[BX+SI+0x55] ...........;13 40 55
ADC AX,[BX+DI+0x55] ...........;13 41 55
ADC AX,[BP+SI+0x55] ...........;13 42 55
ADC AX,[BP+DI+0x55] ...........;13 43 55
ADC AX,[SI+0x55] ..............;13 44 55
ADC AX,[DI+0x55] ..............;13 45 55
ADC AX,[BP+0x55] ..............;13 46 55
ADC AX,[BX+0x55] ..............;13 47 55
ADC CX,[BX+SI+0x55] ...........;13 48 55
ADC CX,[BX+DI+0x55] ...........;13 49 55
ADC CX,[BP+SI+0x55] ...........;13 4a 55
ADC CX,[BP+DI+0x55] ...........;13 4b 55
ADC CX,[SI+0x55] ..............;13 4c 55
ADC CX,[DI+0x55] ..............;13 4d 55
ADC CX,[BP+0x55] ..............;13 4e 55
ADC CX,[BX+0x55] ..............;13 4f 55
ADC DX,[BX+SI+0x55] ...........;13 50 55
ADC DX,[BX+DI+0x55] ...........;13 51 55
ADC DX,[BP+SI+0x55] ...........;13 52 55
ADC DX,[BP+DI+0x55] ...........;13 53 55
ADC DX,[SI+0x55] ..............;13 54 55
ADC DX,[DI+0x55] ..............;13 55 55
ADC DX,[BP+0x55] ..............;13 56 55
ADC DX,[BX+0x55] ..............;13 57 55
ADC BX,[BX+SI+0x55] ...........;13 58 55
ADC BX,[BX+DI+0x55] ...........;13 59 55
ADC BX,[BP+SI+0x55] ...........;13 5a 55
ADC BX,[BP+DI+0x55] ...........;13 5b 55
ADC BX,[SI+0x55] ..............;13 5c 55
ADC BX,[DI+0x55] ..............;13 5d 55
ADC BX,[BP+0x55] ..............;13 5e 55
ADC BX,[BX+0x55] ..............;13 5f 55
ADC SP,[BX+SI+0x55] ...........;13 60 55
ADC SP,[BX+DI+0x55] ...........;13 61 55
ADC SP,[BP+SI+0x55] ...........;13 62 55
ADC SP,[BP+DI+0x55] ...........;13 63 55
ADC SP,[SI+0x55] ..............;13 64 55
ADC SP,[DI+0x55] ..............;13 65 55
ADC SP,[BP+0x55] ..............;13 66 55
ADC SP,[BX+0x55] ..............;13 67 55
ADC BP,[BX+SI+0x55] ...........;13 68 55
ADC BP,[BX+DI+0x55] ...........;13 69 55
ADC BP,[BP+SI+0x55] ...........;13 6a 55
ADC BP,[BP+DI+0x55] ...........;13 6b 55
ADC BP,[SI+0x55] ..............;13 6c 55
ADC BP,[DI+0x55] ..............;13 6d 55
ADC BP,[BP+0x55] ..............;13 6e 55
ADC BP,[BX+0x55] ..............;13 6f 55
ADC SI,[BX+SI+0x55] ...........;13 70 55
ADC SI,[BX+DI+0x55] ...........;13 71 55
ADC SI,[BP+SI+0x55] ...........;13 72 55
ADC SI,[BP+DI+0x55] ...........;13 73 55
ADC SI,[SI+0x55] ..............;13 74 55
ADC SI,[DI+0x55] ..............;13 75 55
ADC SI,[BP+0x55] ..............;13 76 55
ADC SI,[BX+0x55] ..............;13 77 55
ADC DI,[BX+SI+0x55] ...........;13 78 55
ADC DI,[BX+DI+0x55] ...........;13 79 55
ADC DI,[BP+SI+0x55] ...........;13 7a 55
ADC DI,[BP+DI+0x55] ...........;13 7b 55
ADC DI,[SI+0x55] ..............;13 7c 55
ADC DI,[DI+0x55] ..............;13 7d 55
ADC DI,[BP+0x55] ..............;13 7e 55
ADC DI,[BX+0x55] ..............;13 7f 55
ADC AX,[BX+SI+0x5566] .........;13 80 66 55
ADC AX,[BX+DI+0x5566] .........;13 81 66 55
ADC AX,[BP+SI+0x5566] .........;13 82 66 55
ADC AX,[BP+DI+0x5566] .........;13 83 66 55
ADC AX,[SI+0x5566] ............;13 84 66 55
ADC AX,[DI+0x5566] ............;13 85 66 55
ADC AX,[BP+0x5566] ............;13 86 66 55
ADC AX,[BX+0x5566] ............;13 87 66 55
ADC CX,[BX+SI+0x5566] .........;13 88 66 55
ADC CX,[BX+DI+0x5566] .........;13 89 66 55
ADC CX,[BP+SI+0x5566] .........;13 8a 66 55
ADC CX,[BP+DI+0x5566] .........;13 8b 66 55
ADC CX,[SI+0x5566] ............;13 8c 66 55
ADC CX,[DI+0x5566] ............;13 8d 66 55
ADC CX,[BP+0x5566] ............;13 8e 66 55
ADC CX,[BX+0x5566] ............;13 8f 66 55
ADC DX,[BX+SI+0x5566] .........;13 90 66 55
ADC DX,[BX+DI+0x5566] .........;13 91 66 55
ADC DX,[BP+SI+0x5566] .........;13 92 66 55
ADC DX,[BP+DI+0x5566] .........;13 93 66 55
ADC DX,[SI+0x5566] ............;13 94 66 55
ADC DX,[DI+0x5566] ............;13 95 66 55
ADC DX,[BP+0x5566] ............;13 96 66 55
ADC DX,[BX+0x5566] ............;13 97 66 55
ADC BX,[BX+SI+0x5566] .........;13 98 66 55
ADC BX,[BX+DI+0x5566] .........;13 99 66 55
ADC BX,[BP+SI+0x5566] .........;13 9a 66 55
ADC BX,[BP+DI+0x5566] .........;13 9b 66 55
ADC BX,[SI+0x5566] ............;13 9c 66 55
ADC BX,[DI+0x5566] ............;13 9d 66 55
ADC BX,[BP+0x5566] ............;13 9e 66 55
ADC BX,[BX+0x5566] ............;13 9f 66 55
ADC SP,[BX+SI+0x5566] .........;13 a0 66 55
ADC SP,[BX+DI+0x5566] .........;13 a1 66 55
ADC SP,[BP+SI+0x5566] .........;13 a2 66 55
ADC SP,[BP+DI+0x5566] .........;13 a3 66 55
ADC SP,[SI+0x5566] ............;13 a4 66 55
ADC SP,[DI+0x5566] ............;13 a5 66 55
ADC SP,[BP+0x5566] ............;13 a6 66 55
ADC SP,[BX+0x5566] ............;13 a7 66 55
ADC BP,[BX+SI+0x5566] .........;13 a8 66 55
ADC BP,[BX+DI+0x5566] .........;13 a9 66 55
ADC BP,[BP+SI+0x5566] .........;13 aa 66 55
ADC BP,[BP+DI+0x5566] .........;13 ab 66 55
ADC BP,[SI+0x5566] ............;13 ac 66 55
ADC BP,[DI+0x5566] ............;13 ad 66 55
ADC BP,[BP+0x5566] ............;13 ae 66 55
ADC BP,[BX+0x5566] ............;13 af 66 55
ADC SI,[BX+SI+0x5566] .........;13 b0 66 55
ADC SI,[BX+DI+0x5566] .........;13 b1 66 55
ADC SI,[BP+SI+0x5566] .........;13 b2 66 55
ADC SI,[BP+DI+0x5566] .........;13 b3 66 55
ADC SI,[SI+0x5566] ............;13 b4 66 55
ADC SI,[DI+0x5566] ............;13 b5 66 55
ADC SI,[BP+0x5566] ............;13 b6 66 55
ADC SI,[BX+0x5566] ............;13 b7 66 55
ADC DI,[BX+SI+0x5566] .........;13 b8 66 55
ADC DI,[BX+DI+0x5566] .........;13 b9 66 55
ADC DI,[BP+SI+0x5566] .........;13 ba 66 55
ADC DI,[BP+DI+0x5566] .........;13 bb 66 55
ADC DI,[SI+0x5566] ............;13 bc 66 55
ADC DI,[DI+0x5566] ............;13 bd 66 55
ADC DI,[BP+0x5566] ............;13 be 66 55
ADC DI,[BX+0x5566] ............;13 bf 66 55
ADC AL,0x55 ...................;14 55
ADC AX,0x5566 .................;15 66 55
PUSH SS .......................;16
POP SS ........................;17
SBB [BX+SI],AL ................;18 00
SBB [BX+DI],AL ................;18 01
SBB [BP+SI],AL ................;18 02
SBB [BP+DI],AL ................;18 03
SBB [SI],AL ...................;18 04
SBB [DI],AL ...................;18 05
SBB [0x5566],AL ...............;18 06 66 55
SBB [BX],AL ...................;18 07
SBB [BX+SI],CL ................;18 08
SBB [BX+DI],CL ................;18 09
SBB [BP+SI],CL ................;18 0a
SBB [BP+DI],CL ................;18 0b
SBB [SI],CL ...................;18 0c
SBB [DI],CL ...................;18 0d
SBB [0x5566],CL ...............;18 0e 66 55
SBB [BX],CL ...................;18 0f
SBB [BX+SI],DL ................;18 10
SBB [BX+DI],DL ................;18 11
SBB [BP+SI],DL ................;18 12
SBB [BP+DI],DL ................;18 13
SBB [SI],DL ...................;18 14
SBB [DI],DL ...................;18 15
SBB [0x5566],DL ...............;18 16 66 55
SBB [BX],DL ...................;18 17
SBB [BX+SI],BL ................;18 18
SBB [BX+DI],BL ................;18 19
SBB [BP+SI],BL ................;18 1a
SBB [BP+DI],BL ................;18 1b
SBB [SI],BL ...................;18 1c
SBB [DI],BL ...................;18 1d
SBB [0x5566],BL ...............;18 1e 66 55
SBB [BX],BL ...................;18 1f
SBB [BX+SI],AH ................;18 20
SBB [BX+DI],AH ................;18 21
SBB [BP+SI],AH ................;18 22
SBB [BP+DI],AH ................;18 23
SBB [SI],AH ...................;18 24
SBB [DI],AH ...................;18 25
SBB [0x5566],AH ...............;18 26 66 55
SBB [BX],AH ...................;18 27
SBB [BX+SI],CH ................;18 28
SBB [BX+DI],CH ................;18 29
SBB [BP+SI],CH ................;18 2a
```

```
SBB [BP+DI],CH ...............;18 2b        SBB [SI+0x5566],AL ...........;18 84 66 55
SBB [SI],CH ..................;18 2c        SBB [DI+0x5566],AL ...........;18 85 66 55
SBB [DI],CH ..................;18 2d        SBB [BP+0x5566],AL ...........;18 86 66 55
SBB [0x5566],CH ..............;18 2e 66 55  SBB [BX+0x5566],AL ...........;18 87 66 55
SBB [BX],CH ..................;18 2f        SBB [BX+SI+0x5566],CL ........;18 88 66 55
SBB [BX+SI],DH ...............;18 30        SBB [BX+DI+0x5566],CL ........;18 89 66 55
SBB [BX+DI],DH ...............;18 31        SBB [BP+SI+0x5566],CL ........;18 8a 66 55
SBB [BP+SI],DH ...............;18 32        SBB [BP+DI+0x5566],CL ........;18 8b 66 55
SBB [BP+DI],DH ...............;18 33        SBB [SI+0x5566],CL ...........;18 8c 66 55
SBB [SI],DH ..................;18 34        SBB [DI+0x5566],CL ...........;18 8d 66 55
SBB [DI],DH ..................;18 35        SBB [BP+0x5566],CL ...........;18 8e 66 55
SBB [0x5566],DH ..............;18 36 66 55  SBB [BX+0x5566],CL ...........;18 8f 66 55
SBB [BX],DH ..................;18 37        SBB [BX+SI+0x5566],DL ........;18 90 66 55
SBB [BX+SI],BH ...............;18 38        SBB [BX+DI+0x5566],DL ........;18 91 66 55
SBB [BX+DI],BH ...............;18 39        SBB [BP+SI+0x5566],DL ........;18 92 66 55
SBB [BP+SI],BH ...............;18 3a        SBB [BP+DI+0x5566],DL ........;18 93 66 55
SBB [BP+DI],BH ...............;18 3b        SBB [SI+0x5566],DL ...........;18 94 66 55
SBB [SI],BH ..................;18 3c        SBB [DI+0x5566],DL ...........;18 95 66 55
SBB [DI],BH ..................;18 3d        SBB [BP+0x5566],DL ...........;18 96 66 55
SBB [0x5566],BH ..............;18 3e 66 55  SBB [BX+0x5566],DL ...........;18 97 66 55
SBB [BX],BH ..................;18 3f        SBB [BX+SI+0x5566],BL ........;18 98 66 55
SBB [BX+SI+0x55],AL ..........;18 40 55     SBB [BX+DI+0x5566],BL ........;18 99 66 55
SBB [BX+DI+0x55],AL ..........;18 41 55     SBB [BP+SI+0x5566],BL ........;18 9a 66 55
SBB [BP+SI+0x55],AL ..........;18 42 55     SBB [BP+DI+0x5566],BL ........;18 9b 66 55
SBB [BP+DI+0x55],AL ..........;18 43 55     SBB [SI+0x5566],BL ...........;18 9c 66 55
SBB [SI+0x55],AL .............;18 44 55     SBB [DI+0x5566],BL ...........;18 9d 66 55
SBB [DI+0x55],AL .............;18 45 55     SBB [BP+0x5566],BL ...........;18 9e 66 55
SBB [BP+0x55],AL .............;18 46 55     SBB [BX+0x5566],BL ...........;18 9f 66 55
SBB [BX+0x55],AL .............;18 47 55     SBB [BX+SI+0x5566],AH ........;18 a0 66 55
SBB [BX+SI+0x55],CL ..........;18 48 55     SBB [BX+DI+0x5566],AH ........;18 a1 66 55
SBB [BX+DI+0x55],CL ..........;18 49 55     SBB [BP+SI+0x5566],AH ........;18 a2 66 55
SBB [BP+SI+0x55],CL ..........;18 4a 55     SBB [BP+DI+0x5566],AH ........;18 a3 66 55
SBB [BP+DI+0x55],CL ..........;18 4b 55     SBB [SI+0x5566],AH ...........;18 a4 66 55
SBB [SI+0x55],CL .............;18 4c 55     SBB [DI+0x5566],AH ...........;18 a5 66 55
SBB [DI+0x55],CL .............;18 4d 55     SBB [BP+0x5566],AH ...........;18 a6 66 55
SBB [BP+0x55],CL .............;18 4e 55     SBB [BX+0x5566],AH ...........;18 a7 66 55
SBB [BX+0x55],CL .............;18 4f 55     SBB [BX+SI+0x5566],CH ........;18 a8 66 55
SBB [BX+SI+0x55],DL ..........;18 50 55     SBB [BX+DI+0x5566],CH ........;18 a9 66 55
SBB [BX+DI+0x55],DL ..........;18 51 55     SBB [BP+SI+0x5566],CH ........;18 aa 66 55
SBB [BP+SI+0x55],DL ..........;18 52 55     SBB [BP+DI+0x5566],CH ........;18 ab 66 55
SBB [BP+DI+0x55],DL ..........;18 53 55     SBB [SI+0x5566],CH ...........;18 ac 66 55
SBB [SI+0x55],DL .............;18 54 55     SBB [DI+0x5566],CH ...........;18 ad 66 55
SBB [DI+0x55],DL .............;18 55 55     SBB [BP+0x5566],CH ...........;18 ae 66 55
SBB [BP+0x55],DL .............;18 56 55     SBB [BX+0x5566],CH ...........;18 af 66 55
SBB [BX+0x55],DL .............;18 57 55     SBB [BX+SI+0x5566],DH ........;18 b0 66 55
SBB [BX+SI+0x55],BL ..........;18 58 55     SBB [BX+DI+0x5566],DH ........;18 b1 66 55
SBB [BX+DI+0x55],BL ..........;18 59 55     SBB [BP+SI+0x5566],DH ........;18 b2 66 55
SBB [BP+SI+0x55],BL ..........;18 5a 55     SBB [BP+DI+0x5566],DH ........;18 b3 66 55
SBB [BP+DI+0x55],BL ..........;18 5b 55     SBB [SI+0x5566],DH ...........;18 b4 66 55
SBB [SI+0x55],BL .............;18 5c 55     SBB [DI+0x5566],DH ...........;18 b5 66 55
SBB [DI+0x55],BL .............;18 5d 55     SBB [BP+0x5566],DH ...........;18 b6 66 55
SBB [BP+0x55],BL .............;18 5e 55     SBB [BX+0x5566],DH ...........;18 b7 66 55
SBB [BX+0x55],BL .............;18 5f 55     SBB [BX+SI+0x5566],BH ........;18 b8 66 55
SBB [BX+SI+0x55],AH ..........;18 60 55     SBB [BX+DI+0x5566],BH ........;18 b9 66 55
SBB [BX+DI+0x55],AH ..........;18 61 55     SBB [BP+SI+0x5566],BH ........;18 ba 66 55
SBB [BP+SI+0x55],AH ..........;18 62 55     SBB [BP+DI+0x5566],BH ........;18 bb 66 55
SBB [BP+DI+0x55],AH ..........;18 63 55     SBB [SI+0x5566],BH ...........;18 bc 66 55
SBB [SI+0x55],AH .............;18 64 55     SBB [DI+0x5566],BH ...........;18 bd 66 55
SBB [DI+0x55],AH .............;18 65 55     SBB [BP+0x5566],BH ...........;18 be 66 55
SBB [BP+0x55],AH .............;18 66 55     SBB [BX+0x5566],BH ...........;18 bf 66 55
SBB [BX+0x55],AH .............;18 67 55     SBB AL,AL ....................;18 c0
SBB [BX+SI+0x55],CH ..........;18 68 55     SBB CL,AL ....................;18 c1
SBB [BX+DI+0x55],CH ..........;18 69 55     SBB DL,AL ....................;18 c2
SBB [BP+SI+0x55],CH ..........;18 6a 55     SBB BL,AL ....................;18 c3
SBB [BP+DI+0x55],CH ..........;18 6b 55     SBB AH,AL ....................;18 c4
SBB [SI+0x55],CH .............;18 6c 55     SBB CH,AL ....................;18 c5
SBB [DI+0x55],CH .............;18 6d 55     SBB DH,AL ....................;18 c6
SBB [BP+0x55],CH .............;18 6e 55     SBB BH,AL ....................;18 c7
SBB [BX+0x55],CH .............;18 6f 55     SBB AL,CL ....................;18 c8
SBB [BX+SI+0x55],DH ..........;18 70 55     SBB CL,CL ....................;18 c9
SBB [BX+DI+0x55],DH ..........;18 71 55     SBB DL,CL ....................;18 ca
SBB [BP+SI+0x55],DH ..........;18 72 55     SBB BL,CL ....................;18 cb
SBB [BP+DI+0x55],DH ..........;18 73 55     SBB AH,CL ....................;18 cc
SBB [SI+0x55],DH .............;18 74 55     SBB CH,CL ....................;18 cd
SBB [DI+0x55],DH .............;18 75 55     SBB DH,CL ....................;18 ce
SBB [BP+0x55],DH .............;18 76 55     SBB BH,CL ....................;18 cf
SBB [BX+0x55],DH .............;18 77 55     SBB AL,DL ....................;18 d0
SBB [BX+SI+0x55],BH ..........;18 78 55     SBB CL,DL ....................;18 d1
SBB [BX+DI+0x55],BH ..........;18 79 55     SBB DL,DL ....................;18 d2
SBB [BP+SI+0x55],BH ..........;18 7a 55     SBB BL,DL ....................;18 d3
SBB [BP+DI+0x55],BH ..........;18 7b 55     SBB AH,DL ....................;18 d4
SBB [SI+0x55],BH .............;18 7c 55     SBB CH,DL ....................;18 d5
SBB [DI+0x55],BH .............;18 7d 55     SBB DH,DL ....................;18 d6
SBB [BP+0x55],BH .............;18 7e 55     SBB BH,DL ....................;18 d7
SBB [BX+0x55],BH .............;18 7f 55     SBB AL,BL ....................;18 d8
SBB [BX+SI+0x5566],AL ........;18 80 66 55  SBB CL,BL ....................;18 d9
SBB [BX+DI+0x5566],AL ........;18 81 66 55  SBB DL,BL ....................;18 da
SBB [BP+SI+0x5566],AL ........;18 82 66 55  SBB BL,BL ....................;18 db
SBB [BP+DI+0x5566],AL ........;18 83 66 55  SBB AH,BL ....................;18 dc
```

```
SBB CH,BL .....................;18 dd        SBB [0x5566],SI ...............;19 36 66 55
SBB DH,BL .....................;18 de        SBB [BX],SI ...................;19 37
SBB BH,BL .....................;18 df        SBB [BX+SI],DI ................;19 38
SBB AL,AH .....................;18 e0        SBB [BX+DI],DI ................;19 39
SBB CL,AH .....................;18 e1        SBB [BP+SI],DI ................;19 3a
SBB DL,AH .....................;18 e2        SBB [BP+DI],DI ................;19 3b
SBB BL,AH .....................;18 e3        SBB [SI],DI ...................;19 3c
SBB AH,AH .....................;18 e4        SBB [DI],DI ...................;19 3d
SBB CH,AH .....................;18 e5        SBB [0x5566],DI ...............;19 3e 66 55
SBB DH,AH .....................;18 e6        SBB [BX],DI ...................;19 3f
SBB BH,AH .....................;18 e7        SBB [BX+SI+0x55],AX ...........;19 40 55
SBB AL,CH .....................;18 e8        SBB [BX+DI+0x55],AX ...........;19 41 55
SBB CL,CH .....................;18 e9        SBB [BP+SI+0x55],AX ...........;19 42 55
SBB DL,CH .....................;18 ea        SBB [BP+DI+0x55],AX ...........;19 43 55
SBB BL,CH .....................;18 eb        SBB [SI+0x55],AX ..............;19 44 55
SBB AH,CH .....................;18 ec        SBB [DI+0x55],AX ..............;19 45 55
SBB CH,CH .....................;18 ed        SBB [BP+0x55],AX ..............;19 46 55
SBB DH,CH .....................;18 ee        SBB [BX+0x55],AX ..............;19 47 55
SBB BH,CH .....................;18 ef        SBB [BX+SI+0x55],CX ...........;19 48 55
SBB AL,DH .....................;18 f0        SBB [BX+DI+0x55],CX ...........;19 49 55
SBB CL,DH .....................;18 f1        SBB [BP+SI+0x55],CX ...........;19 4a 55
SBB DL,DH .....................;18 f2        SBB [BP+DI+0x55],CX ...........;19 4b 55
SBB BL,DH .....................;18 f3        SBB [SI+0x55],CX ..............;19 4c 55
SBB AH,DH .....................;18 f4        SBB [DI+0x55],CX ..............;19 4d 55
SBB CH,DH .....................;18 f5        SBB [BP+0x55],CX ..............;19 4e 55
SBB DH,DH .....................;18 f6        SBB [BX+0x55],CX ..............;19 4f 55
SBB BH,DH .....................;18 f7        SBB [BX+SI+0x55],DX ...........;19 50 55
SBB AL,BH .....................;18 f8        SBB [BX+DI+0x55],DX ...........;19 51 55
SBB CL,BH .....................;18 f9        SBB [BP+SI+0x55],DX ...........;19 52 55
SBB DL,BH .....................;18 fa        SBB [BP+DI+0x55],DX ...........;19 53 55
SBB BL,BH .....................;18 fb        SBB [SI+0x55],DX ..............;19 54 55
SBB AH,BH .....................;18 fc        SBB [DI+0x55],DX ..............;19 55 55
SBB CH,BH .....................;18 fd        SBB [BP+0x55],DX ..............;19 56 55
SBB DH,BH .....................;18 fe        SBB [BX+0x55],DX ..............;19 57 55
SBB BH,BH .....................;18 ff        SBB [BX+SI+0x55],BX ...........;19 58 55
SBB [BX+SI],AX ................;19 00        SBB [BX+DI+0x55],BX ...........;19 59 55
SBB [BX+DI],AX ................;19 01        SBB [BP+SI+0x55],BX ...........;19 5a 55
SBB [BP+SI],AX ................;19 02        SBB [BP+DI+0x55],BX ...........;19 5b 55
SBB [BP+DI],AX ................;19 03        SBB [SI+0x55],BX ..............;19 5c 55
SBB [SI],AX ...................;19 04        SBB [DI+0x55],BX ..............;19 5d 55
SBB [DI],AX ...................;19 05        SBB [BP+0x55],BX ..............;19 5e 55
SBB [0x5566],AX ...............;19 06 66 55  SBB [BX+0x55],BX ..............;19 5f 55
SBB [BX],AX ...................;19 07        SBB [BX+SI+0x55],SP ...........;19 60 55
SBB [BX+SI],CX ................;19 08        SBB [BX+DI+0x55],SP ...........;19 61 55
SBB [BX+DI],CX ................;19 09        SBB [BP+SI+0x55],SP ...........;19 62 55
SBB [BP+SI],CX ................;19 0a        SBB [BP+DI+0x55],SP ...........;19 63 55
SBB [BP+DI],CX ................;19 0b        SBB [SI+0x55],SP ..............;19 64 55
SBB [SI],CX ...................;19 0c        SBB [DI+0x55],SP ..............;19 65 55
SBB [DI],CX ...................;19 0d        SBB [BP+0x55],SP ..............;19 66 55
SBB [0x5566],CX ...............;19 0e 66 55  SBB [BX+0x55],SP ..............;19 67 55
SBB [BX],CX ...................;19 0f        SBB [BX+SI+0x55],BP ...........;19 68 55
SBB [BX+SI],DX ................;19 10        SBB [BX+DI+0x55],BP ...........;19 69 55
SBB [BX+DI],DX ................;19 11        SBB [BP+SI+0x55],BP ...........;19 6a 55
SBB [BP+SI],DX ................;19 12        SBB [BP+DI+0x55],BP ...........;19 6b 55
SBB [BP+DI],DX ................;19 13        SBB [SI+0x55],BP ..............;19 6c 55
SBB [SI],DX ...................;19 14        SBB [DI+0x55],BP ..............;19 6d 55
SBB [DI],DX ...................;19 15        SBB [BP+0x55],BP ..............;19 6e 55
SBB [0x5566],DX ...............;19 16 66 55  SBB [BX+0x55],BP ..............;19 6f 55
SBB [BX],DX ...................;19 17        SBB [BX+SI+0x55],SI ...........;19 70 55
SBB [BX+SI],BX ................;19 18        SBB [BX+DI+0x55],SI ...........;19 71 55
SBB [BX+DI],BX ................;19 19        SBB [BP+SI+0x55],SI ...........;19 72 55
SBB [BP+SI],BX ................;19 1a        SBB [BP+DI+0x55],SI ...........;19 73 55
SBB [BP+DI],BX ................;19 1b        SBB [SI+0x55],SI ..............;19 74 55
SBB [SI],BX ...................;19 1c        SBB [DI+0x55],SI ..............;19 75 55
SBB [DI],BX ...................;19 1d        SBB [BP+0x55],SI ..............;19 76 55
SBB [0x5566],BX ...............;19 1e 66 55  SBB [BX+0x55],SI ..............;19 77 55
SBB [BX],BX ...................;19 1f        SBB [BX+SI+0x55],DI ...........;19 78 55
SBB [BX+SI],SP ................;19 20        SBB [BX+DI+0x55],DI ...........;19 79 55
SBB [BX+DI],SP ................;19 21        SBB [BP+SI+0x55],DI ...........;19 7a 55
SBB [BP+SI],SP ................;19 22        SBB [BP+DI+0x55],DI ...........;19 7b 55
SBB [BP+DI],SP ................;19 23        SBB [SI+0x55],DI ..............;19 7c 55
SBB [SI],SP ...................;19 24        SBB [DI+0x55],DI ..............;19 7d 55
SBB [DI],SP ...................;19 25        SBB [BP+0x55],DI ..............;19 7e 55
SBB [0x5566],SP ...............;19 26 66 55  SBB [BX+0x55],DI ..............;19 7f 55
SBB [BX],SP ...................;19 27        SBB [BX+SI+0x5566],AX .........;19 80 66 55
SBB [BX+SI],BP ................;19 28        SBB [BX+DI+0x5566],AX .........;19 81 66 55
SBB [BX+DI],BP ................;19 29        SBB [BP+SI+0x5566],AX .........;19 82 66 55
SBB [BP+SI],BP ................;19 2a        SBB [BP+DI+0x5566],AX .........;19 83 66 55
SBB [BP+DI],BP ................;19 2b        SBB [SI+0x5566],AX ............;19 84 66 55
SBB [SI],BP ...................;19 2c        SBB [DI+0x5566],AX ............;19 85 66 55
SBB [DI],BP ...................;19 2d        SBB [BP+0x5566],AX ............;19 86 66 55
SBB [0x5566],BP ...............;19 2e 66 55  SBB [BX+0x5566],AX ............;19 87 66 55
SBB [BX],BP ...................;19 2f        SBB [BX+SI+0x5566],CX .........;19 88 66 55
SBB [BX+SI],SI ................;19 30        SBB [BX+DI+0x5566],CX .........;19 89 66 55
SBB [BX+DI],SI ................;19 31        SBB [BP+SI+0x5566],CX .........;19 8a 66 55
SBB [BP+SI],SI ................;19 32        SBB [BP+DI+0x5566],CX .........;19 8b 66 55
SBB [BP+DI],SI ................;19 33        SBB [SI+0x5566],CX ............;19 8c 66 55
SBB [SI],SI ...................;19 34        SBB [DI+0x5566],CX ............;19 8d 66 55
SBB [DI],SI ...................;19 35        SBB [BP+0x5566],CX ............;19 8e 66 55
```

```
SBB [BX+0x5566],CX .............;19 8f 66 55      SBB AX,BP .....................;19 e8
SBB [BX+SI+0x5566],DX ..........;19 90 66 55      SBB CX,BP .....................;19 e9
SBB [BX+DI+0x5566],DX ..........;19 91 66 55      SBB DX,BP .....................;19 ea
SBB [BP+SI+0x5566],DX ..........;19 92 66 55      SBB BX,BP .....................;19 eb
SBB [BP+DI+0x5566],DX ..........;19 93 66 55      SBB SP,BP .....................;19 ec
SBB [SI+0x5566],DX .............;19 94 66 55      SBB BP,BP .....................;19 ed
SBB [DI+0x5566],DX .............;19 95 66 55      SBB SI,BP .....................;19 ee
SBB [BP+0x5566],DX .............;19 96 66 55      SBB DI,BP .....................;19 ef
SBB [BX+0x5566],DX .............;19 97 66 55      SBB AX,SI .....................;19 f0
SBB [BX+SI+0x5566],BX ..........;19 98 66 55      SBB CX,SI .....................;19 f1
SBB [BX+DI+0x5566],BX ..........;19 99 66 55      SBB DX,SI .....................;19 f2
SBB [BP+SI+0x5566],BX ..........;19 9a 66 55      SBB BX,SI .....................;19 f3
SBB [BP+DI+0x5566],BX ..........;19 9b 66 55      SBB SP,SI .....................;19 f4
SBB [SI+0x5566],BX .............;19 9c 66 55      SBB BP,SI .....................;19 f5
SBB [DI+0x5566],BX .............;19 9d 66 55      SBB SI,SI .....................;19 f6
SBB [BP+0x5566],BX .............;19 9e 66 55      SBB DI,SI .....................;19 f7
SBB [BX+0x5566],BX .............;19 9f 66 55      SBB AX,DI .....................;19 f8
SBB [BX+SI+0x5566],SP ..........;19 a0 66 55      SBB CX,DI .....................;19 f9
SBB [BX+DI+0x5566],SP ..........;19 a1 66 55      SBB DX,DI .....................;19 fa
SBB [BP+SI+0x5566],SP ..........;19 a2 66 55      SBB BX,DI .....................;19 fb
SBB [BP+DI+0x5566],SP ..........;19 a3 66 55      SBB SP,DI .....................;19 fc
SBB [SI+0x5566],SP .............;19 a4 66 55      SBB BP,DI .....................;19 fd
SBB [DI+0x5566],SP .............;19 a5 66 55      SBB SI,DI .....................;19 fe
SBB [BP+0x5566],SP .............;19 a6 66 55      SBB DI,DI .....................;19 ff
SBB [BX+0x5566],SP .............;19 a7 66 55      SBB AL,[BX+SI] ................;1a 00
SBB [BX+SI+0x5566],BP ..........;19 a8 66 55      SBB AL,[BX+DI] ................;1a 01
SBB [BX+DI+0x5566],BP ..........;19 a9 66 55      SBB AL,[BP+SI] ................;1a 02
SBB [BP+SI+0x5566],BP ..........;19 aa 66 55      SBB AL,[BP+DI] ................;1a 03
SBB [BP+DI+0x5566],BP ..........;19 ab 66 55      SBB AL,[SI] ...................;1a 04
SBB [SI+0x5566],BP .............;19 ac 66 55      SBB AL,[DI] ...................;1a 05
SBB [DI+0x5566],BP .............;19 ad 66 55      SBB AL,[0x5566] ...............;1a 06 66 55
SBB [BP+0x5566],BP .............;19 ae 66 55      SBB AL,[BX] ...................;1a 07
SBB [BX+0x5566],BP .............;19 af 66 55      SBB CL,[BX+SI] ................;1a 08
SBB [BX+SI+0x5566],SI ..........;19 b0 66 55      SBB CL,[BX+DI] ................;1a 09
SBB [BX+DI+0x5566],SI ..........;19 b1 66 55      SBB CL,[BP+SI] ................;1a 0a
SBB [BP+SI+0x5566],SI ..........;19 b2 66 55      SBB CL,[BP+DI] ................;1a 0b
SBB [BP+DI+0x5566],SI ..........;19 b3 66 55      SBB CL,[SI] ...................;1a 0c
SBB [SI+0x5566],SI .............;19 b4 66 55      SBB CL,[DI] ...................;1a 0d
SBB [DI+0x5566],SI .............;19 b5 66 55      SBB CL,[0x5566] ...............;1a 0e 66 55
SBB [BP+0x5566],SI .............;19 b6 66 55      SBB CL,[BX] ...................;1a 0f
SBB [BX+0x5566],SI .............;19 b7 66 55      SBB DL,[BX+SI] ................;1a 10
SBB [BX+SI+0x5566],DI ..........;19 b8 66 55      SBB DL,[BX+DI] ................;1a 11
SBB [BX+DI+0x5566],DI ..........;19 b9 66 55      SBB DL,[BP+SI] ................;1a 12
SBB [BP+SI+0x5566],DI ..........;19 ba 66 55      SBB DL,[BP+DI] ................;1a 13
SBB [BP+DI+0x5566],DI ..........;19 bb 66 55      SBB DL,[SI] ...................;1a 14
SBB [SI+0x5566],DI .............;19 bc 66 55      SBB DL,[DI] ...................;1a 15
SBB [DI+0x5566],DI .............;19 bd 66 55      SBB DL,[0x5566] ...............;1a 16 66 55
SBB [BP+0x5566],DI .............;19 be 66 55      SBB DL,[BX] ...................;1a 17
SBB [BX+0x5566],DI .............;19 bf 66 55      SBB BL,[BX+SI] ................;1a 18
SBB AX,AX .....................;19 c0             SBB BL,[BX+DI] ................;1a 19
SBB CX,AX .....................;19 c1             SBB BL,[BP+SI] ................;1a 1a
SBB DX,AX .....................;19 c2             SBB BL,[BP+DI] ................;1a 1b
SBB BX,AX .....................;19 c3             SBB BL,[SI] ...................;1a 1c
SBB SP,AX .....................;19 c4             SBB BL,[DI] ...................;1a 1d
SBB BP,AX .....................;19 c5             SBB BL,[0x5566] ...............;1a 1e 66 55
SBB SI,AX .....................;19 c6             SBB BL,[BX] ...................;1a 1f
SBB DI,AX .....................;19 c7             SBB AH,[BX+SI] ................;1a 20
SBB AX,CX .....................;19 c8             SBB AH,[BX+DI] ................;1a 21
SBB CX,CX .....................;19 c9             SBB AH,[BP+SI] ................;1a 22
SBB DX,CX .....................;19 ca             SBB AH,[BP+DI] ................;1a 23
SBB BX,CX .....................;19 cb             SBB AH,[SI] ...................;1a 24
SBB SP,CX .....................;19 cc             SBB AH,[DI] ...................;1a 25
SBB BP,CX .....................;19 cd             SBB AH,[0x5566] ...............;1a 26 66 55
SBB SI,CX .....................;19 ce             SBB AH,[BX] ...................;1a 27
SBB DI,CX .....................;19 cf             SBB CH,[BX+SI] ................;1a 28
SBB AX,DX .....................;19 d0             SBB CH,[BX+DI] ................;1a 29
SBB CX,DX .....................;19 d1             SBB CH,[BP+SI] ................;1a 2a
SBB DX,DX .....................;19 d2             SBB CH,[BP+DI] ................;1a 2b
SBB BX,DX .....................;19 d3             SBB CH,[SI] ...................;1a 2c
SBB SP,DX .....................;19 d4             SBB CH,[DI] ...................;1a 2d
SBB BP,DX .....................;19 d5             SBB CH,[0x5566] ...............;1a 2e 66 55
SBB SI,DX .....................;19 d6             SBB CH,[BX] ...................;1a 2f
SBB DI,DX .....................;19 d7             SBB DH,[BX+SI] ................;1a 30
SBB AX,BX .....................;19 d8             SBB DH,[BX+DI] ................;1a 31
SBB CX,BX .....................;19 d9             SBB DH,[BP+SI] ................;1a 32
SBB DX,BX .....................;19 da             SBB DH,[BP+DI] ................;1a 33
SBB BX,BX .....................;19 db             SBB DH,[SI] ...................;1a 34
SBB SP,BX .....................;19 dc             SBB DH,[DI] ...................;1a 35
SBB BP,BX .....................;19 dd             SBB DH,[0x5566] ...............;1a 36 66 55
SBB SI,BX .....................;19 de             SBB DH,[BX] ...................;1a 37
SBB DI,BX .....................;19 df             SBB BH,[BX+SI] ................;1a 38
SBB AX,SP .....................;19 e0             SBB BH,[BX+DI] ................;1a 39
SBB CX,SP .....................;19 e1             SBB BH,[BP+SI] ................;1a 3a
SBB DX,SP .....................;19 e2             SBB BH,[BP+DI] ................;1a 3b
SBB BX,SP .....................;19 e3             SBB BH,[SI] ...................;1a 3c
SBB SP,SP .....................;19 e4             SBB BH,[DI] ...................;1a 3d
SBB BP,SP .....................;19 e5             SBB BH,[0x5566] ...............;1a 3e 66 55
SBB SI,SP .....................;19 e6             SBB BH,[BX] ...................;1a 3f
SBB DI,SP .....................;19 e7             SBB AL,[BX+SI+0x55] ...........;1a 40 55
```

```
SBB AL,[BX+DI+0x55] ............;1a 41 55        SBB BL,[BP+SI+0x5566] ........;1a 9a 66 55
SBB AL,[BP+SI+0x55] ............;1a 42 55        SBB BL,[BP+DI+0x5566] ........;1a 9b 66 55
SBB AL,[BP+DI+0x55] ............;1a 43 55        SBB BL,[SI+0x5566] ...........;1a 9c 66 55
SBB AL,[SI+0x55] ...............;1a 44 55        SBB BL,[DI+0x5566] ...........;1a 9d 66 55
SBB AL,[DI+0x55] ...............;1a 45 55        SBB BL,[BP+0x5566] ...........;1a 9e 66 55
SBB AL,[BP+0x55] ...............;1a 46 55        SBB BL,[BX+0x5566] ...........;1a 9f 66 55
SBB AL,[BX+0x55] ...............;1a 47 55        SBB AH,[BX+SI+0x5566] ........;1a a0 66 55
SBB CL,[BX+SI+0x55] ............;1a 48 55        SBB AH,[BX+DI+0x5566] ........;1a a1 66 55
SBB CL,[BX+DI+0x55] ............;1a 49 55        SBB AH,[BP+SI+0x5566] ........;1a a2 66 55
SBB CL,[BP+SI+0x55] ............;1a 4a 55        SBB AH,[BP+DI+0x5566] ........;1a a3 66 55
SBB CL,[BP+DI+0x55] ............;1a 4b 55        SBB AH,[SI+0x5566] ...........;1a a4 66 55
SBB CL,[SI+0x55] ...............;1a 4c 55        SBB AH,[DI+0x5566] ...........;1a a5 66 55
SBB CL,[DI+0x55] ...............;1a 4d 55        SBB AH,[BP+0x5566] ...........;1a a6 66 55
SBB CL,[BP+0x55] ...............;1a 4e 55        SBB AH,[BX+0x5566] ...........;1a a7 66 55
SBB CL,[BX+0x55] ...............;1a 4f 55        SBB CH,[BX+SI+0x5566] ........;1a a8 66 55
SBB DL,[BX+SI+0x55] ............;1a 50 55        SBB CH,[BX+DI+0x5566] ........;1a a9 66 55
SBB DL,[BX+DI+0x55] ............;1a 51 55        SBB CH,[BP+SI+0x5566] ........;1a aa 66 55
SBB DL,[BP+SI+0x55] ............;1a 52 55        SBB CH,[BP+DI+0x5566] ........;1a ab 66 55
SBB DL,[BP+DI+0x55] ............;1a 53 55        SBB CH,[SI+0x5566] ...........;1a ac 66 55
SBB DL,[SI+0x55] ...............;1a 54 55        SBB CH,[DI+0x5566] ...........;1a ad 66 55
SBB DL,[DI+0x55] ...............;1a 55 55        SBB CH,[BP+0x5566] ...........;1a ae 66 55
SBB DL,[BP+0x55] ...............;1a 56 55        SBB CH,[BX+0x5566] ...........;1a af 66 55
SBB DL,[BX+0x55] ...............;1a 57 55        SBB DH,[BX+SI+0x5566] ........;1a b0 66 55
SBB BL,[BX+SI+0x55] ............;1a 58 55        SBB DH,[BX+DI+0x5566] ........;1a b1 66 55
SBB BL,[BX+DI+0x55] ............;1a 59 55        SBB DH,[BP+SI+0x5566] ........;1a b2 66 55
SBB BL,[BP+SI+0x55] ............;1a 5a 55        SBB DH,[BP+DI+0x5566] ........;1a b3 66 55
SBB BL,[BP+DI+0x55] ............;1a 5b 55        SBB DH,[SI+0x5566] ...........;1a b4 66 55
SBB BL,[SI+0x55] ...............;1a 5c 55        SBB DH,[DI+0x5566] ...........;1a b5 66 55
SBB BL,[DI+0x55] ...............;1a 5d 55        SBB DH,[BP+0x5566] ...........;1a b6 66 55
SBB BL,[BP+0x55] ...............;1a 5e 55        SBB DH,[BX+0x5566] ...........;1a b7 66 55
SBB BL,[BX+0x55] ...............;1a 5f 55        SBB BH,[BX+SI+0x5566] ........;1a b8 66 55
SBB AH,[BX+SI+0x55] ............;1a 60 55        SBB BH,[BX+DI+0x5566] ........;1a b9 66 55
SBB AH,[BX+DI+0x55] ............;1a 61 55        SBB BH,[BP+SI+0x5566] ........;1a ba 66 55
SBB AH,[BP+SI+0x55] ............;1a 62 55        SBB BH,[BP+DI+0x5566] ........;1a bb 66 55
SBB AH,[BP+DI+0x55] ............;1a 63 55        SBB BH,[SI+0x5566] ...........;1a bc 66 55
SBB AH,[SI+0x55] ...............;1a 64 55        SBB BH,[DI+0x5566] ...........;1a bd 66 55
SBB AH,[DI+0x55] ...............;1a 65 55        SBB BH,[BP+0x5566] ...........;1a be 66 55
SBB AH,[BP+0x55] ...............;1a 66 55        SBB BH,[BX+0x5566] ...........;1a bf 66 55
SBB AH,[BX+0x55] ...............;1a 67 55        SBB AX,[BX+SI] ...............;1b 00
SBB CH,[BX+SI+0x55] ............;1a 68 55        SBB AX,[BX+DI] ...............;1b 01
SBB CH,[BX+DI+0x55] ............;1a 69 55        SBB AX,[BP+SI] ...............;1b 02
SBB CH,[BP+SI+0x55] ............;1a 6a 55        SBB AX,[BP+DI] ...............;1b 03
SBB CH,[BP+DI+0x55] ............;1a 6b 55        SBB AX,[SI] ..................;1b 04
SBB CH,[SI+0x55] ...............;1a 6c 55        SBB AX,[DI] ..................;1b 05
SBB CH,[DI+0x55] ...............;1a 6d 55        SBB AX,[0x5566] ..............;1b 06 66 55
SBB CH,[BP+0x55] ...............;1a 6e 55        SBB AX,[BX] ..................;1b 07
SBB CH,[BX+0x55] ...............;1a 6f 55        SBB CX,[BX+SI] ...............;1b 08
SBB DH,[BX+SI+0x55] ............;1a 70 55        SBB CX,[BX+DI] ...............;1b 09
SBB DH,[BX+DI+0x55] ............;1a 71 55        SBB CX,[BP+SI] ...............;1b 0a
SBB DH,[BP+SI+0x55] ............;1a 72 55        SBB CX,[BP+DI] ...............;1b 0b
SBB DH,[BP+DI+0x55] ............;1a 73 55        SBB CX,[SI] ..................;1b 0c
SBB DH,[SI+0x55] ...............;1a 74 55        SBB CX,[DI] ..................;1b 0d
SBB DH,[DI+0x55] ...............;1a 75 55        SBB CX,[0x5566] ..............;1b 0e 66 55
SBB DH,[BP+0x55] ...............;1a 76 55        SBB CX,[BX] ..................;1b 0f
SBB DH,[BX+0x55] ...............;1a 77 55        SBB DX,[BX+SI] ...............;1b 10
SBB BH,[BX+SI+0x55] ............;1a 78 55        SBB DX,[BX+DI] ...............;1b 11
SBB BH,[BX+DI+0x55] ............;1a 79 55        SBB DX,[BP+SI] ...............;1b 12
SBB BH,[BP+SI+0x55] ............;1a 7a 55        SBB DX,[BP+DI] ...............;1b 13
SBB BH,[BP+DI+0x55] ............;1a 7b 55        SBB DX,[SI] ..................;1b 14
SBB BH,[SI+0x55] ...............;1a 7c 55        SBB DX,[DI] ..................;1b 15
SBB BH,[DI+0x55] ...............;1a 7d 55        SBB DX,[0x5566] ..............;1b 16 66 55
SBB BH,[BP+0x55] ...............;1a 7e 55        SBB DX,[BX] ..................;1b 17
SBB BH,[BX+0x55] ...............;1a 7f 55        SBB BX,[BX+SI] ...............;1b 18
SBB AL,[BX+SI+0x5566] ..........;1a 80 66 55     SBB BX,[BX+DI] ...............;1b 19
SBB AL,[BX+DI+0x5566] ..........;1a 81 66 55     SBB BX,[BP+SI] ...............;1b 1a
SBB AL,[BP+SI+0x5566] ..........;1a 82 66 55     SBB BX,[BP+DI] ...............;1b 1b
SBB AL,[BP+DI+0x5566] ..........;1a 83 66 55     SBB BX,[SI] ..................;1b 1c
SBB AL,[SI+0x5566] .............;1a 84 66 55     SBB BX,[DI] ..................;1b 1d
SBB AL,[DI+0x5566] .............;1a 85 66 55     SBB BX,[0x5566] ..............;1b 1e 66 55
SBB AL,[BP+0x5566] .............;1a 86 66 55     SBB BX,[BX] ..................;1b 1f
SBB AL,[BX+0x5566] .............;1a 87 66 55     SBB SP,[BX+SI] ...............;1b 20
SBB CL,[BX+SI+0x5566] ..........;1a 88 66 55     SBB SP,[BX+DI] ...............;1b 21
SBB CL,[BX+DI+0x5566] ..........;1a 89 66 55     SBB SP,[BP+SI] ...............;1b 22
SBB CL,[BP+SI+0x5566] ..........;1a 8a 66 55     SBB SP,[BP+DI] ...............;1b 23
SBB CL,[BP+DI+0x5566] ..........;1a 8b 66 55     SBB SP,[SI] ..................;1b 24
SBB CL,[SI+0x5566] .............;1a 8c 66 55     SBB SP,[DI] ..................;1b 25
SBB CL,[DI+0x5566] .............;1a 8d 66 55     SBB SP,[0x5566] ..............;1b 26 66 55
SBB CL,[BP+0x5566] .............;1a 8e 66 55     SBB SP,[BX] ..................;1b 27
SBB CL,[BX+0x5566] .............;1a 8f 66 55     SBB BP,[BX+SI] ...............;1b 28
SBB DL,[BX+SI+0x5566] ..........;1a 90 66 55     SBB BP,[BX+DI] ...............;1b 29
SBB DL,[BX+DI+0x5566] ..........;1a 91 66 55     SBB BP,[BP+SI] ...............;1b 2a
SBB DL,[BP+SI+0x5566] ..........;1a 92 66 55     SBB BP,[BP+DI] ...............;1b 2b
SBB DL,[BP+DI+0x5566] ..........;1a 93 66 55     SBB BP,[SI] ..................;1b 2c
SBB DL,[SI+0x5566] .............;1a 94 66 55     SBB BP,[DI] ..................;1b 2d
SBB DL,[DI+0x5566] .............;1a 95 66 55     SBB BP,[0x5566] ..............;1b 2e 66 55
SBB DL,[BP+0x5566] .............;1a 96 66 55     SBB BP,[BX] ..................;1b 2f
SBB DL,[BX+0x5566] .............;1a 97 66 55     SBB SI,[BX+SI] ...............;1b 30
SBB BL,[BX+SI+0x5566] ..........;1a 98 66 55     SBB SI,[BX+DI] ...............;1b 31
SBB BL,[BX+DI+0x5566] ..........;1a 99 66 55     SBB SI,[BP+SI] ...............;1b 32
```

```
SBB SI,[BP+DI] .................;1b 33          SBB CX,[SI+0x5566] .............;1b 8c 66 55
SBB SI,[SI] ...................;1b 34          SBB CX,[DI+0x5566] .............;1b 8d 66 55
SBB SI,[DI] ...................;1b 35          SBB CX,[BP+0x5566] .............;1b 8e 66 55
SBB SI,[0x5566] ...............;1b 36 66 55    SBB CX,[BX+0x5566] .............;1b 8f 66 55
SBB SI,[BX] ...................;1b 37          SBB DX,[BX+SI+0x5566] ..........;1b 90 66 55
SBB DI,[BX+SI] ................;1b 38          SBB DX,[BX+DI+0x5566] ..........;1b 91 66 55
SBB DI,[BX+DI] ................;1b 39          SBB DX,[BP+SI+0x5566] ..........;1b 92 66 55
SBB DI,[BP+SI] ................;1b 3a          SBB DX,[BP+DI+0x5566] ..........;1b 93 66 55
SBB DI,[BP+DI] ................;1b 3b          SBB DX,[SI+0x5566] .............;1b 94 66 55
SBB DI,[SI] ...................;1b 3c          SBB DX,[DI+0x5566] .............;1b 95 66 55
SBB DI,[DI] ...................;1b 3d          SBB DX,[BP+0x5566] .............;1b 96 66 55
SBB DI,[0x5566] ...............;1b 3e 66 55    SBB DX,[BX+0x5566] .............;1b 97 66 55
SBB DI,[BX] ...................;1b 3f          SBB BX,[BX+SI+0x5566] ..........;1b 98 66 55
SBB AX,[BX+SI+0x55] ...........;1b 40 55       SBB BX,[BX+DI+0x5566] ..........;1b 99 66 55
SBB AX,[BX+DI+0x55] ...........;1b 41 55       SBB BX,[BP+SI+0x5566] ..........;1b 9a 66 55
SBB AX,[BP+SI+0x55] ...........;1b 42 55       SBB BX,[BP+DI+0x5566] ..........;1b 9b 66 55
SBB AX,[BP+DI+0x55] ...........;1b 43 55       SBB BX,[SI+0x5566] .............;1b 9c 66 55
SBB AX,[SI+0x55] ..............;1b 44 55       SBB BX,[DI+0x5566] .............;1b 9d 66 55
SBB AX,[DI+0x55] ..............;1b 45 55       SBB BX,[BP+0x5566] .............;1b 9e 66 55
SBB AX,[BP+0x55] ..............;1b 46 55       SBB BX,[BX+0x5566] .............;1b 9f 66 55
SBB AX,[BX+0x55] ..............;1b 47 55       SBB SP,[BX+SI+0x5566] ..........;1b a0 66 55
SBB CX,[BX+SI+0x55] ...........;1b 48 55       SBB SP,[BX+DI+0x5566] ..........;1b a1 66 55
SBB CX,[BX+DI+0x55] ...........;1b 49 55       SBB SP,[BP+SI+0x5566] ..........;1b a2 66 55
SBB CX,[BP+SI+0x55] ...........;1b 4a 55       SBB SP,[BP+DI+0x5566] ..........;1b a3 66 55
SBB CX,[BP+DI+0x55] ...........;1b 4b 55       SBB SP,[SI+0x5566] .............;1b a4 66 55
SBB CX,[SI+0x55] ..............;1b 4c 55       SBB SP,[DI+0x5566] .............;1b a5 66 55
SBB CX,[DI+0x55] ..............;1b 4d 55       SBB SP,[BP+0x5566] .............;1b a6 66 55
SBB CX,[BP+0x55] ..............;1b 4e 55       SBB SP,[BX+0x5566] .............;1b a7 66 55
SBB CX,[BX+0x55] ..............;1b 4f 55       SBB BP,[BX+SI+0x5566] ..........;1b a8 66 55
SBB DX,[BX+SI+0x55] ...........;1b 50 55       SBB BP,[BX+DI+0x5566] ..........;1b a9 66 55
SBB DX,[BX+DI+0x55] ...........;1b 51 55       SBB BP,[BP+SI+0x5566] ..........;1b aa 66 55
SBB DX,[BP+SI+0x55] ...........;1b 52 55       SBB BP,[BP+DI+0x5566] ..........;1b ab 66 55
SBB DX,[BP+DI+0x55] ...........;1b 53 55       SBB BP,[SI+0x5566] .............;1b ac 66 55
SBB DX,[SI+0x55] ..............;1b 54 55       SBB BP,[DI+0x5566] .............;1b ad 66 55
SBB DX,[DI+0x55] ..............;1b 55 55       SBB BP,[BP+0x5566] .............;1b ae 66 55
SBB DX,[BP+0x55] ..............;1b 56 55       SBB BP,[BX+0x5566] .............;1b af 66 55
SBB DX,[BX+0x55] ..............;1b 57 55       SBB SI,[BX+SI+0x5566] ..........;1b b0 66 55
SBB BX,[BX+SI+0x55] ...........;1b 58 55       SBB SI,[BX+DI+0x5566] ..........;1b b1 66 55
SBB BX,[BX+DI+0x55] ...........;1b 59 55       SBB SI,[BP+SI+0x5566] ..........;1b b2 66 55
SBB BX,[BP+SI+0x55] ...........;1b 5a 55       SBB SI,[BP+DI+0x5566] ..........;1b b3 66 55
SBB BX,[BP+DI+0x55] ...........;1b 5b 55       SBB SI,[SI+0x5566] .............;1b b4 66 55
SBB BX,[SI+0x55] ..............;1b 5c 55       SBB SI,[DI+0x5566] .............;1b b5 66 55
SBB BX,[DI+0x55] ..............;1b 5d 55       SBB SI,[BP+0x5566] .............;1b b6 66 55
SBB BX,[BP+0x55] ..............;1b 5e 55       SBB SI,[BX+0x5566] .............;1b b7 66 55
SBB BX,[BX+0x55] ..............;1b 5f 55       SBB DI,[BX+SI+0x5566] ..........;1b b8 66 55
SBB SP,[BX+SI+0x55] ...........;1b 60 55       SBB DI,[BX+DI+0x5566] ..........;1b b9 66 55
SBB SP,[BX+DI+0x55] ...........;1b 61 55       SBB DI,[BP+SI+0x5566] ..........;1b ba 66 55
SBB SP,[BP+SI+0x55] ...........;1b 62 55       SBB DI,[BP+DI+0x5566] ..........;1b bb 66 55
SBB SP,[BP+DI+0x55] ...........;1b 63 55       SBB DI,[SI+0x5566] .............;1b bc 66 55
SBB SP,[SI+0x55] ..............;1b 64 55       SBB DI,[DI+0x5566] .............;1b bd 66 55
SBB SP,[DI+0x55] ..............;1b 65 55       SBB DI,[BP+0x5566] .............;1b be 66 55
SBB SP,[BP+0x55] ..............;1b 66 55       SBB DI,[BX+0x5566] .............;1b bf 66 55
SBB SP,[BX+0x55] ..............;1b 67 55       SBB AL,0x55 ....................;1c 55
SBB BP,[BX+SI+0x55] ...........;1b 68 55       SBB AX,0x5566 ..................;1d 66 55
SBB BP,[BX+DI+0x55] ...........;1b 69 55       PUSH DS ........................;1e
SBB BP,[BP+SI+0x55] ...........;1b 6a 55       POP DS .........................;1f
SBB BP,[BP+DI+0x55] ...........;1b 6b 55       AND [BX+SI],AL .................;20 00
SBB BP,[SI+0x55] ..............;1b 6c 55       AND [BX+DI],AL .................;20 01
SBB BP,[DI+0x55] ..............;1b 6d 55       AND [BP+SI],AL .................;20 02
SBB BP,[BP+0x55] ..............;1b 6e 55       AND [BP+DI],AL .................;20 03
SBB BP,[BX+0x55] ..............;1b 6f 55       AND [SI],AL ....................;20 04
SBB SI,[BX+SI+0x55] ...........;1b 70 55       AND [DI],AL ....................;20 05
SBB SI,[BX+DI+0x55] ...........;1b 71 55       AND [0x5566],AL ................;20 06 66 55
SBB SI,[BP+SI+0x55] ...........;1b 72 55       AND [BX],AL ....................;20 07
SBB SI,[BP+DI+0x55] ...........;1b 73 55       AND [BX+SI],CL .................;20 08
SBB SI,[SI+0x55] ..............;1b 74 55       AND [BX+DI],CL .................;20 09
SBB SI,[DI+0x55] ..............;1b 75 55       AND [BP+SI],CL .................;20 0a
SBB SI,[BP+0x55] ..............;1b 76 55       AND [BP+DI],CL .................;20 0b
SBB SI,[BX+0x55] ..............;1b 77 55       AND [SI],CL ....................;20 0c
SBB DI,[BX+SI+0x55] ...........;1b 78 55       AND [DI],CL ....................;20 0d
SBB DI,[BX+DI+0x55] ...........;1b 79 55       AND [0x5566],CL ................;20 0e 66 55
SBB DI,[BP+SI+0x55] ...........;1b 7a 55       AND [BX],CL ....................;20 0f
SBB DI,[BP+DI+0x55] ...........;1b 7b 55       AND [BX+SI],DL .................;20 10
SBB DI,[SI+0x55] ..............;1b 7c 55       AND [BX+DI],DL .................;20 11
SBB DI,[DI+0x55] ..............;1b 7d 55       AND [BP+SI],DL .................;20 12
SBB DI,[BP+0x55] ..............;1b 7e 55       AND [BP+DI],DL .................;20 13
SBB DI,[BX+0x55] ..............;1b 7f 55       AND [SI],DL ....................;20 14
SBB AX,[BX+SI+0x5566] .........;1b 80 66 55    AND [DI],DL ....................;20 15
SBB AX,[BX+DI+0x5566] .........;1b 81 66 55    AND [0x5566],DL ................;20 16 66 55
SBB AX,[BP+SI+0x5566] .........;1b 82 66 55    AND [BX],DL ....................;20 17
SBB AX,[BP+DI+0x5566] .........;1b 83 66 55    AND [BX+SI],BL .................;20 18
SBB AX,[SI+0x5566] ............;1b 84 66 55    AND [BX+DI],BL .................;20 19
SBB AX,[DI+0x5566] ............;1b 85 66 55    AND [BP+SI],BL .................;20 1a
SBB AX,[BP+0x5566] ............;1b 86 66 55    AND [BP+DI],BL .................;20 1b
SBB AX,[BX+0x5566] ............;1b 87 66 55    AND [SI],BL ....................;20 1c
SBB CX,[BX+SI+0x5566] .........;1b 88 66 55    AND [DI],BL ....................;20 1d
SBB CX,[BX+DI+0x5566] .........;1b 89 66 55    AND [0x5566],BL ................;20 1e 66 55
SBB CX,[BP+SI+0x5566] .........;1b 8a 66 55    AND [BX],BL ....................;20 1f
SBB CX,[BP+DI+0x5566] .........;1b 8b 66 55    AND [BX+SI],AH .................;20 20
```

```
AND [BX+DI],AH .................;20 21          AND [BP+SI+0x55],BH ...........;20 7a 55
AND [BP+SI],AH .................;20 22          AND [BP+DI+0x55],BH ...........;20 7b 55
AND [BP+DI],AH .................;20 23          AND [SI+0x55],BH ..............;20 7c 55
AND [SI],AH ....................;20 24          AND [DI+0x55],BH ..............;20 7d 55
AND [DI],AH ....................;20 25          AND [BP+0x55],BH ..............;20 7e 55
AND [0x5566],AH ............;20 26 66 55        AND [BX+0x55],BH ..............;20 7f 55
AND [BX],AH ....................;20 27          AND [BX+SI+0x5566],AL .....;20 80 66 55
AND [BX+SI],CH .................;20 28          AND [BX+DI+0x5566],AL .....;20 81 66 55
AND [BX+DI],CH .................;20 29          AND [BP+SI+0x5566],AL .....;20 82 66 55
AND [BP+SI],CH .................;20 2a          AND [BP+DI+0x5566],AL .....;20 83 66 55
AND [BP+DI],CH .................;20 2b          AND [SI+0x5566],AL ........;20 84 66 55
AND [SI],CH ....................;20 2c          AND [DI+0x5566],AL ........;20 85 66 55
AND [DI],CH ....................;20 2d          AND [BP+0x5566],AL ........;20 86 66 55
AND [0x5566],CH ............;20 2e 66 55        AND [BX+0x5566],AL ........;20 87 66 55
AND [BX],CH ....................;20 2f          AND [BX+SI+0x5566],CL .....;20 88 66 55
AND [BX+SI],DH .................;20 30          AND [BX+DI+0x5566],CL .....;20 89 66 55
AND [BX+DI],DH .................;20 31          AND [BP+SI+0x5566],CL .....;20 8a 66 55
AND [BP+SI],DH .................;20 32          AND [BP+DI+0x5566],CL .....;20 8b 66 55
AND [BP+DI],DH .................;20 33          AND [SI+0x5566],CL ........;20 8c 66 55
AND [SI],DH ....................;20 34          AND [DI+0x5566],CL ........;20 8d 66 55
AND [DI],DH ....................;20 35          AND [BP+0x5566],CL ........;20 8e 66 55
AND [0x5566],DH ............;20 36 66 55        AND [BX+0x5566],CL ........;20 8f 66 55
AND [BX],DH ....................;20 37          AND [BX+SI+0x5566],DL .....;20 90 66 55
AND [BX+SI],BH .................;20 38          AND [BX+DI+0x5566],DL .....;20 91 66 55
AND [BX+DI],BH .................;20 39          AND [BP+SI+0x5566],DL .....;20 92 66 55
AND [BP+SI],BH .................;20 3a          AND [BP+DI+0x5566],DL .....;20 93 66 55
AND [BP+DI],BH .................;20 3b          AND [SI+0x5566],DL ........;20 94 66 55
AND [SI],BH ....................;20 3c          AND [DI+0x5566],DL ........;20 95 66 55
AND [DI],BH ....................;20 3d          AND [BP+0x5566],DL ........;20 96 66 55
AND [0x5566],BH ............;20 3e 66 55        AND [BX+0x5566],DL ........;20 97 66 55
AND [BX],BH ....................;20 3f          AND [BX+SI+0x5566],BL .....;20 98 66 55
AND [BX+SI+0x55],AL ..........;20 40 55         AND [BX+DI+0x5566],BL .....;20 99 66 55
AND [BX+DI+0x55],AL ..........;20 41 55         AND [BP+SI+0x5566],BL .....;20 9a 66 55
AND [BP+SI+0x55],AL ..........;20 42 55         AND [BP+DI+0x5566],BL .....;20 9b 66 55
AND [BP+DI+0x55],AL ..........;20 43 55         AND [SI+0x5566],BL ........;20 9c 66 55
AND [SI+0x55],AL .............;20 44 55         AND [DI+0x5566],BL ........;20 9d 66 55
AND [DI+0x55],AL .............;20 45 55         AND [BP+0x5566],BL ........;20 9e 66 55
AND [BP+0x55],AL .............;20 46 55         AND [BX+0x5566],BL ........;20 9f 66 55
AND [BX+0x55],AL .............;20 47 55         AND [BX+SI+0x5566],AH .....;20 a0 66 55
AND [BX+SI+0x55],CL ..........;20 48 55         AND [BX+DI+0x5566],AH .....;20 a1 66 55
AND [BX+DI+0x55],CL ..........;20 49 55         AND [BP+SI+0x5566],AH .....;20 a2 66 55
AND [BP+SI+0x55],CL ..........;20 4a 55         AND [BP+DI+0x5566],AH .....;20 a3 66 55
AND [BP+DI+0x55],CL ..........;20 4b 55         AND [SI+0x5566],AH ........;20 a4 66 55
AND [SI+0x55],CL .............;20 4c 55         AND [DI+0x5566],AH ........;20 a5 66 55
AND [DI+0x55],CL .............;20 4d 55         AND [BP+0x5566],AH ........;20 a6 66 55
AND [BP+0x55],CL .............;20 4e 55         AND [BX+0x5566],AH ........;20 a7 66 55
AND [BX+0x55],CL .............;20 4f 55         AND [BX+SI+0x5566],CH .....;20 a8 66 55
AND [BX+SI+0x55],DL ..........;20 50 55         AND [BX+DI+0x5566],CH .....;20 a9 66 55
AND [BX+DI+0x55],DL ..........;20 51 55         AND [BP+SI+0x5566],CH .....;20 aa 66 55
AND [BP+SI+0x55],DL ..........;20 52 55         AND [BP+DI+0x5566],CH .....;20 ab 66 55
AND [BP+DI+0x55],DL ..........;20 53 55         AND [SI+0x5566],CH ........;20 ac 66 55
AND [SI+0x55],DL .............;20 54 55         AND [DI+0x5566],CH ........;20 ad 66 55
AND [DI+0x55],DL .............;20 55 55         AND [BP+0x5566],CH ........;20 ae 66 55
AND [BP+0x55],DL .............;20 56 55         AND [BX+0x5566],CH ........;20 af 66 55
AND [BX+0x55],DL .............;20 57 55         AND [BX+SI+0x5566],DH .....;20 b0 66 55
AND [BX+SI+0x55],BL ..........;20 58 55         AND [BX+DI+0x5566],DH .....;20 b1 66 55
AND [BX+DI+0x55],BL ..........;20 59 55         AND [BP+SI+0x5566],DH .....;20 b2 66 55
AND [BP+SI+0x55],BL ..........;20 5a 55         AND [BP+DI+0x5566],DH .....;20 b3 66 55
AND [BP+DI+0x55],BL ..........;20 5b 55         AND [SI+0x5566],DH ........;20 b4 66 55
AND [SI+0x55],BL .............;20 5c 55         AND [DI+0x5566],DH ........;20 b5 66 55
AND [DI+0x55],BL .............;20 5d 55         AND [BP+0x5566],DH ........;20 b6 66 55
AND [BP+0x55],BL .............;20 5e 55         AND [BX+0x5566],DH ........;20 b7 66 55
AND [BX+0x55],BL .............;20 5f 55         AND [BX+SI+0x5566],BH .....;20 b8 66 55
AND [BX+SI+0x55],AH ..........;20 60 55         AND [BX+DI+0x5566],BH .....;20 b9 66 55
AND [BX+DI+0x55],AH ..........;20 61 55         AND [BP+SI+0x5566],BH .....;20 ba 66 55
AND [BP+SI+0x55],AH ..........;20 62 55         AND [BP+DI+0x5566],BH .....;20 bb 66 55
AND [BP+DI+0x55],AH ..........;20 63 55         AND [SI+0x5566],BH ........;20 bc 66 55
AND [SI+0x55],AH .............;20 64 55         AND [DI+0x5566],BH ........;20 bd 66 55
AND [DI+0x55],AH .............;20 65 55         AND [BP+0x5566],BH ........;20 be 66 55
AND [BP+0x55],AH .............;20 66 55         AND [BX+0x5566],BH ........;20 bf 66 55
AND [BX+0x55],AH .............;20 67 55         AND AL,AL .....................;20 c0
AND [BX+SI+0x55],CH ..........;20 68 55         AND CL,AL .....................;20 c1
AND [BX+DI+0x55],CH ..........;20 69 55         AND DL,AL .....................;20 c2
AND [BP+SI+0x55],CH ..........;20 6a 55         AND BL,AL .....................;20 c3
AND [BP+DI+0x55],CH ..........;20 6b 55         AND AH,AL .....................;20 c4
AND [SI+0x55],CH .............;20 6c 55         AND CH,AL .....................;20 c5
AND [DI+0x55],CH .............;20 6d 55         AND DH,AL .....................;20 c6
AND [BP+0x55],CH .............;20 6e 55         AND BH,AL .....................;20 c7
AND [BX+0x55],CH .............;20 6f 55         AND AL,CL .....................;20 c8
AND [BX+SI+0x55],DH ..........;20 70 55         AND CL,CL .....................;20 c9
AND [BX+DI+0x55],DH ..........;20 71 55         AND DL,CL .....................;20 ca
AND [BP+SI+0x55],DH ..........;20 72 55         AND BL,CL .....................;20 cb
AND [BP+DI+0x55],DH ..........;20 73 55         AND AH,CL .....................;20 cc
AND [SI+0x55],DH .............;20 74 55         AND CH,CL .....................;20 cd
AND [DI+0x55],DH .............;20 75 55         AND DH,CL .....................;20 ce
AND [BP+0x55],DH .............;20 76 55         AND BH,CL .....................;20 cf
AND [BX+0x55],DH .............;20 77 55         AND AL,DL .....................;20 d0
AND [BX+SI+0x55],BH ..........;20 78 55         AND CL,DL .....................;20 d1
AND [BX+DI+0x55],BH ..........;20 79 55         AND DL,DL .....................;20 d2
```

```
AND BL,DL ...................;20 d3        AND [SI],BP ...................;21 2c
AND AH,DL ...................;20 d4        AND [DI],BP ...................;21 2d
AND CH,DL ...................;20 d5        AND [0x5566],BP ...............;21 2e 66 55
AND DH,DL ...................;20 d6        AND [BX],BP ...................;21 2f
AND BH,DL ...................;20 d7        AND [BX+SI],SI ...............;21 30
AND AL,BL ...................;20 d8        AND [BX+DI],SI ...............;21 31
AND CL,BL ...................;20 d9        AND [BP+SI],SI ...............;21 32
AND DL,BL ...................;20 da        AND [BP+DI],SI ...............;21 33
AND BL,BL ...................;20 db        AND [SI],SI ...................;21 34
AND AH,BL ...................;20 dc        AND [DI],SI ...................;21 35
AND CH,BL ...................;20 dd        AND [0x5566],SI ...............;21 36 66 55
AND DH,BL ...................;20 de        AND [BX],SI ...................;21 37
AND BH,BL ...................;20 df        AND [BX+SI],DI ...............;21 38
AND AL,AH ...................;20 e0        AND [BX+DI],DI ...............;21 39
AND CL,AH ...................;20 e1        AND [BP+SI],DI ...............;21 3a
AND DL,AH ...................;20 e2        AND [BP+DI],DI ...............;21 3b
AND BL,AH ...................;20 e3        AND [SI],DI ...................;21 3c
AND AH,AH ...................;20 e4        AND [DI],DI ...................;21 3d
AND CH,AH ...................;20 e5        AND [0x5566],DI ...............;21 3e 66 55
AND DH,AH ...................;20 e6        AND [BX],DI ...................;21 3f
AND BH,AH ...................;20 e7        AND [BX+SI+0x55],AX ..........;21 40 55
AND AL,CH ...................;20 e8        AND [BX+DI+0x55],AX ..........;21 41 55
AND CL,CH ...................;20 e9        AND [BP+SI+0x55],AX ..........;21 42 55
AND DL,CH ...................;20 ea        AND [BP+DI+0x55],AX ..........;21 43 55
AND BL,CH ...................;20 eb        AND [SI+0x55],AX .............;21 44 55
AND AH,CH ...................;20 ec        AND [DI+0x55],AX .............;21 45 55
AND CH,CH ...................;20 ed        AND [BP+0x55],AX .............;21 46 55
AND DH,CH ...................;20 ee        AND [BX+0x55],AX .............;21 47 55
AND BH,CH ...................;20 ef        AND [BX+SI+0x55],CX ..........;21 48 55
AND AL,DH ...................;20 f0        AND [BX+DI+0x55],CX ..........;21 49 55
AND CL,DH ...................;20 f1        AND [BP+SI+0x55],CX ..........;21 4a 55
AND DL,DH ...................;20 f2        AND [BP+DI+0x55],CX ..........;21 4b 55
AND BL,DH ...................;20 f3        AND [SI+0x55],CX .............;21 4c 55
AND AH,DH ...................;20 f4        AND [DI+0x55],CX .............;21 4d 55
AND CH,DH ...................;20 f5        AND [BP+0x55],CX .............;21 4e 55
AND DH,DH ...................;20 f6        AND [BX+0x55],CX .............;21 4f 55
AND BH,DH ...................;20 f7        AND [BX+SI+0x55],DX ..........;21 50 55
AND AL,BH ...................;20 f8        AND [BX+DI+0x55],DX ..........;21 51 55
AND CL,BH ...................;20 f9        AND [BP+SI+0x55],DX ..........;21 52 55
AND DL,BH ...................;20 fa        AND [BP+DI+0x55],DX ..........;21 53 55
AND BL,BH ...................;20 fb        AND [SI+0x55],DX .............;21 54 55
AND AH,BH ...................;20 fc        AND [DI+0x55],DX .............;21 55 55
AND CH,BH ...................;20 fd        AND [BP+0x55],DX .............;21 56 55
AND DH,BH ...................;20 fe        AND [BX+0x55],DX .............;21 57 55
AND BH,BH ...................;20 ff        AND [BX+SI+0x55],BX ..........;21 58 55
AND [BX+SI],AX ..............;21 00        AND [BX+DI+0x55],BX ..........;21 59 55
AND [BX+DI],AX ..............;21 01        AND [BP+SI+0x55],BX ..........;21 5a 55
AND [BP+SI],AX ..............;21 02        AND [BP+DI+0x55],BX ..........;21 5b 55
AND [BP+DI],AX ..............;21 03        AND [SI+0x55],BX .............;21 5c 55
AND [SI],AX ...................;21 04      AND [DI+0x55],BX .............;21 5d 55
AND [DI],AX ...................;21 05      AND [BP+0x55],BX .............;21 5e 55
AND [0x5566],AX ..............;21 06 66 55 AND [BX+0x55],BX .............;21 5f 55
AND [BX],AX ...................;21 07      AND [BX+SI+0x55],SP ..........;21 60 55
AND [BX+SI],CX ..............;21 08        AND [BX+DI+0x55],SP ..........;21 61 55
AND [BX+DI],CX ..............;21 09        AND [BP+SI+0x55],SP ..........;21 62 55
AND [BP+SI],CX ..............;21 0a        AND [BP+DI+0x55],SP ..........;21 63 55
AND [BP+DI],CX ..............;21 0b        AND [SI+0x55],SP .............;21 64 55
AND [SI],CX ...................;21 0c      AND [DI+0x55],SP .............;21 65 55
AND [DI],CX ...................;21 0d      AND [BP+0x55],SP .............;21 66 55
AND [0x5566],CX ..............;21 0e 66 55 AND [BX+0x55],SP .............;21 67 55
AND [BX],CX ...................;21 0f      AND [BX+SI+0x55],BP ..........;21 68 55
AND [BX+SI],DX ..............;21 10        AND [BX+DI+0x55],BP ..........;21 69 55
AND [BX+DI],DX ..............;21 11        AND [BP+SI+0x55],BP ..........;21 6a 55
AND [BP+SI],DX ..............;21 12        AND [BP+DI+0x55],BP ..........;21 6b 55
AND [BP+DI],DX ..............;21 13        AND [SI+0x55],BP .............;21 6c 55
AND [SI],DX ...................;21 14      AND [DI+0x55],BP .............;21 6d 55
AND [DI],DX ...................;21 15      AND [BP+0x55],BP .............;21 6e 55
AND [0x5566],DX ..............;21 16 66 55 AND [BX+0x55],BP .............;21 6f 55
AND [BX],DX ...................;21 17      AND [BX+SI+0x55],SI ..........;21 70 55
AND [BX+SI],BX ..............;21 18        AND [BX+DI+0x55],SI ..........;21 71 55
AND [BX+DI],BX ..............;21 19        AND [BP+SI+0x55],SI ..........;21 72 55
AND [BP+SI],BX ..............;21 1a        AND [BP+DI+0x55],SI ..........;21 73 55
AND [BP+DI],BX ..............;21 1b        AND [SI+0x55],SI .............;21 74 55
AND [SI],BX ...................;21 1c      AND [DI+0x55],SI .............;21 75 55
AND [DI],BX ...................;21 1d      AND [BP+0x55],SI .............;21 76 55
AND [0x5566],BX ..............;21 1e 66 55 AND [BX+0x55],SI .............;21 77 55
AND [BX],BX ...................;21 1f      AND [BX+SI+0x55],DI ..........;21 78 55
AND [BX+SI],SP ..............;21 20        AND [BX+DI+0x55],DI ..........;21 79 55
AND [BX+DI],SP ..............;21 21        AND [BP+SI+0x55],DI ..........;21 7a 55
AND [BP+SI],SP ..............;21 22        AND [BP+DI+0x55],DI ..........;21 7b 55
AND [BP+DI],SP ..............;21 23        AND [SI+0x55],DI .............;21 7c 55
AND [SI],SP ...................;21 24      AND [DI+0x55],DI .............;21 7d 55
AND [DI],SP ...................;21 25      AND [BP+0x55],DI .............;21 7e 55
AND [0x5566],SP ..............;21 26 66 55 AND [BX+0x55],DI .............;21 7f 55
AND [BX],SP ...................;21 27      AND [BX+SI+0x5566],AX ........;21 80 66 55
AND [BX+SI],BP ..............;21 28        AND [BX+DI+0x5566],AX ........;21 81 66 55
AND [BX+DI],BP ..............;21 29        AND [BP+SI+0x5566],AX ........;21 82 66 55
AND [BP+SI],BP ..............;21 2a        AND [BP+DI+0x5566],AX ........;21 83 66 55
AND [BP+DI],BP ..............;21 2b        AND [SI+0x5566],AX ...........;21 84 66 55
```

```
AND [DI+0x5566],AX .............;21 85 66 55        AND SI,BX .....................;21 de
AND [BP+0x5566],AX .............;21 86 66 55        AND DI,BX .....................;21 df
AND [BX+0x5566],AX .............;21 87 66 55        AND AX,SP .....................;21 e0
AND [BX+SI+0x5566],CX ..........;21 88 66 55        AND CX,SP .....................;21 e1
AND [BX+DI+0x5566],CX ..........;21 89 66 55        AND DX,SP .....................;21 e2
AND [BP+SI+0x5566],CX ..........;21 8a 66 55        AND BX,SP .....................;21 e3
AND [BP+DI+0x5566],CX ..........;21 8b 66 55        AND SP,SP .....................;21 e4
AND [SI+0x5566],CX .............;21 8c 66 55        AND BP,SP .....................;21 e5
AND [DI+0x5566],CX .............;21 8d 66 55        AND SI,SP .....................;21 e6
AND [BP+0x5566],CX .............;21 8e 66 55        AND DI,SP .....................;21 e7
AND [BX+0x5566],CX .............;21 8f 66 55        AND AX,BP .....................;21 e8
AND [BX+SI+0x5566],DX ..........;21 90 66 55        AND CX,BP .....................;21 e9
AND [BX+DI+0x5566],DX ..........;21 91 66 55        AND DX,BP .....................;21 ea
AND [BP+SI+0x5566],DX ..........;21 92 66 55        AND BX,BP .....................;21 eb
AND [BP+DI+0x5566],DX ..........;21 93 66 55        AND SP,BP .....................;21 ec
AND [SI+0x5566],DX .............;21 94 66 55        AND BP,BP .....................;21 ed
AND [DI+0x5566],DX .............;21 95 66 55        AND SI,BP .....................;21 ee
AND [BP+0x5566],DX .............;21 96 66 55        AND DI,BP .....................;21 ef
AND [BX+0x5566],DX .............;21 97 66 55        AND AX,SI .....................;21 f0
AND [BX+SI+0x5566],BX ..........;21 98 66 55        AND CX,SI .....................;21 f1
AND [BX+DI+0x5566],BX ..........;21 99 66 55        AND DX,SI .....................;21 f2
AND [BP+SI+0x5566],BX ..........;21 9a 66 55        AND BX,SI .....................;21 f3
AND [BP+DI+0x5566],BX ..........;21 9b 66 55        AND SP,SI .....................;21 f4
AND [SI+0x5566],BX .............;21 9c 66 55        AND BP,SI .....................;21 f5
AND [DI+0x5566],BX .............;21 9d 66 55        AND SI,SI .....................;21 f6
AND [BP+0x5566],BX .............;21 9e 66 55        AND DI,SI .....................;21 f7
AND [BX+0x5566],BX .............;21 9f 66 55        AND AX,DI .....................;21 f8
AND [BX+SI+0x5566],SP ..........;21 a0 66 55        AND CX,DI .....................;21 f9
AND [BX+DI+0x5566],SP ..........;21 a1 66 55        AND DX,DI .....................;21 fa
AND [BP+SI+0x5566],SP ..........;21 a2 66 55        AND BX,DI .....................;21 fb
AND [BP+DI+0x5566],SP ..........;21 a3 66 55        AND SP,DI .....................;21 fc
AND [SI+0x5566],SP .............;21 a4 66 55        AND BP,DI .....................;21 fd
AND [DI+0x5566],SP .............;21 a5 66 55        AND SI,DI .....................;21 fe
AND [BP+0x5566],SP .............;21 a6 66 55        AND DI,DI .....................;21 ff
AND [BX+0x5566],SP .............;21 a7 66 55        AND AL,[BX+SI] ................;22 00
AND [BX+SI+0x5566],BP ..........;21 a8 66 55        AND AL,[BX+DI] ................;22 01
AND [BX+DI+0x5566],BP ..........;21 a9 66 55        AND AL,[BP+SI] ................;22 02
AND [BP+SI+0x5566],BP ..........;21 aa 66 55        AND AL,[BP+DI] ................;22 03
AND [BP+DI+0x5566],BP ..........;21 ab 66 55        AND AL,[SI] ...................;22 04
AND [SI+0x5566],BP .............;21 ac 66 55        AND AL,[DI] ...................;22 05
AND [DI+0x5566],BP .............;21 ad 66 55        AND AL,[0x5566] ...............;22 06 66 55
AND [BP+0x5566],BP .............;21 ae 66 55        AND AL,[BX] ...................;22 07
AND [BX+0x5566],BP .............;21 af 66 55        AND CL,[BX+SI] ................;22 08
AND [BX+SI+0x5566],SI ..........;21 b0 66 55        AND CL,[BX+DI] ................;22 09
AND [BX+DI+0x5566],SI ..........;21 b1 66 55        AND CL,[BP+SI] ................;22 0a
AND [BP+SI+0x5566],SI ..........;21 b2 66 55        AND CL,[BP+DI] ................;22 0b
AND [BP+DI+0x5566],SI ..........;21 b3 66 55        AND CL,[SI] ...................;22 0c
AND [SI+0x5566],SI .............;21 b4 66 55        AND CL,[DI] ...................;22 0d
AND [DI+0x5566],SI .............;21 b5 66 55        AND CL,[0x5566] ...............;22 0e 66 55
AND [BP+0x5566],SI .............;21 b6 66 55        AND CL,[BX] ...................;22 0f
AND [BX+0x5566],SI .............;21 b7 66 55        AND DL,[BX+SI] ................;22 10
AND [BX+SI+0x5566],DI ..........;21 b8 66 55        AND DL,[BX+DI] ................;22 11
AND [BX+DI+0x5566],DI ..........;21 b9 66 55        AND DL,[BP+SI] ................;22 12
AND [BP+SI+0x5566],DI ..........;21 ba 66 55        AND DL,[BP+DI] ................;22 13
AND [BP+DI+0x5566],DI ..........;21 bb 66 55        AND DL,[SI] ...................;22 14
AND [SI+0x5566],DI .............;21 bc 66 55        AND DL,[DI] ...................;22 15
AND [DI+0x5566],DI .............;21 bd 66 55        AND DL,[0x5566] ...............;22 16 66 55
AND [BP+0x5566],DI .............;21 be 66 55        AND DL,[BX] ...................;22 17
AND [BX+0x5566],DI .............;21 bf 66 55        AND BL,[BX+SI] ................;22 18
AND AX,AX .....................;21 c0             AND BL,[BX+DI] ................;22 19
AND CX,AX .....................;21 c1             AND BL,[BP+SI] ................;22 1a
AND DX,AX .....................;21 c2             AND BL,[BP+DI] ................;22 1b
AND BX,AX .....................;21 c3             AND BL,[SI] ...................;22 1c
AND SP,AX .....................;21 c4             AND BL,[DI] ...................;22 1d
AND BP,AX .....................;21 c5             AND BL,[0x5566] ...............;22 1e 66 55
AND SI,AX .....................;21 c6             AND BL,[BX] ...................;22 1f
AND DI,AX .....................;21 c7             AND AH,[BX+SI] ................;22 20
AND AX,CX .....................;21 c8             AND AH,[BX+DI] ................;22 21
AND CX,CX .....................;21 c9             AND AH,[BP+SI] ................;22 22
AND DX,CX .....................;21 ca             AND AH,[BP+DI] ................;22 23
AND BX,CX .....................;21 cb             AND AH,[SI] ...................;22 24
AND SP,CX .....................;21 cc             AND AH,[DI] ...................;22 25
AND BP,CX .....................;21 cd             AND AH,[0x5566] ...............;22 26 66 55
AND SI,CX .....................;21 ce             AND AH,[BX] ...................;22 27
AND DI,CX .....................;21 cf             AND CH,[BX+SI] ................;22 28
AND AX,DX .....................;21 d0             AND CH,[BX+DI] ................;22 29
AND CX,DX .....................;21 d1             AND CH,[BP+SI] ................;22 2a
AND DX,DX .....................;21 d2             AND CH,[BP+DI] ................;22 2b
AND BX,DX .....................;21 d3             AND CH,[SI] ...................;22 2c
AND SP,DX .....................;21 d4             AND CH,[DI] ...................;22 2d
AND BP,DX .....................;21 d5             AND CH,[0x5566] ...............;22 2e 66 55
AND SI,DX .....................;21 d6             AND CH,[BX] ...................;22 2f
AND DI,DX .....................;21 d7             AND DH,[BX+SI] ................;22 30
AND AX,BX .....................;21 d8             AND DH,[BX+DI] ................;22 31
AND CX,BX .....................;21 d9             AND DH,[BP+SI] ................;22 32
AND DX,BX .....................;21 da             AND DH,[BP+DI] ................;22 33
AND BX,BX .....................;21 db             AND DH,[SI] ...................;22 34
AND SP,BX .....................;21 dc             AND DH,[DI] ...................;22 35
AND BP,BX .....................;21 dd             AND DH,[0x5566] ...............;22 36 66 55
```

```
AND DH,[BX] ...................;22 37            AND DL,[BX+SI+0x5566] ..........;22 90 66 55
AND BH,[BX+SI] ................;22 38            AND DL,[BX+DI+0x5566] ..........;22 91 66 55
AND BH,[BX+DI] ................;22 39            AND DL,[BP+SI+0x5566] ..........;22 92 66 55
AND BH,[BP+SI] ................;22 3a            AND DL,[BP+DI+0x5566] ..........;22 93 66 55
AND BH,[BP+DI] ................;22 3b            AND DL,[SI+0x5566] .............;22 94 66 55
AND BH,[SI] ...................;22 3c            AND DL,[DI+0x5566] .............;22 95 66 55
AND BH,[DI] ...................;22 3d            AND DL,[BP+0x5566] .............;22 96 66 55
AND BH,[0x5566] ...............;22 3e 66 55      AND DL,[BX+0x5566] .............;22 97 66 55
AND BH,[BX] ...................;22 3f            AND BL,[BX+SI+0x5566] ..........;22 98 66 55
AND AL,[BX+SI+0x55] ...........;22 40 55         AND BL,[BX+DI+0x5566] ..........;22 99 66 55
AND AL,[BX+DI+0x55] ...........;22 41 55         AND BL,[BP+SI+0x5566] ..........;22 9a 66 55
AND AL,[BP+SI+0x55] ...........;22 42 55         AND BL,[BP+DI+0x5566] ..........;22 9b 66 55
AND AL,[BP+DI+0x55] ...........;22 43 55         AND BL,[SI+0x5566] .............;22 9c 66 55
AND AL,[SI+0x55] ..............;22 44 55         AND BL,[DI+0x5566] .............;22 9d 66 55
AND AL,[DI+0x55] ..............;22 45 55         AND BL,[BP+0x5566] .............;22 9e 66 55
AND AL,[BP+0x55] ..............;22 46 55         AND BL,[BX+0x5566] .............;22 9f 66 55
AND AL,[BX+0x55] ..............;22 47 55         AND AH,[BX+SI+0x5566] ..........;22 a0 66 55
AND CL,[BX+SI+0x55] ...........;22 48 55         AND AH,[BX+DI+0x5566] ..........;22 a1 66 55
AND CL,[BX+DI+0x55] ...........;22 49 55         AND AH,[BP+SI+0x5566] ..........;22 a2 66 55
AND CL,[BP+SI+0x55] ...........;22 4a 55         AND AH,[BP+DI+0x5566] ..........;22 a3 66 55
AND CL,[BP+DI+0x55] ...........;22 4b 55         AND AH,[SI+0x5566] .............;22 a4 66 55
AND CL,[SI+0x55] ..............;22 4c 55         AND AH,[DI+0x5566] .............;22 a5 66 55
AND CL,[DI+0x55] ..............;22 4d 55         AND AH,[BP+0x5566] .............;22 a6 66 55
AND CL,[BP+0x55] ..............;22 4e 55         AND AH,[BX+0x5566] .............;22 a7 66 55
AND CL,[BX+0x55] ..............;22 4f 55         AND CH,[BX+SI+0x5566] ..........;22 a8 66 55
AND DL,[BX+SI+0x55] ...........;22 50 55         AND CH,[BX+DI+0x5566] ..........;22 a9 66 55
AND DL,[BX+DI+0x55] ...........;22 51 55         AND CH,[BP+SI+0x5566] ..........;22 aa 66 55
AND DL,[BP+SI+0x55] ...........;22 52 55         AND CH,[BP+DI+0x5566] ..........;22 ab 66 55
AND DL,[BP+DI+0x55] ...........;22 53 55         AND CH,[SI+0x5566] .............;22 ac 66 55
AND DL,[SI+0x55] ..............;22 54 55         AND CH,[DI+0x5566] .............;22 ad 66 55
AND DL,[DI+0x55] ..............;22 55 55         AND CH,[BP+0x5566] .............;22 ae 66 55
AND DL,[BP+0x55] ..............;22 56 55         AND CH,[BX+0x5566] .............;22 af 66 55
AND DL,[BX+0x55] ..............;22 57 55         AND DH,[BX+SI+0x5566] ..........;22 b0 66 55
AND BL,[BX+SI+0x55] ...........;22 58 55         AND DH,[BX+DI+0x5566] ..........;22 b1 66 55
AND BL,[BX+DI+0x55] ...........;22 59 55         AND DH,[BP+SI+0x5566] ..........;22 b2 66 55
AND BL,[BP+SI+0x55] ...........;22 5a 55         AND DH,[BP+DI+0x5566] ..........;22 b3 66 55
AND BL,[BP+DI+0x55] ...........;22 5b 55         AND DH,[SI+0x5566] .............;22 b4 66 55
AND BL,[SI+0x55] ..............;22 5c 55         AND DH,[DI+0x5566] .............;22 b5 66 55
AND BL,[DI+0x55] ..............;22 5d 55         AND DH,[BP+0x5566] .............;22 b6 66 55
AND BL,[BP+0x55] ..............;22 5e 55         AND DH,[BX+0x5566] .............;22 b7 66 55
AND BL,[BX+0x55] ..............;22 5f 55         AND BH,[BX+SI+0x5566] ..........;22 b8 66 55
AND AH,[BX+SI+0x55] ...........;22 60 55         AND BH,[BX+DI+0x5566] ..........;22 b9 66 55
AND AH,[BX+DI+0x55] ...........;22 61 55         AND BH,[BP+SI+0x5566] ..........;22 ba 66 55
AND AH,[BP+SI+0x55] ...........;22 62 55         AND BH,[BP+DI+0x5566] ..........;22 bb 66 55
AND AH,[BP+DI+0x55] ...........;22 63 55         AND BH,[SI+0x5566] .............;22 bc 66 55
AND AH,[SI+0x55] ..............;22 64 55         AND BH,[DI+0x5566] .............;22 bd 66 55
AND AH,[DI+0x55] ..............;22 65 55         AND BH,[BP+0x5566] .............;22 be 66 55
AND AH,[BP+0x55] ..............;22 66 55         AND BH,[BX+0x5566] .............;22 bf 66 55
AND AH,[BX+0x55] ..............;22 67 55         AND AX,[BX+SI] ................;23 00
AND CH,[BX+SI+0x55] ...........;22 68 55         AND AX,[BX+DI] ................;23 01
AND CH,[BX+DI+0x55] ...........;22 69 55         AND AX,[BP+SI] ................;23 02
AND CH,[BP+SI+0x55] ...........;22 6a 55         AND AX,[BP+DI] ................;23 03
AND CH,[BP+DI+0x55] ...........;22 6b 55         AND AX,[SI] ...................;23 04
AND CH,[SI+0x55] ..............;22 6c 55         AND AX,[DI] ...................;23 05
AND CH,[DI+0x55] ..............;22 6d 55         AND AX,[0x5566] ...............;23 06 66 55
AND CH,[BP+0x55] ..............;22 6e 55         AND AX,[BX] ...................;23 07
AND CH,[BX+0x55] ..............;22 6f 55         AND CX,[BX+SI] ................;23 08
AND DH,[BX+SI+0x55] ...........;22 70 55         AND CX,[BX+DI] ................;23 09
AND DH,[BX+DI+0x55] ...........;22 71 55         AND CX,[BP+SI] ................;23 0a
AND DH,[BP+SI+0x55] ...........;22 72 55         AND CX,[BP+DI] ................;23 0b
AND DH,[BP+DI+0x55] ...........;22 73 55         AND CX,[SI] ...................;23 0c
AND DH,[SI+0x55] ..............;22 74 55         AND CX,[DI] ...................;23 0d
AND DH,[DI+0x55] ..............;22 75 55         AND CX,[0x5566] ...............;23 0e 66 55
AND DH,[BP+0x55] ..............;22 76 55         AND CX,[BX] ...................;23 0f
AND DH,[BX+0x55] ..............;22 77 55         AND DX,[BX+SI] ................;23 10
AND BH,[BX+SI+0x55] ...........;22 78 55         AND DX,[BX+DI] ................;23 11
AND BH,[BX+DI+0x55] ...........;22 79 55         AND DX,[BP+SI] ................;23 12
AND BH,[BP+SI+0x55] ...........;22 7a 55         AND DX,[BP+DI] ................;23 13
AND BH,[BP+DI+0x55] ...........;22 7b 55         AND DX,[SI] ...................;23 14
AND BH,[SI+0x55] ..............;22 7c 55         AND DX,[DI] ...................;23 15
AND BH,[DI+0x55] ..............;22 7d 55         AND DX,[0x5566] ...............;23 16 66 55
AND BH,[BP+0x55] ..............;22 7e 55         AND DX,[BX] ...................;23 17
AND BH,[BX+0x55] ..............;22 7f 55         AND BX,[BX+SI] ................;23 18
AND AL,[BX+SI+0x5566] .........;22 80 66 55      AND BX,[BX+DI] ................;23 19
AND AL,[BX+DI+0x5566] .........;22 81 66 55      AND BX,[BP+SI] ................;23 1a
AND AL,[BP+SI+0x5566] .........;22 82 66 55      AND BX,[BP+DI] ................;23 1b
AND AL,[BP+DI+0x5566] .........;22 83 66 55      AND BX,[SI] ...................;23 1c
AND AL,[SI+0x5566] ............;22 84 66 55      AND BX,[DI] ...................;23 1d
AND AL,[DI+0x5566] ............;22 85 66 55      AND BX,[0x5566] ...............;23 1e 66 55
AND AL,[BP+0x5566] ............;22 86 66 55      AND BX,[BX] ...................;23 1f
AND AL,[BX+0x5566] ............;22 87 66 55      AND SP,[BX+SI] ................;23 20
AND CL,[BX+SI+0x5566] .........;22 88 66 55      AND SP,[BX+DI] ................;23 21
AND CL,[BX+DI+0x5566] .........;22 89 66 55      AND SP,[BP+SI] ................;23 22
AND CL,[BP+SI+0x5566] .........;22 8a 66 55      AND SP,[BP+DI] ................;23 23
AND CL,[BP+DI+0x5566] .........;22 8b 66 55      AND SP,[SI] ...................;23 24
AND CL,[SI+0x5566] ............;22 8c 66 55      AND SP,[DI] ...................;23 25
AND CL,[DI+0x5566] ............;22 8d 66 55      AND SP,[0x5566] ...............;23 26 66 55
AND CL,[BP+0x5566] ............;22 8e 66 55      AND SP,[BX] ...................;23 27
AND CL,[BX+0x5566] ............;22 8f 66 55      AND BP,[BX+SI] ................;23 28
```

```
AND BP,[BX+DI] ................ ;23 29
AND BP,[BP+SI] ................ ;23 2a
AND BP,[BP+DI] ................ ;23 2b
AND BP,[SI] ................ ;23 2c
AND BP,[DI] ................ ;23 2d
AND BP,[0x5566] ................ ;23 2e 66 55
AND BP,[BX] ................ ;23 2f
AND SI,[BX+SI] ................ ;23 30
AND SI,[BX+DI] ................ ;23 31
AND SI,[BP+SI] ................ ;23 32
AND SI,[BP+DI] ................ ;23 33
AND SI,[SI] ................ ;23 34
AND SI,[DI] ................ ;23 35
AND SI,[0x5566] ................ ;23 36 66 55
AND SI,[BX] ................ ;23 37
AND DI,[BX+SI] ................ ;23 38
AND DI,[BX+DI] ................ ;23 39
AND DI,[BP+SI] ................ ;23 3a
AND DI,[BP+DI] ................ ;23 3b
AND DI,[SI] ................ ;23 3c
AND DI,[DI] ................ ;23 3d
AND DI,[0x5566] ................ ;23 3e 66 55
AND DI,[BX] ................ ;23 3f
AND AX,[BX+SI+0x55] ................ ;23 40 55
AND AX,[BX+DI+0x55] ................ ;23 41 55
AND AX,[BP+SI+0x55] ................ ;23 42 55
AND AX,[BP+DI+0x55] ................ ;23 43 55
AND AX,[SI+0x55] ................ ;23 44 55
AND AX,[DI+0x55] ................ ;23 45 55
AND AX,[BP+0x55] ................ ;23 46 55
AND AX,[BX+0x55] ................ ;23 47 55
AND CX,[BX+SI+0x55] ................ ;23 48 55
AND CX,[BX+DI+0x55] ................ ;23 49 55
AND CX,[BP+SI+0x55] ................ ;23 4a 55
AND CX,[BP+DI+0x55] ................ ;23 4b 55
AND CX,[SI+0x55] ................ ;23 4c 55
AND CX,[DI+0x55] ................ ;23 4d 55
AND CX,[BP+0x55] ................ ;23 4e 55
AND CX,[BX+0x55] ................ ;23 4f 55
AND DX,[BX+SI+0x55] ................ ;23 50 55
AND DX,[BX+DI+0x55] ................ ;23 51 55
AND DX,[BP+SI+0x55] ................ ;23 52 55
AND DX,[BP+DI+0x55] ................ ;23 53 55
AND DX,[SI+0x55] ................ ;23 54 55
AND DX,[DI+0x55] ................ ;23 55 55
AND DX,[BP+0x55] ................ ;23 56 55
AND DX,[BX+0x55] ................ ;23 57 55
AND BX,[BX+SI+0x55] ................ ;23 58 55
AND BX,[BX+DI+0x55] ................ ;23 59 55
AND BX,[BP+SI+0x55] ................ ;23 5a 55
AND BX,[BP+DI+0x55] ................ ;23 5b 55
AND BX,[SI+0x55] ................ ;23 5c 55
AND BX,[DI+0x55] ................ ;23 5d 55
AND BX,[BP+0x55] ................ ;23 5e 55
AND BX,[BX+0x55] ................ ;23 5f 55
AND SP,[BX+SI+0x55] ................ ;23 60 55
AND SP,[BX+DI+0x55] ................ ;23 61 55
AND SP,[BP+SI+0x55] ................ ;23 62 55
AND SP,[BP+DI+0x55] ................ ;23 63 55
AND SP,[SI+0x55] ................ ;23 64 55
AND SP,[DI+0x55] ................ ;23 65 55
AND SP,[BP+0x55] ................ ;23 66 55
AND SP,[BX+0x55] ................ ;23 67 55
AND BP,[BX+SI+0x55] ................ ;23 68 55
AND BP,[BX+DI+0x55] ................ ;23 69 55
AND BP,[BP+SI+0x55] ................ ;23 6a 55
AND BP,[BP+DI+0x55] ................ ;23 6b 55
AND BP,[SI+0x55] ................ ;23 6c 55
AND BP,[DI+0x55] ................ ;23 6d 55
AND BP,[BP+0x55] ................ ;23 6e 55
AND BP,[BX+0x55] ................ ;23 6f 55
AND SI,[BX+SI+0x55] ................ ;23 70 55
AND SI,[BX+DI+0x55] ................ ;23 71 55
AND SI,[BP+SI+0x55] ................ ;23 72 55
AND SI,[BP+DI+0x55] ................ ;23 73 55
AND SI,[SI+0x55] ................ ;23 74 55
AND SI,[DI+0x55] ................ ;23 75 55
AND SI,[BP+0x55] ................ ;23 76 55
AND SI,[BX+0x55] ................ ;23 77 55
AND DI,[BX+SI+0x55] ................ ;23 78 55
AND DI,[BX+DI+0x55] ................ ;23 79 55
AND DI,[BP+SI+0x55] ................ ;23 7a 55
AND DI,[BP+DI+0x55] ................ ;23 7b 55
AND DI,[SI+0x55] ................ ;23 7c 55
AND DI,[DI+0x55] ................ ;23 7d 55
AND DI,[BP+0x55] ................ ;23 7e 55
AND DI,[BX+0x55] ................ ;23 7f 55
AND AX,[BX+SI+0x5566] ................ ;23 80 66 55
AND AX,[BX+DI+0x5566] ................ ;23 81 66 55
AND AX,[BP+SI+0x5566] ................ ;23 82 66 55
AND AX,[BP+DI+0x5566] ................ ;23 83 66 55
AND AX,[SI+0x5566] ................ ;23 84 66 55
AND AX,[DI+0x5566] ................ ;23 85 66 55
AND AX,[BP+0x5566] ................ ;23 86 66 55
AND AX,[BX+0x5566] ................ ;23 87 66 55
AND CX,[BX+SI+0x5566] ................ ;23 88 66 55
AND CX,[BX+DI+0x5566] ................ ;23 89 66 55
AND CX,[BP+SI+0x5566] ................ ;23 8a 66 55
AND CX,[BP+DI+0x5566] ................ ;23 8b 66 55
AND CX,[SI+0x5566] ................ ;23 8c 66 55
AND CX,[DI+0x5566] ................ ;23 8d 66 55
AND CX,[BP+0x5566] ................ ;23 8e 66 55
AND CX,[BX+0x5566] ................ ;23 8f 66 55
AND DX,[BX+SI+0x5566] ................ ;23 90 66 55
AND DX,[BX+DI+0x5566] ................ ;23 91 66 55
AND DX,[BP+SI+0x5566] ................ ;23 92 66 55
AND DX,[BP+DI+0x5566] ................ ;23 93 66 55
AND DX,[SI+0x5566] ................ ;23 94 66 55
AND DX,[DI+0x5566] ................ ;23 95 66 55
AND DX,[BP+0x5566] ................ ;23 96 66 55
AND DX,[BX+0x5566] ................ ;23 97 66 55
AND BX,[BX+SI+0x5566] ................ ;23 98 66 55
AND BX,[BX+DI+0x5566] ................ ;23 99 66 55
AND BX,[BP+SI+0x5566] ................ ;23 9a 66 55
AND BX,[BP+DI+0x5566] ................ ;23 9b 66 55
AND BX,[SI+0x5566] ................ ;23 9c 66 55
AND BX,[DI+0x5566] ................ ;23 9d 66 55
AND BX,[BP+0x5566] ................ ;23 9e 66 55
AND BX,[BX+0x5566] ................ ;23 9f 66 55
AND SP,[BX+SI+0x5566] ................ ;23 a0 66 55
AND SP,[BX+DI+0x5566] ................ ;23 a1 66 55
AND SP,[BP+SI+0x5566] ................ ;23 a2 66 55
AND SP,[BP+DI+0x5566] ................ ;23 a3 66 55
AND SP,[SI+0x5566] ................ ;23 a4 66 55
AND SP,[DI+0x5566] ................ ;23 a5 66 55
AND SP,[BP+0x5566] ................ ;23 a6 66 55
AND SP,[BX+0x5566] ................ ;23 a7 66 55
AND BP,[BX+SI+0x5566] ................ ;23 a8 66 55
AND BP,[BX+DI+0x5566] ................ ;23 a9 66 55
AND BP,[BP+SI+0x5566] ................ ;23 aa 66 55
AND BP,[BP+DI+0x5566] ................ ;23 ab 66 55
AND BP,[SI+0x5566] ................ ;23 ac 66 55
AND BP,[DI+0x5566] ................ ;23 ad 66 55
AND BP,[BP+0x5566] ................ ;23 ae 66 55
AND BP,[BX+0x5566] ................ ;23 af 66 55
AND SI,[BX+SI+0x5566] ................ ;23 b0 66 55
AND SI,[BX+DI+0x5566] ................ ;23 b1 66 55
AND SI,[BP+SI+0x5566] ................ ;23 b2 66 55
AND SI,[BP+DI+0x5566] ................ ;23 b3 66 55
AND SI,[SI+0x5566] ................ ;23 b4 66 55
AND SI,[DI+0x5566] ................ ;23 b5 66 55
AND SI,[BP+0x5566] ................ ;23 b6 66 55
AND SI,[BX+0x5566] ................ ;23 b7 66 55
AND DI,[BX+SI+0x5566] ................ ;23 b8 66 55
AND DI,[BX+DI+0x5566] ................ ;23 b9 66 55
AND DI,[BP+SI+0x5566] ................ ;23 ba 66 55
AND DI,[BP+DI+0x5566] ................ ;23 bb 66 55
AND DI,[SI+0x5566] ................ ;23 bc 66 55
AND DI,[DI+0x5566] ................ ;23 bd 66 55
AND DI,[BP+0x5566] ................ ;23 be 66 55
AND DI,[BX+0x5566] ................ ;23 bf 66 55
AND AL,0x55 ................ ;24 55
AND AX,0x5566 ................ ;25 66 55
ES ................ ;26
DAA ................ ;27
SUB [BX+SI],AL ................ ;28 00
SUB [BX+DI],AL ................ ;28 01
SUB [BP+SI],AL ................ ;28 02
SUB [BP+DI],AL ................ ;28 03
SUB [SI],AL ................ ;28 04
SUB [DI],AL ................ ;28 05
SUB [0x5566],AL ................ ;28 06 66 55
SUB [BX],AL ................ ;28 07
SUB [BX+SI],CL ................ ;28 08
SUB [BX+DI],CL ................ ;28 09
SUB [BP+SI],CL ................ ;28 0a
SUB [BP+DI],CL ................ ;28 0b
SUB [SI],CL ................ ;28 0c
SUB [DI],CL ................ ;28 0d
SUB [0x5566],CL ................ ;28 0e 66 55
SUB [BX],CL ................ ;28 0f
SUB [BX+SI],DL ................ ;28 10
SUB [BX+DI],DL ................ ;28 11
SUB [BP+SI],DL ................ ;28 12
SUB [BP+DI],DL ................ ;28 13
SUB [SI],DL ................ ;28 14
SUB [DI],DL ................ ;28 15
SUB [0x5566],DL ................ ;28 16 66 55
```

```
SUB [BX],DL  .....................;28 17          SUB [BX+SI+0x55],DH  ...........;28 70 55
SUB [BX+SI],BL  ..................;28 18          SUB [BX+DI+0x55],DH  ...........;28 71 55
SUB [BX+DI],BL  ..................;28 19          SUB [BP+SI+0x55],DH  ...........;28 72 55
SUB [BP+SI],BL  ..................;28 1a          SUB [BP+DI+0x55],DH  ...........;28 73 55
SUB [BP+DI],BL  ..................;28 1b          SUB [SI+0x55],DH  ..............;28 74 55
SUB [SI],BL  .....................;28 1c          SUB [DI+0x55],DH  ..............;28 75 55
SUB [DI],BL  .....................;28 1d          SUB [BP+0x55],DH  ..............;28 76 55
SUB [0x5566],BL  .................;28 1e 66 55     SUB [BX+0x55],DH  ..............;28 77 55
SUB [BX],BL  .....................;28 1f          SUB [BX+SI+0x55],BH  ...........;28 78 55
SUB [BX+SI],AH  ..................;28 20          SUB [BX+DI+0x55],BH  ...........;28 79 55
SUB [BX+DI],AH  ..................;28 21          SUB [BP+SI+0x55],BH  ...........;28 7a 55
SUB [BP+SI],AH  ..................;28 22          SUB [BP+DI+0x55],BH  ...........;28 7b 55
SUB [BP+DI],AH  ..................;28 23          SUB [SI+0x55],BH  ..............;28 7c 55
SUB [SI],AH  .....................;28 24          SUB [DI+0x55],BH  ..............;28 7d 55
SUB [DI],AH  .....................;28 25          SUB [BP+0x55],BH  ..............;28 7e 55
SUB [0x5566],AH  .................;28 26 66 55     SUB [BX+0x55],BH  ..............;28 7f 55
SUB [BX],AH  .....................;28 27          SUB [BX+SI+0x5566],AL  .........;28 80 66 55
SUB [BX+SI],CH  ..................;28 28          SUB [BX+DI+0x5566],AL  .........;28 81 66 55
SUB [BX+DI],CH  ..................;28 29          SUB [BP+SI+0x5566],AL  .........;28 82 66 55
SUB [BP+SI],CH  ..................;28 2a          SUB [BP+DI+0x5566],AL  .........;28 83 66 55
SUB [BP+DI],CH  ..................;28 2b          SUB [SI+0x5566],AL  ............;28 84 66 55
SUB [SI],CH  .....................;28 2c          SUB [DI+0x5566],AL  ............;28 85 66 55
SUB [DI],CH  .....................;28 2d          SUB [BP+0x5566],AL  ............;28 86 66 55
SUB [0x5566],CH  .................;28 2e 66 55     SUB [BX+0x5566],AL  ............;28 87 66 55
SUB [BX],CH  .....................;28 2f          SUB [BX+SI+0x5566],CL  .........;28 88 66 55
SUB [BX+SI],DH  ..................;28 30          SUB [BX+DI+0x5566],CL  .........;28 89 66 55
SUB [BX+DI],DH  ..................;28 31          SUB [BP+SI+0x5566],CL  .........;28 8a 66 55
SUB [BP+SI],DH  ..................;28 32          SUB [BP+DI+0x5566],CL  .........;28 8b 66 55
SUB [BP+DI],DH  ..................;28 33          SUB [SI+0x5566],CL  ............;28 8c 66 55
SUB [SI],DH  .....................;28 34          SUB [DI+0x5566],CL  ............;28 8d 66 55
SUB [DI],DH  .....................;28 35          SUB [BP+0x5566],CL  ............;28 8e 66 55
SUB [0x5566],DH  .................;28 36 66 55     SUB [BX+0x5566],CL  ............;28 8f 66 55
SUB [BX],DH  .....................;28 37          SUB [BX+SI+0x5566],DL  .........;28 90 66 55
SUB [BX+SI],BH  ..................;28 38          SUB [BX+DI+0x5566],DL  .........;28 91 66 55
SUB [BX+DI],BH  ..................;28 39          SUB [BP+SI+0x5566],DL  .........;28 92 66 55
SUB [BP+SI],BH  ..................;28 3a          SUB [BP+DI+0x5566],DL  .........;28 93 66 55
SUB [BP+DI],BH  ..................;28 3b          SUB [SI+0x5566],DL  ............;28 94 66 55
SUB [SI],BH  .....................;28 3c          SUB [DI+0x5566],DL  ............;28 95 66 55
SUB [DI],BH  .....................;28 3d          SUB [BP+0x5566],DL  ............;28 96 66 55
SUB [0x5566],BH  .................;28 3e 66 55     SUB [BX+0x5566],DL  ............;28 97 66 55
SUB [BX],BH  .....................;28 3f          SUB [BX+SI+0x5566],BL  .........;28 98 66 55
SUB [BX+SI+0x55],AL  .............;28 40 55       SUB [BX+DI+0x5566],BL  .........;28 99 66 55
SUB [BX+DI+0x55],AL  .............;28 41 55       SUB [BP+SI+0x5566],BL  .........;28 9a 66 55
SUB [BP+SI+0x55],AL  .............;28 42 55       SUB [BP+DI+0x5566],BL  .........;28 9b 66 55
SUB [BP+DI+0x55],AL  .............;28 43 55       SUB [SI+0x5566],BL  ............;28 9c 66 55
SUB [SI+0x55],AL  ................;28 44 55       SUB [DI+0x5566],BL  ............;28 9d 66 55
SUB [DI+0x55],AL  ................;28 45 55       SUB [BP+0x5566],BL  ............;28 9e 66 55
SUB [BP+0x55],AL  ................;28 46 55       SUB [BX+0x5566],BL  ............;28 9f 66 55
SUB [BX+0x55],AL  ................;28 47 55       SUB [BX+SI+0x5566],AH  .........;28 a0 66 55
SUB [BX+SI+0x55],CL  .............;28 48 55       SUB [BX+DI+0x5566],AH  .........;28 a1 66 55
SUB [BX+DI+0x55],CL  .............;28 49 55       SUB [BP+SI+0x5566],AH  .........;28 a2 66 55
SUB [BP+SI+0x55],CL  .............;28 4a 55       SUB [BP+DI+0x5566],AH  .........;28 a3 66 55
SUB [BP+DI+0x55],CL  .............;28 4b 55       SUB [SI+0x5566],AH  ............;28 a4 66 55
SUB [SI+0x55],CL  ................;28 4c 55       SUB [DI+0x5566],AH  ............;28 a5 66 55
SUB [DI+0x55],CL  ................;28 4d 55       SUB [BP+0x5566],AH  ............;28 a6 66 55
SUB [BP+0x55],CL  ................;28 4e 55       SUB [BX+0x5566],AH  ............;28 a7 66 55
SUB [BX+0x55],CL  ................;28 4f 55       SUB [BX+SI+0x5566],CH  .........;28 a8 66 55
SUB [BX+SI+0x55],DL  .............;28 50 55       SUB [BX+DI+0x5566],CH  .........;28 a9 66 55
SUB [BX+DI+0x55],DL  .............;28 51 55       SUB [BP+SI+0x5566],CH  .........;28 aa 66 55
SUB [BP+SI+0x55],DL  .............;28 52 55       SUB [BP+DI+0x5566],CH  .........;28 ab 66 55
SUB [BP+DI+0x55],DL  .............;28 53 55       SUB [SI+0x5566],CH  ............;28 ac 66 55
SUB [SI+0x55],DL  ................;28 54 55       SUB [DI+0x5566],CH  ............;28 ad 66 55
SUB [DI+0x55],DL  ................;28 55 55       SUB [BP+0x5566],CH  ............;28 ae 66 55
SUB [BP+0x55],DL  ................;28 56 55       SUB [BX+0x5566],CH  ............;28 af 66 55
SUB [BX+0x55],DL  ................;28 57 55       SUB [BX+SI+0x5566],DH  .........;28 b0 66 55
SUB [BX+SI+0x55],BL  .............;28 58 55       SUB [BX+DI+0x5566],DH  .........;28 b1 66 55
SUB [BX+DI+0x55],BL  .............;28 59 55       SUB [BP+SI+0x5566],DH  .........;28 b2 66 55
SUB [BP+SI+0x55],BL  .............;28 5a 55       SUB [BP+DI+0x5566],DH  .........;28 b3 66 55
SUB [BP+DI+0x55],BL  .............;28 5b 55       SUB [SI+0x5566],DH  ............;28 b4 66 55
SUB [SI+0x55],BL  ................;28 5c 55       SUB [DI+0x5566],DH  ............;28 b5 66 55
SUB [DI+0x55],BL  ................;28 5d 55       SUB [BP+0x5566],DH  ............;28 b6 66 55
SUB [BP+0x55],BL  ................;28 5e 55       SUB [BX+0x5566],DH  ............;28 b7 66 55
SUB [BX+0x55],BL  ................;28 5f 55       SUB [BX+SI+0x5566],BH  .........;28 b8 66 55
SUB [BX+SI+0x55],AH  .............;28 60 55       SUB [BX+DI+0x5566],BH  .........;28 b9 66 55
SUB [BX+DI+0x55],AH  .............;28 61 55       SUB [BP+SI+0x5566],BH  .........;28 ba 66 55
SUB [BP+SI+0x55],AH  .............;28 62 55       SUB [BP+DI+0x5566],BH  .........;28 bb 66 55
SUB [BP+DI+0x55],AH  .............;28 63 55       SUB [SI+0x5566],BH  ............;28 bc 66 55
SUB [SI+0x55],AH  ................;28 64 55       SUB [DI+0x5566],BH  ............;28 bd 66 55
SUB [DI+0x55],AH  ................;28 65 55       SUB [BP+0x5566],BH  ............;28 be 66 55
SUB [BP+0x55],AH  ................;28 66 55       SUB [BX+0x5566],BH  ............;28 bf 66 55
SUB [BX+0x55],AH  ................;28 67 55       SUB AL,AL  .....................;28 c0
SUB [BX+SI+0x55],CH  .............;28 68 55       SUB CL,AL  .....................;28 c1
SUB [BX+DI+0x55],CH  .............;28 69 55       SUB DL,AL  .....................;28 c2
SUB [BP+SI+0x55],CH  .............;28 6a 55       SUB BL,AL  .....................;28 c3
SUB [BP+DI+0x55],CH  .............;28 6b 55       SUB AH,AL  .....................;28 c4
SUB [SI+0x55],CH  ................;28 6c 55       SUB CH,AL  .....................;28 c5
SUB [DI+0x55],CH  ................;28 6d 55       SUB DH,AL  .....................;28 c6
SUB [BP+0x55],CH  ................;28 6e 55       SUB BH,AL  .....................;28 c7
SUB [BX+0x55],CH  ................;28 6f 55       SUB AL,CL  .....................;28 c8
```

```
SUB CL,CL ....................;28 c9        SUB [BP+SI],SP ...............;29 22
SUB DL,CL ....................;28 ca        SUB [BP+DI],SP ...............;29 23
SUB BL,CL ....................;28 cb        SUB [SI],SP ..................;29 24
SUB AH,CL ....................;28 cc        SUB [DI],SP ..................;29 25
SUB CH,CL ....................;28 cd        SUB [0x5566],SP ..............;29 26 66 55
SUB DH,CL ....................;28 ce        SUB [BX],SP ..................;29 27
SUB BH,CL ....................;28 cf        SUB [BX+SI],BP ...............;29 28
SUB AL,DL ....................;28 d0        SUB [BX+DI],BP ...............;29 29
SUB CL,DL ....................;28 d1        SUB [BP+SI],BP ...............;29 2a
SUB DL,DL ....................;28 d2        SUB [BP+DI],BP ...............;29 2b
SUB BL,DL ....................;28 d3        SUB [SI],BP ..................;29 2c
SUB AH,DL ....................;28 d4        SUB [DI],BP ..................;29 2d
SUB CH,DL ....................;28 d5        SUB [0x5566],BP ..............;29 2e 66 55
SUB DH,DL ....................;28 d6        SUB [BX],BP ..................;29 2f
SUB BH,DL ....................;28 d7        SUB [BX+SI],SI ...............;29 30
SUB AL,BL ....................;28 d8        SUB [BX+DI],SI ...............;29 31
SUB CL,BL ....................;28 d9        SUB [BP+SI],SI ...............;29 32
SUB DL,BL ....................;28 da        SUB [BP+DI],SI ...............;29 33
SUB BL,BL ....................;28 db        SUB [SI],SI ..................;29 34
SUB AH,BL ....................;28 dc        SUB [DI],SI ..................;29 35
SUB CH,BL ....................;28 dd        SUB [0x5566],SI ..............;29 36 66 55
SUB DH,BL ....................;28 de        SUB [BX],SI ..................;29 37
SUB BH,BL ....................;28 df        SUB [BX+SI],DI ...............;29 38
SUB AL,AH ....................;28 e0        SUB [BX+DI],DI ...............;29 39
SUB CL,AH ....................;28 e1        SUB [BP+SI],DI ...............;29 3a
SUB DL,AH ....................;28 e2        SUB [BP+DI],DI ...............;29 3b
SUB BL,AH ....................;28 e3        SUB [SI],DI ..................;29 3c
SUB AH,AH ....................;28 e4        SUB [DI],DI ..................;29 3d
SUB CH,AH ....................;28 e5        SUB [0x5566],DI ..............;29 3e 66 55
SUB DH,AH ....................;28 e6        SUB [BX],DI ..................;29 3f
SUB BH,AH ....................;28 e7        SUB [BX+SI+0x55],AX ..........;29 40 55
SUB AL,CH ....................;28 e8        SUB [BX+DI+0x55],AX ..........;29 41 55
SUB CL,CH ....................;28 e9        SUB [BP+SI+0x55],AX ..........;29 42 55
SUB DL,CH ....................;28 ea        SUB [BP+DI+0x55],AX ..........;29 43 55
SUB BL,CH ....................;28 eb        SUB [SI+0x55],AX .............;29 44 55
SUB AH,CH ....................;28 ec        SUB [DI+0x55],AX .............;29 45 55
SUB CH,CH ....................;28 ed        SUB [BP+0x55],AX .............;29 46 55
SUB DH,CH ....................;28 ee        SUB [BX+0x55],AX .............;29 47 55
SUB BH,CH ....................;28 ef        SUB [BX+SI+0x55],CX ..........;29 48 55
SUB AL,DH ....................;28 f0        SUB [BX+DI+0x55],CX ..........;29 49 55
SUB CL,DH ....................;28 f1        SUB [BP+SI+0x55],CX ..........;29 4a 55
SUB DL,DH ....................;28 f2        SUB [BP+DI+0x55],CX ..........;29 4b 55
SUB BL,DH ....................;28 f3        SUB [SI+0x55],CX .............;29 4c 55
SUB AH,DH ....................;28 f4        SUB [DI+0x55],CX .............;29 4d 55
SUB CH,DH ....................;28 f5        SUB [BP+0x55],CX .............;29 4e 55
SUB DH,DH ....................;28 f6        SUB [BX+0x55],CX .............;29 4f 55
SUB BH,DH ....................;28 f7        SUB [BX+SI+0x55],DX ..........;29 50 55
SUB AL,BH ....................;28 f8        SUB [BX+DI+0x55],DX ..........;29 51 55
SUB CL,BH ....................;28 f9        SUB [BP+SI+0x55],DX ..........;29 52 55
SUB DL,BH ....................;28 fa        SUB [BP+DI+0x55],DX ..........;29 53 55
SUB BL,BH ....................;28 fb        SUB [SI+0x55],DX .............;29 54 55
SUB AH,BH ....................;28 fc        SUB [DI+0x55],DX .............;29 55 55
SUB CH,BH ....................;28 fd        SUB [BP+0x55],DX .............;29 56 55
SUB DH,BH ....................;28 fe        SUB [BX+0x55],DX .............;29 57 55
SUB BH,BH ....................;28 ff        SUB [BX+SI+0x55],BX ..........;29 58 55
SUB [BX+SI],AX ...............;29 00        SUB [BX+DI+0x55],BX ..........;29 59 55
SUB [BX+DI],AX ...............;29 01        SUB [BP+SI+0x55],BX ..........;29 5a 55
SUB [BP+SI],AX ...............;29 02        SUB [BP+DI+0x55],BX ..........;29 5b 55
SUB [BP+DI],AX ...............;29 03        SUB [SI+0x55],BX .............;29 5c 55
SUB [SI],AX ..................;29 04        SUB [DI+0x55],BX .............;29 5d 55
SUB [DI],AX ..................;29 05        SUB [BP+0x55],BX .............;29 5e 55
SUB [0x5566],AX ..............;29 06 66 55  SUB [BX+0x55],BX .............;29 5f 55
SUB [BX],AX ..................;29 07        SUB [BX+SI+0x55],SP ..........;29 60 55
SUB [BX+SI],CX ...............;29 08        SUB [BX+DI+0x55],SP ..........;29 61 55
SUB [BX+DI],CX ...............;29 09        SUB [BP+SI+0x55],SP ..........;29 62 55
SUB [BP+SI],CX ...............;29 0a        SUB [BP+DI+0x55],SP ..........;29 63 55
SUB [BP+DI],CX ...............;29 0b        SUB [SI+0x55],SP .............;29 64 55
SUB [SI],CX ..................;29 0c        SUB [DI+0x55],SP .............;29 65 55
SUB [DI],CX ..................;29 0d        SUB [BP+0x55],SP .............;29 66 55
SUB [0x5566],CX ..............;29 0e 66 55  SUB [BX+0x55],SP .............;29 67 55
SUB [BX],CX ..................;29 0f        SUB [BX+SI+0x55],BP ..........;29 68 55
SUB [BX+SI],DX ...............;29 10        SUB [BX+DI+0x55],BP ..........;29 69 55
SUB [BX+DI],DX ...............;29 11        SUB [BP+SI+0x55],BP ..........;29 6a 55
SUB [BP+SI],DX ...............;29 12        SUB [BP+DI+0x55],BP ..........;29 6b 55
SUB [BP+DI],DX ...............;29 13        SUB [SI+0x55],BP .............;29 6c 55
SUB [SI],DX ..................;29 14        SUB [DI+0x55],BP .............;29 6d 55
SUB [DI],DX ..................;29 15        SUB [BP+0x55],BP .............;29 6e 55
SUB [0x5566],DX ..............;29 16 66 55  SUB [BX+0x55],BP .............;29 6f 55
SUB [BX],DX ..................;29 17        SUB [BX+SI+0x55],SI ..........;29 70 55
SUB [BX+SI],BX ...............;29 18        SUB [BX+DI+0x55],SI ..........;29 71 55
SUB [BX+DI],BX ...............;29 19        SUB [BP+SI+0x55],SI ..........;29 72 55
SUB [BP+SI],BX ...............;29 1a        SUB [BP+DI+0x55],SI ..........;29 73 55
SUB [BP+DI],BX ...............;29 1b        SUB [SI+0x55],SI .............;29 74 55
SUB [SI],BX ..................;29 1c        SUB [DI+0x55],SI .............;29 75 55
SUB [DI],BX ..................;29 1d        SUB [BP+0x55],SI .............;29 76 55
SUB [0x5566],BX ..............;29 1e 66 55  SUB [BX+0x55],SI .............;29 77 55
SUB [BX],BX ..................;29 1f        SUB [BX+SI+0x55],DI ..........;29 78 55
SUB [BX+SI],SP ...............;29 20        SUB [BX+DI+0x55],DI ..........;29 79 55
SUB [BX+DI],SP ...............;29 21        SUB [BP+SI+0x55],DI ..........;29 7a 55
```

```
SUB [BP+DI+0x55],DI ............ ;29 7b 55        SUB SP,DX ..................... ;29 d4
SUB [SI+0x55],DI .............. ;29 7c 55         SUB BP,DX ..................... ;29 d5
SUB [DI+0x55],DI .............. ;29 7d 55         SUB SI,DX ..................... ;29 d6
SUB [BP+0x55],DI .............. ;29 7e 55         SUB DI,DX ..................... ;29 d7
SUB [BX+0x55],DI .............. ;29 7f 55         SUB AX,BX ..................... ;29 d8
SUB [BX+SI+0x5566],AX ......... ;29 80 66 55      SUB CX,BX ..................... ;29 d9
SUB [BX+DI+0x5566],AX ......... ;29 81 66 55      SUB DX,BX ..................... ;29 da
SUB [BP+SI+0x5566],AX ......... ;29 82 66 55      SUB BX,BX ..................... ;29 db
SUB [BP+DI+0x5566],AX ......... ;29 83 66 55      SUB SP,BX ..................... ;29 dc
SUB [SI+0x5566],AX ............ ;29 84 66 55      SUB BP,BX ..................... ;29 dd
SUB [DI+0x5566],AX ............ ;29 85 66 55      SUB SI,BX ..................... ;29 de
SUB [BP+0x5566],AX ............ ;29 86 66 55      SUB DI,BX ..................... ;29 df
SUB [BX+0x5566],AX ............ ;29 87 66 55      SUB AX,SP ..................... ;29 e0
SUB [BX+SI+0x5566],CX ......... ;29 88 66 55      SUB CX,SP ..................... ;29 e1
SUB [BX+DI+0x5566],CX ......... ;29 89 66 55      SUB DX,SP ..................... ;29 e2
SUB [BP+SI+0x5566],CX ......... ;29 8a 66 55      SUB BX,SP ..................... ;29 e3
SUB [BP+DI+0x5566],CX ......... ;29 8b 66 55      SUB SP,SP ..................... ;29 e4
SUB [SI+0x5566],CX ............ ;29 8c 66 55      SUB BP,SP ..................... ;29 e5
SUB [DI+0x5566],CX ............ ;29 8d 66 55      SUB SI,SP ..................... ;29 e6
SUB [BP+0x5566],CX ............ ;29 8e 66 55      SUB DI,SP ..................... ;29 e7
SUB [BX+0x5566],CX ............ ;29 8f 66 55      SUB AX,BP ..................... ;29 e8
SUB [BX+SI+0x5566],DX ......... ;29 90 66 55      SUB CX,BP ..................... ;29 e9
SUB [BX+DI+0x5566],DX ......... ;29 91 66 55      SUB DX,BP ..................... ;29 ea
SUB [BP+SI+0x5566],DX ......... ;29 92 66 55      SUB BX,BP ..................... ;29 eb
SUB [BP+DI+0x5566],DX ......... ;29 93 66 55      SUB SP,BP ..................... ;29 ec
SUB [SI+0x5566],DX ............ ;29 94 66 55      SUB BP,BP ..................... ;29 ed
SUB [DI+0x5566],DX ............ ;29 95 66 55      SUB SI,BP ..................... ;29 ee
SUB [BP+0x5566],DX ............ ;29 96 66 55      SUB DI,BP ..................... ;29 ef
SUB [BX+0x5566],DX ............ ;29 97 66 55      SUB AX,SI ..................... ;29 f0
SUB [BX+SI+0x5566],BX ......... ;29 98 66 55      SUB CX,SI ..................... ;29 f1
SUB [BX+DI+0x5566],BX ......... ;29 99 66 55      SUB DX,SI ..................... ;29 f2
SUB [BP+SI+0x5566],BX ......... ;29 9a 66 55      SUB BX,SI ..................... ;29 f3
SUB [BP+DI+0x5566],BX ......... ;29 9b 66 55      SUB SP,SI ..................... ;29 f4
SUB [SI+0x5566],BX ............ ;29 9c 66 55      SUB BP,SI ..................... ;29 f5
SUB [DI+0x5566],BX ............ ;29 9d 66 55      SUB SI,SI ..................... ;29 f6
SUB [BP+0x5566],BX ............ ;29 9e 66 55      SUB DI,SI ..................... ;29 f7
SUB [BX+0x5566],BX ............ ;29 9f 66 55      SUB AX,DI ..................... ;29 f8
SUB [BX+SI+0x5566],SP ......... ;29 a0 66 55      SUB CX,DI ..................... ;29 f9
SUB [BX+DI+0x5566],SP ......... ;29 a1 66 55      SUB DX,DI ..................... ;29 fa
SUB [BP+SI+0x5566],SP ......... ;29 a2 66 55      SUB BX,DI ..................... ;29 fb
SUB [BP+DI+0x5566],SP ......... ;29 a3 66 55      SUB SP,DI ..................... ;29 fc
SUB [SI+0x5566],SP ............ ;29 a4 66 55      SUB BP,DI ..................... ;29 fd
SUB [DI+0x5566],SP ............ ;29 a5 66 55      SUB SI,DI ..................... ;29 fe
SUB [BP+0x5566],SP ............ ;29 a6 66 55      SUB DI,DI ..................... ;29 ff
SUB [BX+0x5566],SP ............ ;29 a7 66 55      SUB AL,[BX+SI] ................ ;2a 00
SUB [BX+SI+0x5566],BP ......... ;29 a8 66 55      SUB AL,[BX+DI] ................ ;2a 01
SUB [BX+DI+0x5566],BP ......... ;29 a9 66 55      SUB AL,[BP+SI] ................ ;2a 02
SUB [BP+SI+0x5566],BP ......... ;29 aa 66 55      SUB AL,[BP+DI] ................ ;2a 03
SUB [BP+DI+0x5566],BP ......... ;29 ab 66 55      SUB AL,[SI] ................... ;2a 04
SUB [SI+0x5566],BP ............ ;29 ac 66 55      SUB AL,[DI] ................... ;2a 05
SUB [DI+0x5566],BP ............ ;29 ad 66 55      SUB AL,[0x5566] .............. ;2a 06 66 55
SUB [BP+0x5566],BP ............ ;29 ae 66 55      SUB AL,[BX] ................... ;2a 07
SUB [BX+0x5566],BP ............ ;29 af 66 55      SUB CL,[BX+SI] ................ ;2a 08
SUB [BX+SI+0x5566],SI ......... ;29 b0 66 55      SUB CL,[BX+DI] ................ ;2a 09
SUB [BX+DI+0x5566],SI ......... ;29 b1 66 55      SUB CL,[BP+SI] ................ ;2a 0a
SUB [BP+SI+0x5566],SI ......... ;29 b2 66 55      SUB CL,[BP+DI] ................ ;2a 0b
SUB [BP+DI+0x5566],SI ......... ;29 b3 66 55      SUB CL,[SI] ................... ;2a 0c
SUB [SI+0x5566],SI ............ ;29 b4 66 55      SUB CL,[DI] ................... ;2a 0d
SUB [DI+0x5566],SI ............ ;29 b5 66 55      SUB CL,[0x5566] .............. ;2a 0e 66 55
SUB [BP+0x5566],SI ............ ;29 b6 66 55      SUB CL,[BX] ................... ;2a 0f
SUB [BX+0x5566],SI ............ ;29 b7 66 55      SUB DL,[BX+SI] ................ ;2a 10
SUB [BX+SI+0x5566],DI ......... ;29 b8 66 55      SUB DL,[BX+DI] ................ ;2a 11
SUB [BX+DI+0x5566],DI ......... ;29 b9 66 55      SUB DL,[BP+SI] ................ ;2a 12
SUB [BP+SI+0x5566],DI ......... ;29 ba 66 55      SUB DL,[BP+DI] ................ ;2a 13
SUB [BP+DI+0x5566],DI ......... ;29 bb 66 55      SUB DL,[SI] ................... ;2a 14
SUB [SI+0x5566],DI ............ ;29 bc 66 55      SUB DL,[DI] ................... ;2a 15
SUB [DI+0x5566],DI ............ ;29 bd 66 55      SUB DL,[0x5566] .............. ;2a 16 66 55
SUB [BP+0x5566],DI ............ ;29 be 66 55      SUB DL,[BX] ................... ;2a 17
SUB [BX+0x5566],DI ............ ;29 bf 66 55      SUB BL,[BX+SI] ................ ;2a 18
SUB AX,AX ..................... ;29 c0           SUB BL,[BX+DI] ................ ;2a 19
SUB CX,AX ..................... ;29 c1           SUB BL,[BP+SI] ................ ;2a 1a
SUB DX,AX ..................... ;29 c2           SUB BL,[BP+DI] ................ ;2a 1b
SUB BX,AX ..................... ;29 c3           SUB BL,[SI] ................... ;2a 1c
SUB SP,AX ..................... ;29 c4           SUB BL,[DI] ................... ;2a 1d
SUB BP,AX ..................... ;29 c5           SUB BL,[0x5566] .............. ;2a 1e 66 55
SUB SI,AX ..................... ;29 c6           SUB BL,[BX] ................... ;2a 1f
SUB DI,AX ..................... ;29 c7           SUB AH,[BX+SI] ................ ;2a 20
SUB AX,CX ..................... ;29 c8           SUB AH,[BX+DI] ................ ;2a 21
SUB CX,CX ..................... ;29 c9           SUB AH,[BP+SI] ................ ;2a 22
SUB DX,CX ..................... ;29 ca           SUB AH,[BP+DI] ................ ;2a 23
SUB BX,CX ..................... ;29 cb           SUB AH,[SI] ................... ;2a 24
SUB SP,CX ..................... ;29 cc           SUB AH,[DI] ................... ;2a 25
SUB BP,CX ..................... ;29 cd           SUB AH,[0x5566] .............. ;2a 26 66 55
SUB SI,CX ..................... ;29 ce           SUB AH,[BX] ................... ;2a 27
SUB DI,CX ..................... ;29 cf           SUB CH,[BX+SI] ................ ;2a 28
SUB AX,DX ..................... ;29 d0           SUB CH,[BX+DI] ................ ;2a 29
SUB CX,DX ..................... ;29 d1           SUB CH,[BP+SI] ................ ;2a 2a
SUB DX,DX ..................... ;29 d2           SUB CH,[BP+DI] ................ ;2a 2b
SUB BX,DX ..................... ;29 d3           SUB CH,[SI] ................... ;2a 2c
```

```
SUB CH,[DI] ...................;2a 2d          SUB AL,[BP+0x5566] .............;2a 86 66 55
SUB CH,[0x5566] ...............;2a 2e 66 55    SUB AL,[BX+0x5566] .............;2a 87 66 55
SUB CH,[BX] ...................;2a 2f          SUB CL,[BX+SI+0x5566] .........;2a 88 66 55
SUB DH,[BX+SI] ................;2a 30          SUB CL,[BX+DI+0x5566] .........;2a 89 66 55
SUB DH,[BX+DI] ................;2a 31          SUB CL,[BP+SI+0x5566] .........;2a 8a 66 55
SUB DH,[BP+SI] ................;2a 32          SUB CL,[BP+DI+0x5566] .........;2a 8b 66 55
SUB DH,[BP+DI] ................;2a 33          SUB CL,[SI+0x5566] .............;2a 8c 66 55
SUB DH,[SI] ...................;2a 34          SUB CL,[DI+0x5566] .............;2a 8d 66 55
SUB DH,[DI] ...................;2a 35          SUB CL,[BP+0x5566] .............;2a 8e 66 55
SUB DH,[0x5566] ...............;2a 36 66 55    SUB CL,[BX+0x5566] .............;2a 8f 66 55
SUB DH,[BX] ...................;2a 37          SUB DL,[BX+SI+0x5566] .........;2a 90 66 55
SUB BH,[BX+SI] ................;2a 38          SUB DL,[BX+DI+0x5566] .........;2a 91 66 55
SUB BH,[BX+DI] ................;2a 39          SUB DL,[BP+SI+0x5566] .........;2a 92 66 55
SUB BH,[BP+SI] ................;2a 3a          SUB DL,[BP+DI+0x5566] .........;2a 93 66 55
SUB BH,[BP+DI] ................;2a 3b          SUB DL,[SI+0x5566] .............;2a 94 66 55
SUB BH,[SI] ...................;2a 3c          SUB DL,[DI+0x5566] .............;2a 95 66 55
SUB BH,[DI] ...................;2a 3d          SUB DL,[BP+0x5566] .............;2a 96 66 55
SUB BH,[0x5566] ...............;2a 3e 66 55    SUB DL,[BX+0x5566] .............;2a 97 66 55
SUB BH,[BX] ...................;2a 3f          SUB BL,[BX+SI+0x5566] .........;2a 98 66 55
SUB AL,[BX+SI+0x55] ...........;2a 40 55       SUB BL,[BX+DI+0x5566] .........;2a 99 66 55
SUB AL,[BX+DI+0x55] ...........;2a 41 55       SUB BL,[BP+SI+0x5566] .........;2a 9a 66 55
SUB AL,[BP+SI+0x55] ...........;2a 42 55       SUB BL,[BP+DI+0x5566] .........;2a 9b 66 55
SUB AL,[BP+DI+0x55] ...........;2a 43 55       SUB BL,[SI+0x5566] .............;2a 9c 66 55
SUB AL,[SI+0x55] ..............;2a 44 55       SUB BL,[DI+0x5566] .............;2a 9d 66 55
SUB AL,[DI+0x55] ..............;2a 45 55       SUB BL,[BP+0x5566] .............;2a 9e 66 55
SUB AL,[BP+0x55] ..............;2a 46 55       SUB BL,[BX+0x5566] .............;2a 9f 66 55
SUB AL,[BX+0x55] ..............;2a 47 55       SUB AH,[BX+SI+0x5566] .........;2a a0 66 55
SUB CL,[BX+SI+0x55] ...........;2a 48 55       SUB AH,[BX+DI+0x5566] .........;2a a1 66 55
SUB CL,[BX+DI+0x55] ...........;2a 49 55       SUB AH,[BP+SI+0x5566] .........;2a a2 66 55
SUB CL,[BP+SI+0x55] ...........;2a 4a 55       SUB AH,[BP+DI+0x5566] .........;2a a3 66 55
SUB CL,[BP+DI+0x55] ...........;2a 4b 55       SUB AH,[SI+0x5566] .............;2a a4 66 55
SUB CL,[SI+0x55] ..............;2a 4c 55       SUB AH,[DI+0x5566] .............;2a a5 66 55
SUB CL,[DI+0x55] ..............;2a 4d 55       SUB AH,[BP+0x5566] .............;2a a6 66 55
SUB CL,[BP+0x55] ..............;2a 4e 55       SUB AH,[BX+0x5566] .............;2a a7 66 55
SUB CL,[BX+0x55] ..............;2a 4f 55       SUB CH,[BX+SI+0x5566] .........;2a a8 66 55
SUB DL,[BX+SI+0x55] ...........;2a 50 55       SUB CH,[BX+DI+0x5566] .........;2a a9 66 55
SUB DL,[BX+DI+0x55] ...........;2a 51 55       SUB CH,[BP+SI+0x5566] .........;2a aa 66 55
SUB DL,[BP+SI+0x55] ...........;2a 52 55       SUB CH,[BP+DI+0x5566] .........;2a ab 66 55
SUB DL,[BP+DI+0x55] ...........;2a 53 55       SUB CH,[SI+0x5566] .............;2a ac 66 55
SUB DL,[SI+0x55] ..............;2a 54 55       SUB CH,[DI+0x5566] .............;2a ad 66 55
SUB DL,[DI+0x55] ..............;2a 55 55       SUB CH,[BP+0x5566] .............;2a ae 66 55
SUB DL,[BP+0x55] ..............;2a 56 55       SUB CH,[BX+0x5566] .............;2a af 66 55
SUB DL,[BX+0x55] ..............;2a 57 55       SUB DH,[BX+SI+0x5566] .........;2a b0 66 55
SUB BL,[BX+SI+0x55] ...........;2a 58 55       SUB DH,[BX+DI+0x5566] .........;2a b1 66 55
SUB BL,[BX+DI+0x55] ...........;2a 59 55       SUB DH,[BP+SI+0x5566] .........;2a b2 66 55
SUB BL,[BP+SI+0x55] ...........;2a 5a 55       SUB DH,[BP+DI+0x5566] .........;2a b3 66 55
SUB BL,[BP+DI+0x55] ...........;2a 5b 55       SUB DH,[SI+0x5566] .............;2a b4 66 55
SUB BL,[SI+0x55] ..............;2a 5c 55       SUB DH,[DI+0x5566] .............;2a b5 66 55
SUB BL,[DI+0x55] ..............;2a 5d 55       SUB DH,[BP+0x5566] .............;2a b6 66 55
SUB BL,[BP+0x55] ..............;2a 5e 55       SUB DH,[BX+0x5566] .............;2a b7 66 55
SUB BL,[BX+0x55] ..............;2a 5f 55       SUB BH,[BX+SI+0x5566] .........;2a b8 66 55
SUB AH,[BX+SI+0x55] ...........;2a 60 55       SUB BH,[BX+DI+0x5566] .........;2a b9 66 55
SUB AH,[BX+DI+0x55] ...........;2a 61 55       SUB BH,[BP+SI+0x5566] .........;2a ba 66 55
SUB AH,[BP+SI+0x55] ...........;2a 62 55       SUB BH,[BP+DI+0x5566] .........;2a bb 66 55
SUB AH,[BP+DI+0x55] ...........;2a 63 55       SUB BH,[SI+0x5566] .............;2a bc 66 55
SUB AH,[SI+0x55] ..............;2a 64 55       SUB BH,[DI+0x5566] .............;2a bd 66 55
SUB AH,[DI+0x55] ..............;2a 65 55       SUB BH,[BP+0x5566] .............;2a be 66 55
SUB AH,[BP+0x55] ..............;2a 66 55       SUB BH,[BX+0x5566] .............;2a bf 66 55
SUB AH,[BX+0x55] ..............;2a 67 55       SUB AX,[BX+SI] ................;2b 00
SUB CH,[BX+SI+0x55] ...........;2a 68 55       SUB AX,[BX+DI] ................;2b 01
SUB CH,[BX+DI+0x55] ...........;2a 69 55       SUB AX,[BP+SI] ................;2b 02
SUB CH,[BP+SI+0x55] ...........;2a 6a 55       SUB AX,[BP+DI] ................;2b 03
SUB CH,[BP+DI+0x55] ...........;2a 6b 55       SUB AX,[SI] ...................;2b 04
SUB CH,[SI+0x55] ..............;2a 6c 55       SUB AX,[DI] ...................;2b 05
SUB CH,[DI+0x55] ..............;2a 6d 55       SUB AX,[0x5566] ...............;2b 06 66 55
SUB CH,[BP+0x55] ..............;2a 6e 55       SUB AX,[BX] ...................;2b 07
SUB CH,[BX+0x55] ..............;2a 6f 55       SUB CX,[BX+SI] ................;2b 08
SUB DH,[BX+SI+0x55] ...........;2a 70 55       SUB CX,[BX+DI] ................;2b 09
SUB DH,[BX+DI+0x55] ...........;2a 71 55       SUB CX,[BP+SI] ................;2b 0a
SUB DH,[BP+SI+0x55] ...........;2a 72 55       SUB CX,[BP+DI] ................;2b 0b
SUB DH,[BP+DI+0x55] ...........;2a 73 55       SUB CX,[SI] ...................;2b 0c
SUB DH,[SI+0x55] ..............;2a 74 55       SUB CX,[DI] ...................;2b 0d
SUB DH,[DI+0x55] ..............;2a 75 55       SUB CX,[0x5566] ...............;2b 0e 66 55
SUB DH,[BP+0x55] ..............;2a 76 55       SUB CX,[BX] ...................;2b 0f
SUB DH,[BX+0x55] ..............;2a 77 55       SUB DX,[BX+SI] ................;2b 10
SUB BH,[BX+SI+0x55] ...........;2a 78 55       SUB DX,[BX+DI] ................;2b 11
SUB BH,[BX+DI+0x55] ...........;2a 79 55       SUB DX,[BP+SI] ................;2b 12
SUB BH,[BP+SI+0x55] ...........;2a 7a 55       SUB DX,[BP+DI] ................;2b 13
SUB BH,[BP+DI+0x55] ...........;2a 7b 55       SUB DX,[SI] ...................;2b 14
SUB BH,[SI+0x55] ..............;2a 7c 55       SUB DX,[DI] ...................;2b 15
SUB BH,[DI+0x55] ..............;2a 7d 55       SUB DX,[0x5566] ...............;2b 16 66 55
SUB BH,[BP+0x55] ..............;2a 7e 55       SUB DX,[BX] ...................;2b 17
SUB BH,[BX+0x55] ..............;2a 7f 55       SUB BX,[BX+SI] ................;2b 18
SUB AL,[BX+SI+0x5566] .........;2a 80 66 55    SUB BX,[BX+DI] ................;2b 19
SUB AL,[BX+DI+0x5566] .........;2a 81 66 55    SUB BX,[BP+SI] ................;2b 1a
SUB AL,[BP+SI+0x5566] .........;2a 82 66 55    SUB BX,[BP+DI] ................;2b 1b
SUB AL,[BP+DI+0x5566] .........;2a 83 66 55    SUB BX,[SI] ...................;2b 1c
SUB AL,[SI+0x5566] ............;2a 84 66 55    SUB BX,[DI] ...................;2b 1d
SUB AL,[DI+0x5566] ............;2a 85 66 55    SUB BX,[0x5566] ...............;2b 1e 66 55
```

```
SUB BX,[BX] ....................;2b 1f        SUB DI,[BX+SI+0x55] ...........;2b 78 55
SUB SP,[BX+SI] ................;2b 20         SUB DI,[BX+DI+0x55] ...........;2b 79 55
SUB SP,[BX+DI] ................;2b 21         SUB DI,[BP+SI+0x55] ...........;2b 7a 55
SUB SP,[BP+SI] ................;2b 22         SUB DI,[BP+DI+0x55] ...........;2b 7b 55
SUB SP,[BP+DI] ................;2b 23         SUB DI,[SI+0x55] ..............;2b 7c 55
SUB SP,[SI] ...................;2b 24         SUB DI,[DI+0x55] ..............;2b 7d 55
SUB SP,[DI] ...................;2b 25         SUB DI,[BP+0x55] ..............;2b 7e 55
SUB SP,[0x5566] ...............;2b 26 66 55   SUB DI,[BX+0x55] ..............;2b 7f 55
SUB SP,[BX] ...................;2b 27         SUB AX,[BX+SI+0x5566] .........;2b 80 66 55
SUB BP,[BX+SI] ................;2b 28         SUB AX,[BX+DI+0x5566] .........;2b 81 66 55
SUB BP,[BX+DI] ................;2b 29         SUB AX,[BP+SI+0x5566] .........;2b 82 66 55
SUB BP,[BP+SI] ................;2b 2a         SUB AX,[BP+DI+0x5566] .........;2b 83 66 55
SUB BP,[BP+DI] ................;2b 2b         SUB AX,[SI+0x5566] ............;2b 84 66 55
SUB BP,[SI] ...................;2b 2c         SUB AX,[DI+0x5566] ............;2b 85 66 55
SUB BP,[DI] ...................;2b 2d         SUB AX,[BP+0x5566] ............;2b 86 66 55
SUB BP,[0x5566] ...............;2b 2e 66 55   SUB AX,[BX+0x5566] ............;2b 87 66 55
SUB BP,[BX] ...................;2b 2f         SUB CX,[BX+SI+0x5566] .........;2b 88 66 55
SUB SI,[BX+SI] ................;2b 30         SUB CX,[BX+DI+0x5566] .........;2b 89 66 55
SUB SI,[BX+DI] ................;2b 31         SUB CX,[BP+SI+0x5566] .........;2b 8a 66 55
SUB SI,[BP+SI] ................;2b 32         SUB CX,[BP+DI+0x5566] .........;2b 8b 66 55
SUB SI,[BP+DI] ................;2b 33         SUB CX,[SI+0x5566] ............;2b 8c 66 55
SUB SI,[SI] ...................;2b 34         SUB CX,[DI+0x5566] ............;2b 8d 66 55
SUB SI,[DI] ...................;2b 35         SUB CX,[BP+0x5566] ............;2b 8e 66 55
SUB SI,[0x5566] ...............;2b 36 66 55   SUB CX,[BX+0x5566] ............;2b 8f 66 55
SUB SI,[BX] ...................;2b 37         SUB DX,[BX+SI+0x5566] .........;2b 90 66 55
SUB DI,[BX+SI] ................;2b 38         SUB DX,[BX+DI+0x5566] .........;2b 91 66 55
SUB DI,[BX+DI] ................;2b 39         SUB DX,[BP+SI+0x5566] .........;2b 92 66 55
SUB DI,[BP+SI] ................;2b 3a         SUB DX,[BP+DI+0x5566] .........;2b 93 66 55
SUB DI,[BP+DI] ................;2b 3b         SUB DX,[SI+0x5566] ............;2b 94 66 55
SUB DI,[SI] ...................;2b 3c         SUB DX,[DI+0x5566] ............;2b 95 66 55
SUB DI,[DI] ...................;2b 3d         SUB DX,[BP+0x5566] ............;2b 96 66 55
SUB DI,[0x5566] ...............;2b 3e 66 55   SUB DX,[BX+0x5566] ............;2b 97 66 55
SUB DI,[BX] ...................;2b 3f         SUB BX,[BX+SI+0x5566] .........;2b 98 66 55
SUB AX,[BX+SI+0x55] ...........;2b 40 55      SUB BX,[BX+DI+0x5566] .........;2b 99 66 55
SUB AX,[BX+DI+0x55] ...........;2b 41 55      SUB BX,[BP+SI+0x5566] .........;2b 9a 66 55
SUB AX,[BP+SI+0x55] ...........;2b 42 55      SUB BX,[BP+DI+0x5566] .........;2b 9b 66 55
SUB AX,[BP+DI+0x55] ...........;2b 43 55      SUB BX,[SI+0x5566] ............;2b 9c 66 55
SUB AX,[SI+0x55] ..............;2b 44 55      SUB BX,[DI+0x5566] ............;2b 9d 66 55
SUB AX,[DI+0x55] ..............;2b 45 55      SUB BX,[BP+0x5566] ............;2b 9e 66 55
SUB AX,[BP+0x55] ..............;2b 46 55      SUB BX,[BX+0x5566] ............;2b 9f 66 55
SUB AX,[BX+0x55] ..............;2b 47 55      SUB SP,[BX+SI+0x5566] .........;2b a0 66 55
SUB CX,[BX+SI+0x55] ...........;2b 48 55      SUB SP,[BX+DI+0x5566] .........;2b a1 66 55
SUB CX,[BX+DI+0x55] ...........;2b 49 55      SUB SP,[BP+SI+0x5566] .........;2b a2 66 55
SUB CX,[BP+SI+0x55] ...........;2b 4a 55      SUB SP,[BP+DI+0x5566] .........;2b a3 66 55
SUB CX,[BP+DI+0x55] ...........;2b 4b 55      SUB SP,[SI+0x5566] ............;2b a4 66 55
SUB CX,[SI+0x55] ..............;2b 4c 55      SUB SP,[DI+0x5566] ............;2b a5 66 55
SUB CX,[DI+0x55] ..............;2b 4d 55      SUB SP,[BP+0x5566] ............;2b a6 66 55
SUB CX,[BP+0x55] ..............;2b 4e 55      SUB SP,[BX+0x5566] ............;2b a7 66 55
SUB CX,[BX+0x55] ..............;2b 4f 55      SUB BP,[BX+SI+0x5566] .........;2b a8 66 55
SUB DX,[BX+SI+0x55] ...........;2b 50 55      SUB BP,[BX+DI+0x5566] .........;2b a9 66 55
SUB DX,[BX+DI+0x55] ...........;2b 51 55      SUB BP,[BP+SI+0x5566] .........;2b aa 66 55
SUB DX,[BP+SI+0x55] ...........;2b 52 55      SUB BP,[BP+DI+0x5566] .........;2b ab 66 55
SUB DX,[BP+DI+0x55] ...........;2b 53 55      SUB BP,[SI+0x5566] ............;2b ac 66 55
SUB DX,[SI+0x55] ..............;2b 54 55      SUB BP,[DI+0x5566] ............;2b ad 66 55
SUB DX,[DI+0x55] ..............;2b 55 55      SUB BP,[BP+0x5566] ............;2b ae 66 55
SUB DX,[BP+0x55] ..............;2b 56 55      SUB BP,[BX+0x5566] ............;2b af 66 55
SUB DX,[BX+0x55] ..............;2b 57 55      SUB SI,[BX+SI+0x5566] .........;2b b0 66 55
SUB BX,[BX+SI+0x55] ...........;2b 58 55      SUB SI,[BX+DI+0x5566] .........;2b b1 66 55
SUB BX,[BX+DI+0x55] ...........;2b 59 55      SUB SI,[BP+SI+0x5566] .........;2b b2 66 55
SUB BX,[BP+SI+0x55] ...........;2b 5a 55      SUB SI,[BP+DI+0x5566] .........;2b b3 66 55
SUB BX,[BP+DI+0x55] ...........;2b 5b 55      SUB SI,[SI+0x5566] ............;2b b4 66 55
SUB BX,[SI+0x55] ..............;2b 5c 55      SUB SI,[DI+0x5566] ............;2b b5 66 55
SUB BX,[DI+0x55] ..............;2b 5d 55      SUB SI,[BP+0x5566] ............;2b b6 66 55
SUB BX,[BP+0x55] ..............;2b 5e 55      SUB SI,[BX+0x5566] ............;2b b7 66 55
SUB BX,[BX+0x55] ..............;2b 5f 55      SUB DI,[BX+SI+0x5566] .........;2b b8 66 55
SUB SP,[BX+SI+0x55] ...........;2b 60 55      SUB DI,[BX+DI+0x5566] .........;2b b9 66 55
SUB SP,[BX+DI+0x55] ...........;2b 61 55      SUB DI,[BP+SI+0x5566] .........;2b ba 66 55
SUB SP,[BP+SI+0x55] ...........;2b 62 55      SUB DI,[BP+DI+0x5566] .........;2b bb 66 55
SUB SP,[BP+DI+0x55] ...........;2b 63 55      SUB DI,[SI+0x5566] ............;2b bc 66 55
SUB SP,[SI+0x55] ..............;2b 64 55      SUB DI,[DI+0x5566] ............;2b bd 66 55
SUB SP,[DI+0x55] ,.............;2b 65 55      SUB DI,[BP+0x5566] ............;2b be 66 55
SUB SP,[BP+0x55] ..............;2b 66 55      SUB DI,[BX+0x5566] ............;2b bf 66 55
SUB SP,[BX+0x55] ..............;2b 67 55      SUB AL,0x55 ...................;2c 55
SUB BP,[BX+SI+0x55] ...........;2b 68 55      SUB AX,0x5566 .................;2d 66 55
SUB BP,[BX+DI+0x55] ...........;2b 69 55      CS ............................;2e
SUB BP,[BP+SI+0x55] ...........;2b 6a 55      DAS ...........................;2f
SUB BP,[BP+DI+0x55] ...........;2b 6b 55      XOR [BX+SI],AL ................;30 00
SUB BP,[SI+0x55] ..............;2b 6c 55      XOR [BX+DI],AL ................;30 01
SUB BP,[DI+0x55] ..............;2b 6d 55      XOR [BP+SI],AL ................;30 02
SUB BP,[BP+0x55] ..............;2b 6e 55      XOR [BP+DI],AL ................;30 03
SUB BP,[BX+0x55] ..............;2b 6f 55      XOR [SI],AL ...................;30 04
SUB SI,[BX+SI+0x55] ...........;2b 70 55      XOR [DI],AL ...................;30 05
SUB SI,[BX+DI+0x55] ...........;2b 71 55      XOR [0x5566],AL ...............;30 06 66 55
SUB SI,[BP+SI+0x55] ...........;2b 72 55      XOR [BX],AL ...................;30 07
SUB SI,[BP+DI+0x55] ...........;2b 73 55      XOR [BX+SI],CL ................;30 08
SUB SI,[SI+0x55] ..............;2b 74 55      XOR [BX+DI],CL ................;30 09
SUB SI,[DI+0x55] ..............;2b 75 55      XOR [BP+SI],CL ................;30 0a
SUB SI,[BP+0x55] ..............;2b 76 55      XOR [BP+DI],CL ................;30 0b
SUB SI,[BX+0x55] ..............;2b 77 55      XOR [SI],CL ...................;30 0c
```

214

```
XOR [DI],CL .................;30 0d
XOR [0x5566],CL .............;30 0e 66 55
XOR [BX],CL .................;30 0f
XOR [BX+SI],DL ..............;30 10
XOR [BX+DI],DL ..............;30 11
XOR [BP+SI],DL ..............;30 12
XOR [BP+DI],DL ..............;30 13
XOR [SI],DL .................;30 14
XOR [DI],DL .................;30 15
XOR [0x5566],DL .............;30 16 66 55
XOR [BX],DL .................;30 17
XOR [BX+SI],BL ..............;30 18
XOR [BX+DI],BL ..............;30 19
XOR [BP+SI],BL ..............;30 1a
XOR [BP+DI],BL ..............;30 1b
XOR [SI],BL .................;30 1c
XOR [DI],BL .................;30 1d
XOR [0x5566],BL .............;30 1e 66 55
XOR [BX],BL .................;30 1f
XOR [BX+SI],AH ..............;30 20
XOR [BX+DI],AH ..............;30 21
XOR [BP+SI],AH ..............;30 22
XOR [BP+DI],AH ..............;30 23
XOR [SI],AH .................;30 24
XOR [DI],AH .................;30 25
XOR [0x5566],AH .............;30 26 66 55
XOR [BX],AH .................;30 27
XOR [BX+SI],CH ..............;30 28
XOR [BX+DI],CH ..............;30 29
XOR [BP+SI],CH ..............;30 2a
XOR [BP+DI],CH ..............;30 2b
XOR [SI],CH .................;30 2c
XOR [DI],CH .................;30 2d
XOR [0x5566],CH .............;30 2e 66 55
XOR [BX],CH .................;30 2f
XOR [BX+SI],DH ..............;30 30
XOR [BX+DI],DH ..............;30 31
XOR [BP+SI],DH ..............;30 32
XOR [BP+DI],DH ..............;30 33
XOR [SI],DH .................;30 34
XOR [DI],DH .................;30 35
XOR [0x5566],DH .............;30 36 66 55
XOR [BX],DH .................;30 37
XOR [BX+SI],BH ..............;30 38
XOR [BX+DI],BH ..............;30 39
XOR [BP+SI],BH ..............;30 3a
XOR [BP+DI],BH ..............;30 3b
XOR [SI],BH .................;30 3c
XOR [DI],BH .................;30 3d
XOR [0x5566],BH .............;30 3e 66 55
XOR [BX],BH .................;30 3f
XOR [BX+SI+0x55],AL .........;30 40 55
XOR [BX+DI+0x55],AL .........;30 41 55
XOR [BP+SI+0x55],AL .........;30 42 55
XOR [BP+DI+0x55],AL .........;30 43 55
XOR [SI+0x55],AL ............;30 44 55
XOR [DI+0x55],AL ............;30 45 55
XOR [BP+0x55],AL ............;30 46 55
XOR [BX+0x55],AL ............;30 47 55
XOR [BX+SI+0x55],CL .........;30 48 55
XOR [BX+DI+0x55],CL .........;30 49 55
XOR [BP+SI+0x55],CL .........;30 4a 55
XOR [BP+DI+0x55],CL .........;30 4b 55
XOR [SI+0x55],CL ............;30 4c 55
XOR [DI+0x55],CL ............;30 4d 55
XOR [BP+0x55],CL ............;30 4e 55
XOR [BX+0x55],CL ............;30 4f 55
XOR [BX+SI+0x55],DL .........;30 50 55
XOR [BX+DI+0x55],DL .........;30 51 55
XOR [BP+SI+0x55],DL .........;30 52 55
XOR [BP+DI+0x55],DL .........;30 53 55
XOR [SI+0x55],DL ............;30 54 55
XOR [DI+0x55],DL ............;30 55 55
XOR [BP+0x55],DL ............;30 56 55
XOR [BX+0x55],DL ............;30 57 55
XOR [BX+SI+0x55],BL .........;30 58 55
XOR [BX+DI+0x55],BL .........;30 59 55
XOR [BP+SI+0x55],BL .........;30 5a 55
XOR [BP+DI+0x55],BL .........;30 5b 55
XOR [SI+0x55],BL ............;30 5c 55
XOR [DI+0x55],BL ............;30 5d 55
XOR [BP+0x55],BL ............;30 5e 55
XOR [BX+0x55],BL ............;30 5f 55
XOR [BX+SI+0x55],AH .........;30 60 55
XOR [BX+DI+0x55],AH .........;30 61 55
XOR [BP+SI+0x55],AH .........;30 62 55
XOR [BP+DI+0x55],AH .........;30 63 55
XOR [SI+0x55],AH ............;30 64 55
XOR [DI+0x55],AH ............;30 65 55
XOR [BP+0x55],AH ............;30 66 55
XOR [BX+0x55],AH ............;30 67 55
XOR [BX+SI+0x55],CH .........;30 68 55
XOR [BX+DI+0x55],CH .........;30 69 55
XOR [BP+SI+0x55],CH .........;30 6a 55
XOR [BP+DI+0x55],CH .........;30 6b 55
XOR [SI+0x55],CH ............;30 6c 55
XOR [DI+0x55],CH ............;30 6d 55
XOR [BP+0x55],CH ............;30 6e 55
XOR [BX+0x55],CH ............;30 6f 55
XOR [BX+SI+0x55],DH .........;30 70 55
XOR [BX+DI+0x55],DH .........;30 71 55
XOR [BP+SI+0x55],DH .........;30 72 55
XOR [BP+DI+0x55],DH .........;30 73 55
XOR [SI+0x55],DH ............;30 74 55
XOR [DI+0x55],DH ............;30 75 55
XOR [BP+0x55],DH ............;30 76 55
XOR [BX+0x55],DH ............;30 77 55
XOR [BX+SI+0x55],BH .........;30 78 55
XOR [BX+DI+0x55],BH .........;30 79 55
XOR [BP+SI+0x55],BH .........;30 7a 55
XOR [BP+DI+0x55],BH .........;30 7b 55
XOR [SI+0x55],BH ............;30 7c 55
XOR [DI+0x55],BH ............;30 7d 55
XOR [BP+0x55],BH ............;30 7e 55
XOR [BX+0x55],BH ............;30 7f 55
XOR [BX+SI+0x5566],AL .......;30 80 66 55
XOR [BX+DI+0x5566],AL .......;30 81 66 55
XOR [BP+SI+0x5566],AL .......;30 82 66 55
XOR [BP+DI+0x5566],AL .......;30 83 66 55
XOR [SI+0x5566],AL ..........;30 84 66 55
XOR [DI+0x5566],AL ..........;30 85 66 55
XOR [BP+0x5566],AL ..........;30 86 66 55
XOR [BX+0x5566],AL ..........;30 87 66 55
XOR [BX+SI+0x5566],CL .......;30 88 66 55
XOR [BX+DI+0x5566],CL .......;30 89 66 55
XOR [BP+SI+0x5566],CL .......;30 8a 66 55
XOR [BP+DI+0x5566],CL .......;30 8b 66 55
XOR [SI+0x5566],CL ..........;30 8c 66 55
XOR [DI+0x5566],CL ..........;30 8d 66 55
XOR [BP+0x5566],CL ..........;30 8e 66 55
XOR [BX+0x5566],CL ..........;30 8f 66 55
XOR [BX+SI+0x5566],DL .......;30 90 66 55
XOR [BX+DI+0x5566],DL .......;30 91 66 55
XOR [BP+SI+0x5566],DL .......;30 92 66 55
XOR [BP+DI+0x5566],DL .......;30 93 66 55
XOR [SI+0x5566],DL ..........;30 94 66 55
XOR [DI+0x5566],DL ..........;30 95 66 55
XOR [BP+0x5566],DL ..........;30 96 66 55
XOR [BX+0x5566],DL ..........;30 97 66 55
XOR [BX+SI+0x5566],BL .......;30 98 66 55
XOR [BX+DI+0x5566],BL .......;30 99 66 55
XOR [BP+SI+0x5566],BL .......;30 9a 66 55
XOR [BP+DI+0x5566],BL .......;30 9b 66 55
XOR [SI+0x5566],BL ..........;30 9c 66 55
XOR [DI+0x5566],BL ..........;30 9d 66 55
XOR [BP+0x5566],BL ..........;30 9e 66 55
XOR [BX+0x5566],BL ..........;30 9f 66 55
XOR [BX+SI+0x5566],AH .......;30 a0 66 55
XOR [BX+DI+0x5566],AH .......;30 a1 66 55
XOR [BP+SI+0x5566],AH .......;30 a2 66 55
XOR [BP+DI+0x5566],AH .......;30 a3 66 55
XOR [SI+0x5566],AH ..........;30 a4 66 55
XOR [DI+0x5566],AH ..........;30 a5 66 55
XOR [BP+0x5566],AH ..........;30 a6 66 55
XOR [BX+0x5566],AH ..........;30 a7 66 55
XOR [BX+SI+0x5566],CH .......;30 a8 66 55
XOR [BX+DI+0x5566],CH .......;30 a9 66 55
XOR [BP+SI+0x5566],CH .......;30 aa 66 55
XOR [BP+DI+0x5566],CH .......;30 ab 66 55
XOR [SI+0x5566],CH ..........;30 ac 66 55
XOR [DI+0x5566],CH ..........;30 ad 66 55
XOR [BP+0x5566],CH ..........;30 ae 66 55
XOR [BX+0x5566],CH ..........;30 af 66 55
XOR [BX+SI+0x5566],DH .......;30 b0 66 55
XOR [BX+DI+0x5566],DH .......;30 b1 66 55
XOR [BP+SI+0x5566],DH .......;30 b2 66 55
XOR [BP+DI+0x5566],DH .......;30 b3 66 55
XOR [SI+0x5566],DH ..........;30 b4 66 55
XOR [DI+0x5566],DH ..........;30 b5 66 55
XOR [BP+0x5566],DH ..........;30 b6 66 55
XOR [BX+0x5566],DH ..........;30 b7 66 55
XOR [BX+SI+0x5566],BH .......;30 b8 66 55
XOR [BX+DI+0x5566],BH .......;30 b9 66 55
XOR [BP+SI+0x5566],BH .......;30 ba 66 55
XOR [BP+DI+0x5566],BH .......;30 bb 66 55
XOR [SI+0x5566],BH ..........;30 bc 66 55
XOR [DI+0x5566],BH ..........;30 bd 66 55
XOR [BP+0x5566],BH ..........;30 be 66 55
```

```
XOR [BX+0x5566],BH ............;30 bf 66 55        XOR [BX+SI],BX ................;31 18
XOR AL,AL .....................;30 c0             XOR [BX+DI],BX ................;31 19
XOR CL,AL .....................;30 c1             XOR [BP+SI],BX ................;31 1a
XOR DL,AL .....................;30 c2             XOR [BP+DI],BX ................;31 1b
XOR BL,AL .....................;30 c3             XOR [SI],BX ...................;31 1c
XOR AH,AL .....................;30 c4             XOR [DI],BX ...................;31 1d
XOR CH,AL .....................;30 c5             XOR [0x5566],BX ...............;31 1e 66 55
XOR DH,AL .....................;30 c6             XOR [BX],BX ...................;31 1f
XOR BH,AL .....................;30 c7             XOR [BX+SI],SP ................;31 20
XOR AL,CL .....................;30 c8             XOR [BX+DI],SP ................;31 21
XOR CL,CL .....................;30 c9             XOR [BP+SI],SP ................;31 22
XOR DL,CL .....................;30 ca             XOR [BP+DI],SP ................;31 23
XOR BL,CL .....................;30 cb             XOR [SI],SP ...................;31 24
XOR AH,CL .....................;30 cc             XOR [DI],SP ...................;31 25
XOR CH,CL .....................;30 cd             XOR [0x5566],SP ...............;31 26 66 55
XOR DH,CL .....................;30 ce             XOR [BX],SP ...................;31 27
XOR BH,CL .....................;30 cf             XOR [BX+SI],BP ................;31 28
XOR AL,DL .....................;30 d0             XOR [BX+DI],BP ................;31 29
XOR CL,DL .....................;30 d1             XOR [BP+SI],BP ................;31 2a
XOR DL,DL .....................;30 d2             XOR [BP+DI],BP ................;31 2b
XOR BL,DL .....................;30 d3             XOR [SI],BP ...................;31 2c
XOR AH,DL .....................;30 d4             XOR [DI],BP ...................;31 2d
XOR CH,DL .....................;30 d5             XOR [0x5566],BP ...............;31 2e 66 55
XOR DH,DL .....................;30 d6             XOR [BX],BP ...................;31 2f
XOR BH,DL .....................;30 d7             XOR [BX+SI],SI ................;31 30
XOR AL,BL .....................;30 d8             XOR [BX+DI],SI ................;31 31
XOR CL,BL .....................;30 d9             XOR [BP+SI],SI ................;31 32
XOR DL,BL .....................;30 da             XOR [BP+DI],SI ................;31 33
XOR BL,BL .....................;30 db             XOR [SI],SI ...................;31 34
XOR AH,BL .....................;30 dc             XOR [DI],SI ...................;31 35
XOR CH,BL .....................;30 dd             XOR [0x5566],SI ...............;31 36 66 55
XOR DH,BL .....................;30 de             XOR [BX],SI ...................;31 37
XOR BH,BL .....................;30 df             XOR [BX+SI],DI ................;31 38
XOR AL,AH .....................;30 e0             XOR [BX+DI],DI ................;31 39
XOR CL,AH .....................;30 e1             XOR [BP+SI],DI ................;31 3a
XOR DL,AH .....................;30 e2             XOR [BP+DI],DI ................;31 3b
XOR BL,AH .....................;30 e3             XOR [SI],DI ...................;31 3c
XOR AH,AH .....................;30 e4             XOR [DI],DI ...................;31 3d
XOR CH,AH .....................;30 e5             XOR [0x5566],DI ...............;31 3e 66 55
XOR DH,AH .....................;30 e6             XOR [BX],DI ...................;31 3f
XOR BH,AH .....................;30 e7             XOR [BX+SI+0x55],AX ...........;31 40 55
XOR AL,CH .....................;30 e8             XOR [BX+DI+0x55],AX ...........;31 41 55
XOR CL,CH .....................;30 e9             XOR [BP+SI+0x55],AX ...........;31 42 55
XOR DL,CH .....................;30 ea             XOR [BP+DI+0x55],AX ...........;31 43 55
XOR BL,CH .....................;30 eb             XOR [SI+0x55],AX ..............;31 44 55
XOR AH,CH .....................;30 ec             XOR [DI+0x55],AX ..............;31 45 55
XOR CH,CH .....................;30 ed             XOR [BP+0x55],AX ..............;31 46 55
XOR DH,CH .....................;30 ee             XOR [BX+0x55],AX ..............;31 47 55
XOR BH,CH .....................;30 ef             XOR [BX+SI+0x55],CX ...........;31 48 55
XOR AL,DH .....................;30 f0             XOR [BX+DI+0x55],CX ...........;31 49 55
XOR CL,DH .....................;30 f1             XOR [BP+SI+0x55],CX ...........;31 4a 55
XOR DL,DH .....................;30 f2             XOR [BP+DI+0x55],CX ...........;31 4b 55
XOR BL,DH .....................;30 f3             XOR [SI+0x55],CX ..............;31 4c 55
XOR AH,DH .....................;30 f4             XOR [DI+0x55],CX ..............;31 4d 55
XOR CH,DH .....................;30 f5             XOR [BP+0x55],CX ..............;31 4e 55
XOR DH,DH .....................;30 f6             XOR [BX+0x55],CX ..............;31 4f 55
XOR BH,DH .....................;30 f7             XOR [BX+SI+0x55],DX ...........;31 50 55
XOR AL,BH .....................;30 f8             XOR [BX+DI+0x55],DX ...........;31 51 55
XOR CL,BH .....................;30 f9             XOR [BP+SI+0x55],DX ...........;31 52 55
XOR DL,BH .....................;30 fa             XOR [BP+DI+0x55],DX ...........;31 53 55
XOR BL,BH .....................;30 fb             XOR [SI+0x55],DX ..............;31 54 55
XOR AH,BH .....................;30 fc             XOR [DI+0x55],DX ..............;31 55 55
XOR CH,BH .....................;30 fd             XOR [BP+0x55],DX ..............;31 56 55
XOR DH,BH .....................;30 fe             XOR [BX+0x55],DX ..............;31 57 55
XOR BH,BH .....................;30 ff             XOR [BX+SI+0x55],BX ...........;31 58 55
XOR [BX+SI],AX ................;31 00             XOR [BX+DI+0x55],BX ...........;31 59 55
XOR [BX+DI],AX ................;31 01             XOR [BP+SI+0x55],BX ...........;31 5a 55
XOR [BP+SI],AX ................;31 02             XOR [BP+DI+0x55],BX ...........;31 5b 55
XOR [BP+DI],AX ................;31 03             XOR [SI+0x55],BX ..............;31 5c 55
XOR [SI],AX ...................;31 04             XOR [DI+0x55],BX ..............;31 5d 55
XOR [DI],AX ...................;31 05             XOR [BP+0x55],BX ..............;31 5e 55
XOR [0x5566],AX ...............;31 06 66 55       XOR [BX+0x55],BX ..............;31 5f 55
XOR [BX],AX ...................;31 07             XOR [BX+SI+0x55],SP ...........;31 60 55
XOR [BX+SI],CX ................;31 08             XOR [BX+DI+0x55],SP ...........;31 61 55
XOR [BX+DI],CX ................;31 09             XOR [BP+SI+0x55],SP ...........;31 62 55
XOR [BP+SI],CX ................;31 0a             XOR [BP+DI+0x55],SP ...........;31 63 55
XOR [BP+DI],CX ................;31 0b             XOR [SI+0x55],SP ..............;31 64 55
XOR [SI],CX ...................;31 0c             XOR [DI+0x55],SP ..............;31 65 55
XOR [DI],CX ...................;31 0d             XOR [BP+0x55],SP ..............;31 66 55
XOR [0x5566],CX ...............;31 0e 66 55       XOR [BX+0x55],SP ..............;31 67 55
XOR [BX],CX ...................;31 0f             XOR [BX+SI+0x55],BP ...........;31 68 55
XOR [BX+SI],DX ................;31 10             XOR [BX+DI+0x55],BP ...........;31 69 55
XOR [BX+DI],DX ................;31 11             XOR [BP+SI+0x55],BP ...........;31 6a 55
XOR [BP+SI],DX ................;31 12             XOR [BP+DI+0x55],BP ...........;31 6b 55
XOR [BP+DI],DX ................;31 13             XOR [SI+0x55],BP ..............;31 6c 55
XOR [SI],DX ...................;31 14             XOR [DI+0x55],BP ..............;31 6d 55
XOR [DI],DX ...................;31 15             XOR [BP+0x55],BP ..............;31 6e 55
XOR [0x5566],DX ...............;31 16 66 55       XOR [BX+0x55],BP ..............;31 6f 55
XOR [BX],DX ...................;31 17             XOR [BX+SI+0x55],SI ...........;31 70 55
```

```
XOR [BX+DI+0x55],SI ...........;31 71 55      XOR DX,CX .....................;31 ca
XOR [BP+SI+0x55],SI ...........;31 72 55      XOR BX,CX .....................;31 cb
XOR [BP+DI+0x55],SI ...........;31 73 55      XOR SP,CX .....................;31 cc
XOR [SI+0x55],SI ..............;31 74 55      XOR BP,CX .....................;31 cd
XOR [DI+0x55],SI ..............;31 75 55      XOR SI,CX .....................;31 ce
XOR [BP+0x55],SI ..............;31 76 55      XOR DI,CX .....................;31 cf
XOR [BX+0x55],SI ..............;31 77 55      XOR AX,DX .....................;31 d0
XOR [BX+SI+0x55],DI ...........;31 78 55      XOR CX,DX .....................;31 d1
XOR [BX+DI+0x55],DI ...........;31 79 55      XOR DX,DX .....................;31 d2
XOR [BP+SI+0x55],DI ...........;31 7a 55      XOR BX,DX .....................;31 d3
XOR [BP+DI+0x55],DI ...........;31 7b 55      XOR SP,DX .....................;31 d4
XOR [SI+0x55],DI ..............;31 7c 55      XOR BP,DX .....................;31 d5
XOR [DI+0x55],DI ..............;31 7d 55      XOR SI,DX .....................;31 d6
XOR [BP+0x55],DI ..............;31 7e 55      XOR DI,DX .....................;31 d7
XOR [BX+0x55],DI ..............;31 7f 55      XOR AX,BX .....................;31 d8
XOR [BX+SI+0x5566],AX .........;31 80 66 55   XOR CX,BX .....................;31 d9
XOR [BX+DI+0x5566],AX .........;31 81 66 55   XOR DX,BX .....................;31 da
XOR [BP+SI+0x5566],AX .........;31 82 66 55   XOR BX,BX .....................;31 db
XOR [BP+DI+0x5566],AX .........;31 83 66 55   XOR SP,BX .....................;31 dc
XOR [SI+0x5566],AX ............;31 84 66 55   XOR BP,BX .....................;31 dd
XOR [DI+0x5566],AX ............;31 85 66 55   XOR SI,BX .....................;31 de
XOR [BP+0x5566],AX ............;31 86 66 55   XOR DI,BX .....................;31 df
XOR [BX+0x5566],AX ............;31 87 66 55   XOR AX,SP .....................;31 e0
XOR [BX+SI+0x5566],CX .........;31 88 66 55   XOR CX,SP .....................;31 e1
XOR [BX+DI+0x5566],CX .........;31 89 66 55   XOR DX,SP .....................;31 e2
XOR [BP+SI+0x5566],CX .........;31 8a 66 55   XOR BX,SP .....................;31 e3
XOR [BP+DI+0x5566],CX .........;31 8b 66 55   XOR SP,SP .....................;31 e4
XOR [SI+0x5566],CX ............;31 8c 66 55   XOR BP,SP .....................;31 e5
XOR [DI+0x5566],CX ............;31 8d 66 55   XOR SI,SP .....................;31 e6
XOR [BP+0x5566],CX ............;31 8e 66 55   XOR DI,SP .....................;31 e7
XOR [BX+0x5566],CX ............;31 8f 66 55   XOR AX,BP .....................;31 e8
XOR [BX+SI+0x5566],DX .........;31 90 66 55   XOR CX,BP .....................;31 e9
XOR [BX+DI+0x5566],DX .........;31 91 66 55   XOR DX,BP .....................;31 ea
XOR [BP+SI+0x5566],DX .........;31 92 66 55   XOR BX,BP .....................;31 eb
XOR [BP+DI+0x5566],DX .........;31 93 66 55   XOR SP,BP .....................;31 ec
XOR [SI+0x5566],DX ............;31 94 66 55   XOR BP,BP .....................;31 ed
XOR [DI+0x5566],DX ............;31 95 66 55   XOR SI,BP .....................;31 ee
XOR [BP+0x5566],DX ............;31 96 66 55   XOR DI,BP .....................;31 ef
XOR [BX+0x5566],DX ............;31 97 66 55   XOR AX,SI .....................;31 f0
XOR [BX+SI+0x5566],BX .........;31 98 66 55   XOR CX,SI .....................;31 f1
XOR [BX+DI+0x5566],BX .........;31 99 66 55   XOR DX,SI .....................;31 f2
XOR [BP+SI+0x5566],BX .........;31 9a 66 55   XOR BX,SI .....................;31 f3
XOR [BP+DI+0x5566],BX .........;31 9b 66 55   XOR SP,SI .....................;31 f4
XOR [SI+0x5566],BX ............;31 9c 66 55   XOR BP,SI .....................;31 f5
XOR [DI+0x5566],BX ............;31 9d 66 55   XOR SI,SI .....................;31 f6
XOR [BP+0x5566],BX ............;31 9e 66 55   XOR DI,SI .....................;31 f7
XOR [BX+0x5566],BX ............;31 9f 66 55   XOR AX,DI .....................;31 f8
XOR [BX+SI+0x5566],SP .........;31 a0 66 55   XOR CX,DI .....................;31 f9
XOR [BX+DI+0x5566],SP .........;31 a1 66 55   XOR DX,DI .....................;31 fa
XOR [BP+SI+0x5566],SP .........;31 a2 66 55   XOR BX,DI .....................;31 fb
XOR [BP+DI+0x5566],SP .........;31 a3 66 55   XOR SP,DI .....................;31 fc
XOR [SI+0x5566],SP ............;31 a4 66 55   XOR BP,DI .....................;31 fd
XOR [DI+0x5566],SP ............;31 a5 66 55   XOR SI,DI .....................;31 fe
XOR [BP+0x5566],SP ............;31 a6 66 55   XOR DI,DI .....................;31 ff
XOR [BX+0x5566],SP ............;31 a7 66 55   XOR AL,[BX+SI] ................;32 00
XOR [BX+SI+0x5566],BP .........;31 a8 66 55   XOR AL,[BX+DI] ................;32 01
XOR [BX+DI+0x5566],BP .........;31 a9 66 55   XOR AL,[BP+SI] ................;32 02
XOR [BP+SI+0x5566],BP .........;31 aa 66 55   XOR AL,[BP+DI] ................;32 03
XOR [BP+DI+0x5566],BP .........;31 ab 66 55   XOR AL,[SI] ...................;32 04
XOR [SI+0x5566],BP ............;31 ac 66 55   XOR AL,[DI] ...................;32 05
XOR [DI+0x5566],BP ............;31 ad 66 55   XOR AL,[0x5566] ...............;32 06 66 55
XOR [BP+0x5566],BP ............;31 ae 66 55   XOR AL,[BX] ...................;32 07
XOR [BX+0x5566],BP ............;31 af 66 55   XOR CL,[BX+SI] ................;32 08
XOR [BX+SI+0x5566],SI .........;31 b0 66 55   XOR CL,[BX+DI] ................;32 09
XOR [BX+DI+0x5566],SI .........;31 b1 66 55   XOR CL,[BP+SI] ................;32 0a
XOR [BP+SI+0x5566],SI .........;31 b2 66 55   XOR CL,[BP+DI] ................;32 0b
XOR [BP+DI+0x5566],SI .........;31 b3 66 55   XOR CL,[SI] ...................;32 0c
XOR [SI+0x5566],SI ............;31 b4 66 55   XOR CL,[DI] ...................;32 0d
XOR [DI+0x5566],SI ............;31 b5 66 55   XOR CL,[0x5566] ...............;32 0e 66 55
XOR [BP+0x5566],SI ............;31 b6 66 55   XOR CL,[BX] ...................;32 0f
XOR [BX+0x5566],SI ............;31 b7 66 55   XOR DL,[BX+SI] ................;32 10
XOR [BX+SI+0x5566],DI .........;31 b8 66 55   XOR DL,[BX+DI] ................;32 11
XOR [BX+DI+0x5566],DI .........;31 b9 66 55   XOR DL,[BP+SI] ................;32 12
XOR [BP+SI+0x5566],DI .........;31 ba 66 55   XOR DL,[BP+DI] ................;32 13
XOR [BP+DI+0x5566],DI .........;31 bb 66 55   XOR DL,[SI] ...................;32 14
XOR [SI+0x5566],DI ............;31 bc 66 55   XOR DL,[DI] ...................;32 15
XOR [DI+0x5566],DI ............;31 bd 66 55   XOR DL,[0x5566] ...............;32 16 66 55
XOR [BP+0x5566],DI ............;31 be 66 55   XOR DL,[BX] ...................;32 17
XOR [BX+0x5566],DI ............;31 bf 66 55   XOR BL,[BX+SI] ................;32 18
XOR AX,AX .....................;31 c0         XOR BL,[BX+DI] ................;32 19
XOR CX,AX .....................;31 c1         XOR BL,[BP+SI] ................;32 1a
XOR DX,AX .....................;31 c2         XOR BL,[BP+DI] ................;32 1b
XOR BX,AX .....................;31 c3         XOR BL,[SI] ...................;32 1c
XOR SP,AX .....................;31 c4         XOR BL,[DI] ...................;32 1d
XOR BP,AX .....................;31 c5         XOR BL,[0x5566] ...............;32 1e 66 55
XOR SI,AX .....................;31 c6         XOR BL,[BX] ...................;32 1f
XOR DI,AX .....................;31 c7         XOR AH,[BX+SI] ................;32 20
XOR AX,CX .....................;31 c8         XOR AH,[BX+DI] ................;32 21
XOR CX,CX .....................;31 c9         XOR AH,[BP+SI] ................;32 22
```

```
XOR AH,[BP+DI] .................;32 23
XOR AH,[SI] ....................;32 24
XOR AH,[DI] ....................;32 25
XOR AH,[0x5566] ................;32 26 66 55
XOR AH,[BX] ....................;32 27
XOR CH,[BX+SI] .................;32 28
XOR CH,[BX+DI] .................;32 29
XOR CH,[BP+SI] .................;32 2a
XOR CH,[BP+DI] .................;32 2b
XOR CH,[SI] ....................;32 2c
XOR CH,[DI] ....................;32 2d
XOR CH,[0x5566] ................;32 2e 66 55
XOR CH,[BX] ....................;32 2f
XOR DH,[BX+SI] .................;32 30
XOR DH,[BX+DI] .................;32 31
XOR DH,[BP+SI] .................;32 32
XOR DH,[BP+DI] .................;32 33
XOR DH,[SI] ....................;32 34
XOR DH,[DI] ....................;32 35
XOR DH,[0x5566] ................;32 36 66 55
XOR DH,[BX] ....................;32 37
XOR BH,[BX+SI] .................;32 38
XOR BH,[BX+DI] .................;32 39
XOR BH,[BP+SI] .................;32 3a
XOR BH,[BP+DI] .................;32 3b
XOR BH,[SI] ....................;32 3c
XOR BH,[DI] ....................;32 3d
XOR BH,[0x5566] ................;32 3e 66 55
XOR BH,[BX] ....................;32 3f
XOR AL,[BX+SI+0x55] ............;32 40 55
XOR AL,[BX+DI+0x55] ............;32 41 55
XOR AL,[BP+SI+0x55] ............;32 42 55
XOR AL,[BP+DI+0x55] ............;32 43 55
XOR AL,[SI+0x55] ...............;32 44 55
XOR AL,[DI+0x55] ...............;32 45 55
XOR AL,[BP+0x55] ...............;32 46 55
XOR AL,[BX+0x55] ...............;32 47 55
XOR CL,[BX+SI+0x55] ............;32 48 55
XOR CL,[BX+DI+0x55] ............;32 49 55
XOR CL,[BP+SI+0x55] ............;32 4a 55
XOR CL,[BP+DI+0x55] ............;32 4b 55
XOR CL,[SI+0x55] ...............;32 4c 55
XOR CL,[DI+0x55] ...............;32 4d 55
XOR CL,[BP+0x55] ...............;32 4e 55
XOR CL,[BX+0x55] ...............;32 4f 55
XOR DL,[BX+SI+0x55] ............;32 50 55
XOR DL,[BX+DI+0x55] ............;32 51 55
XOR DL,[BP+SI+0x55] ............;32 52 55
XOR DL,[BP+DI+0x55] ............;32 53 55
XOR DL,[SI+0x55] ...............;32 54 55
XOR DL,[DI+0x55] ...............;32 55 55
XOR DL,[BP+0x55] ...............;32 56 55
XOR DL,[BX+0x55] ...............;32 57 55
XOR BL,[BX+SI+0x55] ............;32 58 55
XOR BL,[BX+DI+0x55] ............;32 59 55
XOR BL,[BP+SI+0x55] ............;32 5a 55
XOR BL,[BP+DI+0x55] ............;32 5b 55
XOR BL,[SI+0x55] ...............;32 5c 55
XOR BL,[DI+0x55] ...............;32 5d 55
XOR BL,[BP+0x55] ...............;32 5e 55
XOR BL,[BX+0x55] ...............;32 5f 55
XOR AH,[BX+SI+0x55] ............;32 60 55
XOR AH,[BX+DI+0x55] ............;32 61 55
XOR AH,[BP+SI+0x55] ............;32 62 55
XOR AH,[BP+DI+0x55] ............;32 63 55
XOR AH,[SI+0x55] ...............;32 64 55
XOR AH,[DI+0x55] ...............;32 65 55
XOR AH,[BP+0x55] ...............;32 66 55
XOR AH,[BX+0x55] ...............;32 67 55
XOR CH,[BX+SI+0x55] ............;32 68 55
XOR CH,[BX+DI+0x55] ............;32 69 55
XOR CH,[BP+SI+0x55] ............;32 6a 55
XOR CH,[BP+DI+0x55] ............;32 6b 55
XOR CH,[SI+0x55] ...............;32 6c 55
XOR CH,[DI+0x55] ...............;32 6d 55
XOR CH,[BP+0x55] ...............;32 6e 55
XOR CH,[BX+0x55] ...............;32 6f 55
XOR DH,[BX+SI+0x55] ............;32 70 55
XOR DH,[BX+DI+0x55] ............;32 71 55
XOR DH,[BP+SI+0x55] ............;32 72 55
XOR DH,[BP+DI+0x55] ............;32 73 55
XOR DH,[SI+0x55] ...............;32 74 55
XOR DH,[DI+0x55] ...............;32 75 55
XOR DH,[BP+0x55] ...............;32 76 55
XOR DH,[BX+0x55] ...............;32 77 55
XOR BH,[BX+SI+0x55] ............;32 78 55
XOR BH,[BX+DI+0x55] ............;32 79 55
XOR BH,[BP+SI+0x55] ............;32 7a 55
XOR BH,[BP+DI+0x55] ............;32 7b 55
XOR BH,[SI+0x55] ...............;32 7c 55
XOR BH,[DI+0x55] ...............;32 7d 55
XOR BH,[BP+0x55] ...............;32 7e 55
XOR BH,[BX+0x55] ...............;32 7f 55
XOR AL,[BX+SI+0x5566] ..........;32 80 66 55
XOR AL,[BX+DI+0x5566] ..........;32 81 66 55
XOR AL,[BP+SI+0x5566] ..........;32 82 66 55
XOR AL,[BP+DI+0x5566] ..........;32 83 66 55
XOR AL,[SI+0x5566] .............;32 84 66 55
XOR AL,[DI+0x5566] .............;32 85 66 55
XOR AL,[BP+0x5566] .............;32 86 66 55
XOR AL,[BX+0x5566] .............;32 87 66 55
XOR CL,[BX+SI+0x5566] ..........;32 88 66 55
XOR CL,[BX+DI+0x5566] ..........;32 89 66 55
XOR CL,[BP+SI+0x5566] ..........;32 8a 66 55
XOR CL,[BP+DI+0x5566] ..........;32 8b 66 55
XOR CL,[SI+0x5566] .............;32 8c 66 55
XOR CL,[DI+0x5566] .............;32 8d 66 55
XOR CL,[BP+0x5566] .............;32 8e 66 55
XOR CL,[BX+0x5566] .............;32 8f 66 55
XOR DL,[BX+SI+0x5566] ..........;32 90 66 55
XOR DL,[BX+DI+0x5566] ..........;32 91 66 55
XOR DL,[BP+SI+0x5566] ..........;32 92 66 55
XOR DL,[BP+DI+0x5566] ..........;32 93 66 55
XOR DL,[SI+0x5566] .............;32 94 66 55
XOR DL,[DI+0x5566] .............;32 95 66 55
XOR DL,[BP+0x5566] .............;32 96 66 55
XOR DL,[BX+0x5566] .............;32 97 66 55
XOR BL,[BX+SI+0x5566] ..........;32 98 66 55
XOR BL,[BX+DI+0x5566] ..........;32 99 66 55
XOR BL,[BP+SI+0x5566] ..........;32 9a 66 55
XOR BL,[BP+DI+0x5566] ..........;32 9b 66 55
XOR BL,[SI+0x5566] .............;32 9c 66 55
XOR BL,[DI+0x5566] .............;32 9d 66 55
XOR BL,[BP+0x5566] .............;32 9e 66 55
XOR BL,[BX+0x5566] .............;32 9f 66 55
XOR AH,[BX+SI+0x5566] ..........;32 a0 66 55
XOR AH,[BX+DI+0x5566] ..........;32 a1 66 55
XOR AH,[BP+SI+0x5566] ..........;32 a2 66 55
XOR AH,[BP+DI+0x5566] ..........;32 a3 66 55
XOR AH,[SI+0x5566] .............;32 a4 66 55
XOR AH,[DI+0x5566] .............;32 a5 66 55
XOR AH,[BP+0x5566] .............;32 a6 66 55
XOR AH,[BX+0x5566] .............;32 a7 66 55
XOR CH,[BX+SI+0x5566] ..........;32 a8 66 55
XOR CH,[BX+DI+0x5566] ..........;32 a9 66 55
XOR CH,[BP+SI+0x5566] ..........;32 aa 66 55
XOR CH,[BP+DI+0x5566] ..........;32 ab 66 55
XOR CH,[SI+0x5566] .............;32 ac 66 55
XOR CH,[DI+0x5566] .............;32 ad 66 55
XOR CH,[BP+0x5566] .............;32 ae 66 55
XOR CH,[BX+0x5566] .............;32 af 66 55
XOR DH,[BX+SI+0x5566] ..........;32 b0 66 55
XOR DH,[BX+DI+0x5566] ..........;32 b1 66 55
XOR DH,[BP+SI+0x5566] ..........;32 b2 66 55
XOR DH,[BP+DI+0x5566] ..........;32 b3 66 55
XOR DH,[SI+0x5566] .............;32 b4 66 55
XOR DH,[DI+0x5566] .............;32 b5 66 55
XOR DH,[BP+0x5566] .............;32 b6 66 55
XOR DH,[BX+0x5566] .............;32 b7 66 55
XOR BH,[BX+SI+0x5566] ..........;32 b8 66 55
XOR BH,[BX+DI+0x5566] ..........;32 b9 66 55
XOR BH,[BP+SI+0x5566] ..........;32 ba 66 55
XOR BH,[BP+DI+0x5566] ..........;32 bb 66 55
XOR BH,[SI+0x5566] .............;32 bc 66 55
XOR BH,[DI+0x5566] .............;32 bd 66 55
XOR BH,[BP+0x5566] .............;32 be 66 55
XOR BH,[BX+0x5566] .............;32 bf 66 55
XOR AX,[BX+SI] .................;33 00
XOR AX,[BX+DI] .................;33 01
XOR AX,[BP+SI] .................;33 02
XOR AX,[BP+DI] .................;33 03
XOR AX,[SI] ....................;33 04
XOR AX,[DI] ....................;33 05
XOR AX,[0x5566] ................;33 06 66 55
XOR AX,[BX] ....................;33 07
XOR CX,[BX+SI] .................;33 08
XOR CX,[BX+DI] .................;33 09
XOR CX,[BP+SI] .................;33 0a
XOR CX,[BP+DI] .................;33 0b
XOR CX,[SI] ....................;33 0c
XOR CX,[DI] ....................;33 0d
XOR CX,[0x5566] ................;33 0e 66 55
XOR CX,[BX] ....................;33 0f
XOR DX,[BX+SI] .................;33 10
XOR DX,[BX+DI] .................;33 11
XOR DX,[BP+SI] .................;33 12
XOR DX,[BP+DI] .................;33 13
XOR DX,[SI] ....................;33 14
```

```
XOR DX,[DI] .............;33 15          XOR BP,[BP+0x55] .............;33 6e 55
XOR DX,[0x5566] .........;33 16 66 55    XOR BP,[BX+0x55] .............;33 6f 55
XOR DX,[BX] .............;33 17          XOR SI,[BX+SI+0x55] ..........;33 70 55
XOR BX,[BX+SI] ..........;33 18          XOR SI,[BX+DI+0x55] ..........;33 71 55
XOR BX,[BX+DI] ..........;33 19          XOR SI,[BP+SI+0x55] ..........;33 72 55
XOR BX,[BP+SI] ..........;33 1a          XOR SI,[BP+DI+0x55] ..........;33 73 55
XOR BX,[BP+DI] ..........;33 1b          XOR SI,[SI+0x55] .............;33 74 55
XOR BX,[SI] .............;33 1c          XOR SI,[DI+0x55] .............;33 75 55
XOR BX,[DI] .............;33 1d          XOR SI,[BP+0x55] .............;33 76 55
XOR BX,[0x5566] .........;33 1e 66 55    XOR SI,[BX+0x55] .............;33 77 55
XOR BX,[BX] .............;33 1f          XOR DI,[BX+SI+0x55] ..........;33 78 55
XOR SP,[BX+SI] ..........;33 20          XOR DI,[BX+DI+0x55] ..........;33 79 55
XOR SP,[BX+DI] ..........;33 21          XOR DI,[BP+SI+0x55] ..........;33 7a 55
XOR SP,[BP+SI] ..........;33 22          XOR DI,[BP+DI+0x55] ..........;33 7b 55
XOR SP,[BP+DI] ..........;33 23          XOR DI,[SI+0x55] .............;33 7c 55
XOR SP,[SI] .............;33 24          XOR DI,[DI+0x55] .............;33 7d 55
XOR SP,[DI] .............;33 25          XOR DI,[BP+0x55] .............;33 7e 55
XOR SP,[0x5566] .........;33 26 66 55    XOR DI,[BX+0x55] .............;33 7f 55
XOR SP,[BX] .............;33 27          XOR AX,[BX+SI+0x5566] ........;33 80 66 55
XOR BP,[BX+SI] ..........;33 28          XOR AX,[BX+DI+0x5566] ........;33 81 66 55
XOR BP,[BX+DI] ..........;33 29          XOR AX,[BP+SI+0x5566] ........;33 82 66 55
XOR BP,[BP+SI] ..........;33 2a          XOR AX,[BP+DI+0x5566] ........;33 83 66 55
XOR BP,[BP+DI] ..........;33 2b          XOR AX,[SI+0x5566] ...........;33 84 66 55
XOR BP,[SI] .............;33 2c          XOR AX,[DI+0x5566] ...........;33 85 66 55
XOR BP,[DI] .............;33 2d          XOR AX,[BP+0x5566] ...........;33 86 66 55
XOR BP,[0x5566] .........;33 2e 66 55    XOR AX,[BX+0x5566] ...........;33 87 66 55
XOR BP,[BX] .............;33 2f          XOR CX,[BX+SI+0x5566] ........;33 88 66 55
XOR SI,[BX+SI] ..........;33 30          XOR CX,[BX+DI+0x5566] ........;33 89 66 55
XOR SI,[BX+DI] ..........;33 31          XOR CX,[BP+SI+0x5566] ........;33 8a 66 55
XOR SI,[BP+SI] ..........;33 32          XOR CX,[BP+DI+0x5566] ........;33 8b 66 55
XOR SI,[BP+DI] ..........;33 33          XOR CX,[SI+0x5566] ...........;33 8c 66 55
XOR SI,[SI] .............;33 34          XOR CX,[DI+0x5566] ...........;33 8d 66 55
XOR SI,[DI] .............;33 35          XOR CX,[BP+0x5566] ...........;33 8e 66 55
XOR SI,[0x5566] .........;33 36 66 55    XOR CX,[BX+0x5566] ...........;33 8f 66 55
XOR SI,[BX] .............;33 37          XOR DX,[BX+SI+0x5566] ........;33 90 66 55
XOR DI,[BX+SI] ..........;33 38          XOR DX,[BX+DI+0x5566] ........;33 91 66 55
XOR DI,[BX+DI] ..........;33 39          XOR DX,[BP+SI+0x5566] ........;33 92 66 55
XOR DI,[BP+SI] ..........;33 3a          XOR DX,[BP+DI+0x5566] ........;33 93 66 55
XOR DI,[BP+DI] ..........;33 3b          XOR DX,[SI+0x5566] ...........;33 94 66 55
XOR DI,[SI] .............;33 3c          XOR DX,[DI+0x5566] ...........;33 95 66 55
XOR DI,[DI] .............;33 3d          XOR DX,[BP+0x5566] ...........;33 96 66 55
XOR DI,[0x5566] .........;33 3e 66 55    XOR DX,[BX+0x5566] ...........;33 97 66 55
XOR DI,[BX] .............;33 3f          XOR BX,[BX+SI+0x5566] ........;33 98 66 55
XOR AX,[BX+SI+0x55] .....;33 40 55       XOR BX,[BX+DI+0x5566] ........;33 99 66 55
XOR AX,[BX+DI+0x55] .....;33 41 55       XOR BX,[BP+SI+0x5566] ........;33 9a 66 55
XOR AX,[BP+SI+0x55] .....;33 42 55       XOR BX,[BP+DI+0x5566] ........;33 9b 66 55
XOR AX,[BP+DI+0x55] .....;33 43 55       XOR BX,[SI+0x5566] ...........;33 9c 66 55
XOR AX,[SI+0x55] ........;33 44 55       XOR BX,[DI+0x5566] ...........;33 9d 66 55
XOR AX,[DI+0x55] ........;33 45 55       XOR BX,[BP+0x5566] ...........;33 9e 66 55
XOR AX,[BP+0x55] ........;33 46 55       XOR BX,[BX+0x5566] ...........;33 9f 66 55
XOR AX,[BX+0x55] ........;33 47 55       XOR SP,[BX+SI+0x5566] ........;33 a0 66 55
XOR CX,[BX+SI+0x55] .....;33 48 55       XOR SP,[BX+DI+0x5566] ........;33 a1 66 55
XOR CX,[BX+DI+0x55] .....;33 49 55       XOR SP,[BP+SI+0x5566] ........;33 a2 66 55
XOR CX,[BP+SI+0x55] .....;33 4a 55       XOR SP,[BP+DI+0x5566] ........;33 a3 66 55
XOR CX,[BP+DI+0x55] .....;33 4b 55       XOR SP,[SI+0x5566] ...........;33 a4 66 55
XOR CX,[SI+0x55] ........;33 4c 55       XOR SP,[DI+0x5566] ...........;33 a5 66 55
XOR CX,[DI+0x55] ........;33 4d 55       XOR SP,[BP+0x5566] ...........;33 a6 66 55
XOR CX,[BP+0x55] ........;33 4e 55       XOR SP,[BX+0x5566] ...........;33 a7 66 55
XOR CX,[BX+0x55] ........;33 4f 55       XOR BP,[BX+SI+0x5566] ........;33 a8 66 55
XOR DX,[BX+SI+0x55] .....;33 50 55       XOR BP,[BX+DI+0x5566] ........;33 a9 66 55
XOR DX,[BX+DI+0x55] .....;33 51 55       XOR BP,[BP+SI+0x5566] ........;33 aa 66 55
XOR DX,[BP+SI+0x55] .....;33 52 55       XOR BP,[BP+DI+0x5566] ........;33 ab 66 55
XOR DX,[BP+DI+0x55] .....;33 53 55       XOR BP,[SI+0x5566] ...........;33 ac 66 55
XOR DX,[SI+0x55] ........;33 54 55       XOR BP,[DI+0x5566] ...........;33 ad 66 55
XOR DX,[DI+0x55] ........;33 55 55       XOR BP,[BP+0x5566] ...........;33 ae 66 55
XOR DX,[BP+0x55] ........;33 56 55       XOR BP,[BX+0x5566] ...........;33 af 66 55
XOR DX,[BX+0x55] ........;33 57 55       XOR SI,[BX+SI+0x5566] ........;33 b0 66 55
XOR BX,[BX+SI+0x55] .....;33 58 55       XOR SI,[BX+DI+0x5566] ........;33 b1 66 55
XOR BX,[BX+DI+0x55] .....;33 59 55       XOR SI,[BP+SI+0x5566] ........;33 b2 66 55
XOR BX,[BP+SI+0x55] .....;33 5a 55       XOR SI,[BP+DI+0x5566] ........;33 b3 66 55
XOR BX,[BP+DI+0x55] .....;33 5b 55       XOR SI,[SI+0x5566] ...........;33 b4 66 55
XOR BX,[SI+0x55] ........;33 5c 55       XOR SI,[DI+0x5566] ...........;33 b5 66 55
XOR BX,[DI+0x55] ........;33 5d 55       XOR SI,[BP+0x5566] ...........;33 b6 66 55
XOR BX,[BP+0x55] ........;33 5e 55       XOR SI,[BX+0x5566] ...........;33 b7 66 55
XOR BX,[BX+0x55] ........;33 5f 55       XOR DI,[BX+SI+0x5566] ........;33 b8 66 55
XOR SP,[BX+SI+0x55] .....;33 60 55       XOR DI,[BX+DI+0x5566] ........;33 b9 66 55
XOR SP,[BX+DI+0x55] .....;33 61 55       XOR DI,[BP+SI+0x5566] ........;33 ba 66 55
XOR SP,[BP+SI+0x55] .....;33 62 55       XOR DI,[BP+DI+0x5566] ........;33 bb 66 55
XOR SP,[BP+DI+0x55] .....;33 63 55       XOR DI,[SI+0x5566] ...........;33 bc 66 55
XOR SP,[SI+0x55] ........;33 64 55       XOR DI,[DI+0x5566] ...........;33 bd 66 55
XOR SP,[DI+0x55] ........;33 65 55       XOR DI,[BP+0x5566] ...........;33 be 66 55
XOR SP,[BP+0x55] ........;33 66 55       XOR DI,[BX+0x5566] ...........;33 bf 66 55
XOR SP,[BX+0x55] ........;33 67 55       XOR AL,0x55 ..................;34 55
XOR BP,[BX+SI+0x55] .....;33 68 55       XOR AX,0x5566 ................;35 66 55
XOR BP,[BX+DI+0x55] .....;33 69 55       SS ...........................;36
XOR BP,[BP+SI+0x55] .....;33 6a 55       AAA ..........................;37
XOR BP,[BP+DI+0x55] .....;33 6b 55       CMP [BX+SI],AL ...............;38 00
XOR BP,[SI+0x55] ........;33 6c 55       CMP [BX+DI],AL ...............;38 01
XOR BP,[DI+0x55] ........;33 6d 55       CMP [BP+SI],AL ...............;38 02
```

```
CMP [BP+DI],AL .................;38 03
CMP [SI],AL ....................;38 04
CMP [DI],AL ....................;38 05
CMP [0x5566],AL ...............;38 06 66 55
CMP [BX],AL ....................;38 07
CMP [BX+SI],CL .................;38 08
CMP [BX+DI],CL .................;38 09
CMP [BP+SI],CL .................;38 0a
CMP [BP+DI],CL .................;38 0b
CMP [SI],CL ....................;38 0c
CMP [DI],CL ....................;38 0d
CMP [0x5566],CL ...............;38 0e 66 55
CMP [BX],CL ....................;38 0f
CMP [BX+SI],DL .................;38 10
CMP [BX+DI],DL .................;38 11
CMP [BP+SI],DL .................;38 12
CMP [BP+DI],DL .................;38 13
CMP [SI],DL ....................;38 14
CMP [DI],DL ....................;38 15
CMP [0x5566],DL ...............;38 16 66 55
CMP [BX],DL ....................;38 17
CMP [BX+SI],BL .................;38 18
CMP [BX+DI],BL .................;38 19
CMP [BP+SI],BL .................;38 1a
CMP [BP+DI],BL .................;38 1b
CMP [SI],BL ....................;38 1c
CMP [DI],BL ....................;38 1d
CMP [0x5566],BL ...............;38 1e 66 55
CMP [BX],BL ....................;38 1f
CMP [BX+SI],AH .................;38 20
CMP [BX+DI],AH .................;38 21
CMP [BP+SI],AH .................;38 22
CMP [BP+DI],AH .................;38 23
CMP [SI],AH ....................;38 24
CMP [DI],AH ....................;38 25
CMP [0x5566],AH ...............;38 26 66 55
CMP [BX],AH ....................;38 27
CMP [BX+SI],CH .................;38 28
CMP [BX+DI],CH .................;38 29
CMP [BP+SI],CH .................;38 2a
CMP [BP+DI],CH .................;38 2b
CMP [SI],CH ....................;38 2c
CMP [DI],CH ....................;38 2d
CMP [0x5566],CH ...............;38 2e 66 55
CMP [BX],CH ....................;38 2f
CMP [BX+SI],DH .................;38 30
CMP [BX+DI],DH .................;38 31
CMP [BP+SI],DH .................;38 32
CMP [BP+DI],DH .................;38 33
CMP [SI],DH ....................;38 34
CMP [DI],DH ....................;38 35
CMP [0x5566],DH ...............;38 36 66 55
CMP [BX],DH ....................;38 37
CMP [BX+SI],BH .................;38 38
CMP [BX+DI],BH .................;38 39
CMP [BP+SI],BH .................;38 3a
CMP [BP+DI],BH .................;38 3b
CMP [SI],BH ....................;38 3c
CMP [DI],BH ....................;38 3d
CMP [0x5566],BH ...............;38 3e 66 55
CMP [BX],BH ....................;38 3f
CMP [BX+SI+0x55],AL ...........;38 40 55
CMP [BX+DI+0x55],AL ...........;38 41 55
CMP [BP+SI+0x55],AL ...........;38 42 55
CMP [BP+DI+0x55],AL ...........;38 43 55
CMP [SI+0x55],AL ..............;38 44 55
CMP [DI+0x55],AL ..............;38 45 55
CMP [BP+0x55],AL ..............;38 46 55
CMP [BX+0x55],AL ..............;38 47 55
CMP [BX+SI+0x55],CL ...........;38 48 55
CMP [BX+DI+0x55],CL ...........;38 49 55
CMP [BP+SI+0x55],CL ...........;38 4a 55
CMP [BP+DI+0x55],CL ...........;38 4b 55
CMP [SI+0x55],CL ..............;38 4c 55
CMP [DI+0x55],CL ..............;38 4d 55
CMP [BP+0x55],CL ..............;38 4e 55
CMP [BX+0x55],CL ..............;38 4f 55
CMP [BX+SI+0x55],DL ...........;38 50 55
CMP [BX+DI+0x55],DL ...........;38 51 55
CMP [BP+SI+0x55],DL ...........;38 52 55
CMP [BP+DI+0x55],DL ...........;38 53 55
CMP [SI+0x55],DL ..............;38 54 55
CMP [DI+0x55],DL ..............;38 55 55
CMP [BP+0x55],DL ..............;38 56 55
CMP [BX+0x55],DL ..............;38 57 55
CMP [BX+SI+0x55],BL ...........;38 58 55
CMP [BX+DI+0x55],BL ...........;38 59 55
CMP [BP+SI+0x55],BL ...........;38 5a 55
CMP [BP+DI+0x55],BL ...........;38 5b 55

CMP [SI+0x55],BL ..............;38 5c 55
CMP [DI+0x55],BL ..............;38 5d 55
CMP [BP+0x55],BL ..............;38 5e 55
CMP [BX+0x55],BL ..............;38 5f 55
CMP [BX+SI+0x55],AH ...........;38 60 55
CMP [BX+DI+0x55],AH ...........;38 61 55
CMP [BP+SI+0x55],AH ...........;38 62 55
CMP [BP+DI+0x55],AH ...........;38 63 55
CMP [SI+0x55],AH ..............;38 64 55
CMP [DI+0x55],AH ..............;38 65 55
CMP [BP+0x55],AH ..............;38 66 55
CMP [BX+0x55],AH ..............;38 67 55
CMP [BX+SI+0x55],CH ...........;38 68 55
CMP [BX+DI+0x55],CH ...........;38 69 55
CMP [BP+SI+0x55],CH ...........;38 6a 55
CMP [BP+DI+0x55],CH ...........;38 6b 55
CMP [SI+0x55],CH ..............;38 6c 55
CMP [DI+0x55],CH ..............;38 6d 55
CMP [BP+0x55],CH ..............;38 6e 55
CMP [BX+0x55],CH ..............;38 6f 55
CMP [BX+SI+0x55],DH ...........;38 70 55
CMP [BX+DI+0x55],DH ...........;38 71 55
CMP [BP+SI+0x55],DH ...........;38 72 55
CMP [BP+DI+0x55],DH ...........;38 73 55
CMP [SI+0x55],DH ..............;38 74 55
CMP [DI+0x55],DH ..............;38 75 55
CMP [BP+0x55],DH ..............;38 76 55
CMP [BX+0x55],DH ..............;38 77 55
CMP [BX+SI+0x55],BH ...........;38 78 55
CMP [BX+DI+0x55],BH ...........;38 79 55
CMP [BP+SI+0x55],BH ...........;38 7a 55
CMP [BP+DI+0x55],BH ...........;38 7b 55
CMP [SI+0x55],BH ..............;38 7c 55
CMP [DI+0x55],BH ..............;38 7d 55
CMP [BP+0x55],BH ..............;38 7e 55
CMP [BX+0x55],BH ..............;38 7f 55
CMP [BX+SI+0x5566],AL .........;38 80 66 55
CMP [BX+DI+0x5566],AL .........;38 81 66 55
CMP [BP+SI+0x5566],AL .........;38 82 66 55
CMP [BP+DI+0x5566],AL .........;38 83 66 55
CMP [SI+0x5566],AL ............;38 84 66 55
CMP [DI+0x5566],AL ............;38 85 66 55
CMP [BP+0x5566],AL ............;38 86 66 55
CMP [BX+0x5566],AL ............;38 87 66 55
CMP [BX+SI+0x5566],CL .........;38 88 66 55
CMP [BX+DI+0x5566],CL .........;38 89 66 55
CMP [BP+SI+0x5566],CL .........;38 8a 66 55
CMP [BP+DI+0x5566],CL .........;38 8b 66 55
CMP [SI+0x5566],CL ............;38 8c 66 55
CMP [DI+0x5566],CL ............;38 8d 66 55
CMP [BP+0x5566],CL ............;38 8e 66 55
CMP [BX+0x5566],CL ............;38 8f 66 55
CMP [BX+SI+0x5566],DL .........;38 90 66 55
CMP [BX+DI+0x5566],DL .........;38 91 66 55
CMP [BP+SI+0x5566],DL .........;38 92 66 55
CMP [BP+DI+0x5566],DL .........;38 93 66 55
CMP [SI+0x5566],DL ............;38 94 66 55
CMP [DI+0x5566],DL ............;38 95 66 55
CMP [BP+0x5566],DL ............;38 96 66 55
CMP [BX+0x5566],DL ............;38 97 66 55
CMP [BX+SI+0x5566],BL .........;38 98 66 55
CMP [BX+DI+0x5566],BL .........;38 99 66 55
CMP [BP+SI+0x5566],BL .........;38 9a 66 55
CMP [BP+DI+0x5566],BL .........;38 9b 66 55
CMP [SI+0x5566],BL ............;38 9c 66 55
CMP [DI+0x5566],BL ............;38 9d 66 55
CMP [BP+0x5566],BL ............;38 9e 66 55
CMP [BX+0x5566],BL ............;38 9f 66 55
CMP [BX+SI+0x5566],AH .........;38 a0 66 55
CMP [BX+DI+0x5566],AH .........;38 a1 66 55
CMP [BP+SI+0x5566],AH .........;38 a2 66 55
CMP [BP+DI+0x5566],AH .........;38 a3 66 55
CMP [SI+0x5566],AH ............;38 a4 66 55
CMP [DI+0x5566],AH ............;38 a5 66 55
CMP [BP+0x5566],AH ............;38 a6 66 55
CMP [BX+0x5566],AH ............;38 a7 66 55
CMP [BX+SI+0x5566],CH .........;38 a8 66 55
CMP [BX+DI+0x5566],CH .........;38 a9 66 55
CMP [BP+SI+0x5566],CH .........;38 aa 66 55
CMP [BP+DI+0x5566],CH .........;38 ab 66 55
CMP [SI+0x5566],CH ............;38 ac 66 55
CMP [DI+0x5566],CH ............;38 ad 66 55
CMP [BP+0x5566],CH ............;38 ae 66 55
CMP [BX+0x5566],CH ............;38 af 66 55
CMP [BX+SI+0x5566],DH .........;38 b0 66 55
CMP [BX+DI+0x5566],DH .........;38 b1 66 55
CMP [BP+SI+0x5566],DH .........;38 b2 66 55
CMP [BP+DI+0x5566],DH .........;38 b3 66 55
CMP [SI+0x5566],DH ............;38 b4 66 55
```

```
CMP [DI+0x5566],DH .............;38 b5 66 55      CMP [0x5566],CX ................;39 0e 66 55
CMP [BP+0x5566],DH .............;38 b6 66 55      CMP [BX],CX ....................;39 0f
CMP [BX+0x5566],DH .............;38 b7 66 55      CMP [BX+SI],DX .................;39 10
CMP [BX+SI+0x5566],BH ..........;38 b8 66 55      CMP [BX+DI],DX .................;39 11
CMP [BX+DI+0x5566],BH ..........;38 b9 66 55      CMP [BP+SI],DX .................;39 12
CMP [BP+SI+0x5566],BH ..........;38 ba 66 55      CMP [BP+DI],DX .................;39 13
CMP [BP+DI+0x5566],BH ..........;38 bb 66 55      CMP [SI],DX ....................;39 14
CMP [SI+0x5566],BH .............;38 bc 66 55      CMP [DI],DX ....................;39 15
CMP [DI+0x5566],BH .............;38 bd 66 55      CMP [0x5566],DX ................;39 16 66 55
CMP [BP+0x5566],BH .............;38 be 66 55      CMP [BX],DX ....................;39 17
CMP [BX+0x5566],BH .............;38 bf 66 55      CMP [BX+SI],BX .................;39 18
CMP AL,AL .....................;38 c0             CMP [BX+DI],BX .................;39 19
CMP CL,AL .....................;38 c1             CMP [BP+SI],BX .................;39 1a
CMP DL,AL .....................;38 c2             CMP [BP+DI],BX .................;39 1b
CMP BL,AL .....................;38 c3             CMP [SI],BX ....................;39 1c
CMP AH,AL .....................;38 c4             CMP [DI],BX ....................;39 1d
CMP CH,AL .....................;38 c5             CMP [0x5566],BX ................;39 1e 66 55
CMP DH,AL .....................;38 c6             CMP [BX],BX ....................;39 1f
CMP BH,AL .....................;38 c7             CMP [BX+SI],SP .................;39 20
CMP AL,CL .....................;38 c8             CMP [BX+DI],SP .................;39 21
CMP CL,CL .....................;38 c9             CMP [BP+SI],SP .................;39 22
CMP DL,CL .....................;38 ca             CMP [BP+DI],SP .................;39 23
CMP BL,CL .....................;38 cb             CMP [SI],SP ....................;39 24
CMP AH,CL .....................;38 cc             CMP [DI],SP ....................;39 25
CMP CH,CL .....................;38 cd             CMP [0x5566],SP ................;39 26 66 55
CMP DH,CL .....................;38 ce             CMP [BX],SP ....................;39 27
CMP BH,CL .....................;38 cf             CMP [BX+SI],BP .................;39 28
CMP AL,DL .....................;38 d0             CMP [BX+DI],BP .................;39 29
CMP CL,DL .....................;38 d1             CMP [BP+SI],BP .................;39 2a
CMP DL,DL .....................;38 d2             CMP [BP+DI],BP .................;39 2b
CMP BL,DL .....................;38 d3             CMP [SI],BP ....................;39 2c
CMP AH,DL .....................;38 d4             CMP [DI],BP ....................;39 2d
CMP CH,DL .....................;38 d5             CMP [0x5566],BP ................;39 2e 66 55
CMP DH,DL .....................;38 d6             CMP [BX],BP ....................;39 2f
CMP BH,DL .....................;38 d7             CMP [BX+SI],SI .................;39 30
CMP AL,BL .....................;38 d8             CMP [BX+DI],SI .................;39 31
CMP CL,BL .....................;38 d9             CMP [BP+SI],SI .................;39 32
CMP DL,BL .....................;38 da             CMP [BP+DI],SI .................;39 33
CMP BL,BL .....................;38 db             CMP [SI],SI ....................;39 34
CMP AH,BL .....................;38 dc             CMP [DI],SI ....................;39 35
CMP CH,BL .....................;38 dd             CMP [0x5566],SI ................;39 36 66 55
CMP DH,BL .....................;38 de             CMP [BX],SI ....................;39 37
CMP BH,BL .....................;38 df             CMP [BX+SI],DI .................;39 38
CMP AL,AH .....................;38 e0             CMP [BX+DI],DI .................;39 39
CMP CL,AH .....................;38 e1             CMP [BP+SI],DI .................;39 3a
CMP DL,AH .....................;38 e2             CMP [BP+DI],DI .................;39 3b
CMP BL,AH .....................;38 e3             CMP [SI],DI ....................;39 3c
CMP AH,AH .....................;38 e4             CMP [DI],DI ....................;39 3d
CMP CH,AH .....................;38 e5             CMP [0x5566],DI ................;39 3e 66 55
CMP DH,AH .....................;38 e6             CMP [BX],DI ....................;39 3f
CMP BH,AH .....................;38 e7             CMP [BX+SI+0x55],AX ...........;39 40 55
CMP AL,CH .....................;38 e8             CMP [BX+DI+0x55],AX ...........;39 41 55
CMP CL,CH .....................;38 e9             CMP [BP+SI+0x55],AX ...........;39 42 55
CMP DL,CH .....................;38 ea             CMP [BP+DI+0x55],AX ...........;39 43 55
CMP BL,CH .....................;38 eb             CMP [SI+0x55],AX ..............;39 44 55
CMP AH,CH .....................;38 ec             CMP [DI+0x55],AX ..............;39 45 55
CMP CH,CH .....................;38 ed             CMP [BP+0x55],AX ..............;39 46 55
CMP DH,CH .....................;38 ee             CMP [BX+0x55],AX ..............;39 47 55
CMP BH,CH .....................;38 ef             CMP [BX+SI+0x55],CX ...........;39 48 55
CMP AL,DH .....................;38 f0             CMP [BX+DI+0x55],CX ...........;39 49 55
CMP CL,DH .....................;38 f1             CMP [BP+SI+0x55],CX ...........;39 4a 55
CMP DL,DH .....................;38 f2             CMP [BP+DI+0x55],CX ...........;39 4b 55
CMP BL,DH .....................;38 f3             CMP [SI+0x55],CX ..............;39 4c 55
CMP AH,DH .....................;38 f4             CMP [DI+0x55],CX ..............;39 4d 55
CMP CH,DH .....................;38 f5             CMP [BP+0x55],CX ..............;39 4e 55
CMP DH,DH .....................;38 f6             CMP [BX+0x55],CX ..............;39 4f 55
CMP BH,DH .....................;38 f7             CMP [BX+SI+0x55],DX ...........;39 50 55
CMP AL,BH .....................;38 f8             CMP [BX+DI+0x55],DX ...........;39 51 55
CMP CL,BH .....................;38 f9             CMP [BP+SI+0x55],DX ...........;39 52 55
CMP DL,BH .....................;38 fa             CMP [BP+DI+0x55],DX ...........;39 53 55
CMP BL,BH .....................;38 fb             CMP [SI+0x55],DX ..............;39 54 55
CMP AH,BH .....................;38 fc             CMP [DI+0x55],DX ..............;39 55 55
CMP CH,BH .....................;38 fd             CMP [BP+0x55],DX ..............;39 56 55
CMP DH,BH .....................;38 fe             CMP [BX+0x55],DX ..............;39 57 55
CMP BH,BH .....................;38 ff             CMP [BX+SI+0x55],BX ...........;39 58 55
CMP [BX+SI],AX ................;39 00             CMP [BX+DI+0x55],BX ...........;39 59 55
CMP [BX+DI],AX ................;39 01             CMP [BP+SI+0x55],BX ...........;39 5a 55
CMP [BP+SI],AX ................;39 02             CMP [BP+DI+0x55],BX ...........;39 5b 55
CMP [BP+DI],AX ................;39 03             CMP [SI+0x55],BX ..............;39 5c 55
CMP [SI],AX ...................;39 04             CMP [DI+0x55],BX ..............;39 5d 55
CMP [DI],AX ...................;39 05             CMP [BP+0x55],BX ..............;39 5e 55
CMP [0x5566],AX ...............;39 06 66 55       CMP [BX+0x55],BX ..............;39 5f 55
CMP [BX],AX ...................;39 07             CMP [BX+SI+0x55],SP ...........;39 60 55
CMP [BX+SI],CX ................;39 08             CMP [BX+DI+0x55],SP ...........;39 61 55
CMP [BX+DI],CX ................;39 09             CMP [BP+SI+0x55],SP ...........;39 62 55
CMP [BP+SI],CX ................;39 0a             CMP [BP+DI+0x55],SP ...........;39 63 55
CMP [BP+DI],CX ................;39 0b             CMP [SI+0x55],SP ..............;39 64 55
CMP [SI],CX ...................;39 0c             CMP [DI+0x55],SP ..............;39 65 55
CMP [DI],CX ...................;39 0d             CMP [BP+0x55],SP ..............;39 66 55
```

```
CMP [BX+0x55],SP .............;39 67 55        CMP AX,AX .....................;39 c0
CMP [BX+SI+0x55],BP ..........;39 68 55        CMP CX,AX .....................;39 c1
CMP [BX+SI+0x55],BP ..........;39 69 55        CMP DX,AX .....................;39 c2
CMP [BP+SI+0x55],BP ..........;39 6a 55        CMP BX,AX .....................;39 c3
CMP [BP+DI+0x55],BP ..........;39 6b 55        CMP SP,AX .....................;39 c4
CMP [SI+0x55],BP .............;39 6c 55        CMP BP,AX .....................;39 c5
CMP [DI+0x55],BP .............;39 6d 55        CMP SI,AX .....................;39 c6
CMP [BX+0x55],BP .............;39 6e 55        CMP DI,AX .....................;39 c7
CMP [BX+0x55],BP .............;39 6f 55        CMP AX,CX .....................;39 c8
CMP [BX+SI+0x55],SI ..........;39 70 55        CMP CX,CX .....................;39 c9
CMP [BX+SI+0x55],SI ..........;39 71 55        CMP DX,CX .....................;39 ca
CMP [BP+SI+0x55],SI ..........;39 72 55        CMP BX,CX .....................;39 cb
CMP [BP+DI+0x55],SI ..........;39 73 55        CMP SP,CX .....................;39 cc
CMP [SI+0x55],SI .............;39 74 55        CMP BP,CX .....................;39 cd
CMP [DI+0x55],SI .............;39 75 55        CMP SI,CX .....................;39 ce
CMP [BP+0x55],SI .............;39 76 55        CMP DI,CX .....................;39 cf
CMP [BX+0x55],SI .............;39 77 55        CMP AX,DX .....................;39 d0
CMP [BX+SI+0x55],DI ..........;39 78 55        CMP CX,DX .....................;39 d1
CMP [BX+SI+0x55],DI ..........;39 79 55        CMP DX,DX .....................;39 d2
CMP [BP+SI+0x55],DI ..........;39 7a 55        CMP BX,DX .....................;39 d3
CMP [BP+DI+0x55],DI ..........;39 7b 55        CMP SP,DX .....................;39 d4
CMP [SI+0x55],DI .............;39 7c 55        CMP BP,DX .....................;39 d5
CMP [DI+0x55],DI .............;39 7d 55        CMP SI,DX .....................;39 d6
CMP [BP+0x55],DI .............;39 7e 55        CMP DI,DX .....................;39 d7
CMP [BX+0x55],DI .............;39 7f 55        CMP AX,BX .....................;39 d8
CMP [BX+SI+0x5566],AX ........;39 80 66 55     CMP CX,BX .....................;39 d9
CMP [BX+SI+0x5566],AX ........;39 81 66 55     CMP DX,BX .....................;39 da
CMP [BP+SI+0x5566],AX ........;39 82 66 55     CMP BX,BX .....................;39 db
CMP [BP+DI+0x5566],AX ........;39 83 66 55     CMP SP,BX .....................;39 dc
CMP [SI+0x5566],AX ...........;39 84 66 55     CMP BP,BX .....................;39 dd
CMP [DI+0x5566],AX ...........;39 85 66 55     CMP SI,BX .....................;39 de
CMP [BP+0x5566],AX ...........;39 86 66 55     CMP DI,BX .....................;39 df
CMP [BX+0x5566],AX ...........;39 87 66 55     CMP AX,SP .....................;39 e0
CMP [BX+SI+0x5566],CX ........;39 88 66 55     CMP CX,SP .....................;39 e1
CMP [BX+DI+0x5566],CX ........;39 89 66 55     CMP DX,SP .....................;39 e2
CMP [BP+SI+0x5566],CX ........;39 8a 66 55     CMP BX,SP .....................;39 e3
CMP [BP+DI+0x5566],CX ........;39 8b 66 55     CMP SP,SP .....................;39 e4
CMP [SI+0x5566],CX ...........;39 8c 66 55     CMP BP,SP .....................;39 e5
CMP [DI+0x5566],CX ...........;39 8d 66 55     CMP SI,SP .....................;39 e6
CMP [BP+0x5566],CX ...........;39 8e 66 55     CMP DI,SP .....................;39 e7
CMP [BX+0x5566],CX ...........;39 8f 66 55     CMP AX,BP .....................;39 e8
CMP [BX+SI+0x5566],DX ........;39 90 66 55     CMP CX,BP .....................;39 e9
CMP [BX+DI+0x5566],DX ........;39 91 66 55     CMP DX,BP .....................;39 ea
CMP [BP+SI+0x5566],DX ........;39 92 66 55     CMP BX,BP .....................;39 eb
CMP [BP+DI+0x5566],DX ........;39 93 66 55     CMP SP,BP .....................;39 ec
CMP [SI+0x5566],DX ...........;39 94 66 55     CMP BP,BP .....................;39 ed
CMP [DI+0x5566],DX ...........;39 95 66 55     CMP SI,BP .....................;39 ee
CMP [BP+0x5566],DX ...........;39 96 66 55     CMP DI,BP .....................;39 ef
CMP [BX+0x5566],DX ...........;39 97 66 55     CMP AX,SI .....................;39 f0
CMP [BX+SI+0x5566],BX ........;39 98 66 55     CMP CX,SI .....................;39 f1
CMP [BX+DI+0x5566],BX ........;39 99 66 55     CMP DX,SI .....................;39 f2
CMP [BP+SI+0x5566],BX ........;39 9a 66 55     CMP BX,SI .....................;39 f3
CMP [BP+DI+0x5566],BX ........;39 9b 66 55     CMP SP,SI .....................;39 f4
CMP [SI+0x5566],BX ...........;39 9c 66 55     CMP BP,SI .....................;39 f5
CMP [DI+0x5566],BX ...........;39 9d 66 55     CMP SI,SI .....................;39 f6
CMP [BP+0x5566],BX ...........;39 9e 66 55     CMP DI,SI .....................;39 f7
CMP [BX+0x5566],BX ...........;39 9f 66 55     CMP AX,DI .....................;39 f8
CMP [BX+SI+0x5566],SP ........;39 a0 66 55     CMP CX,DI .....................;39 f9
CMP [BX+DI+0x5566],SP ........;39 a1 66 55     CMP DX,DI .....................;39 fa
CMP [BP+SI+0x5566],SP ........;39 a2 66 55     CMP BX,DI .....................;39 fb
CMP [BP+DI+0x5566],SP ........;39 a3 66 55     CMP SP,DI .....................;39 fc
CMP [SI+0x5566],SP ...........;39 a4 66 55     CMP BP,DI .....................;39 fd
CMP [DI+0x5566],SP ...........;39 a5 66 55     CMP SI,DI .....................;39 fe
CMP [BP+0x5566],SP ...........;39 a6 66 55     CMP DI,DI .....................;39 ff
CMP [BX+0x5566],SP ...........;39 a7 66 55     CMP AL,[BX+SI] ................;3a 00
CMP [BX+SI+0x5566],BP ........;39 a8 66 55     CMP AL,[BX+DI] ................;3a 01
CMP [BX+DI+0x5566],BP ........;39 a9 66 55     CMP AL,[BP+SI] ................;3a 02
CMP [BP+SI+0x5566],BP ........;39 aa 66 55     CMP AL,[BP+DI] ................;3a 03
CMP [BP+DI+0x5566],BP ........;39 ab 66 55     CMP AL,[SI] ...................;3a 04
CMP [SI+0x5566],BP ...........;39 ac 66 55     CMP AL,[DI] ...................;3a 05
CMP [DI+0x5566],BP ...........;39 ad 66 55     CMP AL,[0x5566] ...............;3a 06 66 55
CMP [BP+0x5566],BP ...........;39 ae 66 55     CMP AL,[BX] ...................;3a 07
CMP [BX+0x5566],BP ...........;39 af 66 55     CMP CL,[BX+SI] ................;3a 08
CMP [BX+SI+0x5566],SI ........;39 b0 66 55     CMP CL,[BX+DI] ................;3a 09
CMP [BX+DI+0x5566],SI ........;39 b1 66 55     CMP CL,[BP+SI] ................;3a 0a
CMP [BP+SI+0x5566],SI ........;39 b2 66 55     CMP CL,[BP+DI] ................;3a 0b
CMP [BP+DI+0x5566],SI ........;39 b3 66 55     CMP CL,[SI] ...................;3a 0c
CMP [SI+0x5566],SI ...........;39 b4 66 55     CMP CL,[DI] ...................;3a 0d
CMP [DI+0x5566],SI ...........;39 b5 66 55     CMP CL,[0x5566] ...............;3a 0e 66 55
CMP [BP+0x5566],SI ...........;39 b6 66 55     CMP CL,[BX] ...................;3a 0f
CMP [BX+0x5566],SI ...........;39 b7 66 55     CMP DL,[BX+SI] ................;3a 10
CMP [BX+SI+0x5566],DI ........;39 b8 66 55     CMP DL,[BX+DI] ................;3a 11
CMP [BX+DI+0x5566],DI ........;39 b9 66 55     CMP DL,[BP+SI] ................;3a 12
CMP [BP+SI+0x5566],DI ........;39 ba 66 55     CMP DL,[BP+DI] ................;3a 13
CMP [BP+DI+0x5566],DI ........;39 bb 66 55     CMP DL,[SI] ...................;3a 14
CMP [SI+0x5566],DI ...........;39 bc 66 55     CMP DL,[DI] ...................;3a 15
CMP [DI+0x5566],DI ...........;39 bd 66 55     CMP DL,[0x5566] ...............;3a 16 66 55
CMP [BP+0x5566],DI ...........;39 be 66 55     CMP DL,[BX] ...................;3a 17
CMP [BX+0x5566],DI ...........;39 bf 66 55     CMP BL,[BX+SI] ................;3a 18
```

```
CMP BL,[BX+DI] ................;3a 19
CMP BL,[BP+SI] ................;3a 1a
CMP BL,[BP+DI] ................;3a 1b
CMP BL,[SI] ...................;3a 1c
CMP BL,[DI] ...................;3a 1d
CMP BL,[0x5566] ...............;3a 1e 66 55
CMP BL,[BX] ...................;3a 1f
CMP AH,[BX+SI] ................;3a 20
CMP AH,[BX+DI] ................;3a 21
CMP AH,[BP+SI] ................;3a 22
CMP AH,[BP+DI] ................;3a 23
CMP AH,[SI] ...................;3a 24
CMP AH,[DI] ...................;3a 25
CMP AH,[0x5566] ...............;3a 26 66 55
CMP AH,[BX] ...................;3a 27
CMP CH,[BX+SI] ................;3a 28
CMP CH,[BX+DI] ................;3a 29
CMP CH,[BP+SI] ................;3a 2a
CMP CH,[BP+DI] ................;3a 2b
CMP CH,[SI] ...................;3a 2c
CMP CH,[DI] ...................;3a 2d
CMP CH,[0x5566] ...............;3a 2e 66 55
CMP CH,[BX] ...................;3a 2f
CMP DH,[BX+SI] ................;3a 30
CMP DH,[BX+DI] ................;3a 31
CMP DH,[BP+SI] ................;3a 32
CMP DH,[BP+DI] ................;3a 33
CMP DH,[SI] ...................;3a 34
CMP DH,[DI] ...................;3a 35
CMP DH,[0x5566] ...............;3a 36 66 55
CMP DH,[BX] ...................;3a 37
CMP BH,[BX+SI] ................;3a 38
CMP BH,[BX+DI] ................;3a 39
CMP BH,[BP+SI] ................;3a 3a
CMP BH,[BP+DI] ................;3a 3b
CMP BH,[SI] ...................;3a 3c
CMP BH,[DI] ...................;3a 3d
CMP BH,[0x5566] ...............;3a 3e 66 55
CMP BH,[BX] ...................;3a 3f
CMP AL,[BX+SI+0x55] ...........;3a 40 55
CMP AL,[BX+DI+0x55] ...........;3a 41 55
CMP AL,[BP+SI+0x55] ...........;3a 42 55
CMP AL,[BP+DI+0x55] ...........;3a 43 55
CMP AL,[SI+0x55] ..............;3a 44 55
CMP AL,[DI+0x55] ..............;3a 45 55
CMP AL,[BP+0x55] ..............;3a 46 55
CMP AL,[BX+0x55] ..............;3a 47 55
CMP CL,[BX+SI+0x55] ...........;3a 48 55
CMP CL,[BX+DI+0x55] ...........;3a 49 55
CMP CL,[BP+SI+0x55] ...........;3a 4a 55
CMP CL,[BP+DI+0x55] ...........;3a 4b 55
CMP CL,[SI+0x55] ..............;3a 4c 55
CMP CL,[DI+0x55] ..............;3a 4d 55
CMP CL,[BP+0x55] ..............;3a 4e 55
CMP CL,[BX+0x55] ..............;3a 4f 55
CMP DL,[BX+SI+0x55] ...........;3a 50 55
CMP DL,[BX+DI+0x55] ...........;3a 51 55
CMP DL,[BP+SI+0x55] ...........;3a 52 55
CMP DL,[BP+DI+0x55] ...........;3a 53 55
CMP DL,[SI+0x55] ..............;3a 54 55
CMP DL,[DI+0x55] ..............;3a 55 55
CMP DL,[BP+0x55] ..............;3a 56 55
CMP DL,[BX+0x55] ..............;3a 57 55
CMP BL,[BX+SI+0x55] ...........;3a 58 55
CMP BL,[BX+DI+0x55] ...........;3a 59 55
CMP BL,[BP+SI+0x55] ...........;3a 5a 55
CMP BL,[BP+DI+0x55] ...........;3a 5b 55
CMP BL,[SI+0x55] ..............;3a 5c 55
CMP BL,[DI+0x55] ..............;3a 5d 55
CMP BL,[BP+0x55] ..............;3a 5e 55
CMP BL,[BX+0x55] ..............;3a 5f 55
CMP AH,[BX+SI+0x55] ...........;3a 60 55
CMP AH,[BX+DI+0x55] ...........;3a 61 55
CMP AH,[BP+SI+0x55] ...........;3a 62 55
CMP AH,[BP+DI+0x55] ...........;3a 63 55
CMP AH,[SI+0x55] ..............;3a 64 55
CMP AH,[DI+0x55] ..............;3a 65 55
CMP AH,[BP+0x55] ..............;3a 66 55
CMP AH,[BX+0x55] ..............;3a 67 55
CMP CH,[BX+SI+0x55] ...........;3a 68 55
CMP CH,[BX+DI+0x55] ...........;3a 69 55
CMP CH,[BP+SI+0x55] ...........;3a 6a 55
CMP CH,[BP+DI+0x55] ...........;3a 6b 55
CMP CH,[SI+0x55] ..............;3a 6c 55
CMP CH,[DI+0x55] ..............;3a 6d 55
CMP CH,[BP+0x55] ..............;3a 6e 55
CMP CH,[BX+0x55] ..............;3a 6f 55
CMP DH,[BX+SI+0x55] ...........;3a 70 55
CMP DH,[BX+DI+0x55] ...........;3a 71 55
CMP DH,[BP+SI+0x55] ...........;3a 72 55
CMP DH,[BP+DI+0x55] ...........;3a 73 55
CMP DH,[SI+0x55] ..............;3a 74 55
CMP DH,[DI+0x55] ..............;3a 75 55
CMP DH,[BP+0x55] ..............;3a 76 55
CMP DH,[BX+0x55] ..............;3a 77 55
CMP BH,[BX+SI+0x55] ...........;3a 78 55
CMP BH,[BX+DI+0x55] ...........;3a 79 55
CMP BH,[BP+SI+0x55] ...........;3a 7a 55
CMP BH,[BP+DI+0x55] ...........;3a 7b 55
CMP BH,[SI+0x55] ..............;3a 7c 55
CMP BH,[DI+0x55] ..............;3a 7d 55
CMP BH,[BP+0x55] ..............;3a 7e 55
CMP BH,[BX+0x55] ..............;3a 7f 55
CMP AL,[BX+SI+0x5566] .........;3a 80 66 55
CMP AL,[BX+DI+0x5566] .........;3a 81 66 55
CMP AL,[BP+SI+0x5566] .........;3a 82 66 55
CMP AL,[BP+DI+0x5566] .........;3a 83 66 55
CMP AL,[SI+0x5566] ............;3a 84 66 55
CMP AL,[DI+0x5566] ............;3a 85 66 55
CMP AL,[BP+0x5566] ............;3a 86 66 55
CMP AL,[BX+0x5566] ............;3a 87 66 55
CMP CL,[BX+SI+0x5566] .........;3a 88 66 55
CMP CL,[BX+DI+0x5566] .........;3a 89 66 55
CMP CL,[BP+SI+0x5566] .........;3a 8a 66 55
CMP CL,[BP+DI+0x5566] .........;3a 8b 66 55
CMP CL,[SI+0x5566] ............;3a 8c 66 55
CMP CL,[DI+0x5566] ............;3a 8d 66 55
CMP CL,[BP+0x5566] ............;3a 8e 66 55
CMP CL,[BX+0x5566] ............;3a 8f 66 55
CMP DL,[BX+SI+0x5566] .........;3a 90 66 55
CMP DL,[BX+DI+0x5566] .........;3a 91 66 55
CMP DL,[BP+SI+0x5566] .........;3a 92 66 55
CMP DL,[BP+DI+0x5566] .........;3a 93 66 55
CMP DL,[SI+0x5566] ............;3a 94 66 55
CMP DL,[DI+0x5566] ............;3a 95 66 55
CMP DL,[BP+0x5566] ............;3a 96 66 55
CMP DL,[BX+0x5566] ............;3a 97 66 55
CMP BL,[BX+SI+0x5566] .........;3a 98 66 55
CMP BL,[BX+DI+0x5566] .........;3a 99 66 55
CMP BL,[BP+SI+0x5566] .........;3a 9a 66 55
CMP BL,[BP+DI+0x5566] .........;3a 9b 66 55
CMP BL,[SI+0x5566] ............;3a 9c 66 55
CMP BL,[DI+0x5566] ............;3a 9d 66 55
CMP BL,[BP+0x5566] ............;3a 9e 66 55
CMP BL,[BX+0x5566] ............;3a 9f 66 55
CMP AH,[BX+SI+0x5566] .........;3a a0 66 55
CMP AH,[BX+DI+0x5566] .........;3a a1 66 55
CMP AH,[BP+SI+0x5566] .........;3a a2 66 55
CMP AH,[BP+DI+0x5566] .........;3a a3 66 55
CMP AH,[SI+0x5566] ............;3a a4 66 55
CMP AH,[DI+0x5566] ............;3a a5 66 55
CMP AH,[BP+0x5566] ............;3a a6 66 55
CMP AH,[BX+0x5566] ............;3a a7 66 55
CMP CH,[BX+SI+0x5566] .........;3a a8 66 55
CMP CH,[BX+DI+0x5566] .........;3a a9 66 55
CMP CH,[BP+SI+0x5566] .........;3a aa 66 55
CMP CH,[BP+DI+0x5566] .........;3a ab 66 55
CMP CH,[SI+0x5566] ............;3a ac 66 55
CMP CH,[DI+0x5566] ............;3a ad 66 55
CMP CH,[BP+0x5566] ............;3a ae 66 55
CMP CH,[BX+0x5566] ............;3a af 66 55
CMP DH,[BX+SI+0x5566] .........;3a b0 66 55
CMP DH,[BX+DI+0x5566] .........;3a b1 66 55
CMP DH,[BP+SI+0x5566] .........;3a b2 66 55
CMP DH,[BP+DI+0x5566] .........;3a b3 66 55
CMP DH,[SI+0x5566] ............;3a b4 66 55
CMP DH,[DI+0x5566] ............;3a b5 66 55
CMP DH,[BP+0x5566] ............;3a b6 66 55
CMP DH,[BX+0x5566] ............;3a b7 66 55
CMP BH,[BX+SI+0x5566] .........;3a b8 66 55
CMP BH,[BX+DI+0x5566] .........;3a b9 66 55
CMP BH,[BP+SI+0x5566] .........;3a ba 66 55
CMP BH,[BP+DI+0x5566] .........;3a bb 66 55
CMP BH,[SI+0x5566] ............;3a bc 66 55
CMP BH,[DI+0x5566] ............;3a bd 66 55
CMP BH,[BP+0x5566] ............;3a be 66 55
CMP BH,[BX+0x5566] ............;3a bf 66 55
CMP AX,[BX+SI] ................;3b 00
CMP AX,[BX+DI] ................;3b 01
CMP AX,[BP+SI] ................;3b 02
CMP AX,[BP+DI] ................;3b 03
CMP AX,[SI] ...................;3b 04
CMP AX,[DI] ...................;3b 05
CMP AX,[0x5566] ...............;3b 06 66 55
CMP AX,[BX] ...................;3b 07
CMP CX,[BX+SI] ................;3b 08
CMP CX,[BX+DI] ................;3b 09
CMP CX,[BP+SI] ................;3b 0a
```

```
CMP CX,[BP+DI] ................;3b 0b          CMP SP,[SI+0x55] ...............;3b 64 55
CMP CX,[SI] ....................;3b 0c          CMP SP,[DI+0x55] ...............;3b 65 55
CMP CX,[DI] ....................;3b 0d          CMP SP,[BP+0x55] ...............;3b 66 55
CMP CX,[0x5566] ...........;3b 0e 66 55         CMP SP,[BX+0x55] ...............;3b 67 55
CMP CX,[BX] ....................;3b 0f          CMP BP,[BX+SI+0x55] ............;3b 68 55
CMP DX,[BX+SI] .................;3b 10          CMP BP,[BX+DI+0x55] ............;3b 69 55
CMP DX,[BX+DI] .................;3b 11          CMP BP,[BP+SI+0x55] ............;3b 6a 55
CMP DX,[BP+SI] .................;3b 12          CMP BP,[BP+DI+0x55] ............;3b 6b 55
CMP DX,[BP+DI] .................;3b 13          CMP BP,[SI+0x55] ...............;3b 6c 55
CMP DX,[SI] ....................;3b 14          CMP BP,[DI+0x55] ...............;3b 6d 55
CMP DX,[DI] ....................;3b 15          CMP BP,[BP+0x55] ...............;3b 6e 55
CMP DX,[0x5566] ...........;3b 16 66 55         CMP BP,[BX+0x55] ...............;3b 6f 55
CMP DX,[BX] ....................;3b 17          CMP SI,[BX+SI+0x55] ............;3b 70 55
CMP BX,[BX+SI] .................;3b 18          CMP SI,[BX+DI+0x55] ............;3b 71 55
CMP BX,[BX+DI] .................;3b 19          CMP SI,[BP+SI+0x55] ............;3b 72 55
CMP BX,[BP+SI] .................;3b 1a          CMP SI,[BP+DI+0x55] ............;3b 73 55
CMP BX,[BP+DI] .................;3b 1b          CMP SI,[SI+0x55] ...............;3b 74 55
CMP BX,[SI] ....................;3b 1c          CMP SI,[DI+0x55] ...............;3b 75 55
CMP BX,[DI] ....................;3b 1d          CMP SI,[BP+0x55] ...............;3b 76 55
CMP BX,[0x5566] ...........;3b 1e 66 55         CMP SI,[BX+0x55] ...............;3b 77 55
CMP BX,[BX] ....................;3b 1f          CMP DI,[BX+SI+0x55] ............;3b 78 55
CMP SP,[BX+SI] .................;3b 20          CMP DI,[BX+DI+0x55] ............;3b 79 55
CMP SP,[BX+DI] .................;3b 21          CMP DI,[BP+SI+0x55] ............;3b 7a 55
CMP SP,[BP+SI] .................;3b 22          CMP DI,[BP+DI+0x55] ............;3b 7b 55
CMP SP,[BP+DI] .................;3b 23          CMP DI,[SI+0x55] ...............;3b 7c 55
CMP SP,[SI] ....................;3b 24          CMP DI,[DI+0x55] ...............;3b 7d 55
CMP SP,[DI] ....................;3b 25          CMP DI,[BP+0x55] ...............;3b 7e 55
CMP SP,[0x5566] ...........;3b 26 66 55         CMP DI,[BX+0x55] ...............;3b 7f 55
CMP SP,[BX] ....................;3b 27          CMP AX,[BX+SI+0x5566] ......;3b 80 66 55
CMP BP,[BX+SI] .................;3b 28          CMP AX,[BX+DI+0x5566] ......;3b 81 66 55
CMP BP,[BX+DI] .................;3b 29          CMP AX,[BP+SI+0x5566] ......;3b 82 66 55
CMP BP,[BP+SI] .................;3b 2a          CMP AX,[BP+DI+0x5566] ......;3b 83 66 55
CMP BP,[BP+DI] .................;3b 2b          CMP AX,[SI+0x5566] .........;3b 84 66 55
CMP BP,[SI] ....................;3b 2c          CMP AX,[DI+0x5566] .........;3b 85 66 55
CMP BP,[DI] ....................;3b 2d          CMP AX,[BP+0x5566] .........;3b 86 66 55
CMP BP,[0x5566] ...........;3b 2e 66 55         CMP AX,[BX+0x5566] .........;3b 87 66 55
CMP BP,[BX] ....................;3b 2f          CMP CX,[BX+SI+0x5566] ......;3b 88 66 55
CMP SI,[BX+SI] .................;3b 30          CMP CX,[BX+DI+0x5566] ......;3b 89 66 55
CMP SI,[BX+DI] .................;3b 31          CMP CX,[BP+SI+0x5566] ......;3b 8a 66 55
CMP SI,[BP+SI] .................;3b 32          CMP CX,[BP+DI+0x5566] ......;3b 8b 66 55
CMP SI,[BP+DI] .................;3b 33          CMP CX,[SI+0x5566] .........;3b 8c 66 55
CMP SI,[SI] ....................;3b 34          CMP CX,[DI+0x5566] .........;3b 8d 66 55
CMP SI,[DI] ....................;3b 35          CMP CX,[BP+0x5566] .........;3b 8e 66 55
CMP SI,[0x5566] ...........;3b 36 66 55         CMP CX,[BX+0x5566] .........;3b 8f 66 55
CMP SI,[BX] ....................;3b 37          CMP DX,[BX+SI+0x5566] ......;3b 90 66 55
CMP DI,[BX+SI] .................;3b 38          CMP DX,[BX+DI+0x5566] ......;3b 91 66 55
CMP DI,[BX+DI] .................;3b 39          CMP DX,[BP+SI+0x5566] ......;3b 92 66 55
CMP DI,[BP+SI] .................;3b 3a          CMP DX,[BP+DI+0x5566] ......;3b 93 66 55
CMP DI,[BP+DI] .................;3b 3b          CMP DX,[SI+0x5566] .........;3b 94 66 55
CMP DI,[SI] ....................;3b 3c          CMP DX,[DI+0x5566] .........;3b 95 66 55
CMP DI,[DI] ....................;3b 3d          CMP DX,[BP+0x5566] .........;3b 96 66 55
CMP DI,[0x5566] ...........;3b 3e 66 55         CMP DX,[BX+0x5566] .........;3b 97 66 55
CMP DI,[BX] ....................;3b 3f          CMP BX,[BX+SI+0x5566] ......;3b 98 66 55
CMP AX,[BX+SI+0x55] ............;3b 40 55       CMP BX,[BX+DI+0x5566] ......;3b 99 66 55
CMP AX,[BX+DI+0x55] ............;3b 41 55       CMP BX,[BP+SI+0x5566] ......;3b 9a 66 55
CMP AX,[BP+SI+0x55] ............;3b 42 55       CMP BX,[BP+DI+0x5566] ......;3b 9b 66 55
CMP AX,[BP+DI+0x55] ............;3b 43 55       CMP BX,[SI+0x5566] .........;3b 9c 66 55
CMP AX,[SI+0x55] ...............;3b 44 55       CMP BX,[DI+0x5566] .........;3b 9d 66 55
CMP AX,[DI+0x55] ...............;3b 45 55       CMP BX,[BP+0x5566] .........;3b 9e 66 55
CMP AX,[BP+0x55] ...............;3b 46 55       CMP BX,[BX+0x5566] .........;3b 9f 66 55
CMP AX,[BX+0x55] ...............;3b 47 55       CMP SP,[BX+SI+0x5566] ......;3b a0 66 55
CMP CX,[BX+SI+0x55] ............;3b 48 55       CMP SP,[BX+DI+0x5566] ......;3b a1 66 55
CMP CX,[BX+DI+0x55] ............;3b 49 55       CMP SP,[BP+SI+0x5566] ......;3b a2 66 55
CMP CX,[BP+SI+0x55] ............;3b 4a 55       CMP SP,[BP+DI+0x5566] ......;3b a3 66 55
CMP CX,[BP+DI+0x55] ............;3b 4b 55       CMP SP,[SI+0x5566] .........;3b a4 66 55
CMP CX,[SI+0x55] ...............;3b 4c 55       CMP SP,[DI+0x5566] .........;3b a5 66 55
CMP CX,[DI+0x55] ...............;3b 4d 55       CMP SP,[BP+0x5566] .........;3b a6 66 55
CMP CX,[BP+0x55] ...............;3b 4e 55       CMP SP,[BX+0x5566] .........;3b a7 66 55
CMP CX,[BX+0x55] ...............;3b 4f 55       CMP BP,[BX+SI+0x5566] ......;3b a8 66 55
CMP DX,[BX+SI+0x55] ............;3b 50 55       CMP BP,[BX+DI+0x5566] ......;3b a9 66 55
CMP DX,[BX+DI+0x55] ............;3b 51 55       CMP BP,[BP+SI+0x5566] ......;3b aa 66 55
CMP DX,[BP+SI+0x55] ............;3b 52 55       CMP BP,[BP+DI+0x5566] ......;3b ab 66 55
CMP DX,[BP+DI+0x55] ............;3b 53 55       CMP BP,[SI+0x5566] .........;3b ac 66 55
CMP DX,[SI+0x55] ...............;3b 54 55       CMP BP,[DI+0x5566] .........;3b ad 66 55
CMP DX,[DI+0x55] ...............;3b 55 55       CMP BP,[BP+0x5566] .........;3b ae 66 55
CMP DX,[BP+0x55] ...............;3b 56 55       CMP BP,[BX+0x5566] .........;3b af 66 55
CMP DX,[BX+0x55] ...............;3b 57 55       CMP SI,[BX+SI+0x5566] ......;3b b0 66 55
CMP BX,[BX+SI+0x55] ............;3b 58 55       CMP SI,[BX+DI+0x5566] ......;3b b1 66 55
CMP BX,[BX+DI+0x55] ............;3b 59 55       CMP SI,[BP+SI+0x5566] ......;3b b2 66 55
CMP BX,[BP+SI+0x55] ............;3b 5a 55       CMP SI,[BP+DI+0x5566] ......;3b b3 66 55
CMP BX,[BP+DI+0x55] ............;3b 5b 55       CMP SI,[SI+0x5566] .........;3b b4 66 55
CMP BX,[SI+0x55] ...............;3b 5c 55       CMP SI,[DI+0x5566] .........;3b b5 66 55
CMP BX,[DI+0x55] ...............;3b 5d 55       CMP SI,[BP+0x5566] .........;3b b6 66 55
CMP BX,[BP+0x55] ...............;3b 5e 55       CMP SI,[BX+0x5566] .........;3b b7 66 55
CMP BX,[BX+0x55] ...............;3b 5f 55       CMP DI,[BX+SI+0x5566] ......;3b b8 66 55
CMP SP,[BX+SI+0x55] ............;3b 60 55       CMP DI,[BX+DI+0x5566] ......;3b b9 66 55
CMP SP,[BX+DI+0x55] ............;3b 61 55       CMP DI,[BP+SI+0x5566] ......;3b ba 66 55
CMP SP,[BP+SI+0x55] ............;3b 62 55       CMP DI,[BP+DI+0x5566] ......;3b bb 66 55
CMP SP,[BP+DI+0x55] ............;3b 63 55       CMP DI,[SI+0x5566] .........;3b bc 66 55
```

```
CMP DI,[DI+0x5566] .............;3b bd 66 55
CMP DI,[BP+0x5566] .............;3b be 66 55
CMP DI,[BX+0x5566] .............;3b bf 66 55
CMP AL,0x55 ...................;3c 55
CMP AX,0x5566 .................;3d 66 55
DS ...........................;3e
AAS ..........................;3f
INC AX .......................;40
INC CX .......................;41
INC DX .......................;42
INC BX .......................;43
INC SP .......................;44
INC BP .......................;45
INC SI .......................;46
INC DI .......................;47
DEC AX .......................;48
DEC CX .......................;49
DEC DX .......................;4a
DEC BX .......................;4b
DEC SP .......................;4c
DEC BP .......................;4d
DEC SI .......................;4e
DEC DI .......................;4f
PUSH AX ......................;50
PUSH CX ......................;51
PUSH DX ......................;52
PUSH BX ......................;53
PUSH SP ......................;54
PUSH BP ......................;55
PUSH SI ......................;56
PUSH DI ......................;57
POP AX .......................;58
POP CX .......................;59
POP DX .......................;5a
POP BX .......................;5b
POP SP .......................;5c
POP BP .......................;5d
POP SI .......................;5e
POP DI .......................;5f
JO 0x55 ......................;70 55
JNO 0x55 .....................;71 55
JB 0x55 ......................;72 55
JNB 0x55 .....................;73 55
JZ 0x55 ......................;74 55
JNZ 0x55 .....................;75 55
JBE 0x55 .....................;76 55
JA 0x55 ......................;77 55
JS 0x55 ......................;78 55
JNS 0x55 .....................;79 55
JPE 0x55 .....................;7a 55
JPO 0x55 .....................;7b 55
JL 0x55 ......................;7c 55
JGE 0x55 .....................;7d 55
JLE 0x55 .....................;7e 55
JG 0x55 ......................;7f 55
ADD BYTE [BX+SI],0x88 .........;80 00 88
ADD BYTE [BX+DI],0x88 .........;80 01 88
ADD BYTE [BP+SI],0x88 .........;80 02 88
ADD BYTE [BP+DI],0x88 .........;80 03 88
ADD BYTE [SI],0x88 ...........;80 04 88
ADD BYTE [DI],0x88 ...........;80 05 88
ADD BYTE [0x5566],0x88 ........;80 06 66 55 88
ADD BYTE [BX],0x88 ...........;80 07 88
OR BYTE [BX+SI],0x88 .........;80 08 88
OR BYTE [BX+DI],0x88 .........;80 09 88
OR BYTE [BP+SI],0x88 .........;80 0a 88
OR BYTE [BP+DI],0x88 .........;80 0b 88
OR BYTE [SI],0x88 ...........;80 0c 88
OR BYTE [DI],0x88 ...........;80 0d 88
OR BYTE [0x5566],0x88 ........;80 0e 66 55 88
OR BYTE [BX],0x88 ...........;80 0f 88
ADC BYTE [BX+SI],0x88 .........;80 10 88
ADC BYTE [BX+DI],0x88 .........;80 11 88
ADC BYTE [BP+SI],0x88 .........;80 12 88
ADC BYTE [BP+DI],0x88 .........;80 13 88
ADC BYTE [SI],0x88 ...........;80 14 88
ADC BYTE [DI],0x88 ...........;80 15 88
ADC BYTE [0x5566],0x88 ........;80 16 66 55 88
ADC BYTE [BX],0x88 ...........;80 17 88
SBB BYTE [BX+SI],0x88 .........;80 18 88
SBB BYTE [BX+DI],0x88 .........;80 19 88
SBB BYTE [BP+SI],0x88 .........;80 1a 88
SBB BYTE [BP+DI],0x88 .........;80 1b 88
SBB BYTE [SI],0x88 ...........;80 1c 88
SBB BYTE [DI],0x88 ...........;80 1d 88
SBB BYTE [0x5566],0x88 ........;80 1e 66 55 88
SBB BYTE [BX],0x88 ...........;80 1f 88
AND BYTE [BX+SI],0x88 .........;80 20 88
AND BYTE [BX+DI],0x88 .........;80 21 88
AND BYTE [BP+SI],0x88 .........;80 22 88
AND BYTE [BP+DI],0x88 .........;80 23 88
AND BYTE [SI],0x88 ...........;80 24 88
AND BYTE [DI],0x88 ...........;80 25 88
AND BYTE [0x5566],0x88 ........;80 26 66 55 88
AND BYTE [BX],0x88 ...........;80 27 88
SUB BYTE [BX+SI],0x88 .........;80 28 88
SUB BYTE [BX+DI],0x88 .........;80 29 88
SUB BYTE [BP+SI],0x88 .........;80 2a 88
SUB BYTE [BP+DI],0x88 .........;80 2b 88
SUB BYTE [SI],0x88 ...........;80 2c 88
SUB BYTE [DI],0x88 ...........;80 2d 88
SUB BYTE [0x5566],0x88 ........;80 2e 66 55 88
SUB BYTE [BX],0x88 ...........;80 2f 88
XOR BYTE [BX+SI],0x88 .........;80 30 88
XOR BYTE [BX+DI],0x88 .........;80 31 88
XOR BYTE [BP+SI],0x88 .........;80 32 88
XOR BYTE [BP+DI],0x88 .........;80 33 88
XOR BYTE [SI],0x88 ...........;80 34 88
XOR BYTE [DI],0x88 ...........;80 35 88
XOR BYTE [0x5566],0x88 ........;80 36 66 55 88
XOR BYTE [BX],0x88 ...........;80 37 88
CMP BYTE [BX+SI],0x88 .........;80 38 88
CMP BYTE [BX+DI],0x88 .........;80 39 88
CMP BYTE [BP+SI],0x88 .........;80 3a 88
CMP BYTE [BP+DI],0x88 .........;80 3b 88
CMP BYTE [SI],0x88 ...........;80 3c 88
CMP BYTE [DI],0x88 ...........;80 3d 88
CMP BYTE [0x5566],0x88 ........;80 3e 66 55 88
CMP BYTE [BX],0x88 ...........;80 3f 88
ADD BYTE [BX+SI+0x55],0x88 ....;80 40 55 88
ADD BYTE [BX+DI+0x55],0x88 ....;80 41 55 88
ADD BYTE [BP+SI+0x55],0x88 ....;80 42 55 88
ADD BYTE [BP+DI+0x55],0x88 ....;80 43 55 88
ADD BYTE [SI+0x55],0x88 ......;80 44 55 88
ADD BYTE [DI+0x55],0x88 ......;80 45 55 88
ADD BYTE [BP+0x55],0x88 ......;80 46 55 88
ADD BYTE [BX+0x55],0x88 ......;80 47 55 88
OR BYTE [BX+SI+0x55],0x88 ....;80 48 55 88
OR BYTE [BX+DI+0x55],0x88 ....;80 49 55 88
OR BYTE [BP+SI+0x55],0x88 ....;80 4a 55 88
OR BYTE [BP+DI+0x55],0x88 ....;80 4b 55 88
OR BYTE [SI+0x55],0x88 ......;80 4c 55 88
OR BYTE [DI+0x55],0x88 ......;80 4d 55 88
OR BYTE [BP+0x55],0x88 ......;80 4e 55 88
OR BYTE [BX+0x55],0x88 ......;80 4f 55 88
ADC BYTE [BX+SI+0x55],0x88 ....;80 50 55 88
ADC BYTE [BX+DI+0x55],0x88 ....;80 51 55 88
ADC BYTE [BP+SI+0x55],0x88 ....;80 52 55 88
ADC BYTE [BP+DI+0x55],0x88 ....;80 53 55 88
ADC BYTE [SI+0x55],0x88 ......;80 54 55 88
ADC BYTE [DI+0x55],0x88 ......;80 55 55 88
ADC BYTE [BP+0x55],0x88 ......;80 56 55 88
ADC BYTE [BX+0x55],0x88 ......;80 57 55 88
SBB BYTE [BX+SI+0x55],0x88 ....;80 58 55 88
SBB BYTE [BX+DI+0x55],0x88 ....;80 59 55 88
SBB BYTE [BP+SI+0x55],0x88 ....;80 5a 55 88
SBB BYTE [BP+DI+0x55],0x88 ....;80 5b 55 88
SBB BYTE [SI+0x55],0x88 ......;80 5c 55 88
SBB BYTE [DI+0x55],0x88 ......;80 5d 55 88
SBB BYTE [BP+0x55],0x88 ......;80 5e 55 88
SBB BYTE [BX+0x55],0x88 ......;80 5f 55 88
AND BYTE [BX+SI+0x55],0x88 ....;80 60 55 88
AND BYTE [BX+DI+0x55],0x88 ....;80 61 55 88
AND BYTE [BP+SI+0x55],0x88 ....;80 62 55 88
AND BYTE [BP+DI+0x55],0x88 ....;80 63 55 88
AND BYTE [SI+0x55],0x88 ......;80 64 55 88
AND BYTE [DI+0x55],0x88 ......;80 65 55 88
AND BYTE [BP+0x55],0x88 ......;80 66 55 88
AND BYTE [BX+0x55],0x88 ......;80 67 55 88
SUB BYTE [BX+SI+0x55],0x88 ....;80 68 55 88
SUB BYTE [BX+DI+0x55],0x88 ....;80 69 55 88
SUB BYTE [BP+SI+0x55],0x88 ....;80 6a 55 88
SUB BYTE [BP+DI+0x55],0x88 ....;80 6b 55 88
SUB BYTE [SI+0x55],0x88 ......;80 6c 55 88
SUB BYTE [DI+0x55],0x88 ......;80 6d 55 88
SUB BYTE [BP+0x55],0x88 ......;80 6e 55 88
SUB BYTE [BX+0x55],0x88 ......;80 6f 55 88
XOR BYTE [BX+SI+0x55],0x88 ....;80 70 55 88
XOR BYTE [BX+DI+0x55],0x88 ....;80 71 55 88
XOR BYTE [BP+SI+0x55],0x88 ....;80 72 55 88
XOR BYTE [BP+DI+0x55],0x88 ....;80 73 55 88
XOR BYTE [SI+0x55],0x88 ......;80 74 55 88
XOR BYTE [DI+0x55],0x88 ......;80 75 55 88
XOR BYTE [BP+0x55],0x88 ......;80 76 55 88
XOR BYTE [BX+0x55],0x88 ......;80 77 55 88
CMP BYTE [BX+SI+0x55],0x88 ....;80 78 55 88
CMP BYTE [BX+DI+0x55],0x88 ....;80 79 55 88
CMP BYTE [BP+SI+0x55],0x88 ....;80 7a 55 88
```

```
CMP BYTE [BP+DI+0x55],0x88 .....;80 7b 55 88
CMP BYTE [SI+0x55],0x88 ........;80 7c 55 88
CMP BYTE [DI+0x55],0x88 ........;80 7d 55 88
CMP BYTE [BP+0x55],0x88 ........;80 7e 55 88
CMP BYTE [BX+0x55],0x88 ........;80 7f 55 88
ADD BYTE [BX+SI+0x5566],0x88 ...;80 80 66 55 88
ADD BYTE [BX+DI+0x5566],0x88 ...;80 81 66 55 88
ADD BYTE [BP+SI+0x5566],0x88 ...;80 82 66 55 88
ADD BYTE [BP+DI+0x5566],0x88 ...;80 83 66 55 88
ADD BYTE [SI+0x5566],0x88 ......;80 84 66 55 88
ADD BYTE [DI+0x5566],0x88 ......;80 85 66 55 88
ADD BYTE [BP+0x5566],0x88 ......;80 86 66 55 88
ADD BYTE [BX+0x5566],0x88 ......;80 87 66 55 88
OR BYTE [BX+SI+0x5566],0x88 ....;80 88 66 55 88
OR BYTE [BX+DI+0x5566],0x88 ....;80 89 66 55 88
OR BYTE [BP+SI+0x5566],0x88 ....;80 8a 66 55 88
OR BYTE [BP+DI+0x5566],0x88 ....;80 8b 66 55 88
OR BYTE [SI+0x5566],0x88 .......;80 8c 66 55 88
OR BYTE [DI+0x5566],0x88 .......;80 8d 66 55 88
OR BYTE [BP+0x5566],0x88 .......;80 8e 66 55 88
OR BYTE [BX+0x5566],0x88 .......;80 8f 66 55 88
ADC BYTE [BX+SI+0x5566],0x88 ...;80 90 66 55 88
ADC BYTE [BX+DI+0x5566],0x88 ...;80 91 66 55 88
ADC BYTE [BP+SI+0x5566],0x88 ...;80 92 66 55 88
ADC BYTE [BP+DI+0x5566],0x88 ...;80 93 66 55 88
ADC BYTE [SI+0x5566],0x88 ......;80 94 66 55 88
ADC BYTE [DI+0x5566],0x88 ......;80 95 66 55 88
ADC BYTE [BP+0x5566],0x88 ......;80 96 66 55 88
ADC BYTE [BX+0x5566],0x88 ......;80 97 66 55 88
SBB BYTE [BX+SI+0x5566],0x88 ...;80 98 66 55 88
SBB BYTE [BX+DI+0x5566],0x88 ...;80 99 66 55 88
SBB BYTE [BP+SI+0x5566],0x88 ...;80 9a 66 55 88
SBB BYTE [BP+DI+0x5566],0x88 ...;80 9b 66 55 88
SBB BYTE [SI+0x5566],0x88 ......;80 9c 66 55 88
SBB BYTE [DI+0x5566],0x88 ......;80 9d 66 55 88
SBB BYTE [BP+0x5566],0x88 ......;80 9e 66 55 88
SBB BYTE [BX+0x5566],0x88 ......;80 9f 66 55 88
AND BYTE [BX+SI+0x5566],0x88 ...;80 a0 66 55 88
AND BYTE [BX+DI+0x5566],0x88 ...;80 a1 66 55 88
AND BYTE [BP+SI+0x5566],0x88 ...;80 a2 66 55 88
AND BYTE [BP+DI+0x5566],0x88 ...;80 a3 66 55 88
AND BYTE [SI+0x5566],0x88 ......;80 a4 66 55 88
AND BYTE [DI+0x5566],0x88 ......;80 a5 66 55 88
AND BYTE [BP+0x5566],0x88 ......;80 a6 66 55 88
AND BYTE [BX+0x5566],0x88 ......;80 a7 66 55 88
SUB BYTE [BX+SI+0x5566],0x88 ...;80 a8 66 55 88
SUB BYTE [BX+DI+0x5566],0x88 ...;80 a9 66 55 88
SUB BYTE [BP+SI+0x5566],0x88 ...;80 aa 66 55 88
SUB BYTE [BP+DI+0x5566],0x88 ...;80 ab 66 55 88
SUB BYTE [SI+0x5566],0x88 ......;80 ac 66 55 88
SUB BYTE [DI+0x5566],0x88 ......;80 ad 66 55 88
SUB BYTE [BP+0x5566],0x88 ......;80 ae 66 55 88
SUB BYTE [BX+0x5566],0x88 ......;80 af 66 55 88
XOR BYTE [BX+SI+0x5566],0x88 ...;80 b0 66 55 88
XOR BYTE [BX+DI+0x5566],0x88 ...;80 b1 66 55 88
XOR BYTE [BP+SI+0x5566],0x88 ...;80 b2 66 55 88
XOR BYTE [BP+DI+0x5566],0x88 ...;80 b3 66 55 88
XOR BYTE [SI+0x5566],0x88 ......;80 b4 66 55 88
XOR BYTE [DI+0x5566],0x88 ......;80 b5 66 55 88
XOR BYTE [BP+0x5566],0x88 ......;80 b6 66 55 88
XOR BYTE [BX+0x5566],0x88 ......;80 b7 66 55 88
CMP BYTE [BX+SI+0x5566],0x88 ...;80 b8 66 55 88
CMP BYTE [BX+DI+0x5566],0x88 ...;80 b9 66 55 88
CMP BYTE [BP+SI+0x5566],0x88 ...;80 ba 66 55 88
CMP BYTE [BP+DI+0x5566],0x88 ...;80 bb 66 55 88
CMP BYTE [SI+0x5566],0x88 ......;80 bc 66 55 88
CMP BYTE [DI+0x5566],0x88 ......;80 bd 66 55 88
CMP BYTE [BP+0x5566],0x88 ......;80 be 66 55 88
CMP BYTE [BX+0x5566],0x88 ......;80 bf 66 55 88
ADD AL,0x88 ...................;80 c0 88
ADD CL,0x88 ...................;80 c1 88
ADD DL,0x88 ...................;80 c2 88
ADD BL,0x88 ...................;80 c3 88
ADD AH,0x88 ...................;80 c4 88
ADD CH,0x88 ...................;80 c5 88
ADD DH,0x88 ...................;80 c6 88
ADD BH,0x88 ...................;80 c7 88
OR AL,0x88 ....................;80 c8 88
OR CL,0x88 ....................;80 c9 88
OR DL,0x88 ....................;80 ca 88
OR BL,0x88 ....................;80 cb 88
OR AH,0x88 ....................;80 cc 88
OR CH,0x88 ....................;80 cd 88
OR DH,0x88 ....................;80 ce 88
OR BH,0x88 ....................;80 cf 88
ADC AL,0x88 ...................;80 d0 88
ADC CL,0x88 ...................;80 d1 88
ADC DL,0x88 ...................;80 d2 88
ADC BL,0x88 ...................;80 d3 88

ADC AH,0x88 ...................;80 d4 88
ADC CH,0x88 ...................;80 d5 88
ADC DH,0x88 ...................;80 d6 88
ADC BH,0x88 ...................;80 d7 88
SBB AL,0x88 ...................;80 d8 88
SBB CL,0x88 ...................;80 d9 88
SBB DL,0x88 ...................;80 da 88
SBB BL,0x88 ...................;80 db 88
SBB AH,0x88 ...................;80 dc 88
SBB CH,0x88 ...................;80 dd 88
SBB DH,0x88 ...................;80 de 88
SBB BH,0x88 ...................;80 df 88
AND AL,0x88 ...................;80 e0 88
AND CL,0x88 ...................;80 e1 88
AND DL,0x88 ...................;80 e2 88
AND BL,0x88 ...................;80 e3 88
AND AH,0x88 ...................;80 e4 88
AND CH,0x88 ...................;80 e5 88
AND DH,0x88 ...................;80 e6 88
AND BH,0x88 ...................;80 e7 88
SUB AL,0x88 ...................;80 e8 88
SUB CL,0x88 ...................;80 e9 88
SUB DL,0x88 ...................;80 ea 88
SUB BL,0x88 ...................;80 eb 88
SUB AH,0x88 ...................;80 ec 88
SUB CH,0x88 ...................;80 ed 88
SUB DH,0x88 ...................;80 ee 88
SUB BH,0x88 ...................;80 ef 88
XOR AL,0x88 ...................;80 f0 88
XOR CL,0x88 ...................;80 f1 88
XOR DL,0x88 ...................;80 f2 88
XOR BL,0x88 ...................;80 f3 88
XOR AH,0x88 ...................;80 f4 88
XOR CH,0x88 ...................;80 f5 88
XOR DH,0x88 ...................;80 f6 88
XOR BH,0x88 ...................;80 f7 88
CMP AL,0x88 ...................;80 f8 88
CMP CL,0x88 ...................;80 f9 88
CMP DL,0x88 ...................;80 fa 88
CMP BL,0x88 ...................;80 fb 88
CMP AH,0x88 ...................;80 fc 88
CMP CH,0x88 ...................;80 fd 88
CMP DH,0x88 ...................;80 fe 88
CMP BH,0x88 ...................;80 ff 88
ADD WORD [BX+SI],0x7788 .......;81 00 88 77
ADD WORD [BX+DI],0x7788 .......;81 01 88 77
ADD WORD [BP+SI],0x7788 .......;81 02 88 77
ADD WORD [BP+DI],0x7788 .......;81 03 88 77
ADD WORD [SI],0x7788 ..........;81 04 88 77
ADD WORD [DI],0x7788 ..........;81 05 88 77
ADD WORD [0x5566],0x7788 ......;81 06 66 55 88 77
ADD WORD [BX],0x7788 ..........;81 07 88 77
OR WORD [BX+SI],0x7788 ........;81 08 88 77
OR WORD [BX+DI],0x7788 ........;81 09 88 77
OR WORD [BP+SI],0x7788 ........;81 0a 88 77
OR WORD [BP+DI],0x7788 ........;81 0b 88 77
OR WORD [SI],0x7788 ...........;81 0c 88 77
OR WORD [DI],0x7788 ...........;81 0d 88 77
OR WORD [0x5566],0x7788 .......;81 0e 66 55 88 77
OR WORD [BX],0x7788 ...........;81 0f 88 77
ADC WORD [BX+SI],0x7788 .......;81 10 88 77
ADC WORD [BX+DI],0x7788 .......;81 11 88 77
ADC WORD [BP+SI],0x7788 .......;81 12 88 77
ADC WORD [BP+DI],0x7788 .......;81 13 88 77
ADC WORD [SI],0x7788 ..........;81 14 88 77
ADC WORD [DI],0x7788 ..........;81 15 88 77
ADC WORD [0x5566],0x7788 ......;81 16 66 55 88 77
ADC WORD [BX],0x7788 ..........;81 17 88 77
SBB WORD [BX+SI],0x7788 .......;81 18 88 77
SBB WORD [BX+DI],0x7788 .......;81 19 88 77
SBB WORD [BP+SI],0x7788 .......;81 1a 88 77
SBB WORD [BP+DI],0x7788 .......;81 1b 88 77
SBB WORD [SI],0x7788 ..........;81 1c 88 77
SBB WORD [DI],0x7788 ..........;81 1d 88 77
SBB WORD [0x5566],0x7788 ......;81 1e 66 55 88 77
SBB WORD [BX],0x7788 ..........;81 1f 88 77
AND WORD [BX+SI],0x7788 .......;81 20 88 77
AND WORD [BX+DI],0x7788 .......;81 21 88 77
AND WORD [BP+SI],0x7788 .......;81 22 88 77
AND WORD [BP+DI],0x7788 .......;81 23 88 77
AND WORD [SI],0x7788 ..........;81 24 88 77
AND WORD [DI],0x7788 ..........;81 25 88 77
AND WORD [0x5566],0x7788 ......;81 26 66 55 88 77
AND WORD [BX],0x7788 ..........;81 27 88 77
SUB WORD [BX+SI],0x7788 .......;81 28 88 77
SUB WORD [BX+DI],0x7788 .......;81 29 88 77
SUB WORD [BP+SI],0x7788 .......;81 2a 88 77
SUB WORD [BP+DI],0x7788 .......;81 2b 88 77
SUB WORD [SI],0x7788 ..........;81 2c 88 77
```

```
SUB WORD [DI],0x7788 ...........;81 2d 88 77
SUB WORD [0x5566],0x7788 ......;81 2e 66 55 88 77
SUB WORD [BX],0x7788 ..........;81 2f 88 77
XOR WORD [BX+SI],0x7788 .......;81 30 88 77
XOR WORD [BX+DI],0x7788 .......;81 31 88 77
XOR WORD [BP+SI],0x7788 .......;81 32 88 77
XOR WORD [BP+DI],0x7788 .......;81 33 88 77
XOR WORD [SI],0x7788 ..........;81 34 88 77
XOR WORD [DI],0x7788 ..........;81 35 88 77
XOR WORD [0x5566],0x7788 ......;81 36 66 55 88 77
XOR WORD [BX],0x7788 ..........;81 37 88 77
CMP WORD [BX+SI],0x7788 .......;81 38 88 77
CMP WORD [BX+DI],0x7788 .......;81 39 88 77
CMP WORD [BP+SI],0x7788 .......;81 3a 88 77
CMP WORD [BP+DI],0x7788 .......;81 3b 88 77
CMP WORD [SI],0x7788 ..........;81 3c 88 77
CMP WORD [DI],0x7788 ..........;81 3d 88 77
CMP WORD [0x5566],0x7788 ......;81 3e 66 55 88 77
CMP WORD [BX],0x7788 ..........;81 3f 88 77
ADD WORD [BX+SI+0x55],0x7788 ...;81 40 55 88 77
ADD WORD [BX+DI+0x55],0x7788 ...;81 41 55 88 77
ADD WORD [BP+SI+0x55],0x7788 ...;81 42 55 88 77
ADD WORD [BP+DI+0x55],0x7788 ...;81 43 55 88 77
ADD WORD [SI+0x55],0x7788 .....;81 44 55 88 77
ADD WORD [DI+0x55],0x7788 .....;81 45 55 88 77
ADD WORD [BP+0x55],0x7788 .....;81 46 55 88 77
ADD WORD [BX+0x55],0x7788 .....;81 47 55 88 77
OR WORD [BX+SI+0x55],0x7788 ....;81 48 55 88 77
OR WORD [BX+DI+0x55],0x7788 ....;81 49 55 88 77
OR WORD [BP+SI+0x55],0x7788 ....;81 4a 55 88 77
OR WORD [BP+DI+0x55],0x7788 ....;81 4b 55 88 77
OR WORD [SI+0x55],0x7788 ......;81 4c 55 88 77
OR WORD [DI+0x55],0x7788 ......;81 4d 55 88 77
OR WORD [BP+0x55],0x7788 ......;81 4e 55 88 77
OR WORD [BX+0x55],0x7788 ......;81 4f 55 88 77
ADC WORD [BX+SI+0x55],0x7788 ...;81 50 55 88 77
ADC WORD [BX+DI+0x55],0x7788 ...;81 51 55 88 77
ADC WORD [BP+SI+0x55],0x7788 ...;81 52 55 88 77
ADC WORD [BP+DI+0x55],0x7788 ...;81 53 55 88 77
ADC WORD [SI+0x55],0x7788 .....;81 54 55 88 77
ADC WORD [DI+0x55],0x7788 .....;81 55 55 88 77
ADC WORD [BP+0x55],0x7788 .....;81 56 55 88 77
ADC WORD [BX+0x55],0x7788 .....;81 57 55 88 77
SBB WORD [BX+SI+0x55],0x7788 ...;81 58 55 88 77
SBB WORD [BX+DI+0x55],0x7788 ...;81 59 55 88 77
SBB WORD [BP+SI+0x55],0x7788 ...;81 5a 55 88 77
SBB WORD [BP+DI+0x55],0x7788 ...;81 5b 55 88 77
SBB WORD [SI+0x55],0x7788 .....;81 5c 55 88 77
SBB WORD [DI+0x55],0x7788 .....;81 5d 55 88 77
SBB WORD [BP+0x55],0x7788 .....;81 5e 55 88 77
SBB WORD [BX+0x55],0x7788 .....;81 5f 55 88 77
AND WORD [BX+SI+0x55],0x7788 ...;81 60 55 88 77
AND WORD [BX+DI+0x55],0x7788 ...;81 61 55 88 77
AND WORD [BP+SI+0x55],0x7788 ...;81 62 55 88 77
AND WORD [BP+DI+0x55],0x7788 ...;81 63 55 88 77
AND WORD [SI+0x55],0x7788 .....;81 64 55 88 77
AND WORD [DI+0x55],0x7788 .....;81 65 55 88 77
AND WORD [BP+0x55],0x7788 .....;81 66 55 88 77
AND WORD [BX+0x55],0x7788 .....;81 67 55 88 77
SUB WORD [BX+SI+0x55],0x7788 ...;81 68 55 88 77
SUB WORD [BX+DI+0x55],0x7788 ...;81 69 55 88 77
SUB WORD [BP+SI+0x55],0x7788 ...;81 6a 55 88 77
SUB WORD [BP+DI+0x55],0x7788 ...;81 6b 55 88 77
SUB WORD [SI+0x55],0x7788 .....;81 6c 55 88 77
SUB WORD [DI+0x55],0x7788 .....;81 6d 55 88 77
SUB WORD [BP+0x55],0x7788 .....;81 6e 55 88 77
SUB WORD [BX+0x55],0x7788 .....;81 6f 55 88 77
XOR WORD [BX+SI+0x55],0x7788 ...;81 70 55 88 77
XOR WORD [BX+DI+0x55],0x7788 ...;81 71 55 88 77
XOR WORD [BP+SI+0x55],0x7788 ...;81 72 55 88 77
XOR WORD [BP+DI+0x55],0x7788 ...;81 73 55 88 77
XOR WORD [SI+0x55],0x7788 .....;81 74 55 88 77
XOR WORD [DI+0x55],0x7788 .....;81 75 55 88 77
XOR WORD [BP+0x55],0x7788 .....;81 76 55 88 77
XOR WORD [BX+0x55],0x7788 .....;81 77 55 88 77
CMP WORD [BX+SI+0x55],0x7788 ...;81 78 55 88 77
CMP WORD [BX+DI+0x55],0x7788 ...;81 79 55 88 77
CMP WORD [BP+SI+0x55],0x7788 ...;81 7a 55 88 77
CMP WORD [BP+DI+0x55],0x7788 ...;81 7b 55 88 77
CMP WORD [SI+0x55],0x7788 .....;81 7c 55 88 77
CMP WORD [DI+0x55],0x7788 .....;81 7d 55 88 77
CMP WORD [BP+0x55],0x7788 .....;81 7e 55 88 77
CMP WORD [BX+0x55],0x7788 .....;81 7f 55 88 77
ADD WORD [BX+SI+0x5566],0x7788 .;81 80 66 55 88 77
ADD WORD [BX+DI+0x5566],0x7788 .;81 81 66 55 88 77
ADD WORD [BP+SI+0x5566],0x7788 .;81 82 66 55 88 77
ADD WORD [BP+DI+0x5566],0x7788 .;81 83 66 55 88 77
ADD WORD [SI+0x5566],0x7788 ....;81 84 66 55 88 77
ADD WORD [DI+0x5566],0x7788 ....;81 85 66 55 88 77
ADD WORD [BP+0x5566],0x7788 ....;81 86 66 55 88 77
ADD WORD [BX+0x5566],0x7788 ....;81 87 66 55 88 77
OR WORD [BX+SI+0x5566],0x7788 ..;81 88 66 55 88 77
OR WORD [BX+DI+0x5566],0x7788 ..;81 89 66 55 88 77
OR WORD [BP+SI+0x5566],0x7788 ..;81 8a 66 55 88 77
OR WORD [BP+DI+0x5566],0x7788 ..;81 8b 66 55 88 77
OR WORD [SI+0x5566],0x7788 .....;81 8c 66 55 88 77
OR WORD [DI+0x5566],0x7788 .....;81 8d 66 55 88 77
OR WORD [BP+0x5566],0x7788 .....;81 8e 66 55 88 77
OR WORD [BX+0x5566],0x7788 .....;81 8f 66 55 88 77
ADC WORD [BX+SI+0x5566],0x7788 .;81 90 66 55 88 77
ADC WORD [BX+DI+0x5566],0x7788 .;81 91 66 55 88 77
ADC WORD [BP+SI+0x5566],0x7788 .;81 92 66 55 88 77
ADC WORD [BP+DI+0x5566],0x7788 .;81 93 66 55 88 77
ADC WORD [SI+0x5566],0x7788 ....;81 94 66 55 88 77
ADC WORD [DI+0x5566],0x7788 ....;81 95 66 55 88 77
ADC WORD [BP+0x5566],0x7788 ....;81 96 66 55 88 77
ADC WORD [BX+0x5566],0x7788 ....;81 97 66 55 88 77
SBB WORD [BX+SI+0x5566],0x7788 .;81 98 66 55 88 77
SBB WORD [BX+DI+0x5566],0x7788 .;81 99 66 55 88 77
SBB WORD [BP+SI+0x5566],0x7788 .;81 9a 66 55 88 77
SBB WORD [BP+DI+0x5566],0x7788 .;81 9b 66 55 88 77
SBB WORD [SI+0x5566],0x7788 ....;81 9c 66 55 88 77
SBB WORD [DI+0x5566],0x7788 ....;81 9d 66 55 88 77
SBB WORD [BP+0x5566],0x7788 ....;81 9e 66 55 88 77
SBB WORD [BX+0x5566],0x7788 ....;81 9f 66 55 88 77
AND WORD [BX+SI+0x5566],0x7788 .;81 a0 66 55 88 77
AND WORD [BX+DI+0x5566],0x7788 .;81 a1 66 55 88 77
AND WORD [BP+SI+0x5566],0x7788 .;81 a2 66 55 88 77
AND WORD [BP+DI+0x5566],0x7788 .;81 a3 66 55 88 77
AND WORD [SI+0x5566],0x7788 ....;81 a4 66 55 88 77
AND WORD [DI+0x5566],0x7788 ....;81 a5 66 55 88 77
AND WORD [BP+0x5566],0x7788 ....;81 a6 66 55 88 77
AND WORD [BX+0x5566],0x7788 ....;81 a7 66 55 88 77
SUB WORD [BX+SI+0x5566],0x7788 .;81 a8 66 55 88 77
SUB WORD [BX+DI+0x5566],0x7788 .;81 a9 66 55 88 77
SUB WORD [BP+SI+0x5566],0x7788 .;81 aa 66 55 88 77
SUB WORD [BP+DI+0x5566],0x7788 .;81 ab 66 55 88 77
SUB WORD [SI+0x5566],0x7788 ....;81 ac 66 55 88 77
SUB WORD [DI+0x5566],0x7788 ....;81 ad 66 55 88 77
SUB WORD [BP+0x5566],0x7788 ....;81 ae 66 55 88 77
SUB WORD [BX+0x5566],0x7788 ....;81 af 66 55 88 77
XOR WORD [BX+SI+0x5566],0x7788 .;81 b0 66 55 88 77
XOR WORD [BX+DI+0x5566],0x7788 .;81 b1 66 55 88 77
XOR WORD [BP+SI+0x5566],0x7788 .;81 b2 66 55 88 77
XOR WORD [BP+DI+0x5566],0x7788 .;81 b3 66 55 88 77
XOR WORD [SI+0x5566],0x7788 ....;81 b4 66 55 88 77
XOR WORD [DI+0x5566],0x7788 ....;81 b5 66 55 88 77
XOR WORD [BP+0x5566],0x7788 ....;81 b6 66 55 88 77
XOR WORD [BX+0x5566],0x7788 ....;81 b7 66 55 88 77
CMP WORD [BX+SI+0x5566],0x7788 .;81 b8 66 55 88 77
CMP WORD [BX+DI+0x5566],0x7788 .;81 b9 66 55 88 77
CMP WORD [BP+SI+0x5566],0x7788 .;81 ba 66 55 88 77
CMP WORD [BP+DI+0x5566],0x7788 .;81 bb 66 55 88 77
CMP WORD [SI+0x5566],0x7788 ....;81 bc 66 55 88 77
CMP WORD [DI+0x5566],0x7788 ....;81 bd 66 55 88 77
CMP WORD [BP+0x5566],0x7788 ....;81 be 66 55 88 77
CMP WORD [BX+0x5566],0x7788 ....;81 bf 66 55 88 77
ADD AX,0x7788 ................;81 c0 88 77
ADD CX,0x7788 ................;81 c1 88 77
ADD DX,0x7788 ................;81 c2 88 77
ADD BX,0x7788 ................;81 c3 88 77
ADD SP,0x7788 ................;81 c4 88 77
ADD BP,0x7788 ................;81 c5 88 77
ADD SI,0x7788 ................;81 c6 88 77
ADD DI,0x7788 ................;81 c7 88 77
OR AX,0x7788 .................;81 c8 88 77
OR CX,0x7788 .................;81 c9 88 77
OR DX,0x7788 .................;81 ca 88 77
OR BX,0x7788 .................;81 cb 88 77
OR SP,0x7788 .................;81 cc 88 77
OR BP,0x7788 .................;81 cd 88 77
OR SI,0x7788 .................;81 ce 88 77
OR DI,0x7788 .................;81 cf 88 77
ADC AX,0x7788 ................;81 d0 88 77
ADC CX,0x7788 ................;81 d1 88 77
ADC DX,0x7788 ................;81 d2 88 77
ADC BX,0x7788 ................;81 d3 88 77
ADC SP,0x7788 ................;81 d4 88 77
ADC BP,0x7788 ................;81 d5 88 77
ADC SI,0x7788 ................;81 d6 88 77
ADC DI,0x7788 ................;81 d7 88 77
SBB AX,0x7788 ................;81 d8 88 77
SBB CX,0x7788 ................;81 d9 88 77
SBB DX,0x7788 ................;81 da 88 77
SBB BX,0x7788 ................;81 db 88 77
SBB SP,0x7788 ................;81 dc 88 77
SBB BP,0x7788 ................;81 dd 88 77
SBB SI,0x7788 ................;81 de 88 77
```

```
SBB DI,0x7788 ................;81 df 88 77        CMP WORD [BX+SI],0x77 ........;83 38 77
AND AX,0x7788 ................;81 e0 88 77        CMP WORD [BX+DI],0x77 ........;83 39 77
AND CX,0x7788 ................;81 e1 88 77        CMP WORD [BP+SI],0x77 ........;83 3a 77
AND DX,0x7788 ................;81 e2 88 77        CMP WORD [BP+DI],0x77 ........;83 3b 77
AND BX,0x7788 ................;81 e3 88 77        CMP WORD [SI],0x77 ...........;83 3c 77
AND SP,0x7788 ................;81 e4 88 77        CMP WORD [DI],0x77 ...........;83 3d 77
AND BP,0x7788 ................;81 e5 88 77        CMP WORD [0x5566],0x77 .......;83 3e 66 55 77
AND SI,0x7788 ................;81 e6 88 77        CMP WORD [BX],0x77 ...........;83 3f 77
AND DI,0x7788 ................;81 e7 88 77        ADD WORD [BX+SI+0x55],0x77 ...;83 40 55 77
SUB AX,0x7788 ................;81 e8 88 77        ADD WORD [BX+DI+0x55],0x77 ...;83 41 55 77
SUB CX,0x7788 ................;81 e9 88 77        ADD WORD [BP+SI+0x55],0x77 ...;83 42 55 77
SUB DX,0x7788 ................;81 ea 88 77        ADD WORD [BP+DI+0x55],0x77 ...;83 43 55 77
SUB BX,0x7788 ................;81 eb 88 77        ADD WORD [SI+0x55],0x77 ......;83 44 55 77
SUB SP,0x7788 ................;81 ec 88 77        ADD WORD [DI+0x55],0x77 ......;83 45 55 77
SUB BP,0x7788 ................;81 ed 88 77        ADD WORD [BP+0x55],0x77 ......;83 46 55 77
SUB SI,0x7788 ................;81 ee 88 77        ADD WORD [BX+0x55],0x77 ......;83 47 55 77
SUB DI,0x7788 ................;81 ef 88 77        OR WORD [BX+SI+0x55],0x77 ....;83 48 55 77
XOR AX,0x7788 ................;81 f0 88 77        OR WORD [BX+DI+0x55],0x77 ....;83 49 55 77
XOR CX,0x7788 ................;81 f1 88 77        OR WORD [BP+SI+0x55],0x77 ....;83 4a 55 77
XOR DX,0x7788 ................;81 f2 88 77        OR WORD [BP+DI+0x55],0x77 ....;83 4b 55 77
XOR BX,0x7788 ................;81 f3 88 77        OR WORD [SI+0x55],0x77 .......;83 4c 55 77
XOR SP,0x7788 ................;81 f4 88 77        OR WORD [DI+0x55],0x77 .......;83 4d 55 77
XOR BP,0x7788 ................;81 f5 88 77        OR WORD [BP+0x55],0x77 .......;83 4e 55 77
XOR SI,0x7788 ................;81 f6 88 77        OR WORD [BX+0x55],0x77 .......;83 4f 55 77
XOR DI,0x7788 ................;81 f7 88 77        ADC WORD [BX+SI+0x55],0x77 ...;83 50 55 77
CMP AX,0x7788 ................;81 f8 88 77        ADC WORD [BX+DI+0x55],0x77 ...;83 51 55 77
CMP CX,0x7788 ................;81 f9 88 77        ADC WORD [BP+SI+0x55],0x77 ...;83 52 55 77
CMP DX,0x7788 ................;81 fa 88 77        ADC WORD [BP+DI+0x55],0x77 ...;83 53 55 77
CMP BX,0x7788 ................;81 fb 88 77        ADC WORD [SI+0x55],0x77 ......;83 54 55 77
CMP SP,0x7788 ................;81 fc 88 77        ADC WORD [DI+0x55],0x77 ......;83 55 55 77
CMP BP,0x7788 ................;81 fd 88 77        ADC WORD [BP+0x55],0x77 ......;83 56 55 77
CMP SI,0x7788 ................;81 fe 88 77        ADC WORD [BX+0x55],0x77 ......;83 57 55 77
CMP DI,0x7788 ................;81 ff 88 77        SBB WORD [BX+SI+0x55],0x77 ...;83 58 55 77
ADD WORD [BX+SI],0x77 ........;83 00 77           SBB WORD [BX+DI+0x55],0x77 ...;83 59 55 77
ADD WORD [BX+DI],0x77 ........;83 01 77           SBB WORD [BP+SI+0x55],0x77 ...;83 5a 55 77
ADD WORD [BP+SI],0x77 ........;83 02 77           SBB WORD [BP+DI+0x55],0x77 ...;83 5b 55 77
ADD WORD [BP+DI],0x77 ........;83 03 77           SBB WORD [SI+0x55],0x77 ......;83 5c 55 77
ADD WORD [SI],0x77 ...........;83 04 77           SBB WORD [DI+0x55],0x77 ......;83 5d 55 77
ADD WORD [DI],0x77 ...........;83 05 77           SBB WORD [BP+0x55],0x77 ......;83 5e 55 77
ADD WORD [0x5566],0x77 .......;83 06 66 55 77     SBB WORD [BX+0x55],0x77 ......;83 5f 55 77
ADD WORD [BX],0x77 ...........;83 07 77           AND WORD [BX+SI+0x55],0x77 ...;83 60 55 77
OR WORD [BX+SI],0x77 .........;83 08 77           AND WORD [BX+DI+0x55],0x77 ...;83 61 55 77
OR WORD [BX+DI],0x77 .........;83 09 77           AND WORD [BP+SI+0x55],0x77 ...;83 62 55 77
OR WORD [BP+SI],0x77 .........;83 0a 77           AND WORD [BP+DI+0x55],0x77 ...;83 63 55 77
OR WORD [BP+DI],0x77 .........;83 0b 77           AND WORD [SI+0x55],0x77 ......;83 64 55 77
OR WORD [SI],0x77 ............;83 0c 77           AND WORD [DI+0x55],0x77 ......;83 65 55 77
OR WORD [DI],0x77 ............;83 0d 77           AND WORD [BP+0x55],0x77 ......;83 66 55 77
OR WORD [0x5566],0x77 ........;83 0e 66 55 77     AND WORD [BX+0x55],0x77 ......;83 67 55 77
OR WORD [BX],0x77 ............;83 0f 77           SUB WORD [BX+SI+0x55],0x77 ...;83 68 55 77
ADC WORD [BX+SI],0x77 ........;83 10 77           SUB WORD [BX+DI+0x55],0x77 ...;83 69 55 77
ADC WORD [BX+DI],0x77 ........;83 11 77           SUB WORD [BP+SI+0x55],0x77 ...;83 6a 55 77
ADC WORD [BP+SI],0x77 ........;83 12 77           SUB WORD [BP+DI+0x55],0x77 ...;83 6b 55 77
ADC WORD [BP+DI],0x77 ........;83 13 77           SUB WORD [SI+0x55],0x77 ......;83 6c 55 77
ADC WORD [SI],0x77 ...........;83 14 77           SUB WORD [DI+0x55],0x77 ......;83 6d 55 77
ADC WORD [DI],0x77 ...........;83 15 77           SUB WORD [BP+0x55],0x77 ......;83 6e 55 77
ADC WORD [0x5566],0x77 .......;83 16 66 55 77     SUB WORD [BX+0x55],0x77 ......;83 6f 55 77
ADC WORD [BX],0x77 ...........;83 17 77           XOR WORD [BX+SI+0x55],0x77 ...;83 70 55 77
SBB WORD [BX+SI],0x77 ........;83 18 77           XOR WORD [BX+DI+0x55],0x77 ...;83 71 55 77
SBB WORD [BX+DI],0x77 ........;83 19 77           XOR WORD [BP+SI+0x55],0x77 ...;83 72 55 77
SBB WORD [BP+SI],0x77 ........;83 1a 77           XOR WORD [BP+DI+0x55],0x77 ...;83 73 55 77
SBB WORD [BP+DI],0x77 ........;83 1b 77           XOR WORD [SI+0x55],0x77 ......;83 74 55 77
SBB WORD [SI],0x77 ...........;83 1c 77           XOR WORD [DI+0x55],0x77 ......;83 75 55 77
SBB WORD [DI],0x77 ...........;83 1d 77           XOR WORD [BP+0x55],0x77 ......;83 76 55 77
SBB WORD [0x5566],0x77 .......;83 1e 66 55 77     XOR WORD [BX+0x55],0x77 ......;83 77 55 77
SBB WORD [BX],0x77 ...........;83 1f 77           CMP WORD [BX+SI+0x55],0x77 ...;83 78 55 77
AND WORD [BX+SI],0x77 ........;83 20 77           CMP WORD [BX+DI+0x55],0x77 ...;83 79 55 77
AND WORD [BX+DI],0x77 ........;83 21 77           CMP WORD [BP+SI+0x55],0x77 ...;83 7a 55 77
AND WORD [BP+SI],0x77 ........;83 22 77           CMP WORD [BP+DI+0x55],0x77 ...;83 7b 55 77
AND WORD [BP+DI],0x77 ........;83 23 77           CMP WORD [SI+0x55],0x77 ......;83 7c 55 77
AND WORD [SI],0x77 ...........;83 24 77           CMP WORD [DI+0x55],0x77 ......;83 7d 55 77
AND WORD [DI],0x77 ...........;83 25 77           CMP WORD [BP+0x55],0x77 ......;83 7e 55 77
AND WORD [0x5566],0x77 .......;83 26 66 55 77     CMP WORD [BX+0x55],0x77 ......;83 7f 55 77
AND WORD [BX],0x77 ...........;83 27 77           ADD WORD [BX+SI+0x5566],0x77 ...;83 80 66 55 77
SUB WORD [BX+SI],0x77 ........;83 28 77           ADD WORD [BX+DI+0x5566],0x77 ...;83 81 66 55 77
SUB WORD [BX+DI],0x77 ........;83 29 77           ADD WORD [BP+SI+0x5566],0x77 ...;83 82 66 55 77
SUB WORD [BP+SI],0x77 ........;83 2a 77           ADD WORD [BP+DI+0x5566],0x77 ...;83 83 66 55 77
SUB WORD [BP+DI],0x77 ........;83 2b 77           ADD WORD [SI+0x5566],0x77 ......;83 84 66 55 77
SUB WORD [SI],0x77 ...........;83 2c 77           ADD WORD [DI+0x5566],0x77 ......;83 85 66 55 77
SUB WORD [DI],0x77 ...........;83 2d 77           ADD WORD [BP+0x5566],0x77 ......;83 86 66 55 77
SUB WORD [0x5566],0x77 .......;83 2e 66 55 77     ADD WORD [BX+0x5566],0x77 ......;83 87 66 55 77
SUB WORD [BX],0x77 ...........;83 2f 77           OR WORD [BX+SI+0x5566],0x77 ...;83 88 66 55 77
XOR WORD [BX+SI],0x77 ........;83 30 77           OR WORD [BX+DI+0x5566],0x77 ...;83 89 66 55 77
XOR WORD [BX+DI],0x77 ........;83 31 77           OR WORD [BP+SI+0x5566],0x77 ...;83 8a 66 55 77
XOR WORD [BP+SI],0x77 ........;83 32 77           OR WORD [BP+DI+0x5566],0x77 ...;83 8b 66 55 77
XOR WORD [BP+DI],0x77 ........;83 33 77           OR WORD [SI+0x5566],0x77 ......;83 8c 66 55 77
XOR WORD [SI],0x77 ...........;83 34 77           OR WORD [DI+0x5566],0x77 ......;83 8d 66 55 77
XOR WORD [DI],0x77 ...........;83 35 77           OR WORD [BP+0x5566],0x77 ......;83 8e 66 55 77
XOR WORD [0x5566],0x77 .......;83 36 66 55 77     OR WORD [BX+0x5566],0x77 ......;83 8f 66 55 77
XOR WORD [BX],0x77 ...........;83 37 77           ADC WORD [BX+SI+0x5566],0x77 ...;83 90 66 55 77
```

```
ADC WORD [BX+DI+0x5566],0x77 ...;83 91 66 55 77
ADC WORD [BP+SI+0x5566],0x77 ...;83 92 66 55 77
ADC WORD [BP+DI+0x5566],0x77 ...;83 93 66 55 77
ADC WORD [SI+0x5566],0x77 ......;83 94 66 55 77
ADC WORD [DI+0x5566],0x77 ......;83 95 66 55 77
ADC WORD [BP+0x5566],0x77 ......;83 96 66 55 77
ADC WORD [BX+0x5566],0x77 ......;83 97 66 55 77
SBB WORD [BX+SI+0x5566],0x77 ...;83 98 66 55 77
SBB WORD [BX+DI+0x5566],0x77 ...;83 99 66 55 77
SBB WORD [BP+SI+0x5566],0x77 ...;83 9a 66 55 77
SBB WORD [BP+DI+0x5566],0x77 ...;83 9b 66 55 77
SBB WORD [SI+0x5566],0x77 ......;83 9c 66 55 77
SBB WORD [DI+0x5566],0x77 ......;83 9d 66 55 77
SBB WORD [BP+0x5566],0x77 ......;83 9e 66 55 77
SBB WORD [BX+0x5566],0x77 ......;83 9f 66 55 77
AND WORD [BX+SI+0x5566],0x77 ...;83 a0 66 55 77
AND WORD [BX+DI+0x5566],0x77 ...;83 a1 66 55 77
AND WORD [BP+SI+0x5566],0x77 ...;83 a2 66 55 77
AND WORD [BP+DI+0x5566],0x77 ...;83 a3 66 55 77
AND WORD [SI+0x5566],0x77 ......;83 a4 66 55 77
AND WORD [DI+0x5566],0x77 ......;83 a5 66 55 77
AND WORD [BP+0x5566],0x77 ......;83 a6 66 55 77
AND WORD [BX+0x5566],0x77 ......;83 a7 66 55 77
SUB WORD [BX+SI+0x5566],0x77 ...;83 a8 66 55 77
SUB WORD [BX+DI+0x5566],0x77 ...;83 a9 66 55 77
SUB WORD [BP+SI+0x5566],0x77 ...;83 aa 66 55 77
SUB WORD [BP+DI+0x5566],0x77 ...;83 ab 66 55 77
SUB WORD [SI+0x5566],0x77 ......;83 ac 66 55 77
SUB WORD [DI+0x5566],0x77 ......;83 ad 66 55 77
SUB WORD [BP+0x5566],0x77 ......;83 ae 66 55 77
SUB WORD [BX+0x5566],0x77 ......;83 af 66 55 77
XOR WORD [BX+SI+0x5566],0x77 ...;83 b0 66 55 77
XOR WORD [BX+DI+0x5566],0x77 ...;83 b1 66 55 77
XOR WORD [BP+SI+0x5566],0x77 ...;83 b2 66 55 77
XOR WORD [BP+DI+0x5566],0x77 ...;83 b3 66 55 77
XOR WORD [SI+0x5566],0x77 ......;83 b4 66 55 77
XOR WORD [DI+0x5566],0x77 ......;83 b5 66 55 77
XOR WORD [BP+0x5566],0x77 ......;83 b6 66 55 77
XOR WORD [BX+0x5566],0x77 ......;83 b7 66 55 77
CMP WORD [BX+SI+0x5566],0x77 ...;83 b8 66 55 77
CMP WORD [BX+DI+0x5566],0x77 ...;83 b9 66 55 77
CMP WORD [BP+SI+0x5566],0x77 ...;83 ba 66 55 77
CMP WORD [BP+DI+0x5566],0x77 ...;83 bb 66 55 77
CMP WORD [SI+0x5566],0x77 ......;83 bc 66 55 77
CMP WORD [DI+0x5566],0x77 ......;83 bd 66 55 77
CMP WORD [BP+0x5566],0x77 ......;83 be 66 55 77
CMP WORD [BX+0x5566],0x77 ......;83 bf 66 55 77
ADD AX,0x77 ....................;83 c0 77
ADD CX,0x77 ....................;83 c1 77
ADD DX,0x77 ....................;83 c2 77
ADD BX,0x77 ....................;83 c3 77
ADD SP,0x77 ....................;83 c4 77
ADD BP,0x77 ....................;83 c5 77
ADD SI,0x77 ....................;83 c6 77
ADD DI,0x77 ....................;83 c7 77
OR AX,0x77 .....................;83 c8 77
OR CX,0x77 .....................;83 c9 77
OR DX,0x77 .....................;83 ca 77
OR BX,0x77 .....................;83 cb 77
OR SP,0x77 .....................;83 cc 77
OR BP,0x77 .....................;83 cd 77
OR SI,0x77 .....................;83 ce 77
OR DI,0x77 .....................;83 cf 77
ADC AX,0x77 ....................;83 d0 77
ADC CX,0x77 ....................;83 d1 77
ADC DX,0x77 ....................;83 d2 77
ADC BX,0x77 ....................;83 d3 77
ADC SP,0x77 ....................;83 d4 77
ADC BP,0x77 ....................;83 d5 77
ADC SI,0x77 ....................;83 d6 77
ADC DI,0x77 ....................;83 d7 77
SBB AX,0x77 ....................;83 d8 77
SBB CX,0x77 ....................;83 d9 77
SBB DX,0x77 ....................;83 da 77
SBB BX,0x77 ....................;83 db 77
SBB SP,0x77 ....................;83 dc 77
SBB BP,0x77 ....................;83 dd 77
SBB SI,0x77 ....................;83 de 77
SBB DI,0x77 ....................;83 df 77
AND AX,0x77 ....................;83 e0 77
AND CX,0x77 ....................;83 e1 77
AND DX,0x77 ....................;83 e2 77
AND BX,0x77 ....................;83 e3 77
AND SP,0x77 ....................;83 e4 77
AND BP,0x77 ....................;83 e5 77
AND SI,0x77 ....................;83 e6 77
AND DI,0x77 ....................;83 e7 77
SUB AX,0x77 ....................;83 e8 77
SUB CX,0x77 ....................;83 e9 77

SUB DX,0x77 ....................;83 ea 77
SUB BX,0x77 ....................;83 eb 77
SUB SP,0x77 ....................;83 ec 77
SUB BP,0x77 ....................;83 ed 77
SUB SI,0x77 ....................;83 ee 77
SUB DI,0x77 ....................;83 ef 77
XOR AX,0x77 ....................;83 f0 77
XOR CX,0x77 ....................;83 f1 77
XOR DX,0x77 ....................;83 f2 77
XOR BX,0x77 ....................;83 f3 77
XOR SP,0x77 ....................;83 f4 77
XOR BP,0x77 ....................;83 f5 77
XOR SI,0x77 ....................;83 f6 77
XOR DI,0x77 ....................;83 f7 77
CMP AX,0x77 ....................;83 f8 77
CMP CX,0x77 ....................;83 f9 77
CMP DX,0x77 ....................;83 fa 77
CMP BX,0x77 ....................;83 fb 77
CMP SP,0x77 ....................;83 fc 77
CMP BP,0x77 ....................;83 fd 77
CMP SI,0x77 ....................;83 fe 77
CMP DI,0x77 ....................;83 ff 77
TEST [BX+SI],AL ................;84 00
TEST [BX+DI],AL ................;84 01
TEST [BP+SI],AL ................;84 02
TEST [BP+DI],AL ................;84 03
TEST [SI],AL ...................;84 04
TEST [DI],AL ...................;84 05
TEST [0x5566],AL ...............;84 06 66 55
TEST [BX],AL ...................;84 07
TEST [BX+SI],CL ................;84 08
TEST [BX+DI],CL ................;84 09
TEST [BP+SI],CL ................;84 0a
TEST [BP+DI],CL ................;84 0b
TEST [SI],CL ...................;84 0c
TEST [DI],CL ...................;84 0d
TEST [0x5566],CL ...............;84 0e 66 55
TEST [BX],CL ...................;84 0f
TEST [BX+SI],DL ................;84 10
TEST [BX+DI],DL ................;84 11
TEST [BP+SI],DL ................;84 12
TEST [BP+DI],DL ................;84 13
TEST [SI],DL ...................;84 14
TEST [DI],DL ...................;84 15
TEST [0x5566],DL ...............;84 16 66 55
TEST [BX],DL ...................;84 17
TEST [BX+SI],BL ................;84 18
TEST [BX+DI],BL ................;84 19
TEST [BP+SI],BL ................;84 1a
TEST [BP+DI],BL ................;84 1b
TEST [SI],BL ...................;84 1c
TEST [DI],BL ...................;84 1d
TEST [0x5566],BL ...............;84 1e 66 55
TEST [BX],BL ...................;84 1f
TEST [BX+SI],AH ................;84 20
TEST [BX+DI],AH ................;84 21
TEST [BP+SI],AH ................;84 22
TEST [BP+DI],AH ................;84 23
TEST [SI],AH ...................;84 24
TEST [DI],AH ...................;84 25
TEST [0x5566],AH ...............;84 26 66 55
TEST [BX],AH ...................;84 27
TEST [BX+SI],CH ................;84 28
TEST [BX+DI],CH ................;84 29
TEST [BP+SI],CH ................;84 2a
TEST [BP+DI],CH ................;84 2b
TEST [SI],CH ...................;84 2c
TEST [DI],CH ...................;84 2d
TEST [0x5566],CH ...............;84 2e 66 55
TEST [BX],CH ...................;84 2f
TEST [BX+SI],DH ................;84 30
TEST [BX+DI],DH ................;84 31
TEST [BP+SI],DH ................;84 32
TEST [BP+DI],DH ................;84 33
TEST [SI],DH ...................;84 34
TEST [DI],DH ...................;84 35
TEST [0x5566],DH ...............;84 36 66 55
TEST [BX],DH ...................;84 37
TEST [BX+SI],BH ................;84 38
TEST [BX+DI],BH ................;84 39
TEST [BP+SI],BH ................;84 3a
TEST [BP+DI],BH ................;84 3b
TEST [SI],BH ...................;84 3c
TEST [DI],BH ...................;84 3d
TEST [0x5566],BH ...............;84 3e 66 55
TEST [BX],BH ...................;84 3f
TEST [BX+SI+0x55],AL ...........;84 40 55
TEST [BX+DI+0x55],AL ...........;84 41 55
TEST [BP+SI+0x55],AL ...........;84 42 55
```

```
TEST [BP+DI+0x55],AL ...........;84 43 55        TEST [SI+0x5566],BL ............;84 9c 66 55
TEST [SI+0x55],AL .............;84 44 55         TEST [DI+0x5566],BL ............;84 9d 66 55
TEST [DI+0x55],AL .............;84 45 55         TEST [BP+0x5566],BL ............;84 9e 66 55
TEST [BP+0x55],AL .............;84 46 55         TEST [BX+0x5566],BL ............;84 9f 66 55
TEST [BX+0x55],AL .............;84 47 55         TEST [BX+SI+0x5566],AH .........;84 a0 66 55
TEST [BX+SI+0x55],CL ..........;84 48 55         TEST [BX+DI+0x5566],AH .........;84 a1 66 55
TEST [BX+DI+0x55],CL ..........;84 49 55         TEST [BP+SI+0x5566],AH .........;84 a2 66 55
TEST [BP+SI+0x55],CL ..........;84 4a 55         TEST [BP+DI+0x5566],AH .........;84 a3 66 55
TEST [BP+DI+0x55],CL ..........;84 4b 55         TEST [SI+0x5566],AH ............;84 a4 66 55
TEST [SI+0x55],CL .............;84 4c 55         TEST [DI+0x5566],AH ............;84 a5 66 55
TEST [DI+0x55],CL .............;84 4d 55         TEST [BP+0x5566],AH ............;84 a6 66 55
TEST [BP+0x55],CL .............;84 4e 55         TEST [BX+0x5566],AH ............;84 a7 66 55
TEST [BX+0x55],CL .............;84 4f 55         TEST [BX+SI+0x5566],CH .........;84 a8 66 55
TEST [BX+SI+0x55],DL ..........;84 50 55         TEST [BX+DI+0x5566],CH .........;84 a9 66 55
TEST [BX+DI+0x55],DL ..........;84 51 55         TEST [BP+SI+0x5566],CH .........;84 aa 66 55
TEST [BP+SI+0x55],DL ..........;84 52 55         TEST [BP+DI+0x5566],CH .........;84 ab 66 55
TEST [BP+DI+0x55],DL ..........;84 53 55         TEST [SI+0x5566],CH ............;84 ac 66 55
TEST [SI+0x55],DL .............;84 54 55         TEST [DI+0x5566],CH ............;84 ad 66 55
TEST [DI+0x55],DL .............;84 55 55         TEST [BP+0x5566],CH ............;84 ae 66 55
TEST [BP+0x55],DL .............;84 56 55         TEST [BX+0x5566],CH ............;84 af 66 55
TEST [BX+0x55],DL .............;84 57 55         TEST [BX+SI+0x5566],DH .........;84 b0 66 55
TEST [BX+SI+0x55],BL ..........;84 58 55         TEST [BX+DI+0x5566],DH .........;84 b1 66 55
TEST [BX+DI+0x55],BL ..........;84 59 55         TEST [BP+SI+0x5566],DH .........;84 b2 66 55
TEST [BP+SI+0x55],BL ..........;84 5a 55         TEST [BP+DI+0x5566],DH .........;84 b3 66 55
TEST [BP+DI+0x55],BL ..........;84 5b 55         TEST [SI+0x5566],DH ............;84 b4 66 55
TEST [SI+0x55],BL .............;84 5c 55         TEST [DI+0x5566],DH ............;84 b5 66 55
TEST [DI+0x55],BL .............;84 5d 55         TEST [BP+0x5566],DH ............;84 b6 66 55
TEST [BP+0x55],BL .............;84 5e 55         TEST [BX+0x5566],DH ............;84 b7 66 55
TEST [BX+0x55],BL .............;84 5f 55         TEST [BX+SI+0x5566],BH .........;84 b8 66 55
TEST [BX+SI+0x55],AH ..........;84 60 55         TEST [BX+DI+0x5566],BH .........;84 b9 66 55
TEST [BX+DI+0x55],AH ..........;84 61 55         TEST [BP+SI+0x5566],BH .........;84 ba 66 55
TEST [BP+SI+0x55],AH ..........;84 62 55         TEST [BP+DI+0x5566],BH .........;84 bb 66 55
TEST [BP+DI+0x55],AH ..........;84 63 55         TEST [SI+0x5566],BH ............;84 bc 66 55
TEST [SI+0x55],AH .............;84 64 55         TEST [DI+0x5566],BH ............;84 bd 66 55
TEST [DI+0x55],AH .............;84 65 55         TEST [BP+0x5566],BH ............;84 be 66 55
TEST [BP+0x55],AH .............;84 66 55         TEST [BX+0x5566],BH ............;84 bf 66 55
TEST [BX+0x55],AH .............;84 67 55         TEST AL,AL ....................;84 c0
TEST [BX+SI+0x55],CH ..........;84 68 55         TEST CL,AL ....................;84 c1
TEST [BX+DI+0x55],CH ..........;84 69 55         TEST DL,AL ....................;84 c2
TEST [BP+SI+0x55],CH ..........;84 6a 55         TEST BL,AL ....................;84 c3
TEST [BP+DI+0x55],CH ..........;84 6b 55         TEST AH,AL ....................;84 c4
TEST [SI+0x55],CH .............;84 6c 55         TEST CH,AL ....................;84 c5
TEST [DI+0x55],CH .............;84 6d 55         TEST DH,AL ....................;84 c6
TEST [BP+0x55],CH .............;84 6e 55         TEST BH,AL ....................;84 c7
TEST [BX+0x55],CH .............;84 6f 55         TEST AL,CL ....................;84 c8
TEST [BX+SI+0x55],DH ..........;84 70 55         TEST CL,CL ....................;84 c9
TEST [BX+DI+0x55],DH ..........;84 71 55         TEST DL,CL ....................;84 ca
TEST [BP+SI+0x55],DH ..........;84 72 55         TEST BL,CL ....................;84 cb
TEST [BP+DI+0x55],DH ..........;84 73 55         TEST AH,CL ....................;84 cc
TEST [SI+0x55],DH .............;84 74 55         TEST CH,CL ....................;84 cd
TEST [DI+0x55],DH .............;84 75 55         TEST DH,CL ....................;84 ce
TEST [BP+0x55],DH .............;84 76 55         TEST BH,CL ....................;84 cf
TEST [BX+0x55],DH .............;84 77 55         TEST AL,DL ....................;84 d0
TEST [BX+SI+0x55],BH ..........;84 78 55         TEST CL,DL ....................;84 d1
TEST [BX+DI+0x55],BH ..........;84 79 55         TEST DL,DL ....................;84 d2
TEST [BP+SI+0x55],BH ..........;84 7a 55         TEST BL,DL ....................;84 d3
TEST [BP+DI+0x55],BH ..........;84 7b 55         TEST AH,DL ....................;84 d4
TEST [SI+0x55],BH .............;84 7c 55         TEST CH,DL ....................;84 d5
TEST [DI+0x55],BH .............;84 7d 55         TEST DH,DL ....................;84 d6
TEST [BP+0x55],BH .............;84 7e 55         TEST BH,DL ....................;84 d7
TEST [BX+0x55],BH .............;84 7f 55         TEST AL,BL ....................;84 d8
TEST [BX+SI+0x5566],AL .........;84 80 66 55     TEST CL,BL ....................;84 d9
TEST [BX+DI+0x5566],AL .........;84 81 66 55     TEST DL,BL ....................;84 da
TEST [BP+SI+0x5566],AL .........;84 82 66 55     TEST BL,BL ....................;84 db
TEST [BP+DI+0x5566],AL .........;84 83 66 55     TEST AH,BL ....................;84 dc
TEST [SI+0x5566],AL ............;84 84 66 55     TEST CH,BL ....................;84 dd
TEST [DI+0x5566],AL ............;84 85 66 55     TEST DH,BL ....................;84 de
TEST [BP+0x5566],AL ............;84 86 66 55     TEST BH,BL ....................;84 df
TEST [BX+0x5566],AL ............;84 87 66 55     TEST AL,AH ....................;84 e0
TEST [BX+SI+0x5566],CL .........;84 88 66 55     TEST CL,AH ....................;84 e1
TEST [BX+DI+0x5566],CL .........;84 89 66 55     TEST DL,AH ....................;84 e2
TEST [BP+SI+0x5566],CL .........;84 8a 66 55     TEST BL,AH ....................;84 e3
TEST [BP+DI+0x5566],CL .........;84 8b 66 55     TEST AH,AH ....................;84 e4
TEST [SI+0x5566],CL ............;84 8c 66 55     TEST CH,AH ....................;84 e5
TEST [DI+0x5566],CL ............;84 8d 66 55     TEST DH,AH ....................;84 e6
TEST [BP+0x5566],CL ............;84 8e 66 55     TEST BH,AH ....................;84 e7
TEST [BX+0x5566],CL ............;84 8f 66 55     TEST AL,CH ....................;84 e8
TEST [BX+SI+0x5566],DL .........;84 90 66 55     TEST CL,CH ....................;84 e9
TEST [BX+DI+0x5566],DL .........;84 91 66 55     TEST DL,CH ....................;84 ea
TEST [BP+SI+0x5566],DL .........;84 92 66 55     TEST BL,CH ....................;84 eb
TEST [BP+DI+0x5566],DL .........;84 93 66 55     TEST AH,CH ....................;84 ec
TEST [SI+0x5566],DL ............;84 94 66 55     TEST CH,CH ....................;84 ed
TEST [DI+0x5566],DL ............;84 95 66 55     TEST DH,CH ....................;84 ee
TEST [BP+0x5566],DL ............;84 96 66 55     TEST BH,CH ....................;84 ef
TEST [BX+0x5566],DL ............;84 97 66 55     TEST AL,DH ....................;84 f0
TEST [BX+SI+0x5566],BL .........;84 98 66 55     TEST CL,DH ....................;84 f1
TEST [BX+DI+0x5566],BL .........;84 99 66 55     TEST DL,DH ....................;84 f2
TEST [BP+SI+0x5566],BL .........;84 9a 66 55     TEST BL,DH ....................;84 f3
TEST [BP+DI+0x5566],BL .........;84 9b 66 55     TEST AH,DH ....................;84 f4
```

```
TEST CH,DH .....................;84 f5
TEST DH,DH .....................;84 f6
TEST BH,DH .....................;84 f7
TEST AL,BH .....................;84 f8
TEST CL,BH .....................;84 f9
TEST DL,BH .....................;84 fa
TEST BL,BH .....................;84 fb
TEST AH,BH .....................;84 fc
TEST CH,BH .....................;84 fd
TEST DH,BH .....................;84 fe
TEST BH,BH .....................;84 ff
TEST [BX+SI],AX ...............;85 00
TEST [BX+DI],AX ...............;85 01
TEST [BP+SI],AX ...............;85 02
TEST [BP+DI],AX ...............;85 03
TEST [SI],AX ..................;85 04
TEST [DI],AX ..................;85 05
TEST [0x5566],AX ..............;85 06 66 55
TEST [BX],AX ..................;85 07
TEST [BX+SI],CX ...............;85 08
TEST [BX+DI],CX ...............;85 09
TEST [BP+SI],CX ...............;85 0a
TEST [BP+DI],CX ...............;85 0b
TEST [SI],CX ..................;85 0c
TEST [DI],CX ..................;85 0d
TEST [0x5566],CX ..............;85 0e 66 55
TEST [BX],CX ..................;85 0f
TEST [BX+SI],DX ...............;85 10
TEST [BX+DI],DX ...............;85 11
TEST [BP+SI],DX ...............;85 12
TEST [BP+DI],DX ...............;85 13
TEST [SI],DX ..................;85 14
TEST [DI],DX ..................;85 15
TEST [0x5566],DX ..............;85 16 66 55
TEST [BX],DX ..................;85 17
TEST [BX+SI],BX ...............;85 18
TEST [BX+DI],BX ...............;85 19
TEST [BP+SI],BX ...............;85 1a
TEST [BP+DI],BX ...............;85 1b
TEST [SI],BX ..................;85 1c
TEST [DI],BX ..................;85 1d
TEST [0x5566],BX ..............;85 1e 66 55
TEST [BX],BX ..................;85 1f
TEST [BX+SI],SP ...............;85 20
TEST [BX+DI],SP ...............;85 21
TEST [BP+SI],SP ...............;85 22
TEST [BP+DI],SP ...............;85 23
TEST [SI],SP ..................;85 24
TEST [DI],SP ..................;85 25
TEST [0x5566],SP ..............;85 26 66 55
TEST [BX],SP ..................;85 27
TEST [BX+SI],BP ...............;85 28
TEST [BX+DI],BP ...............;85 29
TEST [BP+SI],BP ...............;85 2a
TEST [BP+DI],BP ...............;85 2b
TEST [SI],BP ..................;85 2c
TEST [DI],BP ..................;85 2d
TEST [0x5566],BP ..............;85 2e 66 55
TEST [BX],BP ..................;85 2f
TEST [BX+SI],SI ...............;85 30
TEST [BX+DI],SI ...............;85 31
TEST [BP+SI],SI ...............;85 32
TEST [BP+DI],SI ...............;85 33
TEST [SI],SI ..................;85 34
TEST [DI],SI ..................;85 35
TEST [0x5566],SI ..............;85 36 66 55
TEST [BX],SI ..................;85 37
TEST [BX+SI],DI ...............;85 38
TEST [BX+DI],DI ...............;85 39
TEST [BP+SI],DI ...............;85 3a
TEST [BP+DI],DI ...............;85 3b
TEST [SI],DI ..................;85 3c
TEST [DI],DI ..................;85 3d
TEST [0x5566],DI ..............;85 3e 66 55
TEST [BX],DI ..................;85 3f
TEST [BX+SI+0x55],AX ..........;85 40 55
TEST [BX+DI+0x55],AX ..........;85 41 55
TEST [BP+SI+0x55],AX ..........;85 42 55
TEST [BP+DI+0x55],AX ..........;85 43 55
TEST [SI+0x55],AX .............;85 44 55
TEST [DI+0x55],AX .............;85 45 55
TEST [BP+0x55],AX .............;85 46 55
TEST [BX+0x55],AX .............;85 47 55
TEST [BX+SI+0x55],CX ..........;85 48 55
TEST [BX+DI+0x55],CX ..........;85 49 55
TEST [BP+SI+0x55],CX ..........;85 4a 55
TEST [BP+DI+0x55],CX ..........;85 4b 55
TEST [SI+0x55],CX .............;85 4c 55
TEST [DI+0x55],CX .............;85 4d 55

TEST [BP+0x55],CX .............;85 4e 55
TEST [BX+0x55],CX .............;85 4f 55
TEST [BX+SI+0x55],DX ..........;85 50 55
TEST [BX+DI+0x55],DX ..........;85 51 55
TEST [BP+SI+0x55],DX ..........;85 52 55
TEST [BP+DI+0x55],DX ..........;85 53 55
TEST [SI+0x55],DX .............;85 54 55
TEST [DI+0x55],DX .............;85 55 55
TEST [BP+0x55],DX .............;85 56 55
TEST [BX+0x55],DX .............;85 57 55
TEST [BX+SI+0x55],BX ..........;85 58 55
TEST [BX+DI+0x55],BX ..........;85 59 55
TEST [BP+SI+0x55],BX ..........;85 5a 55
TEST [BP+DI+0x55],BX ..........;85 5b 55
TEST [SI+0x55],BX .............;85 5c 55
TEST [DI+0x55],BX .............;85 5d 55
TEST [BP+0x55],BX .............;85 5e 55
TEST [BX+0x55],BX .............;85 5f 55
TEST [BX+SI+0x55],SP ..........;85 60 55
TEST [BX+DI+0x55],SP ..........;85 61 55
TEST [BP+SI+0x55],SP ..........;85 62 55
TEST [BP+DI+0x55],SP ..........;85 63 55
TEST [SI+0x55],SP .............;85 64 55
TEST [DI+0x55],SP .............;85 65 55
TEST [BP+0x55],SP .............;85 66 55
TEST [BX+0x55],SP .............;85 67 55
TEST [BX+SI+0x55],BP ..........;85 68 55
TEST [BX+DI+0x55],BP ..........;85 69 55
TEST [BP+SI+0x55],BP ..........;85 6a 55
TEST [BP+DI+0x55],BP ..........;85 6b 55
TEST [SI+0x55],BP .............;85 6c 55
TEST [DI+0x55],BP .............;85 6d 55
TEST [BP+0x55],BP .............;85 6e 55
TEST [BX+0x55],BP .............;85 6f 55
TEST [BX+SI+0x55],SI ..........;85 70 55
TEST [BX+DI+0x55],SI ..........;85 71 55
TEST [BP+SI+0x55],SI ..........;85 72 55
TEST [BP+DI+0x55],SI ..........;85 73 55
TEST [SI+0x55],SI .............;85 74 55
TEST [DI+0x55],SI .............;85 75 55
TEST [BP+0x55],SI .............;85 76 55
TEST [BX+0x55],SI .............;85 77 55
TEST [BX+SI+0x55],DI ..........;85 78 55
TEST [BX+DI+0x55],DI ..........;85 79 55
TEST [BP+SI+0x55],DI ..........;85 7a 55
TEST [BP+DI+0x55],DI ..........;85 7b 55
TEST [SI+0x55],DI .............;85 7c 55
TEST [DI+0x55],DI .............;85 7d 55
TEST [BP+0x55],DI .............;85 7e 55
TEST [BX+0x55],DI .............;85 7f 55
TEST [BX+SI+0x5566],AX ........;85 80 66 55
TEST [BX+DI+0x5566],AX ........;85 81 66 55
TEST [BP+SI+0x5566],AX ........;85 82 66 55
TEST [BP+DI+0x5566],AX ........;85 83 66 55
TEST [SI+0x5566],AX ...........;85 84 66 55
TEST [DI+0x5566],AX ...........;85 85 66 55
TEST [BP+0x5566],AX ...........;85 86 66 55
TEST [BX+0x5566],AX ...........;85 87 66 55
TEST [BX+SI+0x5566],CX ........;85 88 66 55
TEST [BX+DI+0x5566],CX ........;85 89 66 55
TEST [BP+SI+0x5566],CX ........;85 8a 66 55
TEST [BP+DI+0x5566],CX ........;85 8b 66 55
TEST [SI+0x5566],CX ...........;85 8c 66 55
TEST [DI+0x5566],CX ...........;85 8d 66 55
TEST [BP+0x5566],CX ...........;85 8e 66 55
TEST [BX+0x5566],CX ...........;85 8f 66 55
TEST [BX+SI+0x5566],DX ........;85 90 66 55
TEST [BX+DI+0x5566],DX ........;85 91 66 55
TEST [BP+SI+0x5566],DX ........;85 92 66 55
TEST [BP+DI+0x5566],DX ........;85 93 66 55
TEST [SI+0x5566],DX ...........;85 94 66 55
TEST [DI+0x5566],DX ...........;85 95 66 55
TEST [BP+0x5566],DX ...........;85 96 66 55
TEST [BX+0x5566],DX ...........;85 97 66 55
TEST [BX+SI+0x5566],BX ........;85 98 66 55
TEST [BX+DI+0x5566],BX ........;85 99 66 55
TEST [BP+SI+0x5566],BX ........;85 9a 66 55
TEST [BP+DI+0x5566],BX ........;85 9b 66 55
TEST [SI+0x5566],BX ...........;85 9c 66 55
TEST [DI+0x5566],BX ...........;85 9d 66 55
TEST [BP+0x5566],BX ...........;85 9e 66 55
TEST [BX+0x5566],BX ...........;85 9f 66 55
TEST [BX+SI+0x5566],SP ........;85 a0 66 55
TEST [BX+DI+0x5566],SP ........;85 a1 66 55
TEST [BP+SI+0x5566],SP ........;85 a2 66 55
TEST [BP+DI+0x5566],SP ........;85 a3 66 55
TEST [SI+0x5566],SP ...........;85 a4 66 55
TEST [DI+0x5566],SP ...........;85 a5 66 55
TEST [BP+0x5566],SP ...........;85 a6 66 55
```

```
TEST [BX+0x5566],SP ...........;85 a7 66 55      XCHG [BX+SI],AL ...............;86 00
TEST [BX+SI+0x5566],BP ........;85 a8 66 55      XCHG [BX+DI],AL ...............;86 01
TEST [BX+DI+0x5566],BP ........;85 a9 66 55      XCHG [BP+SI],AL ...............;86 02
TEST [BP+SI+0x5566],BP ........;85 aa 66 55      XCHG [BP+DI],AL ...............;86 03
TEST [BP+DI+0x5566],BP ........;85 ab 66 55      XCHG [SI],AL ..................;86 04
TEST [SI+0x5566],BP ...........;85 ac 66 55      XCHG [DI],AL ..................;86 05
TEST [DI+0x5566],BP ...........;85 ad 66 55      XCHG [0x5566],AL ..............;86 06 66 55
TEST [BP+0x5566],BP ...........;85 ae 66 55      XCHG [BX],AL ..................;86 07
TEST [BX+0x5566],BP ...........;85 af 66 55      XCHG [BX+SI],CL ...............;86 08
TEST [BX+SI+0x5566],SI ........;85 b0 66 55      XCHG [BX+DI],CL ...............;86 09
TEST [BX+DI+0x5566],SI ........;85 b1 66 55      XCHG [BP+SI],CL ...............;86 0a
TEST [BP+SI+0x5566],SI ........;85 b2 66 55      XCHG [BP+DI],CL ...............;86 0b
TEST [BP+DI+0x5566],SI ........;85 b3 66 55      XCHG [SI],CL ..................;86 0c
TEST [SI+0x5566],SI ...........;85 b4 66 55      XCHG [DI],CL ..................;86 0d
TEST [DI+0x5566],SI ...........;85 b5 66 55      XCHG [0x5566],CL ..............;86 0e 66 55
TEST [BP+0x5566],SI ...........;85 b6 66 55      XCHG [BX],CL ..................;86 0f
TEST [BX+0x5566],SI ...........;85 b7 66 55      XCHG [BX+SI],DL ...............;86 10
TEST [BX+SI+0x5566],DI ........;85 b8 66 55      XCHG [BX+DI],DL ...............;86 11
TEST [BX+DI+0x5566],DI ........;85 b9 66 55      XCHG [BP+SI],DL ...............;86 12
TEST [BP+SI+0x5566],DI ........;85 ba 66 55      XCHG [BP+DI],DL ...............;86 13
TEST [BP+DI+0x5566],DI ........;85 bb 66 55      XCHG [SI],DL ..................;86 14
TEST [SI+0x5566],DI ...........;85 bc 66 55      XCHG [DI],DL ..................;86 15
TEST [DI+0x5566],DI ...........;85 bd 66 55      XCHG [0x5566],DL ..............;86 16 66 55
TEST [BP+0x5566],DI ...........;85 be 66 55      XCHG [BX],DL ..................;86 17
TEST [BX+0x5566],DI ...........;85 bf 66 55      XCHG [BX+SI],BL ...............;86 18
TEST AX,AX ....................;85 c0            XCHG [BX+DI],BL ...............;86 19
TEST CX,AX ....................;85 c1            XCHG [BP+SI],BL ...............;86 1a
TEST DX,AX ....................;85 c2            XCHG [BP+DI],BL ...............;86 1b
TEST BX,AX ....................;85 c3            XCHG [SI],BL ..................;86 1c
TEST SP,AX ....................;85 c4            XCHG [DI],BL ..................;86 1d
TEST BP,AX ....................;85 c5            XCHG [0x5566],BL ..............;86 1e 66 55
TEST SI,AX ....................;85 c6            XCHG [BX],BL ..................;86 1f
TEST DI,AX ....................;85 c7            XCHG [BX+SI],AH ...............;86 20
TEST AX,CX ....................;85 c8            XCHG [BX+DI],AH ...............;86 21
TEST CX,CX ....................;85 c9            XCHG [BP+SI],AH ...............;86 22
TEST DX,CX ....................;85 ca            XCHG [BP+DI],AH ...............;86 23
TEST BX,CX ....................;85 cb            XCHG [SI],AH ..................;86 24
TEST SP,CX ....................;85 cc            XCHG [DI],AH ..................;86 25
TEST BP,CX ....................;85 cd            XCHG [0x5566],AH ..............;86 26 66 55
TEST SI,CX ....................;85 ce            XCHG [BX],AH ..................;86 27
TEST DI,CX ....................;85 cf            XCHG [BX+SI],CH ...............;86 28
TEST AX,DX ....................;85 d0            XCHG [BX+DI],CH ...............;86 29
TEST CX,DX ....................;85 d1            XCHG [BP+SI],CH ...............;86 2a
TEST DX,DX ....................;85 d2            XCHG [BP+DI],CH ...............;86 2b
TEST BX,DX ....................;85 d3            XCHG [SI],CH ..................;86 2c
TEST SP,DX ....................;85 d4            XCHG [DI],CH ..................;86 2d
TEST BP,DX ....................;85 d5            XCHG [0x5566],CH ..............;86 2e 66 55
TEST SI,DX ....................;85 d6            XCHG [BX],CH ..................;86 2f
TEST DI,DX ....................;85 d7            XCHG [BX+SI],DH ...............;86 30
TEST AX,BX ....................;85 d8            XCHG [BX+DI],DH ...............;86 31
TEST CX,BX ....................;85 d9            XCHG [BP+SI],DH ...............;86 32
TEST DX,BX ....................;85 da            XCHG [BP+DI],DH ...............;86 33
TEST BX,BX ....................;85 db            XCHG [SI],DH ..................;86 34
TEST SP,BX ....................;85 dc            XCHG [DI],DH ..................;86 35
TEST BP,BX ....................;85 dd            XCHG [0x5566],DH ..............;86 36 66 55
TEST SI,BX ....................;85 de            XCHG [BX],DH ..................;86 37
TEST DI,BX ....................;85 df            XCHG [BX+SI],BH ...............;86 38
TEST AX,SP ....................;85 e0            XCHG [BX+DI],BH ...............;86 39
TEST CX,SP ....................;85 e1            XCHG [BP+SI],BH ...............;86 3a
TEST DX,SP ....................;85 e2            XCHG [BP+DI],BH ...............;86 3b
TEST BX,SP ....................;85 e3            XCHG [SI],BH ..................;86 3c
TEST SP,SP ....................;85 e4            XCHG [DI],BH ..................;86 3d
TEST BP,SP ....................;85 e5            XCHG [0x5566],BH ..............;86 3e 66 55
TEST SI,SP ....................;85 e6            XCHG [BX],BH ..................;86 3f
TEST DI,SP ....................;85 e7            XCHG [BX+SI+0x55],AL ..........;86 40 55
TEST AX,BP ....................;85 e8            XCHG [BX+DI+0x55],AL ..........;86 41 55
TEST CX,BP ....................;85 e9            XCHG [BP+SI+0x55],AL ..........;86 42 55
TEST DX,BP ....................;85 ea            XCHG [BP+DI+0x55],AL ..........;86 43 55
TEST BX,BP ....................;85 eb            XCHG [SI+0x55],AL .............;86 44 55
TEST SP,BP ....................;85 ec            XCHG [DI+0x55],AL .............;86 45 55
TEST BP,BP ....................;85 ed            XCHG [BP+0x55],AL .............;86 46 55
TEST SI,BP ....................;85 ee            XCHG [BX+0x55],AL .............;86 47 55
TEST DI,BP ....................;85 ef            XCHG [BX+SI+0x55],CL ..........;86 48 55
TEST AX,SI ....................;85 f0            XCHG [BX+DI+0x55],CL ..........;86 49 55
TEST CX,SI ....................;85 f1            XCHG [BP+SI+0x55],CL ..........;86 4a 55
TEST DX,SI ....................;85 f2            XCHG [BP+DI+0x55],CL ..........;86 4b 55
TEST BX,SI ....................;85 f3            XCHG [SI+0x55],CL .............;86 4c 55
TEST SP,SI ....................;85 f4            XCHG [DI+0x55],CL .............;86 4d 55
TEST BP,SI ....................;85 f5            XCHG [BP+0x55],CL .............;86 4e 55
TEST SI,SI ....................;85 f6            XCHG [BX+0x55],CL .............;86 4f 55
TEST DI,SI ....................;85 f7            XCHG [BX+SI+0x55],DL ..........;86 50 55
TEST AX,DI ....................;85 f8            XCHG [BX+DI+0x55],DL ..........;86 51 55
TEST CX,DI ....................;85 f9            XCHG [BP+SI+0x55],DL ..........;86 52 55
TEST DX,DI ....................;85 fa            XCHG [BP+DI+0x55],DL ..........;86 53 55
TEST BX,DI ....................;85 fb            XCHG [SI+0x55],DL .............;86 54 55
TEST SP,DI ....................;85 fc            XCHG [DI+0x55],DL .............;86 55 55
TEST BP,DI ....................;85 fd            XCHG [BP+0x55],DL .............;86 56 55
TEST SI,DI ....................;85 fe            XCHG [BX+0x55],DL .............;86 57 55
TEST DI,DI ....................;85 ff            XCHG [BX+SI+0x55],BL ..........;86 58 55
```

```
XCHG [BX+DI+0x55],BL ..........;86 59 55      XCHG [BP+SI+0x5566],DH ........;86 b2 66 55
XCHG [BP+SI+0x55],BL ..........;86 5a 55      XCHG [BP+DI+0x5566],DH ........;86 b3 66 55
XCHG [BP+DI+0x55],BL ..........;86 5b 55      XCHG [SI+0x5566],DH ...........;86 b4 66 55
XCHG [SI+0x55],BL .............;86 5c 55       XCHG [DI+0x5566],DH ...........;86 b5 66 55
XCHG [DI+0x55],BL .............;86 5d 55       XCHG [BP+0x5566],DH ...........;86 b6 66 55
XCHG [BP+0x55],BL .............;86 5e 55       XCHG [BX+0x5566],DH ...........;86 b7 66 55
XCHG [BX+0x55],BL .............;86 5f 55       XCHG [BX+SI+0x5566],BH ........;86 b8 66 55
XCHG [BX+SI+0x55],AH ..........;86 60 55       XCHG [BX+DI+0x5566],BH ........;86 b9 66 55
XCHG [BX+DI+0x55],AH ..........;86 61 55       XCHG [BP+SI+0x5566],BH ........;86 ba 66 55
XCHG [BP+SI+0x55],AH ..........;86 62 55       XCHG [BP+DI+0x5566],BH ........;86 bb 66 55
XCHG [BP+DI+0x55],AH ..........;86 63 55       XCHG [SI+0x5566],BH ...........;86 bc 66 55
XCHG [SI+0x55],AH .............;86 64 55       XCHG [DI+0x5566],BH ...........;86 bd 66 55
XCHG [DI+0x55],AH .............;86 65 55       XCHG [BP+0x5566],BH ...........;86 be 66 55
XCHG [BP+0x55],AH .............;86 66 55       XCHG [BX+0x5566],BH ...........;86 bf 66 55
XCHG [BX+0x55],AH .............;86 67 55       XCHG AL,AL ....................;86 c0
XCHG [BX+SI+0x55],CH ..........;86 68 55       XCHG CL,AL ....................;86 c1
XCHG [BX+DI+0x55],CH ..........;86 69 55       XCHG DL,AL ....................;86 c2
XCHG [BP+SI+0x55],CH ..........;86 6a 55       XCHG BL,AL ....................;86 c3
XCHG [BP+DI+0x55],CH ..........;86 6b 55       XCHG AH,AL ....................;86 c4
XCHG [SI+0x55],CH .............;86 6c 55       XCHG CH,AL ....................;86 c5
XCHG [DI+0x55],CH .............;86 6d 55       XCHG DH,AL ....................;86 c6
XCHG [BP+0x55],CH .............;86 6e 55       XCHG BH,AL ....................;86 c7
XCHG [BX+0x55],CH .............;86 6f 55       XCHG AL,CL ....................;86 c8
XCHG [BX+SI+0x55],DH ..........;86 70 55       XCHG CL,CL ....................;86 c9
XCHG [BX+DI+0x55],DH ..........;86 71 55       XCHG DL,CL ....................;86 ca
XCHG [BP+SI+0x55],DH ..........;86 72 55       XCHG BL,CL ....................;86 cb
XCHG [BP+DI+0x55],DH ..........;86 73 55       XCHG AH,CL ....................;86 cc
XCHG [SI+0x55],DH .............;86 74 55       XCHG CH,CL ....................;86 cd
XCHG [DI+0x55],DH .............;86 75 55       XCHG DH,CL ....................;86 ce
XCHG [BP+0x55],DH .............;86 76 55       XCHG BH,CL ....................;86 cf
XCHG [BX+0x55],DH .............;86 77 55       XCHG AL,DL ....................;86 d0
XCHG [BX+SI+0x55],BH ..........;86 78 55       XCHG CL,DL ....................;86 d1
XCHG [BX+DI+0x55],BH ..........;86 79 55       XCHG DL,DL ....................;86 d2
XCHG [BP+SI+0x55],BH ..........;86 7a 55       XCHG BL,DL ....................;86 d3
XCHG [BP+DI+0x55],BH ..........;86 7b 55       XCHG AH,DL ....................;86 d4
XCHG [SI+0x55],BH .............;86 7c 55       XCHG CH,DL ....................;86 d5
XCHG [DI+0x55],BH .............;86 7d 55       XCHG DH,DL ....................;86 d6
XCHG [BP+0x55],BH .............;86 7e 55       XCHG BH,DL ....................;86 d7
XCHG [BX+0x55],BH .............;86 7f 55       XCHG AL,BL ....................;86 d8
XCHG [BX+SI+0x5566],AL ........;86 80 66 55    XCHG CL,BL ....................;86 d9
XCHG [BX+DI+0x5566],AL ........;86 81 66 55    XCHG DL,BL ....................;86 da
XCHG [BP+SI+0x5566],AL ........;86 82 66 55    XCHG BL,BL ....................;86 db
XCHG [BP+DI+0x5566],AL ........;86 83 66 55    XCHG AH,BL ....................;86 dc
XCHG [SI+0x5566],AL ...........;86 84 66 55    XCHG CH,BL ....................;86 dd
XCHG [DI+0x5566],AL ...........;86 85 66 55    XCHG DH,BL ....................;86 de
XCHG [BP+0x5566],AL ...........;86 86 66 55    XCHG BH,BL ....................;86 df
XCHG [BX+0x5566],AL ...........;86 87 66 55    XCHG AL,AH ....................;86 e0
XCHG [BX+SI+0x5566],CL ........;86 88 66 55    XCHG CL,AH ....................;86 e1
XCHG [BX+DI+0x5566],CL ........;86 89 66 55    XCHG DL,AH ....................;86 e2
XCHG [BP+SI+0x5566],CL ........;86 8a 66 55    XCHG BL,AH ....................;86 e3
XCHG [BP+DI+0x5566],CL ........;86 8b 66 55    XCHG AH,AH ....................;86 e4
XCHG [SI+0x5566],CL ...........;86 8c 66 55    XCHG CH,AH ....................;86 e5
XCHG [DI+0x5566],CL ...........;86 8d 66 55    XCHG DH,AH ....................;86 e6
XCHG [BP+0x5566],CL ...........;86 8e 66 55    XCHG BH,AH ....................;86 e7
XCHG [BX+0x5566],CL ...........;86 8f 66 55    XCHG AL,CH ....................;86 e8
XCHG [BX+SI+0x5566],DL ........;86 90 66 55    XCHG CL,CH ....................;86 e9
XCHG [BX+DI+0x5566],DL ........;86 91 66 55    XCHG DL,CH ....................;86 ea
XCHG [BP+SI+0x5566],DL ........;86 92 66 55    XCHG BL,CH ....................;86 eb
XCHG [BP+DI+0x5566],DL ........;86 93 66 55    XCHG AH,CH ....................;86 ec
XCHG [SI+0x5566],DL ...........;86 94 66 55    XCHG CH,CH ....................;86 ed
XCHG [DI+0x5566],DL ...........;86 95 66 55    XCHG DH,CH ....................;86 ee
XCHG [BP+0x5566],DL ...........;86 96 66 55    XCHG BH,CH ....................;86 ef
XCHG [BX+0x5566],DL ...........;86 97 66 55    XCHG AL,DH ....................;86 f0
XCHG [BX+SI+0x5566],BL ........;86 98 66 55    XCHG CL,DH ....................;86 f1
XCHG [BX+DI+0x5566],BL ........;86 99 66 55    XCHG DL,DH ....................;86 f2
XCHG [BP+SI+0x5566],BL ........;86 9a 66 55    XCHG BL,DH ....................;86 f3
XCHG [BP+DI+0x5566],BL ........;86 9b 66 55    XCHG AH,DH ....................;86 f4
XCHG [SI+0x5566],BL ...........;86 9c 66 55    XCHG CH,DH ....................;86 f5
XCHG [DI+0x5566],BL ...........;86 9d 66 55    XCHG DH,DH ....................;86 f6
XCHG [BP+0x5566],BL ...........;86 9e 66 55    XCHG BH,DH ....................;86 f7
XCHG [BX+0x5566],BL ...........;86 9f 66 55    XCHG AL,BH ....................;86 f8
XCHG [BX+SI+0x5566],AH ........;86 a0 66 55    XCHG CL,BH ....................;86 f9
XCHG [BX+DI+0x5566],AH ........;86 a1 66 55    XCHG DL,BH ....................;86 fa
XCHG [BP+SI+0x5566],AH ........;86 a2 66 55    XCHG BL,BH ....................;86 fb
XCHG [BP+DI+0x5566],AH ........;86 a3 66 55    XCHG AH,BH ....................;86 fc
XCHG [SI+0x5566],AH ...........;86 a4 66 55    XCHG CH,BH ....................;86 fd
XCHG [DI+0x5566],AH ...........;86 a5 66 55    XCHG DH,BH ....................;86 fe
XCHG [BP+0x5566],AH ...........;86 a6 66 55    XCHG BH,BH ....................;86 ff
XCHG [BX+0x5566],AH ...........;86 a7 66 55    XCHG [BX+SI],AX ...............;87 00
XCHG [BX+SI+0x5566],CH ........;86 a8 66 55    XCHG [BX+DI],AX ...............;87 01
XCHG [BX+DI+0x5566],CH ........;86 a9 66 55    XCHG [BP+SI],AX ...............;87 02
XCHG [BP+SI+0x5566],CH ........;86 aa 66 55    XCHG [BP+DI],AX ...............;87 03
XCHG [BP+DI+0x5566],CH ........;86 ab 66 55    XCHG [SI],AX ..................;87 04
XCHG [SI+0x5566],CH ...........;86 ac 66 55    XCHG [DI],AX ..................;87 05
XCHG [DI+0x5566],CH ...........;86 ad 66 55    XCHG [0x5566],AX ..............;87 06 66 55
XCHG [BP+0x5566],CH ...........;86 ae 66 55    XCHG [BX],AX ..................;87 07
XCHG [BX+0x5566],CH ...........;86 af 66 55    XCHG [BX+SI],CX ...............;87 08
XCHG [BX+SI+0x5566],DH ........;86 b0 66 55    XCHG [BX+DI],CX ...............;87 09
XCHG [BX+DI+0x5566],DH ........;86 b1 66 55    XCHG [BP+SI],CX ...............;87 0a
```

```
XCHG [BP+DI],CX ................;87 0b          XCHG [SI+0x55],SP ...............;87 64 55
XCHG [SI],CX ...................;87 0c          XCHG [DI+0x55],SP ...............;87 65 55
XCHG [DI],CX ...................;87 0d          XCHG [BP+0x55],SP ...............;87 66 55
XCHG [0x5566],CX ...........;87 0e 66 55        XCHG [BX+0x55],SP ...............;87 67 55
XCHG [BX],CX ...................;87 0f          XCHG [BX+SI+0x55],BP ............;87 68 55
XCHG [BX+SI],DX ................;87 10          XCHG [BX+DI+0x55],BP ............;87 69 55
XCHG [BX+DI],DX ................;87 11          XCHG [BP+SI+0x55],BP ............;87 6a 55
XCHG [BP+SI],DX ................;87 12          XCHG [BP+DI+0x55],BP ............;87 6b 55
XCHG [BP+DI],DX ................;87 13          XCHG [SI+0x55],BP ...............;87 6c 55
XCHG [SI],DX ...................;87 14          XCHG [DI+0x55],BP ...............;87 6d 55
XCHG [DI],DX ...................;87 15          XCHG [BP+0x55],BP ...............;87 6e 55
XCHG [0x5566],DX ...........;87 16 66 55        XCHG [BX+0x55],BP ...............;87 6f 55
XCHG [BX],DX ...................;87 17          XCHG [BX+SI+0x55],SI ............;87 70 55
XCHG [BX+SI],BX ................;87 18          XCHG [BX+DI+0x55],SI ............;87 71 55
XCHG [BX+DI],BX ................;87 19          XCHG [BP+SI+0x55],SI ............;87 72 55
XCHG [BP+SI],BX ................;87 1a          XCHG [BP+DI+0x55],SI ............;87 73 55
XCHG [BP+DI],BX ................;87 1b          XCHG [SI+0x55],SI ...............;87 74 55
XCHG [SI],BX ...................;87 1c          XCHG [DI+0x55],SI ...............;87 75 55
XCHG [DI],BX ...................;87 1d          XCHG [BP+0x55],SI ...............;87 76 55
XCHG [0x5566],BX ...........;87 1e 66 55        XCHG [BX+0x55],SI ...............;87 77 55
XCHG [BX],BX ...................;87 1f          XCHG [BX+SI+0x55],DI ............;87 78 55
XCHG [BX+SI],SP ................;87 20          XCHG [BX+DI+0x55],DI ............;87 79 55
XCHG [BX+DI],SP ................;87 21          XCHG [BP+SI+0x55],DI ............;87 7a 55
XCHG [BP+SI],SP ................;87 22          XCHG [BP+DI+0x55],DI ............;87 7b 55
XCHG [BP+DI],SP ................;87 23          XCHG [SI+0x55],DI ...............;87 7c 55
XCHG [SI],SP ...................;87 24          XCHG [DI+0x55],DI ...............;87 7d 55
XCHG [DI],SP ...................;87 25          XCHG [BP+0x55],DI ...............;87 7e 55
XCHG [0x5566],SP ...........;87 26 66 55        XCHG [BX+0x55],DI ...............;87 7f 55
XCHG [BX],SP ...................;87 27          XCHG [BX+SI+0x5566],AX .......;87 80 66 55
XCHG [BX+SI],BP ................;87 28          XCHG [BX+DI+0x5566],AX .......;87 81 66 55
XCHG [BX+DI],BP ................;87 29          XCHG [BP+SI+0x5566],AX .......;87 82 66 55
XCHG [BP+SI],BP ................;87 2a          XCHG [BP+DI+0x5566],AX .......;87 83 66 55
XCHG [BP+DI],BP ................;87 2b          XCHG [SI+0x5566],AX ..........;87 84 66 55
XCHG [SI],BP ...................;87 2c          XCHG [DI+0x5566],AX ..........;87 85 66 55
XCHG [DI],BP ...................;87 2d          XCHG [BP+0x5566],AX ..........;87 86 66 55
XCHG [0x5566],BP ...........;87 2e 66 55        XCHG [BX+0x5566],AX ..........;87 87 66 55
XCHG [BX],BP ...................;87 2f          XCHG [BX+SI+0x5566],CX .......;87 88 66 55
XCHG [BX+SI],SI ................;87 30          XCHG [BX+DI+0x5566],CX .......;87 89 66 55
XCHG [BX+DI],SI ................;87 31          XCHG [BP+SI+0x5566],CX .......;87 8a 66 55
XCHG [BP+SI],SI ................;87 32          XCHG [BP+DI+0x5566],CX .......;87 8b 66 55
XCHG [BP+DI],SI ................;87 33          XCHG [SI+0x5566],CX ..........;87 8c 66 55
XCHG [SI],SI ...................;87 34          XCHG [DI+0x5566],CX ..........;87 8d 66 55
XCHG [DI],SI ...................;87 35          XCHG [BP+0x5566],CX ..........;87 8e 66 55
XCHG [0x5566],SI ...........;87 36 66 55        XCHG [BX+0x5566],CX ..........;87 8f 66 55
XCHG [BX],SI ...................;87 37          XCHG [BX+SI+0x5566],DX .......;87 90 66 55
XCHG [BX+SI],DI ................;87 38          XCHG [BX+DI+0x5566],DX .......;87 91 66 55
XCHG [BX+DI],DI ................;87 39          XCHG [BP+SI+0x5566],DX .......;87 92 66 55
XCHG [BP+SI],DI ................;87 3a          XCHG [BP+DI+0x5566],DX .......;87 93 66 55
XCHG [BP+DI],DI ................;87 3b          XCHG [SI+0x5566],DX ..........;87 94 66 55
XCHG [SI],DI ...................;87 3c          XCHG [DI+0x5566],DX ..........;87 95 66 55
XCHG [DI],DI ...................;87 3d          XCHG [BP+0x5566],DX ..........;87 96 66 55
XCHG [0x5566],DI ...........;87 3e 66 55        XCHG [BX+0x5566],DX ..........;87 97 66 55
XCHG [BX],DI ...................;87 3f          XCHG [BX+SI+0x5566],BX .......;87 98 66 55
XCHG [BX+SI+0x55],AX ...........;87 40 55       XCHG [BX+DI+0x5566],BX .......;87 99 66 55
XCHG [BX+DI+0x55],AX ...........;87 41 55       XCHG [BP+SI+0x5566],BX .......;87 9a 66 55
XCHG [BP+SI+0x55],AX ...........;87 42 55       XCHG [BP+DI+0x5566],BX .......;87 9b 66 55
XCHG [BP+DI+0x55],AX ...........;87 43 55       XCHG [SI+0x5566],BX ..........;87 9c 66 55
XCHG [SI+0x55],AX ..............;87 44 55       XCHG [DI+0x5566],BX ..........;87 9d 66 55
XCHG [DI+0x55],AX ..............;87 45 55       XCHG [BP+0x5566],BX ..........;87 9e 66 55
XCHG [BP+0x55],AX ..............;87 46 55       XCHG [BX+0x5566],BX ..........;87 9f 66 55
XCHG [BX+0x55],AX ..............;87 47 55       XCHG [BX+SI+0x5566],SP .......;87 a0 66 55
XCHG [BX+SI+0x55],CX ...........;87 48 55       XCHG [BX+DI+0x5566],SP .......;87 a1 66 55
XCHG [BX+DI+0x55],CX ...........;87 49 55       XCHG [BP+SI+0x5566],SP .......;87 a2 66 55
XCHG [BP+SI+0x55],CX ...........;87 4a 55       XCHG [BP+DI+0x5566],SP .......;87 a3 66 55
XCHG [BP+DI+0x55],CX ...........;87 4b 55       XCHG [SI+0x5566],SP ..........;87 a4 66 55
XCHG [SI+0x55],CX ..............;87 4c 55       XCHG [DI+0x5566],SP ..........;87 a5 66 55
XCHG [DI+0x55],CX ..............;87 4d 55       XCHG [BP+0x5566],SP ..........;87 a6 66 55
XCHG [BP+0x55],CX ..............;87 4e 55       XCHG [BX+0x5566],SP ..........;87 a7 66 55
XCHG [BX+0x55],CX ..............;87 4f 55       XCHG [BX+SI+0x5566],BP .......;87 a8 66 55
XCHG [BX+SI+0x55],DX ...........;87 50 55       XCHG [BX+DI+0x5566],BP .......;87 a9 66 55
XCHG [BX+DI+0x55],DX ...........;87 51 55       XCHG [BP+SI+0x5566],BP .......;87 aa 66 55
XCHG [BP+SI+0x55],DX ...........;87 52 55       XCHG [BP+DI+0x5566],BP .......;87 ab 66 55
XCHG [BP+DI+0x55],DX ...........;87 53 55       XCHG [SI+0x5566],BP ..........;87 ac 66 55
XCHG [SI+0x55],DX ..............;87 54 55       XCHG [DI+0x5566],BP ..........;87 ad 66 55
XCHG [DI+0x55],DX ..............;87 55 55       XCHG [BP+0x5566],BP ..........;87 ae 66 55
XCHG [BP+0x55],DX ..............;87 56 55       XCHG [BX+0x5566],BP ..........;87 af 66 55
XCHG [BX+0x55],DX ..............;87 57 55       XCHG [BX+SI+0x5566],SI .......;87 b0 66 55
XCHG [BX+SI+0x55],BX ...........;87 58 55       XCHG [BX+DI+0x5566],SI .......;87 b1 66 55
XCHG [BX+DI+0x55],BX ...........;87 59 55       XCHG [BP+SI+0x5566],SI .......;87 b2 66 55
XCHG [BP+SI+0x55],BX ...........;87 5a 55       XCHG [BP+DI+0x5566],SI .......;87 b3 66 55
XCHG [BP+DI+0x55],BX ...........;87 5b 55       XCHG [SI+0x5566],SI ..........;87 b4 66 55
XCHG [SI+0x55],BX ..............;87 5c 55       XCHG [DI+0x5566],SI ..........;87 b5 66 55
XCHG [DI+0x55],BX ..............;87 5d 55       XCHG [BP+0x5566],SI ..........;87 b6 66 55
XCHG [BP+0x55],BX ..............;87 5e 55       XCHG [BX+0x5566],SI ..........;87 b7 66 55
XCHG [BX+0x55],BX ..............;87 5f 55       XCHG [BX+SI+0x5566],DI .......;87 b8 66 55
XCHG [BX+SI+0x55],SP ...........;87 60 55       XCHG [BX+DI+0x5566],DI .......;87 b9 66 55
XCHG [BX+DI+0x55],SP ...........;87 61 55       XCHG [BP+SI+0x5566],DI .......;87 ba 66 55
XCHG [BP+SI+0x55],SP ...........;87 62 55       XCHG [BP+DI+0x5566],DI .......;87 bb 66 55
XCHG [BP+DI+0x55],SP ...........;87 63 55       XCHG [SI+0x5566],DI ..........;87 bc 66 55
```

```
XCHG [DI+0x5566],DI ...........;87 bd 66 55        MOV [0x5566],DL ................;88 16 66 55
XCHG [BP+0x5566],DI ...........;87 be 66 55        MOV [BX],DL ...................;88 17
XCHG [BX+0x5566],DI ...........;87 bf 66 55        MOV [BX+SI],BL ................;88 18
XCHG AX,AX ...................;87 c0               MOV [BX+DI],BL ................;88 19
XCHG CX,AX ...................;87 c1               MOV [BP+SI],BL ................;88 1a
XCHG DX,AX ...................;87 c2               MOV [BP+DI],BL ................;88 1b
XCHG BX,AX ...................;87 c3               MOV [SI],BL ...................;88 1c
XCHG SP,AX ...................;87 c4               MOV [DI],BL ...................;88 1d
XCHG BP,AX ...................;87 c5               MOV [0x5566],BL ...............;88 1e 66 55
XCHG SI,AX ...................;87 c6               MOV [BX],BL ...................;88 1f
XCHG DI,AX ...................;87 c7               MOV [BX+SI],AH ................;88 20
XCHG AX,CX ...................;87 c8               MOV [BX+DI],AH ................;88 21
XCHG CX,CX ...................;87 c9               MOV [BP+SI],AH ................;88 22
XCHG DX,CX ...................;87 ca               MOV [BP+DI],AH ................;88 23
XCHG BX,CX ...................;87 cb               MOV [SI],AH ...................;88 24
XCHG SP,CX ...................;87 cc               MOV [DI],AH ...................;88 25
XCHG BP,CX ...................;87 cd               MOV [0x5566],AH ...............;88 26 66 55
XCHG SI,CX ...................;87 ce               MOV [BX],AH ...................;88 27
XCHG DI,CX ...................;87 cf               MOV [BX+SI],CH ................;88 28
XCHG AX,DX ...................;87 d0               MOV [BX+DI],CH ................;88 29
XCHG CX,DX ...................;87 d1               MOV [BP+SI],CH ................;88 2a
XCHG DX,DX ...................;87 d2               MOV [BP+DI],CH ................;88 2b
XCHG BX,DX ...................;87 d3               MOV [SI],CH ...................;88 2c
XCHG SP,DX ...................;87 d4               MOV [DI],CH ...................;88 2d
XCHG BP,DX ...................;87 d5               MOV [0x5566],CH ...............;88 2e 66 55
XCHG SI,DX ...................;87 d6               MOV [BX],CH ...................;88 2f
XCHG DI,DX ...................;87 d7               MOV [BX+SI],DH ................;88 30
XCHG AX,BX ...................;87 d8               MOV [BX+DI],DH ................;88 31
XCHG CX,BX ...................;87 d9               MOV [BP+SI],DH ................;88 32
XCHG DX,BX ...................;87 da               MOV [BP+DI],DH ................;88 33
XCHG BX,BX ...................;87 db               MOV [SI],DH ...................;88 34
XCHG SP,BX ...................;87 dc               MOV [DI],DH ...................;88 35
XCHG BP,BX ...................;87 dd               MOV [0x5566],DH ...............;88 36 66 55
XCHG SI,BX ...................;87 de               MOV [BX],DH ...................;88 37
XCHG DI,BX ...................;87 df               MOV [BX+SI],BH ................;88 38
XCHG AX,SP ...................;87 e0               MOV [BX+DI],BH ................;88 39
XCHG CX,SP ...................;87 e1               MOV [BP+SI],BH ................;88 3a
XCHG DX,SP ...................;87 e2               MOV [BP+DI],BH ................;88 3b
XCHG BX,SP ...................;87 e3               MOV [SI],BH ...................;88 3c
XCHG SP,SP ...................;87 e4               MOV [DI],BH ...................;88 3d
XCHG BP,SP ...................;87 e5               MOV [0x5566],BH ...............;88 3e 66 55
XCHG SI,SP ...................;87 e6               MOV [BX],BH ...................;88 3f
XCHG DI,SP ...................;87 e7               MOV [BX+SI+0x55],AL ...........;88 40 55
XCHG AX,BP ...................;87 e8               MOV [BX+DI+0x55],AL ...........;88 41 55
XCHG CX,BP ...................;87 e9               MOV [BP+SI+0x55],AL ...........;88 42 55
XCHG DX,BP ...................;87 ea               MOV [BP+DI+0x55],AL ...........;88 43 55
XCHG BX,BP ...................;87 eb               MOV [SI+0x55],AL ..............;88 44 55
XCHG SP,BP ...................;87 ec               MOV [DI+0x55],AL ..............;88 45 55
XCHG BP,BP ...................;87 ed               MOV [BP+0x55],AL ..............;88 46 55
XCHG SI,BP ...................;87 ee               MOV [BX+0x55],AL ..............;88 47 55
XCHG DI,BP ...................;87 ef               MOV [BX+SI+0x55],CL ...........;88 48 55
XCHG AX,SI ...................;87 f0               MOV [BX+DI+0x55],CL ...........;88 49 55
XCHG CX,SI ...................;87 f1               MOV [BP+SI+0x55],CL ...........;88 4a 55
XCHG DX,SI ...................;87 f2               MOV [BP+DI+0x55],CL ...........;88 4b 55
XCHG BX,SI ...................;87 f3               MOV [SI+0x55],CL ..............;88 4c 55
XCHG SP,SI ...................;87 f4               MOV [DI+0x55],CL ..............;88 4d 55
XCHG BP,SI ...................;87 f5               MOV [BP+0x55],CL ..............;88 4e 55
XCHG SI,SI ...................;87 f6               MOV [BX+0x55],CL ..............;88 4f 55
XCHG DI,SI ...................;87 f7               MOV [BX+SI+0x55],DL ...........;88 50 55
XCHG AX,DI ...................;87 f8               MOV [BX+DI+0x55],DL ...........;88 51 55
XCHG CX,DI ...................;87 f9               MOV [BP+SI+0x55],DL ...........;88 52 55
XCHG DX,DI ...................;87 fa               MOV [BP+DI+0x55],DL ...........;88 53 55
XCHG BX,DI ...................;87 fb               MOV [SI+0x55],DL ..............;88 54 55
XCHG SP,DI ...................;87 fc               MOV [DI+0x55],DL ..............;88 55 55
XCHG BP,DI ...................;87 fd               MOV [BP+0x55],DL ..............;88 56 55
XCHG SI,DI ...................;87 fe               MOV [BX+0x55],DL ..............;88 57 55
XCHG DI,DI ...................;87 ff               MOV [BX+SI+0x55],BL ...........;88 58 55
MOV [BX+SI],AL ...............;88 00               MOV [BX+DI+0x55],BL ...........;88 59 55
MOV [BX+DI],AL ...............;88 01               MOV [BP+SI+0x55],BL ...........;88 5a 55
MOV [BP+SI],AL ...............;88 02               MOV [BP+DI+0x55],BL ...........;88 5b 55
MOV [BP+DI],AL ...............;88 03               MOV [SI+0x55],BL ..............;88 5c 55
MOV [SI],AL ..................;88 04               MOV [DI+0x55],BL ..............;88 5d 55
MOV [DI],AL ..................;88 05               MOV [BP+0x55],BL ..............;88 5e 55
MOV [0x5566],AL ..............;88 06 66 55         MOV [BX+0x55],BL ..............;88 5f 55
MOV [BX],AL ..................;88 07               MOV [BX+SI+0x55],AH ...........;88 60 55
MOV [BX+SI],CL ...............;88 08               MOV [BX+DI+0x55],AH ...........;88 61 55
MOV [BX+DI],CL ...............;88 09               MOV [BP+SI+0x55],AH ...........;88 62 55
MOV [BP+SI],CL ...............;88 0a               MOV [BP+DI+0x55],AH ...........;88 63 55
MOV [BP+DI],CL ...............;88 0b               MOV [SI+0x55],AH ..............;88 64 55
MOV [SI],CL ..................;88 0c               MOV [DI+0x55],AH ..............;88 65 55
MOV [DI],CL ..................;88 0d               MOV [BP+0x55],AH ..............;88 66 55
MOV [0x5566],CL ..............;88 0e 66 55         MOV [BX+0x55],AH ..............;88 67 55
MOV [BX],CL ..................;88 0f               MOV [BX+SI+0x55],CH ...........;88 68 55
MOV [BX+SI],DL ...............;88 10               MOV [BX+DI+0x55],CH ...........;88 69 55
MOV [BX+DI],DL ...............;88 11               MOV [BP+SI+0x55],CH ...........;88 6a 55
MOV [BP+SI],DL ...............;88 12               MOV [BP+DI+0x55],CH ...........;88 6b 55
MOV [BP+DI],DL ...............;88 13               MOV [SI+0x55],CH ..............;88 6c 55
MOV [SI],DL ..................;88 14               MOV [DI+0x55],CH ..............;88 6d 55
MOV [DI],DL ..................;88 15               MOV [BP+0x55],CH ..............;88 6e 55
```

```
MOV [BX+0x55],CH ..............;88 6f 55          MOV AL,CL .....................;88 c8
MOV [BX+SI+0x55],DH ...........;88 70 55          MOV CL,CL .....................;88 c9
MOV [BX+DI+0x55],DH ...........;88 71 55          MOV DL,CL .....................;88 ca
MOV [BP+SI+0x55],DH ...........;88 72 55          MOV BL,CL .....................;88 cb
MOV [BP+DI+0x55],DH ...........;88 73 55          MOV AH,CL .....................;88 cc
MOV [SI+0x55],DH ..............;88 74 55          MOV CH,CL .....................;88 cd
MOV [DI+0x55],DH ..............;88 75 55          MOV DH,CL .....................;88 ce
MOV [BP+0x55],DH ..............;88 76 55          MOV BH,CL .....................;88 cf
MOV [BX+0x55],DH ..............;88 77 55          MOV AL,DL .....................;88 d0
MOV [BX+SI+0x55],BH ...........;88 78 55          MOV CL,DL .....................;88 d1
MOV [BX+DI+0x55],BH ...........;88 79 55          MOV DL,DL .....................;88 d2
MOV [BP+SI+0x55],BH ...........;88 7a 55          MOV BL,DL .....................;88 d3
MOV [BP+DI+0x55],BH ...........;88 7b 55          MOV AH,DL .....................;88 d4
MOV [SI+0x55],BH ..............;88 7c 55          MOV CH,DL .....................;88 d5
MOV [DI+0x55],BH ..............;88 7d 55          MOV DH,DL .....................;88 d6
MOV [BP+0x55],BH ..............;88 7e 55          MOV BH,DL .....................;88 d7
MOV [BX+0x55],BH ..............;88 7f 55          MOV AL,BL .....................;88 d8
MOV [BX+SI+0x5566],AL .........;88 80 66 55       MOV CL,BL .....................;88 d9
MOV [BX+DI+0x5566],AL .........;88 81 66 55       MOV DL,BL .....................;88 da
MOV [BP+SI+0x5566],AL .........;88 82 66 55       MOV BL,BL .....................;88 db
MOV [BP+DI+0x5566],AL .........;88 83 66 55       MOV AH,BL .....................;88 dc
MOV [SI+0x5566],AL ............;88 84 66 55       MOV CH,BL .....................;88 dd
MOV [DI+0x5566],AL ............;88 85 66 55       MOV DH,BL .....................;88 de
MOV [BP+0x5566],AL ............;88 86 66 55       MOV BH,BL .....................;88 df
MOV [BX+0x5566],AL ............;88 87 66 55       MOV AL,AH .....................;88 e0
MOV [BX+SI+0x5566],CL .........;88 88 66 55       MOV CL,AH .....................;88 e1
MOV [BX+DI+0x5566],CL .........;88 89 66 55       MOV DL,AH .....................;88 e2
MOV [BP+SI+0x5566],CL .........;88 8a 66 55       MOV BL,AH .....................;88 e3
MOV [BP+DI+0x5566],CL .........;88 8b 66 55       MOV AH,AH .....................;88 e4
MOV [SI+0x5566],CL ............;88 8c 66 55       MOV CH,AH .....................;88 e5
MOV [DI+0x5566],CL ............;88 8d 66 55       MOV DH,AH .....................;88 e6
MOV [BP+0x5566],CL ............;88 8e 66 55       MOV BH,AH .....................;88 e7
MOV [BX+0x5566],CL ............;88 8f 66 55       MOV AL,CH .....................;88 e8
MOV [BX+SI+0x5566],DL .........;88 90 66 55       MOV CL,CH .....................;88 e9
MOV [BX+DI+0x5566],DL .........;88 91 66 55       MOV DL,CH .....................;88 ea
MOV [BP+SI+0x5566],DL .........;88 92 66 55       MOV BL,CH .....................;88 eb
MOV [BP+DI+0x5566],DL .........;88 93 66 55       MOV AH,CH .....................;88 ec
MOV [SI+0x5566],DL ............;88 94 66 55       MOV CH,CH .....................;88 ed
MOV [DI+0x5566],DL ............;88 95 66 55       MOV DH,CH .....................;88 ee
MOV [BP+0x5566],DL ............;88 96 66 55       MOV BH,CH .....................;88 ef
MOV [BX+0x5566],DL ............;88 97 66 55       MOV AL,DH .....................;88 f0
MOV [BX+SI+0x5566],BL .........;88 98 66 55       MOV CL,DH .....................;88 f1
MOV [BX+DI+0x5566],BL .........;88 99 66 55       MOV DL,DH .....................;88 f2
MOV [BP+SI+0x5566],BL .........;88 9a 66 55       MOV BL,DH .....................;88 f3
MOV [BP+DI+0x5566],BL .........;88 9b 66 55       MOV AH,DH .....................;88 f4
MOV [SI+0x5566],BL ............;88 9c 66 55       MOV CH,DH .....................;88 f5
MOV [DI+0x5566],BL ............;88 9d 66 55       MOV DH,DH .....................;88 f6
MOV [BP+0x5566],BL ............;88 9e 66 55       MOV BH,DH .....................;88 f7
MOV [BX+0x5566],BL ............;88 9f 66 55       MOV AL,BH .....................;88 f8
MOV [BX+SI+0x5566],AH .........;88 a0 66 55       MOV CL,BH .....................;88 f9
MOV [BX+DI+0x5566],AH .........;88 a1 66 55       MOV DL,BH .....................;88 fa
MOV [BP+SI+0x5566],AH .........;88 a2 66 55       MOV BL,BH .....................;88 fb
MOV [BP+DI+0x5566],AH .........;88 a3 66 55       MOV AH,BH .....................;88 fc
MOV [SI+0x5566],AH ............;88 a4 66 55       MOV CH,BH .....................;88 fd
MOV [DI+0x5566],AH ............;88 a5 66 55       MOV DH,BH .....................;88 fe
MOV [BP+0x5566],AH ............;88 a6 66 55       MOV BH,BH .....................;88 ff
MOV [BX+0x5566],AH ............;88 a7 66 55       MOV [BX+SI],AX ................;89 00
MOV [BX+SI+0x5566],CH .........;88 a8 66 55       MOV [BX+DI],AX ................;89 01
MOV [BX+DI+0x5566],CH .........;88 a9 66 55       MOV [BP+SI],AX ................;89 02
MOV [BP+SI+0x5566],CH .........;88 aa 66 55       MOV [BP+DI],AX ................;89 03
MOV [BP+DI+0x5566],CH .........;88 ab 66 55       MOV [SI],AX ...................;89 04
MOV [SI+0x5566],CH ............;88 ac 66 55       MOV [DI],AX ...................;89 05
MOV [DI+0x5566],CH ............;88 ad 66 55       MOV [0x5566],AX ...............;89 06 66 55
MOV [BP+0x5566],CH ............;88 ae 66 55       MOV [BX],AX ...................;89 07
MOV [BX+0x5566],CH ............;88 af 66 55       MOV [BX+SI],CX ................;89 08
MOV [BX+SI+0x5566],DH .........;88 b0 66 55       MOV [BX+DI],CX ................;89 09
MOV [BX+DI+0x5566],DH .........;88 b1 66 55       MOV [BP+SI],CX ................;89 0a
MOV [BP+SI+0x5566],DH .........;88 b2 66 55       MOV [BP+DI],CX ................;89 0b
MOV [BP+DI+0x5566],DH .........;88 b3 66 55       MOV [SI],CX ...................;89 0c
MOV [SI+0x5566],DH ............;88 b4 66 55       MOV [DI],CX ...................;89 0d
MOV [DI+0x5566],DH ............;88 b5 66 55       MOV [0x5566],CX ...............;89 0e 66 55
MOV [BP+0x5566],DH ............;88 b6 66 55       MOV [BX],CX ...................;89 0f
MOV [BX+0x5566],DH ............;88 b7 66 55       MOV [BX+SI],DX ................;89 10
MOV [BX+SI+0x5566],BH .........;88 b8 66 55       MOV [BX+DI],DX ................;89 11
MOV [BX+DI+0x5566],BH .........;88 b9 66 55       MOV [BP+SI],DX ................;89 12
MOV [BP+SI+0x5566],BH .........;88 ba 66 55       MOV [BP+DI],DX ................;89 13
MOV [BP+DI+0x5566],BH .........;88 bb 66 55       MOV [SI],DX ...................;89 14
MOV [SI+0x5566],BH ............;88 bc 66 55       MOV [DI],DX ...................;89 15
MOV [DI+0x5566],BH ............;88 bd 66 55       MOV [0x5566],DX ...............;89 16 66 55
MOV [BP+0x5566],BH ............;88 be 66 55       MOV [BX],DX ...................;89 17
MOV [BX+0x5566],BH ............;88 bf 66 55       MOV [BX+SI],BX ................;89 18
MOV AL,AL .....................;88 c0             MOV [BX+DI],BX ................;89 19
MOV CL,AL .....................;88 c1             MOV [BP+SI],BX ................;89 1a
MOV DL,AL .....................;88 c2             MOV [BP+DI],BX ................;89 1b
MOV BL,AL .....................;88 c3             MOV [SI],BX ...................;89 1c
MOV AH,AL .....................;88 c4             MOV [DI],BX ...................;89 1d
MOV CH,AL .....................;88 c5             MOV [0x5566],BX ...............;89 1e 66 55
MOV DH,AL .....................;88 c6             MOV [BX],BX ...................;89 1f
MOV BH,AL .....................;88 c7             MOV [BX+SI],SP ................;89 20
```

```
MOV [BX+DI],SP ...............;89 21
MOV [BP+SI],SP ...............;89 22
MOV [BP+DI],SP ...............;89 23
MOV [SI],SP ..................;89 24
MOV [DI],SP ..................;89 25
MOV [0x5566],SP .........;89 26 66 55
MOV [BX],SP ..................;89 27
MOV [BX+SI],BP ...............;89 28
MOV [BX+DI],BP ...............;89 29
MOV [BP+SI],BP ...............;89 2a
MOV [BP+DI],BP ...............;89 2b
MOV [SI],BP ..................;89 2c
MOV [DI],BP ..................;89 2d
MOV [0x5566],BP .........;89 2e 66 55
MOV [BX],BP ..................;89 2f
MOV [BX+SI],SI ...............;89 30
MOV [BX+DI],SI ...............;89 31
MOV [BP+SI],SI ...............;89 32
MOV [BP+DI],SI ...............;89 33
MOV [SI],SI ..................;89 34
MOV [DI],SI ..................;89 35
MOV [0x5566],SI .........;89 36 66 55
MOV [BX],SI ..................;89 37
MOV [BX+SI],DI ...............;89 38
MOV [BX+DI],DI ...............;89 39
MOV [BP+SI],DI ...............;89 3a
MOV [BP+DI],DI ...............;89 3b
MOV [SI],DI ..................;89 3c
MOV [DI],DI ..................;89 3d
MOV [0x5566],DI .........;89 3e 66 55
MOV [BX],DI ..................;89 3f
MOV [BX+SI+0x55],AX ..........;89 40 55
MOV [BX+DI+0x55],AX ..........;89 41 55
MOV [BP+SI+0x55],AX ..........;89 42 55
MOV [BP+DI+0x55],AX ..........;89 43 55
MOV [SI+0x55],AX .............;89 44 55
MOV [DI+0x55],AX .............;89 45 55
MOV [BP+0x55],AX .............;89 46 55
MOV [BX+0x55],AX .............;89 47 55
MOV [BX+SI+0x55],CX ..........;89 48 55
MOV [BX+DI+0x55],CX ..........;89 49 55
MOV [BP+SI+0x55],CX ..........;89 4a 55
MOV [BP+DI+0x55],CX ..........;89 4b 55
MOV [SI+0x55],CX .............;89 4c 55
MOV [DI+0x55],CX .............;89 4d 55
MOV [BP+0x55],CX .............;89 4e 55
MOV [BX+0x55],CX .............;89 4f 55
MOV [BX+SI+0x55],DX ..........;89 50 55
MOV [BX+DI+0x55],DX ..........;89 51 55
MOV [BP+SI+0x55],DX ..........;89 52 55
MOV [BP+DI+0x55],DX ..........;89 53 55
MOV [SI+0x55],DX .............;89 54 55
MOV [DI+0x55],DX .............;89 55 55
MOV [BP+0x55],DX .............;89 56 55
MOV [BX+0x55],DX .............;89 57 55
MOV [BX+SI+0x55],BX ..........;89 58 55
MOV [BX+DI+0x55],BX ..........;89 59 55
MOV [BP+SI+0x55],BX ..........;89 5a 55
MOV [BP+DI+0x55],BX ..........;89 5b 55
MOV [SI+0x55],BX .............;89 5c 55
MOV [DI+0x55],BX .............;89 5d 55
MOV [BP+0x55],BX .............;89 5e 55
MOV [BX+0x55],BX .............;89 5f 55
MOV [BX+SI+0x55],SP ..........;89 60 55
MOV [BX+DI+0x55],SP ..........;89 61 55
MOV [BP+SI+0x55],SP ..........;89 62 55
MOV [BP+DI+0x55],SP ..........;89 63 55
MOV [SI+0x55],SP .............;89 64 55
MOV [DI+0x55],SP .............;89 65 55
MOV [BP+0x55],SP .............;89 66 55
MOV [BX+0x55],SP .............;89 67 55
MOV [BX+SI+0x55],BP ..........;89 68 55
MOV [BX+DI+0x55],BP ..........;89 69 55
MOV [BP+SI+0x55],BP ..........;89 6a 55
MOV [BP+DI+0x55],BP ..........;89 6b 55
MOV [SI+0x55],BP .............;89 6c 55
MOV [DI+0x55],BP .............;89 6d 55
MOV [BP+0x55],BP .............;89 6e 55
MOV [BX+0x55],BP .............;89 6f 55
MOV [BX+SI+0x55],SI ..........;89 70 55
MOV [BX+DI+0x55],SI ..........;89 71 55
MOV [BP+SI+0x55],SI ..........;89 72 55
MOV [BP+DI+0x55],SI ..........;89 73 55
MOV [SI+0x55],SI .............;89 74 55
MOV [DI+0x55],SI .............;89 75 55
MOV [BP+0x55],SI .............;89 76 55
MOV [BX+0x55],SI .............;89 77 55
MOV [BX+SI+0x55],DI ..........;89 78 55
MOV [BX+DI+0x55],DI ..........;89 79 55

MOV [BP+SI+0x55],DI ..........;89 7a 55
MOV [BP+DI+0x55],DI ..........;89 7b 55
MOV [SI+0x55],DI .............;89 7c 55
MOV [DI+0x55],DI .............;89 7d 55
MOV [BP+0x55],DI .............;89 7e 55
MOV [BX+0x55],DI .............;89 7f 55
MOV [BX+SI+0x5566],AX ....;89 80 66 55
MOV [BX+DI+0x5566],AX ....;89 81 66 55
MOV [BP+SI+0x5566],AX ....;89 82 66 55
MOV [BP+DI+0x5566],AX ....;89 83 66 55
MOV [SI+0x5566],AX .......;89 84 66 55
MOV [DI+0x5566],AX .......;89 85 66 55
MOV [BP+0x5566],AX .......;89 86 66 55
MOV [BX+0x5566],AX .......;89 87 66 55
MOV [BX+SI+0x5566],CX ....;89 88 66 55
MOV [BX+DI+0x5566],CX ....;89 89 66 55
MOV [BP+SI+0x5566],CX ....;89 8a 66 55
MOV [BP+DI+0x5566],CX ....;89 8b 66 55
MOV [SI+0x5566],CX .......;89 8c 66 55
MOV [DI+0x5566],CX .......;89 8d 66 55
MOV [BP+0x5566],CX .......;89 8e 66 55
MOV [BX+0x5566],CX .......;89 8f 66 55
MOV [BX+SI+0x5566],DX ....;89 90 66 55
MOV [BX+DI+0x5566],DX ....;89 91 66 55
MOV [BP+SI+0x5566],DX ....;89 92 66 55
MOV [BP+DI+0x5566],DX ....;89 93 66 55
MOV [SI+0x5566],DX .......;89 94 66 55
MOV [DI+0x5566],DX .......;89 95 66 55
MOV [BP+0x5566],DX .......;89 96 66 55
MOV [BX+0x5566],DX .......;89 97 66 55
MOV [BX+SI+0x5566],BX ....;89 98 66 55
MOV [BX+DI+0x5566],BX ....;89 99 66 55
MOV [BP+SI+0x5566],BX ....;89 9a 66 55
MOV [BP+DI+0x5566],BX ....;89 9b 66 55
MOV [SI+0x5566],BX .......;89 9c 66 55
MOV [DI+0x5566],BX .......;89 9d 66 55
MOV [BP+0x5566],BX .......;89 9e 66 55
MOV [BX+0x5566],BX .......;89 9f 66 55
MOV [BX+SI+0x5566],SP ....;89 a0 66 55
MOV [BX+DI+0x5566],SP ....;89 a1 66 55
MOV [BP+SI+0x5566],SP ....;89 a2 66 55
MOV [BP+DI+0x5566],SP ....;89 a3 66 55
MOV [SI+0x5566],SP .......;89 a4 66 55
MOV [DI+0x5566],SP .......;89 a5 66 55
MOV [BP+0x5566],SP .......;89 a6 66 55
MOV [BX+0x5566],SP .......;89 a7 66 55
MOV [BX+SI+0x5566],BP ....;89 a8 66 55
MOV [BX+DI+0x5566],BP ....;89 a9 66 55
MOV [BP+SI+0x5566],BP ....;89 aa 66 55
MOV [BP+DI+0x5566],BP ....;89 ab 66 55
MOV [SI+0x5566],BP .......;89 ac 66 55
MOV [DI+0x5566],BP .......;89 ad 66 55
MOV [BP+0x5566],BP .......;89 ae 66 55
MOV [BX+0x5566],BP .......;89 af 66 55
MOV [BX+SI+0x5566],SI ....;89 b0 66 55
MOV [BX+DI+0x5566],SI ....;89 b1 66 55
MOV [BP+SI+0x5566],SI ....;89 b2 66 55
MOV [BP+DI+0x5566],SI ....;89 b3 66 55
MOV [SI+0x5566],SI .......;89 b4 66 55
MOV [DI+0x5566],SI .......;89 b5 66 55
MOV [BP+0x5566],SI .......;89 b6 66 55
MOV [BX+0x5566],SI .......;89 b7 66 55
MOV [BX+SI+0x5566],DI ....;89 b8 66 55
MOV [BX+DI+0x5566],DI ....;89 b9 66 55
MOV [BP+SI+0x5566],DI ....;89 ba 66 55
MOV [BP+DI+0x5566],DI ....;89 bb 66 55
MOV [SI+0x5566],DI .......;89 bc 66 55
MOV [DI+0x5566],DI .......;89 bd 66 55
MOV [BP+0x5566],DI .......;89 be 66 55
MOV [BX+0x5566],DI .......;89 bf 66 55
MOV AX,AX ....................;89 c0
MOV CX,AX ....................;89 c1
MOV DX,AX ....................;89 c2
MOV BX,AX ....................;89 c3
MOV SP,AX ....................;89 c4
MOV BP,AX ....................;89 c5
MOV SI,AX ....................;89 c6
MOV DI,AX ....................;89 c7
MOV AX,CX ....................;89 c8
MOV CX,CX ....................;89 c9
MOV DX,CX ....................;89 ca
MOV BX,CX ....................;89 cb
MOV SP,CX ....................;89 cc
MOV BP,CX ....................;89 cd
MOV SI,CX ....................;89 ce
MOV DI,CX ....................;89 cf
MOV AX,DX ....................;89 d0
MOV CX,DX ....................;89 d1
MOV DX,DX ....................;89 d2
```

```
MOV BX,DX .......................;89 d3      MOV CH,[SI] ...................;8a 2c
MOV SP,DX .......................;89 d4      MOV CH,[DI] ...................;8a 2d
MOV BP,DX .......................;89 d5      MOV CH,[0x5566] ...............;8a 2e 66 55
MOV SI,DX .......................;89 d6      MOV CH,[BX] ...................;8a 2f
MOV DI,DX .......................;89 d7      MOV DH,[BX+SI] ................;8a 30
MOV AX,BX .......................;89 d8      MOV DH,[BX+DI] ................;8a 31
MOV CX,BX .......................;89 d9      MOV DH,[BP+SI] ................;8a 32
MOV DX,BX .......................;89 da      MOV DH,[BP+DI] ................;8a 33
MOV BX,BX .......................;89 db      MOV DH,[SI] ...................;8a 34
MOV SP,BX .......................;89 dc      MOV DH,[DI] ...................;8a 35
MOV BP,BX .......................;89 dd      MOV DH,[0x5566] ...............;8a 36 66 55
MOV SI,BX .......................;89 de      MOV DH,[BX] ...................;8a 37
MOV DI,BX .......................;89 df      MOV BH,[BX+SI] ................;8a 38
MOV AX,SP .......................;89 e0      MOV BH,[BX+DI] ................;8a 39
MOV CX,SP .......................;89 e1      MOV BH,[BP+SI] ................;8a 3a
MOV DX,SP .......................;89 e2      MOV BH,[BP+DI] ................;8a 3b
MOV BX,SP .......................;89 e3      MOV BH,[SI] ...................;8a 3c
MOV SP,SP .......................;89 e4      MOV BH,[DI] ...................;8a 3d
MOV BP,SP .......................;89 e5      MOV BH,[0x5566] ...............;8a 3e 66 55
MOV SI,SP .......................;89 e6      MOV BH,[BX] ...................;8a 3f
MOV DI,SP .......................;89 e7      MOV AL,[BX+SI+0x55] ...........;8a 40 55
MOV AX,BP .......................;89 e8      MOV AL,[BX+DI+0x55] ...........;8a 41 55
MOV CX,BP .......................;89 e9      MOV AL,[BP+SI+0x55] ...........;8a 42 55
MOV DX,BP .......................;89 ea      MOV AL,[BP+DI+0x55] ...........;8a 43 55
MOV BX,BP .......................;89 eb      MOV AL,[SI+0x55] ..............;8a 44 55
MOV SP,BP .......................;89 ec      MOV AL,[DI+0x55] ..............;8a 45 55
MOV BP,BP .......................;89 ed      MOV AL,[BP+0x55] ..............;8a 46 55
MOV SI,BP .......................;89 ee      MOV AL,[BX+0x55] ..............;8a 47 55
MOV DI,BP .......................;89 ef      MOV CL,[BX+SI+0x55] ...........;8a 48 55
MOV AX,SI .......................;89 f0      MOV CL,[BX+DI+0x55] ...........;8a 49 55
MOV CX,SI .......................;89 f1      MOV CL,[BP+SI+0x55] ...........;8a 4a 55
MOV DX,SI .......................;89 f2      MOV CL,[BP+DI+0x55] ...........;8a 4b 55
MOV BX,SI .......................;89 f3      MOV CL,[SI+0x55] ..............;8a 4c 55
MOV SP,SI .......................;89 f4      MOV CL,[DI+0x55] ..............;8a 4d 55
MOV BP,SI .......................;89 f5      MOV CL,[BP+0x55] ..............;8a 4e 55
MOV SI,SI .......................;89 f6      MOV CL,[BX+0x55] ..............;8a 4f 55
MOV DI,SI .......................;89 f7      MOV DL,[BX+SI+0x55] ...........;8a 50 55
MOV AX,DI .......................;89 f8      MOV DL,[BX+DI+0x55] ...........;8a 51 55
MOV CX,DI .......................;89 f9      MOV DL,[BP+SI+0x55] ...........;8a 52 55
MOV DX,DI .......................;89 fa      MOV DL,[BP+DI+0x55] ...........;8a 53 55
MOV BX,DI .......................;89 fb      MOV DL,[SI+0x55] ..............;8a 54 55
MOV SP,DI .......................;89 fc      MOV DL,[DI+0x55] ..............;8a 55 55
MOV BP,DI .......................;89 fd      MOV DL,[BP+0x55] ..............;8a 56 55
MOV SI,DI .......................;89 fe      MOV DL,[BX+0x55] ..............;8a 57 55
MOV DI,DI .......................;89 ff      MOV BL,[BX+SI+0x55] ...........;8a 58 55
MOV AL,[BX+SI] ..................;8a 00      MOV BL,[BX+DI+0x55] ...........;8a 59 55
MOV AL,[BX+DI] ..................;8a 01      MOV BL,[BP+SI+0x55] ...........;8a 5a 55
MOV AL,[BP+SI] ..................;8a 02      MOV BL,[BP+DI+0x55] ...........;8a 5b 55
MOV AL,[BP+DI] ..................;8a 03      MOV BL,[SI+0x55] ..............;8a 5c 55
MOV AL,[SI] .....................;8a 04      MOV BL,[DI+0x55] ..............;8a 5d 55
MOV AL,[DI] .....................;8a 05      MOV BL,[BP+0x55] ..............;8a 5e 55
MOV AL,[0x5566] .................;8a 06 66 55 MOV BL,[BX+0x55] ..............;8a 5f 55
MOV AL,[BX] .....................;8a 07      MOV AH,[BX+SI+0x55] ...........;8a 60 55
MOV CL,[BX+SI] ..................;8a 08      MOV AH,[BX+DI+0x55] ...........;8a 61 55
MOV CL,[BX+DI] ..................;8a 09      MOV AH,[BP+SI+0x55] ...........;8a 62 55
MOV CL,[BP+SI] ..................;8a 0a      MOV AH,[BP+DI+0x55] ...........;8a 63 55
MOV CL,[BP+DI] ..................;8a 0b      MOV AH,[SI+0x55] ..............;8a 64 55
MOV CL,[SI] .....................;8a 0c      MOV AH,[DI+0x55] ..............;8a 65 55
MOV CL,[DI] .....................;8a 0d      MOV AH,[BP+0x55] ..............;8a 66 55
MOV CL,[0x5566] .................;8a 0e 66 55 MOV AH,[BX+0x55] ..............;8a 67 55
MOV CL,[BX] .....................;8a 0f      MOV CH,[BX+SI+0x55] ...........;8a 68 55
MOV DL,[BX+SI] ..................;8a 10      MOV CH,[BX+DI+0x55] ...........;8a 69 55
MOV DL,[BX+DI] ..................;8a 11      MOV CH,[BP+SI+0x55] ...........;8a 6a 55
MOV DL,[BP+SI] ..................;8a 12      MOV CH,[BP+DI+0x55] ...........;8a 6b 55
MOV DL,[BP+DI] ..................;8a 13      MOV CH,[SI+0x55] ..............;8a 6c 55
MOV DL,[SI] .....................;8a 14      MOV CH,[DI+0x55] ..............;8a 6d 55
MOV DL,[DI] .....................;8a 15      MOV CH,[BP+0x55] ..............;8a 6e 55
MOV DL,[0x5566] .................;8a 16 66 55 MOV CH,[BX+0x55] ..............;8a 6f 55
MOV DL,[BX] .....................;8a 17      MOV DH,[BX+SI+0x55] ...........;8a 70 55
MOV BL,[BX+SI] ..................;8a 18      MOV DH,[BX+DI+0x55] ...........;8a 71 55
MOV BL,[BX+DI] ..................;8a 19      MOV DH,[BP+SI+0x55] ...........;8a 72 55
MOV BL,[BP+SI] ..................;8a 1a      MOV DH,[BP+DI+0x55] ...........;8a 73 55
MOV BL,[BP+DI] ..................;8a 1b      MOV DH,[SI+0x55] ..............;8a 74 55
MOV BL,[SI] .....................;8a 1c      MOV DH,[DI+0x55] ..............;8a 75 55
MOV BL,[DI] .....................;8a 1d      MOV DH,[BP+0x55] ..............;8a 76 55
MOV BL,[0x5566] .................;8a 1e 66 55 MOV DH,[BX+0x55] ..............;8a 77 55
MOV BL,[BX] .....................;8a 1f      MOV BH,[BX+SI+0x55] ...........;8a 78 55
MOV AH,[BX+SI] ..................;8a 20      MOV BH,[BX+DI+0x55] ...........;8a 79 55
MOV AH,[BX+DI] ..................;8a 21      MOV BH,[BP+SI+0x55] ...........;8a 7a 55
MOV AH,[BP+SI] ..................;8a 22      MOV BH,[BP+DI+0x55] ...........;8a 7b 55
MOV AH,[BP+DI] ..................;8a 23      MOV BH,[SI+0x55] ..............;8a 7c 55
MOV AH,[SI] .....................;8a 24      MOV BH,[DI+0x55] ..............;8a 7d 55
MOV AH,[DI] .....................;8a 25      MOV BH,[BP+0x55] ..............;8a 7e 55
MOV AH,[0x5566] .................;8a 26 66 55 MOV BH,[BX+0x55] ..............;8a 7f 55
MOV AH,[BX] .....................;8a 27      MOV AL,[BX+SI+0x5566] .........;8a 80 66 55
MOV CH,[BX+SI] ..................;8a 28      MOV AL,[BX+DI+0x5566] .........;8a 81 66 55
MOV CH,[BX+DI] ..................;8a 29      MOV AL,[BP+SI+0x5566] .........;8a 82 66 55
MOV CH,[BP+SI] ..................;8a 2a      MOV AL,[BP+DI+0x5566] .........;8a 83 66 55
MOV CH,[BP+DI] ..................;8a 2b      MOV AL,[SI+0x5566] ............;8a 84 66 55
```

```
MOV AL,[DI+0x5566] .............;8a 85 66 55      MOV BX,[0x5566] .................;8b 1e 66 55
MOV AL,[BP+0x5566] .............;8a 86 66 55      MOV BX,[BX] ....................;8b 1f
MOV AL,[BX+0x5566] .............;8a 87 66 55      MOV SP,[BX+SI] .................;8b 20
MOV CL,[BX+SI+0x5566] ..........;8a 88 66 55      MOV SP,[BX+DI] .................;8b 21
MOV CL,[BX+DI+0x5566] ..........;8a 89 66 55      MOV SP,[BP+SI] .................;8b 22
MOV CL,[BP+SI+0x5566] ..........;8a 8a 66 55      MOV SP,[BP+DI] .................;8b 23
MOV CL,[BP+DI+0x5566] ..........;8a 8b 66 55      MOV SP,[SI] ....................;8b 24
MOV CL,[SI+0x5566] .............;8a 8c 66 55      MOV SP,[DI] ....................;8b 25
MOV CL,[DI+0x5566] .............;8a 8d 66 55      MOV SP,[0x5566] ................;8b 26 66 55
MOV CL,[BP+0x5566] .............;8a 8e 66 55      MOV SP,[BX] ....................;8b 27
MOV CL,[BX+0x5566] .............;8a 8f 66 55      MOV BP,[BX+SI] .................;8b 28
MOV DL,[BX+SI+0x5566] ..........;8a 90 66 55      MOV BP,[BX+DI] .................;8b 29
MOV DL,[BX+DI+0x5566] ..........;8a 91 66 55      MOV BP,[BP+SI] .................;8b 2a
MOV DL,[BP+SI+0x5566] ..........;8a 92 66 55      MOV BP,[BP+DI] .................;8b 2b
MOV DL,[BP+DI+0x5566] ..........;8a 93 66 55      MOV BP,[SI] ....................;8b 2c
MOV DL,[SI+0x5566] .............;8a 94 66 55      MOV BP,[DI] ....................;8b 2d
MOV DL,[DI+0x5566] .............;8a 95 66 55      MOV BP,[0x5566] ................;8b 2e 66 55
MOV DL,[BP+0x5566] .............;8a 96 66 55      MOV BP,[BX] ....................;8b 2f
MOV DL,[BX+0x5566] .............;8a 97 66 55      MOV SI,[BX+SI] .................;8b 30
MOV BL,[BX+SI+0x5566] ..........;8a 98 66 55      MOV SI,[BX+DI] .................;8b 31
MOV BL,[BX+DI+0x5566] ..........;8a 99 66 55      MOV SI,[BP+SI] .................;8b 32
MOV BL,[BP+SI+0x5566] ..........;8a 9a 66 55      MOV SI,[BP+DI] .................;8b 33
MOV BL,[BP+DI+0x5566] ..........;8a 9b 66 55      MOV SI,[SI] ....................;8b 34
MOV BL,[SI+0x5566] .............;8a 9c 66 55      MOV SI,[DI] ....................;8b 35
MOV BL,[DI+0x5566] .............;8a 9d 66 55      MOV SI,[0x5566] ................;8b 36 66 55
MOV BL,[BP+0x5566] .............;8a 9e 66 55      MOV SI,[BX] ....................;8b 37
MOV BL,[BX+0x5566] .............;8a 9f 66 55      MOV DI,[BX+SI] .................;8b 38
MOV AH,[BX+SI+0x5566] ..........;8a a0 66 55      MOV DI,[BX+DI] .................;8b 39
MOV AH,[BX+DI+0x5566] ..........;8a a1 66 55      MOV DI,[BP+SI] .................;8b 3a
MOV AH,[BP+SI+0x5566] ..........;8a a2 66 55      MOV DI,[BP+DI] .................;8b 3b
MOV AH,[BP+DI+0x5566] ..........;8a a3 66 55      MOV DI,[SI] ....................;8b 3c
MOV AH,[SI+0x5566] .............;8a a4 66 55      MOV DI,[DI] ....................;8b 3d
MOV AH,[DI+0x5566] .............;8a a5 66 55      MOV DI,[0x5566] ................;8b 3e 66 55
MOV AH,[BP+0x5566] .............;8a a6 66 55      MOV DI,[BX] ....................;8b 3f
MOV AH,[BX+0x5566] .............;8a a7 66 55      MOV AX,[BX+SI+0x55] ............;8b 40 55
MOV CH,[BX+SI+0x5566] ..........;8a a8 66 55      MOV AX,[BX+DI+0x55] ............;8b 41 55
MOV CH,[BX+DI+0x5566] ..........;8a a9 66 55      MOV AX,[BP+SI+0x55] ............;8b 42 55
MOV CH,[BP+SI+0x5566] ..........;8a aa 66 55      MOV AX,[BP+DI+0x55] ............;8b 43 55
MOV CH,[BP+DI+0x5566] ..........;8a ab 66 55      MOV AX,[SI+0x55] ...............;8b 44 55
MOV CH,[SI+0x5566] .............;8a ac 66 55      MOV AX,[DI+0x55] ...............;8b 45 55
MOV CH,[DI+0x5566] .............;8a ad 66 55      MOV AX,[BP+0x55] ...............;8b 46 55
MOV CH,[BP+0x5566] .............;8a ae 66 55      MOV AX,[BX+0x55] ...............;8b 47 55
MOV CH,[BX+0x5566] .............;8a af 66 55      MOV CX,[BX+SI+0x55] ............;8b 48 55
MOV DH,[BX+SI+0x5566] ..........;8a b0 66 55      MOV CX,[BX+DI+0x55] ............;8b 49 55
MOV DH,[BX+DI+0x5566] ..........;8a b1 66 55      MOV CX,[BP+SI+0x55] ............;8b 4a 55
MOV DH,[BP+SI+0x5566] ..........;8a b2 66 55      MOV CX,[BP+DI+0x55] ............;8b 4b 55
MOV DH,[BP+DI+0x5566] ..........;8a b3 66 55      MOV CX,[SI+0x55] ...............;8b 4c 55
MOV DH,[SI+0x5566] .............;8a b4 66 55      MOV CX,[DI+0x55] ...............;8b 4d 55
MOV DH,[DI+0x5566] .............;8a b5 66 55      MOV CX,[BP+0x55] ...............;8b 4e 55
MOV DH,[BP+0x5566] .............;8a b6 66 55      MOV CX,[BX+0x55] ...............;8b 4f 55
MOV DH,[BX+0x5566] .............;8a b7 66 55      MOV DX,[BX+SI+0x55] ............;8b 50 55
MOV BH,[BX+SI+0x5566] ..........;8a b8 66 55      MOV DX,[BX+DI+0x55] ............;8b 51 55
MOV BH,[BX+DI+0x5566] ..........;8a b9 66 55      MOV DX,[BP+SI+0x55] ............;8b 52 55
MOV BH,[BP+SI+0x5566] ..........;8a ba 66 55      MOV DX,[BP+DI+0x55] ............;8b 53 55
MOV BH,[BP+DI+0x5566] ..........;8a bb 66 55      MOV DX,[SI+0x55] ...............;8b 54 55
MOV BH,[SI+0x5566] .............;8a bc 66 55      MOV DX,[DI+0x55] ...............;8b 55 55
MOV BH,[DI+0x5566] .............;8a bd 66 55      MOV DX,[BP+0x55] ...............;8b 56 55
MOV BH,[BP+0x5566] .............;8a be 66 55      MOV DX,[BX+0x55] ...............;8b 57 55
MOV BH,[BX+0x5566] .............;8a bf 66 55      MOV BX,[BX+SI+0x55] ............;8b 58 55
MOV AX,[BX+SI] .................;8b 00             MOV BX,[BX+DI+0x55] ............;8b 59 55
MOV AX,[BX+DI] .................;8b 01             MOV BX,[BP+SI+0x55] ............;8b 5a 55
MOV AX,[BP+SI] .................;8b 02             MOV BX,[BP+DI+0x55] ............;8b 5b 55
MOV AX,[BP+DI] .................;8b 03             MOV BX,[SI+0x55] ...............;8b 5c 55
MOV AX,[SI] ....................;8b 04             MOV BX,[DI+0x55] ...............;8b 5d 55
MOV AX,[DI] ....................;8b 05             MOV BX,[BP+0x55] ...............;8b 5e 55
MOV AX,[0x5566] ................;8b 06 66 55       MOV BX,[BX+0x55] ...............;8b 5f 55
MOV AX,[BX] ....................;8b 07             MOV SP,[BX+SI+0x55] ............;8b 60 55
MOV CX,[BX+SI] .................;8b 08             MOV SP,[BX+DI+0x55] ............;8b 61 55
MOV CX,[BX+DI] .................;8b 09             MOV SP,[BP+SI+0x55] ............;8b 62 55
MOV CX,[BP+SI] .................;8b 0a             MOV SP,[BP+DI+0x55] ............;8b 63 55
MOV CX,[BP+DI] .................;8b 0b             MOV SP,[SI+0x55] ...............;8b 64 55
MOV CX,[SI] ....................;8b 0c             MOV SP,[DI+0x55] ...............;8b 65 55
MOV CX,[DI] ....................;8b 0d             MOV SP,[BP+0x55] ...............;8b 66 55
MOV CX,[0x5566] ................;8b 0e 66 55       MOV SP,[BX+0x55] ...............;8b 67 55
MOV CX,[BX] ....................;8b 0f             MOV BP,[BX+SI+0x55] ............;8b 68 55
MOV DX,[BX+SI] .................;8b 10             MOV BP,[BX+DI+0x55] ............;8b 69 55
MOV DX,[BX+DI] .................;8b 11             MOV BP,[BP+SI+0x55] ............;8b 6a 55
MOV DX,[BP+SI] .................;8b 12             MOV BP,[BP+DI+0x55] ............;8b 6b 55
MOV DX,[BP+DI] .................;8b 13             MOV BP,[SI+0x55] ...............;8b 6c 55
MOV DX,[SI] ....................;8b 14             MOV BP,[DI+0x55] ...............;8b 6d 55
MOV DX,[DI] ....................;8b 15             MOV BP,[BP+0x55] ...............;8b 6e 55
MOV DX,[0x5566] ................;8b 16 66 55       MOV BP,[BX+0x55] ...............;8b 6f 55
MOV DX,[BX] ....................;8b 17             MOV SI,[BX+SI+0x55] ............;8b 70 55
MOV BX,[BX+SI] .................;8b 18             MOV SI,[BX+DI+0x55] ............;8b 71 55
MOV BX,[BX+DI] .................;8b 19             MOV SI,[BP+SI+0x55] ............;8b 72 55
MOV BX,[BP+SI] .................;8b 1a             MOV SI,[BP+DI+0x55] ............;8b 73 55
MOV BX,[BP+DI] .................;8b 1b             MOV SI,[SI+0x55] ...............;8b 74 55
MOV BX,[SI] ....................;8b 1c             MOV SI,[DI+0x55] ...............;8b 75 55
MOV BX,[DI] ....................;8b 1d             MOV SI,[BP+0x55] ...............;8b 76 55
```

```
MOV SI,[BX+0x55] ...............;8b 77 55          MOV [BX+SI],SS ................;8c 10
MOV DI,[BX+SI+0x55] ...........;8b 78 55          MOV [BX+DI],SS ................;8c 11
MOV DI,[BX+DI+0x55] ...........;8b 79 55          MOV [BP+SI],SS ................;8c 12
MOV DI,[BP+SI+0x55] ...........;8b 7a 55          MOV [BP+DI],SS ................;8c 13
MOV DI,[BP+DI+0x55] ...........;8b 7b 55          MOV [SI],SS ...................;8c 14
MOV DI,[SI+0x55] ..............;8b 7c 55          MOV [DI],SS ...................;8c 15
MOV DI,[DI+0x55] ..............;8b 7d 55          MOV [0x5566],SS ...............;8c 16 66 55
MOV DI,[BP+0x55] ..............;8b 7e 55          MOV [BX],SS ...................;8c 17
MOV DI,[BX+0x55] ..............;8b 7f 55          MOV [BX+SI],DS ................;8c 18
MOV AX,[BX+SI+0x5566] .........;8b 80 66 55       MOV [BX+DI],DS ................;8c 19
MOV AX,[BX+DI+0x5566] .........;8b 81 66 55       MOV [BP+SI],DS ................;8c 1a
MOV AX,[BP+SI+0x5566] .........;8b 82 66 55       MOV [BP+DI],DS ................;8c 1b
MOV AX,[BP+DI+0x5566] .........;8b 83 66 55       MOV [SI],DS ...................;8c 1c
MOV AX,[SI+0x5566] ............;8b 84 66 55       MOV [DI],DS ...................;8c 1d
MOV AX,[DI+0x5566] ............;8b 85 66 55       MOV [0x5566],DS ...............;8c 1e 66 55
MOV AX,[BP+0x5566] ............;8b 86 66 55       MOV [BX],DS ...................;8c 1f
MOV AX,[BX+0x5566] ............;8b 87 66 55       MOV [BX+SI+0x55],ES ...........;8c 40 55
MOV CX,[BX+SI+0x5566] .........;8b 88 66 55       MOV [BX+DI+0x55],ES ...........;8c 41 55
MOV CX,[BX+DI+0x5566] .........;8b 89 66 55       MOV [BP+SI+0x55],ES ...........;8c 42 55
MOV CX,[BP+SI+0x5566] .........;8b 8a 66 55       MOV [BP+DI+0x55],ES ...........;8c 43 55
MOV CX,[BP+DI+0x5566] .........;8b 8b 66 55       MOV [SI+0x55],ES ..............;8c 44 55
MOV CX,[SI+0x5566] ............;8b 8c 66 55       MOV [DI+0x55],ES ..............;8c 45 55
MOV CX,[DI+0x5566] ............;8b 8d 66 55       MOV [BP+0x55],ES ..............;8c 46 55
MOV CX,[BP+0x5566] ............;8b 8e 66 55       MOV [BX+0x55],ES ..............;8c 47 55
MOV CX,[BX+0x5566] ............;8b 8f 66 55       MOV [BX+SI+0x55],CS ...........;8c 48 55
MOV DX,[BX+SI+0x5566] .........;8b 90 66 55       MOV [BX+DI+0x55],CS ...........;8c 49 55
MOV DX,[BX+DI+0x5566] .........;8b 91 66 55       MOV [BP+SI+0x55],CS ...........;8c 4a 55
MOV DX,[BP+SI+0x5566] .........;8b 92 66 55       MOV [BP+DI+0x55],CS ...........;8c 4b 55
MOV DX,[BP+DI+0x5566] .........;8b 93 66 55       MOV [SI+0x55],CS ..............;8c 4c 55
MOV DX,[SI+0x5566] ............;8b 94 66 55       MOV [DI+0x55],CS ..............;8c 4d 55
MOV DX,[DI+0x5566] ............;8b 95 66 55       MOV [BP+0x55],CS ..............;8c 4e 55
MOV DX,[BP+0x5566] ............;8b 96 66 55       MOV [BX+0x55],CS ..............;8c 4f 55
MOV DX,[BX+0x5566] ............;8b 97 66 55       MOV [BX+SI+0x55],SS ...........;8c 50 55
MOV BX,[BX+SI+0x5566] .........;8b 98 66 55       MOV [BX+DI+0x55],SS ...........;8c 51 55
MOV BX,[BX+DI+0x5566] .........;8b 99 66 55       MOV [BP+SI+0x55],SS ...........;8c 52 55
MOV BX,[BP+SI+0x5566] .........;8b 9a 66 55       MOV [BP+DI+0x55],SS ...........;8c 53 55
MOV BX,[BP+DI+0x5566] .........;8b 9b 66 55       MOV [SI+0x55],SS ..............;8c 54 55
MOV BX,[SI+0x5566] ............;8b 9c 66 55       MOV [DI+0x55],SS ..............;8c 55 55
MOV BX,[DI+0x5566] ............;8b 9d 66 55       MOV [BP+0x55],SS ..............;8c 56 55
MOV BX,[BP+0x5566] ............;8b 9e 66 55       MOV [BX+0x55],SS ..............;8c 57 55
MOV BX,[BX+0x5566] ............;8b 9f 66 55       MOV [BX+SI+0x55],DS ...........;8c 58 55
MOV SP,[BX+SI+0x5566] .........;8b a0 66 55       MOV [BX+DI+0x55],DS ...........;8c 59 55
MOV SP,[BX+DI+0x5566] .........;8b a1 66 55       MOV [BP+SI+0x55],DS ...........;8c 5a 55
MOV SP,[BP+SI+0x5566] .........;8b a2 66 55       MOV [BP+DI+0x55],DS ...........;8c 5b 55
MOV SP,[BP+DI+0x5566] .........;8b a3 66 55       MOV [SI+0x55],DS ..............;8c 5c 55
MOV SP,[SI+0x5566] ............;8b a4 66 55       MOV [DI+0x55],DS ..............;8c 5d 55
MOV SP,[DI+0x5566] ............;8b a5 66 55       MOV [BP+0x55],DS ..............;8c 5e 55
MOV SP,[BP+0x5566] ............;8b a6 66 55       MOV [BX+0x55],DS ..............;8c 5f 55
MOV SP,[BX+0x5566] ............;8b a7 66 55       MOV [BX+SI+0x5566],ES .........;8c 80 66 55
MOV BP,[BX+SI+0x5566] .........;8b a8 66 55       MOV [BX+DI+0x5566],ES .........;8c 81 66 55
MOV BP,[BX+DI+0x5566] .........;8b a9 66 55       MOV [BP+SI+0x5566],ES .........;8c 82 66 55
MOV BP,[BP+SI+0x5566] .........;8b aa 66 55       MOV [BP+DI+0x5566],ES .........;8c 83 66 55
MOV BP,[BP+DI+0x5566] .........;8b ab 66 55       MOV [SI+0x5566],ES ............;8c 84 66 55
MOV BP,[SI+0x5566] ............;8b ac 66 55       MOV [DI+0x5566],ES ............;8c 85 66 55
MOV BP,[DI+0x5566] ............;8b ad 66 55       MOV [BP+0x5566],ES ............;8c 86 66 55
MOV BP,[BP+0x5566] ............;8b ae 66 55       MOV [BX+0x5566],ES ............;8c 87 66 55
MOV BP,[BX+0x5566] ............;8b af 66 55       MOV [BX+SI+0x5566],CS .........;8c 88 66 55
MOV SI,[BX+SI+0x5566] .........;8b b0 66 55       MOV [BX+DI+0x5566],CS .........;8c 89 66 55
MOV SI,[BX+DI+0x5566] .........;8b b1 66 55       MOV [BP+SI+0x5566],CS .........;8c 8a 66 55
MOV SI,[BP+SI+0x5566] .........;8b b2 66 55       MOV [BP+DI+0x5566],CS .........;8c 8b 66 55
MOV SI,[BP+DI+0x5566] .........;8b b3 66 55       MOV [SI+0x5566],CS ............;8c 8c 66 55
MOV SI,[SI+0x5566] ............;8b b4 66 55       MOV [DI+0x5566],CS ............;8c 8d 66 55
MOV SI,[DI+0x5566] ............;8b b5 66 55       MOV [BP+0x5566],CS ............;8c 8e 66 55
MOV SI,[BP+0x5566] ............;8b b6 66 55       MOV [BX+0x5566],CS ............;8c 8f 66 55
MOV SI,[BX+0x5566] ............;8b b7 66 55       MOV [BX+SI+0x5566],SS .........;8c 90 66 55
MOV DI,[BX+SI+0x5566] .........;8b b8 66 55       MOV [BX+DI+0x5566],SS .........;8c 91 66 55
MOV DI,[BX+DI+0x5566] .........;8b b9 66 55       MOV [BP+SI+0x5566],SS .........;8c 92 66 55
MOV DI,[BP+SI+0x5566] .........;8b ba 66 55       MOV [BP+DI+0x5566],SS .........;8c 93 66 55
MOV DI,[BP+DI+0x5566] .........;8b bb 66 55       MOV [SI+0x5566],SS ............;8c 94 66 55
MOV DI,[SI+0x5566] ............;8b bc 66 55       MOV [DI+0x5566],SS ............;8c 95 66 55
MOV DI,[DI+0x5566] ............;8b bd 66 55       MOV [BP+0x5566],SS ............;8c 96 66 55
MOV DI,[BP+0x5566] ............;8b be 66 55       MOV [BX+0x5566],SS ............;8c 97 66 55
MOV DI,[BX+0x5566] ............;8b bf 66 55       MOV [BX+SI+0x5566],DS .........;8c 98 66 55
MOV [BX+SI],ES ................;8c 00             MOV [BX+DI+0x5566],DS .........;8c 99 66 55
MOV [BX+DI],ES ................;8c 01             MOV [BP+SI+0x5566],DS .........;8c 9a 66 55
MOV [BP+SI],ES ................;8c 02             MOV [BP+DI+0x5566],DS .........;8c 9b 66 55
MOV [BP+DI],ES ................;8c 03             MOV [SI+0x5566],DS ............;8c 9c 66 55
MOV [SI],ES ...................;8c 04             MOV [DI+0x5566],DS ............;8c 9d 66 55
MOV [DI],ES ...................;8c 05             MOV [BP+0x5566],DS ............;8c 9e 66 55
MOV [0x5566],ES ...............;8c 06 66 55       MOV [BX+0x5566],DS ............;8c 9f 66 55
MOV [BX],ES ...................;8c 07             MOV AX,ES .....................;8c c0
MOV [BX+SI],CS ................;8c 08             MOV CX,ES .....................;8c c1
MOV [BX+DI],CS ................;8c 09             MOV DX,ES .....................;8c c2
MOV [BP+SI],CS ................;8c 0a             MOV BX,ES .....................;8c c3
MOV [BP+DI],CS ................;8c 0b             MOV SP,ES .....................;8c c4
MOV [SI],CS ...................;8c 0c             MOV BP,ES .....................;8c c5
MOV [DI],CS ...................;8c 0d             MOV SI,ES .....................;8c c6
MOV [0x5566],CS ...............;8c 0e 66 55       MOV DI,ES .....................;8c c7
MOV [BX],CS ...................;8c 0f             MOV AX,CS .....................;8c c8
```

```
MOV CX,CS .....................;8c c9          LEA AX,[BP+SI+0x55] ...........;8d 42 55
MOV DX,CS .....................;8c ca          LEA AX,[BP+DI+0x55] ...........;8d 43 55
MOV BX,CS .....................;8c cb          LEA AX,[SI+0x55] ..............;8d 44 55
MOV SP,CS .....................;8c cc          LEA AX,[DI+0x55] ..............;8d 45 55
MOV BP,CS .....................;8c cd          LEA AX,[BP+0x55] ..............;8d 46 55
MOV SI,CS .....................;8c ce          LEA AX,[BX+0x55] ..............;8d 47 55
MOV DI,CS .....................;8c cf          LEA CX,[BX+SI+0x55] ...........;8d 48 55
MOV AX,SS .....................;8c d0          LEA CX,[BX+DI+0x55] ...........;8d 49 55
MOV CX,SS .....................;8c d1          LEA CX,[BP+SI+0x55] ...........;8d 4a 55
MOV DX,SS .....................;8c d2          LEA CX,[BP+DI+0x55] ...........;8d 4b 55
MOV BX,SS .....................;8c d3          LEA CX,[SI+0x55] ..............;8d 4c 55
MOV SP,SS .....................;8c d4          LEA CX,[DI+0x55] ..............;8d 4d 55
MOV BP,SS .....................;8c d5          LEA CX,[BP+0x55] ..............;8d 4e 55
MOV SI,SS .....................;8c d6          LEA CX,[BX+0x55] ..............;8d 4f 55
MOV DI,SS .....................;8c d7          LEA DX,[BX+SI+0x55] ...........;8d 50 55
MOV AX,DS .....................;8c d8          LEA DX,[BX+DI+0x55] ...........;8d 51 55
MOV CX,DS .....................;8c d9          LEA DX,[BP+SI+0x55] ...........;8d 52 55
MOV DX,DS .....................;8c da          LEA DX,[BP+DI+0x55] ...........;8d 53 55
MOV BX,DS .....................;8c db          LEA DX,[SI+0x55] ..............;8d 54 55
MOV SP,DS .....................;8c dc          LEA DX,[DI+0x55] ..............;8d 55 55
MOV BP,DS .....................;8c dd          LEA DX,[BP+0x55] ..............;8d 56 55
MOV SI,DS .....................;8c de          LEA DX,[BX+0x55] ..............;8d 57 55
MOV DI,DS .....................;8c df          LEA BX,[BX+SI+0x55] ...........;8d 58 55
LEA AX,[BX+SI] ................;8d 00          LEA BX,[BX+DI+0x55] ...........;8d 59 55
LEA AX,[BX+DI] ................;8d 01          LEA BX,[BP+SI+0x55] ...........;8d 5a 55
LEA AX,[BP+SI] ................;8d 02          LEA BX,[BP+DI+0x55] ...........;8d 5b 55
LEA AX,[BP+DI] ................;8d 03          LEA BX,[SI+0x55] ..............;8d 5c 55
LEA AX,[SI] ...................;8d 04          LEA BX,[DI+0x55] ..............;8d 5d 55
LEA AX,[DI] ...................;8d 05          LEA BX,[BP+0x55] ..............;8d 5e 55
LEA AX,[0x5566] ...............;8d 06 66 55    LEA BX,[BX+0x55] ..............;8d 5f 55
LEA AX,[BX] ...................;8d 07          LEA SP,[BX+SI+0x55] ...........;8d 60 55
LEA CX,[BX+SI] ................;8d 08          LEA SP,[BX+DI+0x55] ...........;8d 61 55
LEA CX,[BX+DI] ................;8d 09          LEA SP,[BP+SI+0x55] ...........;8d 62 55
LEA CX,[BP+SI] ................;8d 0a          LEA SP,[BP+DI+0x55] ...........;8d 63 55
LEA CX,[BP+DI] ................;8d 0b          LEA SP,[SI+0x55] ..............;8d 64 55
LEA CX,[SI] ...................;8d 0c          LEA SP,[DI+0x55] ..............;8d 65 55
LEA CX,[DI] ...................;8d 0d          LEA SP,[BP+0x55] ..............;8d 66 55
LEA CX,[0x5566] ...............;8d 0e 66 55    LEA SP,[BX+0x55] ..............;8d 67 55
LEA CX,[BX] ...................;8d 0f          LEA BP,[BX+SI+0x55] ...........;8d 68 55
LEA DX,[BX+SI] ................;8d 10          LEA BP,[BX+DI+0x55] ...........;8d 69 55
LEA DX,[BX+DI] ................;8d 11          LEA BP,[BP+SI+0x55] ...........;8d 6a 55
LEA DX,[BP+SI] ................;8d 12          LEA BP,[BP+DI+0x55] ...........;8d 6b 55
LEA DX,[BP+DI] ................;8d 13          LEA BP,[SI+0x55] ..............;8d 6c 55
LEA DX,[SI] ...................;8d 14          LEA BP,[DI+0x55] ..............;8d 6d 55
LEA DX,[DI] ...................;8d 15          LEA BP,[BP+0x55] ..............;8d 6e 55
LEA DX,[0x5566] ...............;8d 16 66 55    LEA BP,[BX+0x55] ..............;8d 6f 55
LEA DX,[BX] ...................;8d 17          LEA SI,[BX+SI+0x55] ...........;8d 70 55
LEA BX,[BX+SI] ................;8d 18          LEA SI,[BX+DI+0x55] ...........;8d 71 55
LEA BX,[BX+DI] ................;8d 19          LEA SI,[BP+SI+0x55] ...........;8d 72 55
LEA BX,[BP+SI] ................;8d 1a          LEA SI,[BP+DI+0x55] ...........;8d 73 55
LEA BX,[BP+DI] ................;8d 1b          LEA SI,[SI+0x55] ..............;8d 74 55
LEA BX,[SI] ...................;8d 1c          LEA SI,[DI+0x55] ..............;8d 75 55
LEA BX,[DI] ...................;8d 1d          LEA SI,[BP+0x55] ..............;8d 76 55
LEA BX,[0x5566] ...............;8d 1e 66 55    LEA SI,[BX+0x55] ..............;8d 77 55
LEA BX,[BX] ...................;8d 1f          LEA DI,[BX+SI+0x55] ...........;8d 78 55
LEA SP,[BX+SI] ................;8d 20          LEA DI,[BX+DI+0x55] ...........;8d 79 55
LEA SP,[BX+DI] ................;8d 21          LEA DI,[BP+SI+0x55] ...........;8d 7a 55
LEA SP,[BP+SI] ................;8d 22          LEA DI,[BP+DI+0x55] ...........;8d 7b 55
LEA SP,[BP+DI] ................;8d 23          LEA DI,[SI+0x55] ..............;8d 7c 55
LEA SP,[SI] ...................;8d 24          LEA DI,[DI+0x55] ..............;8d 7d 55
LEA SP,[DI] ...................;8d 25          LEA DI,[BP+0x55] ..............;8d 7e 55
LEA SP,[0x5566] ...............;8d 26 66 55    LEA DI,[BX+0x55] ..............;8d 7f 55
LEA SP,[BX] ...................;8d 27          LEA AX,[BX+SI+0x5566] .........;8d 80 66 55
LEA BP,[BX+SI] ................;8d 28          LEA AX,[BX+DI+0x5566] .........;8d 81 66 55
LEA BP,[BX+DI] ................;8d 29          LEA AX,[BP+SI+0x5566] .........;8d 82 66 55
LEA BP,[BP+SI] ................;8d 2a          LEA AX,[BP+DI+0x5566] .........;8d 83 66 55
LEA BP,[BP+DI] ................;8d 2b          LEA AX,[SI+0x5566] ............;8d 84 66 55
LEA BP,[SI] ...................;8d 2c          LEA AX,[DI+0x5566] ............;8d 85 66 55
LEA BP,[DI] ...................;8d 2d          LEA AX,[BP+0x5566] ............;8d 86 66 55
LEA BP,[0x5566] ...............;8d 2e 66 55    LEA AX,[BX+0x5566] ............;8d 87 66 55
LEA BP,[BX] ...................;8d 2f          LEA CX,[BX+SI+0x5566] .........;8d 88 66 55
LEA SI,[BX+SI] ................;8d 30          LEA CX,[BX+DI+0x5566] .........;8d 89 66 55
LEA SI,[BX+DI] ................;8d 31          LEA CX,[BP+SI+0x5566] .........;8d 8a 66 55
LEA SI,[BP+SI] ................;8d 32          LEA CX,[BP+DI+0x5566] .........;8d 8b 66 55
LEA SI,[BP+DI] ................;8d 33          LEA CX,[SI+0x5566] ............;8d 8c 66 55
LEA SI,[SI] ...................;8d 34          LEA CX,[DI+0x5566] ............;8d 8d 66 55
LEA SI,[DI] ...................;8d 35          LEA CX,[BP+0x5566] ............;8d 8e 66 55
LEA SI,[0x5566] ...............;8d 36 66 55    LEA CX,[BX+0x5566] ............;8d 8f 66 55
LEA SI,[BX] ...................;8d 37          LEA DX,[BX+SI+0x5566] .........;8d 90 66 55
LEA DI,[BX+SI] ................;8d 38          LEA DX,[BX+DI+0x5566] .........;8d 91 66 55
LEA DI,[BX+DI] ................;8d 39          LEA DX,[BP+SI+0x5566] .........;8d 92 66 55
LEA DI,[BP+SI] ................;8d 3a          LEA DX,[BP+DI+0x5566] .........;8d 93 66 55
LEA DI,[BP+DI] ................;8d 3b          LEA DX,[SI+0x5566] ............;8d 94 66 55
LEA DI,[SI] ...................;8d 3c          LEA DX,[DI+0x5566] ............;8d 95 66 55
LEA DI,[DI] ...................;8d 3d          LEA DX,[BP+0x5566] ............;8d 96 66 55
LEA DI,[0x5566] ...............;8d 3e 66 55    LEA DX,[BX+0x5566] ............;8d 97 66 55
LEA DI,[BX] ...................;8d 3f          LEA BX,[BX+SI+0x5566] .........;8d 98 66 55
LEA AX,[BX+SI+0x55] ...........;8d 40 55       LEA BX,[BX+DI+0x5566] .........;8d 99 66 55
LEA AX,[BX+DI+0x55] ...........;8d 41 55       LEA BX,[BP+SI+0x5566] .........;8d 9a 66 55
```

```
LEA BX,[BP+DI+0x5566] ..........;8d 9b 66 55
LEA BX,[SI+0x5566] ............;8d 9c 66 55
LEA BX,[DI+0x5566] ............;8d 9d 66 55
LEA BX,[BP+0x5566] ............;8d 9e 66 55
LEA BX,[BX+0x5566] ............;8d 9f 66 55
LEA SP,[BX+SI+0x5566] .........;8d a0 66 55
LEA SP,[BX+DI+0x5566] .........;8d a1 66 55
LEA SP,[BP+SI+0x5566] .........;8d a2 66 55
LEA SP,[BP+DI+0x5566] .........;8d a3 66 55
LEA SP,[SI+0x5566] ............;8d a4 66 55
LEA SP,[DI+0x5566] ............;8d a5 66 55
LEA SP,[BP+0x5566] ............;8d a6 66 55
LEA SP,[BX+0x5566] ............;8d a7 66 55
LEA BP,[BX+SI+0x5566] .........;8d a8 66 55
LEA BP,[BX+DI+0x5566] .........;8d a9 66 55
LEA BP,[BP+SI+0x5566] .........;8d aa 66 55
LEA BP,[BP+DI+0x5566] .........;8d ab 66 55
LEA BP,[SI+0x5566] ............;8d ac 66 55
LEA BP,[DI+0x5566] ............;8d ad 66 55
LEA BP,[BP+0x5566] ............;8d ae 66 55
LEA BP,[BX+0x5566] ............;8d af 66 55
LEA SI,[BX+SI+0x5566] .........;8d b0 66 55
LEA SI,[BX+DI+0x5566] .........;8d b1 66 55
LEA SI,[BP+SI+0x5566] .........;8d b2 66 55
LEA SI,[BP+DI+0x5566] .........;8d b3 66 55
LEA SI,[SI+0x5566] ............;8d b4 66 55
LEA SI,[DI+0x5566] ............;8d b5 66 55
LEA SI,[BP+0x5566] ............;8d b6 66 55
LEA SI,[BX+0x5566] ............;8d b7 66 55
LEA DI,[BX+SI+0x5566] .........;8d b8 66 55
LEA DI,[BX+DI+0x5566] .........;8d b9 66 55
LEA DI,[BP+SI+0x5566] .........;8d ba 66 55
LEA DI,[BP+DI+0x5566] .........;8d bb 66 55
LEA DI,[SI+0x5566] ............;8d bc 66 55
LEA DI,[DI+0x5566] ............;8d bd 66 55
LEA DI,[BP+0x5566] ............;8d be 66 55
LEA DI,[BX+0x5566] ............;8d bf 66 55
MOV ES,[BX+SI] ................;8e 00
MOV ES,[BX+DI] ................;8e 01
MOV ES,[BP+SI] ................;8e 02
MOV ES,[BP+DI] ................;8e 03
MOV ES,[SI] ...................;8e 04
MOV ES,[DI] ...................;8e 05
MOV ES,[0x5566] ...............;8e 06 66 55
MOV ES,[BX] ...................;8e 07
MOV CS,[BX+SI] ................;8e 08
MOV CS,[BX+DI] ................;8e 09
MOV CS,[BP+SI] ................;8e 0a
MOV CS,[BP+DI] ................;8e 0b
MOV CS,[SI] ...................;8e 0c
MOV CS,[DI] ...................;8e 0d
MOV CS,[0x5566] ...............;8e 0e 66 55
MOV CS,[BX] ...................;8e 0f
MOV SS,[BX+SI] ................;8e 10
MOV SS,[BX+DI] ................;8e 11
MOV SS,[BP+SI] ................;8e 12
MOV SS,[BP+DI] ................;8e 13
MOV SS,[SI] ...................;8e 14
MOV SS,[DI] ...................;8e 15
MOV SS,[0x5566] ...............;8e 16 66 55
MOV SS,[BX] ...................;8e 17
MOV DS,[BX+SI] ................;8e 18
MOV DS,[BX+DI] ................;8e 19
MOV DS,[BP+SI] ................;8e 1a
MOV DS,[BP+DI] ................;8e 1b
MOV DS,[SI] ...................;8e 1c
MOV DS,[DI] ...................;8e 1d
MOV DS,[0x5566] ...............;8e 1e 66 55
MOV DS,[BX] ...................;8e 1f
MOV ES,[BX+SI+0x55] ...........;8e 40 55
MOV ES,[BX+DI+0x55] ...........;8e 41 55
MOV ES,[BP+SI+0x55] ...........;8e 42 55
MOV ES,[BP+DI+0x55] ...........;8e 43 55
MOV ES,[SI+0x55] ..............;8e 44 55
MOV ES,[DI+0x55] ..............;8e 45 55
MOV ES,[BP+0x55] ..............;8e 46 55
MOV ES,[BX+0x55] ..............;8e 47 55
MOV CS,[BX+SI+0x55] ...........;8e 48 55
MOV CS,[BX+DI+0x55] ...........;8e 49 55
MOV CS,[BP+SI+0x55] ...........;8e 4a 55
MOV CS,[BP+DI+0x55] ...........;8e 4b 55
MOV CS,[SI+0x55] ..............;8e 4c 55
MOV CS,[DI+0x55] ..............;8e 4d 55
MOV CS,[BP+0x55] ..............;8e 4e 55
MOV CS,[BX+0x55] ..............;8e 4f 55
MOV SS,[BX+SI+0x55] ...........;8e 50 55
MOV SS,[BX+DI+0x55] ...........;8e 51 55
MOV SS,[BP+SI+0x55] ...........;8e 52 55
MOV SS,[BP+DI+0x55] ...........;8e 53 55
MOV SS,[SI+0x55] ..............;8e 54 55
MOV SS,[DI+0x55] ..............;8e 55 55
MOV SS,[BP+0x55] ..............;8e 56 55
MOV SS,[BX+0x55] ..............;8e 57 55
MOV DS,[BX+SI+0x55] ...........;8e 58 55
MOV DS,[BX+DI+0x55] ...........;8e 59 55
MOV DS,[BP+SI+0x55] ...........;8e 5a 55
MOV DS,[BP+DI+0x55] ...........;8e 5b 55
MOV DS,[SI+0x55] ..............;8e 5c 55
MOV DS,[DI+0x55] ..............;8e 5d 55
MOV DS,[BP+0x55] ..............;8e 5e 55
MOV DS,[BX+0x55] ..............;8e 5f 55
MOV ES,[BX+SI+0x5566] .........;8e 80 66 55
MOV ES,[BX+DI+0x5566] .........;8e 81 66 55
MOV ES,[BP+SI+0x5566] .........;8e 82 66 55
MOV ES,[BP+DI+0x5566] .........;8e 83 66 55
MOV ES,[SI+0x5566] ............;8e 84 66 55
MOV ES,[DI+0x5566] ............;8e 85 66 55
MOV ES,[BP+0x5566] ............;8e 86 66 55
MOV ES,[BX+0x5566] ............;8e 87 66 55
MOV CS,[BX+SI+0x5566] .........;8e 88 66 55
MOV CS,[BX+DI+0x5566] .........;8e 89 66 55
MOV CS,[BP+SI+0x5566] .........;8e 8a 66 55
MOV CS,[BP+DI+0x5566] .........;8e 8b 66 55
MOV CS,[SI+0x5566] ............;8e 8c 66 55
MOV CS,[DI+0x5566] ............;8e 8d 66 55
MOV CS,[BP+0x5566] ............;8e 8e 66 55
MOV CS,[BX+0x5566] ............;8e 8f 66 55
MOV SS,[BX+SI+0x5566] .........;8e 90 66 55
MOV SS,[BX+DI+0x5566] .........;8e 91 66 55
MOV SS,[BP+SI+0x5566] .........;8e 92 66 55
MOV SS,[BP+DI+0x5566] .........;8e 93 66 55
MOV SS,[SI+0x5566] ............;8e 94 66 55
MOV SS,[DI+0x5566] ............;8e 95 66 55
MOV SS,[BP+0x5566] ............;8e 96 66 55
MOV SS,[BX+0x5566] ............;8e 97 66 55
MOV DS,[BX+SI+0x5566] .........;8e 98 66 55
MOV DS,[BX+DI+0x5566] .........;8e 99 66 55
MOV DS,[BP+SI+0x5566] .........;8e 9a 66 55
MOV DS,[BP+DI+0x5566] .........;8e 9b 66 55
MOV DS,[SI+0x5566] ............;8e 9c 66 55
MOV DS,[DI+0x5566] ............;8e 9d 66 55
MOV DS,[BP+0x5566] ............;8e 9e 66 55
MOV DS,[BX+0x5566] ............;8e 9f 66 55
MOV ES,AX .....................;8e c0
MOV ES,CX .....................;8e c1
MOV ES,DX .....................;8e c2
MOV ES,BX .....................;8e c3
MOV ES,SP .....................;8e c4
MOV ES,BP .....................;8e c5
MOV ES,SI .....................;8e c6
MOV ES,DI .....................;8e c7
MOV CS,AX .....................;8e c8
MOV CS,CX .....................;8e c9
MOV CS,DX .....................;8e ca
MOV CS,BX .....................;8e cb
MOV CS,SP .....................;8e cc
MOV CS,BP .....................;8e cd
MOV CS,SI .....................;8e ce
MOV CS,DI .....................;8e cf
MOV SS,AX .....................;8e d0
MOV SS,CX .....................;8e d1
MOV SS,DX .....................;8e d2
MOV SS,BX .....................;8e d3
MOV SS,SP .....................;8e d4
MOV SS,BP .....................;8e d5
MOV SS,SI .....................;8e d6
MOV SS,DI .....................;8e d7
MOV DS,AX .....................;8e d8
MOV DS,CX .....................;8e d9
MOV DS,DX .....................;8e da
MOV DS,BX .....................;8e db
MOV DS,SP .....................;8e dc
MOV DS,BP .....................;8e dd
MOV DS,SI .....................;8e de
MOV DS,DI .....................;8e df
POP WORD [BX+SI] ..............;8f 00
POP WORD [BX+DI] ..............;8f 01
POP WORD [BP+SI] ..............;8f 02
POP WORD [BP+DI] ..............;8f 03
POP WORD [SI] .................;8f 04
POP WORD [DI] .................;8f 05
POP WORD [0x5566] .............;8f 06 66 55
POP WORD [BX] .................;8f 07
POP WORD [BX+SI+0x55] .........;8f 40 55
POP WORD [BX+DI+0x55] .........;8f 41 55
POP WORD [BP+SI+0x55] .........;8f 42 55
POP WORD [BP+DI+0x55] .........;8f 43 55
POP WORD [SI+0x55] ............;8f 44 55
```

```
POP WORD [DI+0x55] .............;8f 45 55        LES BX,[SI] ....................;c4 1c
POP WORD [BP+0x55] .............;8f 46 55        LES BX,[DI] ....................;c4 1d
POP WORD [BX+0x55] .............;8f 47 55        LES BX,[0x5566] ................;c4 1e 66 55
POP WORD [BX+SI+0x5566] .......;8f 80 66 55      LES BX,[BX] ....................;c4 1f
POP WORD [BX+DI+0x5566] .......;8f 81 66 55      LES SP,[BX+SI] .................;c4 20
POP WORD [BP+SI+0x5566] .......;8f 82 66 55      LES SP,[BX+DI] .................;c4 21
POP WORD [BP+DI+0x5566] .......;8f 83 66 55      LES SP,[BP+SI] .................;c4 22
POP WORD [SI+0x5566] ..........;8f 84 66 55      LES SP,[BP+DI] .................;c4 23
POP WORD [DI+0x5566] ..........;8f 85 66 55      LES SP,[SI] ....................;c4 24
POP WORD [BP+0x5566] ..........;8f 86 66 55      LES SP,[DI] ....................;c4 25
POP WORD [BX+0x5566] ..........;8f 87 66 55      LES SP,[0x5566] ................;c4 26 66 55
NOP ...........................;90               LES SP,[BX] ....................;c4 27
XCHG AX,CX ....................;91               LES BP,[BX+SI] .................;c4 28
XCHG AX,DX ....................;92               LES BP,[BX+DI] .................;c4 29
XCHG AX,BX ....................;93               LES BP,[BP+SI] .................;c4 2a
XCHG AX,SP ....................;94               LES BP,[BP+DI] .................;c4 2b
XCHG AX,BP ....................;95               LES BP,[SI] ....................;c4 2c
XCHG AX,SI ....................;96               LES BP,[DI] ....................;c4 2d
XCHG AX,DI ....................;97               LES BP,[0x5566] ................;c4 2e 66 55
CBW ...........................;98               LES BP,[BX] ....................;c4 2f
CWD ...........................;99               LES SI,[BX+SI] .................;c4 30
CALL 0x5566:0x7788 ............;9a 66 55 88 77   LES SI,[BX+DI] .................;c4 31
WAIT ..........................;9b               LES SI,[BP+SI] .................;c4 32
PUSHF .........................;9c               LES SI,[BP+DI] .................;c4 33
POPF ..........................;9d               LES SI,[SI] ....................;c4 34
SAHF ..........................;9e               LES SI,[DI] ....................;c4 35
LAHF ..........................;9f               LES SI,[0x5566] ................;c4 36 66 55
MOV AL,[0x5566] ...............;a0 66 55         LES SI,[BX] ....................;c4 37
MOV AX,[0x5566] ...............;a1 66 55         LES DI,[BX+SI] .................;c4 38
MOV [0x5566],AL ...............;a2 66 55         LES DI,[BX+DI] .................;c4 39
MOV [0x5566],AX ...............;a3 66 55         LES DI,[BP+SI] .................;c4 3a
MOVSB .........................;a4               LES DI,[BP+DI] .................;c4 3b
MOVSW .........................;a5               LES DI,[SI] ....................;c4 3c
CMPSB .........................;a6               LES DI,[DI] ....................;c4 3d
CMPSW .........................;a7               LES DI,[0x5566] ................;c4 3e 66 55
TEST AL,0x55 ..................;a8 55            LES DI,[BX] ....................;c4 3f
TEST AX,0x5566 ................;a9 66 55         LES AX,[BX+SI+0x55] ............;c4 40 55
STOSB .........................;aa               LES AX,[BX+DI+0x55] ............;c4 41 55
STOSW .........................;ab               LES AX,[BP+SI+0x55] ............;c4 42 55
LODSB .........................;ac               LES AX,[BP+DI+0x55] ............;c4 43 55
LODSW .........................;ad               LES AX,[SI+0x55] ...............;c4 44 55
SCASB .........................;ae               LES AX,[DI+0x55] ...............;c4 45 55
SCASW .........................;af               LES AX,[BP+0x55] ...............;c4 46 55
MOV AL,0x55 ...................;b0 55            LES AX,[BX+0x55] ...............;c4 47 55
MOV CL,0x55 ...................;b1 55            LES CX,[BX+SI+0x55] ............;c4 48 55
MOV DL,0x55 ...................;b2 55            LES CX,[BX+DI+0x55] ............;c4 49 55
MOV BL,0x55 ...................;b3 55            LES CX,[BP+SI+0x55] ............;c4 4a 55
MOV AH,0x55 ...................;b4 55            LES CX,[BP+DI+0x55] ............;c4 4b 55
MOV CH,0x55 ...................;b5 55            LES CX,[SI+0x55] ...............;c4 4c 55
MOV DH,0x55 ...................;b6 55            LES CX,[DI+0x55] ...............;c4 4d 55
MOV BH,0x55 ...................;b7 55            LES CX,[BP+0x55] ...............;c4 4e 55
MOV AX,0x5566 .................;b8 66 55         LES CX,[BX+0x55] ...............;c4 4f 55
MOV CX,0x5566 .................;b9 66 55         LES DX,[BX+SI+0x55] ............;c4 50 55
MOV DX,0x5566 .................;ba 66 55         LES DX,[BX+DI+0x55] ............;c4 51 55
MOV BX,0x5566 .................;bb 66 55         LES DX,[BP+SI+0x55] ............;c4 52 55
MOV SP,0x5566 .................;bc 66 55         LES DX,[BP+DI+0x55] ............;c4 53 55
MOV BP,0x5566 .................;bd 66 55         LES DX,[SI+0x55] ...............;c4 54 55
MOV SI,0x5566 .................;be 66 55         LES DX,[DI+0x55] ...............;c4 55 55
MOV DI,0x5566 .................;bf 66 55         LES DX,[BP+0x55] ...............;c4 56 55
RET 0x5566 ....................;c2 66 55         LES DX,[BX+0x55] ...............;c4 57 55
RET ...........................;c3               LES BX,[BX+SI+0x55] ............;c4 58 55
LES AX,[BX+SI] .................;c4 00           LES BX,[BX+DI+0x55] ............;c4 59 55
LES AX,[BX+DI] .................;c4 01           LES BX,[BP+SI+0x55] ............;c4 5a 55
LES AX,[BP+SI] .................;c4 02           LES BX,[BP+DI+0x55] ............;c4 5b 55
LES AX,[BP+DI] .................;c4 03           LES BX,[SI+0x55] ...............;c4 5c 55
LES AX,[SI] ....................;c4 04           LES BX,[DI+0x55] ...............;c4 5d 55
LES AX,[DI] ....................;c4 05           LES BX,[BP+0x55] ...............;c4 5e 55
LES AX,[0x5566] ................;c4 06 66 55     LES BX,[BX+0x55] ...............;c4 5f 55
LES AX,[BX] ....................;c4 07           LES SP,[BX+SI+0x55] ............;c4 60 55
LES CX,[BX+SI] .................;c4 08           LES SP,[BX+DI+0x55] ............;c4 61 55
LES CX,[BX+DI] .................;c4 09           LES SP,[BP+SI+0x55] ............;c4 62 55
LES CX,[BP+SI] .................;c4 0a           LES SP,[BP+DI+0x55] ............;c4 63 55
LES CX,[BP+DI] .................;c4 0b           LES SP,[SI+0x55] ...............;c4 64 55
LES CX,[SI] ....................;c4 0c           LES SP,[DI+0x55] ...............;c4 65 55
LES CX,[DI] ....................;c4 0d           LES SP,[BP+0x55] ...............;c4 66 55
LES CX,[0x5566] ................;c4 0e 66 55     LES SP,[BX+0x55] ...............;c4 67 55
LES CX,[BX] ....................;c4 0f           LES BP,[BX+SI+0x55] ............;c4 68 55
LES DX,[BX+SI] .................;c4 10           LES BP,[BX+DI+0x55] ............;c4 69 55
LES DX,[BX+DI] .................;c4 11           LES BP,[BP+SI+0x55] ............;c4 6a 55
LES DX,[BP+SI] .................;c4 12           LES BP,[BP+DI+0x55] ............;c4 6b 55
LES DX,[BP+DI] .................;c4 13           LES BP,[SI+0x55] ...............;c4 6c 55
LES DX,[SI] ....................;c4 14           LES BP,[DI+0x55] ...............;c4 6d 55
LES DX,[DI] ....................;c4 15           LES BP,[BP+0x55] ...............;c4 6e 55
LES DX,[0x5566] ................;c4 16 66 55     LES BP,[BX+0x55] ...............;c4 6f 55
LES DX,[BX] ....................;c4 17           LES SI,[BX+SI+0x55] ............;c4 70 55
LES BX,[BX+SI] .................;c4 18           LES SI,[BX+DI+0x55] ............;c4 71 55
LES BX,[BX+DI] .................;c4 19           LES SI,[BP+SI+0x55] ............;c4 72 55
LES BX,[BP+SI] .................;c4 1a           LES SI,[BP+DI+0x55] ............;c4 73 55
LES BX,[BP+DI] .................;c4 1b           LES SI,[SI+0x55] ...............;c4 74 55
```

```
LES SI,[DI+0x55] ................;c4 75 55
LES SI,[BP+0x55] ................;c4 76 55
LES SI,[BX+0x55] ................;c4 77 55
LES DI,[BX+SI+0x55] .............;c4 78 55
LES DI,[BX+DI+0x55] .............;c4 79 55
LES DI,[BP+SI+0x55] .............;c4 7a 55
LES DI,[BP+DI+0x55] .............;c4 7b 55
LES DI,[SI+0x55] ................;c4 7c 55
LES DI,[DI+0x55] ................;c4 7d 55
LES DI,[BP+0x55] ................;c4 7e 55
LES DI,[BX+0x55] ................;c4 7f 55
LES AX,[BX+SI+0x5566] ...........;c4 80 66 55
LES AX,[BX+DI+0x5566] ...........;c4 81 66 55
LES AX,[BP+SI+0x5566] ...........;c4 82 66 55
LES AX,[BP+DI+0x5566] ...........;c4 83 66 55
LES AX,[SI+0x5566] ..............;c4 84 66 55
LES AX,[DI+0x5566] ..............;c4 85 66 55
LES AX,[BP+0x5566] ..............;c4 86 66 55
LES AX,[BX+0x5566] ..............;c4 87 66 55
LES CX,[BX+SI+0x5566] ...........;c4 88 66 55
LES CX,[BX+DI+0x5566] ...........;c4 89 66 55
LES CX,[BP+SI+0x5566] ...........;c4 8a 66 55
LES CX,[BP+DI+0x5566] ...........;c4 8b 66 55
LES CX,[SI+0x5566] ..............;c4 8c 66 55
LES CX,[DI+0x5566] ..............;c4 8d 66 55
LES CX,[BP+0x5566] ..............;c4 8e 66 55
LES CX,[BX+0x5566] ..............;c4 8f 66 55
LES DX,[BX+SI+0x5566] ...........;c4 90 66 55
LES DX,[BX+DI+0x5566] ...........;c4 91 66 55
LES DX,[BP+SI+0x5566] ...........;c4 92 66 55
LES DX,[BP+DI+0x5566] ...........;c4 93 66 55
LES DX,[SI+0x5566] ..............;c4 94 66 55
LES DX,[DI+0x5566] ..............;c4 95 66 55
LES DX,[BP+0x5566] ..............;c4 96 66 55
LES DX,[BX+0x5566] ..............;c4 97 66 55
LES BX,[BX+SI+0x5566] ...........;c4 98 66 55
LES BX,[BX+DI+0x5566] ...........;c4 99 66 55
LES BX,[BP+SI+0x5566] ...........;c4 9a 66 55
LES BX,[BP+DI+0x5566] ...........;c4 9b 66 55
LES BX,[SI+0x5566] ..............;c4 9c 66 55
LES BX,[DI+0x5566] ..............;c4 9d 66 55
LES BX,[BP+0x5566] ..............;c4 9e 66 55
LES BX,[BX+0x5566] ..............;c4 9f 66 55
LES SP,[BX+SI+0x5566] ...........;c4 a0 66 55
LES SP,[BX+DI+0x5566] ...........;c4 a1 66 55
LES SP,[BP+SI+0x5566] ...........;c4 a2 66 55
LES SP,[BP+DI+0x5566] ...........;c4 a3 66 55
LES SP,[SI+0x5566] ..............;c4 a4 66 55
LES SP,[DI+0x5566] ..............;c4 a5 66 55
LES SP,[BP+0x5566] ..............;c4 a6 66 55
LES SP,[BX+0x5566] ..............;c4 a7 66 55
LES BP,[BX+SI+0x5566] ...........;c4 a8 66 55
LES BP,[BX+DI+0x5566] ...........;c4 a9 66 55
LES BP,[BP+SI+0x5566] ...........;c4 aa 66 55
LES BP,[BP+DI+0x5566] ...........;c4 ab 66 55
LES BP,[SI+0x5566] ..............;c4 ac 66 55
LES BP,[DI+0x5566] ..............;c4 ad 66 55
LES BP,[BP+0x5566] ..............;c4 ae 66 55
LES BP,[BX+0x5566] ..............;c4 af 66 55
LES SI,[BX+SI+0x5566] ...........;c4 b0 66 55
LES SI,[BX+DI+0x5566] ...........;c4 b1 66 55
LES SI,[BP+SI+0x5566] ...........;c4 b2 66 55
LES SI,[BP+DI+0x5566] ...........;c4 b3 66 55
LES SI,[SI+0x5566] ..............;c4 b4 66 55
LES SI,[DI+0x5566] ..............;c4 b5 66 55
LES SI,[BP+0x5566] ..............;c4 b6 66 55
LES SI,[BX+0x5566] ..............;c4 b7 66 55
LES DI,[BX+SI+0x5566] ...........;c4 b8 66 55
LES DI,[BX+DI+0x5566] ...........;c4 b9 66 55
LES DI,[BP+SI+0x5566] ...........;c4 ba 66 55
LES DI,[BP+DI+0x5566] ...........;c4 bb 66 55
LES DI,[SI+0x5566] ..............;c4 bc 66 55
LES DI,[DI+0x5566] ..............;c4 bd 66 55
LES DI,[BP+0x5566] ..............;c4 be 66 55
LES DI,[BX+0x5566] ..............;c4 bf 66 55
LDS AX,[BX+SI] ..................;c5 00
LDS AX,[BX+DI] ..................;c5 01
LDS AX,[BP+SI] ..................;c5 02
LDS AX,[BP+DI] ..................;c5 03
LDS AX,[SI] .....................;c5 04
LDS AX,[DI] .....................;c5 05
LDS AX,[0x5566] .................;c5 06 66 55
LDS AX,[BX] .....................;c5 07
LDS CX,[BX+SI] ..................;c5 08
LDS CX,[BX+DI] ..................;c5 09
LDS CX,[BP+SI] ..................;c5 0a
LDS CX,[BP+DI] ..................;c5 0b
LDS CX,[SI] .....................;c5 0c
LDS CX,[DI] .....................;c5 0d
LDS CX,[0x5566] .................;c5 0e 66 55
LDS CX,[BX] .....................;c5 0f
LDS DX,[BX+SI] ..................;c5 10
LDS DX,[BX+DI] ..................;c5 11
LDS DX,[BP+SI] ..................;c5 12
LDS DX,[BP+DI] ..................;c5 13
LDS DX,[SI] .....................;c5 14
LDS DX,[DI] .....................;c5 15
LDS DX,[0x5566] .................;c5 16 66 55
LDS DX,[BX] .....................;c5 17
LDS BX,[BX+SI] ..................;c5 18
LDS BX,[BX+DI] ..................;c5 19
LDS BX,[BP+SI] ..................;c5 1a
LDS BX,[BP+DI] ..................;c5 1b
LDS BX,[SI] .....................;c5 1c
LDS BX,[DI] .....................;c5 1d
LDS BX,[0x5566] .................;c5 1e 66 55
LDS BX,[BX] .....................;c5 1f
LDS SP,[BX+SI] ..................;c5 20
LDS SP,[BX+DI] ..................;c5 21
LDS SP,[BP+SI] ..................;c5 22
LDS SP,[BP+DI] ..................;c5 23
LDS SP,[SI] .....................;c5 24
LDS SP,[DI] .....................;c5 25
LDS SP,[0x5566] .................;c5 26 66 55
LDS SP,[BX] .....................;c5 27
LDS BP,[BX+SI] ..................;c5 28
LDS BP,[BX+DI] ..................;c5 29
LDS BP,[BP+SI] ..................;c5 2a
LDS BP,[BP+DI] ..................;c5 2b
LDS BP,[SI] .....................;c5 2c
LDS BP,[DI] .....................;c5 2d
LDS BP,[0x5566] .................;c5 2e 66 55
LDS BP,[BX] .....................;c5 2f
LDS SI,[BX+SI] ..................;c5 30
LDS SI,[BX+DI] ..................;c5 31
LDS SI,[BP+SI] ..................;c5 32
LDS SI,[BP+DI] ..................;c5 33
LDS SI,[SI] .....................;c5 34
LDS SI,[DI] .....................;c5 35
LDS SI,[0x5566] .................;c5 36 66 55
LDS SI,[BX] .....................;c5 37
LDS DI,[BX+SI] ..................;c5 38
LDS DI,[BX+DI] ..................;c5 39
LDS DI,[BP+SI] ..................;c5 3a
LDS DI,[BP+DI] ..................;c5 3b
LDS DI,[SI] .....................;c5 3c
LDS DI,[DI] .....................;c5 3d
LDS DI,[0x5566] .................;c5 3e 66 55
LDS DI,[BX] .....................;c5 3f
LDS AX,[BX+SI+0x55] .............;c5 40 55
LDS AX,[BX+DI+0x55] .............;c5 41 55
LDS AX,[BP+SI+0x55] .............;c5 42 55
LDS AX,[BP+DI+0x55] .............;c5 43 55
LDS AX,[SI+0x55] ................;c5 44 55
LDS AX,[DI+0x55] ................;c5 45 55
LDS AX,[BP+0x55] ................;c5 46 55
LDS AX,[BX+0x55] ................;c5 47 55
LDS CX,[BX+SI+0x55] .............;c5 48 55
LDS CX,[BX+DI+0x55] .............;c5 49 55
LDS CX,[BP+SI+0x55] .............;c5 4a 55
LDS CX,[BP+DI+0x55] .............;c5 4b 55
LDS CX,[SI+0x55] ................;c5 4c 55
LDS CX,[DI+0x55] ................;c5 4d 55
LDS CX,[BP+0x55] ................;c5 4e 55
LDS CX,[BX+0x55] ................;c5 4f 55
LDS DX,[BX+SI+0x55] .............;c5 50 55
LDS DX,[BX+DI+0x55] .............;c5 51 55
LDS DX,[BP+SI+0x55] .............;c5 52 55
LDS DX,[BP+DI+0x55] .............;c5 53 55
LDS DX,[SI+0x55] ................;c5 54 55
LDS DX,[DI+0x55] ................;c5 55 55
LDS DX,[BP+0x55] ................;c5 56 55
LDS DX,[BX+0x55] ................;c5 57 55
LDS BX,[BX+SI+0x55] .............;c5 58 55
LDS BX,[BX+DI+0x55] .............;c5 59 55
LDS BX,[BP+SI+0x55] .............;c5 5a 55
LDS BX,[BP+DI+0x55] .............;c5 5b 55
LDS BX,[SI+0x55] ................;c5 5c 55
LDS BX,[DI+0x55] ................;c5 5d 55
LDS BX,[BP+0x55] ................;c5 5e 55
LDS BX,[BX+0x55] ................;c5 5f 55
LDS SP,[BX+SI+0x55] .............;c5 60 55
LDS SP,[BX+DI+0x55] .............;c5 61 55
LDS SP,[BP+SI+0x55] .............;c5 62 55
LDS SP,[BP+DI+0x55] .............;c5 63 55
LDS SP,[SI+0x55] ................;c5 64 55
LDS SP,[DI+0x55] ................;c5 65 55
LDS SP,[BP+0x55] ................;c5 66 55
```

```
LDS SP,[BX+0x55]  ..............;c5 67 55        MOV BYTE [BX+SI],0x88  .........;c6 00 88
LDS BP,[BX+SI+0x55]  ...........;c5 68 55        MOV BYTE [BX+DI],0x88  .........;c6 01 88
LDS BP,[BX+DI+0x55]  ...........;c5 69 55        MOV BYTE [BP+SI],0x88  .........;c6 02 88
LDS BP,[BP+SI+0x55]  ...........;c5 6a 55        MOV BYTE [BP+DI],0x88  .........;c6 03 88
LDS BP,[BP+DI+0x55]  ...........;c5 6b 55        MOV BYTE [SI],0x88  ............;c6 04 88
LDS BP,[SI+0x55]  ..............;c5 6c 55        MOV BYTE [DI],0x88  ............;c6 05 88
LDS BP,[DI+0x55]  ..............;c5 6d 55        MOV BYTE [0x5566],0x88  ........;c6 06 66 55 88
LDS BP,[BP+0x55]  ..............;c5 6e 55        MOV BYTE [BX],0x88  ............;c6 07 88
LDS BP,[BX+0x55]  ..............;c5 6f 55        MOV BYTE [BX+SI+0x55],0x88  ....;c6 40 55 88
LDS SI,[BX+SI+0x55]  ...........;c5 70 55        MOV BYTE [BX+DI+0x55],0x88  ....;c6 41 55 88
LDS SI,[BX+DI+0x55]  ...........;c5 71 55        MOV BYTE [BP+SI+0x55],0x88  ....;c6 42 55 88
LDS SI,[BP+SI+0x55]  ...........;c5 72 55        MOV BYTE [BP+DI+0x55],0x88  ....;c6 43 55 88
LDS SI,[BP+DI+0x55]  ...........;c5 73 55        MOV BYTE [SI+0x55],0x88  .......;c6 44 55 88
LDS SI,[SI+0x55]  ..............;c5 74 55        MOV BYTE [DI+0x55],0x88  .......;c6 45 55 88
LDS SI,[DI+0x55]  ..............;c5 75 55        MOV BYTE [BP+0x55],0x88  .......;c6 46 55 88
LDS SI,[BP+0x55]  ..............;c5 76 55        MOV BYTE [BX+0x55],0x88  .......;c6 47 55 88
LDS SI,[BX+0x55]  ..............;c5 77 55        MOV BYTE [BX+SI+0x5566],0x88  ..;c6 80 66 55 88
LDS DI,[BX+SI+0x55]  ...........;c5 78 55        MOV BYTE [BX+DI+0x5566],0x88  ..;c6 81 66 55 88
LDS DI,[BX+DI+0x55]  ...........;c5 79 55        MOV BYTE [BP+SI+0x5566],0x88  ..;c6 82 66 55 88
LDS DI,[BP+SI+0x55]  ...........;c5 7a 55        MOV BYTE [BP+DI+0x5566],0x88  ..;c6 83 66 55 88
LDS DI,[BP+DI+0x55]  ...........;c5 7b 55        MOV BYTE [SI+0x5566],0x88  .....;c6 84 66 55 88
LDS DI,[SI+0x55]  ..............;c5 7c 55        MOV BYTE [DI+0x5566],0x88  .....;c6 85 66 55 88
LDS DI,[DI+0x55]  ..............;c5 7d 55        MOV BYTE [BP+0x5566],0x88  .....;c6 86 66 55 88
LDS DI,[BP+0x55]  ..............;c5 7e 55        MOV BYTE [BX+0x5566],0x88  .....;c6 87 66 55 88
LDS DI,[BX+0x55]  ..............;c5 7f 55        MOV WORD [BX+SI],0x7788  .......;c7 00 88 77
LDS AX,[BX+SI+0x5566]  .........;c5 80 66 55     MOV WORD [BX+DI],0x7788  .......;c7 01 88 77
LDS AX,[BX+DI+0x5566]  .........;c5 81 66 55     MOV WORD [BP+SI],0x7788  .......;c7 02 88 77
LDS AX,[BP+SI+0x5566]  .........;c5 82 66 55     MOV WORD [BP+DI],0x7788  .......;c7 03 88 77
LDS AX,[BP+DI+0x5566]  .........;c5 83 66 55     MOV WORD [SI],0x7788  ..........;c7 04 88 77
LDS AX,[SI+0x5566]  ............;c5 84 66 55     MOV WORD [DI],0x7788  ..........;c7 05 88 77
LDS AX,[DI+0x5566]  ............;c5 85 66 55     MOV WORD [0x5566],0x7788  ......;c7 06 66 55 88 77
LDS AX,[BP+0x5566]  ............;c5 86 66 55     MOV WORD [BX],0x7788  ..........;c7 07 88 77
LDS AX,[BX+0x5566]  ............;c5 87 66 55     MOV WORD [BX+SI+0x55],0x7788  ..;c7 40 55 88 77
LDS CX,[BX+SI+0x5566]  .........;c5 88 66 55     MOV WORD [BX+DI+0x55],0x7788  ..;c7 41 55 88 77
LDS CX,[BX+DI+0x5566]  .........;c5 89 66 55     MOV WORD [BP+SI+0x55],0x7788  ..;c7 42 55 88 77
LDS CX,[BP+SI+0x5566]  .........;c5 8a 66 55     MOV WORD [BP+DI+0x55],0x7788  ..;c7 43 55 88 77
LDS CX,[BP+DI+0x5566]  .........;c5 8b 66 55     MOV WORD [SI+0x55],0x7788  .....;c7 44 55 88 77
LDS CX,[SI+0x5566]  ............;c5 8c 66 55     MOV WORD [DI+0x55],0x7788  .....;c7 45 55 88 77
LDS CX,[DI+0x5566]  ............;c5 8d 66 55     MOV WORD [BP+0x55],0x7788  .....;c7 46 55 88 77
LDS CX,[BP+0x5566]  ............;c5 8e 66 55     MOV WORD [BX+0x55],0x7788  .....;c7 47 55 88 77
LDS CX,[BX+0x5566]  ............;c5 8f 66 55     MOV WORD [BX+SI+0x5566],0x7788  ;c7 80 66 55 88 77
LDS DX,[BX+SI+0x5566]  .........;c5 90 66 55     MOV WORD [BX+DI+0x5566],0x7788  ;c7 81 66 55 88 77
LDS DX,[BX+DI+0x5566]  .........;c5 91 66 55     MOV WORD [BP+SI+0x5566],0x7788  ;c7 82 66 55 88 77
LDS DX,[BP+SI+0x5566]  .........;c5 92 66 55     MOV WORD [BP+DI+0x5566],0x7788  ;c7 83 66 55 88 77
LDS DX,[BP+DI+0x5566]  .........;c5 93 66 55     MOV WORD [SI+0x5566],0x7788  ...;c7 84 66 55 88 77
LDS DX,[SI+0x5566]  ............;c5 94 66 55     MOV WORD [DI+0x5566],0x7788  ...;c7 85 66 55 88 77
LDS DX,[DI+0x5566]  ............;c5 95 66 55     MOV WORD [BP+0x5566],0x7788  ...;c7 86 66 55 88 77
LDS DX,[BP+0x5566]  ............;c5 96 66 55     MOV WORD [BX+0x5566],0x7788  ...;c7 87 66 55 88 77
LDS DX,[BX+0x5566]  ............;c5 97 66 55     RETF 0x5566  ..................;ca 66 55
LDS BX,[BX+SI+0x5566]  .........;c5 98 66 55     RETF  .........................;cb
LDS BX,[BX+DI+0x5566]  .........;c5 99 66 55     INT3  .........................;cc
LDS BX,[BP+SI+0x5566]  .........;c5 9a 66 55     INT 0x55  .....................;cd 55
LDS BX,[BP+DI+0x5566]  .........;c5 9b 66 55     INTO  .........................;ce
LDS BX,[SI+0x5566]  ............;c5 9c 66 55     IRET  .........................;cf
LDS BX,[DI+0x5566]  ............;c5 9d 66 55     ROL BYTE [BX+SI],1  ............;d0 00
LDS BX,[BP+0x5566]  ............;c5 9e 66 55     ROL BYTE [BX+DI],1  ............;d0 01
LDS BX,[BX+0x5566]  ............;c5 9f 66 55     ROL BYTE [BP+SI],1  ............;d0 02
LDS SP,[BX+SI+0x5566]  .........;c5 a0 66 55     ROL BYTE [BP+DI],1  ............;d0 03
LDS SP,[BX+DI+0x5566]  .........;c5 a1 66 55     ROL BYTE [SI],1  ...............;d0 04
LDS SP,[BP+SI+0x5566]  .........;c5 a2 66 55     ROL BYTE [DI],1  ...............;d0 05
LDS SP,[BP+DI+0x5566]  .........;c5 a3 66 55     ROL BYTE [0x5566],1  ...........;d0 06 66 55
LDS SP,[SI+0x5566]  ............;c5 a4 66 55     ROL BYTE [BX],1  ...............;d0 07
LDS SP,[DI+0x5566]  ............;c5 a5 66 55     ROR BYTE [BX+SI],1  ............;d0 08
LDS SP,[BP+0x5566]  ............;c5 a6 66 55     ROR BYTE [BX+DI],1  ............;d0 09
LDS SP,[BX+0x5566]  ............;c5 a7 66 55     ROR BYTE [BP+SI],1  ............;d0 0a
LDS BP,[BX+SI+0x5566]  .........;c5 a8 66 55     ROR BYTE [BP+DI],1  ............;d0 0b
LDS BP,[BX+DI+0x5566]  .........;c5 a9 66 55     ROR BYTE [SI],1  ...............;d0 0c
LDS BP,[BP+SI+0x5566]  .........;c5 aa 66 55     ROR BYTE [DI],1  ...............;d0 0d
LDS BP,[BP+DI+0x5566]  .........;c5 ab 66 55     ROR BYTE [0x5566],1  ...........;d0 0e 66 55
LDS BP,[SI+0x5566]  ............;c5 ac 66 55     ROR BYTE [BX],1  ...............;d0 0f
LDS BP,[DI+0x5566]  ............;c5 ad 66 55     RCL BYTE [BX+SI],1  ............;d0 10
LDS BP,[BP+0x5566]  ............;c5 ae 66 55     RCL BYTE [BX+DI],1  ............;d0 11
LDS BP,[BX+0x5566]  ............;c5 af 66 55     RCL BYTE [BP+SI],1  ............;d0 12
LDS SI,[BX+SI+0x5566]  .........;c5 b0 66 55     RCL BYTE [BP+DI],1  ............;d0 13
LDS SI,[BX+DI+0x5566]  .........;c5 b1 66 55     RCL BYTE [SI],1  ...............;d0 14
LDS SI,[BP+SI+0x5566]  .........;c5 b2 66 55     RCL BYTE [DI],1  ...............;d0 15
LDS SI,[BP+DI+0x5566]  .........;c5 b3 66 55     RCL BYTE [0x5566],1  ...........;d0 16 66 55
LDS SI,[SI+0x5566]  ............;c5 b4 66 55     RCL BYTE [BX],1  ...............;d0 17
LDS SI,[DI+0x5566]  ............;c5 b5 66 55     RCR BYTE [BX+SI],1  ............;d0 18
LDS SI,[BP+0x5566]  ............;c5 b6 66 55     RCR BYTE [BX+DI],1  ............;d0 19
LDS SI,[BX+0x5566]  ............;c5 b7 66 55     RCR BYTE [BP+SI],1  ............;d0 1a
LDS DI,[BX+SI+0x5566]  .........;c5 b8 66 55     RCR BYTE [BP+DI],1  ............;d0 1b
LDS DI,[BX+DI+0x5566]  .........;c5 b9 66 55     RCR BYTE [SI],1  ...............;d0 1c
LDS DI,[BP+SI+0x5566]  .........;c5 ba 66 55     RCR BYTE [DI],1  ...............;d0 1d
LDS DI,[BP+DI+0x5566]  .........;c5 bb 66 55     RCR BYTE [0x5566],1  ...........;d0 1e 66 55
LDS DI,[SI+0x5566]  ............;c5 bc 66 55     RCR BYTE [BX],1  ...............;d0 1f
LDS DI,[DI+0x5566]  ............;c5 bd 66 55     SHL BYTE [BX+SI],1  ............;d0 20
LDS DI,[BP+0x5566]  ............;c5 be 66 55     SHL BYTE [BX+DI],1  ............;d0 21
LDS DI,[BX+0x5566]  ............;c5 bf 66 55     SHL BYTE [BP+SI],1  ............;d0 22
```

```
SHL BYTE [BP+DI],1 ............;d0 23              ROR BYTE [SI+0x5566],1 .........;d0 8c 66 55
SHL BYTE [SI],1 ...............;d0 24              ROR BYTE [DI+0x5566],1 .........;d0 8d 66 55
SHL BYTE [DI],1 ...............;d0 25              ROR BYTE [BP+0x5566],1 .........;d0 8e 66 55
SHL BYTE [0x5566],1 ...........;d0 26 66 55        ROR BYTE [BX+0x5566],1 .........;d0 8f 66 55
SHL BYTE [BX],1 ...............;d0 27              RCL BYTE [BX+SI+0x5566],1 ......;d0 90 66 55
SHR BYTE [BX+SI],1 ............;d0 28              RCL BYTE [BX+DI+0x5566],1 ......;d0 91 66 55
SHR BYTE [BX+DI],1 ............;d0 29              RCL BYTE [BP+SI+0x5566],1 ......;d0 92 66 55
SHR BYTE [BP+SI],1 ............;d0 2a              RCL BYTE [BP+DI+0x5566],1 ......;d0 93 66 55
SHR BYTE [BP+DI],1 ............;d0 2b              RCL BYTE [SI+0x5566],1 .........;d0 94 66 55
SHR BYTE [SI],1 ...............;d0 2c              RCL BYTE [DI+0x5566],1 .........;d0 95 66 55
SHR BYTE [DI],1 ...............;d0 2d              RCL BYTE [BP+0x5566],1 .........;d0 96 66 55
SHR BYTE [0x5566],1 ...........;d0 2e 66 55        RCL BYTE [BX+0x5566],1 .........;d0 97 66 55
SHR BYTE [BX],1 ...............;d0 2f              RCR BYTE [BX+SI+0x5566],1 ......;d0 98 66 55
SAR BYTE [BX+SI],1 ............;d0 38              RCR BYTE [BX+DI+0x5566],1 ......;d0 99 66 55
SAR BYTE [BX+DI],1 ............;d0 39              RCR BYTE [BP+SI+0x5566],1 ......;d0 9a 66 55
SAR BYTE [BP+SI],1 ............;d0 3a              RCR BYTE [BP+DI+0x5566],1 ......;d0 9b 66 55
SAR BYTE [BP+DI],1 ............;d0 3b              RCR BYTE [SI+0x5566],1 .........;d0 9c 66 55
SAR BYTE [SI],1 ...............;d0 3c              RCR BYTE [DI+0x5566],1 .........;d0 9d 66 55
SAR BYTE [DI],1 ...............;d0 3d              RCR BYTE [BP+0x5566],1 .........;d0 9e 66 55
SAR BYTE [0x5566],1 ...........;d0 3e 66 55        RCR BYTE [BX+0x5566],1 .........;d0 9f 66 55
SAR BYTE [BX],1 ...............;d0 3f              SHL BYTE [BX+SI+0x5566],1 ......;d0 a0 66 55
ROL BYTE [BX+SI+0x55],1 .......;d0 40 55           SHL BYTE [BX+DI+0x5566],1 ......;d0 a1 66 55
ROL BYTE [BX+DI+0x55],1 .......;d0 41 55           SHL BYTE [BP+SI+0x5566],1 ......;d0 a2 66 55
ROL BYTE [BP+SI+0x55],1 .......;d0 42 55           SHL BYTE [BP+DI+0x5566],1 ......;d0 a3 66 55
ROL BYTE [BP+DI+0x55],1 .......;d0 43 55           SHL BYTE [SI+0x5566],1 .........;d0 a4 66 55
ROL BYTE [SI+0x55],1 ..........;d0 44 55           SHL BYTE [DI+0x5566],1 .........;d0 a5 66 55
ROL BYTE [DI+0x55],1 ..........;d0 45 55           SHL BYTE [BP+0x5566],1 .........;d0 a6 66 55
ROL BYTE [BP+0x55],1 ..........;d0 46 55           SHL BYTE [BX+0x5566],1 .........;d0 a7 66 55
ROL BYTE [BX+0x55],1 ..........;d0 47 55           SHR BYTE [BX+SI+0x5566],1 ......;d0 a8 66 55
ROR BYTE [BX+SI+0x55],1 .......;d0 48 55           SHR BYTE [BX+DI+0x5566],1 ......;d0 a9 66 55
ROR BYTE [BX+DI+0x55],1 .......;d0 49 55           SHR BYTE [BP+SI+0x5566],1 ......;d0 aa 66 55
ROR BYTE [BP+SI+0x55],1 .......;d0 4a 55           SHR BYTE [BP+DI+0x5566],1 ......;d0 ab 66 55
ROR BYTE [BP+DI+0x55],1 .......;d0 4b 55           SHR BYTE [SI+0x5566],1 .........;d0 ac 66 55
ROR BYTE [SI+0x55],1 ..........;d0 4c 55           SHR BYTE [DI+0x5566],1 .........;d0 ad 66 55
ROR BYTE [DI+0x55],1 ..........;d0 4d 55           SHR BYTE [BP+0x5566],1 .........;d0 ae 66 55
ROR BYTE [BP+0x55],1 ..........;d0 4e 55           SHR BYTE [BX+0x5566],1 .........;d0 af 66 55
ROR BYTE [BX+0x55],1 ..........;d0 4f 55           SAR BYTE [BX+SI+0x5566],1 ......;d0 b8 66 55
RCL BYTE [BX+SI+0x55],1 .......;d0 50 55           SAR BYTE [BX+DI+0x5566],1 ......;d0 b9 66 55
RCL BYTE [BX+DI+0x55],1 .......;d0 51 55           SAR BYTE [BP+SI+0x5566],1 ......;d0 ba 66 55
RCL BYTE [BP+SI+0x55],1 .......;d0 52 55           SAR BYTE [BP+DI+0x5566],1 ......;d0 bb 66 55
RCL BYTE [BP+DI+0x55],1 .......;d0 53 55           SAR BYTE [SI+0x5566],1 .........;d0 bc 66 55
RCL BYTE [SI+0x55],1 ..........;d0 54 55           SAR BYTE [DI+0x5566],1 .........;d0 bd 66 55
RCL BYTE [DI+0x55],1 ..........;d0 55 55           SAR BYTE [BP+0x5566],1 .........;d0 be 66 55
RCL BYTE [BP+0x55],1 ..........;d0 56 55           SAR BYTE [BX+0x5566],1 .........;d0 bf 66 55
RCL BYTE [BX+0x55],1 ..........;d0 57 55           ROL AL,1 .......................;d0 c0
RCR BYTE [BX+SI+0x55],1 .......;d0 58 55           ROL CL,1 .......................;d0 c1
RCR BYTE [BX+DI+0x55],1 .......;d0 59 55           ROL DL,1 .......................;d0 c2
RCR BYTE [BP+SI+0x55],1 .......;d0 5a 55           ROL BL,1 .......................;d0 c3
RCR BYTE [BP+DI+0x55],1 .......;d0 5b 55           ROL AH,1 .......................;d0 c4
RCR BYTE [SI+0x55],1 ..........;d0 5c 55           ROL CH,1 .......................;d0 c5
RCR BYTE [DI+0x55],1 ..........;d0 5d 55           ROL DH,1 .......................;d0 c6
RCR BYTE [BP+0x55],1 ..........;d0 5e 55           ROL BH,1 .......................;d0 c7
RCR BYTE [BX+0x55],1 ..........;d0 5f 55           ROR AL,1 .......................;d0 c8
SHL BYTE [BX+SI+0x55],1 .......;d0 60 55           ROR CL,1 .......................;d0 c9
SHL BYTE [BX+DI+0x55],1 .......;d0 61 55           ROR DL,1 .......................;d0 ca
SHL BYTE [BP+SI+0x55],1 .......;d0 62 55           ROR BL,1 .......................;d0 cb
SHL BYTE [BP+DI+0x55],1 .......;d0 63 55           ROR AH,1 .......................;d0 cc
SHL BYTE [SI+0x55],1 ..........;d0 64 55           ROR CH,1 .......................;d0 cd
SHL BYTE [DI+0x55],1 ..........;d0 65 55           ROR DH,1 .......................;d0 ce
SHL BYTE [BP+0x55],1 ..........;d0 66 55           ROR BH,1 .......................;d0 cf
SHL BYTE [BX+0x55],1 ..........;d0 67 55           RCL AL,1 .......................;d0 d0
SHR BYTE [BX+SI+0x55],1 .......;d0 68 55           RCL CL,1 .......................;d0 d1
SHR BYTE [BX+DI+0x55],1 .......;d0 69 55           RCL DL,1 .......................;d0 d2
SHR BYTE [BP+SI+0x55],1 .......;d0 6a 55           RCL BL,1 .......................;d0 d3
SHR BYTE [BP+DI+0x55],1 .......;d0 6b 55           RCL AH,1 .......................;d0 d4
SHR BYTE [SI+0x55],1 ..........;d0 6c 55           RCL CH,1 .......................;d0 d5
SHR BYTE [DI+0x55],1 ..........;d0 6d 55           RCL DH,1 .......................;d0 d6
SHR BYTE [BP+0x55],1 ..........;d0 6e 55           RCL BH,1 .......................;d0 d7
SHR BYTE [BX+0x55],1 ..........;d0 6f 55           RCR AL,1 .......................;d0 d8
SAR BYTE [BX+SI+0x55],1 .......;d0 78 55           RCR CL,1 .......................;d0 d9
SAR BYTE [BX+DI+0x55],1 .......;d0 79 55           RCR DL,1 .......................;d0 da
SAR BYTE [BP+SI+0x55],1 .......;d0 7a 55           RCR BL,1 .......................;d0 db
SAR BYTE [BP+DI+0x55],1 .......;d0 7b 55           RCR AH,1 .......................;d0 dc
SAR BYTE [SI+0x55],1 ..........;d0 7c 55           RCR CH,1 .......................;d0 dd
SAR BYTE [DI+0x55],1 ..........;d0 7d 55           RCR DH,1 .......................;d0 de
SAR BYTE [BP+0x55],1 ..........;d0 7e 55           RCR BH,1 .......................;d0 df
SAR BYTE [BX+0x55],1 ..........;d0 7f 55           SHL AL,1 .......................;d0 e0
ROL BYTE [BX+SI+0x5566],1 .....;d0 80 66 55        SHL CL,1 .......................;d0 e1
ROL BYTE [BX+DI+0x5566],1 .....;d0 81 66 55        SHL DL,1 .......................;d0 e2
ROL BYTE [BP+SI+0x5566],1 .....;d0 82 66 55        SHL BL,1 .......................;d0 e3
ROL BYTE [BP+DI+0x5566],1 .....;d0 83 66 55        SHL AH,1 .......................;d0 e4
ROL BYTE [SI+0x5566],1 ........;d0 84 66 55        SHL CH,1 .......................;d0 e5
ROL BYTE [DI+0x5566],1 ........;d0 85 66 55        SHL DH,1 .......................;d0 e6
ROL BYTE [BP+0x5566],1 ........;d0 86 66 55        SHL BH,1 .......................;d0 e7
ROL BYTE [BX+0x5566],1 ........;d0 87 66 55        SHR AL,1 .......................;d0 e8
ROR BYTE [BX+SI+0x5566],1 .....;d0 88 66 55        SHR CL,1 .......................;d0 e9
ROR BYTE [BX+DI+0x5566],1 .....;d0 89 66 55        SHR DL,1 .......................;d0 ea
ROR BYTE [BP+SI+0x5566],1 .....;d0 8a 66 55        SHR BL,1 .......................;d0 eb
ROR BYTE [BP+DI+0x5566],1 .....;d0 8b 66 55        SHR AH,1 .......................;d0 ec
```

```
SHR CH,1 .......................;d0 ed
SHR DH,1 .......................;d0 ee
SHR BH,1 .......................;d0 ef
SAR AL,1 .......................;d0 f8
SAR CL,1 .......................;d0 f9
SAR DL,1 .......................;d0 fa
SAR BL,1 .......................;d0 fb
SAR AH,1 .......................;d0 fc
SAR CH,1 .......................;d0 fd
SAR DH,1 .......................;d0 fe
SAR BH,1 .......................;d0 ff
ROL WORD [BX+SI],1 .............;d1 00
ROL WORD [BX+DI],1 .............;d1 01
ROL WORD [BP+SI],1 .............;d1 02
ROL WORD [BP+DI],1 .............;d1 03
ROL WORD [SI],1 ................;d1 04
ROL WORD [DI],1 ................;d1 05
ROL WORD [0x5566],1 ............;d1 06 66 55
ROL WORD [BX],1 ................;d1 07
ROR WORD [BX+SI],1 .............;d1 08
ROR WORD [BX+DI],1 .............;d1 09
ROR WORD [BP+SI],1 .............;d1 0a
ROR WORD [BP+DI],1 .............;d1 0b
ROR WORD [SI],1 ................;d1 0c
ROR WORD [DI],1 ................;d1 0d
ROR WORD [0x5566],1 ............;d1 0e 66 55
ROR WORD [BX],1 ................;d1 0f
RCL WORD [BX+SI],1 .............;d1 10
RCL WORD [BX+DI],1 .............;d1 11
RCL WORD [BP+SI],1 .............;d1 12
RCL WORD [BP+DI],1 .............;d1 13
RCL WORD [SI],1 ................;d1 14
RCL WORD [DI],1 ................;d1 15
RCL WORD [0x5566],1 ............;d1 16 66 55
RCL WORD [BX],1 ................;d1 17
RCR WORD [BX+SI],1 .............;d1 18
RCR WORD [BX+DI],1 .............;d1 19
RCR WORD [BP+SI],1 .............;d1 1a
RCR WORD [BP+DI],1 .............;d1 1b
RCR WORD [SI],1 ................;d1 1c
RCR WORD [DI],1 ................;d1 1d
RCR WORD [0x5566],1 ............;d1 1e 66 55
RCR WORD [BX],1 ................;d1 1f
SHL WORD [BX+SI],1 .............;d1 20
SHL WORD [BX+DI],1 .............;d1 21
SHL WORD [BP+SI],1 .............;d1 22
SHL WORD [BP+DI],1 .............;d1 23
SHL WORD [SI],1 ................;d1 24
SHL WORD [DI],1 ................;d1 25
SHL WORD [0x5566],1 ............;d1 26 66 55
SHL WORD [BX],1 ................;d1 27
SHR WORD [BX+SI],1 .............;d1 28
SHR WORD [BX+DI],1 .............;d1 29
SHR WORD [BP+SI],1 .............;d1 2a
SHR WORD [BP+DI],1 .............;d1 2b
SHR WORD [SI],1 ................;d1 2c
SHR WORD [DI],1 ................;d1 2d
SHR WORD [0x5566],1 ............;d1 2e 66 55
SHR WORD [BX],1 ................;d1 2f
SAR WORD [BX+SI],1 .............;d1 38
SAR WORD [BX+DI],1 .............;d1 39
SAR WORD [BP+SI],1 .............;d1 3a
SAR WORD [BP+DI],1 .............;d1 3b
SAR WORD [SI],1 ................;d1 3c
SAR WORD [DI],1 ................;d1 3d
SAR WORD [0x5566],1 ............;d1 3e 66 55
SAR WORD [BX],1 ................;d1 3f
ROL WORD [BX+SI+0x55],1 ........;d1 40 55
ROL WORD [BX+DI+0x55],1 ........;d1 41 55
ROL WORD [BP+SI+0x55],1 ........;d1 42 55
ROL WORD [BP+DI+0x55],1 ........;d1 43 55
ROL WORD [SI+0x55],1 ...........;d1 44 55
ROL WORD [DI+0x55],1 ...........;d1 45 55
ROL WORD [BP+0x55],1 ...........;d1 46 55
ROL WORD [BX+0x55],1 ...........;d1 47 55
ROR WORD [BX+SI+0x55],1 ........;d1 48 55
ROR WORD [BX+DI+0x55],1 ........;d1 49 55
ROR WORD [BP+SI+0x55],1 ........;d1 4a 55
ROR WORD [BP+DI+0x55],1 ........;d1 4b 55
ROR WORD [SI+0x55],1 ...........;d1 4c 55
ROR WORD [DI+0x55],1 ...........;d1 4d 55
ROR WORD [BP+0x55],1 ...........;d1 4e 55
ROR WORD [BX+0x55],1 ...........;d1 4f 55
RCL WORD [BX+SI+0x55],1 ........;d1 50 55
RCL WORD [BX+DI+0x55],1 ........;d1 51 55
RCL WORD [BP+SI+0x55],1 ........;d1 52 55
RCL WORD [BP+DI+0x55],1 ........;d1 53 55
RCL WORD [SI+0x55],1 ...........;d1 54 55
RCL WORD [DI+0x55],1 ...........;d1 55 55
```

```
RCL WORD [BP+0x55],1 ...........;d1 56 55
RCL WORD [BX+0x55],1 ...........;d1 57 55
RCR WORD [BX+SI+0x55],1 ........;d1 58 55
RCR WORD [BX+DI+0x55],1 ........;d1 59 55
RCR WORD [BP+SI+0x55],1 ........;d1 5a 55
RCR WORD [BP+DI+0x55],1 ........;d1 5b 55
RCR WORD [SI+0x55],1 ...........;d1 5c 55
RCR WORD [DI+0x55],1 ...........;d1 5d 55
RCR WORD [BP+0x55],1 ...........;d1 5e 55
RCR WORD [BX+0x55],1 ...........;d1 5f 55
SHL WORD [BX+SI+0x55],1 ........;d1 60 55
SHL WORD [BX+DI+0x55],1 ........;d1 61 55
SHL WORD [BP+SI+0x55],1 ........;d1 62 55
SHL WORD [BP+DI+0x55],1 ........;d1 63 55
SHL WORD [SI+0x55],1 ...........;d1 64 55
SHL WORD [DI+0x55],1 ...........;d1 65 55
SHL WORD [BP+0x55],1 ...........;d1 66 55
SHL WORD [BX+0x55],1 ...........;d1 67 55
SHR WORD [BX+SI+0x55],1 ........;d1 68 55
SHR WORD [BX+DI+0x55],1 ........;d1 69 55
SHR WORD [BP+SI+0x55],1 ........;d1 6a 55
SHR WORD [BP+DI+0x55],1 ........;d1 6b 55
SHR WORD [SI+0x55],1 ...........;d1 6c 55
SHR WORD [DI+0x55],1 ...........;d1 6d 55
SHR WORD [BP+0x55],1 ...........;d1 6e 55
SHR WORD [BX+0x55],1 ...........;d1 6f 55
SAR WORD [BX+SI+0x55],1 ........;d1 78 55
SAR WORD [BX+DI+0x55],1 ........;d1 79 55
SAR WORD [BP+SI+0x55],1 ........;d1 7a 55
SAR WORD [BP+DI+0x55],1 ........;d1 7b 55
SAR WORD [SI+0x55],1 ...........;d1 7c 55
SAR WORD [DI+0x55],1 ...........;d1 7d 55
SAR WORD [BP+0x55],1 ...........;d1 7e 55
SAR WORD [BX+0x55],1 ...........;d1 7f 55
ROL WORD [BX+SI+0x5566],1 ......;d1 80 66 55
ROL WORD [BX+DI+0x5566],1 ......;d1 81 66 55
ROL WORD [BP+SI+0x5566],1 ......;d1 82 66 55
ROL WORD [BP+DI+0x5566],1 ......;d1 83 66 55
ROL WORD [SI+0x5566],1 .........;d1 84 66 55
ROL WORD [DI+0x5566],1 .........;d1 85 66 55
ROL WORD [BP+0x5566],1 .........;d1 86 66 55
ROL WORD [BX+0x5566],1 .........;d1 87 66 55
ROR WORD [BX+SI+0x5566],1 ......;d1 88 66 55
ROR WORD [BX+DI+0x5566],1 ......;d1 89 66 55
ROR WORD [BP+SI+0x5566],1 ......;d1 8a 66 55
ROR WORD [BP+DI+0x5566],1 ......;d1 8b 66 55
ROR WORD [SI+0x5566],1 .........;d1 8c 66 55
ROR WORD [DI+0x5566],1 .........;d1 8d 66 55
ROR WORD [BP+0x5566],1 .........;d1 8e 66 55
ROR WORD [BX+0x5566],1 .........;d1 8f 66 55
RCL WORD [BX+SI+0x5566],1 ......;d1 90 66 55
RCL WORD [BX+DI+0x5566],1 ......;d1 91 66 55
RCL WORD [BP+SI+0x5566],1 ......;d1 92 66 55
RCL WORD [BP+DI+0x5566],1 ......;d1 93 66 55
RCL WORD [SI+0x5566],1 .........;d1 94 66 55
RCL WORD [DI+0x5566],1 .........;d1 95 66 55
RCL WORD [BP+0x5566],1 .........;d1 96 66 55
RCL WORD [BX+0x5566],1 .........;d1 97 66 55
RCR WORD [BX+SI+0x5566],1 ......;d1 98 66 55
RCR WORD [BX+DI+0x5566],1 ......;d1 99 66 55
RCR WORD [BP+SI+0x5566],1 ......;d1 9a 66 55
RCR WORD [BP+DI+0x5566],1 ......;d1 9b 66 55
RCR WORD [SI+0x5566],1 .........;d1 9c 66 55
RCR WORD [DI+0x5566],1 .........;d1 9d 66 55
RCR WORD [BP+0x5566],1 .........;d1 9e 66 55
RCR WORD [BX+0x5566],1 .........;d1 9f 66 55
SHL WORD [BX+SI+0x5566],1 ......;d1 a0 66 55
SHL WORD [BX+DI+0x5566],1 ......;d1 a1 66 55
SHL WORD [BP+SI+0x5566],1 ......;d1 a2 66 55
SHL WORD [BP+DI+0x5566],1 ......;d1 a3 66 55
SHL WORD [SI+0x5566],1 .........;d1 a4 66 55
SHL WORD [DI+0x5566],1 .........;d1 a5 66 55
SHL WORD [BP+0x5566],1 .........;d1 a6 66 55
SHL WORD [BX+0x5566],1 .........;d1 a7 66 55
SHR WORD [BX+SI+0x5566],1 ......;d1 a8 66 55
SHR WORD [BX+DI+0x5566],1 ......;d1 a9 66 55
SHR WORD [BP+SI+0x5566],1 ......;d1 aa 66 55
SHR WORD [BP+DI+0x5566],1 ......;d1 ab 66 55
SHR WORD [SI+0x5566],1 .........;d1 ac 66 55
SHR WORD [DI+0x5566],1 .........;d1 ad 66 55
SHR WORD [BP+0x5566],1 .........;d1 ae 66 55
SHR WORD [BX+0x5566],1 .........;d1 af 66 55
SAR WORD [BX+SI+0x5566],1 ......;d1 b8 66 55
SAR WORD [BX+DI+0x5566],1 ......;d1 b9 66 55
SAR WORD [BP+SI+0x5566],1 ......;d1 ba 66 55
SAR WORD [BP+DI+0x5566],1 ......;d1 bb 66 55
SAR WORD [SI+0x5566],1 .........;d1 bc 66 55
SAR WORD [DI+0x5566],1 .........;d1 bd 66 55
SAR WORD [BP+0x5566],1 .........;d1 be 66 55
```

```
SAR WORD [BX+0x5566],1 ........;d1 bf 66 55
ROL AX,1 ......................;d1 c0
ROL CX,1 ......................;d1 c1
ROL DX,1 ......................;d1 c2
ROL BX,1 ......................;d1 c3
ROL SP,1 ......................;d1 c4
ROL BP,1 ......................;d1 c5
ROL SI,1 ......................;d1 c6
ROL DI,1 ......................;d1 c7
ROR AX,1 ......................;d1 c8
ROR CX,1 ......................;d1 c9
ROR DX,1 ......................;d1 ca
ROR BX,1 ......................;d1 cb
ROR SP,1 ......................;d1 cc
ROR BP,1 ......................;d1 cd
ROR SI,1 ......................;d1 ce
ROR DI,1 ......................;d1 cf
RCL AX,1 ......................;d1 d0
RCL CX,1 ......................;d1 d1
RCL DX,1 ......................;d1 d2
RCL BX,1 ......................;d1 d3
RCL SP,1 ......................;d1 d4
RCL BP,1 ......................;d1 d5
RCL SI,1 ......................;d1 d6
RCL DI,1 ......................;d1 d7
RCR AX,1 ......................;d1 d8
RCR CX,1 ......................;d1 d9
RCR DX,1 ......................;d1 da
RCR BX,1 ......................;d1 db
RCR SP,1 ......................;d1 dc
RCR BP,1 ......................;d1 dd
RCR SI,1 ......................;d1 de
RCR DI,1 ......................;d1 df
SHL AX,1 ......................;d1 e0
SHL CX,1 ......................;d1 e1
SHL DX,1 ......................;d1 e2
SHL BX,1 ......................;d1 e3
SHL SP,1 ......................;d1 e4
SHL BP,1 ......................;d1 e5
SHL SI,1 ......................;d1 e6
SHL DI,1 ......................;d1 e7
SHR AX,1 ......................;d1 e8
SHR CX,1 ......................;d1 e9
SHR DX,1 ......................;d1 ea
SHR BX,1 ......................;d1 eb
SHR SP,1 ......................;d1 ec
SHR BP,1 ......................;d1 ed
SHR SI,1 ......................;d1 ee
SHR DI,1 ......................;d1 ef
SAR AX,1 ......................;d1 f8
SAR CX,1 ......................;d1 f9
SAR DX,1 ......................;d1 fa
SAR BX,1 ......................;d1 fb
SAR SP,1 ......................;d1 fc
SAR BP,1 ......................;d1 fd
SAR SI,1 ......................;d1 fe
SAR DI,1 ......................;d1 ff
ROL BYTE [BX+SI],CL ..........;d2 00
ROL BYTE [BX+DI],CL ..........;d2 01
ROL BYTE [BP+SI],CL ..........;d2 02
ROL BYTE [BP+DI],CL ..........;d2 03
ROL BYTE [SI],CL .............;d2 04
ROL BYTE [DI],CL .............;d2 05
ROL BYTE [0x5566],CL .........;d2 06 66 55
ROL BYTE [BX],CL .............;d2 07
ROR BYTE [BX+SI],CL ..........;d2 08
ROR BYTE [BX+DI],CL ..........;d2 09
ROR BYTE [BP+SI],CL ..........;d2 0a
ROR BYTE [BP+DI],CL ..........;d2 0b
ROR BYTE [SI],CL .............;d2 0c
ROR BYTE [DI],CL .............;d2 0d
ROR BYTE [0x5566],CL .........;d2 0e 66 55
ROR BYTE [BX],CL .............;d2 0f
RCL BYTE [BX+SI],CL ..........;d2 10
RCL BYTE [BX+DI],CL ..........;d2 11
RCL BYTE [BP+SI],CL ..........;d2 12
RCL BYTE [BP+DI],CL ..........;d2 13
RCL BYTE [SI],CL .............;d2 14
RCL BYTE [DI],CL .............;d2 15
RCL BYTE [0x5566],CL .........;d2 16 66 55
RCL BYTE [BX],CL .............;d2 17
RCR BYTE [BX+SI],CL ..........;d2 18
RCR BYTE [BX+DI],CL ..........;d2 19
RCR BYTE [BP+SI],CL ..........;d2 1a
RCR BYTE [BP+DI],CL ..........;d2 1b
RCR BYTE [SI],CL .............;d2 1c
RCR BYTE [DI],CL .............;d2 1d
RCR BYTE [0x5566],CL .........;d2 1e 66 55
RCR BYTE [BX],CL .............;d2 1f
SHL BYTE [BX+SI],CL ..........;d2 20
SHL BYTE [BX+DI],CL ..........;d2 21
SHL BYTE [BP+SI],CL ..........;d2 22
SHL BYTE [BP+DI],CL ..........;d2 23
SHL BYTE [SI],CL .............;d2 24
SHL BYTE [DI],CL .............;d2 25
SHL BYTE [0x5566],CL .........;d2 26 66 55
SHL BYTE [BX],CL .............;d2 27
SHR BYTE [BX+SI],CL ..........;d2 28
SHR BYTE [BX+DI],CL ..........;d2 29
SHR BYTE [BP+SI],CL ..........;d2 2a
SHR BYTE [BP+DI],CL ..........;d2 2b
SHR BYTE [SI],CL .............;d2 2c
SHR BYTE [DI],CL .............;d2 2d
SHR BYTE [0x5566],CL .........;d2 2e 66 55
SHR BYTE [BX],CL .............;d2 2f
SAR BYTE [BX+SI],CL ..........;d2 38
SAR BYTE [BX+DI],CL ..........;d2 39
SAR BYTE [BP+SI],CL ..........;d2 3a
SAR BYTE [BP+DI],CL ..........;d2 3b
SAR BYTE [SI],CL .............;d2 3c
SAR BYTE [DI],CL .............;d2 3d
SAR BYTE [0x5566],CL .........;d2 3e 66 55
SAR BYTE [BX],CL .............;d2 3f
ROL BYTE [BX+SI+0x55],CL .....;d2 40 55
ROL BYTE [BX+DI+0x55],CL .....;d2 41 55
ROL BYTE [BP+SI+0x55],CL .....;d2 42 55
ROL BYTE [BP+DI+0x55],CL .....;d2 43 55
ROL BYTE [SI+0x55],CL ........;d2 44 55
ROL BYTE [DI+0x55],CL ........;d2 45 55
ROL BYTE [BP+0x55],CL ........;d2 46 55
ROL BYTE [BX+0x55],CL ........;d2 47 55
ROR BYTE [BX+SI+0x55],CL .....;d2 48 55
ROR BYTE [BX+DI+0x55],CL .....;d2 49 55
ROR BYTE [BP+SI+0x55],CL .....;d2 4a 55
ROR BYTE [BP+DI+0x55],CL .....;d2 4b 55
ROR BYTE [SI+0x55],CL ........;d2 4c 55
ROR BYTE [DI+0x55],CL ........;d2 4d 55
ROR BYTE [BP+0x55],CL ........;d2 4e 55
ROR BYTE [BX+0x55],CL ........;d2 4f 55
RCL BYTE [BX+SI+0x55],CL .....;d2 50 55
RCL BYTE [BX+DI+0x55],CL .....;d2 51 55
RCL BYTE [BP+SI+0x55],CL .....;d2 52 55
RCL BYTE [BP+DI+0x55],CL .....;d2 53 55
RCL BYTE [SI+0x55],CL ........;d2 54 55
RCL BYTE [DI+0x55],CL ........;d2 55 55
RCL BYTE [BP+0x55],CL ........;d2 56 55
RCL BYTE [BX+0x55],CL ........;d2 57 55
RCR BYTE [BX+SI+0x55],CL .....;d2 58 55
RCR BYTE [BX+DI+0x55],CL .....;d2 59 55
RCR BYTE [BP+SI+0x55],CL .....;d2 5a 55
RCR BYTE [BP+DI+0x55],CL .....;d2 5b 55
RCR BYTE [SI+0x55],CL ........;d2 5c 55
RCR BYTE [DI+0x55],CL ........;d2 5d 55
RCR BYTE [BP+0x55],CL ........;d2 5e 55
RCR BYTE [BX+0x55],CL ........;d2 5f 55
SHL BYTE [BX+SI+0x55],CL .....;d2 60 55
SHL BYTE [BX+DI+0x55],CL .....;d2 61 55
SHL BYTE [BP+SI+0x55],CL .....;d2 62 55
SHL BYTE [BP+DI+0x55],CL .....;d2 63 55
SHL BYTE [SI+0x55],CL ........;d2 64 55
SHL BYTE [DI+0x55],CL ........;d2 65 55
SHL BYTE [BP+0x55],CL ........;d2 66 55
SHL BYTE [BX+0x55],CL ........;d2 67 55
SHR BYTE [BX+SI+0x55],CL .....;d2 68 55
SHR BYTE [BX+DI+0x55],CL .....;d2 69 55
SHR BYTE [BP+SI+0x55],CL .....;d2 6a 55
SHR BYTE [BP+DI+0x55],CL .....;d2 6b 55
SHR BYTE [SI+0x55],CL ........;d2 6c 55
SHR BYTE [DI+0x55],CL ........;d2 6d 55
SHR BYTE [BP+0x55],CL ........;d2 6e 55
SHR BYTE [BX+0x55],CL ........;d2 6f 55
SAR BYTE [BX+SI+0x55],CL .....;d2 78 55
SAR BYTE [BX+DI+0x55],CL .....;d2 79 55
SAR BYTE [BP+SI+0x55],CL .....;d2 7a 55
SAR BYTE [BP+DI+0x55],CL .....;d2 7b 55
SAR BYTE [SI+0x55],CL ........;d2 7c 55
SAR BYTE [DI+0x55],CL ........;d2 7d 55
SAR BYTE [BP+0x55],CL ........;d2 7e 55
SAR BYTE [BX+0x55],CL ........;d2 7f 55
ROL BYTE [BX+SI+0x5566],CL ...;d2 80 66 55
ROL BYTE [BX+DI+0x5566],CL ...;d2 81 66 55
ROL BYTE [BP+SI+0x5566],CL ...;d2 82 66 55
ROL BYTE [BP+DI+0x5566],CL ...;d2 83 66 55
ROL BYTE [SI+0x5566],CL ......;d2 84 66 55
ROL BYTE [DI+0x5566],CL ......;d2 85 66 55
ROL BYTE [BP+0x5566],CL ......;d2 86 66 55
ROL BYTE [BX+0x5566],CL ......;d2 87 66 55
ROR BYTE [BX+SI+0x5566],CL ...;d2 88 66 55
```

```
ROR BYTE [BX+DI+0x5566],CL .....;d2 89 66 55      SHR DL,CL ....................;d2 ea
ROR BYTE [BP+SI+0x5566],CL .....;d2 8a 66 55      SHR BL,CL ....................;d2 eb
ROR BYTE [BP+DI+0x5566],CL .....;d2 8b 66 55      SHR AH,CL ....................;d2 ec
ROR BYTE [SI+0x5566],CL ........;d2 8c 66 55      SHR CH,CL ....................;d2 ed
ROR BYTE [DI+0x5566],CL ........;d2 8d 66 55      SHR DH,CL ....................;d2 ee
ROR BYTE [BP+0x5566],CL ........;d2 8e 66 55      SHR BH,CL ....................;d2 ef
ROR BYTE [BX+0x5566],CL ........;d2 8f 66 55      SAR AL,CL ....................;d2 f8
RCL BYTE [BX+SI+0x5566],CL .....;d2 90 66 55      SAR CL,CL ....................;d2 f9
RCL BYTE [BX+DI+0x5566],CL .....;d2 91 66 55      SAR DL,CL ....................;d2 fa
RCL BYTE [BP+SI+0x5566],CL .....;d2 92 66 55      SAR BL,CL ....................;d2 fb
RCL BYTE [BP+DI+0x5566],CL .....;d2 93 66 55      SAR AH,CL ....................;d2 fc
RCL BYTE [SI+0x5566],CL ........;d2 94 66 55      SAR CH,CL ....................;d2 fd
RCL BYTE [DI+0x5566],CL ........;d2 95 66 55      SAR DH,CL ....................;d2 fe
RCL BYTE [BP+0x5566],CL ........;d2 96 66 55      SAR BH,CL ....................;d2 ff
RCL BYTE [BX+0x5566],CL ........;d2 97 66 55      ROL WORD [BX+SI],CL ..........;d3 00
RCR BYTE [BX+SI+0x5566],CL .....;d2 98 66 55      ROL WORD [BX+DI],CL ..........;d3 01
RCR BYTE [BX+DI+0x5566],CL .....;d2 99 66 55      ROL WORD [BP+SI],CL ..........;d3 02
RCR BYTE [BP+SI+0x5566],CL .....;d2 9a 66 55      ROL WORD [BP+DI],CL ..........;d3 03
RCR BYTE [BP+DI+0x5566],CL .....;d2 9b 66 55      ROL WORD [SI],CL .............;d3 04
RCR BYTE [SI+0x5566],CL ........;d2 9c 66 55      ROL WORD [DI],CL .............;d3 05
RCR BYTE [DI+0x5566],CL ........;d2 9d 66 55      ROL WORD [0x5566],CL .........;d3 06 66 55
RCR BYTE [BP+0x5566],CL ........;d2 9e 66 55      ROL WORD [BX],CL .............;d3 07
RCR BYTE [BX+0x5566],CL ........;d2 9f 66 55      ROR WORD [BX+SI],CL ..........;d3 08
SHL BYTE [BX+SI+0x5566],CL .....;d2 a0 66 55      ROR WORD [BX+DI],CL ..........;d3 09
SHL BYTE [BX+DI+0x5566],CL .....;d2 a1 66 55      ROR WORD [BP+SI],CL ..........;d3 0a
SHL BYTE [BP+SI+0x5566],CL .....;d2 a2 66 55      ROR WORD [BP+DI],CL ..........;d3 0b
SHL BYTE [BP+DI+0x5566],CL .....;d2 a3 66 55      ROR WORD [SI],CL .............;d3 0c
SHL BYTE [SI+0x5566],CL ........;d2 a4 66 55      ROR WORD [DI],CL .............;d3 0d
SHL BYTE [DI+0x5566],CL ........;d2 a5 66 55      ROR WORD [0x5566],CL .........;d3 0e 66 55
SHL BYTE [BP+0x5566],CL ........;d2 a6 66 55      ROR WORD [BX],CL .............;d3 0f
SHL BYTE [BX+0x5566],CL ........;d2 a7 66 55      RCL WORD [BX+SI],CL ..........;d3 10
SHR BYTE [BX+SI+0x5566],CL .....;d2 a8 66 55      RCL WORD [BX+DI],CL ..........;d3 11
SHR BYTE [BX+DI+0x5566],CL .....;d2 a9 66 55      RCL WORD [BP+SI],CL ..........;d3 12
SHR BYTE [BP+SI+0x5566],CL .....;d2 aa 66 55      RCL WORD [BP+DI],CL ..........;d3 13
SHR BYTE [BP+DI+0x5566],CL .....;d2 ab 66 55      RCL WORD [SI],CL .............;d3 14
SHR BYTE [SI+0x5566],CL ........;d2 ac 66 55      RCL WORD [DI],CL .............;d3 15
SHR BYTE [DI+0x5566],CL ........;d2 ad 66 55      RCL WORD [0x5566],CL .........;d3 16 66 55
SHR BYTE [BP+0x5566],CL ........;d2 ae 66 55      RCL WORD [BX],CL .............;d3 17
SHR BYTE [BX+0x5566],CL ........;d2 af 66 55      RCR WORD [BX+SI],CL ..........;d3 18
SAR BYTE [BX+SI+0x5566],CL .....;d2 b8 66 55      RCR WORD [BX+DI],CL ..........;d3 19
SAR BYTE [BX+DI+0x5566],CL .....;d2 b9 66 55      RCR WORD [BP+SI],CL ..........;d3 1a
SAR BYTE [BP+SI+0x5566],CL .....;d2 ba 66 55      RCR WORD [BP+DI],CL ..........;d3 1b
SAR BYTE [BP+DI+0x5566],CL .....;d2 bb 66 55      RCR WORD [SI],CL .............;d3 1c
SAR BYTE [SI+0x5566],CL ........;d2 bc 66 55      RCR WORD [DI],CL .............;d3 1d
SAR BYTE [DI+0x5566],CL ........;d2 bd 66 55      RCR WORD [0x5566],CL .........;d3 1e 66 55
SAR BYTE [BP+0x5566],CL ........;d2 be 66 55      RCR WORD [BX],CL .............;d3 1f
SAR BYTE [BX+0x5566],CL ........;d2 bf 66 55      SHL WORD [BX+SI],CL ..........;d3 20
ROL AL,CL ....................;d2 c0              SHL WORD [BX+DI],CL ..........;d3 21
ROL CL,CL ....................;d2 c1              SHL WORD [BP+SI],CL ..........;d3 22
ROL DL,CL ....................;d2 c2              SHL WORD [BP+DI],CL ..........;d3 23
ROL BL,CL ....................;d2 c3              SHL WORD [SI],CL .............;d3 24
ROL AH,CL ....................;d2 c4              SHL WORD [DI],CL .............;d3 25
ROL CH,CL ....................;d2 c5              SHL WORD [0x5566],CL .........;d3 26 66 55
ROL DH,CL ....................;d2 c6              SHL WORD [BX],CL .............;d3 27
ROL BH,CL ....................;d2 c7              SHR WORD [BX+SI],CL ..........;d3 28
ROR AL,CL ....................;d2 c8              SHR WORD [BX+DI],CL ..........;d3 29
ROR CL,CL ....................;d2 c9              SHR WORD [BP+SI],CL ..........;d3 2a
ROR DL,CL ....................;d2 ca              SHR WORD [BP+DI],CL ..........;d3 2b
ROR BL,CL ....................;d2 cb              SHR WORD [SI],CL .............;d3 2c
ROR AH,CL ....................;d2 cc              SHR WORD [DI],CL .............;d3 2d
ROR CH,CL ....................;d2 cd              SHR WORD [0x5566],CL .........;d3 2e 66 55
ROR DH,CL ....................;d2 ce              SHR WORD [BX],CL .............;d3 2f
ROR BH,CL ....................;d2 cf              SAR WORD [BX+SI],CL ..........;d3 38
RCL AL,CL ....................;d2 d0              SAR WORD [BX+DI],CL ..........;d3 39
RCL CL,CL ....................;d2 d1              SAR WORD [BP+SI],CL ..........;d3 3a
RCL DL,CL ....................;d2 d2              SAR WORD [BP+DI],CL ..........;d3 3b
RCL BL,CL ....................;d2 d3              SAR WORD [SI],CL .............;d3 3c
RCL AH,CL ....................;d2 d4              SAR WORD [DI],CL .............;d3 3d
RCL CH,CL ....................;d2 d5              SAR WORD [0x5566],CL .........;d3 3e 66 55
RCL DH,CL ....................;d2 d6              SAR WORD [BX],CL .............;d3 3f
RCL BH,CL ....................;d2 d7              ROL WORD [BX+SI+0x55],CL .....;d3 40 55
RCR AL,CL ....................;d2 d8              ROL WORD [BX+DI+0x55],CL .....;d3 41 55
RCR CL,CL ....................;d2 d9              ROL WORD [BP+SI+0x55],CL .....;d3 42 55
RCR DL,CL ....................;d2 da              ROL WORD [BP+DI+0x55],CL .....;d3 43 55
RCR BL,CL ....................;d2 db              ROL WORD [SI+0x55],CL ........;d3 44 55
RCR AH,CL ....................;d2 dc              ROL WORD [DI+0x55],CL ........;d3 45 55
RCR CH,CL ....................;d2 dd              ROL WORD [BP+0x55],CL ........;d3 46 55
RCR DH,CL ....................;d2 de              ROL WORD [BX+0x55],CL ........;d3 47 55
RCR BH,CL ....................;d2 df              ROR WORD [BX+SI+0x55],CL .....;d3 48 55
SHL AL,CL ....................;d2 e0              ROR WORD [BX+DI+0x55],CL .....;d3 49 55
SHL CL,CL ....................;d2 e1              ROR WORD [BP+SI+0x55],CL .....;d3 4a 55
SHL DL,CL ....................;d2 e2              ROR WORD [BP+DI+0x55],CL .....;d3 4b 55
SHL BL,CL ....................;d2 e3              ROR WORD [SI+0x55],CL ........;d3 4c 55
SHL AH,CL ....................;d2 e4              ROR WORD [DI+0x55],CL ........;d3 4d 55
SHL CH,CL ....................;d2 e5              ROR WORD [BP+0x55],CL ........;d3 4e 55
SHL DH,CL ....................;d2 e6              ROR WORD [BX+0x55],CL ........;d3 4f 55
SHL BH,CL ....................;d2 e7              RCL WORD [BX+SI+0x55],CL .....;d3 50 55
SHR AL,CL ....................;d2 e8              RCL WORD [BX+DI+0x55],CL .....;d3 51 55
SHR CL,CL ....................;d2 e9              RCL WORD [BP+SI+0x55],CL .....;d3 52 55
```

```
RCL WORD [BP+DI+0x55],CL .......;d3 53 55        SAR WORD [SI+0x5566],CL .........;d3 bc 66 55
RCL WORD [SI+0x55],CL ..........;d3 54 55        SAR WORD [DI+0x5566],CL .........;d3 bd 66 55
RCL WORD [DI+0x55],CL ..........;d3 55 55        SAR WORD [BP+0x5566],CL .........;d3 be 66 55
RCL WORD [BP+0x55],CL ..........;d3 56 55        SAR WORD [BX+0x5566],CL .........;d3 bf 66 55
RCL WORD [BX+0x55],CL ..........;d3 57 55        ROL AX,CL ......................;d3 c0
RCR WORD [BX+SI+0x55],CL .......;d3 58 55        ROL CX,CL ......................;d3 c1
RCR WORD [BX+DI+0x55],CL .......;d3 59 55        ROL DX,CL ......................;d3 c2
RCR WORD [BP+SI+0x55],CL .......;d3 5a 55        ROL BX,CL ......................;d3 c3
RCR WORD [BP+DI+0x55],CL .......;d3 5b 55        ROL SP,CL ......................;d3 c4
RCR WORD [SI+0x55],CL ..........;d3 5c 55        ROL BP,CL ......................;d3 c5
RCR WORD [DI+0x55],CL ..........;d3 5d 55        ROL SI,CL ......................;d3 c6
RCR WORD [BP+0x55],CL ..........;d3 5e 55        ROL DI,CL ......................;d3 c7
RCR WORD [BX+0x55],CL ..........;d3 5f 55        ROR AX,CL ......................;d3 c8
SHL WORD [BX+SI+0x55],CL .......;d3 60 55        ROR CX,CL ......................;d3 c9
SHL WORD [BX+DI+0x55],CL .......;d3 61 55        ROR DX,CL ......................;d3 ca
SHL WORD [BP+SI+0x55],CL .......;d3 62 55        ROR BX,CL ......................;d3 cb
SHL WORD [BP+DI+0x55],CL .......;d3 63 55        ROR SP,CL ......................;d3 cc
SHL WORD [SI+0x55],CL ..........;d3 64 55        ROR BP,CL ......................;d3 cd
SHL WORD [DI+0x55],CL ..........;d3 65 55        ROR SI,CL ......................;d3 ce
SHL WORD [BP+0x55],CL ..........;d3 66 55        ROR DI,CL ......................;d3 cf
SHL WORD [BX+0x55],CL ..........;d3 67 55        RCL AX,CL ......................;d3 d0
SHR WORD [BX+SI+0x55],CL .......;d3 68 55        RCL CX,CL ......................;d3 d1
SHR WORD [BX+DI+0x55],CL .......;d3 69 55        RCL DX,CL ......................;d3 d2
SHR WORD [BP+SI+0x55],CL .......;d3 6a 55        RCL BX,CL ......................;d3 d3
SHR WORD [BP+DI+0x55],CL .......;d3 6b 55        RCL SP,CL ......................;d3 d4
SHR WORD [SI+0x55],CL ..........;d3 6c 55        RCL BP,CL ......................;d3 d5
SHR WORD [DI+0x55],CL ..........;d3 6d 55        RCL SI,CL ......................;d3 d6
SHR WORD [BP+0x55],CL ..........;d3 6e 55        RCL DI,CL ......................;d3 d7
SHR WORD [BX+0x55],CL ..........;d3 6f 55        RCR AX,CL ......................;d3 d8
SAR WORD [BX+SI+0x55],CL .......;d3 78 55        RCR CX,CL ......................;d3 d9
SAR WORD [BX+DI+0x55],CL .......;d3 79 55        RCR DX,CL ......................;d3 da
SAR WORD [BP+SI+0x55],CL .......;d3 7a 55        RCR BX,CL ......................;d3 db
SAR WORD [BP+DI+0x55],CL .......;d3 7b 55        RCR SP,CL ......................;d3 dc
SAR WORD [SI+0x55],CL ..........;d3 7c 55        RCR BP,CL ......................;d3 dd
SAR WORD [DI+0x55],CL ..........;d3 7d 55        RCR SI,CL ......................;d3 de
SAR WORD [BP+0x55],CL ..........;d3 7e 55        RCR DI,CL ......................;d3 df
SAR WORD [BX+0x55],CL ..........;d3 7f 55        SHL AX,CL ......................;d3 e0
ROL WORD [BX+SI+0x5566],CL .;d3 80 66 55         SHL CX,CL ......................;d3 e1
ROL WORD [BX+DI+0x5566],CL .;d3 81 66 55         SHL DX,CL ......................;d3 e2
ROL WORD [BP+SI+0x5566],CL .;d3 82 66 55         SHL BX,CL ......................;d3 e3
ROL WORD [BP+DI+0x5566],CL .;d3 83 66 55         SHL SP,CL ......................;d3 e4
ROL WORD [SI+0x5566],CL .;d3 84 66 55            SHL BP,CL ......................;d3 e5
ROL WORD [DI+0x5566],CL .;d3 85 66 55            SHL SI,CL ......................;d3 e6
ROL WORD [BP+0x5566],CL .;d3 86 66 55            SHL DI,CL ......................;d3 e7
ROL WORD [BX+0x5566],CL .;d3 87 66 55            SHR AX,CL ......................;d3 e8
ROR WORD [BX+SI+0x5566],CL .;d3 88 66 55         SHR CX,CL ......................;d3 e9
ROR WORD [BX+DI+0x5566],CL .;d3 89 66 55         SHR DX,CL ......................;d3 ea
ROR WORD [BP+SI+0x5566],CL .;d3 8a 66 55         SHR BX,CL ......................;d3 eb
ROR WORD [BP+DI+0x5566],CL .;d3 8b 66 55         SHR SP,CL ......................;d3 ec
ROR WORD [SI+0x5566],CL .;d3 8c 66 55            SHR BP,CL ......................;d3 ed
ROR WORD [DI+0x5566],CL .;d3 8d 66 55            SHR SI,CL ......................;d3 ee
ROR WORD [BP+0x5566],CL .;d3 8e 66 55            SHR DI,CL ......................;d3 ef
ROR WORD [BX+0x5566],CL .;d3 8f 66 55            SAR AX,CL ......................;d3 f8
RCL WORD [BX+SI+0x5566],CL .;d3 90 66 55         SAR CX,CL ......................;d3 f9
RCL WORD [BX+DI+0x5566],CL .;d3 91 66 55         SAR DX,CL ......................;d3 fa
RCL WORD [BP+SI+0x5566],CL .;d3 92 66 55         SAR BX,CL ......................;d3 fb
RCL WORD [BP+DI+0x5566],CL .;d3 93 66 55         SAR SP,CL ......................;d3 fc
RCL WORD [SI+0x5566],CL .;d3 94 66 55            SAR BP,CL ......................;d3 fd
RCL WORD [DI+0x5566],CL .;d3 95 66 55            SAR SI,CL ......................;d3 fe
RCL WORD [BP+0x5566],CL .;d3 96 66 55            SAR DI,CL ......................;d3 ff
RCL WORD [BX+0x5566],CL .;d3 97 66 55            AAM ............................;d4 0a
RCR WORD [BX+SI+0x5566],CL .;d3 98 66 55         AAD ............................;d5 0a
RCR WORD [BX+DI+0x5566],CL .;d3 99 66 55         XLAT ...........................;d7
RCR WORD [BP+SI+0x5566],CL .;d3 9a 66 55         LOOPNZ 0x55 ....................;e0 55
RCR WORD [BP+DI+0x5566],CL .;d3 9b 66 55         LOOPZ 0x55 .....................;e1 55
RCR WORD [SI+0x5566],CL .;d3 9c 66 55            LOOP 0x55 ......................;e2 55
RCR WORD [DI+0x5566],CL .;d3 9d 66 55            JCXZ 0x55 ......................;e3 55
RCR WORD [BP+0x5566],CL .;d3 9e 66 55            IN AL,(0x55) ...................;e4 55
RCR WORD [BX+0x5566],CL .;d3 9f 66 55            IN AX,(0x55) ...................;e5 55
SHL WORD [BX+SI+0x5566],CL .;d3 a0 66 55         OUT (0x55),AL ..................;e6 55
SHL WORD [BX+DI+0x5566],CL .;d3 a1 66 55         OUT (0x55),AX ..................;e7 55
SHL WORD [BP+SI+0x5566],CL .;d3 a2 66 55         CALL 0x5566 ................;e8 66 55
SHL WORD [BP+DI+0x5566],CL .;d3 a3 66 55         JMP 0x5566 .................;e9 66 55
SHL WORD [SI+0x5566],CL .;d3 a4 66 55            JMP 0x5566:0x7788 ..............;ea 66 55 88 77
SHL WORD [DI+0x5566],CL .;d3 a5 66 55            JMP 0x55 .......................;eb 55
SHL WORD [BP+0x5566],CL .;d3 a6 66 55            IN AL,DX .......................;ec
SHL WORD [BX+0x5566],CL .;d3 a7 66 55            IN AX,DX .......................;ed
SHR WORD [BX+SI+0x5566],CL .;d3 a8 66 55         OUT DX,AL ......................;ee
SHR WORD [BX+DI+0x5566],CL .;d3 a9 66 55         OUT DX,AX ......................;ef
SHR WORD [BP+SI+0x5566],CL .;d3 aa 66 55         LOCK ...........................;f0
SHR WORD [BP+DI+0x5566],CL .;d3 ab 66 55         REPNZ ..........................;f2
SHR WORD [SI+0x5566],CL .;d3 ac 66 55            REPZ ...........................;f3
SHR WORD [DI+0x5566],CL .;d3 ad 66 55            HLT ............................;f4
SHR WORD [BP+0x5566],CL .;d3 ae 66 55            CMC ............................;f5
SHR WORD [BX+0x5566],CL .;d3 af 66 55            TEST BYTE [BX+SI],0x77 .........;f6 00 77
SAR WORD [BX+SI+0x5566],CL .;d3 b8 66 55         TEST BYTE [BX+DI],0x77 .........;f6 01 77
SAR WORD [BX+DI+0x5566],CL .;d3 b9 66 55         TEST BYTE [BP+SI],0x77 .........;f6 02 77
SAR WORD [BP+SI+0x5566],CL .;d3 ba 66 55         TEST BYTE [BP+DI],0x77 .........;f6 03 77
SAR WORD [BP+DI+0x5566],CL .;d3 bb 66 55         TEST BYTE [SI],0x77 ............;f6 04 77
```

```
TEST BYTE [DI],0x77 ............;f6 05 77          IMUL BYTE [BP+0x55] ...........;f6 6e 55
TEST BYTE [0x5566],0x77 ........;f6 06 66 55 77    IMUL BYTE [BX+0x55] ...........;f6 6f 55
TEST BYTE [BX],0x77 ............;f6 07 77          DIV BYTE [BX+SI+0x55] .........;f6 70 55
NOT BYTE [BX+SI] ...............;f6 10             DIV BYTE [BX+DI+0x55] .........;f6 71 55
NOT BYTE [BX+DI] ...............;f6 11             DIV BYTE [BP+SI+0x55] .........;f6 72 55
NOT BYTE [BP+SI] ...............;f6 12             DIV BYTE [BP+DI+0x55] .........;f6 73 55
NOT BYTE [BP+DI] ...............;f6 13             DIV BYTE [SI+0x55] ............;f6 74 55
NOT BYTE [SI] ..................;f6 14             DIV BYTE [DI+0x55] ............;f6 75 55
NOT BYTE [DI] ..................;f6 15             DIV BYTE [BP+0x55] ............;f6 76 55
NOT BYTE [0x5566] ..............;f6 16 66 55       DIV BYTE [BX+0x55] ............;f6 77 55
NOT BYTE [BX] ..................;f6 17             IDIV BYTE [BX+SI+0x55] ........;f6 78 55
NEG BYTE [BX+SI] ...............;f6 18             IDIV BYTE [BX+DI+0x55] ........;f6 79 55
NEG BYTE [BX+DI] ...............;f6 19             IDIV BYTE [BP+SI+0x55] ........;f6 7a 55
NEG BYTE [BP+SI] ...............;f6 1a             IDIV BYTE [BP+DI+0x55] ........;f6 7b 55
NEG BYTE [BP+DI] ...............;f6 1b             IDIV BYTE [SI+0x55] ...........;f6 7c 55
NEG BYTE [SI] ..................;f6 1c             IDIV BYTE [DI+0x55] ...........;f6 7d 55
NEG BYTE [DI] ..................;f6 1d             IDIV BYTE [BP+0x55] ...........;f6 7e 55
NEG BYTE [0x5566] ..............;f6 1e 66 55       IDIV BYTE [BX+0x55] ...........;f6 7f 55
NEG BYTE [BX] ..................;f6 1f             TEST BYTE [BX+SI+0x5566],0x77 ..;f6 80 66 55 77
MUL BYTE [BX+SI] ...............;f6 20             TEST BYTE [BX+DI+0x5566],0x77 ..;f6 81 66 55 77
MUL BYTE [BX+DI] ...............;f6 21             TEST BYTE [BP+SI+0x5566],0x77 ..;f6 82 66 55 77
MUL BYTE [BP+SI] ...............;f6 22             TEST BYTE [BP+DI+0x5566],0x77 ..;f6 83 66 55 77
MUL BYTE [BP+DI] ...............;f6 23             TEST BYTE [SI+0x5566],0x77 .....;f6 84 66 55 77
MUL BYTE [SI] ..................;f6 24             TEST BYTE [DI+0x5566],0x77 .....;f6 85 66 55 77
MUL BYTE [DI] ..................;f6 25             TEST BYTE [BP+0x5566],0x77 .....;f6 86 66 55 77
MUL BYTE [0x5566] ..............;f6 26 66 55       TEST BYTE [BX+0x5566],0x77 .....;f6 87 66 55 77
MUL BYTE [BX] ..................;f6 27             NOT BYTE [BX+SI+0x5566] ........;f6 90 66 55
IMUL BYTE [BX+SI] ..............;f6 28             NOT BYTE [BX+DI+0x5566] ........;f6 91 66 55
IMUL BYTE [BX+DI] ..............;f6 29             NOT BYTE [BP+SI+0x5566] ........;f6 92 66 55
IMUL BYTE [BP+SI] ..............;f6 2a             NOT BYTE [BP+DI+0x5566] ........;f6 93 66 55
IMUL BYTE [BP+DI] ..............;f6 2b             NOT BYTE [SI+0x5566] ...........;f6 94 66 55
IMUL BYTE [SI] .................;f6 2c             NOT BYTE [DI+0x5566] ...........;f6 95 66 55
IMUL BYTE [DI] .................;f6 2d             NOT BYTE [BP+0x5566] ...........;f6 96 66 55
IMUL BYTE [0x5566] .............;f6 2e 66 55       NOT BYTE [BX+0x5566] ...........;f6 97 66 55
IMUL BYTE [BX] .................;f6 2f             NEG BYTE [BX+SI+0x5566] ........;f6 98 66 55
DIV BYTE [BX+SI] ...............;f6 30             NEG BYTE [BX+DI+0x5566] ........;f6 99 66 55
DIV BYTE [BX+DI] ...............;f6 31             NEG BYTE [BP+SI+0x5566] ........;f6 9a 66 55
DIV BYTE [BP+SI] ...............;f6 32             NEG BYTE [BP+DI+0x5566] ........;f6 9b 66 55
DIV BYTE [BP+DI] ...............;f6 33             NEG BYTE [SI+0x5566] ...........;f6 9c 66 55
DIV BYTE [SI] ..................;f6 34             NEG BYTE [DI+0x5566] ...........;f6 9d 66 55
DIV BYTE [DI] ..................;f6 35             NEG BYTE [BP+0x5566] ...........;f6 9e 66 55
DIV BYTE [0x5566] ..............;f6 36 66 55       NEG BYTE [BX+0x5566] ...........;f6 9f 66 55
DIV BYTE [BX] ..................;f6 37             MUL BYTE [BX+SI+0x5566] ........;f6 a0 66 55
IDIV BYTE [BX+SI] ..............;f6 38             MUL BYTE [BX+DI+0x5566] ........;f6 a1 66 55
IDIV BYTE [BX+DI] ..............;f6 39             MUL BYTE [BP+SI+0x5566] ........;f6 a2 66 55
IDIV BYTE [BP+SI] ..............;f6 3a             MUL BYTE [BP+DI+0x5566] ........;f6 a3 66 55
IDIV BYTE [BP+DI] ..............;f6 3b             MUL BYTE [SI+0x5566] ...........;f6 a4 66 55
IDIV BYTE [SI] .................;f6 3c             MUL BYTE [DI+0x5566] ...........;f6 a5 66 55
IDIV BYTE [DI] .................;f6 3d             MUL BYTE [BP+0x5566] ...........;f6 a6 66 55
IDIV BYTE [0x5566] .............;f6 3e 66 55       MUL BYTE [BX+0x5566] ...........;f6 a7 66 55
IDIV BYTE [BX] .................;f6 3f             IMUL BYTE [BX+SI+0x5566] .......;f6 a8 66 55
TEST BYTE [BX+SI+0x55],0x77 ....;f6 40 55 77       IMUL BYTE [BX+DI+0x5566] .......;f6 a9 66 55
TEST BYTE [BX+DI+0x55],0x77 ....;f6 41 55 77       IMUL BYTE [BP+SI+0x5566] .......;f6 aa 66 55
TEST BYTE [BP+SI+0x55],0x77 ....;f6 42 55 77       IMUL BYTE [BP+DI+0x5566] .......;f6 ab 66 55
TEST BYTE [BP+DI+0x55],0x77 ....;f6 43 55 77       IMUL BYTE [SI+0x5566] ..........;f6 ac 66 55
TEST BYTE [SI+0x55],0x77 .......;f6 44 55 77       IMUL BYTE [DI+0x5566] ..........;f6 ad 66 55
TEST BYTE [DI+0x55],0x77 .......;f6 45 55 77       IMUL BYTE [BP+0x5566] ..........;f6 ae 66 55
TEST BYTE [BP+0x55],0x77 .......;f6 46 55 77       IMUL BYTE [BX+0x5566] ..........;f6 af 66 55
TEST BYTE [BX+0x55],0x77 .......;f6 47 55 77       DIV BYTE [BX+SI+0x5566] ........;f6 b0 66 55
NOT BYTE [BX+SI+0x55] ..........;f6 50 55          DIV BYTE [BX+DI+0x5566] ........;f6 b1 66 55
NOT BYTE [BX+DI+0x55] ..........;f6 51 55          DIV BYTE [BP+SI+0x5566] ........;f6 b2 66 55
NOT BYTE [BP+SI+0x55] ..........;f6 52 55          DIV BYTE [BP+DI+0x5566] ........;f6 b3 66 55
NOT BYTE [BP+DI+0x55] ..........;f6 53 55          DIV BYTE [SI+0x5566] ...........;f6 b4 66 55
NOT BYTE [SI+0x55] .............;f6 54 55          DIV BYTE [DI+0x5566] ...........;f6 b5 66 55
NOT BYTE [DI+0x55] .............;f6 55 55          DIV BYTE [BP+0x5566] ...........;f6 b6 66 55
NOT BYTE [BP+0x55] .............;f6 56 55          DIV BYTE [BX+0x5566] ...........;f6 b7 66 55
NOT BYTE [BX+0x55] .............;f6 57 55          IDIV BYTE [BX+SI+0x5566] .......;f6 b8 66 55
NEG BYTE [BX+SI+0x55] ..........;f6 58 55          IDIV BYTE [BX+DI+0x5566] .......;f6 b9 66 55
NEG BYTE [BX+DI+0x55] ..........;f6 59 55          IDIV BYTE [BP+SI+0x5566] .......;f6 ba 66 55
NEG BYTE [BP+SI+0x55] ..........;f6 5a 55          IDIV BYTE [BP+DI+0x5566] .......;f6 bb 66 55
NEG BYTE [BP+DI+0x55] ..........;f6 5b 55          IDIV BYTE [SI+0x5566] ..........;f6 bc 66 55
NEG BYTE [SI+0x55] .............;f6 5c 55          IDIV BYTE [DI+0x5566] ..........;f6 bd 66 55
NEG BYTE [DI+0x55] .............;f6 5d 55          IDIV BYTE [BP+0x5566] ..........;f6 be 66 55
NEG BYTE [BP+0x55] .............;f6 5e 55          IDIV BYTE [BX+0x5566] ..........;f6 bf 66 55
NEG BYTE [BX+0x55] .............;f6 5f 55          TEST AL,0x77 ...................;f6 c0 77
MUL BYTE [BX+SI+0x55] ..........;f6 60 55          TEST CL,0x77 ...................;f6 c1 77
MUL BYTE [BX+DI+0x55] ..........;f6 61 55          TEST DL,0x77 ...................;f6 c2 77
MUL BYTE [BP+SI+0x55] ..........;f6 62 55          TEST BL,0x77 ...................;f6 c3 77
MUL BYTE [BP+DI+0x55] ..........;f6 63 55          TEST AH,0x77 ...................;f6 c4 77
MUL BYTE [SI+0x55] .............;f6 64 55          TEST CH,0x77 ...................;f6 c5 77
MUL BYTE [DI+0x55] .............;f6 65 55          TEST DH,0x77 ...................;f6 c6 77
MUL BYTE [BP+0x55] .............;f6 66 55          TEST BH,0x77 ...................;f6 c7 77
MUL BYTE [BX+0x55] .............;f6 67 55          NOT AL .........................;f6 d0
IMUL BYTE [BX+SI+0x55] .........;f6 68 55          NOT CL .........................;f6 d1
IMUL BYTE [BX+DI+0x55] .........;f6 69 55          NOT DL .........................;f6 d2
IMUL BYTE [BP+SI+0x55] .........;f6 6a 55          NOT BL .........................;f6 d3
IMUL BYTE [BP+DI+0x55] .........;f6 6b 55          NOT AH .........................;f6 d4
IMUL BYTE [SI+0x55] ............;f6 6c 55          NOT CH .........................;f6 d5
IMUL BYTE [DI+0x55] ............;f6 6d 55          NOT DH .........................;f6 d6
```

251

```
NOT  BH ........................;f6 d7
NEG  AL ........................;f6 d8
NEG  CL ........................;f6 d9
NEG  DL ........................;f6 da
NEG  BL ........................;f6 db
NEG  AH ........................;f6 dc
NEG  CH ........................;f6 dd
NEG  DH ........................;f6 de
NEG  BH ........................;f6 df
MUL  AL ........................;f6 e0
MUL  CL ........................;f6 e1
MUL  DL ........................;f6 e2
MUL  BL ........................;f6 e3
MUL  AH ........................;f6 e4
MUL  CH ........................;f6 e5
MUL  DH ........................;f6 e6
MUL  BH ........................;f6 e7
IMUL AL ........................;f6 e8
IMUL CL ........................;f6 e9
IMUL DL ........................;f6 ea
IMUL BL ........................;f6 eb
IMUL AH ........................;f6 ec
IMUL CH ........................;f6 ed
IMUL DH ........................;f6 ee
IMUL BH ........................;f6 ef
DIV  AL ........................;f6 f0
DIV  CL ........................;f6 f1
DIV  DL ........................;f6 f2
DIV  BL ........................;f6 f3
DIV  AH ........................;f6 f4
DIV  CH ........................;f6 f5
DIV  DH ........................;f6 f6
DIV  BH ........................;f6 f7
IDIV AL ........................;f6 f8
IDIV CL ........................;f6 f9
IDIV DL ........................;f6 fa
IDIV BL ........................;f6 fb
IDIV AH ........................;f6 fc
IDIV CH ........................;f6 fd
IDIV DH ........................;f6 fe
IDIV BH ........................;f6 ff
TEST WORD [BX+SI],0x7788 .......;f7 00 88 77
TEST WORD [BX+DI],0x7788 .......;f7 01 88 77
TEST WORD [BP+SI],0x7788 .......;f7 02 88 77
TEST WORD [BP+DI],0x7788 .......;f7 03 88 77
TEST WORD [SI],0x7788 ..........;f7 04 88 77
TEST WORD [DI],0x7788 ..........;f7 05 88 77
TEST WORD [0x5566],0x7788 ......;f7 06 66 55 88 77
TEST WORD [BX],0x7788 ..........;f7 07 88 77
NOT  WORD [BX+SI] ..............;f7 10
NOT  WORD [BX+DI] ..............;f7 11
NOT  WORD [BP+SI] ..............;f7 12
NOT  WORD [BP+DI] ..............;f7 13
NOT  WORD [SI] .................;f7 14
NOT  WORD [DI] .................;f7 15
NOT  WORD [0x5566] .............;f7 16 66 55
NOT  WORD [BX] .................;f7 17
NEG  WORD [BX+SI] ..............;f7 18
NEG  WORD [BX+DI] ..............;f7 19
NEG  WORD [BP+SI] ..............;f7 1a
NEG  WORD [BP+DI] ..............;f7 1b
NEG  WORD [SI] .................;f7 1c
NEG  WORD [DI] .................;f7 1d
NEG  WORD [0x5566] .............;f7 1e 66 55
NEG  WORD [BX] .................;f7 1f
MUL  WORD [BX+SI] ..............;f7 20
MUL  WORD [BX+DI] ..............;f7 21
MUL  WORD [BP+SI] ..............;f7 22
MUL  WORD [BP+DI] ..............;f7 23
MUL  WORD [SI] .................;f7 24
MUL  WORD [DI] .................;f7 25
MUL  WORD [0x5566] .............;f7 26 66 55
MUL  WORD [BX] .................;f7 27
IMUL WORD [BX+SI] ..............;f7 28
IMUL WORD [BX+DI] ..............;f7 29
IMUL WORD [BP+SI] ..............;f7 2a
IMUL WORD [BP+DI] ..............;f7 2b
IMUL WORD [SI] .................;f7 2c
IMUL WORD [DI] .................;f7 2d
IMUL WORD [0x5566] .............;f7 2e 66 55
IMUL WORD [BX] .................;f7 2f
DIV  WORD [BX+SI] ..............;f7 30
DIV  WORD [BX+DI] ..............;f7 31
DIV  WORD [BP+SI] ..............;f7 32
DIV  WORD [BP+DI] ..............;f7 33
DIV  WORD [SI] .................;f7 34
DIV  WORD [DI] .................;f7 35
DIV  WORD [0x5566] .............;f7 36 66 55
DIV  WORD [BX] .................;f7 37

IDIV WORD [BX+SI] ..............;f7 38
IDIV WORD [BX+DI] ..............;f7 39
IDIV WORD [BP+SI] ..............;f7 3a
IDIV WORD [BP+DI] ..............;f7 3b
IDIV WORD [SI] .................;f7 3c
IDIV WORD [DI] .................;f7 3d
IDIV WORD [0x5566] .............;f7 3e 66 55
IDIV WORD [BX] .................;f7 3f
TEST WORD [BX+SI+0x55],0x7788 ..;f7 40 55 88 77
TEST WORD [BX+DI+0x55],0x7788 ..;f7 41 55 88 77
TEST WORD [BP+SI+0x55],0x7788 ..;f7 42 55 88 77
TEST WORD [BP+DI+0x55],0x7788 ..;f7 43 55 88 77
TEST WORD [SI+0x55],0x7788 .....;f7 44 55 88 77
TEST WORD [DI+0x55],0x7788 .....;f7 45 55 88 77
TEST WORD [BP+0x55],0x7788 .....;f7 46 55 88 77
TEST WORD [BX+0x55],0x7788 .....;f7 47 55 88 77
NOT  WORD [BX+SI+0x55] .........;f7 50 55
NOT  WORD [BX+DI+0x55] .........;f7 51 55
NOT  WORD [BP+SI+0x55] .........;f7 52 55
NOT  WORD [BP+DI+0x55] .........;f7 53 55
NOT  WORD [SI+0x55] ............;f7 54 55
NOT  WORD [DI+0x55] ............;f7 55 55
NOT  WORD [BP+0x55] ............;f7 56 55
NOT  WORD [BX+0x55] ............;f7 57 55
NEG  WORD [BX+SI+0x55] .........;f7 58 55
NEG  WORD [BX+DI+0x55] .........;f7 59 55
NEG  WORD [BP+SI+0x55] .........;f7 5a 55
NEG  WORD [BP+DI+0x55] .........;f7 5b 55
NEG  WORD [SI+0x55] ............;f7 5c 55
NEG  WORD [DI+0x55] ............;f7 5d 55
NEG  WORD [BP+0x55] ............;f7 5e 55
NEG  WORD [BX+0x55] ............;f7 5f 55
MUL  WORD [BX+SI+0x55] .........;f7 60 55
MUL  WORD [BX+DI+0x55] .........;f7 61 55
MUL  WORD [BP+SI+0x55] .........;f7 62 55
MUL  WORD [BP+DI+0x55] .........;f7 63 55
MUL  WORD [SI+0x55] ............;f7 64 55
MUL  WORD [DI+0x55] ............;f7 65 55
MUL  WORD [BP+0x55] ............;f7 66 55
MUL  WORD [BX+0x55] ............;f7 67 55
IMUL WORD [BX+SI+0x55] .........;f7 68 55
IMUL WORD [BX+DI+0x55] .........;f7 69 55
IMUL WORD [BP+SI+0x55] .........;f7 6a 55
IMUL WORD [BP+DI+0x55] .........;f7 6b 55
IMUL WORD [SI+0x55] ............;f7 6c 55
IMUL WORD [DI+0x55] ............;f7 6d 55
IMUL WORD [BP+0x55] ............;f7 6e 55
IMUL WORD [BX+0x55] ............;f7 6f 55
DIV  WORD [BX+SI+0x55] .........;f7 70 55
DIV  WORD [BX+DI+0x55] .........;f7 71 55
DIV  WORD [BP+SI+0x55] .........;f7 72 55
DIV  WORD [BP+DI+0x55] .........;f7 73 55
DIV  WORD [SI+0x55] ............;f7 74 55
DIV  WORD [DI+0x55] ............;f7 75 55
DIV  WORD [BP+0x55] ............;f7 76 55
DIV  WORD [BX+0x55] ............;f7 77 55
IDIV WORD [BX+SI+0x55] .........;f7 78 55
IDIV WORD [BX+DI+0x55] .........;f7 79 55
IDIV WORD [BP+SI+0x55] .........;f7 7a 55
IDIV WORD [BP+DI+0x55] .........;f7 7b 55
IDIV WORD [SI+0x55] ............;f7 7c 55
IDIV WORD [DI+0x55] ............;f7 7d 55
IDIV WORD [BP+0x55] ............;f7 7e 55
IDIV WORD [BX+0x55] ............;f7 7f 55
TEST WORD [BX+SI+0x5566],0x7788 ;f7 80 66 55 88 77
TEST WORD [BX+DI+0x5566],0x7788 ;f7 81 66 55 88 77
TEST WORD [BP+SI+0x5566],0x7788 ;f7 82 66 55 88 77
TEST WORD [BP+DI+0x5566],0x7788 ;f7 83 66 55 88 77
TEST WORD [SI+0x5566],0x7788 ...;f7 84 66 55 88 77
TEST WORD [DI+0x5566],0x7788 ...;f7 85 66 55 88 77
TEST WORD [BP+0x5566],0x7788 ...;f7 86 66 55 88 77
TEST WORD [BX+0x5566],0x7788 ...;f7 87 66 55 88 77
NOT  WORD [BX+SI+0x5566] .......;f7 90 66 55
NOT  WORD [BX+DI+0x5566] .......;f7 91 66 55
NOT  WORD [BP+SI+0x5566] .......;f7 92 66 55
NOT  WORD [BP+DI+0x5566] .......;f7 93 66 55
NOT  WORD [SI+0x5566] ..........;f7 94 66 55
NOT  WORD [DI+0x5566] ..........;f7 95 66 55
NOT  WORD [BP+0x5566] ..........;f7 96 66 55
NOT  WORD [BX+0x5566] ..........;f7 97 66 55
NEG  WORD [BX+SI+0x5566] .......;f7 98 66 55
NEG  WORD [BX+DI+0x5566] .......;f7 99 66 55
NEG  WORD [BP+SI+0x5566] .......;f7 9a 66 55
NEG  WORD [BP+DI+0x5566] .......;f7 9b 66 55
NEG  WORD [SI+0x5566] ..........;f7 9c 66 55
NEG  WORD [DI+0x5566] ..........;f7 9d 66 55
NEG  WORD [BP+0x5566] ..........;f7 9e 66 55
NEG  WORD [BX+0x5566] ..........;f7 9f 66 55
MUL  WORD [BX+SI+0x5566] .......;f7 a0 66 55
```

```
MUL WORD [BX+DI+0x5566] ........;f7 a1 66 55      CLI .............................;fa
MUL WORD [BP+SI+0x5566] ........;f7 a2 66 55      STI .............................;fb
MUL WORD [BP+DI+0x5566] ........;f7 a3 66 55      CLD .............................;fc
MUL WORD [SI+0x5566] ...........;f7 a4 66 55      STD .............................;fd
MUL WORD [DI+0x5566] ...........;f7 a5 66 55      INC BYTE [BX+SI] ................;fe 00
MUL WORD [BP+0x5566] ...........;f7 a6 66 55      INC BYTE [BX+DI] ................;fe 01
MUL WORD [BX+0x5566] ...........;f7 a7 66 55      INC BYTE [BP+SI] ................;fe 02
IMUL WORD [BX+SI+0x5566] .......;f7 a8 66 55      INC BYTE [BP+DI] ................;fe 03
IMUL WORD [BX+DI+0x5566] .......;f7 a9 66 55      INC BYTE [SI] ...................;fe 04
IMUL WORD [BP+SI+0x5566] .......;f7 aa 66 55      INC BYTE [DI] ...................;fe 05
IMUL WORD [BP+DI+0x5566] .......;f7 ab 66 55      INC BYTE [0x5566] ...............;fe 06 66 55
IMUL WORD [SI+0x5566] ..........;f7 ac 66 55      INC BYTE [BX] ...................;fe 07
IMUL WORD [DI+0x5566] ..........;f7 ad 66 55      DEC BYTE [BX+SI] ................;fe 08
IMUL WORD [BP+0x5566] ..........;f7 ae 66 55      DEC BYTE [BX+DI] ................;fe 09
IMUL WORD [BX+0x5566] ..........;f7 af 66 55      DEC BYTE [BP+SI] ................;fe 0a
DIV WORD [BX+SI+0x5566] ........;f7 b0 66 55      DEC BYTE [BP+DI] ................;fe 0b
DIV WORD [BX+DI+0x5566] ........;f7 b1 66 55      DEC BYTE [SI] ...................;fe 0c
DIV WORD [BP+SI+0x5566] ........;f7 b2 66 55      DEC BYTE [DI] ...................;fe 0d
DIV WORD [BP+DI+0x5566] ........;f7 b3 66 55      DEC BYTE [0x5566] ...............;fe 0e 66 55
DIV WORD [SI+0x5566] ...........;f7 b4 66 55      DEC BYTE [BX] ...................;fe 0f
DIV WORD [DI+0x5566] ...........;f7 b5 66 55      INC BYTE [BX+SI+0x55] ...........;fe 40 55
DIV WORD [BP+0x5566] ...........;f7 b6 66 55      INC BYTE [BX+DI+0x55] ...........;fe 41 55
DIV WORD [BX+0x5566] ...........;f7 b7 66 55      INC BYTE [BP+SI+0x55] ...........;fe 42 55
IDIV WORD [BX+SI+0x5566] .......;f7 b8 66 55      INC BYTE [BP+DI+0x55] ...........;fe 43 55
IDIV WORD [BX+DI+0x5566] .......;f7 b9 66 55      INC BYTE [SI+0x55] ..............;fe 44 55
IDIV WORD [BP+SI+0x5566] .......;f7 ba 66 55      INC BYTE [DI+0x55] ..............;fe 45 55
IDIV WORD [BP+DI+0x5566] .......;f7 bb 66 55      INC BYTE [BP+0x55] ..............;fe 46 55
IDIV WORD [SI+0x5566] ..........;f7 bc 66 55      INC BYTE [BX+0x55] ..............;fe 47 55
IDIV WORD [DI+0x5566] ..........;f7 bd 66 55      DEC BYTE [BX+SI+0x55] ...........;fe 48 55
IDIV WORD [BP+0x5566] ..........;f7 be 66 55      DEC BYTE [BX+DI+0x55] ...........;fe 49 55
IDIV WORD [BX+0x5566] ..........;f7 bf 66 55      DEC BYTE [BP+SI+0x55] ...........;fe 4a 55
TEST AX,0x7788 .................;f7 c0 88 77      DEC BYTE [BP+DI+0x55] ...........;fe 4b 55
TEST CX,0x7788 .................;f7 c1 88 77      DEC BYTE [SI+0x55] ..............;fe 4c 55
TEST DX,0x7788 .................;f7 c2 88 77      DEC BYTE [DI+0x55] ..............;fe 4d 55
TEST BX,0x7788 .................;f7 c3 88 77      DEC BYTE [BP+0x55] ..............;fe 4e 55
TEST SP,0x7788 .................;f7 c4 88 77      DEC BYTE [BX+0x55] ..............;fe 4f 55
TEST BP,0x7788 .................;f7 c5 88 77      INC BYTE [BX+SI+0x5566] .........;fe 80 66 55
TEST SI,0x7788 .................;f7 c6 88 77      INC BYTE [BX+DI+0x5566] .........;fe 81 66 55
TEST DI,0x7788 .................;f7 c7 88 77      INC BYTE [BP+SI+0x5566] .........;fe 82 66 55
NOT AX .........................;f7 d0            INC BYTE [BP+DI+0x5566] .........;fe 83 66 55
NOT CX .........................;f7 d1            INC BYTE [SI+0x5566] ............;fe 84 66 55
NOT DX .........................;f7 d2            INC BYTE [DI+0x5566] ............;fe 85 66 55
NOT BX .........................;f7 d3            INC BYTE [BP+0x5566] ............;fe 86 66 55
NOT SP .........................;f7 d4            INC BYTE [BX+0x5566] ............;fe 87 66 55
NOT BP .........................;f7 d5            DEC BYTE [BX+SI+0x5566] .........;fe 88 66 55
NOT SI .........................;f7 d6            DEC BYTE [BX+DI+0x5566] .........;fe 89 66 55
NOT DI .........................;f7 d7            DEC BYTE [BP+SI+0x5566] .........;fe 8a 66 55
NEG AX .........................;f7 d8            DEC BYTE [BP+DI+0x5566] .........;fe 8b 66 55
NEG CX .........................;f7 d9            DEC BYTE [SI+0x5566] ............;fe 8c 66 55
NEG DX .........................;f7 da            DEC BYTE [DI+0x5566] ............;fe 8d 66 55
NEG BX .........................;f7 db            DEC BYTE [BP+0x5566] ............;fe 8e 66 55
NEG SP .........................;f7 dc            DEC BYTE [BX+0x5566] ............;fe 8f 66 55
NEG BP .........................;f7 dd            INC WORD [BX+SI] ................;ff 00
NEG SI .........................;f7 de            INC WORD [BX+DI] ................;ff 01
NEG DI .........................;f7 df            INC WORD [BP+SI] ................;ff 02
MUL AX .........................;f7 e0            INC WORD [BP+DI] ................;ff 03
MUL CX .........................;f7 e1            INC WORD [SI] ...................;ff 04
MUL DX .........................;f7 e2            INC WORD [DI] ...................;ff 05
MUL BX .........................;f7 e3            INC WORD [0x5566] ...............;ff 06 66 55
MUL SP .........................;f7 e4            INC WORD [BX] ...................;ff 07
MUL BP .........................;f7 e5            DEC WORD [BX+SI] ................;ff 08
MUL SI .........................;f7 e6            DEC WORD [BX+DI] ................;ff 09
MUL DI .........................;f7 e7            DEC WORD [BP+SI] ................;ff 0a
IMUL AX ........................;f7 e8            DEC WORD [BP+DI] ................;ff 0b
IMUL CX ........................;f7 e9            DEC WORD [SI] ...................;ff 0c
IMUL DX ........................;f7 ea            DEC WORD [DI] ...................;ff 0d
IMUL BX ........................;f7 eb            DEC WORD [0x5566] ...............;ff 0e 66 55
IMUL SP ........................;f7 ec            DEC WORD [BX] ...................;ff 0f
IMUL BP ........................;f7 ed            CALL [BX+SI] ....................;ff 10
IMUL SI ........................;f7 ee            CALL [BX+DI] ....................;ff 11
IMUL DI ........................;f7 ef            CALL [BP+SI] ....................;ff 12
DIV AX .........................;f7 f0            CALL [BP+DI] ....................;ff 13
DIV CX .........................;f7 f1            CALL [SI] .......................;ff 14
DIV DX .........................;f7 f2            CALL [DI] .......................;ff 15
DIV BX .........................;f7 f3            CALL [0x5566] ...................;ff 16 66 55
DIV SP .........................;f7 f4            CALL [BX] .......................;ff 17
DIV BP .........................;f7 f5            CALL FAR [BX+SI] ................;ff 18
DIV SI .........................;f7 f6            CALL FAR [BX+DI] ................;ff 19
DIV DI .........................;f7 f7            CALL FAR [BP+SI] ................;ff 1a
IDIV AX ........................;f7 f8            CALL FAR [BP+DI] ................;ff 1b
IDIV CX ........................;f7 f9            CALL FAR [SI] ...................;ff 1c
IDIV DX ........................;f7 fa            CALL FAR [DI] ...................;ff 1d
IDIV BX ........................;f7 fb            CALL FAR [0x5566] ...............;ff 1e 66 55
IDIV SP ........................;f7 fc            CALL FAR [BX] ...................;ff 1f
IDIV BP ........................;f7 fd            JMP [BX+SI] .....................;ff 20
IDIV SI ........................;f7 fe            JMP [BX+DI] .....................;ff 21
IDIV DI ........................;f7 ff            JMP [BP+SI] .....................;ff 22
CLC ............................;f8              JMP [BP+DI] .....................;ff 23
STC ............................;f9              JMP [SI] ........................;ff 24
```

```
JMP  [DI] ........................;ff 25
JMP  [0x5566] ...................;ff 26 66 55
JMP  [BX] ........................;ff 27
JMP  FAR [BX+SI] ................;ff 28
JMP  FAR [BX+DI] ................;ff 29
JMP  FAR [BP+SI] ................;ff 2a
JMP  FAR [BP+DI] ................;ff 2b
JMP  FAR [SI] ...................;ff 2c
JMP  FAR [DI] ...................;ff 2d
JMP  FAR [0x5566] ..............;ff 2e 66 55
JMP  FAR [BX] ...................;ff 2f
PUSH WORD [BX+SI] ..............;ff 30
PUSH WORD [BX+DI] ..............;ff 31
PUSH WORD [BP+SI] ..............;ff 32
PUSH WORD [BP+DI] ..............;ff 33
PUSH WORD [SI] .................;ff 34
PUSH WORD [DI] .................;ff 35
PUSH WORD [0x5566] ............;ff 36 66 55
PUSH WORD [BX] .................;ff 37
INC  WORD [BX+SI+0x55] .........;ff 40 55
INC  WORD [BX+DI+0x55] .........;ff 41 55
INC  WORD [BP+SI+0x55] .........;ff 42 55
INC  WORD [BP+DI+0x55] .........;ff 43 55
INC  WORD [SI+0x55] ............;ff 44 55
INC  WORD [DI+0x55] ............;ff 45 55
INC  WORD [BP+0x55] ............;ff 46 55
INC  WORD [BX+0x55] ............;ff 47 55
DEC  WORD [BX+SI+0x55] .........;ff 48 55
DEC  WORD [BX+DI+0x55] .........;ff 49 55
DEC  WORD [BP+SI+0x55] .........;ff 4a 55
DEC  WORD [BP+DI+0x55] .........;ff 4b 55
DEC  WORD [SI+0x55] ............;ff 4c 55
DEC  WORD [DI+0x55] ............;ff 4d 55
DEC  WORD [BP+0x55] ............;ff 4e 55
DEC  WORD [BX+0x55] ............;ff 4f 55
CALL [BX+SI+0x55] ..............;ff 50 55
CALL [BX+DI+0x55] ..............;ff 51 55
CALL [BP+SI+0x55] ..............;ff 52 55
CALL [BP+DI+0x55] ..............;ff 53 55
CALL [SI+0x55] .................;ff 54 55
CALL [DI+0x55] .................;ff 55 55
CALL [BP+0x55] .................;ff 56 55
CALL [BX+0x55] .................;ff 57 55
CALL FAR [BX+SI+0x55] .........;ff 58 55
CALL FAR [BX+DI+0x55] .........;ff 59 55
CALL FAR [BP+SI+0x55] .........;ff 5a 55
CALL FAR [BP+DI+0x55] .........;ff 5b 55
CALL FAR [SI+0x55] ............;ff 5c 55
CALL FAR [DI+0x55] ............;ff 5d 55
CALL FAR [BP+0x55] ............;ff 5e 55
CALL FAR [BX+0x55] ............;ff 5f 55
JMP  [BX+SI+0x55] ..............;ff 60 55
JMP  [BX+DI+0x55] ..............;ff 61 55
JMP  [BP+SI+0x55] ..............;ff 62 55
JMP  [BP+DI+0x55] ..............;ff 63 55
JMP  [SI+0x55] .................;ff 64 55
JMP  [DI+0x55] .................;ff 65 55
JMP  [BP+0x55] .................;ff 66 55
JMP  [BX+0x55] .................;ff 67 55
JMP  FAR [BX+SI+0x55] ..........;ff 68 55
JMP  FAR [BX+DI+0x55] ..........;ff 69 55
JMP  FAR [BP+SI+0x55] ..........;ff 6a 55
JMP  FAR [BP+DI+0x55] ..........;ff 6b 55
JMP  FAR [SI+0x55] .............;ff 6c 55
JMP  FAR [DI+0x55] .............;ff 6d 55
JMP  FAR [BP+0x55] .............;ff 6e 55
JMP  FAR [BX+0x55] .............;ff 6f 55
PUSH WORD [BX+SI+0x55] .........;ff 70 55
PUSH WORD [BX+DI+0x55] .........;ff 71 55
PUSH WORD [BP+SI+0x55] .........;ff 72 55
PUSH WORD [BP+DI+0x55] .........;ff 73 55
PUSH WORD [SI+0x55] ............;ff 74 55
PUSH WORD [DI+0x55] ............;ff 75 55
PUSH WORD [BP+0x55] ............;ff 76 55
PUSH WORD [BX+0x55] ............;ff 77 55
INC  WORD [BX+SI+0x5566] .......;ff 80 66 55
INC  WORD [BX+DI+0x5566] .......;ff 81 66 55
INC  WORD [BP+SI+0x5566] .......;ff 82 66 55
INC  WORD [BP+DI+0x5566] .......;ff 83 66 55
INC  WORD [SI+0x5566] ..........;ff 84 66 55
INC  WORD [DI+0x5566] ..........;ff 85 66 55
INC  WORD [BP+0x5566] ..........;ff 86 66 55
INC  WORD [BX+0x5566] ..........;ff 87 66 55
DEC  WORD [BX+SI+0x5566] .......;ff 88 66 55
DEC  WORD [BX+DI+0x5566] .......;ff 89 66 55
DEC  WORD [BP+SI+0x5566] .......;ff 8a 66 55
DEC  WORD [BP+DI+0x5566] .......;ff 8b 66 55
DEC  WORD [SI+0x5566] ..........;ff 8c 66 55
DEC  WORD [DI+0x5566] ..........;ff 8d 66 55
DEC  WORD [BP+0x5566] ..........;ff 8e 66 55
DEC  WORD [BX+0x5566] ..........;ff 8f 66 55
CALL [BX+SI+0x5566] ............;ff 90 66 55
CALL [BX+DI+0x5566] ............;ff 91 66 55
CALL [BP+SI+0x5566] ............;ff 92 66 55
CALL [BP+DI+0x5566] ............;ff 93 66 55
CALL [SI+0x5566] ...............;ff 94 66 55
CALL [DI+0x5566] ...............;ff 95 66 55
CALL [BP+0x5566] ...............;ff 96 66 55
CALL [BX+0x5566] ...............;ff 97 66 55
CALL FAR [BX+SI+0x5566] .......;ff 98 66 55
CALL FAR [BX+DI+0x5566] .......;ff 99 66 55
CALL FAR [BP+SI+0x5566] .......;ff 9a 66 55
CALL FAR [BP+DI+0x5566] .......;ff 9b 66 55
CALL FAR [SI+0x5566] ..........;ff 9c 66 55
CALL FAR [DI+0x5566] ..........;ff 9d 66 55
CALL FAR [BP+0x5566] ..........;ff 9e 66 55
CALL FAR [BX+0x5566] ..........;ff 9f 66 55
JMP  [BX+SI+0x5566] ............;ff a0 66 55
JMP  [BX+DI+0x5566] ............;ff a1 66 55
JMP  [BP+SI+0x5566] ............;ff a2 66 55
JMP  [BP+DI+0x5566] ............;ff a3 66 55
JMP  [SI+0x5566] ...............;ff a4 66 55
JMP  [DI+0x5566] ...............;ff a5 66 55
JMP  [BP+0x5566] ...............;ff a6 66 55
JMP  [BX+0x5566] ...............;ff a7 66 55
JMP  FAR [BX+SI+0x5566] ........;ff a8 66 55
JMP  FAR [BX+DI+0x5566] ........;ff a9 66 55
JMP  FAR [BP+SI+0x5566] ........;ff aa 66 55
JMP  FAR [BP+DI+0x5566] ........;ff ab 66 55
JMP  FAR [SI+0x5566] ..........;ff ac 66 55
JMP  FAR [DI+0x5566] ..........;ff ad 66 55
JMP  FAR [BP+0x5566] ..........;ff ae 66 55
JMP  FAR [BX+0x5566] ..........;ff af 66 55
PUSH WORD [BX+SI+0x5566] .......;ff b0 66 55
PUSH WORD [BX+DI+0x5566] .......;ff b1 66 55
PUSH WORD [BP+SI+0x5566] .......;ff b2 66 55
PUSH WORD [BP+DI+0x5566] .......;ff b3 66 55
PUSH WORD [SI+0x5566] ..........;ff b4 66 55
PUSH WORD [DI+0x5566] ..........;ff b5 66 55
PUSH WORD [BP+0x5566] ..........;ff b6 66 55
PUSH WORD [BX+0x5566] ..........;ff b7 66 55
```

Appendix D

Optimization tricks

Here are some optimization tricks that can be useful to make your programs shorter.

D.1 Number initialization.

If you set any 16-bit register to zero, it is shortest to write this (using DX as an example):

```
    XOR DX,DX      ; 2 bytes versus 3 for MOV DX,0
```

D.2 Increment/decrement 8-bit register.

If you are using **inc al** then it is suggested to use **inc ax** if you know AL wouldn't overflow over 255. Same for **dec al** (using **dec ax**) if you know AL will never underflow from 0 to 255.

D.3 Moving AX to another register.

If you are going to copy AX to another register, it uses a single byte for the idiom **xchg ax,reg**, while **mov reg,ax** uses 2 bytes. The idiom **push ax / pop reg** also uses 2 bytes.

D.4 Returning information inside flags.

Sometimes we have functions that return only a True or False value. We can use **clc** and **sec** to clear and set the Carry flag, and use **jc** and **jnc** to test for it.

You can use also **cmc** to complement Carry flag and reverse sense.

This saves many bytes in comparison with **mov al,0** and **mov al,1**, and of course the instructions **test al,al, and al,al, or al,al** or **cmp al,0**.

D.5 Doing multiple 8-bit operations.

If you are doing multiple 8-bit operations with constants, it is better to use the register AL. Most arithmetic/logical instructions with constant operand are shorter when the register AL is being used.

For example, **add al,0x05** (2 bytes) versus **add bl,0x05** (3 bytes). Of course the savings are greater over several instructions.

The register AX also has shorter arithmetic/logical instructions with 16-bit constant operand. For example, **add ax,0x1005** (3 bytes) versus **add bx,0x1003** (4 bytes).

Notice that short constants in the range -128 to +127 for arithmetic/logical instructions are optimized to 3 bytes for any 16-bit register (see the instructions starting with opcode 0x83 in appendix C).

D.6 Using the DAA and DAS instructions.

Sometimes it's easier to handle things like scores and level numbers using decimal arithmetic. What is this? It means the numbers are preserved in hexadecimal as they are written. This is called BCD arithmetic. For example, 5678 decimal would be written inside AX as 0x5678 hexadecimal.

The instructions **daa** and **das** help to do these operations but only for 8-bit size. The instruction **daa** is used after **add**, and the instruction **das** is used after **sub**.

For example, if the register AL contains 0x09 and you add 0x01 to the value then it would contain 0x0a; but the **daa** instruction would correct it to 0x10.

```
MOV AL,0x93
ADD AL,0x14    ; Add 0x14 to AL (like 14 decimal)
DAA            ; Decimal Adjust Addition inside AL register.
               ; Result is 0x07 inside AL and Carry = 1

MOV AL,0x23
SUB AL,0x14    ; Subtract 0x14 to AL (like 14 decimal)
DAS            ; Decimal Adjust Subtraction inside AL register.
               ; Result is 0x09 inside AL and Carry = 0
```

D.7 Using the AAD and AAM instructions.

These instructions were used originally to unpack two-digit numbers inside AH (0-9) and AL (0-9). Both instructions occupy 2 bytes. The first byte is the operation code, and the second byte contains 10.

The instruction **aad** does these operations:

$$AL = AH * 10 + AL$$

$$AH = 0$$

While the instruction **aam** does these operations:

$$AH = AL / 10$$

$$AL = AL \text{ modulo } 10$$

In the original 8088 processors, the constant 10 could be changed to anything, and the processor does the operation with that constant. But it is a deprecated feature and it isn't documented in newer processors. In fact some 8088 clones like the V20 and V30 only support the instruction with the constant 10.

This instruction can save precious bytes when you need an 8-bit multiplication or division by 10.

D.8 Using the AAA and AAS instructions.

These instructions have the same operation as **daa** and **das**, with an important variation: the lower digit (0-9) is inside AL, and the higher digit (0-9) is inside AH. Both only operate in 8-bit mode.

So you can add and subtract only values 0 to 9 to AL, and then use **aaa** or **aas** as required.

Appendix E

About the author

Óscar Toledo Gutiérrez (Mexico, 1978) is an experienced computer programmer.

He has written hundreds of programs in several programming languages, collaborates in the design of the Fenix Operating System and the Biyubi Internet Browser, gives talks at universities and does game design and programming consulting.

He is also the creator of the world's smallest chess programs written in C, Java, Javascript, x86 and 6502 machine code, and also the first Mexican to win the IOCCC (International Obfuscated C Code Contest): Best Game (2005), Best of Show (2007), Best Small Program (2007), Most Portable Chess Set (2007) and Best Non-chess Game (2012), and 2nd place winner at the first JS1K contest (2010).

One of his hobbies is working on classic consoles. He has developed games for MSX, Colecovision, Intellivision, TI-99/4A, Atari 2600, PC, Sega Master System, Memotech, Spectravideo and Tatung Einstein. His games Princess Quest and Mecha-8 are included in the Colecovision Flashback retro console by AtGames and he created the IntyBASIC language for programming Intellivision consoles.

He is also the author of the books *Toledo Nanochess: The Commented Source Code*, *Programming Games for Intellivision* and *ColecoVision Games Guide*, and tweetstar with short stories in Spanish published in @historiasmini and now collected in 3 books.